Communications
in Computer and Information Science 94

T0189707

Sanjay Ranka   Arunava Banerjee   Kanad Kishore Biswas
Sumeet Dua   Prabhat Mishra   Rajat Moona
Sheung-Hung Poon   Cho-Li Wang (Eds.)

Contemporary Computing

Third International Conference, IC3 2010
Noida, India, August 9-11, 2010
Proceedings, Part I

 Springer

Volume Editors

Sanjay Ranka
University of Florida, Gainesville, FL, USA
E-mail: ranka@cise.ufl.edu

Arunava Banerjee
University of Florida, Gainesville, FL, USA
E-mail: arunava@cise.ufl.edu

Kanad Kishore Biswas
Indian Institute of Technology, New Delhi, India
E-mail: kkb@cse.iitd.ernet.in

Sumeet Dua
Louisiana Tech University, Ruston, LA, USA
E-mail: sdua@coes.latech.edu

Prabhat Mishra
University of Florida, Gainesville, FL, USA
E-mail: prabhat@cise.ufl.edu

Rajat Moona
Indian Institute of Technology, Kanpur, India
E-mail: moona@iitk.ac.in

Sheung-Hung Poon
National Tsing Hua University, Hsin-Chu, Taiwan, R.O.C.
E-mail: sheung.hung.poon@gmail.com

Cho-Li Wang
The University of Hong Kong, China
E-mail: clwang@cs.hku.hk

Library of Congress Control Number: 2010931449

CR Subject Classification (1998): I.4, I.2, I.5, H.4, C.2, F.1

ISSN   1865-0929
ISBN-10   3-642-14833-6 Springer Berlin Heidelberg New York
ISBN-13   978-3-642-14833-0 Springer Berlin Heidelberg New York

springer.com

© Springer-Verlag Berlin Heidelberg 2010
Printed in Germany

Typesetting: Camera-ready by author, data conversion by Scientific Publishing Services, Chennai, India
Printed on acid-free paper   06/3180   5 4 3 2 1 0

Preface

Welcome to the proceedings of the Third International Conference on Contemporary Computing, which was held in Noida (outskirts of New Delhi), India. Computing is an exciting and evolving area. This conference, which was jointly organized by the Jaypee Institute of Information Technology, Noida, India and the University of Florida, Gainesville, USA, focused on topics that are of contemporary interest to computer and computational scientists and engineers.

The conference had an exciting technical program of 79 papers submitted by researchers and practitioners from academia, industry, and government to advance the algorithmic, systems, applications, and educational aspects of contemporary computing. These papers were selected from 350 submissions (with an overall acceptance rate of around 23%). The technical program was put together by a distinguished international Program Committee consisting of more than 150 members. The Program Committee was led by the following Track Chairs: Arunava Banerjee, Kanad Kishore Biswas, Summet Dua, Prabhat Mishra, Rajat Moona, Sheung-Hung Poon, and Cho-Li Wang. I would like to thank the Program Committee and the Track Chairs for their tremendous effort.

I would like to thank the General Chairs, Prof. Sartaj Sahni and Prof. Sanjay Goel, for giving me the opportunity to lead the technical program.

Sanjay Ranka

Organization

Chief Patron

Shri Jaiprakash Gaur

Patron

Shri Manoj Gaur

Advisory Committee

S.K. Khanna	Jaypee Institute of Information Technology, India
M.N. Farruqui	Jaypee Institute of Information Technology, India
Y. Medury	Jaypee Institute of Information Technology, India
J.P. Gupta	Jaypee Institute of Information Technology, India
T.R. Kakkar	Jaypee Institute of Information Technology, India
S.L. Maskara	Jaypee Institute of Information Technology, India

General Co-chairs

Sartaj Sahni	University of Florida, USA
Sanjay Goel	Jaypee Institute of Information Technology, India

Program Chair

Sanjay Ranka	University of Florida, USA

Track Co-chairs

Algorithms

Arunava Banerjee	University of Florida, Gainesville, USA
Sheung-Hung POON	National Tsing Hua University, Taiwan ROC

Applications

Sumeet Dua	Louisiana Tech, USA
K.K. Biswas	IIT Delhi, India

Systems

Prabhat Mishra   University of Florida, USA
Rajat Moona   Indian Institute of Technology, Kanpur, India
Cho-Li Wang   University of Hong Kong, Hong Kong

Technical Program Committee

Aaron Striegel   University of Notre Dame, Indiana, USA
Alan Chiu   Louisiana Tech University, USA
Amitabha Bagchi   Indian Institute of Technology, Delhi, India
Ananth Kalyanaraman   Washington State University, USA
Anil Tiwari   The LNM IIT, Rajasthan, India
Animesh Pathak   INRIA, Rocquencourt, Paris, France
Anirban Mondal   IIIT Delhi, India
Ankush Mittal   IIT Roorkee, India
Annamalai Annamalai   Prairie View A&M University,Texas, USA
Ansuman Banerjee   National University of Singapore, Singapore
Antoine Vigneron   INRA, France
Arijit Ghosh   CDNetworks, USA
Ashish Sureka   IIIT Delhi, India
Ashok Srinivasan   Florida State University, USA
Bertil Schmidt   Nanyang Technological University, Singapore
Bharat Madan   Applied Research Laboratory - Penn State
                             University, USA
Che-Rung Lee   National Tsing Hua University, Taiwan
Chien-Liang Chen   Aletheia University, Taiwan
Chin-Laung Lei   National Taiwan University, Taipei, Taiwan
Chris Gentle   Avaya Australia, Australia
Christian Duncan   Louisiana Tech University, USA
Christie Fuller   Louisiana Tech University, USA
Chuan Wu   The University of Hong Kong, Hong Kong
Chun-Cheng Lin   Taipei Municipal University of Education, Taipei,
                             Taiwan
Chung-Shou Liao   National Tsing Hua University, Taiwan
Connor Johnson   Louisiana Tech University, USA
Costas Bekas   IBM Zurich Research Laboratory, USA
D. J. Guan   National Sun Yat-Sen University, Taiwan
Devesh Kumar Bhatnagar
   Bhatnagar   Landis&Gyr, Noida, India
Dhiren Patel   National Institute of Technology, Surat, India
Eun-Sung Jung   University of Florida, USA
Francisco Massetto   University of São Paulo, Brazil
G. S. Lehal   Punjabi University, Patiala, India
Gaurav Gupta   IIIT Delhi, India
George Varsamopoulos   School of Computing and Informatics,
                             Bloomington, USA

Mohammad Ali Abam	Dortmund University, Germany
Mohammad Farshi	Yazd University, Iran
Namrata Shekhar	Synopsys, California, USA
Naveen Kandiraju	Yahoo Inc., Sunnyvale, California
Naveen Kumar	Delhi University, India
Ng Yin Kwee	Nanyang Technological University, Singapore
Nigel Gwee	Southern University, Los Angeles, USA
Nirmalya Bandyopadhyay	UFL
P. Pandey	IIT Bombay, India
Pabitra Mitra	Indian Institute of Technology, Kharagpur, India
Paolo Bellavista	University of Bologna, Italy
Parbati Manna	University of Florida, USA
Patrick Mcdowell	South Eastern Louisiana University, USA
Per Kjeldaas	Louisiana Tech University, USA
Peter Rockett	University of Sheffield, UK
Philippe O.A. Navaux	Universidade Federal do Rio Grande do Sul, Brazil
Piyush Kumar	Florida State University, USA
Ponnurangam Kumaraguru	Indian Institute of Information Technology, Delhi, India
Prabhakar T.V.	IIT Kanpur, India
Prabir Kumar Biswas	Indian Institute of Technology Kharagpur
Pradeep Chowriappa	Louisiana Tech University, USA
Pramod Singh	ABV-IIITM, Gwalior, India
Prerna Sethi	Louisiana Tech University, USA
Prerna Sethi	Louisiana Tech University, USA
Prof. Merchant	IIT Bombay, India
Prudence Wong	University of Liverpool, U.K.
Pushpendra Singh	IIIT Delhi, India
Rajeev Kumar	Indian Institute of Technology Kharagpur, India
Rajendra Acharya	Ngee Ann Polytechnic, Singapore
Richa Singh	IIIT Delhi, India
Robert Hsu	Chung Hua University, Taiwan
Roberto Rojas-Cessa	New Jersey Institute of Technology, USA
Rodrigo Mello	Universidade de Sao Paulo, Brazil
Roop Jain	JIIT, Noida, India
Ruppa Thulasiram	University of Manitoba, Canada
S. Hong	University of Sydney, Australia
Saeed Moghaddam	University of Florida, USA
Sandeep Gupta	Arizona State University, USA
Sandip Aine	Mentor Graphics, India
Sanjay Chaudhary	Dhirubhai Ambani Institute of Information and Communication Technology, India
Saroj Kaushik	IIT Delhi, India
S.C. Gupta	National Informatics Centre, India
Seetharama Satyanarayana-Jois	College of Pharmacy, Los Angeles, USA

Shankar Lall Maskara	JIIT, Noida, India
Sheetal Saini	Louisiana Tech University, USA
Shih Yu Chang	National Tsing Hua University of Taiwan
Shireesh Verma	Conexant, California, USA
Shripad Thite	Google Inc., USA
Shyam Gupta	IIT Delhi
Siu Ming Yiu	The University of Hong Kong
Siu-Wing Cheng	Hong Kong University of Science and Technology, Hong Kong
Somitra Sandhya	IIIT Delhi, India
Somnath Sengupta	Indian Institute of Technology, Kharagpur, India
Sonajharia Minz	Jawaharlal Nehru University, India
Song Fu	New Mexico Institute of Mining and Technology, USA
Sridhar Hariharaputran	Bielefeld University, Germany
Stanley P.Y. Fung	University of Leicester, UK
Sudip Seal	Oak Ridge National Laboratory, USA
Sumantra Dutta Roy	Indian Institute of Technology, Delhi, India
Suresh Chandra	IIT Delhi, India
Teng Moh	San Jose State University, Canada
Tianzhou Chen	Zhejiang University, P. R. China
Tien-Ching Lin	Academia Sinica, Taiwan
Ton Kloks	National Chung Cheng University, Taiwan
Travis Atkison	Lousiana Tech University, USA
Tridib Mukherjee	Arizona State University, USA
Tyng-Yeu Liang	National Kaohsiung University of Applied Science, Taiwan
Tzung-Shi Chen	National University of Tainan, Taiwan
Vikram Goyal	IIIT Delhi, India
Vinayak Naik	IIIT Delhi, India
Vir Phoha	Louisiana Tech University, USA
Wang Yinfeng	School of Electronics and Information Engineering, Xi'an Jiaotong University, P.R. China
Wen-Chieh Lin	National Chiao Tung University, Taiwan
Xian Du	Louisiana Tech University, USA
Xiaofeng Song	Nanjing University of Aeronautics and Astronautics, P.R. China
Xiaoyu Yang	University of Southampton, UK
Xuerong Yong	University of Puerto Rico at Mayaguez, USA
Yajun Wang	Microsoft Research Asia, P.R. China
Yeh-Ching Chung	National Tsing Hua University, Taiwan
Yenumula Reddy	Grambling State University, Los Angeles, USA
Yong-Kee Jun	Gyeongsang National University, South Korea
Yo-Sub Han	Yonsei University, Korea
Young Choon Lee	University of Sydney, Australia
Yu-Chee Tseng	National Chiao-Tung University, Taiwan
Yuting Zhao	University of Aberdeen, UK

Zhe Wang   University of Florida, USA
Zhihui Du   Tsinghua University, P.R. China
Zili Shao   Polytechnic University, Hong Kong

Publicity Co-chairs

Bhardwaj Veeravalli   University of Singapore, Singapore
Divakar Yadav   JIIT Noida, India
Koji Nakano   Hiroshima University, Japan
Masoud Sadjadi   Florida International University, USA
Paolo Bellavista   University of Bologna, Italy
Rajkumar Buyya   University of Melbourne, Australia

Publications Committee

Vikas Saxena   JIIT Noida, India *(Publication Chair)*
Abhishek Swaroo   JIIT, India
Alok Aggarwal   JIIT, India
Mukta Goel   JIIT Noida, India
Pawan Kumar Upadhyay   JIIT Noida, India
Rakhi Hemani   JIIT Noida, India

Web Administration

Sandeep K. Singh   JIIT Noida, India
Shikha Mehta   JIIT, Noida, India

Graphic Design

Sangeeta Malik   JIIT Noida, India

Registration Committee

Krishna Asawa   JIIT Noida, India *(Chair)*
Anshul Gakhar   JIIT Noida, India
Archana Purwar   JIIT Noida, India
Indu Chawla   JIIT Noida, India
Manisha Rathi   JIIT Noida, India
Purtee Kohli   JIIT Noida, India

Finance Chair

Bharat Gupta   JIIT, Noida, India

Poster Session Committee

Hima Bindu	JIIT, Noida, India *(Chair)*
Antariksh De	Xerox, USA
Jolly Shah	JIIT, Noida, India
Kumar Lomash	Adobe Systems, India
Nikhil Wason	Orangut (Co-Chair)
Priyank Singh	Firmware Developer at Marvell Semiconductor, India
Rakhi Himani	JIIT, Noida, India
Sangeeta Mittal	JIIT, Noida, India
Siddarth Batra	Co-Founder & CEO at Zunavision, USA

Student Project Exhibition Chair

Alok Aggarwal	JIIT, India

Student Volunteers Coordinator

Manish Thakur	JIIT, Noida, India

Local Arrangements Committee

Prakash Kumar	JIIT, Noida, India *(Chair)*
Adarsh Kumar	JIIT Noida, India
Akhilesh Sachan	JIIT Noida, India
Anuja Arora	JIIT Noida, India
Arti Gupta	JIIT Noida, India
Bharat Gupta	JIIT Noida, India
Gagandeep Kaur	JIIT Noida, India
Hema N.	JIIT Noida, India
Indu Chawla	JIIT Noida, India
K. Raj Lakshmi	JIIT Noida, India
Kavita Pandey	JIIT Noida, India
Manoj Bharadwaj	JIIT, Noida, India
Meenakshi Gujral	JIIT Noida, India
Mukta Goel	JIIT Noida, India
O. N. Singh	JIIT, Noida, India
Parmeet Kaur	JIIT Noida, India
Pawan Kumar Upadhyay	JIIT Noida, India
Prakash Kumar	JIIT Noida, India
Prashant Kaushik	JIIT Noida, India
S. Bhaseen	JIIT Noida, India
S.J.S. Soni	JIIT, Noida, India

Sangeeta Mittal   JIIT Noida, India
Sanjay Kataria   JIIT Noida, India
Shikha Jain   JIIT Noida, India
Suma Dawn   JIIT Noida, India
Tribhuvan K Tiwari   JIIT Noida, India
Vimal Kumar   JIIT Noida, India
Vivek Mishra   JIIT Noida, India

Table of Contents – Part I

Technical Session-3: Algorithm-3 (A-3)

Technical Session-4: Algorithm-4 (A-4)

Technical Session-5: Algorithm-5 (A-5)

Technical Session-6: Application-1 (P-1)

Technical Session-7: Application-2 (P-2)

Technical Session-8: Application-3 (P-3)

Technical Session-9: Application-4 (P-4)

Technical Session-10: Application-5 (P-5)

Technical Session-11: Application-6 (P-6)

Table of Contents – Part II

Technical Session-12: System-1 (S-1)

Technical Session-13: System-2 (S-2)

Technical Session-14: System-3 (S-3)

Technical Session-15: System-4 (S-4)

Technical Session-16: System-6 (S-6)

A PDE-Based Nonlinear Filter Adapted to Rayleigh's Speckle Noise for De-speckling 2D Ultrasound Images

Rajeev Srivastava[1] and J.R.P. Gupta[2]

[1] Department of Computer Engineering, Institute of Technology, Banaras Hindu University (ITBHU), Varanasi-221005, U.P., India
rajeev.cse@itbhu.ac.in, rajeev_sri@yahoo.com
[2] Department of Instrumentation and Control Engineering, Netaji Subhas Institute of Technology (Delhi University), Sector-3, Dwarka, New Delhi-110078, India
jrpg83@yahoo.com

Abstract. The speckle noise present in the acquired ultrasound image may lead to misinterpretation of medical image during diagnosis and therefore, it must be reduced. The speckle noise in ultrasound image is normally multiplicative in nature and distributed according to Rayleigh's probability density function (pdf). In this paper, a nonlinear partial-differential equation (PDE) based speckle reduction model adapted to Rayleigh's noise is proposed in variational framework to reduce the speckle noise from 2D ultrasound (US) images. The initial condition of the PDE is the speckle noised US image and the de-speckled image is obtained after certain iterations of the proposed PDE till its convergence. The performance of the proposed non-linear PDE based filter has been evaluated in terms of mean square error (MSE), peak signal-to-noise ratio (PSNR), correlation parameter (CP) and mean structure similarity index map (MSSIM) for several ultrasound images with varying amount of speckle noise variance. The obtained results justify the applicability of the proposed scheme.

Keywords: Partial differential equation, Speckle noise reduction, 2D B-scan ultrasound images, PDE based model, Rayleigh's probability distribution function, nonlinear PDE based filter.

1 Introduction

The speckle noise occurs in coherent imaging of objects whenever surface roughness of the image being imaged is of the order of the wavelength of the incident radiation [2]. The presence of speckle noise in an imaging system reduces its resolution; especially for low contrast images and suppression of speckle noise is an important consideration in the design of coherent imaging systems. The speckle noise is present in many imaging and vision related applications such as ultrasound imaging, synthetic aperture radar imaging (SAR), digital holography and many more. For correct interpretation of image data it becomes essential to reduce the speckle noise. The speckle noise [2] has complex amplitude given as $a(x, y) = a_R(x, y) + ja_I(x, y)$, where a_R and a_I are zero mean, independent Gaussian random variables for each (x, y) with

S. Ranka et al. (Eds.): IC3 2010, Part I, CCIS 94, pp. 1–12, 2010.

some variance. The intensity field of speckle noise is given as $n(x, y) = |a(x, y)|^2$ $= a_R^2 + a_I^2$. The image observation model [2] for speckle noise reads:

$$I_0(x, y) = I(x, y) * n(x, y) + \eta(x, y) \tag{1}$$

where $I_0(x, y)$ is the observed speckled noised image; $I(x, y)$ is the original noise free image and $n(x, y)$ is the Gaussian noise with zero-mean and known variance σ_n^2 and $\eta(x, y)$ is the detector noise which is additive in nature. Assuming detector noise to be zero, the general observation model reads:

$$I_0(x, y) = I(x, y) * n(x, y) \tag{2}$$

The B-scan or 2D ultrasound images which are used is medical diagnosis are generated by reflected or transmitted coherent ultrasound waves at fixed frequencies that interact with different tissue types and give rise to various interference phenomenon leading to speckle noise. The speckle noise present in the acquired ultrasound image may lead to misinterpretation of medical image during diagnosis and therefore, it must be reduced. The speckle noise present in ultrasound image is normally multiplicative in nature and distributed according to Rayleigh's probability density function (pdf) given as follows [3]:

$$p(I / I_0) = \frac{I_0}{\sigma^2} \exp(-\frac{I^2}{2\sigma^2}) \tag{3}$$

Where I_0 is the observed or recorded ultrasound image containing speckle noise; I is the image to be restored; and σ^2 is the speckle noise variance.

The removal of multiplicative speckle noise is difficult in comparison to the additive noise. The various methods available in literature for speckle noise reduction are N-Look Method, spatial averaging and homomorphic filtering [1, 2]. The N-Look process [2] is usually done during data acquisition stage and speckle reduction by spatial filtering is performed on the image after it is acquired. The homomorphic filtering [1, 2] approach operates in logarithmic domain. Irrespective of the methods used to reduce the speckle noise from images, the ideal speckle reduction method must preserve radiometric information and the textural information i.e. the edges between different areas and spatial signal variability. The spatial filters are of two types which are adaptive and non-adaptive. Non-adaptive filters take the parameters of the whole image signal into consideration and leave out the local properties of the terrain backscatter or the nature of the sensor. These kinds of filters are not appropriate for non-stationary scene signal. Fast Fourier Transform (FFT) is an example of such filter. The adaptive filters accommodate changes in local properties of the tissue backscatter as well as the nature of the sensor. In adaptive filters, the speckle noise is considered as being stationary but the changes in the mean backscatters due to changes in the type of target are taken into consideration. Adaptive filters reduce speckles while preserving the edges and these filters modify the image based on statistics extracted from the local environment of each pixel. Adaptive filter varies the contrast stretch for each pixel depending upon the Digital Number (DN) values in the surrounding moving kernel. A filter that adapts the stretch to the region of interest produces a better enhancement. Examples of adaptive filters are: Mean [2], median [2], Lee [4], Lee-sigma [5], Frost [6] and Gamma MAP [7]. In homomorphic filtering approach, the multiplicative speckle noise is first converted to additive noise by taking the logarithm of equation (2), then one of the additive noise model is applied for noise reduction, and finally the speckle reduced image is obtained by taking the exponential of the image obtained in second step. For additive noise removal the various methods available in literature are based on statistical techniques, wavelet based techniques and PDE based diffusion techniques. The popular methods are simple averaging [1,2], least mean squares [1,2], Weiner filtering [1,2], wavelet based de-noising [8], anisotropic diffusion based techniques [9], total variation (TV) based approach [10-12], complex diffusion based approach [13], fourth order PDE [14] and many more [15-18]. In paper [19], the authors have introduced a method for multiplicative noise removal which can also be used for speckle reduction from images. In paper [20] authors have proposed a speckle reducing anisotropic diffusion (SRAD) filter based on the extended concepts of Lee filter[4,5], frost filter [6] and anisotropic diffusion [9]. In a recent paper [21], the authors have investigated and compiled some of the techniques mostly used in the smoothing or suppression of speckle noise in ultrasound images.

2 Methods and Models

2.1 The Proposed Nonlinear PDE Based Model

The proposed nonlinear PDE based filter is modelled as an energy minimization problem in a variational framework. Since the acquisition speckle noise of the ultrasound image is not Gaussian, a least square fit is not the best choice for such an estimation process. Furthermore, independent pixel estimation does not reflect the spatial regularity of the diffusion function. Hence, it is proposed to tackle these issues with a variational framework which is adaptable to noise distribution and is able to use valuable information given by the neighbour pixels.

The de-speckling and regularization of ultrasound image data is obtained by minimizing the following nonlinear energy functional of the image I within continuous domain Ω :

$$E(I) = \underset{\min \ \Omega}{\arg} \{ \int [L(p(I/I_0)) + \lambda \cdot \phi(\|\nabla I\|)]d\Omega \quad (4)$$

The first term in energy functional given by equation (4) i.e. $L(p(I/I_0))$ is the log likelihood term of Rayleigh's distributed speckle noise in the ultrasound image. This term measures the dissimilarities at a pixel between observed image I_0 and its estimated value I obtained during the filtering process. This term makes the overall restoration process adapted to Rayleigh's distributed speckle noise in ultrasound images.

The probability distribution function of the Rayleigh's speckle noise present in B-Scan ultrasound image is given by equation (3). The log likelihood $L(p(I/I_0))$ of Rayleigh's pdf reads

$$\log(p(I / I_0)) = \log[\frac{I_0}{\sigma^2} \exp(-\frac{I^2}{2\sigma^2})]$$

$$= \log(\frac{I_0}{\sigma^2}) + \log \exp(-\frac{I^2}{2\sigma^2}) \qquad (5)$$

$$= \log(\frac{I_0}{\sigma^2}) - \frac{I^2}{2\sigma^2}$$

For obtaining the maximum likelihood of I, the derivative of log likelihood of Rayleigh's pdf w.r.t. I read

$$\frac{\partial \log(p(I / I_0))}{\partial I} = -\frac{I}{\sigma^2}$$

Let $\qquad\qquad L'(p(I / I_0) = -\frac{I}{\sigma^2} \qquad (6)$

The term $L'(p(I / I_0))$ acts as the data attachment term or data likelihood term.

In second term of equation (4), λ is a regularization parameter and has constant value. The term $\phi(\|\nabla I\|)$ is the gradient norm of the image I and is responsible for regularization and restoration of the noisy speckled image. The advantage of defining the energy of an image in terms of gradient magnitude is that gradient of an image is based on first order derivative which defines the variations in gray level of the image. The noise is associated with large gradient variations. If one is able to minimize these variations defined by the energy functional in gradient magnitude terms then noise can also be minimized in successive iterations and the original image can be restored. The one suitable choice for the energy term $\phi(\|\nabla I\|)$ based on energy functional defined by Perona and Malik [9] for deriving anisotropic diffusion based filter is:

$$\phi(\|\nabla I\|) = \|\nabla I\|^2 \qquad (7)$$

Substituting the $\phi(\|\nabla I\|)$ with Perona and Malik [9] energy functional $\|\nabla I\|^2$ in equation (4), it reads

$$E(I) = \underset{\min \Omega}{\arg} \{ \int [L(p(I / I_0)) + \lambda \cdot \|\nabla I\|^2] d\Omega \qquad (8)$$

To minimize the Rayleigh's speckle noise from ultrasound images, the Euler-Lagrange minimization technique combined with gradient descent approach is used here to minimize the energy functional given by equation (8) and this operation leads to following PDE:

$$\frac{\partial I}{\partial t} = L'(p(I / I_0)) + \lambda \cdot c \nabla^2 I \qquad (9)$$

The first term $L'(p(I / I_0))$ in equation (9) is the first derivative of log likelihood term of Rayleigh's probability distribution function (pdf) that describes the speckle noise in ultrasound images. This term act as the data attachment term and makes the PDE defined by equation (9) adapted to speckle noise. The second term in equation (9) is the 2D isotropic heat equation and it performs 2D diffusion of the image and subsequently de-noises the image [9]. The basic disadvantage of using the isotropic diffusion is that it may lead to blurring and over smoothing of image; edges and fine texture details from the image may be lost. Therefore, to overcome the difficulty associated with isotropic diffusion, in this paper it is proposed to use anisotropic diffusion [9] based filter. By replacing the constant conductivity coefficient c with an adaptive conductivity coefficient defined in terms of image differential structure, the second term in equation (9) can be written in its anisotropic diffusion [9] form and the proposed model adapted to Rayleigh's speckle noise reads:

$$\frac{\partial I}{\partial t} = L'(p(I/I_0)) + \lambda \cdot div(c(\|\nabla I\|)\nabla I) \tag{10a}$$

With initial condition

$$I_{t=0} = I_0 \tag{10b}$$

The PDE given by equation (10a) with the initial condition as the noisy image I_0, generates the filtered de-speckled image after certain iterations till its convergence. The PDE given by equation (10) behaves as a nonlinear anisotropic diffusion based filter adapted to Rayleigh's speckle noise in ultrasound images. The function $c(x, y, t)$ may be defined as $c(x, y, t) = c(\|\nabla I\|)$. The conductivity coefficient $c(x, y, t)$ controls the diffusion process within the image that can be varied according to image structure. The diffusion is lowered where edges occur to preserve the edges and the diffusion is enhanced in smooth region of the image. The diffusion coefficient c is defined as follows [9]:

$$c(\|\nabla I\|) = \frac{1}{1 + \frac{\|\nabla I\|^2}{k^2}} \tag{11}$$

where $k > 0$ is a gradient threshold that differentiates homogeneous area and regions of contours and edges.

Therefore, *the proposed anisotropic diffusion based model adapted to Rayleigh's distributed speckle noise* reads

$$\frac{\partial I}{\partial t} = -\frac{I}{\sigma^2} + \lambda \nabla.(c(\|\nabla I\|)\nabla I) \tag{12a}$$

With initial condition

$$I_{t=0} = I_0 \tag{12b}$$

The first term, which is first derivative of log likelihood of Rayleigh's pdf with respect to estimated image, acts as the data attachment term and measures the dissimilarities at a pixel between observed image and its estimated value obtained during filtering process thereby making the whole filtering process adapted to noise. The second term is responsible for regularization and smoothing of the image data by minimizing the variance of pixels.

2.2 Adaptive Estimation of the Edge Threshold Parameter k

The edge threshold parameter, k used in diffusion coefficient given by Equation (11) is a measure for edge preservation within the image during the diffusion process. The relation $\|\nabla I\| > k$ implies that edges are preserved i.e. diffusion effect is small. In other words, k is a contrast parameter because regions in which $\|\nabla I\| > k$ are considered as edges and the diffusion process has a low effect. For a small diffusion coefficient the image gets smoothed, but details are better preserved with respect to the large k. When k increases the smoothing effect is linear. Normally, the value of k is a positive constant which is set by hand at some fixed value and must be fine tuned according to a particular application. For example, the value of k is set in between 20 to 100 for digital images for anisotropic diffusion based PDE [9] and remains constant throughout the iterations of the PDE as originally proposed in paper [9]. Further, since $\|\nabla I\|$ decreases in successive iterations the value of k should also decrease in successive iterations. Therefore, for best results the value of k should be determined adaptively according to the application in hand rather than fixing it to some constant value throughout the various iterations of the PDE till its convergence. Hence, to make the proposed scheme overall adaptive in nature, the adaptive value of k is proposed to be determined from the speckle scale space function which is also known as speckle index and it is defined as [23]:

$$k = \frac{\sqrt{\sigma_n^2}}{\mu} = \frac{stddev(It)}{mean(It)} \tag{13}$$

where the numerator is the standard deviation and the denominator is the mean of the image, respectively, processed and evolved by the diffusion based PDEs at time t i.e. It over a homogeneous area of the image at time t. The speckle space function is a measure of speckle noise in an image. As the speckle noise decreases in successive iterations of the proposed diffusion based PDEs, the value of edge threshold parameter is also decreased in successive iterations making the overall scheme adaptive in nature. The speckle scale space function can also be regarded as an average reciprocal signal-to-noise ratio, with the image signal being the mean value and the noise being the standard deviation. The values of speckle scale space function i.e. speckle index lies in between 0 (no speckle) and 1(fully developed speckle). Hence, for better speckle reduction, the value of speckle index should be low. Further, k can be approximated as a negative exponential distribution [20]:

$$k \approx k_0 \exp(-\alpha t) \tag{14}$$

where α is a constant and k_0 is the speckle coefficient of variation in the observed image. For fully developed speckle in ultrasound images without compounding the value of k_0 is 1.

2.3 Discretization of the Proposed Model for Digital Implementations

For digital implementations, the proposed model given by equation (12) can be discretized using finite differences schemes [24]. The discretized form of the proposed PDE based model, given by equation (12), reads

$$I^{n+1}(x, y) = I^n(x, y) + \Delta t.[L'(p(I/I_0)) + \lambda \cdot div(c(\|\nabla I^n(x, y)\|)\nabla I^n(x, y))] \quad (15)$$

i.e. $I^{n+1}(x, y) = I^n(x, y) + \Delta t.[-\dfrac{I^n(x, y)}{\sigma^2} + \lambda \cdot div(c(\|\nabla I^n(x, y)\|)\nabla I^n(x, y))]$ (16)

For the numerical scheme, given by equation (16) to be stable, the von Neumann analysis [24], shows that we require $\dfrac{\Delta t}{(\Delta x)^2} < ¼$. If the grid size is set to $\Delta x = 1$, then $\Delta t < ¼$ i.e. $\Delta t < 0.25$. Therefore, the value of Δt is set to 0.24 for stability of equation (16).

3 Results and Performance Analysis

The metrics for comparing the performance of various speckle reduction schemes in considerations from digital ultrasound images are defined as follows:

Mean square error [2]:

$$MSE = \frac{1}{m \times n} \sum_{i=1}^{m} \sum_{j=1}^{n} \left[I'(i, j) - I(i, j) \right]^2 \quad (17)$$

where I is the original image without speckle noise , I' is the filtered speckle reduced image , $m \times n$ is the size of the image and i=1.......m, j=1........n.

Peak signal-to-noise ratio [2]:

$$PSNR = 20 \log_{10} \left[\frac{255}{RMSE} \right] \quad (18)$$

Here RMSE is the root mean square error. For optimal performance, measured values of MSE should be small and that of PSNR should be large.

Correlation parameter (CP) [25]:
Correlation parameter (CP) is a qualitative measure for edge preservation. If one is interested in suppressing speckle noise while at the same time preserving the edges of the original image then this parameter proposed in paper [25] can be used. To

evaluate the performance of the edge preservation or sharpness, the correlation parameter is defined as follows

$$CP = \frac{\sum\limits_{i=1}^{m}\sum\limits_{j=1}^{n}(\Delta I - \overline{\Delta I}) \times (\Delta \hat{I} - \overline{\Delta \hat{I}})}{\sqrt{\sum\limits_{i=1}^{m}\sum\limits_{j=1}^{n}(\Delta I - \overline{\Delta I})^2 \times \sum\limits_{i=1}^{m}\sum\limits_{j=1}^{n}(\Delta \hat{I} - \overline{\Delta \hat{I}})^2}} \qquad (19)$$

Where ΔI and $\Delta \hat{I}$ are high pass filtered versions of original image I and filtered image $\hat{I}$ obtained via a 3x3 pixel standard approximation of the Laplacian operator. The $\overline{\Delta I}$ and $\overline{\Delta \hat{I}}$ are the mean values of I and $\hat{I}$ respectively. The correlation parameter should be closer to unity for an optimal effect of edge preservation.

Structure similarity index map (SSIM) [26]:
SSIM is used to compare luminance, contrast and structure of two different images. It can be treated as a similarity measure of two different images. This similarity measure is a function of luminance, contrast and structure. The SSIM of two images X and Y be calculated as:

$$SSIM(X,Y) = \frac{(2\mu_x\mu_y + C_1) \times (2\sigma_{xy} + C_2)}{(\mu_x^2 + \mu_y^2 + C_1) \times (\sigma_x^2 + \sigma_y^2 + C_2)}. \qquad (20)$$

Where μ_i (i = X or Y) is the mean intensity, σ_i (i=X or Y) is the standard deviation, $\sigma_{xy} = \sigma_x.\sigma_y$ and C_i (i=1 or 2) is the constant to avoid instability when $\mu_x^2 + \mu_y^2$ is very close to zero and is defined as $C_i = (k_iL)^2$ in which $k_i << 1$ and L is the dynamic range of pixel values e.g. L=255 for 8-bit gray scale image. In order to have an overall quality measurement of the entire image, mean SSIM is defined as

$$MSSIM(X,Y) = \frac{1}{mn}\sum\limits_{i=1}^{m}\sum\limits_{j=1}^{n}SSIM(X_{ij},Y_{ij}). \qquad (21)$$

The MSSIM value should be closer to unity for optimal measure of similarity.

3.1 Results and Discussions

The performances of the proposed method with other methods available in literature [4,5,6,20,22] have been compared in terms of MSE, PSNR, CP and MSSIM for varying amount of speckle noise variance. The speckle noise was introduced artificially in all the test cases based on speckle noise model defined by equation (2) and Rayleigh's pdf given by equation (3). During experimentation 20 possible choices of speckle noise variance σ_n^2 with values from 0.002 to 0.04 in steps of 0.02 were used. The value of Δt was set to 0.24 for the proposed anisotropic diffusion based scheme. It has been tested through experimentation that after 25-30 iterations the proposed scheme converge to the desired level of solution i.e. produces acceptable quality of speckle reduced images. After 30 iterations the PSNR values of these schemes start decreasing. Therefore, total numbers of iterations were fixed to 30 for the proposed scheme. The initial condition of the PDE given by equation (12a) is Rayleigh's distributed speckle noised ultrasound image and the final solution is the speckle reduced ultrasound image. The value of the regularization parameter λ was set to one. The threshold parameter used by diffusion coefficient given by equation (11) was determined adaptively by equation (14).

The results for one ultrasound image fetusbrain.jpg of size 225x300 are shown in this paper. Figure 1 shows the comparison of visual results of the proposed scheme with other schemes for the sample ultrasound image fetusbrain.jpg of size 225x300. Figure 2 shows the performance comparison of various schemes in terms of MSE and PSNR with respect to change in speckle variance. Figure 3 shows the performance comparison in terms of CP and MSSIM. From Figure 2 it can be observed that the proposed non-linear PDE-based filter for speckle reduction is associated with minimum MSE and maximum PSNR values in comparison to other schemes for all values for speckle noise variances. Further, from Figure 3 it can be observed that the proposed model for speckle reduction is associated with higher values of CP and MSSIM in comparison to other schemes and is very close to unity indicating that the proposed scheme is well capable of preserving edges and structure of ultrasound images in addition to effective reduction of speckle noise which are essential requirements for medical images. The overall performance trend also remained same for several other ultrasound images. From, the results obtained it can be concluded that the proposed nonlinear PDE-based filter adapted to Rayleigh's speckle noise is a better and optimal choice among all the existing schemes for speckle reduction from ultrasound images.

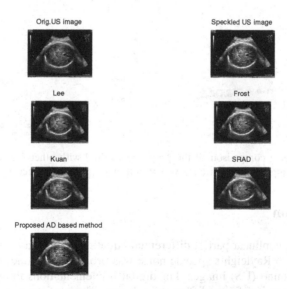

Fig. 1. Comparison of visual results of the proposed scheme with other schemes for the sample ultrasound image fetusbrain.jpg of size 225x300 for speckle variance 0.04

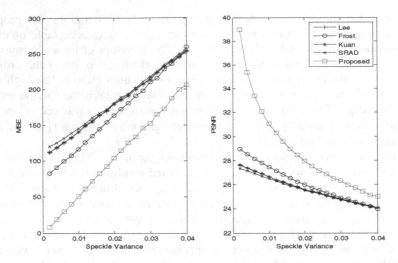

Fig. 2. Performance comparison of the proposed method with other methods for the sample image fetusbrain.jpg; Speckle variance Vs MSE (left) and Speckle variance Vs PSNR (Right)

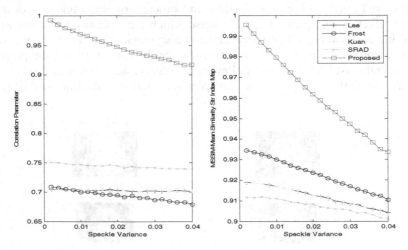

Fig. 3. Performance comparison of the proposed method with other methods for the sample image fetusbrain.jpg; Speckle variance Vs CP (left) and Speckle variance Vs MSSIM (Right)

4   Conclusion

In this paper, a nonlinear partial-differential equation (PDE) based speckle reduction model adapted to Rayleigh's speckle noise was proposed to reduce the speckle noise from 2D ultrasound (US) images. For digital implementations the proposed scheme was discretized using finite difference scheme. The performance of the proposed non-linear PDE based filter was evaluated in terms of mean square error (MSE), peak signal-to-noise ratio (PSNR), correlation parameter (CP) and mean structure similarity index map for several ultrasound images with varying amount of speckle noise variance. The results for one test case are shown in this paper. The proposed scheme was compared with other standard speckle reduction techniques such as Lee filter, Frost Filter, Kuan Filter and SRAD filter. From the obtained results it can be concluded that the proposed scheme is outperforming all other standard schemes and producing the optimal results. In addition to speckle reduction, the proposed scheme is also well capable of preserving the edges, fine structures and other radiometric information such as luminance and contrast of the restored image which are essential requirements for ultrasound images for correct interpretation of the image data.

References

1. Gonzalez, R.C., Wintz, P.: Digital Image Processing, 2nd edn. Academic Press, New York (1987)
2. Jain, A.K.: Fundamentals of Digital Image Processing. PHI, India (2005)
3. Johan, M.: Thijssen: Ultrasonic speckle formation, analysis and processing applied to tissue characterization. Pattern Recognition Letters 24, 659–675 (2003)
4. Lee, J.S.: Speckle Analysis and Smoothing of Synthetic Aperture Radar Images. Computer Graphics and Image Processing 17, 24–32 (1981)
5. Lee, J.S.: Digital Image Smoothing and the Sigma Filter. Computer Vision, Graphics and Image Processing 24, 255–269 (1983)
6. Frost, V.S., Stiles, J.A., Josephine, A., Shanmugan, K.S., Holtzman, J.C.: A Model for Radar Images and Its Application to Adaptive Digital Filtering of Multiplicative Noise. IEEE Transactions on Pattern Analysis and Machine Intelligence PAMI-4 (2), 157–166 (1982)
7. Lopes, A., Nezry, E., Touzi, R., Laur, H.: Maximum a Posteriori Speckle Filtering and First Order Texture Models in SAR Images. In: International Geoscience and Remote Sensing Symposium (IGARSS), Washingaton DC, USA (1990)
8. Donoho, D.L., Johnstone, I.M.: Ideal spatial adaptation via wavelet shrinkage. Biometrika 81, 425–455 (1994)
9. Perona, P., Malik, J.: Scale space and edge detection using anisotropic diffusion. IEEE Transactions on Pattern Analysis and Machine Intelligence 12, 629–639 (1990)
10. Rudin, L., Osher, S., Fatemi, E.: Non linear total variation based noise removal algorithms. Physica D 60, 259–268 (1992)
11. Beck, A., Teboulle, M.: Fast Gradient-Based Algorithms for Constrained Total Variation Image De-noising and Deblurring Problems. IEEE Transactions on Image Processing 18(11), 2419–2434 (2009)
12. Chen, Q., Montesinos, P., Sun, Q.S., Heng, P.A., De Xia, S.: Adaptive total variation denoising based on difference curvature. Image and Vision Computing (2009), doi:10.1016/j.imavis.2009.04.012
13. Giloba, G., Sochen, N., Zeevi, Y.Y.: Image enhancement and de-noising by complex diffusion processes. IEEE Transactions on Pattern Analysis and Machine Intelligence 25(8), 1020–1036 (2004)
14. You, Y.L., Kaveh, M.: Fourth – order partial differential equations for noise Removal. IEEE Transactions on Image Processing 9, 1723–1730 (2000)
15. Witkin, A.P.: Scale-space filtering. In: Proc: Int. Joint Conf. Artificial Intelligence, pp. 1019–1021 (1983)

16. Chambolle, A.: Partial Differential equations and image processing. In: Proc: IEEE Int. Conf. on Image Processing, Austin, TX (November 1994)
17. Caselles, V., Morel, J.M., Sapiro, G.: Introduction to the special issue on partial differential equations and geometry driven diffusions in image processing. IEEE Transactions on Image Processing 7(3), 269–273 (1998)
18. ter Harr Romeny, B. (ed.): Geometry driven diffusion in computer vision. Kluwer, Boston (1994)
19. Shi, J., Osher, S.: A nonlinear scale space method for a convex multiplicative model. SIAM Journal of Imaging Sciences 1(3), 294–321 (2008)
20. Yu, Y., Acton, S.T.: Speckle Reducing Anisotropic Diffusion. IEEE Transactions on Image Processing 11(11), 1260–1270 (2002)
21. Mateo, J.L., Fernández-Caballeró, A.: Finding out general tendencies in speckle noise reduction in ultrasound images. Expert Systems with Application 36, 7786–7797 (2009)
22. Kuan, D.T., Sawchuk, A.A.: Adaptive restoration of images with speckle. IEEE Trans. Acoustics, Speech and Signal Processing ASSP-35, 373–383 (1987)
23. Dewaele, P., Wambacq, P., Oosterlinck, A., Marchand, J.L.: Comparison of some speckle reduction techniques for SAR images. In: Proc: Geoscience and Remote Sensing Symposium, IGARSS 1990, pp. 2417–2422 (1990)
24. Press, W.H., Teukolsky, S.A., Vetterling, W.T., Flannery, B.P.: Numerical Recipes in C: The Art of Scientific Computing, 2nd edn. Cambridge University Press, USA (1992), ISBN 0-521-43108-5
25. Salinas, H.M., Fernandez, D.C.: Comparison of PDE-based nonlinear diffusion approaches for image enhancement and denoising in optical coherence tomography. IEEE Transactions on Medical Imaging 26(6), 761–771 (2007)
26. Wang, Z., Bovik, A.C., Sheikh, H.R., Simon-celli, E.P.: Image quality assessment- from error visibility to structural similarity. IEEE Transactions on Image Processing 13(4), 1–14 (2004)

Face Recognition Using Kernel Fisher Linear Discriminant Analysis and RBF Neural Network

S. Thakur[1], J.K. Sing[2,*], D.K. Basu[2,3] and M. Nasipuri[2]

[1] Department of Computer Science & Engineering, GCELT, Kolkata, India
[2] Department of Computer Science & Engineering, Jadavpur University, Kolkata, India
[3] AICTE Emeritus Fellow
jksing@ieee.org

Abstract. A new face recognition method is presented based on Kernel Fisher's Linear Discriminant Analysis (KFLDA) and Radial Basis Function Neural Network (RBFNN). First, the principal component analysis (PCA) technique is used to reduce the dimension of the facial image. Next, the reduced images are further processed by the KFLDA. Here, KFLDA is used for extraction of most discriminating features in appearance-based face recognition. KFLDA provides better generalizations taking higher order correlations into account rather than FLDA, which projects directions, based on second order statistics. RBFNN is used as a classifier, which classify the face images based on these extracted features. We have tested the potential of the proposed method on the ORL face database. The experimental results show that the proposed method provides higher recognition rates in comparison to some other existing methods.

Keywords: Face Recognition, PCA, FLD, KFLDA, RBFNN, ORL.

1 Introduction

Face recognition is one of the important areas in the field of pattern recognition, computer vision and artificial intelligence. It can be used in wide range of applications such as credit cards, passport, biometrics, law enforcement, identity authentication and surveillance. Surveys on face recognition may be found in [1]-[2]. The image data are always high dimensional in the face recognition area, and it require considerable amount of computing time for recognition. That's why the feature extraction is very important for improving classifier's accuracy and reducing the run time for classification. Principal component analysis (PCA) and Fisher's linear discriminant analysis (FLDA) are two powerful methods used for data reduction as well as feature extraction in appearance-based face recognition approaches. The PCA method is based on linearly projecting the image space into a low dimensional feature space for dimensionality reduction [3]. It yields projection directions that maximize the total scatter across all classes, i.e., across all images of all training images. Thus, PCA retains unwanted variations due to lighting and facial expression [4]. The FLDA technique projects the face images from high-dimensional image space to a relatively

---

* Corresponding author.

S. Ranka et al. (Eds.): IC3 2010, Part I, CCIS 94, pp. 13–20, 2010.

low-dimensional space linearly by maximizing the ratio of between-class scatter matrix to that of within-class scatter matrix [4]. A nonlinear version of the FLDA, called the kernel FLDA is proposed by Mika *et al.* [5] and Baudat *et al.* [6]. The results showed that KFLDA is able to extract the most discriminant features in the features space, which is equivalent to extracting the most discriminant nonlinear features in the original input space. The KFLDA method extracts the higher order statistics of samples as features and at the same time it also maximizes the class separation of different classes and compacted the same classes of patterns as possible when we project these features to a lower dimensional space.

In this paper, we propose a new method for face recognition using KFLDA and RBF neural networks (RBFNN). First, the face images are reduced by the PCA technique. Then, the face features are extracted by the KFLDA method. The RBF neural networks have been used due to its simple structure and faster learning ability. It has been seen that variations between the images of the same subject due to variation in pose, orientation, etc. are quite high. Therefore, to achieve high recognition rate, structural information of face images of the same subject is to be considered for classification process. This has been realized by identifying sub-clusters corresponding to a subject separately using a clustering algorithm. Then the prototypes of these sub-clusters are used to model the hidden layer neurons of the RBF neural networks. This process also improves its generalization capabilities.

2 Proposed Method

In our proposed method, at first the dimension of the facial images is reduced with the help of PCA technique. Then the features are extracted from these reduced images using the KFLDA technique. The KFLDA technique helps to extract the most discriminant features using higher order statistics. Finally, an RBF neural networks classifier is designed to classify the face images based on these extracted features. The schematic diagram of the proposed method is shown in Fig. 1.

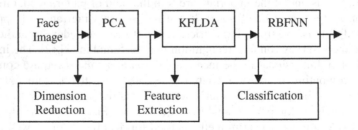

Fig. 1. Schematic diagram of the proposed method

3 Dimension Reduction Using PCA

Firstly, the dimension of the face images reduced using the PCA method. The PCA technique may be summarized as follows:

Let the training set of R images be $X = (X_1, X_2, ..., X_R) \subset \Re^{D \times R}$. Then the covariance matrix is defined as follows:

$$\Gamma = \frac{1}{R} \sum_{i=1}^{R} (X_i - \overline{X})(X_i - \overline{X})^T \tag{1}$$

$$= \Phi\Phi^T$$

where $\Phi = (\Phi_1, \Phi_2, ..., \Phi_R) \subset \Re^{D \times R}$ and $\overline{X} = \frac{1}{R} \sum_{i=1}^{R} X_i$, which is the mean image of the training set. The dimension of the covariance matrix Γ is $D \times D$. Then, the eigenvalues and eigenvectors are calculated from the covariance matrix Γ. Let $Q = (Q_1, Q_2, ..., Q_r) \subset \Re^{D \times R}$ ($r < R$) be the r eigenvectors corresponding to r largest eigenvalues. Each of the r eigenvectors is called an *eigenface*. Now, each of the face images of the training set X_i is projected into the eigenface space to obtain its corresponding eigenface based feature $Z_i \subset \Re^{r \times R}$, which is defined as follows:

$$Z_i = Q^T Y_i, \; i = 1, 2, ..., R \tag{2}$$

where Y_i is the mean-subtracted image of X_i.

4   Kernel Fisher Linear Discriminant Analysis (KFLDA)

The idea of KFLDA is to perform FLDA in an implicit feature space R^f constructed by the nonlinear mapping function $\phi : Z^i \in R^r \rightarrow \phi(Z^i) \in R^f$. In implementation, kernel tricks are applied in input space to perform inner product of two vectors in R^f with the following kernel function:

$$k(y, z) = \phi(y) \cdot \phi(z) \tag{3}$$

The between-class scatter matrix and within-class scatter matrix in R^f are defined as follows:

$$S_B^\phi = \sum_{i=1}^{c} (\mu_i^\phi - \mu^\phi)(\mu_i^\phi - \mu^\phi)^T \tag{4}$$

$$S_W^\phi = \sum_{i=1}^{c} \frac{1}{l_i} \sum_{j=1}^{l_i} (\phi(z_j) - \mu_i^\phi)(\phi(z_j) - \mu_i^\phi)^T \tag{5}$$

where μ^ϕ and μ_i^ϕ are the mean of all samples and mean of class i in R^f, respectively. l_i is the number of samples belonging to class i.

The Fisher's criteria in R^f is defined as follows:

$$F(\phi) = \frac{|w^T S_B^\phi w|}{|w^T S_W^\phi w|} \tag{6}$$

If the S_W^ϕ is a nonsingular matrix then this ratio is maximized when the column vectors of the projection matrix ϕ are the eigenvectors of $S_B^\phi \, S_W^{\phi \, -1}$. The optimal projection matrix ϕ_{opt} is defined as follows :

$$\phi_{opt} = \arg \max_w \; |S_B^\phi \, S_W^{\phi \, -1}|$$

(7)

$$= [q_1, q_2, ..., q_m]$$

where $\{q_i \mid i=1, 2, ..., m\}$ is the set of normalized eigenvectors of $S_B^\phi \, S_W^{\phi \, -1}$ corresponding to m largest eigenvalues $\{\lambda_i \mid i=1, 2, ..., m\}$.

Now, each of the reduced face images of the training set Z_i is projected into the lower-dimensional space spanned by the m normalized eigenvectors to obtain its corresponding KFLDA-based features F_i, which is defined as follows:

$$F_i = \phi_{opt}^T Z_i , \; i = 1,2,.........,R$$

(8)

In order to recognize the test images, features are extracted from each of the test images by reducing its dimension using the equation (2) and then applying the equation (8).

5 RBF Neural Networks

We have used RBF neural networks for classifying the images due to its simple structure and faster learning abilities in the same way as in [7]. In the face recognition problem, since the variations between the face images of a person, taken by varying pose, orientation, etc., are quite high, it is reasonable to find the sub-clusters from the feature space associated with each person. This process helps to acquire structural information more appropriately from the feature space spanned by the training set. The prototypes of these sub-clusters are modeled as the hidden layer neurons of the RBFNN. To realize the above process we have clustered the training images associated with each person separately. The clustering process is defined as follows:

1) Let there are R images of a person in the training set. We have to find K $(K < R)$ sub-clusters from the image space spanned by the R training images.
2) Initially, all the training images are assigned as R distinct clusters. Set $k = R$.
3) Compute inter-cluster distance d(i, j) by the following equation:

$$d(i, j) = \left\| C_i - C_j \right\|; i, j = 1,2,..., k$$
$$\scriptstyle i \neq j$$

(9)

where C_i and C_j are the ith and jth clusters. $\|\cdot\|$ is the Euclidean norm.

4) Find the two closest clusters C_i and C_j by the following equation:

$$d_{\min}(i, j) = \arg \min_{i,j} \{d(i, j)\}; i, j = 1,2,..., R, i \neq j$$

(10)

5) Find a new cluster by averaging the above two closest clusters and set $k = k-1$.
6) Repeat the steps 3 - 5 until $k = K$.
7) Repeat steps 1 - 6 for all the subjects in the training set separately.

The width of the Gaussian function (basis function) associated with each of the hidden layer neurons is estimated in such a way, that minimizes the overlapping between different classes and maximizes the generalization ability of the RBFNN. The weights of the links between hidden layer and output layer are estimated using least-mean-square (LMS) algorithm. The values for β and η are selected for which RBFNN provides best performance. In our experiments, we have found $\beta=2.0$ and $\eta=0.03$ after many experimental runs.

6   Experimental Results

The performance of the proposed method was carried out on the Cambridge ORL face database [4]. The ORL database contains 400 grayscale images of 40 persons. Each person has 10 images, each having a resolution of 112x92 and 256 gray levels. Images of the individuals have been taken varying light intensity, facial expressions (open/closed eyes, smiling/not smiling) and facial details (glasses/no glasses). All the images were taken against a dark homogeneous background, with tilt and rotation up to 20° and scale variation up to 10%. Sample face images of a person are shown in Fig. 1. To reduce the computational complexity, each image is down sampled into a size of 16x16.

The recognition rate is defined as the ratio of the total number of correct recognition by the method to the total number of images in the test set for a single experimental run. Therefore, the average recognition rate, R_{avg}, of the method is defined as follows:

$$R_{avg} = \frac{\sum_{i=1}^{p} n_{cls}^{i}}{p * n_{tot}} \tag{11}$$

where p is the number of experimental runs. The n_{cls}^{i} is the number of correct recognition in the ith run and n_{tot} is the total number of faces under test in each run.

Fig. 2. Sample images of a person from the ORL database

6.1   Randomly Partitioning the Database

In our first experiment, we have selected randomly s images per person from the database to form the *training set*. Remaining images are selected to form the corresponding *test set*. It should be noted that there is no overlap between the training and test images. In this way ten (p=10) different training and test sets has been generated for each value of s.

Table 1. Average recognition rates of the proposed methods by varying the number of features

No. of Features	Recognition Rate
25	97
35	97.5
45	97.5
55	97.5
65	98
75	98.5
85	98.5
95	99
105	99
115	**99.5**
125	99
135	99.5
145	99.5
155	99.5
165	99.5

Average recognition rates by varying number of features for s=5 are shown in Table 1. From the above Table 1 it may be noted that the best recognition rate (99.50%) is obtained when the number of features is 115. In the case of s=4, we have also considered 115 features. The average, maximum and minimum recognition rates for s=4 and 5 are shown in Table 2.

Table 2. Average recognition rates of the proposed methods by randomly partitioning the database

s	4	5
# training samples	160	200
R_{avg} (%)	**99.63**	**98.5**
Maximum (%)	100	100
Minimum (%)	96.88	95

We have compared the average recognition rates (%) of the proposed method with the FLDA-based methods reported in [9] and [10] on the ORL database. The comparisons are shown in Table 3. It can be seen from the table that the proposed method is superior to those reported in [9], [10] and [11]. In [11] the features considered were 150 while in our proposed method we comparatively considered less number of features.

Table 3. Comparison of the average recognition rates (%) of different FLDA-based approaches on the ORL database

s	4	5
DLDA [9]	91.77	94.55
2DFLD [9]	93.46	95.40
PCA+FLD [9]	89.42	90.98
LDA [10]	-	88.87
LDA+RBF [10]	-	94.00
FLDA [11]	96.75	97.80
Proposed Method	**99.63**	**98.5**

7 Conclusion

In this paper, we have presented a new method for face recognition based on KFLDA and an RBFNN classifier. The face images are reduced with the PCA, and then the facial features are extracted using the KFLDA. The average recognition rates we obtained with our proposed method are 99.63% and 99.50% in case of four and five samples per subject, respectively. The experimental results on the ORL database show that the proposed method achieves higher recognition rates in comparison with the other FLDA and KFLDA-based methods reported in the literature.

Acknowledgments. This work was partially supported by the CMATER and the SRUVM projects of the Department of Computer Science & Engineering, Jadavpur University, Kolkata, India. The author, S. Thakur would like to thank Government College of Engineering & Technology, Kolkata for providing computing facilities and allowing time for conducting research works. The author, D. K. Basu would also like to thank the AICTE for providing him the Emeritus Fellowship (F.No.: 1-51/RID/EF(13)/2007-08, dated 28-02-2008).

References

1. Zhao, W., Chellappa, R., Phillops, P.J., Rosenfeld, A.: Face recognition: A literature survey. ACM Computing Surveys 35, 399–458 (2003)
2. Tolba, A.S., El-Baz, A.H., El-Harby, A.A.: Face recognition: A literature review. Int'l Journal of Signal Processing 2, 88–103 (2006)
3. Turk, M., Pentland, A.: Eigenface for recognition. J. Cognitive Neuroscience 3, 71–86 (1991)
4. Belhumeur, P.N., Hespanha, J.P., Kriegman, D.J.: Eigenfaces versus fisherfaces recognition using class specific linear projection. J. IEEE Trans. Pattern Anal. Mach. Intell. 23, 711–720 (1997)
5. Mika, S., Ratsch, G., Weston, J.: Fisher discriminant analysis with kernels. In: Proc. Neural Networks Signal ProcessingWorkshop, pp. 41–48 (1999)

6. Baudat, G., Anouar, F.: Generalized discriminant analysis using a kernel approach. Neural Comput. 12(10), 2385–2404 (2000)
7. Thakur, S., Sing, J.K., Basu, D.K., Nasipuri, M.: Face recognition using Principal Component Analysis and RBF Neural Networks. In: ICETET, India, pp. 695–700 (2008)
8. ORL face database. AT&T Laboratories, Cambridge, U. K.
   http://www.uk.research.att.com/facedatabase.html
9. Xiong, H., Swamy, M.N.S., Ahmad, M.O.: Two-dimensional FLD for face recognition. J. Pattern Recognition 38, 1121–1124 (2005)
10. Pan, Y.Q., Liu, Y., Zheng, Y.W.: Face recognition using kernel PCA and hybrid flexible neural tree. In: International Conference on Wavelet Analysis and Pattern Recognition, China, pp. 1361–1366 (2007)
11. Thakur, S., Sing, J.K., Basu, D.K., Nasipuri, M.: Face recognition by integrating RBF neural networks and a distance measure. In: IC3IT, India, pp. 264–269 (2009)

Parallel Enumeration Sort on OTIS-Hypercube

Keny T. Lucas

Xavier Institute of Social Service,
Department of Information Management,
Dr. Camil Bulcke Path, Ranchi - 834001, Jharkhand, India
kenny.lucas@gmail.com
http://www.xiss.ac.in

Abstract. OTIS (optical transpose interconnection system), as a model of optoelectronic parallel computers, has gained tremendous popularity and is widely accepted among researchers. A rich literature on various parallel algorithms proposed for different OTIS models is available. In this paper, we propose a parallel algorithm for enumeration sort on N-processor OTIS-Hypercube architecture. The first algorithm Sort1 is for sparse enumeration sort of $\sqrt{N}$ data elements. Algorithm Sort2, the second algorithm, is for sorting N data elements on the same architecture. Here, the time complexity of the algorithms are analyzed by the number of data movements required on the electronic links and optical links. The data movements required through electronic link and that required through optical link are expressed as electronic moves and optical moves respectively. The first proposed algorithm, Sort1, requires $4\log \sqrt{N}$ electronic moves and 3 OTIS moves. Sort2, the second algorithm requires $\sqrt{N} + (N + 10\sqrt{N})\log \sqrt{N}$ electronic moves and $3\sqrt{N}$ OTIS moves.

Keywords: Parallel algorithm, OTIS-Hypercube, enumeration sort, time complexity.

1 Introduction

An electronic link is superior to optical link when the distance between processors is up to a few millimeters and the free space optics is better than electronic link for longer interconnects in terms of power, speed and bandwidth [9,14]. The limitations of electronic links in multiprocessor systems, motivated researchers to explore various alternatives for long interconnect distance. The OTIS model was suggested by [10,23,42] and has been extensively explored in the last few years. In this hybrid architecture, the processors are arranged in groups and it is assumed that the processors within a group are packaged in a single microchip. The processors in a microchip are connected through electronic links whereas the inter-chip links are established through the free space optics. The bandwidth is maximized and the power is minimized when the number of processors in each group equals the number of groups in the overall OTIS architecture [15]. Several studies have been reported in [12,18,19,20,21,22,23,28,30,31,38,39,40,41] for the case where the number of processors in each group equals the number of groups

S. Ranka et al. (Eds.): IC3 2010, Part I, CCIS 94, pp. 21–31, 2010.

in the respective OTIS models. However, a more general OTIS architecture has been reported in [4] where the number of groups does not equal the number of processors within each group. Here, the author has emphasized more on the ways to minimize the number of lenses required in OTIS architectures.

The interconnection pattern of each group in the architecture determines the nature of that OTIS model. There have been quite a number of models available such as OTIS-Ring, OTIS-Mesh, OTIS-mesh of trees, OTIS-Hypercube, OTIS-Torus, OTIS-Perfect shuffle, OTIS-Triangular array and OTIS-k-ary n-cube. The OTIS architecture has become increasingly popular in the recent years as it efficiently utilizes the benefits of optical and electronic link in its architecture. Many parallel algorithms for various problems such as image processing [38], matrix multiplication [39], basic operations [40], prefix computation [13,21], BPC permutation [30], randomized routing, selection and sorting [20,22,28], gossiping [18], polynomial interpolation and root finding [12], data rearrangement [37], construction of conflict graph [19] have been proposed on variety of OTIS architectures.

Sorting is one of the most studied problems in computer science for the following reasons: first, because it is used as a substep in many applications. second, it is a combinatorial problem with many interesting and diverse solutions. Sorting is also an important benchmark for parallel computers. Enumeration sort is a rank-based method. This method sorts the data elements by determining the rank (position) for each element in the sorted sequence. Sparse enumeration sort is a class of sorting, where the number of data elements to be sorted is much less than the network size. For a network of size p, the number of elements is typically $p^\in$, for $0 <\in< 1$. In this paper, we present two algorithms for enumeration sort. First algorithm is presented for $\in= \frac{1}{2}$ and the second one for $\in= 1$.

Several authors have studied sorting on various interconnection networks. Batcher's odd-even merge sort for N data elements was shown to run in $O(\log^2 N)$ time on a hypercube [11]. Randomized sorting algorithms on hypercubic networks were presented in $O(\log N)$ time [29]. Thompson and Kung [35], Schnorr and Shamir [32], Leighton [16] reported sorting algorithms for mesh like architectures all in $O(N)$ time. De et al. [8] proposed a sorting algorithm on Multi-Mesh network based on shear-sort requiring $58N^{1/4} + o(N^{1/4})$ time. Another algorithm on Multi-Mesh proposed by Sinha et al. [33] was shown to be an improvement over [8] by reducing the associated constant from 58 to 54. Many parallel algorithms have been developed on optoelectronics platform as well. The sorting algorithm [40] on OTIS-Mesh based on Leighton's column sort [17] was shown to run in $22\sqrt{N} + o(\sqrt{N})$ electronic moves $+ O(N^{3/8})$ OTIS moves for MIMD model. Rajasekaran ans Sahni [28] developed randomized sorting algorithm on OTIS-Mesh with $8\sqrt{N} + o(\sqrt{N})$ steps. Osterloh [27] proposed k-k sorting on the same model that performs in $8N^{1/2} + o(N^{1/3})$ time for for $k \leq 4$ and $kN^{1/2} + o(kN^{1/3})$ for $k \geq 4$.

various works have also been reported on sparse enumeration sort on various interconnection networks. Davila and Rajasekaran [5] developed sparse enumeration sorting of $d^\in$ keys, $0 <\in< 1$ in $\tilde{O}(\lceil\frac{d}{r}\rceil+\log r)$ time on POPS (d,r) network with $N = dr$ processors. Sinha et al. [34] reported an $O(\log^2 N)$ time algorithm on the OMULT network. Nassimi and Sahni [24] presented the sparse enumeration sorting of N elements on a hypercube with $N^{1+\frac{1}{k}}$ processors, $1 < k < \log N$ in $O(k\log N)$ time. An algorithm on OTIS-Ring has been presented in [22] with an AT cost of $O(N^{2.5})$ electronic move $+ O(N^2)$ OTIS moves. Similarly, sparse enumeration sort on OTIS-MOT with an AT cost of $O(N\log \sqrt{N})$ electronic moves $+ O(N)$ OTIS moves has been presented in [20].

This paper is organized as follows. The section 2 describes the architecture of the OTIS-Hypercube parallel computer. The proposed algorithms, Sort1 and Sort2 are discussed in Section 3. Finally conclusion is given in section 4.

2   Topology of OTIS-Hypercube

The hypercube architecture has been a popular interconnection network for multiprocessor systems. The iPSC/2 [26] and iPSC/860 [36] parallel machines are based on this Interconnection pattern. This is a special case of k-ary n-cube where $k = 2$. Various works on k-ary n-cube have been reported in [3,6,7]. An OTIS model is hybrid architecture consisting of both the electronic and optical

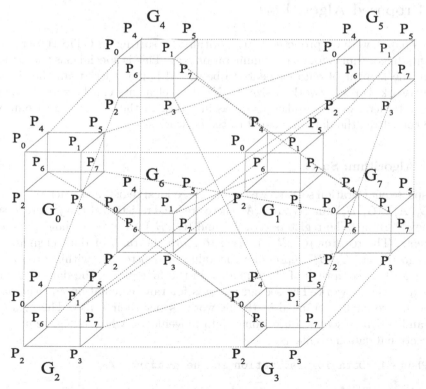

Fig. 1. Topology of $2^3 \times 2^3$-processor OTIS-Hypercube. The solid lines denote electronic links and the dotted lines represent optical links.

communication systems [10,23,42]. The processors in this architecture are divided into groups where the number of groups equals the number of processors within each group. All the processors within the group (binary hypercube) are connected through electronic link whereas the processors of different hypercubes are connected through free space optics as suggested in [42].

An OTIS-Hypercube, having $N(=2^d \times 2^d)$ processors, is organized into $\sqrt{N}(=2^d)$ binary hypercubes and each hypercube consists of $\sqrt{N}(=2^d)$ processors. The processors in each binary hypercube form a d-dimensional hypercube in which a ring can be easily embedded. Let (G_i, P_j) denote the jth processor within the jth group, where $1 \le i, j \le \sqrt{N}$. Each processor (G_i, P_j) is connected to all the adjacent processors within the group through bidirectional electronic links. The bidirectional optical links connect all pair of processors, (G_i, P_j) and (G_j, P_i), each from different group. The diameter of the N-processor OTIS-Hypercube computer is $2d + 1$. The algorithmic properties for OTIS-Hypercube have been developed in [31] and some algorithms have been reported in [25,31]. In analyzing our proposed algorithms, we count data moves along the electronic links as electronic moves and that on optical links as optical moves separately. The graph topology of a 2^3-processor OTIS-Hypercube is shown in Fig. 1.

3   Proposed Algorithms

In this paper, we have proposed two algorithms for sorting on OTIS-Hypercube. The first algorithm is for sparse enumeration sort. This is special class of sorting where the number of data elements to be sorted is much less than the size of the network. For a network of size N, $N^\in$ data elements can be sorted, where $0 <\in< 1$. Here, we have taken $\in= \frac{1}{2}$ as in [1,11]. In the second algorithm, we have considered the data size equal to the network size.

3.1   Algorithm: Sort1

For sparse enumeration sorting, we assume three local registers at each processor as (G_i, A_j), (G_i, B_j) and (G_i, R_j). All these are local resisters at the jth processor of the ith group. The registers (G_i, A_j) and (G_i, B_j) are used to hold the data elements. The register (G_i, R_j) is used to store the rank of data element. In the algorithms, (G_i, B_j) represents the value of register B_j within group G_i. The algorithm comprises of three phases. In the first phase, the data elements are fed to the network. The second phase is for rank calculation and the data elements are finally arranged in the network as per their ranks. The symbols '←' and '→' represent unidirectional data movements, whereas '↔' represents bidirectional data movements.

/* Phase 1: Data initialization in the network */

Data Initialization: The initial data is populated in the network as $(G_i, A_j) \leftarrow x_{i+j}$, where $0 \le i \le 2^d - 1$ and $j = 0$.

This is illustrated in Table 1.

```
/* Phase 2: Calculating ranks of all the data elements */
```

$\forall i, 0 \le i \le 2^d - 1$, Do in parallel
{
    $(G_i, B_j) := (G_i, A_j)$
    Broadcast (G_i, A_j) and (G_i, B_j) locally within the group
    $(G_i, B_j) \leftrightarrow (G_j, B_i)$
}
$\forall i, j, \ 0 \le i, j \le 2^d - 1$, Do in parallel
{
      If $(G_i, A_j) \ge (G_i, B_j)$ then
        $(G_i, R_j) := 1$
      Else
        $(G_i, R_j) := 0$
}
$\forall i, \ 0 \le i \le 2^d - 1$, Do in parallel
    Sum the values of all (G_i, R_j)'s, $0 \le j \le 2^d - 1$, and store
      the result in (G_i, R_0)

The contents of registers (G_i, A_j) and (G_i, B_j) are shown in Table 2.

```
/* Phase 3: Data rearrangement */
```

$\forall i, 0 \le i \le 2^d - 1$, Do in parallel
    Broadcast (G_i, A_0) and (G_i, R_0) locally within the group
$\forall i, j, \ 0 \le i, j \le 2^d - 1$, Do in parallel
{
      If $(G_i, R_j) \ne i + 1$, where $0 \le i, j \le 2^d - 1$, then do in parallel
      {
        $(G_i, R_j) \rightarrow (G_{(G_i, R_j)}, R_i)$ and broadcast locally within the group
        $(G_i, A_j) \rightarrow (G_{(G_i, R_j)}, A_i)$ and broadcast locally within the group
      }
}
$\forall i, j, \ 0 \le i, j \le 2^d - 1$, Do in parallel
{
      $(G_i, R_j) \leftrightarrow (G_j, R_i)$
      $(G_i, A_j) \leftrightarrow (G_j, A_i)$
}

Time complexity: Data initialization phase takes constant time. Phase 2 requires $2\log \sqrt{N}$ electronic moves and one OTIS move. Phase 3 needs $2\log \sqrt{N}$ electronic moves + two OTIS moves. Thus, the overall requirement of algorithm Sort1 is of $4\log \sqrt{N}$ electronic moves + three OTIS moves.

Table 1. Initial data in (G_i, A_j)

Group	Register	P_0	P_1	P_2	P_3	P_4	P_5	P_6	P_7
G_0	A	x_0	-	-	-	-	-	-	-
G_1	A	x_1	-	-	-	-	-	-	-
G_2	A	x_2	-	-	-	-	-	-	-
G_3	A	x_3	-	-	-	-	-	-	-
G_4	A	x_4	-	-	-	-	-	-	-
G_5	A	x_5	-	-	-	-	-	-	-
G_6	A	x_6	-	-	-	-	-	-	-
G_7	A	x_7	-	-	-	-	-	-	-

Table 2. The contents of (G_i, A_j) and (G_i, B_j) in phase 2

Group	Register	P_0	P_1	P_2	P_3	P_4	P_5	P_6	P_7
G_0	A	x_0	x_0	x_0	x_0	x_0	x_0	x_0	x_0
	B	x_0	x_1	x_2	x_3	x_4	x_5	x_6	x_7
G_1	A	x_1	x_1	x_1	x_1	x_1	x_1	x_1	x_1
	B	x_0	x_1	x_2	x_3	x_4	x_5	x_6	x_7
G_2	A	x_2	x_2	x_2	x_2	x_2	x_2	x_2	x_2
	B	x_0	x_1	x_2	x_3	x_4	x_5	x_6	x_7
G_3	A	x_3	x_3	x_3	x_3	x_3	x_3	x_3	x_3
	B	x_0	x_1	x_2	x_3	x_4	x_5	x_6	x_7
G_4	A	x_4	x_4	x_4	x_4	x_4	x_4	x_4	x_4
	B	x_0	x_1	x_2	x_3	x_4	x_5	x_6	x_7
G_5	A	x_5	x_5	x_5	x_5	x_5	x_5	x_5	x_5
	B	x_0	x_1	x_2	x_3	x_4	x_5	x_6	x_7
G_6	A	x_6	x_6	x_6	x_6	x_6	x_6	x_6	x_6
	B	x_0	x_1	x_2	x_3	x_4	x_5	x_6	x_7
G_7	A	x_7	x_7	x_7	x_7	x_7	x_7	x_7	x_7
	B	x_0	x_1	x_2	x_3	x_4	x_5	x_6	x_7

3.2   Algorithm 2: Sort2

In this case, we use five registers at each processor (G_i, A_j), (G_i, B_j), (G_i, C_j), (G_i, D_j) and (G_i, R_j). The registers (G_i, A_j), (G_i, B_j) and (G_i, C_j) are used to hold the data elements. The registers (G_i, D_j) and (G_i, R_j) are used to store the rank of data element. The algorithm comprises of three phases. In the first phase, the data elements are fed to the network. The second phase is for rank calculation and the data elements are finally arranged in the network as per their ranks.

```
/* Phase 1: Data initialization */
```

Data Initialization: The initial data is populated in the network as $(G_i, A_j) \leftarrow 2^d(i-1)+j$, where $1 \le i,j \le 2^d$. This is illustrated in Table 3.

Phase 2: /* Rank calculating */

Step 1: /* Intra-group rank calculation */
$\forall i, 0 \leq i \leq 2^d - 1$, Do in parallel
{
  For $j = 0$ to $2^d - 1$ do
     $(G_i, B_j) := (G_i, A_j)$
     Broadcast (G_i, B_j) locally within the group
     $\forall k$, where $0 \leq k \leq 2^d - 1$, Do in parallel
        If $(G_i, B_k) \geq (G_i, A_k)$ then
          $(G_i, R_k) := 1$
        Else
          $(G_i, R_k) := 0$
     Sum the values of all (G_i, R_k)'s, where $0 \leq k \leq 2^d - 1$
     and store the result in (G_i, R_j)
  End For
}

The result of broadcasting (G_i, B_0) is shown in Table 4.

Step 2: /* Inter-group rank calculation */

For $t = 1$ to $2^d - 1$ Do
  $\forall i, j,\ 0 \leq i, j \leq 2^d - 1$, Do in parallel
  {
      $(G_i, C_j) := (G_i, A_j)$
      Group move on (G_i, C_j) and (G_i, R_j)
  }
  For $j = 0$ to $2^d - 1$ do
     $\forall i,\ 0 \leq i \leq 2^d - 1$, Do in parallel
     {
        $(G_i, B_j) := (G_i, C_j)$
        Broadcast (G_i, B_j) locally within the group
     }
     $\forall i, k,\ 0 \leq i, k \leq 2^d - 1$, Do in parallel
     {
        If $(G_i, B_k) \geq (G_i, A_k)$ then
          $(G_i, D_k) := (G_i, D_k)$+1
     }
     $\forall i,\ 0 \leq k \leq 2^d - 1$, Do in parallel
        Sum the values of (G_i, D_k)'s and add to (G_i, R_j)
  End For
End For

The result after performing group move on (G_i, C_j) is shown
in Table 5.

Phase 3: /* Data rearrangement */

$\forall i, 0 \le i \le 2^d - 1$, Do in parallel
{
   For $j = 0$ to $2^d - 1$
      Broadcast (G_i, R_j) and (G_i, C_j) locally within the group
      If $(G_i, R_j) \ne 2^d i + j + 1$ then do in parallel
         $(G_i, R_j) \to (G_q, R_i)$, where $\lfloor \frac{(G_i, R_j)}{2^d} \rfloor + 1 = q$
         $(G_i, C_j) \to (G_q, C_i)$, where $\lfloor \frac{(G_i, R_j)}{2^d} \rfloor + 1 = q$
         move (G_q, R_i) to (G_q, R_l) where $(G_q, R_l) \bmod 2^d = l - 1$
         move (G_q, C_i) to (G_q, C_l) where $(G_q, R_l) \bmod 2^d = l - 1$
      End If
   End For
}

Table 3. Initial data in (G_i, A_j)

Group	Register	P_0	P_1	P_2	P_3	P_4	P_5	P_6	P_7
G_0	A	x_0	x_1	x_2	x_3	x_4	x_5	x_6	x_7
G_1	A	x_8	x_9	x_{10}	x_{11}	x_{12}	x_{13}	x_{14}	x_{15}
G_2	A	x_{16}	x_{17}	x_{18}	x_{19}	x_{20}	x_{21}	x_{22}	x_{23}
G_3	A	x_{24}	x_{25}	x_{26}	x_{27}	x_{28}	x_{29}	x_{30}	x_{31}
G_4	A	x_{32}	x_{33}	x_{34}	x_{35}	x_{36}	x_{37}	x_{38}	x_{39}
G_5	A	x_{40}	x_{41}	x_{42}	x_{43}	x_{44}	x_{45}	x_{46}	x_{47}
G_6	A	x_{48}	x_{49}	x_{50}	x_{51}	x_{52}	x_{53}	x_{54}	x_{55}
G_7	A	x_{56}	x_{57}	x_{58}	x_{59}	x_{60}	x_{61}	x_{62}	x_{63}

Table 4. The result after broadcasting (G_i, B_0)

Group	Register	P_0	P_1	P_2	P_3	P_4	P_5	P_6	P_7
G_0	A	x_0	x_1	x_2	x_3	x_4	x_5	x_6	x_7
	B	x_0	x_0	x_0	x_0	x_0	x_0	x_0	x_0
G_1	A	x_8	x_9	x_{10}	x_{11}	x_{12}	x_{13}	x_{14}	x_{15}
	B	x_8	x_8	x_8	x_8	x_8	x_8	x_8	x_8
G_2	A	x_{16}	x_{17}	x_{18}	x_{19}	x_{20}	x_{21}	x_{22}	x_{23}
	B	x_{16}	x_{16}	x_{16}	x_{16}	x_{16}	x_{16}	x_{16}	x_{16}
G_3	A	x_{24}	x_{25}	x_{26}	x_{27}	x_{28}	x_{29}	x_{30}	x_{31}
	B	x_{24}	x_{24}	x_{24}	x_{24}	x_{24}	x_{24}	x_{24}	x_{24}
G_4	A	x_{32}	x_{33}	x_{34}	x_{35}	x_{36}	x_{37}	x_{38}	x_{39}
	B	x_{32}	x_{32}	x_{32}	x_{32}	x_{32}	x_{32}	x_{32}	x_{32}
G_5	A	x_{40}	x_{41}	x_{42}	x_{43}	x_{44}	x_{45}	x_{46}	x_{47}
	B	x_{40}	x_{40}	x_{40}	x_{40}	x_{40}	x_{40}	x_{40}	x_{40}
G_6	A	x_{48}	x_{49}	x_{50}	x_{51}	x_{52}	x_{53}	x_{54}	x_{55}
	B	x_{48}	x_{48}	x_{48}	x_{48}	x_{48}	x_{48}	x_{48}	x_{48}
G_7	A	x_{56}	x_{57}	x_{58}	x_{59}	x_{60}	x_{61}	x_{62}	x_{63}
	B	x_{56}	x_{56}	x_{56}	x_{56}	x_{56}	x_{56}	x_{56}	x_{56}

Table 5. After performing group move on (G_i, C_j)

Group	Register	P_0	P_1	P_2	P_3	P_4	P_5	P_6	P_7
G_0	A	x_0	x_1	x_2	x_3	x_4	x_5	x_6	x_7
G_0	C	x_{32}	x_{33}	x_{34}	x_{35}	x_{36}	x_{37}	x_{38}	x_{39}
G_1	A	x_8	x_9	x_{10}	x_{11}	x_{12}	x_{13}	x_{14}	x_{15}
G_1	C	x_0	x_1	x_2	x_3	x_4	x_5	x_6	x_7
G_2	A	x_{16}	x_{17}	x_{18}	x_{19}	x_{20}	x_{21}	x_{22}	x_{23}
G_2	C	x_{24}	x_{25}	x_{26}	x_{27}	x_{28}	x_{29}	x_{30}	x_{31}
G_3	A	x_{24}	x_{25}	x_{26}	x_{27}	x_{28}	x_{29}	x_{30}	x_{31}
G_3	C	x_8	x_9	x_{10}	x_{11}	x_{12}	x_{13}	x_{14}	x_{15}
G_4	A	x_{32}	x_{33}	x_{34}	x_{35}	x_{36}	x_{37}	x_{38}	x_{39}
G_4	C	x_{40}	x_{41}	x_{42}	x_{43}	x_{44}	x_{45}	x_{46}	x_{47}
G_5	A	x_{40}	x_{41}	x_{42}	x_{43}	x_{44}	x_{45}	x_{46}	x_{47}
G_5	C	x_{56}	x_{57}	x_{58}	x_{59}	x_{60}	x_{61}	x_{62}	x_{63}
G_6	A	x_{48}	x_{49}	x_{50}	x_{51}	x_{52}	x_{53}	x_{54}	x_{55}
G_6	C	x_{16}	x_{17}	x_{18}	x_{19}	x_{20}	x_{21}	x_{22}	x_{23}
G_7	A	x_{56}	x_{57}	x_{58}	x_{59}	x_{60}	x_{61}	x_{62}	x_{63}
G_7	C	x_{48}	x_{49}	x_{50}	x_{51}	x_{52}	x_{53}	x_{54}	x_{55}

Time complexity: Data initialization phase requires constant time. Step 1 of phase 2 requires $2\sqrt{N}(\log \sqrt{N})$ electronic moves. Step 2 of phase 2 requires $2\sqrt{N}$ OTIS moves $+ \sqrt{N} + (N+3\sqrt{N})\log \sqrt{N}$ electronic move. Phase 3 requires $2\sqrt{N}\log \sqrt{N}$ electronic moves $+ \sqrt{N}$ OTIS moves. Thus the overall communication requirement for the proposed algorithm Sort2 is $\sqrt{N} + (N + 10\sqrt{N})\log \sqrt{N}$ electronic moves $+ 3\sqrt{N}$ OTIS moves.

4   Conclusion

In this paper, we have proposed parallel algorithms for enumeration sort on OTIS-Hypercube model. The first algorithm 1 (Sort1), proposed for sparse enumeration sort, needs $4\log \sqrt{N}$ electronic moves $+$ three OTIS moves. Hence, the AT cost of the first algorithm is $O(N\log \sqrt{N})$ electronic moves $+ O(N)$ OTIS moves. This algorithm has the same AT cost as that presented in [20]. The algorithm 2 (Sort2) requires $\sqrt{N} + (N + 10\sqrt{N})\log \sqrt{N}$ electronic moves $+ 3\sqrt{N}$ OTIS moves. Thus, the AT cost of Algorithm 2 is $O(N^2\log \sqrt{N})$ electronic moves $+ O(N\sqrt{N})$ OTIS moves. The second algorithm has better AT cost compared to that presented in [22].

References

1. Akl, S.G.: Parallel Sorting Algorithms. Academic Press, Orlando (1985)
2. Batcher, K.: Sorting networks and their applications. In: AFIPS Spring Joint Computing Conference (1968)
3. Bose, B., Broeg, B., Kwon, Y., Ashir, Y.: Lee Distance and Topological Properties of k-ary n-cubes. IEEE Trans. Comput. 44, 1021–1030 (1995)

4. Cosnard, M., Fraigniaud, P.: Finding the Roots of a Polynomial on an MIMD Multicomputer. Parallel Comput. 15, 75–85 (1990)
5. Davila, J., Rajasekaran, S.: Randomized Sorting on the POPS network. Intl. J. Found. Comp. Sci. 16, 105–116 (2005)
6. Day, K.: Topological Properties of OTIS-Networks. IEEE Trans. Paral. Distr. Syst. 13, 359–366 (2002)
7. Day, K.: Optical Transpose k-ary n-cube networks. J. Syst. Arch. 5, 697–705 (2004)
8. De, M., Das, D., Ghosh, M., Sinha, B.P.: An efficient sorting algorithm on multi-mesh network. IEEE Trans. Comput. 46, 1132–1137 (1997)
9. Feldman, M., Esener, S., Guest, C., Lee, S.: Comparison between Electrical and Free Space Optical Interconnects based on Power and Speed Consideration. Appl. Optic. 27, 1742–1751 (1988)
10. Hendrick, W., Kibar, O., Marchand, P., Fan, C., Blerkom, D.V., McCormick, F., Cogkor, I., Hansen, M., Esener, S.: Modeling and Optimization of the Optical Transpose Interconnection System. Optoelectronic Technology Center (1995)
11. Horowitz, E., Sahni, S., Rajasekaran, S.: Fundamentals of Computer Algorithms. Galgotia Publications Pvt. Ltd., New Delhi (2002)
12. Jana, P.K.: Polynomial Interpolation and Polynomial Root Finding on OTIS-Mesh. Parall. Comput. 32, 301–312 (2006)
13. Jana, P.K., Sinha, B.P.: An Improved Parallel Prefix Algorithm on OTIS-Mesh. Parall. Proc. Lett. 16, 429–440 (2006)
14. Kaimilev, F., Marchand, P., Krishnamoorthy, A., Esener, S., Lee, S.: Performance Comparison between Optoelectronic and VLSI Multistage Interconnection Networks. J. Light. Tech. 9, 1674–1692 (1991)
15. Krishnamoorthy, A., Marchand, P., Kiamilev, F., Esener, S.: Grain-size Considerations for Optoelectronic Multistage Interconnection Networks. Appl. Optic. 31, 5480–5507 (1992)
16. Leighton, F.T.: Tight bounds on the complexity of parallel sorting. IEEE Trans. Comput. 34, 344–354 (1995)
17. Leighton, F.T.: Introduction to Parallel Algorithms and Architectures: Array, Trees and Hypercubes. Morgan Kaufman, San Mateo (1992)
18. Lucas, K.T.: The gossiping on OTIS-Hypercube Optoelectronic Parallel Computer. In: International Conference on Parallel and Distributed Techniques and Applications, pp. 185–189. CSREA Press, Nevada (2007)
19. Lucas, K.T., Mallick, D.K., Jana, P.K.: Parallel Algorithm for the Conflict Graph on OTIS-Triangular Array. In: Rao, S., Chatterjee, M., Jayanti, P., Murthy, C.S.R., Saha, S.K. (eds.) ICDCN 2008. LNCS, vol. 4904, pp. 274–279. Springer, Heidelberg (2008)
20. Lucas, K.T., Jana, P.K.: An Efficient Parallel Sorting Algorithm on OTIS-Mesh of Trees. In: IEEE International Advance Computing Conference, India, pp. 175–180 (2009)
21. Lucas, K.T.: Parallel Algorithm for Prefix Computation on OTIS k-ary n-Cube Parallel Computer. Intl. J. Recen. Trend. in Eng. 1, 560–562 (2009)
22. Lucas, K.T.: Parallel algorithm for sorting on OTIS-ring Multicomputer. In: The 2nd Annual Compute Conference, pp. 1–5. ACM, New York (2009)
23. Marsden, G.C., Marchand, P., Harvey, P., Esener, S.: Optical Transpose Interconnection System Architectures. Optic. Lett. 18, 1083–1085 (1993)
24. Nassimi, D., Sahni, S.: Parallel permutation and sorting algorithms and a new generalized connection network. J. ACM 29, 642–667 (1982)
25. Nassimi, D., Sahni, S.: Optimal BPC Permutations on a Cube Connected Computer. IEEE Trans. Comput. 34, 338–341 (1982)

26. Nugent, S.F.: The iPSC/2 Direct-connect Communication Technology. In: 3rd International Conference on Hypercube Concurrent Computers and Applications, pp. 51–60 (1988)
27. Osterloh, A.: Sorting on OTIS-Mesh. In: IPDPS (2000)
28. Rajasekaran, S., Sahni, S.: Randomized Routing, Selection and Sorting on the OTIS-Mesh. IEEE Trans. Parall. Distr. Syst. 9, 833–840 (1998)
29. Reif, J., Valiant, L.: A Logarithmic Time Sort for Linear Size Networks. J. ACM. 34, 60–76 (1987)
30. Sahni, S., Wang, C.-F.: BPC Permutation on the OTIS-Mesh Optoelectronic Computer. In: 4th International Conference on Massively Parallel Processing using Optical Interconnections, pp. 130–135 (1997)
31. Sahni, S., Wang, C.-F.: BPC Permutation on the OTIS-Hypercube Optoelectronic Computer. Informat. 22, 263–269 (1998)
32. Schnorr, C.P., Shamir, A.: An Optimal Sorting Algorithm for Mesh Connected Computers. In: 18th ACM STOC (1986)
33. Sinha, B.P., Mukherjee, A.: Parallel Sorting Algorithm using Multiway Merge and its Implementation on a Multimesh Network. J. Parall. Distr. Comput. 60, 891–907 (2000)
34. Sinha, B.P., Bandyopadhyay, S.: OMULT:An Optical Interconnection System for Parallel Computing. In: ICCDC (2004)
35. Thompson, C.D., Kung, H.T.: Sorting on a Mesh-connected Parallel Computer. Comm. ACM 20, 263–271 (1977)
36. Vanvoorst, B., Seidel, S., Barsez, E.: Workload of an iPSC/860. In: Scalable High-Performance Computing Conference, pp. 1–31 (1994)
37. Wang, C.-F.: Algorithms for the OTIS optoelectronic computer, Ph.D. Thesis, Department of Computer Science, University of Florida (1998)
38. Wang, C.-F., Sahni, S.: Image Processing on the OTIS-Mesh Optoelectronic Computer. IEEE Trans. Parall. Distr. Syst. 11, 97–109 (2000)
39. Wang, C.-F., Sahni, S.: Matrix Multiplication on the OTIS-Mesh Optoelectronic Computer. IEEE Trans. Comput. 50, 635–646 (2001)
40. Wang, C.-F., Sahni, S.: Basic Operations on the OTIS-Mesh Optoelectronic Computer. IEEE Trans. Parall. Distr. Syst. 9, 1226–1236 (1998)
41. Wang, C.-F., Sahni, S.: OTIS Optoelectronic Computers. In: Li, K., Pan, Y., Zhang, S.Q. (eds.) Parallel Computation Using Optical Interconnections, pp. 99–116. Kluwer Academic, Dordrecht (1998)
42. Zane, F., Marchend, P., Paturi, R., Esener, S.: Scalable Network Architecture using the Optical Transpose Interconnection System (OTIS). In: 2nd International Conference on Massively Parallel Processing using Optical Interconnections (MPPOI 1996), San Antonio, Texas, pp. 114–121 (1996)

A Robust Trust Mechanism Algorithm for Secure Power Aware AODV Routing in Mobile Ad Hoc Networks

Naga Sathish Gidijala, Sanketh Datla, and R.C. Joshi

Department of Electronics and Computers Engineering,
Indian Institue of Technology Roorkee,
Roorkee, India
nagasathish007@gmail.com,
{sankipec,rcjosfec}@iitr.ernet.in

Abstract. MANET refers to a network formed by a group of wireless mobile nodes that can communicate with each other and also mobile at the same time. MANET is an infrastructure-less network in which all the mobile nodes cooperate with each other in routing packets from source node to the destination nodes, in accordance with some routing protocol. The main goal of this paper is to provide secure energy efficient routing protocol for mobile ad hoc networks, since the critical limiting factors for a mobile node is its operation time, restricted by battery capacity and trusted third party, the absence of which may result in nodes deviating from the routing protocol for selfish or malicious reasons. This paper addresses both these problems in MANETs by proposing a new robust trust mechanism against route misbehavior attacks over energy efficient AODV routing. The performance of the proposed methodology has been studied on simulated environment using JiST-SWANS with ad hoc network comprising of route misbehavior attacks.

Keywords: MANET, AODV, DSR, Blackhole, Multi-hop.

1 Introduction

A Mobile Ad hoc NETwork (MANET) is a collection of wireless mobile nodes which may form a temporary network, without the use of any fixed infrastructure or centralized administration [1]. Nodes rely on multi-hop routing protocols to forward data packets sent from a source node to a destination node which is out of its transmission range. Every node may function as both a data source and a router that forward data for other nodes. A lot of routing protocols have been proposed in the literature [2], including proactive, reactive, and hybrid solutions. Broch et al. [3] gives a simulation study of MANET routing protocols on different mobility and traffic scenarios. Djenouri et al. [4] have shown that reactive protocols are more adaptable to MANET environments than proactive protocols. Ad hoc On Demand Distance Vector (AODV) [5] is one of the reactive routing protocol which is largely adopted.

Security is an essential service for wired and wireless network communications [6]. Moreover, the components of MANETs are mostly battery operated devices. The

S. Ranka et al. (Eds.): IC3 2010, Part I, CCIS 94, pp. 32–41, 2010.
© Springer-Verlag Berlin Heidelberg 2010

battery lifetime is one of the central issues. As each node acts as both host and router of packets, the battery of the host runs down very quickly if high traffic is routed through it, leading to non functioning of the node and hence the broken link in the network. As the Battery Lifetime cannot be significantly improved, there is a need for designing energy-efficient software and hardware which minimizes the battery usage. Our proposed secure power aware trust Mechanism addresses both these problems in the world of Mobile Ad hoc Networks effectively and efficiently.

2 Related Work

The first secure routing based on Trust Management in MANETs is targeted at various malicious packet forwarding attacks [8]. This is an extension of DSR algorithm for Routing. Paul et al.[9] built a reputation based Trust Model targeting packet modification and masquerading attacks. This is also an extension of DSR routing algorithm; however, No experimental results have been showed [10]. Trust against False recommendation attacks and Newcomer attacks have been discussed in detail by Sun et al[11]. The methodology used is the direct observation on packet dropping rate at malicious nodes in the network and the trust model proposed is a Probability based trust model. However authors suggest that higher mobility of the nodes can lead to higher false alarm rates when the detection rate is fixed with this approach.

Golbeck [12] discusses the three main properties of trust in the context of a social network perspective: transitivity, asymmetry, and personalization. First, trust is not perfectly transitive in a mathematical sense. That is, if A trusts B, and B trusts C, it does not guarantee that A trusts C. Second, trust is not necessarily symmetric, meaning not identical in both directions. Third, trust is inherently a personal opinion. Two people often evaluate trustworthiness about the same entity differently. Jiang and Baras [13] proposed a trust distribution scheme called ABED (Ant-Based trust Evidence Distribution) based on the *swarm intelligence paradigm*, which is claimed to be highly distributed and adaptive to mobility. The key principle is called *stigmergy*, indirect communication through the environment. However, no specific attacks were considered in [13].

Although a lot of research has been done in the area of routing for MANETs, the available routing mechanisms are not sufficient in the following aspects: From the application point of view, the performance is still far from what is achieved in fixed networks [15]. From the algorithmic point of view, they require information about the context of the single network node within routing algorithms [16]. Furthermore, routing protocols should consider energy constraints, security constraint (e.g. don't route through an insecure area) and in some applications, real-time constraints (delivery in time).

3 Routing Attack Models

The default AODV protocol without any improvisations considers that all the nodes in the network work properly and assumes the absence of any malicious or selfish nodes. However, if there are any malicious or selfish nodes in the network, the standard AODV does not cope up with the anomalous behavior of the network. In order to test the behavior of the network in the presence of malicious nodes and to observe how

the trust model reduces the effect of these malicious nodes, two types of Route Misbehavior attacks namely Blackhole and Greyhole Attacks have been chosen. There are
several possible mechanisms [17] to implement these attacks within AODV, and we
use the following definitions.

In Blackhole Attack, we consider two varieties of attacks namely Blackhole-
OnRoute and Blackhole-FakeDest Attacks. Blackhole-OnRoute Attack operates by
replying to every RREQ that it receives, claiming that it has the fresh enough route to
the Destination, regardless of whether it actually knows a route. A Blackhole-
OnRoute node claims to have an existing fresh route to the destination and so the generated RREP has the same sequence number as the RREQ, causing it to be accepted
by the original sender, which subsequently creates a route with the blackhole as an
intermediate node. From the results shown, one can easily deduce the fact that Blackhole-OnRoute effects the network performance considerably. However, Blackhole-
FakeDest Attack is more malicious than Blackhole-OnRoute, since in addition to
claiming that it has the most recent route,it also increases the sequence number in the
RREP which prevents the Malicious route formed to be overwritten by the original
route.

A greyhole can be viewed as a faulty node, rather than explicitly malicious. Grey-
holes do not falsify route replies, but instead will periodically drop packets. This
might be due to a fault or due to malicious intentions. Regardless of the reason, grey-
holes appear as intermittently faulty nodes to the rest of the network.

4 Energy Consumption Model

Every node in network periodically calculates its energy consumed because of Transmission and Reception of Packets. For this purpose, a simple energy consumption
model[18] has been chosen to evaluate the performance of trust mechanism on power
aware AODV protocol. Energy consumption of a node after time t is calculated as

$$E_{cons}(t) = x*N_t + y*N_r \qquad (1)$$

Where,

$E_{cons}(t)$ is the energy consumed by node at time t

N_t is the number of packets Transmitted by node after time t

N_r is the number of packets Received by node after time t

x and y are constants such that $0 \leq x, y \leq 1$

The Total energy consumed is calculated independently [18] by taking into account
the amount of energy spent on Transmission or Reception of packets as follows

In Transmission mode, the power consumed for transmitting a packet is given by
the Eq (2)

$$\text{Consumed energy} = P_t * T \qquad (2)$$

Where P_t is the transmitting power and T is transmission time.

In Reception mode, the power consumed for receiving a packet is given by Eq (3)

$$\text{Consumed energy} = P_r * T \qquad (3)$$

Where P_r is the reception power and T is the reception time.

The value T can be calculated as

$$T= \text{Data size} / \text{Data rate} \qquad (4)$$

Hence, the remaining energy of each node can be calculated using Eq (2) or Eq(3)

$$\text{Rem energy } E_{rem} = \text{Current energy} - \text{Consumed energy} \qquad (5)$$

Initially all the nodes are assigned with the maximum battery capacity. With each packet reception and transmission, the battery energy associated with the node decreases. If the residual energy associated with the node falls below the threshold value, the node stops functioning there by opting itself out of the routing process.

5 Proposed Methodology

Trustworthiness of the nodes in the network has been calculated using the method of Passive Acknowledgement. Using Passive Acknowledgement, we make sure that the network works in promiscuous mode in order to monitor the channel [19]. The packets which are forwarded for the neighboring node will be observed if they are indeed forwarded by the node or not, irrespective of their actual destination in this mode. In computing, **promiscuous mode** or *promisc mode* is a configuration of a network card that makes the card pass all traffic it receives to the kernel rather than just frames addressed to it — a feature normally used for packet sniffing, and bridged networking for hardware virtualization. Each frame includes the hardware (Media Access Control) address. When a network card receives a frame, it normally drops it unless the frame is addressed to that card. In promiscuous mode, however, the card allows all frames through, thus allowing the computer to read frame intended for other machines or network devices [20].

Many operating systems require superuser privileges to enable promiscuous mode. A non-routing node in promiscuous mode can generally only monitor traffic to and from other nodes within the same collision domain (for Ethernet and Wireless LAN) or ring (for Token ring or FDDI). Computers attached to the same network hub satisfy this requirement, which is why network switches are used to combat malicious use of promiscuous mode. A router may monitor all traffic that it routes. Promiscuous mode is often used to diagnose network connectivity issues. There are programs that make use of this feature to show the user all the data being transferred over the network. Some protocols like FTP and Telnet transfer data and passwords in clear text, without encryption, and network scanners can see this data. Therefore, computer users are encouraged to stay away from insecure protocols like telnet and use more secure ones such as SSH. Promiscuous mode is also used by transparent network bridges in order to capture all traffic that needs to pass the bridge so that it can be retransmitted on the other side of the bridge.

For evaluating trust over power aware AODV protocol we take a data structure called GetTrust with the Fields of TrustPres, TrustThres, TrustLowest which will be maintained by all the nodes for each of their neighboring nodes. To detect whether a packet is successfully forwarded, the packets that have been recently sent for forwarding are stored in the packetBuff. This is a circular buffer, meaning that if packets are not removed frequently enough the buffer will cycle, erasing the oldest elements.

Thus, if a node is dropping packets or is being unacceptably slow at forwarding packets then the buffer will cycle. Initially, TrustPres for each node will be initiated to 0. If the node is detected to forward packets, TrustPres is incremented. If it is not forwarding or unacceptably slow, TrustPres value is Decremented. We calculate the Residual Energy of each node E_{res} using the previous theory. Now at each Intermediate Node, we first check for the TrustPres value of that node to be higher than the TrustThres. If so, it means that the node is trusted and can be used for forwarding packets. Then we check whether the Residual Energy of the neighboring node is higher than the Energy Threshold. If both these conditions are met, then only the RREQ is forwarded to the next neighboring node by updating TrustLowest and EnergyLowest Variables, else it is discarded as the node does not have enough energy reserves to forward the packets.

At the destination, a timer is started when the first RREQ is received. After receiving all the RREQ till the timer expires, TrustLowest and EnergyLowest values in each RREQ are checked against the Thresholds. If both are above the respective thresholds, their average is calculated and stored in DecisionAvg of that RREQ. If any of the Thresholds is not satisfied, the RREQ is discarded. The Highest of these DecisionAvg values is chosen to be the desired route among the available routes and the RREP will be sent with the route as the Obtained route in RREQ with highest DecisionAvg. When receiving a RREP the first hop node is checked and if it is untrusted then the reply is disregarded. Thus, only routes where the first hop is trusted are established.

The selection of route is made as shown in Figure 1 by taking each of the features into consideration. The number of hops between source node and destination node, the residual energy of the route and the amount of trust in the route are the three important factors taken into account while making a routing decision as shown. In the figure, the route S-F-B-H-C-D is the most efficient route off all available ones and will be chosen for routing data packets according to the proposed methodology.

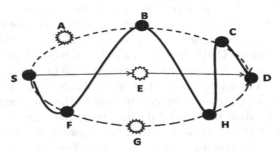

S->Source Node, D -> Destination Node
E,G -> Low Energy Nodes , A-> Blackhole Node

S-E-D Shortest Route but not Energy Efficient
S-A-B-C-D Non Trustable
S-F-G-H-D Non Energy Efficient
S-F-B-H-C-D Efficient and Trustable Route

Fig. 1. Selection of Shortest, Most Trustable and Energy Efficient Route out of available routes

Various steps involved in the total work carried out has been listed out in the following flow chart.

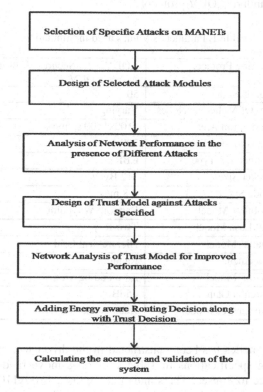

Fig. 2. Flow Chart showing the overall work done in the Implementation

6 Simulation Setup and Implementation Details

To evaluate the performance of Power-Aware Trusted AODV in the presence of route misbehavior attacks, a Java based network simulator namely JiST-SWANS is used. JIST is a high-performance discrete event simulation engine that runs over a standard Java virtual machine. SWANS is a scalable wireless network simulator built atop the JiST platform. It was created primarily because existing network simulation tools are not sufficient for current research needs, and its performance serves as a validation of the virtual machine-based approach to simulator construction. SWANS is organized as independent software components that can be composed to form complete wireless network or sensor network configurations. Its capabilities are similar to ns2 and Glo-MoSim, but is able to simulate much larger networks. SWANS leverages the JiST design to achieve high simulation throughput, save memory, and run standard Java network applications over simulated networks. In addition, SWANS implements a data structure, called hierarchical binning, for efficient computation of signal propagation. The conventional code of AODV implemented in JiST has been modified in accordance with the attack models explained. Hence a new AODV for each of the three attacks have been designed. A new power-aware Trusted AODV is developed in order to test the performance of network in the presence of attacks. Malicious nodes in the network follow any one of the attack models designed and the remaining fair nodes follow the standard AODV protocol.

Table 1. Parameters Values used in Simulation

Routing Protocol	AODV / Secure Power Aware AODV
No. of Nodes	50
No. Of Malicious Nodes	Varying
Simulation Area	1100x1100 sq.mtrs
Transmission Range	200m
Connection Type	CBR
Packet Size	512 Bytes
Node Speed	2-8 m/sec
Mobility Model	Random Waypoint
PathLoss Model	Two-Ray
Spatial Model	Hierarchical Grid
Placement	Random
Fading Model	Zero Fading Model
Antenna Gain	15dB
Interference Model	RadioNoiseAdditive

A network of 50 nodes has been constructed in the driver to test the Attacks with the field possessing specifications in Table 1. Nodes move randomly with speeds varying from 2m/sec to 8m/sec. The simulation area is a 1100x1100 sq. meters with nodes randomly distributed all throughout the area. RadioNoiseAdditive model includes a cumulative SNR computation (noise accumulates, as opposite to independent noise of RadioNoiseIndep), preamble and PLCP header capture, and frame body capture. RadioNoiseAdditive model is equivalent to the so called "Physical model" of successful reception of a transmission.

According to the RadioNoiseAdditive model in SWANS, when signal A arrives, its power is compared with the cumulative noise level sensed by this node's radio and with a receive threshold. If A's signal strength is above the cumulative noise level by SNR threshold (the signal-to-noise ratio between A and the cumulative noise is above some predefined threshold) and it is above the receive threshold, the radio locks on A and starts receiving it. If the radio is unable to lock on A (the signal is too weak or the noise is too strong), the power level of A is added to the cumulative noise at this node. This setup matches a scenario of an open air, in which there are no obstacles from which the signal can reflect off and fade. The number of malicious nodes is varied in the case of each of the attacks and the packets sent by the source node and those received by the destination are noted down.

Various bugs present in the JiST SWANS free distribution software, have been fixed in order to improve the existing functionality of the simulator.

Inorder to implement Black Hole On Route Attack, AODV has been modified such that the routeToDestExits() and hasFreshRoute() methods always return TRUE irrespective of the route table entries for the required destination, so that the node pretends as if it has the fresh route to the Destination with hop count equal to 1. Hence the node will send the route reply to the source indicating a Fresh Route in the RREP message and drops forwarding the received RREQ packets. For GreyHole Attack, the node Burst Faults for a specific amount of time which is chosen randomly after running out of some specified time which will also be chosen randomly between 0 and MAX_TIME_TO_BURST_FAULT.

7 Results and Analysis

The Packet Throughput of the network has been considered to evaluate the effect of discussed attack models on AODV. Packet Throughput can be defined as the ratio of packets received by the destination to the number of packets sent (%)

These metrics have been observed using standard AODV for each attack type under various proportions of malicious nodes. Later Trusted Power Aware AODV has been

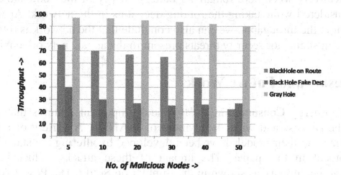

Fig. 3. Throughput comparison with varying number of malicious nodes following specified attacks on AODV

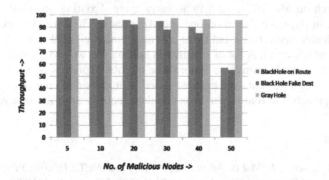

Fig. 4. Throughput comparison with varying number of malicious nodes following specified attacks on Secure Trusted Power Aware AODV

used on the same network for comparison. As shown in Figure 3, as the number of malicious nodes is increased each attack type reduces throughput of the network in standared AODV. A small number of blackhole nodes dramatically reduces throughput, the effect stabilizes for moderate numbers, and for Blackhole-OnRoute falls of for high numbers (Blackhole-FakeDest does not fall off further since throughput has already fallen significantly). The Greyhole attack results in a fairly linear throughput reduction as the number of malicious nodes increases.

As predicted, Blackhole-FakeDest has the most effect. For AODV, increasing the number of Blackhole-FakeDes nodes very soon reduces throughput while a similar number of Blackhole-OnRoute nodes gives better throughput. This clearly indicates the fact that the Blackhole-FakeDest is the one which affects the network the most as it fakes to has the Fresh Route to the Destination everytime it receives the RREQ messages from its neighbours. In Figure 3, the same network with specified attacks has been executed over Secure Trusted Power Aware AODV protocol. We can clearly observe that the number of packets delivered to the destination in this case is far improved when compared to the standard AODV protocol as shown in Figure 4. Thus one can conclude from this explanation that the throughput of the network can be improvised effectively when both remaining battery energy of the node and trust in the node are considered while taking the routing decisions in the network. Apart from the improvement in the throughput, we can also conclude that the network is robust against various route misbehavior security threats present in the ad hoc network environment.

8 Conclusion and Future Work

Security and Energy Consumption are two such important features that they could determine the success and wide deployment of MANET. A variety of attacks have been identified and their models have been developed by altering the standard code of AODV protocol in this paper. The impact of these attacks reduces the overall throughput of the network as shown in the Simulation Study. The Power Aware Trust Mechanism developed increases the throughput of the network considerably even in the presence of attacks. Hence efficient detection techniques such as Trust based Detection Techniques need to be followed in order to identify the malicious nodes in the network and avoid considering them in taking routing decisions.

The research on MANET is still in an early stage. Existing proposals of securing the networks are typically based on one specific attack. They could work well in the presence of designated attacks, but there are many unanticipated or combined attacks that remain undiscovered. A lot of research is still on the way to identify new threats and create secure mechanisms to counter those threats. More research can be done on the robust key management system, trust-based protocols and energy aware routing, integrated approaches to routing security, and data security at different layers.

References

1. Corson, S., Macker, J.: Mobile Ad hoc Networking (MANET): Routing Protocol Performance Issues and Evaluation Considerations. RFC 2501, Informational (1999)
2. Royer, E., Toh, C.: A review of current routing protocols for ad hoc mobile wireless networks. IEEE Personal Communications 6(2), 46–55 (1999)

3. Broch, J., Hu, Y., Johnson, D., Jetcheva, J., Maltz, D.: A performance comparison of multi-hop wireless ad hoc network routing protocols. In: Proceedings of the 4th Annual ACM/IEEE International Conference on Mobile Computing and Networking, pp. 85–97 (1998)
4. Badache, N., Derhab, A., Djenouri, D.: Ad hoc networks routing protocols and mobility. Int. Arab. J. Inf. Technol. 3(2), 126–133 (2006)
5. Belding-Royer, E., Das, S., Perkins, C.: Ad hoc On- Demand Distance Vector (AODV) Routing, RFC 3561, Experimental (2003)
6. Wu, B., Chen, J., Wu, J., Cardei, M.: A survey on Attacks and Countermeasures in Mobile Ad hoc Networks. In: Florida Atlantic University, Wireless/Mobile Network Security, ch. 12. Springer, Heidelberg (2006)
7. Li, J., Li, R., Kato, J.: Future Trust Management Framework for Mobile Ad Hoc Networks: Security in Mobile Ad Hoc Networks. IEEE Communications Magazine 46(4), 108–114 (2008)
8. Blaze, M., Feigenbaum, J., Lacy, J.: Decentralized Trust Management. In: Proceedings of IEEE Symposium on Security and Privacy, pp. 164–173 (1996)
9. Paul, K., Westhoff, D.: Context-Aware Detection of Selfish Nodes in DSR based Ad Hoc Networks. In: Proceedings of IEEE Globecom Conference, Taipeh, Taiwan (2002)
10. Cho, J.-H., Swami, A.: Towards Trust-based Cognitive Networks: A Sur-vey of Trust Management for Mobile Ad Hoc Networks. In: 14th ICCRTS. U.S. Army Research Laboratory (2008)
11. Han, Z., L.Sun, Y., Yu, W., J.R.Liu, K.: Information Theoretic Framework of Trust Modeling and Evaluation for Ad Hoc Networks. IEEE Journal on Selected Areas in Communications 24(2), 305–317 (2006)
12. Golbeck, J.: Computing with Trust: Definition, Properties, and Algorithms. In: Securecomm and Workshops-Security and Privacy for Emerging Areas in Communications Networks, Baltimore, MD, pp. 1–7 (2006)
13. Jiang, T., S.Baras, J.: Ant-based Adaptive Trust Evidence Distribution in MANET. In: Proc. 2nd Int'l Conf. on Mobile Distributed Computing Systems Workshops (MDC), Tokyo, Japan, pp. 588–593 (2004)
14. Theodorakopoulos, S.Baras, J.: On Trust Models and Trust Evaluation Metrics for Ad Hoc Networks. IEEE Journal on Selected Areas in Communications 24(2), 318–328 (2006)
15. Wu, H., Shi, C.: A Trust Management Model for P2P File Sharing System. In: International Conference on Multimedia and Ubiquitous Engineering, IEEE Explore 978-0-7695-3134-2/08 (2008)
16. Fotino, M., Gozzi, A., Cano, J.-C., Calafate, C., De Rango, F., Manzoni, P., Marano, S.: Evaluating Energy Consumption of Proactive and Reactive Routing Protocols in a MANET. In: IFIP International Federation for Information Processing. Wireless Sensor and Adhoc Networks, vol. 248, pp. 119–130. Springer, Heidelberg (2007)
17. Griffiths, N., Jhumka, A., Dawson, A., Myers, R.: A Simple Trust model for On-Demand Routing in Mobile Ad-Hoc Networks. In: IDC 2008, pp. 105–114 (2008)
18. Rishiwal, V., Verma, S., Bajpai, S.K.: QoS Based Power Aware Routing in MANETs. International Journal of Computer Theory and Engineering 1(1), 1793–8201 (2009)
19. Huraj, L., Reiser, H.: VO Intersection Trust in Ad Hoc Grid Environment. In: Proceedings of the 2009 Fifth International Conference on Networking and Services, pp. 456–461 (2009)
20. http://en.wikipedia.org/wiki/Promiscuous_mode

A Heuristic Algorithm for Constrained Redundancy Optimization in Complex Systems

Sudhanshu Aggarwal

Indian National Science Academy, Bahadur Shah Zafar Marg, New Delhi-110002, India
s_aggarwal11@yahoo.com

Abstract. In this paper, a new sensitivity factor in respect of minimal cut sets is defined and used to develop an efficient heuristic algorithm for solving the problem of constrained reliability optimization in complex systems. The algorithm is tested on complex system structures from the literature by solving a set of problems (with both linear and nonlinear constraints), with given and randomly generated data. It is observed that, in comparison to the other existing heuristics, our algorithm can be used as an attractive alternative.

Keywords: Complex Systems, Heuristic Algorithm, Constrained Redundancy Optimization, Minimal Cut Sets, Reliability Importance Measure.

1 Introduction

In general, system reliability optimization problems are nonlinear programming problems and NP-hard. They are more difficult to solve than general nonlinear programming problems, because their solutions are integers. For the past few decades numerous constrained reliability optimization techniques, to meet the basic need of the reliability engineers of finding the best way to increase system reliability subject to constraints on resources such as cost, weight and power, have been proposed in the literature. Generally these techniques can be classified as Dynamic Programming, Integer Programming, Geometric Programming, Lagrange Multipliers Method, Heuristic Algorithms, Meta-Heuristic Algorithms etc. In fact even with Dynamic Programming it is hard to solve problems with more than 3 constraints. As such, any simple and computationally efficient heuristic method may be useful for solving large-scale reliability optimization problems. A good review of all these techniques can be found in Kuo *et al.* [1]. Recently, Coit [2], Shelokar et al. [3], Ramirez-Marquez et al. [4], Zhao and Liu [5], and Agarwal and Gupta [6] and [7] have solved redundancy allocation problems using various approaches. Ha and Kuo [8] developed a algorithm for reliability-redundancy allocation problem using scaling method.

This paper introduces, heuristically, a new sensitivity factor in respect of minimal cut sets. Based on this, it provides an efficient heuristic algorithm for solving the problem of constrained redundancy optimization in complex systems.

The central common feature of all the heuristic optimization methods is that they start off with a more or less arbitrary initial solution, iteratively produce new solutions by some generation rule and evaluate these new solutions, and eventually report the best solution found during the search process [9].

S. Ranka et al. (Eds.): IC3 2010, Part I, CCIS 94, pp. 42–52, 2010.

Almost all the heuristic algorithms developed until 1981 search for the optimal solution iteratively, remaining within the feasible region, in which a redundancy is added to only one subsystem in each iteration; and the selection of the subsystem is based on a sensitivity factor. Thus the solutions obtained are optimal only in 1-neighborhood. It was in 1982 that Kohda & Inoue (KI) [10] presented a heuristic algorithm in which two feasible solutions obtained in successive iterations are in 2-neighborhoods of each other. Shi [11] developed a heuristic algorithm based on minimal path sets in which the feasible solutions obtained in successive iterations are in 1-neighborhood or 2-neighborhoods of each other. Kim &Yum algorithm (KYA) [12] allows excursions over a bounded infeasible region i.e. the search for optimal is made not only in the feasible region but also into the bounded infeasible region.

Agarwal and Aggarwal (A&A) [13], [14] and [15] proposed heuristic algorithms, based on measures of reliability importance, for solving the problem of constrained redundancy optimization in complex systems, applicable to separable monotonically nondecreasing constraint functions. These algorithms following the approach of adjusting unit-increment with time, require determining all minimal path sets / cut sets of the system. A&A [15] defined new measures of reliability importance in respect of minimal path sets and minimal cut sets, respectively, and used them to develop two efficient heuristic algorithms, to be referred as A_1 [15] and A_2 [15]. To study the performance of these algorithms numerical computations have been carried out on complex system structures from literature with linear as well as non-linear constraints. It is observed that all the A&A [13], [14] and [15], algorithms giving solutions that are optimal in 1-neighborhood, perform much better than Shi [11]. KI [10] and KY [12] algorithms perform some what better than these algorithms as they should, since while KI [10] gives solutions optimal in 2-neighborhood, the solutions obtained by KY [12] need not even be in 2-neighborhood.

Agarwal and Aggarwal (A&A) [16] proposed a heuristic in which the solutions obtained are optimal in 3-neighborhood. They have shown that their algorithm performs better than those of KI [10], Shi [11] and KY [12]. However, all these heuristics, except that of KI [10], require the constraint functions to be separable and monotonically nondecreasing. Agarwal and Aggarwal (A&A) [17] further proposed a 3-neighborhood heuristic algorithm, which is an improvement over A&A [16].

Relaxing the condition of separable and monotonically nondecreasing constraint functions, Agarwal and Aggarwal (A&A) [18] further proposed a 3-neighborhood heuristic algorithm which, even without compromising on the solution quality, is much faster than KY [12], and A&A [16] and [17].

Recently Ha and Kuo (HK) [19] proposed a tree heuristic for solving the general redundancy allocation problem in reliability optimization. They have concluded that their algorithm outperforms KY [12].

In this paper an algorithm is developed for constrained reliability optimization problems with separable and monotonically nondecreasing constraint functions, following the approach of adjusting unit-increment with time. In the algorithm, to be referred as P-Alg, a minimal cut set is selected according to a Minimal Cut Set Sensitivity factor as introduced in Section 4 and then one of the stages in the selected cut set is chosen on the basis of a Reliability Importance Measure [20].

To study and compare P-Alg with those of A&A [13], [14], [15], [17] and [18], and HK [19] numerical computations have been carried out. The algorithm is tested on complex system structures from the literature by solving a set of problems (with both linear and nonlinear constraints), with given and randomly generated data. It is observed that P-Alg can be used as an attractive alternative.

2 Notations and Assumptions

n	No. of subsystems
X_i	No. of components in subsystem i
X	$(X_1, \cdots, X_n)$; vector of decision variables
p_i, q_i	Reliability, Unreliability of a single component of subsystem i
$R_i(X_i)$, $Q_i(X_i)$	Reliability, Unreliability of subsystem i with X_i Components
$R_s(X)$, $Q_s(X)$	System Reliability, Unreliability
X^*	Optimal / Near Optimal Solution in 1-neighborhood
m	No. of constraints
$g_i^j(X_i)$	Resource j consumed in subsystem i with X_i Components
C^j	Maximum of resource j
k	No. of minimal cut sets
f_u	Minimal cut set u of the system
ΔR_i	$R_i(X_i + 1) - R_i(X_i)$; Perturbation of $R_i(X_i)$
$\Delta R_s(+i)$	Increment in system reliability for increasing X_i by 1
$\Delta g_i^j(+i)$	Increment in resource j at subsystem i for increasing X_i by 1

Assumptions

1. The system and all of its subsystems are coherent.
2. All constraints are separable and additive among components. Each constraint is a nondecreasing function of X_i for each subsystem.

3 Problem Formulation

Reliability optimization problem is formulated as:

$P\ 1$ Maximize: $R_s(X)$

$$\text{subject to } \sum_{i=1}^{n} g_i^{\,j}(X_i) \leq C^j, \ j=1,\cdots,m$$

X_i are positive integers, for all i.

4 Definitions and Steps of Algorithm

Definitions
A new Minimal Cut Set Sensitivity Factor is defined as given below.

Minimal Cut Set Sensitivity Factor $b_u(X)$. The ratio of the unreliability of the minimal cut set u to the number of components contained.

$$b_u(X) = \left[\frac{\prod\limits_{i \in f_u} Q_i(X_i)}{\sum\limits_{i \in f_u} X_i} \right] \qquad u = 1, 2, ..., k. \tag{1}$$

This Minimal Cut Set Sensitivity Factor gives an approximate idea of contribution of a component towards unreliability of the minimal cut set containing the same. This factor is used to identify minimal cut sets of the system that are the best candidates for efforts leading to improve system reliability.

Reliability Importance Measure for a Component. The Reliability Importance Measure $I_i(X)$ for component i, as defined in Aven and Jenson [20] is:

$$I_i(X) \approx \sum_{u:\, i \in f_u} \prod_{j \in f_u} Q_j(X_j) \tag{2}$$

i.e. $I_i(X)$ is approximately equal to the sum of the unreliabilities of the minimal cut sets that include component i.

Steps of the P-Alg:
1. Find all minimal cut sets of the system.
2. Let $X_i = 1$ for all i.
3. Calculate $b_u(X)$, u = 1, 2, ... , k, for each minimal cut set and find uh such that $b_{uh}(X) = \text{Max}\{ b_u(X) \}$. In case of a tie, choose that minimal cut set, which consumes least resources i.e. for which $\sum\limits_{i \in uh} \sum\limits_{j=1}^{m} g_i^j(X_i)$ is minimum.
4. Within the chosen minimal cut set uh, calculate $I_i(X)$ and choose $I_e(X) = \underset{i \in uh}{\text{Max}}\{ I_i(X) \}$. In case of a tie, subsystem is selected according to the Selection Criterion as given below in (3):

$$\underset{i = e \in uh}{\text{Max}} \left[\Delta R_s(+i) \Big/ \sum_{j=1}^{m} \left\{ \Delta g_i^j(+i) / C^j \right\} \right] \tag{3}$$

Then add a redundant component to the selected subsystem e.

5. Check the constraints:

    (a) If any constraint is violated, go to step 6.

    (b) If no constraint is violated, go to step 3.

    (c) If any constraint is exactly satisfied, stop. The current X_i's are then the optimum configuration of the system. Go to step 7.

6. Remove the redundant component added in step 4. Remove minimal cut set uh from further consideration. If all the minimal cut sets are excluded from further consideration, then $X^* = X$ is the optimal / near optimal solution; else go to step 3.

7. Calculate the system reliability R_s for the optimum X^*.

5 Computational Experiments and Results

To study and compare P-Alg with those of A&A [13], [14], [15], [17] and [18], and HK [19] , the following examples are considered. These algorithms are programmed in C++ and numerical computations have been carried out on a P4-2.40GHz computer.

Example 1
Consider an optimal redundancy allocation Problem of the bridge network system as shown in Fig.1:

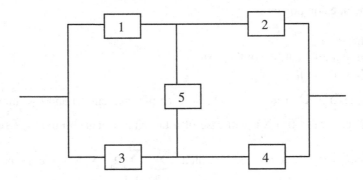

Fig. 1. A Bridge System

The system reliability is:

$$R_s(X) = R_1(X_1)R_2(X_2) + R_3(X_3)R_4(X_4)\{Q_1(X_1) + R_1(X_1)Q_2(X_2)\} +$$
$$R_1(X_1)R_4(X_4)R_5(X_5)Q_2(X_2)Q_3(X_3) + R_2(X_2)R_3(X_3)R_5(X_5)Q_1(X_1)Q_4(X_4)$$

For Linear Constraint:
Problem:
Maximize $R_s(X)$

subject to $\sum_{i=1}^{5} c_i X_i \leq 20$

where X_i, $i = 1,.....,5$ are positive integers.

The subsystems data is:

i	1	2	3	4	5
p_i	0.70	0.85	0.75	0.80	0.90
c_i	2	3	2	3	1

Solution:
There are four minimal cut sets:
$f_1 = \{1,3\}$, $f_2 = \{2,4\}$, $f_3 = \{1,4,5\}$ and $f_4 = \{2,3,5\}$.
    Table 1 shows the procedure to obtain the optimal solution.

Table 1.

Number of components in each subsystem	Consumed Resource	Minimal Cut Set Sensitivity Factor $b_u(X)$				Reliability Importance Measure $I_i(X)$				
X_1 X_2 X_3 X_4 X_5	$C \equiv \sum_{i=1}^{5} c_i X_i$	F_1 $\{1,3\}$	f_2 $\{2,4\}$	f_3 $\{1,4,5\}$	f_4 $\{2,3,5\}$	I_1	I_2	I_3	I_4	I_5
1 1 1 1 1	11	0.0375˙	0.0150	0.0020	0.0012	0.081#	0.079			
2 1 1 1 1	13	0.0075	0.0150˙	0.0004	0.0012		0.03375#	0.0318		
2 2 1 1 1	16	0.0075˙	0.0015	0.0004	0.0001	0.024#	0.023			
3 2 1 1 1	18	0.0017˙	0.0015	0.0001	0.0001	0.00729	0.00731#			
3 2 2 1 1	20									

• This minimal cut set has the highest importance.
\# A redundant component is to be added to this subsystem

    The optimal / near optimal solution is $X^* = (3,2,2,1,1)$ with $R_s(X^*) = 0.993215771$.
    This has also been verified by A&A [13], [14] and [15] and HK [19] algorithm. By using A&A [17] and [18] algorithm the same solution is obtained.

For Nonlinear Constraint:
Problem:
Maximize $R_s(X)$
subject to

$$g_1(X) = \sum_{i=1}^{5} c_i X_i^2 \leq 100$$

$$g_2(X) = \sum_{i=1}^{5} d_i[X_i + \exp(\frac{X_i}{4})] \leq 175$$

$$g_3(X) = \sum_{i=1}^{5} w_i X_i \exp(\frac{X_i}{4}) \leq 200$$

X_i, $i = 1,2,...5$ are positive integers.

The subsystem data is:

i	1	2	3	4	5
p_i	0.7	0.85	0.75	0.8	0.9
c_i	1	2	3	4	2
d_i	0.7	7	15	9	0.4
w_i	0.7	8	8	6	9

The solution obtained by the P-Alg is:

$X^* = (4,3,3,3,1)$ with $R_s(X^*) = 0.999835$.

The solution obtained by A&A [17] and [18] algorithms, respectively, is $X^* = (6,4,2,2,1)$ with $R_s(X^*) = 0.999928$ and $X^* = (1,2,4,3,1)$ with $R_s(X^*) = 0.998409$. By using A&A [13], [14] and A$_2$ [15] algorithms the same solution is obtained. By using A$_1$ [15], and HK [19] algorithms, the solutions $X^* = (7,4,2,1,1)$ with $R_s(X^*) = 0.999878$ and $X^* = (4,4,3,2,2)$ with $R_s(X^*) = 0.999917$, respectively, are obtained.

To compare the performance of the P-Alg with those of A&A [13], [14], [15], [17] and [18], and HK [19] algorithms at depth, more numerical computations for complex systems comprising of 5 (bridge system), 7, and 10 units (A&A [17] and [18]) have been carried out.

The problems in the computation have the same structure as $P1$ except that the constraints are replaced by:

$$\sum_{i=1}^{n} c_{ij} X_i \leq b_j, \quad j = 1,2,...,m.$$

Test problems are generated for the following combinations of the problem parameters:

$n = 5, 7, 10,$
$m = 1, 5.$

This results in 6 sets of problems. For each set, 10 problems are generated randomly:

{c_{ij}} vary from (0, 100),

{p_i} vary from (0.6, 0.95),

{b_j} vary from (20, 100) for $m = 1$ and (50, 1000) for $m = 5$.

For each complex system, an expression for the system reliability is obtained by the improved algorithm for network reliability [21].

The performance of the P-Alg with those of A&A [13], [14], [15], [17] and [18], and HK [19] algorithms is assessed in terms of Average relative error (A), Maximum relative error (M), and Optimality rate (O) of the 10 problems for each system defined as follows:

A_i = Average Relative Error for algorithm i $= \frac{1}{10} [\sum_{j=1}^{10} (R_j^* - R_{ij})/ R_j^*]$.

M_i = Maximum Relative Error for algorithm i $= \max_{1 \leq j \leq 10} \{(R_j^* - R_{ij})/ R_j^*\}$.

O_i = Optimality Rate for algorithm i

= Number of times (out of 10 problems) algorithm i yields the best system reliability.

R_{ij} = System reliability obtained by algorithm i for test problem j; $j = 1,2,...,10$.

R_j^* = The best system reliability obtained by any of the eight algorithms; $j = 1,2,...,10$.

Table 2 contains the values of A, M, and O for the set of 60 problems solved with P-Alg, A&A [13], [14], [15], [17] and [18], and HK [19] algorithms. We further rank the algorithms analyzing these values. Table 3 shows the number of times an algorithm attains a particular rank.

Table 3. Ranking of algorithms

Rank	Algorithms							
	HK [19]	A&A [18]	A&A [17]	A_1 [15]	A_2 [15]	A&A [14]	A&A [13]	P-Alg
1	2	0	4	0	0	0	0	0
2	2	3	1	0	1	1	0	1
3	1	1	0	0	2	2	1	1
4	0	2	0	2	1	1	0	1
5	0	0	1	1	0	0	2	2
6	0	0	0	3	2	2	1	1
7	1	0	0	0	0	0	0	0
8	0	0	0	0	0	0	2	0

From Table 3 it can be observed that P-Alg performs better than A&A [13]. However it performs somewhat worse than A&A [14] and [15]. Obviously A&A [17] and [18] and HK [19] algorithms perform better than P-Alg as they should, since while A&A [17] and [18] give solutions optimal in 3-neighborhood, the solutions by HK [19] need not be in 1-neighborhood. The effectiveness of the P-Alg in comparison to A&A [13], [14], [15], [17] and [18], and HK [19] algorithms in terms of computing time (sec) is shown in Table 4.

Table 2. Comparison of performance measures (A, M, O) for different algorithms

System		HK [19]	A&A [18]	A&A [17]	A₁ [15]	A₂ [15]	A&A [14]	A&A [13]	P-Alg
5×1	A	0.00036800	0.00219230	0.00023540	0.00289410	0.00154500	0.00154500	0.00488870	0.00278110
	M	0.00184400	0.01324200	0.00141000	0.01324200	0.00703100	0.00703100	0.02024800	0.01324200
	O	6/10	6/10	6/10	2/10	4/10	4/10	2/10	3/10
5×5	A	0.00809270	0.00020750	0.00000000	0.00420680	0.00377250	0.00377250	0.00395650	0.00322400
	M	0.04745000	0.00207500	0.00000000	0.02106400	0.01888200	0.01888200	0.01292700	0.01888200
	O	7/10	9/10	10/10	7/10	4/10	4/10	2/10	5/10
7×1	A	0.00037480	0.00245260	0.00024220	0.00549780	0.00669140	0.00669140	0.02346790	0.00636480
	M	0.00177700	0.01362600	0.00166000	0.04375700	0.01424500	0.01424500	0.12968500	0.01424500
	O	6/10	6/10	8/10	6/10	2/10	2/10	0/10	2/10
7×5	A	0.00029770	0.00181030	0.00111980	0.00373100	0.00454910	0.00454910	0.00337570	0.00449220
	M	0.00261000	0.00747800	0.00755700	0.02638100	0.01461800	0.01461800	0.00835600	0.01461800
	O	7/10	6/10	6/10	4/10	3/10	3/10	2/10	3/10
10×1	A	0.00000000	0.00148440	0.00289220	0.01757880	0.00236360	0.00236360	0.01437250	0.00246990
	M	0.00000000	0.01035000	0.01618900	0.03677100	0.01035000	0.01035000	0.06110000	0.01035000
	O	10/10	8/10	7/10	1/10	4/10	4/10	1/10	4/10
10×5	A	0.00093800	0.00186210	0.00051420	0.01488420	0.00068550	0.00068550	0.01483760	0.00068550
	M	0.00871800	0.00893300	0.00351000	0.04336600	0.00274800	0.00274800	0.04334300	0.00274800
	O	8/10	7/10	7/10	0/10	6/10	6/10	2/10	6/10

Table 4. Comparison of computing times (sec)

Problem	HK [19]	A&A [18]	A&A [17]	A_1 [15]	A_2 [15]	A&A [14]	A&A [13]	P Alg
5×1	0.02	0.71	0.84	0*	0*	0*	0*	0*
5×5	0.02	0.88	0.88	0	0	0	0	0
7×1	0.02	1.24	1.21	0	0	0	0	0
7×5	0.02	1.52	1.87	0	0	0	0	0
10×1	0.01	0.99	1.13	0	0	0	0	0
10×5	0.02	1.84	2.07	0	0	0	0	0

* 0 means that computing time is less than 0.001.

Table 4 shows that P-Alg performs as good as A&A [13], [14] and [15] and is much faster than A&A [17] and [18] and HK [19] in terms of computational time.

Based on the set of various problems solved, it may thus be concluded that the proposed algorithm appears to be very efficient in solving highly constrained reliability optimization problems for complex systems and as such, this algorithm would be of interest and importance to the system designers, reliability practitioners, as well as to the researchers in academia, business and industry.

Acknowledgement

The author thanks Prof. Manju Lata Agarwal and Dr. Vikas Sharma for helpful discussions. The author also thanks the referees for their valuable suggestions that led to a better presentation of the paper.

References

1. Kuo, W., Prasad, V.R., Tillman, F.A., Hwang, C.-L.: Optimal Reliability Design: Fundamentals and Applications. Cambridge University Press, Cambridge (2001)
2. Coit, D.W.: Cold-standby redundancy optimization for nonrepairable systems. IIE Transactions 33, 471–478 (2001)
3. Shelokar, P.S., Jayaraman, V.K., Kulkarni, B.D.: Ant algorithm for single and multiobjective reliability optimization problems. Quality and Reliability Engineering International 18, 497–514 (2002)
4. Ramirez-Marquez, J.E., Coit, D.W., Konak, A.: Redundancy allocation for series-parallel systems using a max-min approach. IIE Transactions 36, 891–898 (2004)
5. Zhao, R., Liu, B.: Redundancy optimization problems with uncertainty of combining randomness and fuzziness. European Journal of Operational Research 157, 716–735 (2004)
6. Agarwal, M., Gupta, R.: Penalty guided heuristic algorithm for constrained redundancy optimization. Journal of Mathematical Sciences 2, 72–94 (2003)
7. Agarwal, M., Gupta, R.: Penalty function approach in heuristic algorithm for constrained redundancy reliability optimization. IEEE Transactions on Reliability 54, 549–558 (2005)
8. Ha, C., Kuo, W.: Multi-path approach for reliability-redundancy allocation using a scaling method. Journal of Heuristics 11, 201–217 (2005)
9. Maringer, D.: Portfolio Management with Heuristic Optimization. Springer, Netherlands (2005)

10. Kohda, T., Inoue, K.: A reliability optimization method for complex sys-tems with the criterion of local optimality. IEEE Transactions on Reliability 31, 109–111 (1982)
11. Shi, D.H.: A new heuristic algorithm for constrained redundancy-optimization in complex systems. IEEE Transactions on Reliability 36, 621–623 (1987)
12. Kim, J.H., Yum, B.J.: A heuristic method for solving redundancy opti-mization problems in complex systems. IEEE Trans. Reliability 42, 572–578 (1993)
13. Agarwal, M., Aggarwal, S.: Constrained redundancy optimization in complex systems: A heuristic approach. Statistical Methods 7, 64–80 (2005)
14. Agarwal, M., Aggarwal, S.: A heuristic reliability optimization algorithm for complex systems based on measures of reliability importance. Journal of the Indian Statistical Association 42, 35–48 (2004)
15. Agarwal, M., Aggarwal, S.: Heuristic algorithms for constrained redun-dancy optimization in complex systems based on new measures of importance. OPSEARCH 43, 88–102 (2006)
16. Agarwal, M., Aggarwal, S.: A heuristic 3-neighborhood reliability opti-mization algorithm. In: Rao, M.R., Puri, M.C. (eds.) Operational Research And Its Applications: Recent Trends (APORS 2003), vol. I, pp. 214–222. Allied Publishers Pvt. Ltd, New Delhi (2004)
17. Agarwal, M., Aggarwal, S.: A 3-neighborhood heuristic algorithm for constrained redundancy optimization in complex systems. International Journal of Performability Engineering 2, 331–340 (2006)
18. Agarwal, M., Aggarwal, S.: An improved 3-neighborhood heuristic algo-rithm for constrained reliability optimization. International Journal of Material & Structural Reliability 6, 1–11 (2008)
19. Ha, C., Kuo, W.: Multi-path heuristic for redundancy allocation: the tree heuristic. IEEE Transactions on Reliability 55, 37–43 (2006)
20. Aven, T., Jensen, U.: Stochastic Models in Reliability. Springer, New York (1999)
21. Abraham, J.A.: An improved algorithm for network reliability. IEEE Transactions on Reliability 28, 58–61 (1979)

A Hybrid Genetic Algorithm Based Test Case Generation Using Sequence Diagrams

Mahesh Shirole[1] and Rajeev Kumar[2]

[1] Computer Technology Department, VJTI, Matunga,
Mumbai, 400019, India
mrshirole@vjti.org.in
[2] Department of Computer Science and Engineering,
Indian Institute of Technology Kharagpur,
Kharagpur WB, 721302, India
rajeevkumar.cse@gmail.com

Abstract. This paper presents a hybrid approach of generating test cases using sequence diagram with genetic algorithm. Sequence diagram shows the method call dependencies that exist among the methods that potentially appear in a method call sequence, which is good for integration testing. In this work, we use genetic algorithm to generate interclass method sequences using the sequence diagram. Main focus of the work is to exploit sequence diagram using genetic algorithm to search method sequences leading to usable behavior in application domain. Method sequences generated by this approach are used to generate test cases for dynamic execution. The test cases are generated for integration level testing. This results in a model based testing technique for object oriented software. Experimental results show that a test case covers major scenarios leading to both valid and invalid flows of a given scenario. Test cases generated using genetic algorithm improves the method coverage as well as exception coverage as shown in the result.

Keywords: model-based testing, sequence diagram, genetic algorithm, OO testing, automated test case generation, UML diagram, integration testing.

1 Introduction

Object oriented analysis and design can lead to better system architecture and object-oriented programming enforces a disciplined coding style, though it does not shield against programmers' error or lack of understanding of the specifications and ensures the production of correct and trusted programs by itself. Object oriented software presents many challenges for testing, compared to the testing for procedural language due to its properties such as encapsulation, inheritance, polymorphism, and structured exception handling. This makes testing of object oriented software more challenging, tedious and time consuming.

Techniques and tools for testing traditional structured-oriented software are good but not sufficient to test object-oriented systems. Object oriented software development life cycle produces different types of models. These models are composition of

S. Ranka et al. (Eds.): IC3 2010, Part I, CCIS 94, pp. 53–63, 2010.

different types of structural, behavioral, and process diagrams. A few diagrams of these models allow us to built test-cases early in the development life cycle. A sequence diagram captures the time dependent sequences of interactions between objects. A sequence diagram has two dimensions: the vertical dimension shows the sequences of messages/calls in an order of the time they occur; the horizontal dimension shows the object instances to which messages are sent. The interactions between the classes are realized by method calls from object of one class to object of another class. Integration testing concerned with the testing of the interactions between classes.

Model-based testing is the application of model based design for designing and executing the necessary artifacts to perform software testing. The model describing the System Under Test (SUT) is usually an abstract, and may be partial presentation of the SUT's desired behavior. The test cases derived from this model are functional tests on the same level of abstraction as the model. Here we are considering the UML sequence diagram as model for generating test cases. The effectiveness of model-based testing is primarily due to potential automation it offers. To find test cases, the automation is searched for executable paths. A possible execution path can serve as a test case. Depending on the complexity of the SUT and corresponding model the number of paths can be very large. For finding appropriate test cases, i.e. paths that refer to certain requirement to proof, the search of the path has to be guided. There we found the stochastic search based Genetic Algorithm (GA) has the potential to give superior results and this is experimentally shown in this paper.

The approach presented in this paper employs GA to produce test cases by taking input from sequence diagram. We use GA to search potential method call sequences which find alternative possible paths leading to both valid and invalid paths. Invalid paths lead to error messages or exceptions in a given scenario.

This paper is organized as follows: Section 2 presents a brief survey of the related work. Section 3 includes motivation for test generation using hybridization of sequence diagram with GA. Section 4 discusses the proposed approach for test case generation. Section 5 describes experimental set up and presents the results. Section 6 concludes the paper.

2 Related Work

A sequence diagram in Unified modeling Language (UML) is a kind of interaction diagram that shows how processes operate with one another in order.

A model based testing technique is presented by Emanuela et al. [14]. In their work, the reuse of sequence diagram is done to generate labeled transition system (LTS) graph. LTS is used as an internal model to preciously present functional behavior. Test cases are generated by traversing LTS from initial state using depth first search (DFS).

A fault revealing capability of test sets that are generated from UML state-charts and sequence diagrams is discussed by Abdurazik et al. [15]. Test cases are generated by using sequence diagrams using complete trace of messages during the execution of user level operation. Message sequence path coverage is used as coverage criteria. Experimental study in this paper shows that the sequence diagram test set does better at revealing integration level faults.

A test path generator as well as test class generator from the sequence diagram is presented by Yao-Cheng & Nai-Wei [16]. Test paths are generated by converting a sequence diagram into the message flow graph. The paths are generated to satisfy the flow graph based coverage criteria such as all-node, all-edge, all-path, usage based all nodes, and usage based all edge. To generate test paths from message flow graph, a depth first search (DFS) traversal is used. The tool presented automatically generates Java method(s) that tests the test path. This tool is semiautomatic generation of test cases in integration level testing.

SeDiTeC tool uses sequence diagram to generate Java test programs and stubs [17]. Testable sequence diagram notion is presented using seven requirements which sequence diagram must fulfill. SeDiTeC tool enables testing as early as possible by providing facilities, such as --- (i) Combined sequence diagram, (ii) Autometic test stub generation for selected class, (iii) Source code instrumentation, and (iv) Initialization of objects e.g. setup method of JUnit. Tool supports early automated testing based on testable sequence diagrams and method pre and post conditions.

Evolutionary approaches (EAs) have emerged an interesting area to design the search based test data generation [1]. Genetic Algorithms have been used successfully to automate the generation of test data for procedural software. Various software procedures with different input data structures, and program structures conditions and loops are tested [2]. Currently, researchers are showing interest to apply EA for object-oriented testing at unit and integration level testing [6], [7]. The evolutionary search techniques are offering a promising perspective for object-oriented testing.

In the area of evolutionary structural testing for object-oriented testing, Tonella [7] designed string based chromosome generation and genetic operators to create new chromosomes. The chromosome representation includes specification of sequence of statements for object creation, state change, and method invocation. Resulting chromosomes from GA are transformed into JUnit test methods for execution.

Usage of standard evolutionary algorithm to generate test cases is proposed by Wappler & Lammermann [6]. They proposed use of standard evolutionary algorithm which used basic type values such as integer, float to representation of the chromosome. He has proposed various type of genotype representation to optimize the search at multiple levels.

The Strongly Typed Genetic Programming (STGP) to generate the object oriented test program was investigated by Wappler & Wegener [8]. Wappler & Wegener used tree based representation of chromosome and applied tree based mutation and crossover operators. The call dependencies that exist among the test cluster methods are expressed using method call dependency graph (MCDG). The encapsulated method coverage has been exercised in [9]. While automating the test in object-oriented software one problem is to achieve test adequacy. A model for testing adequacy criteria for object oriented software is discussed by Haworth et al. [10], which focuses on objects and interactions occurring within and between objects in cluster. The coverage criteria based on UML sequence diagrams is discussed by Rountev et al. [11].

There are several testing techniques that make use of interaction diagrams to derive dynamic interactions among the objects. However, to our knowledge, there is no existing work that combines a GA and UML sequence diagram to generate test cases.

3 Motivation: Sequence Diagram and Genetic Algorithm

In this section, we discuss the test case generation using the sequence diagram and the use of genetic algorithms to generate dynamic test cases.

3.1 Sequence Diagram Driven Testing

A usecase model describes a system's functional requirements in terms of usecases. It is a model of systems intended functionality and its environment. A usecase has normal basic flow and several alternative flows, which are regular variants, odd cases, and exceptional flows for handling error situations. A usecase realization is the expression of a particular usecase within the design model. The usecase realization can be presented using a set of diagrams that model the context of the collaboration and interactions of the collaborations. Sequence diagram is one of the diagrams used to describe how a usecase is realized. Sequence diagram captures one entire pass through a usecase showing logic described by the basic course of actions. Sequence diagram captures the time dependent sequences of interactions between objects. Sequence diagrams describe interactions among software components and, thus are considered to be good source for integration testing [18].

Figure 1 shows a book search scenario using sequence diagram. In this diagram one actor customer, and three objects of classes SearchPage, Catalogue, and searchResult are shown. The sequence of messages shows the temporal order of messages exchanged among them. The orders of these messages are important for test case generation. The flow of these ordered messages are represented as a test class. Using this basic scenario there could be many other scenarios which may frequently happen in a problem domain, such as, a customer did not enter search criteria information or requested book is not available in catalogue, etc.

The main feature of the sequence diagram is to show message sequence as the execution occurs. Execution occurrence is used in sequence diagrams to show the period of time during which an object performs an action. Message sequence as identified from sequence diagrams which is a process of finding messages in a given sequence. Let $msg1$ and $msg2$ be two consecutive messages. If the receive event of $msg1$ and send event of $msg2$ sent immediately after $msg1$ lies between the start event occurrence and finish event occurrence of a particular execution occurrence, then these two messages form a message sequence. This sequence of message is used to generate test case. The message sequence for searching book in library extracted from sequence diagram shown in Figure 1 is:

Message sequence1: Search()-> ValidateSearchCriteria() -> Result Search(author)-> create()-> displayResult().

These messages are for different objects and by using this information we can generate test script to check validity of operation performed in the said scenario. This simple examples gives motivation to find different other messages sequences which may find possible path sequences by exploring other possible paths from the given sequence diagram.

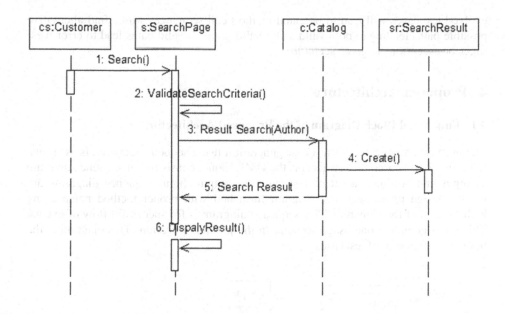

Fig. 1. A sequence diagram to search book

3.2   Genetic Algorithm Driven Testing

Genetic algorithm represents a class of stochastic search techniques and procedures based on the process of natural genetics. They are characterized by an iterative procedure and can work in parallel on the number of potential solutions for a population of individuals. Permissible solution values for the variables of the optimization problem are encoded in each individual.

The fundamental concept of GA is to evolve successive generations of increasingly better combinations of those parameters that significantly affect the overall performance of a design. Starting with selection of good individuals, the GA tries to achieve the (near) optimum solution by stochastically exchange of information among increasingly fitter samples (combination) and by introduction of a probability of independent random change (mutation). The adaptation of the GA is achieved by selection and reinsertion procedure based on fitness. Selection procedure controls the individuals which are selected for reproduction, depending on the individual's fitness values. The reinsertion strategy determines how many and which individuals are taken from the parent and the offspring population to form the next generation.

In order to automate software tests with the aid of GA, the test aim must itself be transformed into an optimization task. For this a numeric representation of the test aim is necessary, from which suitable fitness function for the evaluation of generated test data can be derived. Depending on which test aim is pursued, different fitness functions emerge for test data evaluation. GA could be applied to test case generation if the message sequences are clearly defined and appropriate function related to this goal is built. This motivate to use GA which takes message path from sequence diagram and execute sequence of operators iteratively for test cases to evolve. The evolved test cases will lead to potential method call sequences which find alternative possible paths leading to both valid and invalid paths. Invalid paths lead to error messages or exceptions in given scenario.

4 Proposed Architecture

4.1 Functional Block Diagram of the Proposed Architecture

The proposed architecture of test case generation using sequence diagram is as shown in Figure 2. This architecture accepts the UML model consisting of sequence diagram as input and produces a set of test cases as output. Input sequence diagrams are mostly design phase sequence diagram furnished with proper method name along with the rest of the signature. This sequence diagram is for successful flow of events. This gives complete one usage scenario in the given application. This diagram is the basis for generation of test cases.

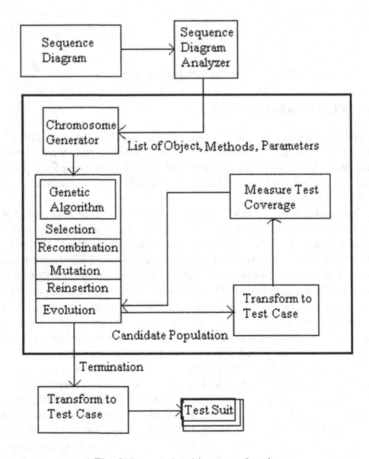

Fig. 2. Proposed architecture of testing

Sequence diagram analyzer is a block which takes the sequence diagram as input and finds the number of objects participating in sequence diagram, methods that are called in the sequenced diagram, and parameters of each method. Next functional block is the chromosome generator, who encodes the input from sequence diagram analyzer into chromosomes. The encoding technique is described in next sub-section. GA which operates on the given chromosome to generate required population and evolve through generations to satisfy the objective function. Every chromosome in the population of each generation is converted into a JUnit test case by Transform to Test Case (TTC) block. The Measure Test Coverage (MTC) block tries to measure the test coverage of each test case according the objective of the testing. This block weight every chromosome according to the coverage achieved. The evaluation stage of GA uses these weights to maximize the fitness value of each chromosome. The fit chromosomes are passed in next generation. This process is iterated till a convergence based on method coverage is achieved. The final population is converted into the test suit by TTC block.

4.2 Chromosome Encoding

Encoding is a crucial stage where we transform the test aim into the optimization task. In test case generation generally three types of statements are written. First type of statement is a constructor, which initializes an instance of the class, whose objects are participating in sequence diagrams. Second type of the statements is simple method invocation, which is message exchange between objects to change state. Third type of statement is value assignment, which invokes the message and returns a value to field variable or object. For each type of statements we have proposed a gene which is distinguished by Gene Type field.

Gene Type		Class Name					Object Name					Method Name					Number of Parameters					Parameter List			
0	0																								

Fig. 3(a). Constructor Call Gene

Gene Type		Return Type					Object Name					Method Name					Number of Parameters					Parameter List			
0	1																								

Fig. 3(b). Simple Method Invocation Gene

Gene Type		Receiving Object					Object Name					Method Name					Number of Parameters					Parameter List		
1	0																							

Fig. 3(c). Object Value Assignment Gene

Fig. 3. Encoding of Gene

The constructor is represented in Constructor Call Gen (CCG) as shown in Figure 3(a). Gene Type field is 00, class name, object name, method name fields are BCD representation of number representing the class, object, and method respectively. Number of Parameters field is a BCD representation of number representing the value of number of parameters for the method, and Parameter List field is BCD representation of number representing the parameter name.

A simple method invocation is encoded as shown in Figure 3(b) as Simple Method Invocation Gene (SMIG).The return type is encoded as BCD representation. Object Value Assignment Gene (OVAG) is represented as shown in Figure 3(c) where, receiving object is encoded as BCD representation of the receiving object.

4.3 Objective Function

Objective function is used to guide the GA to find near optimal values. Objective function is dependent on the coverage criteria for testing. The message sequence path coverage criterion is used to test test-cases generated from the sequence diagram. Each sequence generated is compared with the message sequence of the sequence diagram. Fitness value is increased when the sequence of messages generated from chromosome traverse same path as sequence diagram. Objective function is dependent on the coverage of method sequence in a given sequence diagram.

Fitness function is designed to maximize the coverage mentioned above. The objective function is used to determine the best individual in the given population that lead to the search of the optimum result. This function is applied for each chromosome to get objective value.

5 Experimental Results

We have carried out the experiment on many problems, though in this paper we included two simple cases due to space limitation. This serves as a proof of concept as well as to demonstrate the applicability of concept on a smaller application on an ATM System Simulation [21], as is shown.

The software is designed to control a simulated automated teller machine (ATM) having a magnetic stripe reader for reading an ATM card, a customer console (keyboard and display) for interaction with the customer, a slot for depositing envelopes, a dispenser for cash (in multiples of $20), a printer for printing customer receipts, and a key-operated switch to allow an operator to start or stop the machine. The ATM will communicate with the bank's computer over an appropriate communication link.

For ATM Simulation example test cases are generated for system startup, system shut down, withdraw, deposit , transfer, and inquiry transaction usecases. Figure 4 is a sequence diagram for system startup usecase. This diagram includes four objects --- OperatorPanel, ATM, CashDispenser, and NetworkToBank. Message sequence is as shown from switchOn() to openConnection() completes the system startup functionality. To generate test case an instance of each class which participate in sequence diagram as well as the classes who are appearing as method arguments in methods are instantiated and initialized. Then proper order of method call from legitimate object is called as per the sequence diagram message flow. Figure 5 shows one of the sample test case generated for Figure 4 by decoding chromosome.

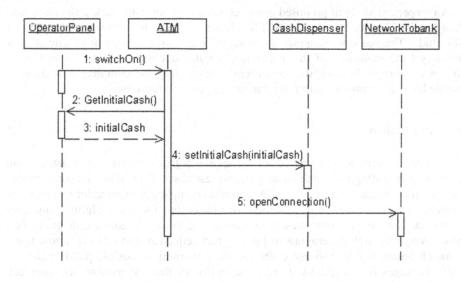

Fig. 4. UML sequence diagram for System Startup use case

```
ATM theATM = new ATM(10,"Matunga","SBI",null);
OperatorPanel op = new OperatorPanel(theATM);
Log lg = new Log();
CashDispenser cd = new CashDispenser(lg);
NetworkToBank nTob = new NetworkToBank(lg,null);
Money initialCash;
theATM.switchOn();
initialCash = op.getInitialCash();
cd.setInitialCash(initialCash);
nTob.openConnection();
```

Fig. 5. Output test case generated from a Sample chromosome

Table 1. Experimental Results

Software Under Test	Number of methods	Number of methods covered		Number of exceptions	Number of exceptions covered		Code coverage		Message Sequence Coverage	
		No-GA	GA		No-GA	GA	No-GA	GA	No-GA	GA
Stack	9	5	8	2	0	1	46.3	81.8	100	100
Calculator	5	5	5	1	0	1	100	100	100	100
SCES	30	22	22	1	0	0	63	68	100	100

An emperical study of proposed approach is carried out with stack, calculator, Student Course Enrollment System (SCES). Table 1 shows the experimental results of this study. The sequence diagramas considered are simple as well as of limited scenarios yet the main aim of this paper to generate superior test cases using GA, is shown to work well. Now we are currently developing the complete tool chain to handle large sysyems and with full scenarios to generate test cases.

6 Conclusion

This paper presents a model based testing approach that combines information from UML sequence diagram with GA to generate test cases. Binary chromosome encoding technique is used in this work. GA generates comparatively superior results when sequence diagram message flow is used for fitness function. Each chromosome generates one test case to cover message sequence according to sequence diagram. Test cases evolve through generations to final correct sequence flows of execution, while some chromosomes lead to test cases covering alternative possible paths leading to error messages or exceptions in given scenario. In this experiment, the approach proved successful to generate test cases leading to full message sequence coverage.

References

1. McMinn, P.: Search-based Test Data Generation: A Survey. Journal on Software Testing, Verification and Reliability 14(2), 105–156 (2004)
2. Sthamer, H.: The Automatic Generation of Software Test Data using Genetic Algorithms. PhD thesis, University of Glamorgan, Pontyprid, Walse, Great Britain (1996)
3. Myers, G., Sandler, C., Badgett, T., Thomas, T.: The Art of Software Testing, 2nd edn. John Wiley & Sons, Chichester (2004)
4. Tsai, B.: A Novel Hybrid Object-oriented Class Testing Method. International Journal of Services and Standards, Inderscience Publishers 1(4), 512–524 (2005)
5. Schlingoff, H., Vos, T., Wegener, J.: Evolutionary Test Generation. Dagstuhl Seminar Proceedings (2008),
   http://drops.dagstuhl.de/opus/volltexte/2009/2022
6. Wappler, S., Lammermann, F.: Using Evolutionary Algorithms for the Unit Testing of the Object-oriented Software. In: Proceedings of the 2005 Conference on Genetic and Evolutionary Computation, pp. 1053–1060. ACM, New York (2005)
7. Tonella, P.: Evolutionary Testing of Classes. In: Proceedings of the 2004 ACM SIGSOFT International Symposium on Software Testing and Analysis, pp. 119–128 (2004)
8. Wappler, S., Wegener, J.: Evolutionary Unit Testing of Object-Oriented Software Using Strongly Typed Genetic programming. In: Proceedings of the 8th Annual Conference on Genetic and Evolutionary Compution, pp. 1925–1932. ACM, New York (2006)
9. Wappler, S., Schieferdecker, I.: Improving Evolutionary Class Testing in the Presence of Non-Public Methods. In: Proceedings of the 22nd IEEE/ACM International Conference on Automated Software Engineering, pp. 381–384. ACM, New York (2007)
10. Haworth, B., Kirsopp, C., Roper, M., Shepperd, M., Webster, S.: Towards the Development of Adequacy Criteria for Object-oriented Systems. In: Proceedings of the 5th European Conference on Software Testing Analysis and Review, Edinburgh, pp. 417–427 (1997)

11. Rountev, A., Kagan, S., Sawin, J.: Coverage Criteria for Testing of Object Interactions in Sequence Diagrams. In: Cerioli, M. (ed.) FASE 2005. LNCS, vol. 3442, pp. 282–297. Springer, Heidelberg (2005)
12. OMG: Unified Modeling Language 2.0 specification, http://www.omg.org/spec/UML/2.2/
13. Fowler, M.: UML Distilled: A Brief Guide to the Standard Object Modeling Language, 3rd edn. Addison Wesley, Reading (2004)
14. Emanuela, G., Franciso, G., Machado, P.: Test Case Generation by means of UML Sequence Diagrams and Labeled Transition Systems. In: IEEE International Conference on System Man and Cybernetics, pp. 1292–1297. IEEE, Los Alamitos (2007)
15. Abdurazik, A., Offutt, J., Baldini, A.: A Controlled Experimental Evaluation of Test Cases Generated from UML Diagrams. Information and Software Engineering Department, George Mason University, Technical Report (2004)
16. Lei, Y.-C., Lin, N.-W.: Semiautomatic Test Case Generation Based on Sequence Diagrams. In: ICS 2008, Taiwan, pp. 349–355 (2008)
17. Fraikin, F., Leonhardt, T.: SeDiTeC - Testing Based on Sequence Diagrams. In: Proceeding of 17th IEEE Conference on Automated Software Engineering. IEEE, Los Alamitos (2002)
18. KansomKeat, S., Offutt, J., Abdurazik, A., Baldini, A.: A Comparative Evaluation of Test Generated from Different UML Diagrams. In: Ninth ACIS International Conference on Software Engineering, Artificial Intelligence, Networking, and Parallel/Distributed Computing, pp. 867–872 (2008)
19. Java Genetic Algorithm Programming Framework, http://jgap.sourceforge.net/
20. Bruegge, B., Dutoit, A.: Object Oriented Software Engineering: Using UML, Patterns and Java. Pearson Education Publication, London (2009)
21. ATM System, http://www.cs.gordon.edu/local/courses/cs211/ATMExample

LACAIS: Learning Automata Based Cooperative Artificial Immune System for Function Optimization

Alireza Rezvanian[1] and Mohammad Reza Meybodi[2]

[1] Department of Computer & IT Engineering, Islamic Azad university, Qazvin branch, Iran
[2] Department of Computer & IT Engineering, Amirkabir University of Technology,
Tehran, Iran
rezvan@qiau.ac.ir, mmeybodi@aut.ac.ir

Abstract. Artificial Immune System (AIS) is taken into account from evolutionary algorithms that have been inspired from defensive mechanism of complex natural immune system. For using this algorithm like other evolutionary algorithms, it should be regulated many parameters, which usually they confront researchers with difficulties. Also another weakness of AIS especially in multimodal problems is trapping in local minima. In basic method, mutation rate changes as only and most important factor results in convergence rate changes and falling in local optima. This paper presented two hybrid algorithm using learning automata to improve the performance of AIS. In the first algorithm entitled LA-AIS has been used one learning automata for tuning the hypermutation rate of AIS and also creating a balance between the process of global and local search. In the second algorithm entitled LA-CAIS has been used two learning automata for cooperative antibodies in the evolution process. Experimental results on several standard functions have shown that the two proposed method are superior to some AIS versions.

Keywords: Artificial Immune System, Hypermutation, Learning Automata, Cooperative, Function Optimization.

1 Introduction

Global optimization problems are used in continuous spaces in various problems of communication, commerce, engineering design and biological sciences. Optimization in nonlinear, non-convex and non-differential functions remained as investigative challenge for researchers on solving of optimization problems [1]. According to applications of these problems from many years ago, several methods have been developed for solving them that can be classified them in two groups: traditional and heuristics (stochastic) methods. In most traditional methods that usually including of numerical methods such as linear programming, gradient based method or analytical methods like differential calculus and lagrange multiplies [12] meantime have answer and enough time, there is limitation like derivation on function. Also, there are other methods that find all of local minimums, finally among which global minimum are

S. Ranka et al. (Eds.): IC3 2010, Part I, CCIS 94, pp. 64–75, 2010.
© Springer-Verlag Berlin Heidelberg 2010

selected [1]. In spite of guaranties of definite methods, because of being time consuming and limitations that they have on function, also, stochastic methods are important. With regard to comparison of mentioned algorithms, there are difficulties, among them, all of them have not examined with similar functions. Some of methods require arrangement of many parameters, and stating about the better methods in many cases depends on input function specifications. For example, for function that they have noises, it have been developed certain methods [13]. Of course, with due attention to [11] performance average of search methods equals on all of functions. It is too easy we cannot produce a search algorithm that relative to other algorithms on all of functions has the better performance. But each of existing algorithms has area of its certain performance.

In set of function optimization methods have been suggested certain heuristic methods that these methods in the proportion of numerical and traditional methods have more flexibility and they are usable in various areas. From heuristic methods in this fields, we can mention that simulated annealing [2], tabu search [3], genetic algorithm [4], evolutionary strategy [5] [6], particle swarm optimization [7], differential evolution algorithm [8] [9], and recently artificial immune system [10]. Among optimization methods which they have been inspired from nature, genetic algorithm is very famous. In genetic algorithm there is possibility of early local optima and it applies mutation for came out from local optima. Also, set of points that they are considered as the next generation candidate is limited.

Artificial immune system algorithms are evolutionary methods and have several powerful features, such as population size dynamically adjustable, effective exploitation exploration of the search space, location of multiple optima, capability of maintaining local optima solutions, and also having the most of genetic algorithm features without difficulties of genetic algorithm [18]. Learning automaton (LA) is a general-purpose stochastic optimization tool, which has been developed as a model for learning systems. The LA tries to determine, iteratively, the optimal action to apply to the environment from a finite number of actions that are available to it. The environment returns a reinforcement signal that shows the relative quality of an action of the LA, and then LA adjusts itself by means of a learning algorithm. LA have been used to enhance the learning capability of other algorithms such as neural networks [17], genetic algorithms [32], particle swarm optimization [14] [31] and ant colony optimization [33].

In this paper, in the first algorithm, it has been used the combination of artificial immune system and learning automata for improvement of standard AIS. But, presence of high learning rate in learning automata is resulted in increasing of convergence speed or falling in local optima and in the event a good accuracy but will reduce convergence speed. Therefore, for removing of this difficulty, in second algorithm we proposed using of cooperation between learning automata with difference learning rate. Also in previously has been introduced the other model of learning concept with cooperative in from of CLA-EC in [34]. But in suggested model in second algorithm has been used combination of two cooperative automatons with various, low and high learning rate, so, high learning rated automatons merely results in speed acceleration of antibodies towards optimum answer and at the same time of learning rated automatons in cooperation with high learning rated automatons with interchanging some of its antibodies prevents falling in local optima.

In this paper, at first it has been introduced AIS in short, in third section it has been presented LA briefly. Proposed two algorithms has discussed in fourth section, and finally, results of experiments on proposed methods and other famous methods have been given in fifth section.

2 Artificial Immune System

Artificial immune system (AIS) is one of the computational intelligence branches in computer sciences, which inspired from natural immune system to present several algorithms for solving computer problems. Natural immune system acts in various levels, which in the first level, immune system tries to prevent enter the external invaders as known pathogen using skins, tears and similar strategies. In the second level as innate immune system encountered with all kind of pathogens in form of public strategy, immune response in this step done for all of antigens similarly. Also, this level of immune system acts very slow and is not enough for encountering with antigens. In the next level has settled adaptive immune which in this level for each antigen is created ideal comparison method. This level of immune acts very fast and it can produce many immune cells for encounter with antigens. The Immune algorithms that have planning in AIS, have modeled adaptive immune and these algorithms have been used for solving many computer problems. AIS algorithms are classified to several groups: negative selection, clonal selection, bone marrow, Immune networks, and danger theory. Each algorithm has modeled part of natural immune system. According to the literature, these algorithms have been used for solving optimization problems, pattern recognition, classification, clustering, intrusion detection, and other computer problems and have obtained good results relative to existing algorithms [14] [16]. Generally, can be consider the AIS as an adaptive, very parallel and distributed system.

Mutation in genetic algorithm is used for preventing premature convergence, recycling and finding unseen and missed solutions, but in the AIS, mutation acts as only and most important operator that called Hypermutation, so acts in form of probable in the affinity is used between antibodies and antigens. Part of the population with high affinity value tolerate the lowest mutation rate and similarly part of antibodies with

---

Algorithm 1: Standard Artificial Immune System Algorithm

Initialize population (randomly)
Individuals (candidate solution)
Evaluation (fitness function) for all antibodies
While (termination criterion not satisfied)
    Select (superior antibodies from parent population)
    Cloning based on fitness value
    Variation operators on clones (**Hypermutation**)
    Evaluating new generated antibodies
    Selection of superior antibodies
    Creation of next generation population
End

Fig. 1. Pseudo-code of standard AIS algorithm

low affinity value tolerate highest mutation rate. Small amount of mutation rate in genetic algorithm is necessary and acts successfully, so it has created diversity in recombination. As a value, increasing cycles approaches the answer, so the rate will reduce until become zero and maintenance of most competent will become to the most amount. But in the artificial immune system algorithm, mutation should acts effectively as only and the most important operator. The general concept of standard AIS algorithm which is mentioned in the various references is given in form of Pseudo-code in figure 1 [15] [29] [30].

Also, several   applications of optimization by AIS reported for solving different problems [10] [19] such as Multi-Modal Optimization, Multi-Objective Optimization, Constrained Optimization, Combinatorial Optimization, Inventory Optimization, Time Dependent Optimization, Job Shop Scheduling, Numerical Function Optimization [20].

3 Learning Automata

Learning Automata (LA) are adaptive decision-making devices operating on unknown random environments. An LA has a finite set of actions and each action has a certain probability (unknown for the automaton) of getting rewarded by the environment. The aim is to learn to choose the optimal action, the action with the highest probability of being rewarded, through repeated interaction of the system. If the LA is chosen properly, the process of interacting with the environment can result in selection of the optimal action. A study reported in [28] illustrates how a stochastic automaton works in feedback connection with a random environment.

Figure 2 shows relation between learning automata and environment and figure 3 pseudo code respectively [21].

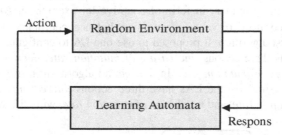

Fig. 2. The interaction between learning automata and environment

Algorithm 2: Learning Automata
Initialize p to [1/s,1/s,...,1/s] where s is the number of actions
While not done
Select an action i a sample realization of distribution p
Evaluate action and return a reinforcement signal β
Update probability vector according to learning algorithm
End While

Fig. 3. Pseudo-code of variable-structure learning automaton

Variable structure LA can be defined as $\{\alpha,\beta,p,T\}$ which $\alpha=\{\alpha_1,...,\alpha_r\}$ is set of automata actions, $\beta=\{\beta_1,...,\beta_m\}$ is set of automata inputs, $p=\{p_1,...,p_r\}$ is vector of each actions and $p(n+1)=T[\alpha(n),\beta(n),p(n)]$ is the learning algorithm.

The following algorithm is a sample of linear learning algorithms. We assume that action α_i is selected at time step n.

In case of desirable response from the environment:

$$p_i(n+1)= p_i(n)+a[1- p_i(n)]$$
$$p_j(n+1)=(1-a)p_j(n) \qquad \forall_j \quad j\neq i \qquad (1)$$

In case of desirable response from the environment:

$$p_i(n+1)=(1-b)p_i(n)$$
$$p_j(n+1)=\left(\frac{b}{r-1}\right)+(1-b)p_j(n)+ \qquad \forall_j \quad j\neq i \qquad (2)$$

In equations (1) and (2), a is the reward parameter and b is the penalty parameter. When a and b are equal, the algorithm is called is called L_{RP}, when b is much smaller than a, the algorithm is $L_{RεP}$, and when b is zero, it is called L_{RI}.

More details and information about learning automata, obtained in [22].

4 Proposed Method

In this section it has been explained proposed method for improvement of AIS algorithm based on learning automata. Our suggestion to improve artificial immune system algorithm is configuration of rate of probability mutation changes. Mutation rate in standard algorithm and some of extended versions in constant and usually take places with reverse of affinity amount in form of adaptive for example in AIGA model [18] also has been used from α value as common balance coefficient in mutation rate changes. In the first algorithm, it proposed to use one LA to configure mutation rate as adaptively. LA has three actions: *increasing of mutation rate, decreasing of mutation rate*, and *no change of mutation rate*. In the second algorithm, it use two LA for two antibodies groups, similarly the LAs have three actions: *increasing of mutation rate, decreasing of mutation rate*, and *no change of mutation rate*, with different learning rate

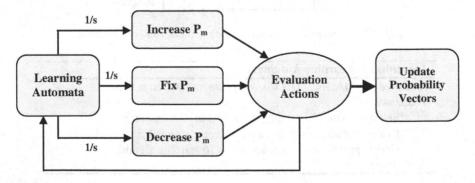

Fig. 4. Structure of proposed learning automata

and similarly actions. In each stage, automatons have selected one of these actions and based on selected action is corrected parameter value of mutation rate, consequently become well. LA updates probability of suitable action (mutation rate change) according to feedback from environment. General structure of LA has been shown in figure 4.

Working of two algorithms is the same but in the second algorithm, cooperative automatons with different LA in each groups exchange some of antibodies randomly in certain period of iterations until to satisfy stopping conditions. Generally we can state stages of these algorithms as follows in figure 5 and figures 6.

Proposed Algorithm 1: LA-AIS

---

1. Initialize antibodies.
2. Initialize LA.
3. Affinity value of antibodies is calculated.
4. According to affinity value of antibodies is accomplished process of clonal selection.
5. Learning automatons select one of actions according to probability vectors of their actions.
6. Based on to selected actions, quality of mutation amount of antibodies is specified and improved new value and hypermutation changes.
7. Affinity values of antibodies are calculated again.
8. Based on updating results by hypermutation in antibodies is studied affinity amount of antibodies and evaluated learning automata performances and update probability vector of selecting learning automata actions.
9. Replacing antibodies is accomplished by colonies with high affinity and some parts of antibodies are eliminated with low and dense fitness.
10. Go to 2 if termination criterion not satisfied

Fig. 5. Proposed algorithm 1: Learning Automata based Artificial Immune System (LA-AIS)

In each algorithm selected action evaluated by average performance of antibodies (fitness average), that it compared in previous situation, in the event that it is being better from current situation, the selected action is evaluated positive otherwise the action is evaluated negative.

The most important benefit of this method especially second algorithm is its high ability to escape from local optimum or settling in suitable convergence. Indeed with increasing mutation rate value, is grew beam of changes and has been accomplished global search and with decreasing mutation rate value, beam of changes becomes small and accomplishing a local search on the search space. In first algorithm, in spite of learning automata with constant learning rate, there were a constant convergence rate, but in second algorithm, presence of two learning automatons with low and high learning rates meantime establishing fast and parallel search is created possibility of cooperation between them with exchanging intermediate solutions.

Proposed Algorithm 2: LA-CAIS

1. Initialize antibodies in two groups with difference learning automata.
2. Initialize LAs in two groups (Low and High learning rate)
3. Affinity value of antibodies is calculated.
4. According to affinity value of antibodies is accomplished process of clonal selection for two groups simultaneously.
5. In each group learning automatons select one of actions according to probability vectors of their actions.
6. Based on to selected actions, quality of mutation amount of antibodies is specified and improved new value and hypermutation changes for two groups simultaneously.
7. Affinity values of antibodies are calculated again for two groups.
8. Based on updating results by hypermutation in antibodies is studied affinity amount of antibodies and evaluated learning automata performances and update probability vector of selecting learning automata actions for two groups simultaneously.
9. Replacing antibodies is accomplished by colonies with high affinity and some parts of antibodies are eliminated with low and dense fitness for each group.
10. Exchange some of their antibodies randomly between two groups when achieving to expected period of iterations.
11. Go to 2 if termination criterion not satisfied

Fig. 6. Proposed algorithm 2: Learning Automata based Cooperative Artificial Immune System (LA-CAIS)

5   Experimental Results

For examining the proposed methods have done experiments on four famous standard functions that usually they are used as criterion of evaluating methods in most of literature [14]. Functions that are used consist of Sphere, Rastrigin, Ackley, and Rosenbrock which have been defined by equations of (3) to (6) respectively [14].

$$f_1(x) = \sum_{i=1}^{n} x_i^{2} \tag{3}$$

$$f_2(x) = \sum_{i=1}^{n} (x_i^{2} - 10\cos(2\pi x_i) + 10) \tag{4}$$

$$f_3(x) = 20 + e - 20e^{-0.2\sqrt{\frac{1}{n}\sum_{i=1}^{n} x_i^{2}}} - e^{\frac{1}{n}\sum_{i=1}^{n}\cos(2\pi x_i)} \tag{5}$$

$$f_4(x) = \sum_{i=1}^{n-1} (100(x_{i+1} - x_i^{2})^2 + (x_i - 1)^2) \tag{6}$$

All of these functions have global optimum with zero values. Initial population size and the number of steps have been considered 20 and 500, respectively.

For comparison, the numerical experiments were performed with six algorithms by results of average and best for Standard Artificial Immune System algorithm as *SAIS* [23], B-Cell Algorithm as *BCA* [24], Clonal Selection Algorithm as *CSA* [25], Adaptive Clonal Selection Algorithm as *ACSA* [26], Optimization Artificial Immune Network as *OAIN* [27], Standard Genetic Algorithm as *SGA* [4], Artificial Immune-Genetic Algorithm as *AIGA* [18], and finally proposed method in algorithm 1, Learning Automata-based Artificial Immune System as *AISLA* and algorithm 2, Learning Automata-based Cooperative Artificial Immune System as *CAISLA*.

In LA_{RP}, penalty and reward rate values have been considered $a=b=0.01$ and for LA_{ReP} $a=0.01$ and $b = 0.001$.

Also cooperation automata has been considered in form of LA_{RI} for which high learning rated automata $a=0.01$ and for low learning rated automata $a=0.001$. And iterations have been considered in each exchange period equal to 10 evaluations, and experimented function dimension has been considered in form of 10 dimensional.

Results of these experiments with given results in other common methods has been compared for *Sphere*, *Rastrigin*, *Ackley*, and *Rosenbrock* in tables 1.

Table 1. Performance of the proposed methods and other methods for benchmark functions

(A) Sphere

Method	Best	Average
SAIS	0.1349	0.6561
BCA	0.0025	1.7112
CSA	0.00526	2.5832
ACSA	6.6806	9.3832
OAIN	24.3793	24.6139
SGA	1.604	3.0526
AISLA$_{RI}$	0.0065	0.1801
AISLA$_{ReP}$	0.0013	0.1958
AISLA$_{RP}$	0.0012	0.1201
CAISLA$_{RI}$	0.000044	0.0026

(B) Rastrigin

Method	Best	Average
SAIS	16.6119	17.1973
BCA	8.3354	16.6878
CSA	16.1979	33.4838
ACSA	77.7343	96.279
OAIN	89.2454	95.2565
SGA	13.9295	17.8693
AISLA$_{RI}$	1.5910	5.3821
AISLA$_{ReP}$	1.4834	5.9271
AISLA$_{RP}$	1.1175	5.0602
CAISLA$_{RI}$	1.0399	4.1466

(C) Ackley

Method	Best	Average
SAIS	3.0271	3.3249
BCA	2.0442	6.0789
CSA	4.1067	5.7433
ACSA	12.8586	13.9453
OAIN	20.2124	20.2534
SGA	0.8392	1.3469
AISLA$_{RI}$	1.6166	1.6503
AISLA$_{ReP}$	1.6143	1.6393
AISLA$_{RP}$	1.6136	1.6240
CAISLA$_{RI}$	1.6131	1.6203

(D) Rosenbrock

Method	Best	Average
SAIS	11.6153	11.6351
BCA	10.8634	73.0078
CSA	15.9718	83.2074
ACSA	100.9198	113.9453
OAIN	591.5480	591.5525
SGA	16.9974	24.3716
AISLA$_{RI}$	10.1321	12.3744
AISLA$_{ReP}$	10.0530	12.9905
AISLA$_{RP}$	10.2448	10.2527
CAISLA$_{RI}$	10.0117	11.2650

For better comparison of proposed method and other methods, comparison graph of converge rate in form of algorithm have been shown in figure 7 for Sphere, Rastrigin, Ackley, and Rosenbrock function.

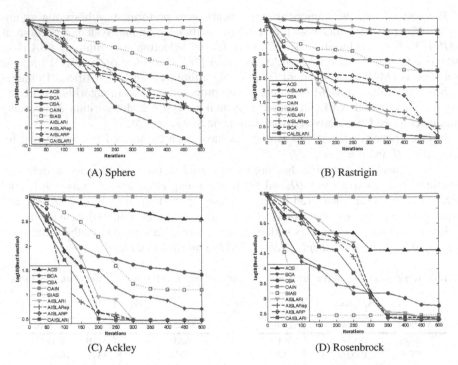

(A) Sphere

(B) Rastrigin

(C) Ackley

(D) Rosenbrock

Fig. 7. Comparison of proposed method and other methods for benchmark functions

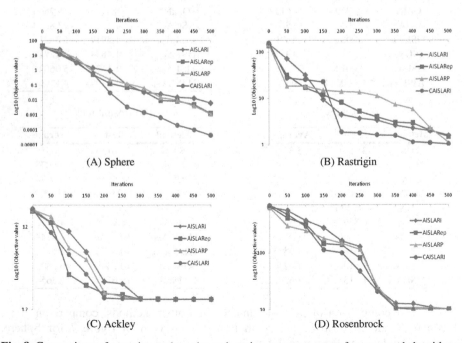

(A) Sphere

(B) Rastrigin

(C) Ackley

(D) Rosenbrock

Fig. 8. Comparison of experimental results on learning automata types for proposed algorithms

Also, for better evaluation between different states of proposed learning automatons, another comparison has been given for proposed methods in form of algorithm in figure of 8 for Sphere, Rastrigin, Ackley, and Rosenbrock.

As shown results, proposed algorithm 2 as learning automata-based cooperative artificial immune system, meantime it have the algorithm 1 features by which feedback that it gets from environment, gives more suitable behavior in search space and it has desirable efficiency, with addition of cooperation concept between automatons are created a good balance among convergence. In fact, in first proposed method Hypermutation as move important and only operator is balanced effectively in artificial immune system algorithm until improves convergence behavior and having better adaptive method to standard state, and with second propose has lower sensitivity to parameter arrangement state and it has better adaption.

6 Conclusion

In this paper, a new two methods have been presented for improvement of AIS algorithm using learning automata and cooperation concept between automatons in optimization. In all versions of AIS, rate of mutation changes as only and most important evolutionary operator is constant and it is with due attention to contrary of antibodies distances. But in proposed method using learning automata with due attention to feedback of environment changes rate is updated and addition of cooperation concept between two automatons with different learning rate is establish on equilibrium between local and global search. We never can give a method which it can cover successful on all functions but at the same time it has been shown in experiment results that proposed methods have had relative improvement to some of the other version of artificial immune system. Moreover improvements in proposed methods with combination of soft computing concepts and emphasizing on the other applications is considered in the future works.

References

1. Wang, Y.J., Zhang, J.S., Zhang, G.Y.: A Dynamic Clustering based Differential Evolution Algorithm for Global Optimization. European Journal of Operational Research 183, 56–73 (2007)
2. Kirkpatrick, S., Gelatt, C.D., Vecchi, M.P.: Optimization by Simulated Annealing. Science 220(4598), 671–680 (1983)
3. Hedar, A.R., Fulushima, M.: Tabu Search Directed by Direct Search Methods for Nonlinear Global Optimization. European Journal of Operational Research 170, 329–349 (2006)
4. Fogel, D.B., Michalwicz, Z.: Evolutionary Computation 1 - Basic Algorithms and Operators. Institute of Physics (IoP) Publishing, Bristol (2000)
5. Herrera, F., Lozano, M., Molina, D.: Continuous Scatter Search: An Analysis of the Integration of Some Combination Methods and Improvement Strategies. European Journal of Operational Research 169(2), 450–476 (2006)
6. Hedar, A., Fukushima, M.: Evolution Strategies Learned with Automatic Termination Criteria. In: SCIS&ISIS 2006, Tokyo, Japan (2006)

7. Kennedy, J., Eberhart, R.C.: Particle Swarm Optimization. In: IEEE International Conference on Neural Networks, Piscataway, NJ, pp. 1942–1948. IEEE Press, Los Alamitos (1995)
8. Price, K., Storn, R., Lampinen, J.: Differential Evolution - A Practical Approach to Global Optimization. Springer, Heidelberg (2005)
9. Qin, A.K., Huang, V.L., Suganthan, P.N.: Differential Evolution Algorithm with Strategy Adaptation for Global Numerical Optimization. IEEE Transactions on Evolutionary Computation 13(2), 398–417 (2009)
10. Gong, M., Jiao, L., Zhang, X.: A Population-based Artificial Immune System for Numerical Optimization. Neurocomputing 72(1-3), 149–161 (2008)
11. Bozorgzadeh, M.A., Rahimi, A., Shiry, S.: A Novel Approach for Global Optimization in High Dimensions. In: 12th Annual CSI Computer Conference of Iran, Tehran, Iran, pp. 1–8 (2007)
12. Vanderplaats, G.N.: Numerical Optimization Techniques for Engineering Design with Applications. McGraw-Hill, New York (1984)
13. Huyer, W., Neumaier, A.: SNOBFIT–Stable Noisy Optimization by Branch and Fit. ACM Transactions on Mathematical Software 35(2), 9 (2008)
14. Hashemi, A.B., Meybodi, M.R.: A Note on the Learning Automata based Algorithms for Adaptive Parameter Selection in PSO. Journal of Applied Soft Computing (2010) (to appear)
15. Timmis, J., Hone, A., Stibor, T., Clark, E.: Theoretical advances in artificial immune systems. Theoretical Computer Science 403(1), 11–32 (2008)
16. Dasgupta, D.: Artificial Immune Systems and their Applications. Springer, New York (1998)
17. Meybodi, M.R., Beigy, H.: A Note on Learning Automata Based Schemes for Adaptation of BP Parameters. Journal of Neurocomputing 48(4), 957–974 (2002)
18. Yongshou, D., Yuanyuan, L., Lei, W., Junling, W., Deling, Z.: Adaptive Immune-Genetic Algorithm for Global Optimization to Multivariable Function. Journal of Systems Engineering and Electronics 18(3), 655–660 (2007)
19. Wang, X., Gao, X.Z., Ovaska, S.J.: Artificial Immune Optimization Methods and Applications - A Survey. In: IEEE International Conference on Systems, Man and Cybernetics, vol. 4, pp. 3415–3420. IEEE Press, Los Alamitos (2004)
20. Campelo, F., Guimaraes, F.G., Igarashi, H.: Overview of Artificial Immune Systems for Multi-objective Optimization. In: Obayashi, S., Deb, K., Poloni, C., Hiroyasu, T., Murata, T. (eds.) EMO 2007. LNCS, vol. 4403, pp. 937–951. Springer, Heidelberg (2007)
21. Sheybani, M., Meybodi, M.R.: PSO-LA: A New Model for Optimization. In: 12th Annual CSI Computer Conference of Iran, Tehran, Iran, pp. 1162–1169 (2007)
22. Meybodi, M.R., Kharazmi, M.R.: Application of Cellular Learning Automata to Image Processing. J. Aut. 14(56A), 1101–1126 (2004)
23. Cutello, V., Nicosia, G.: The Clonal Selection Principle for in Silico and in Vivo Computing. In: Recent Developments in Biologically Inspired Computing, pp. 104–146. Idea Group Publishing (2005)
24. Timmis, J., Edmonds, C., Kelsey, J.: Assessing the Performance of Two Immune Inspired Algorithms and a Hybrid Genetic Algorithm for Function Optimisation. In: IEEE Congress on Evolutionary Computation, Potland, Oregon, USA, vol. 1, pp. 1044–1051. IEEE Press, Los Alamitos (2004)
25. De Castro, L.N., Von Zuben, F.J.: Learning and optimization using the Clonal Selection Principle. IEEE Transactions on Evolutionary Computation 6(3), 239–251 (2002)

26. Garrett, S.M.: Parameter-free, adaptive clonal selection. In: IEEE Congress on Evolutionary Computation, Potland, Oregon, USA, vol. 1, pp. 1052–1058 (2004)
27. Cutello, V., Nicosia, G., Pavone, M.: Real Coded Clonal Selection Algorithm for Unconstrained Global Numerical Optimization using a Hybrid Inversely Proportional Hypermutation Operator. In: 21st Annual ACM Symposium on Applied Computing, Dijon, France, pp. 950–954 (2006)
28. Narendra, K.S., Thathachar, M.A.L.: Learning Automata: An Introduction. Prentice-Hall Inc., Englewood Cliffs (1989)
29. Khilwani, N., Prakash, A., Shankar, R., Tiwari, M.: Fast clonal algorithm. Engineering Applications of Artificial Intelligence 21(1), 106–128 (2008)
30. De Castro, L.N., Von Zuben, F.J.: Recent developments in biologically inspired computing. Igi Global (2004)
31. Sheybani, M., Meybodi, M.R.: CLA-PSO: A New Model for Optimization. In: 15th Conference on Electrical Engineering, Volume on Computer, Telecommunication Research Center, Tehran, Iran (2007)
32. Abtahi, F., Meybodi, M.R., Ebadzadeh, M.M., Maani, R.: Learning Automata-Based Co-Evolutionary Genetic Algorithms for Function Optimization. In: IEEE 6th International Symposium on Intelligent Systems, Subotica, Serbia, pp. 1–5. IEEE Press, Los Alamitos (2008)
33. Ebdali, F., Meybodi, M.R.: Adaptation of Ants colony Parameters Using Learning Automata. In: 10th Annual CSI Computer Conference of Iran, pp. 972–980 (2005)
34. Masoodifar, B., Meybodi, M.R., Hashemi, M.: Cooperative CLA-EC. In: 12th Annual CSI Computer Conference of Iran, pp. 558–559 (2007)

Image Reconstruction from Projection under Periodicity Constraints Using Genetic Algorithm

Narender Kumar and Tanuja Srivastava

Department of Mathematics, Indian Institute of Technology
Roorkee, Uttrakhand, India
narenrawal@gmail.com

Abstract. In this paper we study the problem of image reconstruction from a small number of projections. This type of problem arises in material science during developing the program for the reconstruction of crystalline structure from their projection image, obtained by high-resolution transmission electron microscopy. The problem has large number of solutions due to few projections. To reduce the number of solutions we can use some priori information about the object. This priori information is called constraints. One of these constraints is periodicity constraint. We use genetic algorithm to optimize the solution, which is an evolutionary technique to solve the problem.

Keywords: Discrete Tomography, Reconstruction, Genetic Algorithm, Constraints, Periodicity.

1 Introduction

Image reconstruction from projection or computerized tomography is the technique to find out the density distribution within a physical object from a multiple projections. In computerized tomography we attempt to reconstruct a density function f(x) in R^2 or R^3 from knowledge of its line integral or weighted line sum [1]. This line integral or weighted line sum is the projection of f(x) along line L. The object from the mathematically point of view, corresponds to a density function for which integral or summation in the form of projection data is known. So we can categorize tomography into continuous tomography and discrete tomography. In case of continuous tomography we consider that both the domain and the range of function are continuous. But in discrete tomography the domain of the function could be either continuous or discrete and the range of the function is finite set of real number.

Discrete tomography is used when only few projections for reconstruction are available. But since projection data may be less than the number of unknown variable the problem becomes ill posed. According to Hadmard [2] mathematically problem are termed well posed if they fulfill the following criteria (i) A solution exists (ii) the solution is unique (iii) the solution depend continuously on the data continuously.

On the opposite problems that do not meet these criteria are called ill posed. Image reconstruction from few projections is also ill posed problem because it generates a large number of solutions. To minimize number of solution we require some a-priori

S. Ranka et al. (Eds.): IC3 2010, Part I, CCIS 94, pp. 76–83, 2010.

information about the object geometry. This a-priori information about the object is also called additional constraints on the space of solution. Examples of these are connectivity, convexity and periodicity.

In this paper we use periodicity constraint to minimize the solution space. The periodicity constraint is a natural constraint in crystalline solid object. A polynomial time algorithm for periodicity (p, 1) or periodicity (1, q) is developed by Alberto Del Lungo [3]. But periodicity (p, q) is not yet solved in polynomial time. We try to solve it with the help of genetic algorithm. Genetic algorithm is evolutionary computing technique to find the optimum solution. Inspired by Darwin's theory of evolution - Genetic Algorithms (GAs) are computer programs which create an environment where populations of data can compete and only the fittest survive. Since it is a heuristic approach, the exact solution not known. Most real-life problems are like that: the solutions are not calculated exactly but they are estimated according to some a-priori information. Genetic algorithms are used in the field of tomography, for elliptical object or convexity constraint from a limited number of projections in [4], [5].

2 Notation and Statement of the Problems

Let m and n be the positive integers and define:
Binary matrix $A = [a_{ij}]_{m \times n}$,

Vector $R = (r_1, r_2, ...r_m)$

And $C = (c_1, c_2, ...c_m)$ such that

$$r_i = \sum_{j=1}^{n} a_{ij}, \tag{1}$$

$$c_j = \sum_{i=1}^{m} a_{ij}, \tag{2}$$

$$\sum_{i=1}^{m} r_i = \sum_{j=1}^{n} c_j \tag{3}$$

For all $1 \leq i \leq n$ and $1 \leq j \leq m$.

Here R is the vector of row sums and C is the vector of column sums.

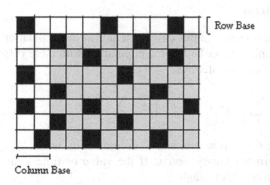

Fig. 1. Showing column base and row base in binary matrix with periodical (1, 2)

A binary matrix A of size $m \times n$ is said to be (p, q)-periodical if $a_{ij} = 1$ implies that

$a_{i+p, j+q} = 1$ if $1 \leq i + p \leq m$ and $1 \leq j + q \leq n$

$a_{i-p, j-q} = 1$ if $1 \leq i - p \leq m$ and $1 \leq j - q \leq n$

Such a matrix is said to have period (p, q).

In (p, q)-periodical binary matrix we can define a Row Base RB, which include set of element a_{ij} where $i \leq p$ and Column Base CB, which include set of elements a_{ij} where $j \leq q$. All other element of binary matrix can be generated by column base and row base. So we try to find out the element of the column base and row base in this paper.

3 Genetic Image Reconstruction

In genetic algorithm we start with a set of possible solutions (represented by chromosomes) the population. Solutions from one population are taken and used to form a new population. This is motivated by a hope that the new population will be better than the old one. New solutions (offspring) are selected according to their fitness - the more suitable they are the more chances they have to reproduce by mating (crossover). Repeat the cycle until some condition is satisfied [7].

Genetic algorithm has been used to reconstruction of circular or elliptical object from small number of projection [4]. A memetic algorithm is used from orthogonal projection [3].

We have used binary image as chromosome and each point in the image as gene. The process creates initial set of random individuals in Row Base and Column Base. Other points in the image are generated using these points of row base and column base. In each generation of chromosome we perform selection, guided crossover, guided mutation, mutation and cloning. This evolutionary process is repeated until a satisfactory result is obtained or number of iteration limits is reached at maximum.

3.1 Selection Criteria

We use steady state selection in this case, best half of the population is used to generate offspring and replace other half of the population with these offspring. The fitness function used for selection criteria is:

$$f = \sum_{i=1}^{n} \left| r_i' - r_i \right| + \sum_{j=1}^{m} \left| c_j' - c_j \right| \tag{4}$$

Here r_i & c_j denote the ith row sum and j^{th} column sum, where as $r_{i'}$ & $c_{j'}$ denote the same from reconstructed binary matrix. If the value of fitness function is low then fitness of binary matrix will be high.

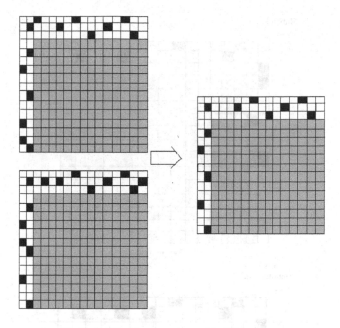

Fig. 2. Arithmetic crossover with AND operator

3.2 Guided Crossover

In the guided crossover we decide which parents will participate in reproduction. Each pair of parents produce only one child and these children replace with worst chromosome in the population. The two parents remain in the next generation. We have randomly chosen two parents from half of the population. An arithmetic crossover is used to generate new offspring, in the given figure crossover by AND operator is done only in row base and column base other part is calculated on the basis of these bases.

3.3 Mutation

The mutation operator changes the black and white points of the same chromosome with a probability Pm, these points are chosen randomly. The fitness of matrix generated by offspring after mutation may be worse then parents matrix.

3.4 Guided Mutation

In a (p, q)-periodical binary matrix if $r_i + r_{i+p} = k$, then (i+ p)th row will contain k number of non zero elements in the first q column i.e. 1,2,…q.

Similarly, if $c_j + c_{j+q} = k$, then (j + q)th column will have k non zero entries in first p rows from row 1 to row p i.e. 1,2,…q. This property can be used in mutation to maintain periodicity constraints. In this type of mutation we change the value of points 0 to 1. This type of mutation is called guided mutation.

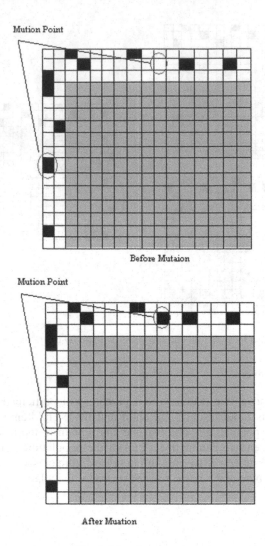

Fig. 3. Mutation operator

3.5 Cloning

This is the standard elitist selection technique. It simply assures that the binary matrix with the best fitness value will be present as more than one copy in the next population too. Although this operation reduces the variability of the hereditary characteristics, but experimentally it can be verified that it increases the accuracy of the final result.

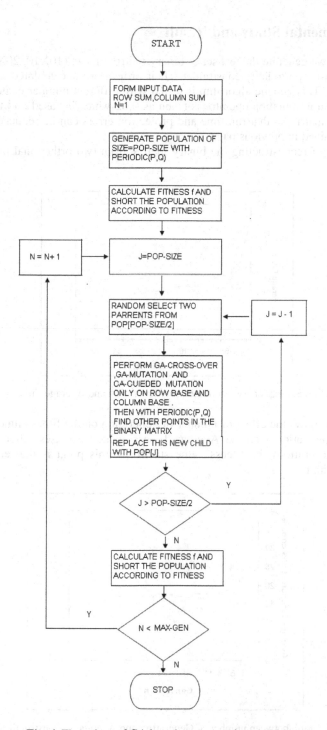

Fig. 4. Flow chart of GA based reconstruction algorithm

4 Experimental Study and Result

In this paper we generate the test set of binary matrix of size (10X10, 20X20, 30X30, and 40X40) with periodicity constraints. Their projections is calculated and stored in the database. This genetic algorithm is tested with different number of iteration. The probability Pm in mutation operator is taken as 0.02 which is based on the input data set of binary matrix so that run time and projection errors can be reduced. The algorithm is explained in previous page.

The result of reconstructing the binary matrix from two orthogonal projections is shown below

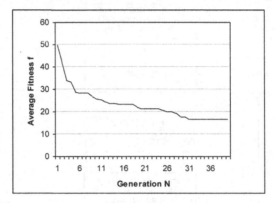

Fig. 5. Graph between number of Generation and Average Fitness

The graph shows the effect of number of generation on the fitness function. As the number of generation increase Average fitness value decreases, after a sufficient number of generations the fitness value stabilized, this point is the termination of genetic algorithm.

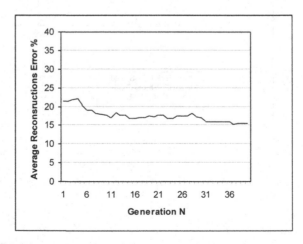

Fig. 6. Graph between number of Generation and Average Reconstruction error

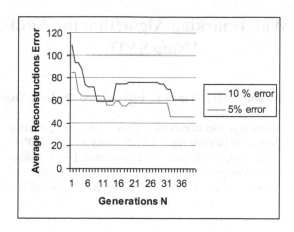

Fig. 7. Graph between number of Generation and Average Reconstruction error with different projection error

The graph in the fig. 6 shows the effect of number of generation on the reconstruction error. As the number of generation increase the average reconstruction error is decrease.

The graph in the fig. 7 shows the effect of the projection error on the reconstruction process. We add 10% and 5% error in the projection data as shown in the graph. The average reconstruction error with these impurities in projection data is shown in the graph.

5 Conclusions

We use genetic algorithm to reconstruct the binary matrix with periodicity (p,q). The genetic algorithm is used first time in the tomographic reconstruction with this type of constraints. We can apply this method for reconstruction of the structure of the crystalline solid, which have the periodicity property.

References

1. Kak, A.C., Slaney, M.: Principles of Computerized Tomographic Imaging. IEEE Press, New York (1988)
2. Hadamard, J.: Lectures on Cauchy's Problem in Linear Partial Differential Equations. Dover Publications, Mineola (1923)
3. Lungo, A.D., Frosini, A., Nivat, M., Vuillon, L.: Discrete Tomography: Reconstruction under Periodicity Constraints. LNCS. Springer, Heidelberg (2002)
4. Venere, M., Liao, H., Clausse, A.: A Genetic algorithm for adaptive tomography of elliptical objects. IEEE Signal Process. Lett. 7(7), 176–178 (2000)
5. Valenti, C.: A genetic algorithm for discrete tomography reconstruction. Genet. Program. Evolvable Mach. 9, 85–96 (2008)
6. Batenburg, K.J.: An evolutionary algorithm for discrete tomography. Discrete Appl. Math. 151, 36–54 (2005)
7. Michalewicz, Z.: Genetic Algorithm + Data Structure = Evolutionary Programs. Springer, Heidelberg (1996)

A Robust Watermarking Algorithm for Audio Signals Using SVD

Malay Kishore Dutta[1], Vinay K. Pathak[2], and Phalguni Gupta[3]

[1] Department of Electronics and Communication Engineering,
Galgotias College of Engineering and Technology, Greater NOIDA, India
[2] Department of Computer Science and Engineering, HBTI -Kanpur, India
[3] Department of Computer Science and Engineering, IIT – Kanpur, India
malay_kishore@rediffmail.com, vinaypathak.hbti@gmail.com,
pg@cse.iitk.ac.in

Abstract. Perceptual transparency and robustness are trade offs in audio watermarking which is an existing research problem. Synchronization attacks are the most challenging attack in audio watermarking. An algorithm is proposed in this paper which has good perceptual transparency and is also robust to synchronization attacks. The watermark embedding regions are selectively chosen in the high energy regions of the audio which makes the embedding process robust to signal processing attacks. The watermark is embedded in the audio in an adaptive manner. The degree of embedding is localized in nature and depends on the audio content of that localized region. The watermark is embedded by quantization of the singular values in the wavelet domain which makes the process perceptually transparent. The experimental results suggest that the proposed method maintains a good perceptual quality of the audio signal and maintains good robustness against signal processing attacks.

Keywords: Audio watermarking, Digital right management, Singular value decomposition, Robustness.

1 Introduction

With the development of high speed internet and transmission of audio files over the internet, there is a need of copyright protection and digital right management. Illegal reproduction and unauthorized distribution of digital audio has become a high alarming problem in protecting the copyright of digital media [1]. Digital watermarking is one of the possible solutions for copyright protection and digital right management. A watermark is designed for residing permanently in the original audio data even after repeated reproduction and distribution. Since human auditory system (HAS) is more sensitive than human visual system (HVS), embedding watermark to the audio signal is more difficult than that in an image. According to IFPI (International Federation of the phonographic Industry) [2], a good audio watermarking algorithm should be such that the addition of watermark should be perceptually transparent, of high security and robust to signal processing attacks.

S. Ranka et al. (Eds.): IC3 2010, Part I, CCIS 94, pp. 84–93, 2010.

These requirements are often contradictory with each other and there is a need to make a trade-off among them. These conflicting requirements create many challenges to design perceptually transparent and robust audio watermarking. The popular watermarking algorithms are in time domain [3], [4] and in frequency domain [5], [6]. There exist some algorithms which are bused on quantization methods and in cepstrum domain [7], [8].

It has been seen in all existing methods that synchronization attacks cause a severe problem in detection and recovery of watermark. In such an attack, the watermark is actually present in the audio signal but cannot be detected because of the synchronization. Synchronization attacks such as MP3 compression and TSM (time-scale modification) cause dislocation between embedding and detection in the time domain and are hence difficult to recover the watermark from the audio signal. Some methods which are proposed to solve the problem of synchronization attacks are exhaustive search [9], peak point extraction with special shaping [10], content based localized watermarking [11], high energy reference points based watermarking [12], and self synchronization for audio watermarking [13]. In these methods the watermarking is done in a uniform way after the region of embedding is decided. In the high energy points used as reference for synchronization [10], [11], [12], the watermark is embedded in the regions decided by the algorithm without taking care of any localization parameters. In doing so, the watermark embedded in the regions is sometimes under-loaded (can absorb more watermark data) and sometimes over-loaded (data embedded may be lost in synchronization attack). So there is a need for methods which can embed the watermark in the host audio signal in such a way that the embedding is done in a justified way according to the localized content of the audio.

This paper proposes a method where the amount of watermark data (degree of embedding) to be embedded in a region is decided by local parameters. In order to do so, the watermark data is embedded in a manner so that it can withstand synchronization attacks and also get accommodated in optimum number of regions for embedding. The proposed method is adaptive, is based on singular value decomposition (SVD) and is localized according to the content of the audio signal. It has been reported in case of image watermarking [14], [15] that the singular values (SV) of the image remain unaltered even if some alterations are made in the host image. It is expected the similar behavior in case of audio signals. The proposed method is designed based on this idea. Accordingly the inverse of this property where the SVs are modified without changing the perceptual property of the audio signal is used to watermark the audio signals.

The paper is organized as follows; Section 2 gives an overview of singular value decomposition (SVD). The method of selection of watermark embedding region is described in Section 3. The watermarking method in the SVD domain is proposed in Section 4. The performance evaluation parameters are discussed in Section 5. The experimental results that consist of subjective evaluation for perceptual transparency and robustness tests against signal processing attacks are analyzed in Section 6 while the last Section concludes the paper.

2 Singular Value Decomposition

Singular value decomposition (SVD) which is used to diagonalize matrices, packs most of the signal energy into a few singular values. The SVD belongs to the group of orthogonal transformations which decompose the input matrix into several matrices, one of which has only nonzero values in the main diagonal. An arbitrary matrix A of size $M{\times}N$ can be represented by its SVD in the form of:

$$A = USV^T$$

where U and V are $M{\times}M$ and $N{\times}N$ matrices respectively. The columns of U and V are mutually orthogonal unit vectors. The $M \times N$ matrix S is a pseudo-diagonal matrix and its diagonal elements, which are arranged by descending gradation, are all non-negative values. They are called SVs, and the first value is far bigger than others. While both U and V are not unique, the singular values are fully determined by A.

To apply the SVD in an audio signal the audio frames (coefficients in time domain or any other domain like DWT, DCT, FFT domain etc.) are converted into two dimensional matrix. The matrix S which has diagonal elements in the descending order can be modified / quantized as per the watermark bit to be embedded. To explain the method let us consider the original audio frame as A and W is the watermark bits to be embedded.

$A = USV^T$
S_W = Modified /Quantized value of S
$A_W = US_wV^T$

where S_W is the modified singular values and A_W is the watermarked audio frame whose SVs are modified.

3 Selection of Watermark Embedding Regions and Degree of Embedding

Finding the watermark embedding region is one of the most important steps in audio watermarking. If the embedding regions are not properly selected, the detection and recovery of the watermark under signal processing attacks is very difficult. This paper proposes the way to select embedding regions on the original audio waveform based on selecting high energy peaks as reference points.

It has been shown in [16] that synchronization attacks like time scale modifications (TSM) are performed on the harmonic components and the residual components separately. The harmonic portion is changed in time scale by modulating each harmonic component to DC, interpolating and decimating the DC signal and then demodulating each component back to its original frequency. The residual portion can be further separated into high energy transients and noise in the wavelet transform domain. In doing so the edges and the relative distances between the edges are preserved and the noise component is time scaled. In contemporary music, there is use of percussion instruments like drum, tabla etc. The beats of these instruments are the high energy music edges which can be used as reference points. Hence we can conclude that the time scale modification method elongates the audio signal in the low energy regions (minimum transients) and tends to conserve the high energy transients.

Thus if the watermark is embedded in audio segments near the high energy peaks, the effect of synchronization attacks become minimum. On the other hand, if the watermark is embedded in the minimum transient regions synchronization attacks may severely effect the detection and recovery of the watermark from the audio signal. If one bit is embedded in one region of embedding (ROE), then the number of reference points required to embed the watermark in case of normal convention (non-adaptive) method may be equal to the number of bits in the watermark. One can get a large number of ROE by decreasing the threshold. To do this data will be embedded in less sharp transients which is more prone to synchronization attack.

Based on the above discussion, the watermark embedding regions are chosen in the regions of high energy transients. The amount of watermark information to be embedded (degree of embedding, DOE) in these regions is kept adaptive according to the localized content. It is intended to embed more information in the more sharp music edges and less information in less sharp music edges which makes the embedding process adaptive in nature. Steps in selection of reference points for watermark embedding are as follows:

1. *Read Audio Signal as vector X.*
2. *Find the max value of the samples max[X (i]) in X.*
3. *Find all the peaks above [(1-n) [max(X (i)] where n is a fraction. Store these values in a vector D.*
4. *A new vector C is created as*

$$for\ n = 1:\ |D|$$
$$if\ D(i+1) - D(i) > |WM|$$
$$then\ C(i) = D(i);$$

where |WM| = length of watermark.

5. *The reference point i is mapped to the degree of embedding as shown in Table 1.*
6. *z=0*

$$for\ i = 1:length(C)$$
$$if\ K(i,j) > 0\ then$$

$$z = z + j;$$
C is the required set of reference points
else
$$n = n + 0.05$$
go to step step 3

The region of watermark embedding (ROE) is given by:

$$ROE(i) = [C(i) - |A|/2) : C(i) + |A|/2] \qquad (1)$$

(Excluding the point i)

The point i (high energy peak) is excluded so that it is not modified in the process of watermark embedding and creates a possibility of not detecting it in the watermark detection process. This point i is used as a reference and not for embedding of watermark. The number of watermark bits to be embedded in the *ROE* is called as degree of embedding *(DOE)*. In this paper the *DOE* is selected from a set of pre-decided ranges as shown in Table 1. However more optimized calculation of *DOE* can be done to suit the requirements for various types of audio files having different types of contents.

Table 1. Degree of Embedding for the Set of Reference Points

	Range of Reference point (i)	Degree of Embedding (j)
1	[max(X(i)] > i • 0.95* [max(X(i)]	10
2	0.95* [max(X(i)] > i • 0.90* [max(X(i)]	9
3	0.90* [max(X(i)] > i • 0.85 *[max(X(i)]	8
4	0.85* [max(X(i)] > i • 0.80 *[max(X(i)]	7
5	0.80* [max(X(i)] > i • 0.75 *[max(X(i)]	6
6	0.75* [max(X(i)] > i • 0.70 *[max(X(i)]	5
7	0.70* [max(X(i)] > i • 0.65 *[max(X(i)]	4
8	0.65* [max(X(i)] > i • 0.60 *[max(X(i)]	3
9	0.60* [max(X(i)] > i • 0.55 *[max(X(i)]	2
10	0.55* [max(X(i)] > i • 0.50 *[max(X(i)]	1

4 Watermark Embedding and Detection

The watermark used is a binary image B of size KxK and is given by

$$B = \{b(n_1, n_2) : 1 \leq n_1 \leq K, 1 \leq n_2 \leq K, \ b(n_1, n_1) \in \{0,1\}$$

The two dimensional binary image B of size KxK is converted into a one-dimensional sequence in order to embed it in the audio signal.

$$WM = \{wm(i) = b(n_1, n_2): 1 \leq n_1 \leq K, 1 \leq n_2 \leq K \qquad (2)$$
$$i = (n_1 - 1) \, x \, M + n_2, \ 1 \leq i \leq KxK$$

4.1 Watermark Embeddding

The watermark embedding steps are as follows:

Step 1: The region of embedding $ROE(i)$ is determined using equation 1.

Step 2: The reference point i is mapped to one of the degree of embedding j as given in Table 1.

Step 3: Third level DWT is applied to the audio segment using Haar wavelet.

Step 4: Divide the low frequency approximate wavelet components of each $ROE(i)$ segment into j equal sub-segments where j is the degree of embedding $DOE(i)$ for that corresponding $ROE(i)$

Step 5: The sub-segments are converted into blocks $ROE(i)(j)$ of size $m \, x \, m$ (blocks are converted into matrix to apply SVD). (Zero padding may be done to achieve $m \, x \, m$ size).

Step 6: SVD for each $ROE(i)(j)$ is calculated as

$$ROE(i)(j) = USV^T$$

Let $S_{ij} = (S_{11} \, S_{22} \, ... S_{mm})$ be the non zero diagonal elements of the matrix S for the jth sub-segment of the ith reference point.

Step 7: The watermark is embedded using Quantization index modulation. The embedding is done as follows:

> *for i = 1: length(wm)*
> *if K[i][j] >0 then*
> $S_{ij}' = |\_S_{ij}/\mu\_|.\mu + 3\mu/4$ *if wm (i) =1*
> $|\_S_{ij}/\mu\_|.\mu + \mu/4$ *if wm (i) =0*
> *i =i +1;*
> *end for*

$|\_\_|$ indicates the floor function and S_{ij} and S_{ij}' the   SVD of DWT coefficients of the low frequency j^{th} sub-segment of the ith reference point of original and watermarked audio data respectively.

By increasing the value of μ the robustness increases but imperceptibility   decreases. This value of μ has to be maximized in such a way so that the watermark maintains perceptual transparency.

Step 8: The watermarked sub-segment $\overline{ROE(i)(j)}$ is obtained by applying inverse SVD to the modified singular values.

Step 9: The modified audio segment is constructed from all the modified sub-segments. The inverse DWT is performed to get the watermarked signal.

4.2 Watermark Detection

The watermark extraction is the reverse process of the watermark embedding process. The first step in this process is to identify the embedding regions (ROE). Once the embedding regions are identified then the watermark detection and recovery can be performed. The synchronization points are to be first determined and then the ROE is to be estimated.

Step 1: Vector C containing the index (i elements) of all the high energy reference points are determined using the same value of threshold that have been used in the embedding process.

Step 2: From this value of i calculate the degree of embedding using Table 1.

Step 3: The $ROE(i)$ is calculated using equation 1. Take DWT of this segment. This DWT segment ROE(i) is divided into j equal sub-segments. The sub-segments are converted into blocks $ROEWM(i)(j)$ of size m X m. (blocks are converted into matrix to apply SVD, Zero padding may be done to achieve m X m size).

Step 4: SVD for each $ROE(i)(j)$ is calculated as
> $ROE(i)(j) = USV^T$

Let $S_{ij} = (S_{11} S_{22} ....S_{mm})$ be the non zero diagonal elements of the matrix S for the jth sub- segment of the ith reference point.

Step 5: The watermark wm is extracted as follows:

> $wm(k) = 1$ *if* $S_{ij}* - |\_ S_{ij}*/S\_| \cdot S \geq S/2$
> $wm(k) = 0$ *if* $S_{ij}* - |\_ S_{ij}*/S\_| \cdot S < S/2$
> $k = 1: length(wm).$

It can be seen from above that the original SVD coefficients are not required in the extraction process and thus the algorithm is blind in nature.

5 Performance Analysis

The performance of the proposed method of audio watermarking is evaluated by some performance coefficients as discussed below:

a. Normalized Correlation (NC)
    The normalized correlation (NC) is used to evaluate the similarity measurement of extracted binary watermark, which can be defined as:

$$NC(W, W^*) = \frac{\sum_{i=1}^{M} W(i) \; W^*(i)}{\sqrt{\sum_{i=1}^{M} W(i)^2} \; \sqrt{\sum_{i=1}^{M} W^*(i)^2}}$$

where W and W^* are original and extracted watermark respectively, i is the index of the watermark and M is the length of the watermark.

b. Bit Error Rate (BER)
    The bit error rate (BER) is used to find the percentage of error bits between original watermark and extracted watermark. The BER is given by:

$$BER = \frac{1}{M} \sum_{i=1}^{1 \leq i \leq M} w(i) \oplus w^*(i)$$

d. Subjective Listening Test
    Ten listeners of different age groups are provided with the original and the watermarked audio signal, and they are asked to classify the difference in terms the mean opinion score (MOS) grades. The MOS grades are defined in Table 2.

Table 2. MOS Definitions

Effect of Watermark	Quality of Audio	Score
Imperceptible	Excellent	0
Perceptible but not annoying	Good	-1
Slightly annoying	Fair	-2
Annoying	Poor	-3
Very Annoying	Very Poor	-4

6 Experimental Results

Experiments have been performed with different types of audio files. As discussed in Section 3 the degree of embedding is dependent on the localized audio characteristics which make a justified method of embedding data in the audio. In case of non-adaptive data embedding more number of ROE are required which can be achieved by decreasing the threshold (which is a fraction of the maximum value of the audio signal, as shown in Table 4). Thus data will be embedded in less sharp music edges which is more prone to synchronization attacks. The binary image used as watermark is given in Fig. 1.The robustness test for the proposed method is compared with non-adaptive method in Table 4. The results of subjective tests are given in Table 3.

Fig. 1. Binary image watermark

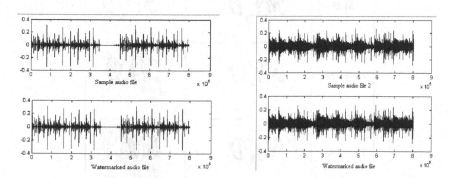

Fig. 2. The original (Sample1 and Sample 2) sampled at 44.1 KHz and the watermarked signal

Table 3. MOS Grades of subjective listening test

Watermarked Audio	MOS
Tabla	0
Classical	0
Multiple Musical Instrument	-1
Country	0
Pop	0

Table 4. Comparison of Performance of the Proposed Adaptive Method against Signal Processing Attacks to Non-Adaptive Method

Non-adaptive method (Uniform DOE)														
Audio Sample	No of ROE used for watermarking	Threshold value required	+ 2% TSM		+5% TSM		-2% TSM		-5% TSM		Low pass filtering		MP3 compression	
			BER	NC	BER	NC	BER	NC	BER	NC	BER	NC	BER	NC
Tabla	4096	0.55	12%	0.92	19%	0.88	13%	0.91	21%	0.86	14%	0.91	17%	0.89
Classical	4096	0.58	14%	0.91	25%	0.82	15%	0.91	23%	0.84	15%	0.90	21%	0.86
Multiple Musical Instruments	4096	0.49	13%	0.91	24%	0.82	13%	0.91	24%	0.83	11%	0.93	19%	0.88
Country	4096	0.51	15%	0.90	27%	0.80	13%	0.91	29%	0.78	12%	0.92	21%	0.86
Pop	4096	0.56	19%	0.88	32%	0.68	20%	0.86	34%	0.66	18%	0.88	27%	0.80
Proposed adaptive method (DOE based on localized property)														
Tabla	887	0.71	7%	0.97	11%	0.93	7%	0.97	12%	0.92	8%	0.97	11%	0.93
Classical	1022	0.69	10%	0.94	14%	0.91	9%	0.95	13%	0.91	6%	0.96	12%	0.92
Multiple Musical Instruments	918	0.72	8%	0.95	16%	0.90	8%	0.95	15%	0.90	8%	0.97	11%	0.93
Country	987	0.77	10%	0.94	15%	0.90	9%	0.95	16%	0.90	7%	0.96	10%	0.94
Pop	891	0.76	17%	0.89	13%	0.91	18%	0.89	14%	0.91	11%	0.94	15%	0.90

Attack	Proposed Method (adaptive DOE)	Non-adaptive DOE
TSM 1%	 *MKD*	 *MKD*
TSM 2%	 *MKD*	 *MKD*
TSM 3%	 *MKD*	 *MKD*
TSM 5%	 *MKD*	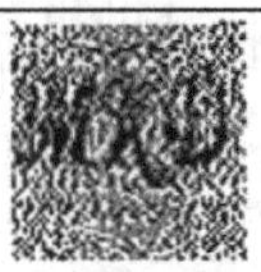 *MKD*

Fig. 4. Binary Watermark Recovered under Signal Processing Attacks

7 Conclusion

A content based adaptive audio watermarking is proposed in this paper. The amount of watermark data to be embedded in a localized region is based on localized parameters of the audio signal. Hence a variable degree of embedding is proposed which embeds the watermark in the audio signal in an optimized way so that the method is robust to signal processing attacks and also perceptually transparent to human auditory system. The watermark is embedded in DWT domain using quantization of SVD coefficients. Experimental results and listening subjective tests confirm that the watermarking method embeds the watermark in an imperceptible way and offer good robustness to common signal processing attacks.

References

1. Bender, W., Gruhl, D., Morimoto, N., Lu, A.: Techniques for data hiding. IBM Systems Journal 35(3-4), 313–336 (1996)
2. Katzenbeisser, S., Petitcolas, F.A.P.: Information Hiding Techniques for Steganography and Digital Watermarking. Artech House Inc. (2000)
3. Gerzon, M.A., Graven, P.G.: A high-rate buried-data channel for audio CD. Journal of the Audio Engineering Society 43(1/2), 3–22 (1995)
4. Gruhl, D., et al.: Echo hiding. In: Anderson, R. (ed.) IH 1996. LNCS, vol. 1174, pp. 295–315. Springer, Heidelberg (1996)

5. Cooperman, M., Moskowitz, S.: Steganographic Method and Device: U.S. Patent 5613004 (1997)
6. Huang, J., Wang, Y., Shi, Y.Q.: A blind audio watermarking algorithm with self-synchronization. IEEE Int. Symp. Circuits and Systems 3, 627–630 (2002)
7. Akhaee, M.A., Saberian, M.J., Feizi, S., Marvasti, F.: Robust Audio Data Hiding Using Correlated Quantization With Histogram-Based Detector. IEEE Transactions on Multimedia, 834–842 (2009)
8. Bhat, V., Sengupta, I., Das, A.: Audio Watermarking Based on Mean Quantizationin Cepstrum Domain. In: International Conference on Advance Computing and Communications, pp. 73–77 (2008)
9. Arnold, M.: Audio watermarking: Features, applications, and algorithms. In: Proc. IEEE Int. Conf. Multimedia & Expo., vol. 2, pp. 1013–1016 (2000)
10. Wei, F.S., Feng, X., Li, M.: A Blind Audio Watermarking Scheme Using Peak Point Extraction. IEEE International Symposium on Circuits and Systems 5, 4409–4412 (2005)
11. Li, X.X., Lu, P.: Localized Audio Watermarking Technique Robust Against Time-Scale Modification. IEEE Transactions on Multimedia 8(1), 60–69 (2006)
12. Dutta, M.K., Gupta, P., Pathak, V.K.: Biometric Based Audio Watermarking. In: Proceedings of International Conference on Multimedia Information Networking and Security, pp. 10–14 (2009)
13. Wu, S., Huang, J., Huang, D.: Efficiently Self-Synchronized Audio Watermarking for Assured Audio Data Transmission. IEEE Transactions on Broadcasting 51(1), 69–76 (2005)
14. Liu, R., Tan, T.: A SVD-Based Watermarking Scheme for Protecting Rightful Ownership. IEEE Transactions on Multimedia 4(1), 121–128 (2002)
15. yavuz, E., Telatar, Z.: Improved SVD-DWT based digital image watermarking against watermark ambiguity. In: ACM Symposium on Applied Computing, pp. 1051–1055 (2007)
16. Duxbury, C., Davies, M.E., Sandier, M.B.: Separation of transient information in audio using multi-resolution analysis techniques. In: Proc. Int. Workshop on Digital Audio Effects, pp. 21–27 (December 2001)

Differential Evolution Using Interpolated Local Search

Musrrat Ali, Millie Pant, and V.P. Singh

Dept. of Paper Technology, Indian Institute of Technology Roorkee, Roorkee, India
musrrat.iitr@gmail.com, millifpt@iitr.ernet.in,
singhvp3@gmail.com

Abstract. In this paper we propose a novel variant of the Differential Evolution (DE) algorithm based on local search. The corresponding algorithm is named as Differential Evolution with Interpolated Local Search (DEILS). In DEILS, the local search operation is applied in an adaptive manner. The adaptive behavior enables the algorithm to search its neighborhood in an effective manner and the interpolation helps in exploiting the solutions. In this way a balance is maintained between the exploration and exploitation factors. The performance of DEILS is investigated and compared with basic differential evolution, modified versions of DE and some other evolutionary algorithms. It is found that the proposed scheme improves the performance of DE in terms of quality of solution without compromising with the convergence rate.

Keywords: global optimization, differential evolution, quadratic interpolation, local search.

1 Introduction

Differential Evolution, proposed by Storn and Price in 1995 [1], has emerged as a popular choice for solving global optimization problems [2]. Using a few parameters, DE exhibits an overall excellent performance for a wide range of benchmark as well as real-world application problems [3]. However, despite several attractive features, it has been observed that the performance of DE is not completely flawless.

DE has certain unique features that distinguish it from other population based evolutionary algorithms (EA). It has a distinctive manner in which it generates the new points and performs selection of points for the next generation. In DE every individual produces a single offspring with the help of directional information. Further, it is designed in such a manner that after the selection process, the points for the next generation are either better or as good as the points of the previous generation. Although these features are there to make DE an effective algorithm, they sometimes hinder its performance by slowing down the convergence rate. Some other drawbacks of DE [4] include premature convergence, where the algorithms stops without even reaching a local optimal solution and stagnation, where the algorithm accepts new points in the population but shows no improvement in fitness function value. Therefore, researchers are now concentrating on improving the performance of the classical DE algorithm by using different heuristics. These modifications mainly consist of;

S. Ranka et al. (Eds.): IC3 2010, Part I, CCIS 94, pp. 94–106, 2010.
© Springer-Verlag Berlin Heidelberg 2010

introducing new mutation strategies, using adaptive control parameters, variation in initial population etc [5] – [15]. Several recent versions of DE can be found in [16].

One of the methods by which the performance of a global optimization algorithm like DE can be enhanced is its hybridization with a local search. This may accelerate the performance of DE by providing it some additional information about the search domain.

Local search (LS) mechanism can be applied in several ways for example the initial population may be generated by using a LS so that the search technique has some a priori knowledge about the domain. It may also be applied during the processing of the algorithm to explore its neighborhood. Noman and Iba in their work [17] pointed out that the adaptive nature of the LS mechanism exploits the neighborhood quite effectively and significantly improves the convergence characteristics of the algorithm. They proposed the use of simplex crossover operator (SPX) as LS and named their algorithm as DEahcSPX, which reportedly gave a good performance on a test suite of global optimization problems. Inspired by the performance DEahcSPX, in the present study we propose a new LS method namely Interpolated Local Search (ILS) and analyze its effect on the convergence of basic DE. We have applied ILS in an adaptive manner and have named the corresponding algorithm as Differential Evolution with Interpolated Local Search (DEILS). Its comparison with basic DE and other algorithms show that the proposed schemes enhance the convergence rate besides maintaining the solution quality.

The remainder of the paper is structured as follows. Section 2 gives the basic Differential Evolution. Section 3 describes the local search ILS, used in this study. Section 4 presents the proposed DEILS algorithm. Experimental setting and Benchmark problems are given in Section 5. Section 6 provides comparisons of results. Finally the paper is concluded in section 7.

2 Differential Evolution

Throughout the present study we shall follow *DE/rand/1/bin* version of DE [1] and shall refer to it as basic version. This particular scheme is briefly described as:

DE starts with a population of NP candidate solutions: $X_{i,G}$, $i = 1, \ldots ,$NP, where the index i denotes the ith individual of the population and G denotes the generation to which the population belongs. The three main operators of DE are mutation, crossover and selection.

Mutation: The mutation operation of DE applies the vector differentials between the existing population members for determining both the degree and direction of perturbation applied to the individual subject of the mutation operation. The mutation process at each generation begins by randomly selecting three individuals $X_{r1,G}$, $X_{r2,G}$ and $X_{r3,G}$,in the population set of (say) NP elements. The ith perturbed individual, $V_{i,G+1}$, is generated based on the three chosen individuals as follows:

$$V_{i,G+1} = X_{r3,G} + F * (X_{r1,G} - X_{r2,G}) \qquad (1)$$

Where, $i = 1. \ldots$ NP, $r_1, r_2, r_3 \in \{1. \ldots$ NP$\}$ are randomly selected such that $r_1 \neq r_2 \neq r_3 \neq i$, F is the control parameter such that $F \in [0, 1]$.

Crossover: once the mutant vector is generated, the perturbed individual, $V_{i,G+1} = (v_{1,i,G+1}, \ldots, v_{n,i,G+1})$, and the current population member, $X_{i,G} = (x_{1,i,G}, \ldots, x_{n,i,G})$, are then subject to the crossover operation, that finally generates the population of candidates, or "trial" vectors, $U_{i,G+1} = (u_{1,i,G+1}, \ldots, u_{n,i,G+1})$, as follows:

$$u_{j,i,G+1} = \begin{cases} v_{j,i,G+1} \ if \ rand_j \leq C_r \vee j = k \\ x_{j,i,G} \qquad\qquad otherwise \end{cases} \tag{2}$$

Where, $j = 1 \ldots n$, $k \in \{1, \ldots, n\}$ is a random parameter's index, chosen once for each i. The crossover rate, $Cr \in [0, 1]$, is set by the user.

Selection: The selection scheme of DE also differs from that of other EAs. The population for the next generation is selected from the individual in current population and its corresponding trial vector according to the following rule:

$$X_{i,G+1} = \begin{cases} U_{i,G+1} \ if \ f(U_{i,G+1}) \leq f(X_{i,G}) \\ X_{i,G} \qquad\qquad otherwise \end{cases} \tag{3}$$

Thus, each individual of the temporary (trial) population is compared with its counterpart in the current population. The one with the lower objective function value will survive from the tournament selection to the population of the next generation. As a result, all the individuals of the next generation are as good as or better than their counterparts in the current generation. In DE trial vector is not compared against all the individuals in the current generation, but only against one individual, its counterpart, in the current generation.

3 Interpolated Local Search (ILS)

The proposed ILS is based on Quadratic Interpolation (QI) method. ILS is one of the simplest and the oldest direct search method used for solving optimization problems. It makes use of gradient in a numerical way. In ILS, three distinct points are chosen randomly from the population. A parabolic curve is fitted into the selected points and the point lying at the minimum of this quadratic curve is then evaluated. Mathematically, the new point (say T) is obtained as follows:

$$T = \frac{1}{2} \frac{(X_{r1,G}^2 - X_{r2,G}^2)f(X_{r3,G}) + (X_{r2,G}^2 - X_{r3,G}^2)f(X_{r1,G}) + (X_{r3,G}^2 - X_{r1,G}^2)f(X_{r2,G})}{(X_{r1,G} - X_{r2,G})f(X_{r3,G}) + (X_{r2,G} - X_{r3,G})f(X_{r1,G}) + (X_{r3,G} - X_{r1,G})f(X_{r2,G})}$$

The symbols have the usual meaning as described in the previous section. Initially, this method was designed to solve problems having a single variable.

ILS has been used in conjugation with several variants of random search/ evolutionary algorithms and has given good results. H. Li [20] proposed a hybrid genetic algorithm (HGA), incorporating QI, for solving constrained optimization problems. Zhang et al [21], used it in DE. Some other papers using QI approach are [18], [19].

4 The Proposed DEILS Algorithm

In this section we give the proposed Differential Evolution with Interpolated Local Search, DEILS, which makes use of ILS in an adaptive manner. Here we would like to mention that in the present study we have made a slight change in ILS. Here, we select one best point and two random points distinct from each other and also from the best point. This is in contrast with the original ILS, where three distinct points are selected randomly. The presence of a best point biases the search in the neighborhood of the individual having the best fitness. DEILS start like the basic DE up to the selection process. Then at the end of every generation, the point having the best fitness is selected and its neighborhood is explored with the help of local search scheme (i.e. ILS). The local search is applied in an adaptive manner. That is to say, the process of LS is repeated till the time there is an improvement in the fitness of the best particle (say X_{Best}). In case there is no improvement in the fitness the algorithm moves on to the next generation. The working of this algorithm is described with the help of a flowchart in Fig. 1.

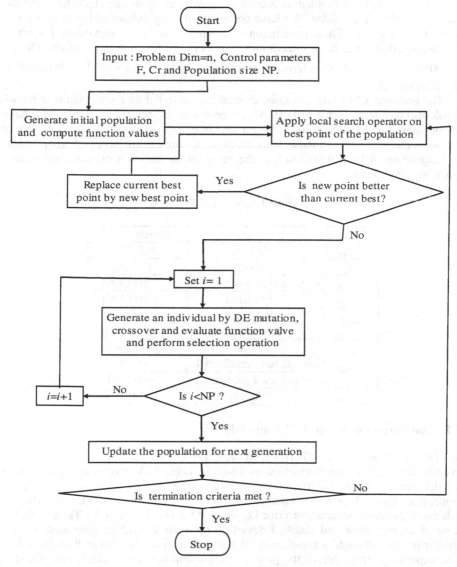

Fig. 1. Flow chart of DEILS

5 Experimental Setup and Benchmark Problems

In order to make a fair comparison of proposed algorithm and basic DE, we have used C++ rand ( ) function to generate initial population for both the algorithms. The number of individuals in the population is taken as the dimension of the problem. Scaling factor F is generally taken within the range [0.4, 1.2]. In general very large values of C_r may end up in premature convergence, while very small values of C_r may slow down the rate of convergence. In the present study, we have taken F=0.5 and Cr=0.5. Both these values were taken after the fine tuning of parameters.

All the algorithms taken in the present study are executed on a PIV PC, using DEV C++. Each problem is executed thirty times by all the algorithms and the average results are recorded. We have compared the algorithms taking two criteria; error and evaluations. Thus, termination criterion is different in both cases. For error, the termination criteria is maximum number of function evaluation (NFE= 10000*Dim). For evaluation termination criterion is $\left| f^* - f_{\min} \right| \le \varepsilon = 10^{-6}$. Where f^* is global optimum.

The performances of the proposed algorithms are tested on a set of ten benchmark problems taken from literature [17]. All the problems are scalable in nature. We have solved them for dimension 30. This test set though small contains a diverse set of problems and serves as a suitable launch pad for testing the efficiency of an optimization algorithm. A brief description of the name of the function, its code and search range are given Table 1.

Table 1. Benchmark Problems

Code	Name	Search range
f_{sph}	Sphere	[-100,100]
f_{ack}	Ackley	[-32,32]
f_{sch}	Generalized Schwefel	[-500,500]
f_{sal}	Salomon	[-100,100]
f_{ras}	Rastrigin	[-5,5]
f_{ros}	Rosenbrock	[-100,100]
f_{grw}	Griewank	[-600,600]
f_{pn1}	Generalized Penalized 1	[-50,50]
f_{pn2}	Generalized Penalized 2	[-50,50]
f_{wht}	Whitely	[-100,100]

5.1 Comparison between DEILS and DE

In this section we compare DEILS with basic DE algorithm. The results in terms of average error and standard deviation are listed in Table 2. Average error is defined as the difference between the true global optimum value and the value obtained by the algorithm. Table 3 provides number of function evaluations (NFE) obtained to achieve the desired accuracy of error i.e. 10^{-06}. As it is clear from the Table 2 that in term of average error and standard deviation both the algorithms give more or less similar results although in some cases DEILS performs slightly better than basic DE. The superior performance of the proposed algorithm is more evident from Table 3, which gives the average number of functions evaluations. Here the maximum NFE is fixed as 300000. From Table 3 we can see that DEILS takes lesser NFE to achieve the required fitness in comparison to the basic DE in five cases and there is a tie in remaining five cases. Performance curves (convergence graphs) of few selected functions are given in Fig2(a) – Fig2(d).From these illustrations also it is evident that the convergence of proposed DEILS is faster than basic DE.

Table 2. Mean error and standard deviation (std) of function in 30 runs

fun	Error			
	DE	DEILS	DE	DEILS
f_{sph}	5.49987e-149	0.00000e+00	4.55330e-147	0.00000e+00
f_{ack}	3.69735e-15	3.69735e-15	8.34353e-23	7.43032e-21
f_{sch}	6.81827e-04	6.81827e-04	7.43300e-07	5.43211e-06
f_{sal}	1.99873e-01	9.99066e-02	5.34343e-02	1.34945e-02
f_{ras}	8.26081e+01	5.46332e+01	1.44733e+01	5.56690e+01
f_{ros}	2.45162e+01	2.05378e+01	3.45332e+02	4.38822e+01
f_{grw}	0.00000e+00	0.00000e+00	4.32382e-31	8.54829e-34
f_{pn1}	1.35360e-19	1.35360e-19	4.32382e-26	5.34933e-28
f_{pn2}	1.29115e-19	1.29115e-19	2.43486e-23	7.54332e-22
f_{wht}	3.62633e+02	3.52693e+02	5.59321e+01	4.43932e+01

Table 3. Mean number of function evaluation to achieve accuracy 10^{-6}

fun	DE	DEILS
f_{sph}	21270	**19482**
f_{ack}	31950	**26839**
f_{sch}	300000	300000
f_{sal}	300000	300000
f_{ras}	300000	300000
f_{ros}	300000	300000
f_{grw}	23370	**19876**
f_{pn1}	20730	**16521**
f_{pn2}	21780	**18445**
f_{wht}	300000	300000

5.2 Comparison between DEILS and Other State of the Art Algorithms

The performance of the proposed DEILS is further compared with two modified versions of DE; DEahcSPX [17] and TDE [14]. We executed these algorithms with same parameter settings as given in relevant literatures. Also we have compared DEILS with some other state of the art evolutionary algorithms like G3+PCX, MGG+UNDX and MGG+SPX. For these three algorithms we have taken the results given in [17]. All these algorithms have reportedly given good performance for a set of benchmark problems. The results obtained are summarized in Tables 4 and 5. In Table 4, the

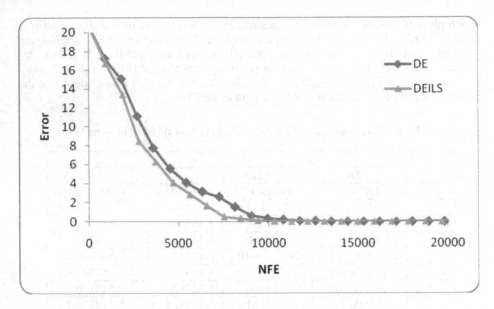

Fig. 2. (a) Performance curves of Ackley function

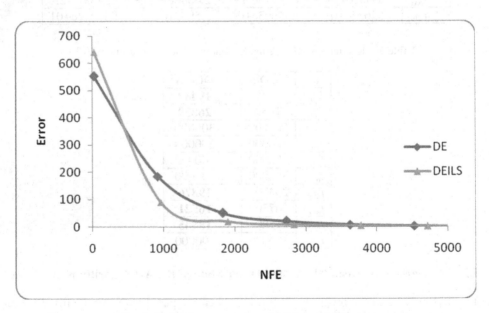

Fig. 2. (b) Performance curves of Griewank function

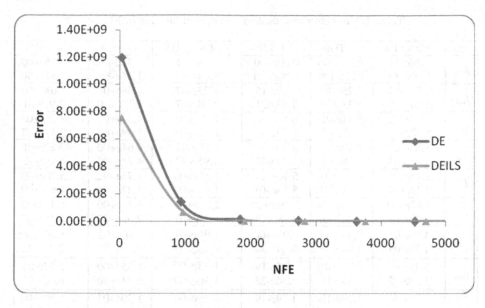

Fig. 2. (c) Performance curves of PN1 function

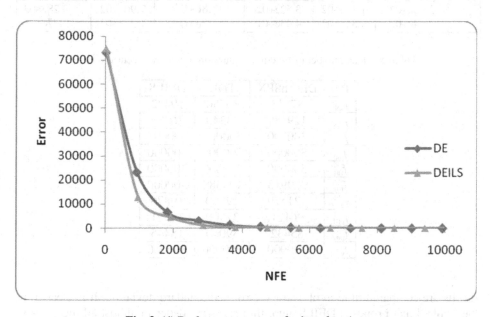

Fig. 2. (d) Performance curves of sphere function

Table 4. Mean error and standard deviation of function in 30 runs

fun	DEahcSPX	TDE	DEILS	MGG+UNDX	G3+PCX	MGG+SPX
f_{sph}	9.50e-31	4.53e-100	0.00e+00	1.73e-11	3.58e-81	8.75e+00
	3.09e-30	4.22e-106	0.00e+00	1.94e-11	1.36e-81	2.87e+00
f_{ack}	1.78e-14	7.25e-13	3.69e-15	8.23e-07	1.48e+01	1.68e+00
	1.01e-32	2.33e-30	7.43e-21	4.64e-07	4.17e+00	2.99e-01
f_{sch}	2.89e+02	6.81e-01	6.81e-04	4.12e+03	4.04e+03	8.70e+03
	5.48e+02	1.23e-01	5.43e-06	1.72e+03	1.09e+03	2.41e+02
f_{sal}	1.83e-01	1.99e-01	9.99e-02	1.50e-01	4.64e+00	3.82e-01
	3.45e-03	9.98e-02	1.34e-02	4.95e-02	4.74e+00	4.29e-02
f_{ras}	2.45e+01	1.29e+01	5.46e+01	1.35e+00	1.75e+02	5.78e+00
	2.43e+01	8.56e+01	5.56e+01	1.03e+00	3.37e+01	1.83e+00
f_{ros}	1.87e+00	2.23e+00	2.058e+01	2.81e+01	4.18e+00	1.38e+03
	5.01e+01	1.026e-01	4.38e+01	1.23e+01	9.68e+01	6.45e+02
f_{grw}	4.94e-03	7.39e-03	0.00e+00	2.96e-04	1.07e-02	1.09e+00
	4.79e-04	1.08e-19	8.54e-34	1.48e-03	1.30e-02	2.24e-02
f_{pn1}	3.45e-06	1.35e-019	1.35e-19	4.93e-02	4.35e+00	2.57e-01
	5.53e-05	1.84e-18	5.34e-28	3.50e-02	6.94e+00	6.90e-02
f_{pn2}	2.39e-30	1.29e-19	1.29e-19	4.39e-04	1.50e+01	2.29e+00
	4.34e-31	7.34e-21	7.54e-22	2.20e-03	1.58e+01	3.72e-01
f_{wht}	3.05e+02	1.49e+02	3.52e+02	4.28e+02	7.90e+02	3.28e+03
	2.34e+02	4.34e+02	4.43e+01	3.82e+01	1.27e+02	2.77e+03

Table 5. Mean number of function evaluation to achieve accuracy 10^{-6}

fun	DEachSPX	TDE	DEILS
f_{sph}	87013	30750	19482
f_{ack}	129189	44340	26839
f_{sch}	300000	300000	300000
f_{sal}	300000	300000	300000
f_{ras}	300000	300000	300000
f_{ros}	299913	193380	300000
f_{grw}	121579	29880	19876
f_{pn1}	96121	37500	16521
f_{pn2}	85432	39060	18445
f_{wht}	300000	300000	300000

results are compared in term of average error and standard deviation. It is clear from the Table 4 that proposed DEILS algorithm performs better in almost all the cases in comparison to the other algorithms. From Table 5 we can see that DEILS takes lesser number of function evaluations in most of the functions to achieve the accuracy given in last column. Performance curves of few selected functions showing the comparison of the DEILS with TDE and DEahcSPX are illustrated in Fig. 3(a) – 3(d).

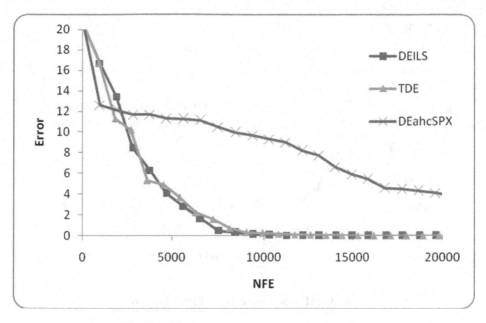

Fig. 3. (a) Performance curves of Ackley function

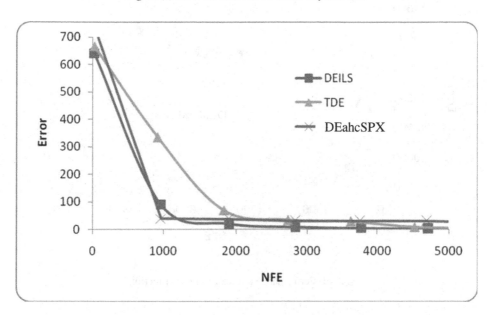

Fig. 3. (b) Performance curves Griewank function

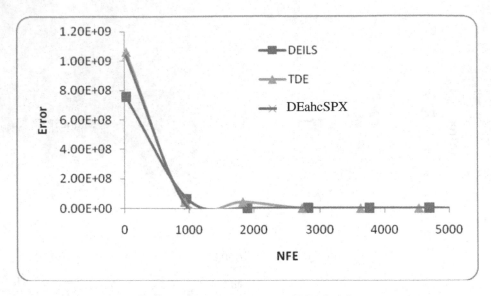

Fig. 3. (c) Performance curves of PN1 function

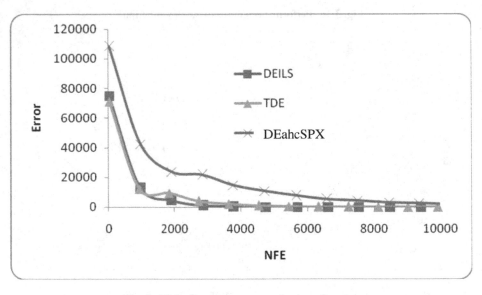

Fig. 3. (d) Performance curves of sphere function

6 Discussions and Conclusions

In this paper we presented a new LS scheme; Interpolated Local Search (ILS) embedded in the structure of basic DE and applied it adaptively to explore the neighborhood of the best individual in the population. The corresponding algorithm is named as DEILS. The ILS scheme makes a judicious use of the exploration and exploitation abilities of the search mechanism and is therefore more likely to avoid false or premature convergence. This scheme is rather greedy in nature as it bias the new trial solution strongly in the direction where the best one of three individuals chosen for the mutation lies and can therefore be viewed as good local search.

The simulation of results showed that the DEILS algorithm is quite competent for solving problems of different dimensions in less number of function evaluations without compromising with the quality of solution.

Its comparison with other variants of DE as well as with some other state of the algorithms (DEahcSPX, TDE, G3+PCX, MGG+UNDX and MGG+SPX) shows the promising nature of DEILS. However, we would like to maintain that the work is still in the preliminary stages and efforts continue for advanced study. We intend to apply it for more complex problems and compare its performance with other versions of DE and with other optimization algorithms.

References

1. Storn, R., Price, K.: Differential evolution – a simple and efficient adaptive scheme for global optimization over continuous spaces.Technical Report TR-95-012, Berkeley, CA (1995)
2. Storn, R., Price, K.V.: Differential evolution—A simple and efficient heuristic for global optimization over continuous spaces. J. Global Opt. 11(4), 341–359 (1997)
3. Price, K.V., Storn, R.M., Lampinen, J.A.: Differential Evolution: A Practical Approach to Global Optimization. Springer, Berlin (2005)
4. Lampinen, J., Zelinka, I.: On stagnation of the differential evolution algorithm. In: Ošmera, P. (ed.) Proc. of MENDEL 2000, 6th International Mendel Conference on Soft Computing, pp. 76–83 (2000)
5. Pant, M., Thangaraj, R., Abraham, A., Grosan, C.: Differential Evolution with Laplace Mutation Operator. IEEE Congress on Evolutionary Computation, 2841–2849 (2009)
6. Ali, M., Pant, M., Abraham, A.: Mixed Strategy Embedded Differential Evolution. IEEE Congress on Evolutionary Computation, 2841–2849 (2009)
7. Brest, J., Zamuda, A., Boskovic, B., Maucec, M.S., Zumer, V.: Dynamic Optimization using Differential Evolution. IEEE Congress on Evolutionary Computation, 415–421 (2009)
8. Epitropakis, M.G., Plagianakos, V.P., Vrahatis, M.N.: Evolutionary Adaption of the Differential Evolution Control Parameters. IEEE Congress on Evolutionary Computation, 1359–1366 (2009)
9. Menchaca-Mendez, A., Coello, C.A.C.: A new proposal to hybridize the Nelder Mead Differential Evolution Algorithm for Constrained Optimization. IEEE Congress on Evolutionary Computation, 2598–2605 (2009)
10. Tasgetiren, M.F., Pan, Q.-K., Suganthan, P.N., Liang, Y.-C.: A Differential Evolution Algorithm with Variable Parameter Search for Real Parameter Continuous Function Optimization. IEEE Congress on Evolutionary Computation, 1247–1254 (2009)
11. Pant, M., Ali, M., Singh, V.P.: Parent centric differential evolution algorithm for global optimization. J. Opsearch 46(2), 153–168 (2009)
12. Lai, J.C.Y., Leung, F.H.F., Ling, S.H.: A new Differential Evolution Algorithm with Wavelet Theory based Mutation operation. IEEE Congress on Evolutionary Computation, 1116–1122 (2009)
13. Omran, G.H.M., Engelbrecht, A.P.: Free Search Differential Evolution. IEEE Congress on Evolutionary Computation, 110–117 (2009)

14. Fan, H.-Y., Lampinen, J.: A Trigonometric Mutation Operation to Differential Evolution. J. of Global Optimization 27, 105–129 (2003)
15. Rahnamayan, S., Tizhoosh, H.R., Salama, M.M.A.: A novel population initialization method for accelerating evolutionary algorithms. J. Computer and Applied Mathematics with Application 53, 1605–1614 (2007)
16. Chakraborty, U.K.: Advances in Differential Evolution. Springer, Heidelberg (2008)
17. Noman, N., Iba, H.: Accelerating differential evolution using an adaptive local search. J. IEEE transactions on evolutionary computation 12(1), 107–125 (2008)
18. Mohan, C., Shanker, K.: A Controlled Random Search Technique For Global Optimization using Quadratic Approximation. J. Asia-Pacific Journal of Operational Research 11, 93–101 (1994)
19. Ali, M.M., Torn, A., Vitanen, D.S.: A numerical comparison of some modified controlled random search algorithms. J. Global Optimization 11, 341–359 (1997)
20. Li, H., Jiao, Y.C., Wang, Y.P.: Integrating the simplified interpolation into the genetic algorithm for constrained optimization problems, pp. 247–254. Springer, Heidelberg (2005)
21. Zhang, L., Jiao, Y.-C., Li, H., Zhang, F.-S.: Hybrid Differential Evolution and the Simplified Quadratic Interpolation for Global Optimization. In: GEC 2009, Shanghai, China, June 12-14. ACM, New York (2009), 978-1-60558-326-6/09/06

A New SVD Based Watermarking Framework in Fractional Fourier Domain

Gaurav Bhatnagar[1] and Balasubramanian Raman[2]

[1] University of Windsor, Windsor-N9C 1M2, ON, Canada
goravb@uwindsor.ca
[2] Indian Institute of Technology Roorkee, Roorkee-247 667, India
balaiitr@ieee.org

Abstract. In this paper, a new robust watermarking scheme is proposed using fractional Fourier transform (FrFT) and singular value decomposition. The core idea of the proposed scheme is to decompose an image using FrFT followed by the non-overlapping block segmentation. A new key matrix is then formed by taking maximum singular values of all non-overlapping blocks. For embedding this key matrix is used and is done by modifying singular values with the singular values of the watermark. The experimental results show better visual imperceptibility and resiliency of the proposed scheme against intentional or un-intentional variety of attacks.

Keywords: Digital Watermarking, Fractional Fourier Transform, Singular Value Decomposition.

1 Introduction

With the rapid exploitation of computer and internet technology, it is easier to manipulate digital media. To ensure the rightful ownership and the authenticity of the original media, digital watermarking [1] is identified as a suitable solution. Digital watermarking is a technique for inserting information into a digital media. The embedding/insertion is made in such a way that it must not cause serious degradation to the original digital media. Embedding must be done either in spatial domain [2,7] or in frequency domain [4,5,6,7]. Frequency Domain Methods are the most popular in comparison with Spatial Domain Methods because when an image is inverse transformed, watermark is distributed irregularly over the image. Recently, for transforming images into frequency domain, Fourier transform, discrete cosine transform, wavelet transform etc are used. Among these transforms wavelet transform proves very popular these days since it is localized in both spatial and frequency domain.

Few years ago, another transform called Singular Value Decomposition (SVD) [8,9] was explored for watermarking. The core idea behind these schemes is to modify the singular values of the image or image blocks with the singular values of watermark. Recently, some researchers present hybrid watermarking schemes

S. Ranka et al. (Eds.): IC3 2010, Part I, CCIS 94, pp. 107–118, 2010.
© Springer-Verlag Berlin Heidelberg 2010

in which they combine SVD with other transforms. SVD based scheme withstands a variety attacks but it is not resistant to geometric attacks like rotation, cropping etc. Hence, for improving the performance of watermarking system, hybridization is needed. In literature, there are two famous hybrid watermarking schemes by Ganic [10] and Sverdlov [11]. Ganic presented hybrid-watermarking scheme based on DWT and SVD. After decomposing the cover image into four bands, SVD is applied on each band and modify the singular values of each band with the singular values of the visual watermark. Sverdlov used the same concept taking DCT and SVD. DCT coefficients are mapped into four quadrants via ZIG-ZAG scan and modify the singular values of each quadrant. In both the approaches, modifications in all frequencies allow the development of a watermarking scheme that is robust to a wide range of attacks. Other hybrid schemes [12,13,14] are the different variants and extensions of these two.

In this paper, a new robust watermarking scheme is proposed which is based on FrFT and SVD. Unlike existing SVD based watermarking scheme, proposed scheme embeds watermark in the singular values of the key matrix which is obtained from non-overlapping blocks segmentation, FrFT and SVD. The original image is first transformed into FrFT domain followed by the segmentation into no-overlapping blocks. The highest singular value of each block is obtained and stacked into an array to form key matrix. The watermark is embedded in the key matrix and embedding is done by modifying its singular values with the watermark singular values. The main benefit of the proposed scheme is that the watermark is embedded in the more robustly in the highest singular values because most of image energy is contained in the highest singular values. Experimental results show the robustness and superiority of the proposed algorithm.

This paper is organized as follows: In section 2, mathematical preliminaries are illustrated followed by the brief description of proposed watermarking scheme in section 3. In section 4, experimental results using proposed watermarking scheme are presented and finally section 5 gives the concluding remarks regarding proposed watermarking scheme.

2   Mathematical Preliminaries

This section reviews the basic mathematical concepts and results which are used in the proposed watermarking scheme. These concepts are as follows.

2.1   Fractional Fourier Transform (FrFT)

The concept of Fractional Fourier transform (FrFT) is introduced by Victor Namias in 1980 [15]. The FrFT is the generalization of Fourier transform. The essence of the generalization is to provide a parameter α and can be interpreted as a rotation by an angle α in the time-frequency plane or decomposition of the signal in terms of chirps. Generally, this parameter is called angle or transform order associated with FrFT. Mathematically, the FrFT of a one dimensional function $s(t)$ is defined as

$$F^{\alpha}[s(t)](x) = \int_{-\infty}^{\infty} s(t)K_{\alpha}(t,x)\ dt \tag{1}$$

where α is the transform order and $K_\alpha(t,x)$ is the transform kernel and is given by:

$$K_\alpha(t,x) = \begin{cases} \sqrt{1-i\cot\alpha} \; e^{i\frac{t^2+x^2}{2}\cot\alpha - ixt \; \csc\alpha} & \alpha \neq n\pi \\ \delta(t-x), & \alpha = 2n\pi \\ \delta(t+x), & \alpha = 2n\pi \pm \pi \end{cases} \tag{2}$$

where n is a given integer. The FrFT of a signal exists under the same conditions in which its Fourier transform exists. The inverse FrFT can be visualized as the FrFT with transform order $-\alpha$. The main property of FrFT is that the signal obtained is in purely time domain if transform order (α) is 0 and in purely frequency domain if transform order (α) is $\pi/2$. Further, due to the separability of the transform, the higher dimensional FrFT can be obtained by successively taking one dimensional FrFT along all the directions.

The main benefit of using FrFT in watermarking is it dependance on the transform orders. These transform orders are used as the keys to the watermark extraction because without using correct transform orders no one can obtain correct transformed domain in which the watermark is embedded. Hence, no one can extract the watermark efficiently with wrong transform orders.

2.2 Singular Value Decomposition

Let A be a general real(complex) matrix of order $m \times n$. The singular value decomposition (SVD)[16] of A is the factorization

$$A = U * S * V^T \tag{3}$$

where U and V are *orthogonal(unitary)* and $S = diag(\sigma_1, \sigma_2, ..., \sigma_r)$, where σ_i, $i = 1(1)r$ are the singular values of the matrix A with $r = min(m,n)$ and satisfying $\sigma_1 \geq \sigma_2 \geq ... \geq \sigma_r$. The first r columns of V are the *right singular vectors* and the first r columns of U are the *left singular vectors*. Use of SVD in digital image processing has some advantages. First, the size of the matrices from SVD transformation is not fixed. It can be a square or rectangular. Secondly, singular values in a digital image are less affected if general image processing is performed. Finally, singular values contain intrinsic algebraic image properties.

3   Proposed Watermarking Algorithm

In this section, we have discussed some motivating factors in design of our approach to watermarking. We have used FrFT and SVD for developing the watermarking scheme. Let us consider F is the host image and W is the watermark. The host and watermark images are gray scale images of size $M \times N$ and $m \times n$ respectively.

3.1 Embedding Process

The embedding process is given as follows.

1. Perform (α_x, α_y)-FrFT on the host image, which is denoted by f, where α_x and α_y are the transform order along x- and y-axis.
2. Segment f into non-overlapping blocks of size $p_1 \times p_2$, which are denoted by f^q, where $p_1 = \lfloor \frac{M}{m} \rfloor$, $p_2 = \lfloor \frac{N}{n} \rfloor$ and $q = mn$ is the total number of blocks.
3. Perform SVD transform on all non-overlapping blocks f^q i.e.

$$f^q = U_{f^q}\, S_{f^q}\, V_{f^q}^T \tag{4}$$

4. Collect the highest singular value of all non-overlapping blocks f^q and stacked into a array of size $m \times n$ to form key matrix (K) as

$$K = \begin{bmatrix} \sigma_1 & \sigma_2 & \sigma_3 & \cdots & \sigma_n \\ \sigma_{n+1} & \sigma_{n+2} & \sigma_{n+3} & \cdots & \sigma_{2n} \\ \vdots & \vdots & \vdots & \ddots & \vdots \\ \sigma_{m(n+1)} & \sigma_{m(n+2)} & \sigma_{m(n+3)} & \cdots & \sigma_{mn} \end{bmatrix} \tag{5}$$

5. Perform SVD transform on K and watermark image W

$$K = U_K\, S_K\, V_K^T \tag{6}$$
$$W = U_W\, S_W\, V_W^T \tag{7}$$

6. Modify the singular values of K with the singular values of the watermark as

$$S_K^* = S_K + \beta\, S_W \tag{8}$$

where β gives the watermark strength.

7. Perform inverse SVD to construct modified K

$$K_{new} = U_K\, S_K^*\, V_K^T \tag{9}$$

8. Map modified highest singular value on their original position followed by inverse SVD to get modified non-overlapping blocks f_{new}^q.
9. Map modified blocks to their original position followed by inverse (α_x, α_y)-FrFT to get watermarked image $\widetilde{F}$.

3.2 Extraction Process

The extraction process is given as follows.

1. Perform (α_x, α_y)-FrFT on the watermarked image $(\widetilde{F})$, which is denoted by $\widetilde{f}$, where α_x and α_y are the transform order along x- and y-axis.
2. Segment $\widetilde{f}$ into non-overlapping blocks of size $p_1 \times p_2$, which are denoted by $\widetilde{f}^q$, where $p_1 = \lfloor \frac{M}{m} \rfloor$, $p_2 = \lfloor \frac{N}{n} \rfloor$ and $q = mn$ is the total number of blocks.

3. Perform SVD transform on all non-overlapping blocks $\widetilde{f}^q$ i.e.

$$\widetilde{f}^q = U_{\widetilde{f}^q} \, S_{\widetilde{f}^q} \, V_{\widetilde{f}^q}^T \tag{10}$$

4. Collect the highest singular value of all non-overlapping blocks $\widetilde{f}^q$ and stacked into a array of size $m \times n$ to form watermarked key matrix $(\widetilde{K})$ as

$$\widetilde{K} = \begin{bmatrix} \widetilde{\sigma}_1 & \widetilde{\sigma}_2 & \widetilde{\sigma}_3 & \cdots & \widetilde{\sigma}_n \\ \widetilde{\sigma}_{n+1} & \widetilde{\sigma}_{n+2} & \widetilde{\sigma}_{n+3} & \cdots & \widetilde{\sigma}_{2n} \\ \vdots & \vdots & \vdots & \ddots & \vdots \\ \widetilde{\sigma}_{m(n+1)} & \widetilde{\sigma}_{m(n+2)} & \widetilde{\sigma}_{m(n+3)} & \cdots & \widetilde{\sigma}_{mn} \end{bmatrix} \tag{11}$$

5. Perform SVD transform on $\widetilde{K}$

$$\widetilde{K} = U_{\widetilde{K}} \, S_{\widetilde{K}} \, V_{\widetilde{K}}^T \tag{12}$$

6. Extract the singular values of watermark from watermarked image as

$$S_W^{ext} = \frac{S_{\widetilde{K}} - S_K}{\beta} \tag{13}$$

7. Obtain the extracted watermark as

$$W_{ext} = U_W \, S_W^{ext} \, V_W^T \tag{14}$$

4   Experimental Results

In order to explore the performance of proposed watermarking algorithm, MAT-LAB platform is used and a number of experiments are performed on standard uncompressed gray-scale Mandrill image of size 512×512. For watermark, 8-bit gray scale CVSS LAB logo is used which is of size 128×128. The watermarked image quality is measured using PSNR (Peak Signal to Noise Ratio), which is given by

$$PSNR(x,y) = 10 \, log_{10} \frac{255^2}{\frac{1}{MN} \sum_{i=1}^{M} \sum_{j=1}^{N} [x_{i,j} - y_{i,j}]^2} \tag{15}$$

where MN is the total number of pixels in the image, $x_{i,j}$ and $y_{i,j}$ are the values of the ij^{th} pixel in original and watermarked image. The PSNR for watermarked Mandrill image is 40.2898 dB. Now, the watermarked image undergoes to different kind of intentional and un-intentional attacks followed by the watermark extraction. In order to verify the quality of extracted watermark, different measures can be used to show the similarity between the original and the extracted singular values. In the proposed algorithm, used correlation coefficient is given by:

$$\rho(w, \bar{w}) = \frac{\sum_{i=1}^{r} w(i) \, \bar{w}(i)}{\sqrt{\sum_{i=1}^{r} \bar{w}^2(i)} \sqrt{\sum_{i=1}^{r} w^2(i)}} \tag{16}$$

where w is the singular values of the original watermark, $\bar{w}$ is the extracted singular values and $r = max(m,n)$. The value of ρ lies between [-1, 1]. If the value of ρ is equal to 1 then the extracted singular values are just equal to original one. If the value of ρ is -1 then the difference is negative for the largest singular values. In this case, the lighter parts of the image become darker and darker parts become lighter i.e constructed watermark looks like negative thin film. According to statistics, the principle range for correlation coefficient is [0, 1]. Hence, the Negative Image Transform (NIT) is performed on the extracted watermark whenever ρ takes negative value, in order to get ρ in the principle range. The NIT with intensity levels in the range [0, L-1] is given by the expression $s = L - 1 - r$, where r is the original intensity and s is the transformed intensity.

To investigate the robustness of the proposed algorithm, the watermarked image is attacked by Average and Median Filtering, Gaussian noise addition, JPEG compression, Cropping, Resizing, Rotation, Histogram Equalization, Contrast adjustment and sharpening attacks. After these attacks on the watermarked image, the extracted watermarks are compared with the original one using Eqn. 16. In figure 1, original host, original watermark, watermarked host and extracted watermark images are shown. If original and watermarked images are observed then no perceptual degradation is found according to the human visual system. The detailed results in order to verify robustness of the proposed algorithm are discussed below.

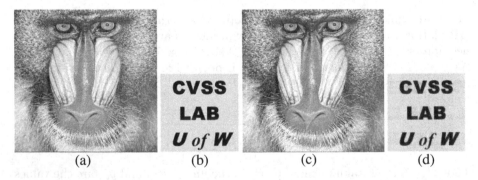

(a)   (b)   (c)   (d)

Fig. 1. a) Original Mandrill Image b) Original CVSS LAB Logo c) Watermarked Mandrill Image d) Extracted Logo

The most common manipulation in digital image is filtering. The watermarked image is filtered by average and median filtering considering 13×13 window and watermark is then extracted from attacked images. The visual results are depicted in the figures 2 and 3 respectively. Another most common method to estimate the robustness of watermark is the addition of noise. In many cases, the degradation and distortion of the image are due to noise addition. Robustness against additive noise is estimated by degrading watermark image by adding 80% Gaussian noise randomly. It is clear from the figure 4 that lot of information is

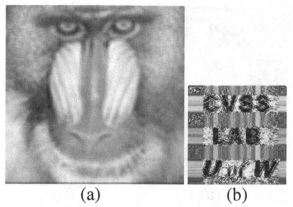

(a)   (b)

Fig. 2. Results for Average filtering (13 × 13) a) Attack Mandrill Image b) Extracted CVSS LAB Logo

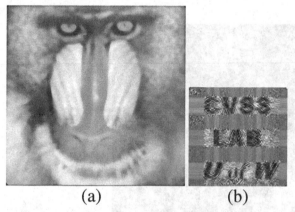

(a)   (b)

Fig. 3. Results for Median filtering (13 × 13) a) Attack Mandrill Image b) Extracted CVSS LAB Logo

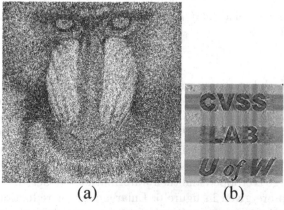

(a)   (b)

Fig. 4. Results for Gaussian Noise Addition (80%) a) Attack Mandrill Image b) Extracted CVSS LAB Logo

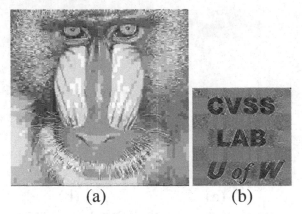

(a)   (b)

Fig. 5. Results for JPEG Compression ($CR = 100$) a) Attack Mandrill Image b) Extracted CVSS LAB Logo

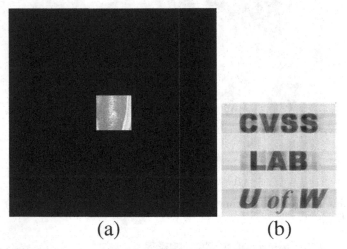

(a)   (b)

Fig. 6. Results for Cropping (95% area cropped) a) Attack Mandrill Image b) Extracted CVSS LAB Logo

lost after this attack but the extracted watermark is still recognizable. To check the robustness against Image Compression, the watermarked image is attacked by JPEG compression attack. The extracted watermark logo from compressed Watermarked host image using JPEG compression with compression ratio 100 is given in figure 5. Image cropping is another most common manipulation in digital image. To check the robustness against Image Cropping, the 95% area of the watermarked image is cropped and then watermark is extracted. The corresponding visual results are given in figure 6. Enlargement or reduction is commonly performed to fit the image into the desired size and there is information loss of the image including embedded watermarks. Hence, the proposed technique

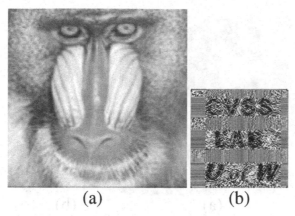

Fig. 7. Results for Resizing (512 → 128 → 512) a) Attack Mandrill Image b) Extracted CVSS LAB Logo

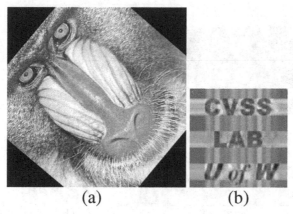

Fig. 8. Results for Rotation (50°) a) Attack Mandrill Image b) Extracted CVSS LAB Logo

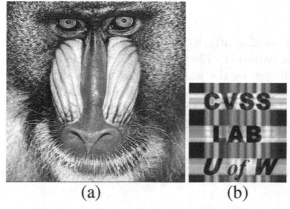

Fig. 9. Results for Histogram Equalization a) Attack Mandrill Image b) Extracted CVSS LAB Logo

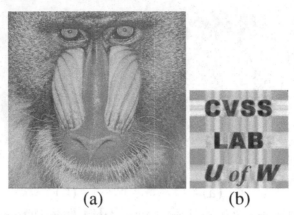

Fig. 10. Results for Contrast Adjustments (decreased by 50%) a) Attack Mandrill Image b) Extracted CVSS LAB Logo

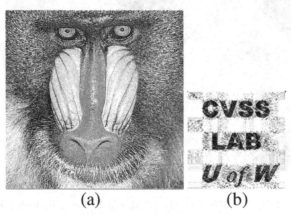

Fig. 11. Results for Sharpening (increased by 80%) a) Attack Mandrill Image b) Extracted CVSS LAB Logo

is also tested for resizing attack. For doing this task, the size of watermarked host image is first reduced to 128 × 128 and then carried back to its original size i.e. 512 × 512 followed by the watermark extraction and corresponding results are shown in figure 7. The proposed technique is also tested for rotation attack. For this purpose, the watermarked image is rotate with 50° (see figure 8). In figures 9, 10 and 11, the results for Histogram equalization, Contrast Adjustment and Sharpening attacks are shown respectively. For Contrast Adjustment, the contrast of the watermarked image is decreased by 50% whereas the sharpness of the watermarked image is increased by 80% for sharpening attack.

Table 1. Correlation Coefficients of Extracted Watermarks after Attacks

Attacks	ρ
No Attack	0.9999
Average Filtering (13×13)	0.8760
Median Filtering (13×13)	0.9090
Gaussian Noise Addition (80%)	0.9550
JPEG Compression ($CR = 100$)	0.9619
Cropping (95% area cropped)	0.9868
Resizing ($512 \rightarrow 128 \rightarrow 512$)	0.8394
Rotation ($50°$)	0.9452
Histogram Equalization	0.8579
Contrast Adjustment (50% decreased)	0.9854
Sharpening (80% increased)	0.9709

5 Conclusions

In this paper, a simple yet efficient watermarking scheme is proposed which is based on fractional Fourier transform and singular value decomposition. The main benefit of the proposed scheme is the use of FrFT because the transform orders plays a vital role of keys. Since, without knowing transform orders one cannot obtain the correct domain in which watermark is embedded and therefore cannot extract the watermark correctly. The experimental results clearly demonstrates the improve performance in terms of imperceptibility and robustness against different kind of attacks. Moreover, proposed scheme is also employed when original image is a color image. In this case, the original color image is transformed into independent colour channels (like YCbCr etc.) from the RGB channels. Then the watermark is embedded in the Luminance channel (like Y in YCbCr). Finally, the watermarked image is obtained by transform modified independent colour channels to RGB channels.

References

1. Cox, I.J., Miller, M.L., Bloom, J.A.: Digital watermarking. Morgan Kaufmann, San Francisco (2001)
2. Kim, W.G., Lee, J.C., Lee, W.D.: An image watermarking scheme with hidden signatures. In: IEEE International Conference on Image Processing, Kobe, Japan, vol. 2, pp. 206–210 (1999)

3. Voyatzis, G., Pitas, I.: Chaotic watermarks for embedding in the spatial digital image domain. In: IEEE International Conference on Image Processing, Chicago, Illinois, USA, vol. 2, pp. 432–435 (1998)
4. Xia, X., Boncelet, C.G., Arce, G.R.: A multiresolution watermark for digital images. In: IEEE International Conference on Image Processing, Santa Barbara, CA, vol. 3, pp. 548–551 (1997)
5. Kundur, D., Hatzinakos, D.: Towards robust logo watermarking using meltiresolution image fusion. IEEE Transcations on Multimedia 6, 185–197 (2004)
6. Dawei, Z., Guanrong, C., Wenbo, L.: A chaos-based robust wavelet-domain watermarking algorithm. J. Chaos Solitons Fractals 22, 47–54 (2004)
7. Djurovic, I., Stankovic, S., Pitas, I.: Digital watermarking in the fractional fourier transformation domain. Journal of Network and Computer Applications 24(4), 167–173 (2001)
8. Liu, R., Tan, T.: An SVD-Based Watermarking Scheme for Protecting Rightful Ownership. IEEE Transactions on Multimedia 4(1), 121–128 (2002)
9. Chandra, D.V.S.: Digital Image Watermarking Using Singular Value Decomposition. In: IEEE Midwest Symposium on Circuits and Systems, Tulsa, Oklahoma, pp. 264–267 (2002)
10. Ganic, E., Eskicioglu, A.M.: Robust Embedding of Visual Watermarks Using DWT-SVD. Journal of Electronic Imaging (2005)
11. Sverldov, A., Dexter, S., Eskicioglu, A.M.: Robust DCT-SVD Domain Image Watermarking for Copyright Protection: Embedding Data in All Frequencies. In: European Signal Processing Conference, Antalya, Turkey, pp. 1–4 (2005)
12. Li, Q., Yuan, C., Zong, Y.Z.: Adaptive DWT-SVD Domain Image Watermarking Using Human Visual Model. In: International Conference on Advanced Communication Technology, Phoenix Park, Korea, pp. 1947–1951 (2007)
13. Lin, C.H., Jen, J.S., Kuo, L.C.: Distributed discrete wavelet transformation for copyright protection. In: Intrnational Workshop on Image Analysis for Multimedia Interactive Services, Incheon, Korea, pp. 53–56 (2006)
14. Qi, X., Brimley, B., Brimley, G.: An adaptive QIM- and SVD-based digital image watermarking scheme in the wavelet domain. In: International Conference on Image Processing, San Diego, California, USA, pp. 421–424 (2008)
15. Namias, V.: The fractional order Fourier transform and its application to quantum mechanics. J. Inst. Math. Appl. 25, 241–265 (1980)
16. Strang, G.: Introduction to Linear Algebra. Wellesley-Cambridge Press (1993)

Mining Frequent and Associated Gene Expression Patterns from Spatial Gene Expression Data: A Proposed Approach

M. Anandhavalli[1,*], M.K. Ghose[1], and K. Gauthaman[2]

[1] Department of Computer Science Engineering, SMIT, East Sikkim, India
anandhigautham@gmail.com
[2] Department of Department of Drug Technology, Higher Institute of Medical Technology, Derna, Libya

Abstract. In recent years interest has grown in "mining" spatial gene expression databases to extract novel and interesting information. Knowledge Discovery in Databases (KDD) has been recognized as an emerging research area. Association rules discovery is an important KDD technique for better data understanding. This paper proposes an enhancement with a fast and memory efficient algorithm to mine association rules from spatial gene expression data. In this paper, the features of Similarity matrix, Boolean matrix and Bit operations are combined to generate frequent gene expression patterns without candidate generation and association rules with fixed antecedent and multiple consequents using Bit operations has been generated. The obtained results accurately reflected knowledge hidden in the datasets under examination.

Keywords: Association rules, Similarity matrix, Spatial Gene Expression Data, Bit AND-OR operations, Fixed antecedent.

1 Introduction

Progress in data acquisition and storage facilitated the explosive growth in the amount of data collected by World Genome Projects. Often the data sets are becoming so huge, that make them difficult to exploit and explore. RNA in situ hybridization and DNA microarray are two primary methods for monitoring gene expression levels on large scale. Microarrays provide a quantitative overview of the relative changes of expression levels of large number of genes [4, 5], but they do not often document the spatial information on individual genes [3]. In contrast, RNA in situ hybridization uses gene-specific probes and can determine the spatial patterns of gene expression precisely. The impetus to effectively harness the increased volumes of data now available has lead to the need for new data analysis techniques to build data characterizations and extract useful patterns and models. Consequently, the research field of KDD, also known as data mining, has arisen with mining association rules becoming one of the most prominent techniques within the context of extracting relationships among items hidden within datasets.

---

* Corresponding author.

S. Ranka et al. (Eds.): IC3 2010, Part I, CCIS 94, pp. 119–130, 2010.

When applying an association rule mining algorithm on the in situ hybridization spatial gene expression data the characteristics like large search space, uninteresting genes and data normalization must be taken into consideration. When Apriori-like algorithm [1, 2] is applied to the spatial gene expression of data which is a similarity matrix of size n × n where n is considered as either probe name or gene name and the size of the itemsets is equal to the number of transactions, the complexity of generating candidate itemsets, number of passes over the database and the space to store the support counts of the itemsets will increase highly.

The objective of this work is to develop an efficient association rule mining algorithm to analyse the spatial gene expression data by taking all the above mentioned complexities and characteristics into consideration. In this paper, the attempt has been made to propose efficient algorithm for discovering frequent item sets without the generation of candidate itemsets and mining association rules with fixed antecedent and multiple consequents for spatial gene expression data.

2 Related Work

In the context of association rules and gene expression data, the previous studies can be classified into two main categories:

a. Association rules over gene expression from micro-array experiments.
b. Association rules over spatial gene expression data.

The first category aims to find rules that show associations between genes, and perhaps other things, such as the type of treatment used in the experiment [4, 5]. In the context of gene expression, biological data set, fuzzy association rules [9] have been proposed to consider simultaneously gene expression data, Gene Ontology (Go) annotations and gene structures. A novel row-wise depth-first algorithm FARMER [10] is used to mine all the interesting rule groups (IRGs) satisfying user-specified minimum measure (support, confidence, chi square value) thresholds, instead of finding individual association rules have been proposed. The Association rules have been used for determining the redundancy of protein and DNA sequences in biological database by [12]. An ant-based Association rules mining (Ant-ARM) algorithm which makes use of natural behaviour of ants such as cooperation and adaptation to allow for a flexible robust search for a good candidate solution, have been proposed for gene expression data analysis by [11].

The second category aims to mine association rules from spatial gene expression data which is a result of in situ gene expression studies and extracts the same type of relationships between genes which are expressed in the form of spatial regions, thereby providing knowledge on how areas in an embryo are linked spatially [8].In earlier studies of spatial gene expression data and association rule mining, Apriori algorithm has been used to extract interesting association rules which gives the same type of relationships between genes [7], thereby providing knowledge on how areas in a mouse embryo are linked spatially in Edinburgh Mouse Atlas gene expression database (EMAGE). When applying an existing Apriori like algorithm for the spatial gene analysis, we will need to modify it to improve the generation of frequently occur items (genes), the number of passes over the data for faster execution of the algorithm and to discover of interesting association rules with efficient usage of memory also.

Here after it may be noted that "gene" refers an item or column and "probe pattern" refers as a transaction or row, for the given database D.

3 Approach

The proposed algorithm comprises three phases as follows.

Phase 1: Transforming the similarity matrix into the Boolean matrix
Phase 2: Generating the set of frequent itemsets with support value greater than a predefined threshold (minimum support).
Phase 3: Generating association rules from the generated frequent itemsets with confidence value greater than a predefined threshold (minimum confidence).

3.1 Approach Decomposition

Let D be a given database. Let $I=\{i_1, i_2, ..., i_n\}$ be a set of items and $D_t =\{ t_1, t_2, ..., t_n\}$ be the transactions, $i_j \in D$. Let $R = \{r_1, r_2,...,r_n\}$ denote a set of rows, and $C=\{c_1,c_2,..., c_n\}$ denote a set of columns. The Table 1 shows that $Gene_1$, $Gene_2$ and $Gene_3$ are expressed in probe pattern $EMAGE_1$ and $Gene_4$ is not expressed in probe pattern $EMAGE_1$.

Table 1. Example of Spatial Gene Expression data

Probe Names/ Gene Name	$Gene_1$	$Gene_2$	$Gene_3$	$Gene_4$
$EMAGE_1$	1	0.033	0.00029	0.00
$EMAGE_2$	0.033	1	0.0031	0.005
$EMAGE_3$	0.00029	0.0031	1	0.23
$EMAGE_4$	0.00	0.005	0.023	1

Definition 1. An association rule is an implication in the form of X→Y, where X,Y⊂I are sets of items called itemsets, and $X \cap Y = \varnothing$. X is called antecedent while Y is called consequent, the rule means X implies Y.

Definition 2. Support count of an item is defined as total number of transactions contains that item.

Definition 3. Support of an association rule is defined as support(X→Y)=Probability $(X \cup Y)$.

Definition 4. Confidence of an association rule is defined as the confidence(X→Y)= Probability(Y|X) = Probability($X \cup Y$) / Probability(X)

Definition 5. A set of items (such as the antecedent or the consequent of a rule) is called an itemset. The number of items in an itemset is called the length of an itemset. Itemsets of length k are referred to as k-itemsets.

Definition 6. The support count is defined as support_count=minsupp× n, where minsupp is the user defined minimum support and n is the number of transactions.

Definition 7. An itemset that contains k items can potentially generate upto 2^k-1 frequent itemsets, excluding the null set.

Definition 8. (Apriori principle) If an itemset is frequent, then all of its subset must also be frequent. For example, given the frequent items $\{c_1, c_2, c_3\}$, the itemset $\{c_1, c_2\}$, $\{c_2, c_3\}$, $\{c_1, c_3\}$ which are subsets of $\{c_1, c_2, c_3\}$ are also frequent itemsets.

Definition 9. Boolean matrix is a matrix with item values of 1 or 0.

Definition 10. If "and" operation is carried out for the k columns vectors of the Boolean matrix, the sum of '1's of the operation result is called k-support of the k columns vector.

Definition 11. For the frequent itemsets X and Y, the association rule   X→{Y-X} holds if the ratio of $\frac{\text{support\_co unt}(Y)}{\text{support\_co unt}(X)} \geq \text{minconf}$ in which minconf is the minimum confidence given by the user.

3.2 Approach Decomposition

Value greater than x% discretization method has been used to transform the values contained in the spatial gene expression data into Boolean values. The set of transactions are constructed by taking, for each probe pattern r, every gene g from which its associated gene expression pattern c satisfies the minimum similarity β, i.e., similarity(r, c) > β, to form the itemsets. The framework for data preprocessing method is given in Figure 1.

```
Input: Raw Database D_r and user_specified_value β
Output: Preprocessed Database D
1.     For all transactions i <= row in D_r do
2.         For all items j <= column in D_r do
3.             if j^th item is present in i^th transaction with value > β then
4.                 set D[i,j] =1
5.             else
6.                 set D[i,j] =0
7.         end for
8.     end for
```

Table 2 shows an example of the preprocessed data matrix after applying the method of value greater than x% with β =0.005 to the spatial gene expression data given in Table 1.

Table 2. Example of Preprocessed Spatial Gene Expression data

Probe Names/ Gene Name	$Gene_1$	$Gene_2$	$Gene_3$	$Gene_4$
$EMAGE_1$	1	1	0	0
$EMAGE_2$	1	1	0	1
$EMAGE_3$	0	0	1	1
$EMAGE_4$	0	1	1	1

3.3 Phase 2: Frequent Itemset Generation

The frequent itemset generation comprises two phases as follows.

a. Generation of the set of frequent 1-itemsets F_1 with support value greater than minimum support as follows.

i. First the Boolean matrix D is scanned to count the support count of the itemsets. The support of all items Ij are computed with help of counting the number of '1's in the jth column of D using function sum(column) in step 9 of MineFI algorithm.

ii. If the support of an item I_j is greater than the support count (by Definition 10), then the itemset $\{I_j\}$ is a frequent 1-itemset and is added to the set of frequent 1-itemset F_1. Otherwise itemset $\{I_j\}$ is not a frequent 1-itemset and the jth column will be deleted from D.

iii. The sum of '1's of each row R_i is recomputed with Boolean AND operation. The rows r_i whose sum of '1's is smaller than 2 are deleted from the matrix D, using Theorem 1.

Theorem 1. R_k is a k-dimensional itemset. If the number of (k-1)-dimensional subsets of all (k-1)-dimensional frequent itemset F_{k-1}, which contains R_k, is less than k, then R_k is not a k-dimensional frequent itemset. In the context of Boolean matrix, if the sum of '1's in a row vector R_k is smaller than k, it is not necessary for R_k to involve in the calculation of the k- supports.

Proof. It is clear that the number of (k-1)-dimensional subsets of R_k is k. If the number of (k-1)-dimensional subsets of all (k-1)-dimensional frequent itemset F_{k-1}, which contains R_k, is less than k, then there exists a (k-1)-dimensional subset of R_k that is not frequent itemset.

The description of the algorithm for generating frequent itemset is as follows.

Algorithm 1: MineFI

```
1.   MineFI( )
2.   Input: Dataset D, the minimum support minsupp. Output: Set of frequent itemsets F.
3.   Phase 1: Normalization
4.   Normalize the data matrix D and transformed into Boolean Matrix B;
5.   Calculate number of rows R and columns C in matrix B.
6.   Calculate support_count = number of rows × minsupp;
7.   Phase 2: Frequent 1- itemset Generation
8.   for each column Cᵢ of B do
9.   { if sum(Cᵢ) ≥ support_count
10.      then F₁ = { Iᵢ};
11.      else delete Cᵢ from B;
12.   endif
13.   }
14.  for each row Rj of B do
15.  {   if sum(Rⱼ) < 2
16.      then delete  Rⱼ from B;
17.      endif
18.  }
19.  Phase 3: Frequent k-itemset generation
20.  for (k=2; | Fₖ₋₁| > k-1; k++) do              // Join Procedure
```

```
21.  {      Produce k-vectors combination for all columns of B;
22.         for each k-vectors combination { Ci1, Ci2,…,Cik} do
23.            {  E = Ci1 ∩ Ci2 ∩ …. ∩ Cik
24.               if sum(E) ≥ support_count
25.               then Fk = { Ii1, Ii2,…Iik}
26.               endif
27.            }
28.            for each item Ii in Fk do                    // Pruning Procedure
29.               If |Fk(Ii)| < k
30.               then delete the column Bi according to item Ii from B;
31.               endif
32.            for each row Rj of B do
33.               if sum(Bj) < k+1
34.               then  delete Rj from B;
35.               endif
36.       k=k+1
37.  }
38.  Return F = F1 ∪ F2,…., ∪ Fk
```

Table 3. Binary Dataset D_{4x4} with support count of 1-itemset

TID/Items	c_1	c_2	c_3	c_4
r_1	1	1	0	1
r_2	1	1	0	1
r_3	0	0	1	1
r_4	1	1	1	1
Support count of items	3	3	2	4

For the dataset given in Table 3, the number of rows and columns =4, minimum support= 80%. So the support count = number of rows * minimum support = 4*0.8 = 3.2 =3.

When k=1, the number of itemset whose support value greater than 3 are considered as frequent itemset and is added to the set of frequent 1-itemset, F_1={{c_1},{c_2}, {c_4}}. Itemset {c_3} is not a frequent 1-itemset and the column c_3 will be deleted from D_{4x4}. Now Boolean AND operation is performed on each row of the dataset to count number of 1's. The result is given in Table 4.

By Theorem 1, the row r_3 whose sum of '1's is smaller than 1 is deleted from the dataset given in Table 3 and the result is given in Table 5.

As a result, the algorithm only needs to compare the count of each item of F_{k-1} with the count of each item C. If the count of the item C equals to k, and then consider C. Otherwise item C must be non-frequent itemset, it should be deleted.

Table 4. Support counting of 1-itemset

TID/Items	c_1	c_2	c_4	Result of Boolean AND operation on columns c_1,c_2 and c_4
r_1	1	1	1	1
r_2	1	1	1	1
r_3	0	0	1	0
r_4	1	1	1	1

Table 5. Example of Dataset D_{3x3}

TID/Items	c_1	c_2	c_4
r_1	1	1	1
r_2	1	1	1
r_4	1	1	1

b. Generation of the set of frequent k-itemsets Fk (where k >1) with pruning of the Boolean matrix if necessary. The second phase involves join and pruning procedures.

i) Join Procedure (step 21 of MineFI algorithm) involves the generation of the set of frequent k-itemsets Fk, k columns vector of the Boolean matrix are combined and frequent k-itemsets are computed with help of AND operation of Boolean matrix. If the Boolean matrix D has 'a' rows and 'b' columns, then the combinations of k column vectors, aCk, will be produced. The AND operation is applied for each combination of k columns vector, if the sum of '1's is not smaller than the support count, then the k-itemsets corresponding to the combination of k column vectors are the frequent k-itemsets and they are added to the set of frequent k-itemsets Fk.

When k=2, column vectors of the dataset given in Table 5 are combined to generate frequent 2-itemsets F2. After combining the columns c1, c2, c4 with Boolean AND operation, we get the result as given in Table 6.

Table 6. Example of column vector combination

TID/Items	$c_1 c_2$	$c_1 c_4$	$c_2 c_4$
r_1	1	1	1
r_2	1	1	1
r_4	1	1	1
Support count of 2-itemset	3	3	3

The number of itemset whose support value greater than 3 are considered as frequent itemset and is added to the set of frequent 2-itemset, so $F_2=\{\{c_1,c_2\},\{c_1,c_4\},\{c_2,c_4\}\}$.

ii) Pruning procedure involves the deletion of some rows and columns from the Boolean matrix D. Let I' be the set of all itemsets in the frequent set F_{k-1}, where k>2. Number of items in $F_{k-1}(j)$ where $j \subset I'$ are computed and delete the column of the corresponding item j if the number of items, $|F_{k-1}(j)|$, is smaller than k-1 using Theorem 2. First the column of the Boolean matrix is pruned according to Theorem 3. Second, the sum of '1's of each row r_i is recomputed. The rows r_i whose sum of '1's is smaller than k are deleted from the matrix D, by Theorem 1.

Theorem 2. $|F_K|$ presents the number of k-itemsets in the frequent set F_K. If $|F_K|$ is smaller than k+1, the maximum length frequent itemsets is k.

Proof. Let X is a Frequent (k+1) itemsets, F_{k+1} and X have k+1 frequent k-subsets. If the number of frequent k-itemsets in the frequent set F_k is smaller than k+1, there are no frequent (k+1)-itemsets in the mined database.

Theorem 3. Suppose Itemsets X is a k-itemsets; $|F_{K-1}(j)|$ presents the number of items 'j' in the frequent set F_{K-1}. There is an item j in X. If $| F_{K-1}(j)|$ is smaller than   k-1, itemset X is not a frequent itemsets.

Proof. If the total number of all '1's in R_k is less than k (dimension of frequent itemset F_k), then we won't find any elements X of frequent itemset F_k in R_k. Obviously as we know that if transaction record R contains two '1's and the dimension of frequent itemset F_3 is 3, then any element X in F_3 will have at least 3 items. If there are only two '1's, we cannot find an element with 3 items in the record with number of '1's is only two.

According to Theorem 2, the number of items in $F_2(j)$ where $j \subset I'$ are computed and then delete the column of the corresponding item j if the number of items, $|F_2(j)|$, is smaller than 2, using Theorem 3. As the number of items, $|F_2(j)|$, is greater than 2 , no column is deleted from the dataset given Table 5.

According to Theorem 2, the second step of the frequent mining process will be continued because there are three frequent 3-itemsets in the set of frequent 2-itemset F_2. When k=3, column vectors of the dataset given in Table 5 are combined to generate frequent 3-itemsets F_3 and the result is given in Table 7.

Table 7. Example of column vector combination

TID/Items	$c_1 c_2 c_4$
r_1	1
r_2	1
r_4	1
Support count of 3-itemset	3

So $F_3=\{\{c_1, c_2, c_4\}\}$. As the number of items, $|F_3(j)|$, is less than 3 , all the columns are deleted from the dataset given in Table 7 and the algorithm is terminated. The frequent items generated for the given example data are $F=\{\{c_1\},\{c_2\},\{c_4\},\{c_1,c_2\}, c_1,c_4\},\{c_2,c_4\},\{c_1, c_2, c_4\}\}$.

We shall use the following example in which the frequent itemsets are sorted in descending order of their support count given in Table 8 for the generation of association rules.

Table 8. Set of frequent itemsets with support count

Frequent itemsets	Support count	Bit representation	Frequent itemsets	Support count	Bit representation
{c4}	4	1000	{c1,c4}	3	1001
{c1}	3	0001	{c2,c4}	3	1010
{c2}	3	0010	{c1,c2,c4}	2	1011
{c1,c2}	3	0011			

3.4 Phase 3: Association Rules Generation

The description of the algorithm for generating association rules is as follows.

Algorithm 2: MineAR
----

1. **MineAR( )**
2. Input: Set of Frequent (F) itemsets with descending order of support count,
        new_support and minimum confidence, *minconf.*
3. Output: Set of Association rules
4. count_frequent_items =0;
5. **for** all f_k, $f_k \in$ F do
6. count_frequent_items = count_frequent_items +1;
7. **for** all f_k, $f_k \in$ F, k=1 to count_frequent_items -1 **do**
8. {   required_support_count = new_support(f_k) $\times$ minconf; total=0
9.   **for** all f_m , $f_m \in$ F, m = k+1 to count_frequent_items **do**
10. {   **if** new_support(F_m) $\geq$ required_support
11.   **then**
12. a = convert f_k into unsigned integer representation;
13.   b = convert f_m into unsigned integer representation;
14.   **If** ($F_k \subset F_m$)
15.   **then**
16.   rule_conf= new_support(F_m)/new_support(F_k) ;
17.   Generate the rule $F_k \rightarrow (F_m-F_k)$ with confidence = rule_conf and
                                    new_support = new_support (F_m);
18.   total =totoal+1;
19.   **endif**
20.   **else**
21.   **if** (total < 2)
22.   **then** continue step1 with next k ;
23.   **else**   total=0 ;
24.   **endif**
25.   **endif**
26.   }
27. }

The working method of the association rules generation procedure is discussed in the following steps:

1. Read all the frequent itemsets along with their support count sorted in decreasing order and user specified minimum confidence value. Count the number of frequent itemsets. The example is given in Table 8 with count=7. The steps 5 and 6 of algorithm MineAR will carry out this calculation.
2. Find the required support count of the first itemset using definition 6.
3. Convert the frequent itemset into bit representation by using number '1' if the itemset is present, otherwise 0 and the result is given in Table 8.
4. Convert second frequent itemset into its bit representation and its support count is checked with required support. If the support count is greater than or equal to required support, then it is again checked that whether the first frequent itemset is a subset of second frequent itemset or not, using bitwise AND operation on bit value of

the frequent itemsets. If the first frequent itemset is a subset of second frequent itemset, then the rule {first itemset} → {second itemset} will be generated (steps 10 through 18 of MineAR). After that the algorithm will continue with the first and third frequent itemset, in step 9 of the algorithm MineAR.

5. Suppose if the support count of the second frequent itemset is less the required support, and if the total number of rules generated with that second frequent itemset is less than 2, according to Theorem 4 to avoid unnecessary checking of the rule, then the algorithm starts with new iteration from the step 7 of the algorithm MineAR. Otherwise it will set the counter for the number of rules generated is equal to 0 and continue with the first and third frequent itemset, in step 9 of the algorithm MineAR as we are generating the association rules with fixed antecedent with multiple consequents.(steps 21 through 24 of MineAR)

Theorem 4. Suppose there exists two rules $X \rightarrow Y$ and $X \rightarrow \{Y \cup Z\}$, where $Z \notin \{X \cup Y\}$, satisfying the minimum confidence threshold, then the confidence of $X \rightarrow \{Y \cup Z\}$ cannot be larger than confidence of $X \rightarrow Y$.

Proof. Let us assume that D is the dataset and n be the number of items, I is a set of items, Z is an item such that $Z \notin D$ but $Z \notin I$, X is a set of items such that $X \notin D$ and $X \subset I$. Let support_count(I)=j;   support_count(Z)=k;   support_count(I $\cup$ Z)=m; support_count(X)=n;

i.e. $m \leq minimum(j,k)$; if $k<j$, then $m<j$; if $k \geq$, then m=j. So $m \leq j$.

$$\Rightarrow support\_count(I \cup Z) \leq support\_count(I) = \frac{support\_count(I \cup Z)}{support\_count(X)} \leq \frac{support\_count(I)}{support\_count(X)}$$

$$\Rightarrow \frac{support\_count(I \cup Z)/n}{support\_count(X)/n} \leq \frac{support\_count(I)/n}{support\_count(X)/n} \Rightarrow \frac{support(I \cup Z)}{support(X)} \leq \frac{support(I)}{support(X)}$$

$$\Rightarrow \quad confidence \quad of \quad X \rightarrow \{(I \cup Z) - X\} \leq confidence \quad of \quad X \rightarrow \{I - X\}$$

So we have concluded that the confidence of $X \rightarrow \{Y \cup Z\}$ cannot be larger than confidence of $X \rightarrow Y$.

The set of association rules generated for the running example with minimum confidence =100% are as follows: $c_1 \rightarrow c_2, c_1 \rightarrow c_4, c_2 \rightarrow c_1, c_2 \rightarrow c_4$.

4   Results and Discussion

The proposed algorithm was implemented in Java and tested on Linux platform. Comprehensive experiments on EMAGE spatial gene expression data [6] has been conducted to study the impact of normalization and to compare the effect of proposed algorithm with Apriori, Srikant and Partition algorithms.

Figure 2 gives the experimental results for execution time (generating frequent itemsets and finding rules) for various user specified minimum supports and shows that response time of the proposed algorithm is much better than that of the other algorithms.

Figure 3 gives the experimental results for memory usage for various user specified minimum supports and results show that proposed algorithm uses less memory than that of other algorithms because of the AND operations and bit representation of itemsets.

The number of association rules decreases along with an increase in minimum support under a given specific minimum confidence, which shows an appropriate Minsupport (or Minconfidence) can constrain the number of association rules and avoid the occurrence of some association rules so that it cannot yield a decision. These results have shown in Figure 4 for EMAGE and market databases. The results are as expected and quite consistent with our intuition.

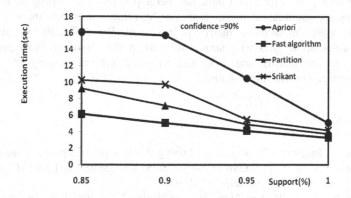

Fig. 2. Run time performance of the algorithms on EMAGE dataset

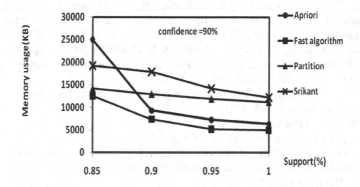

Fig. 3. Performance based on memory usage of the algorithms on EMAGE dataset

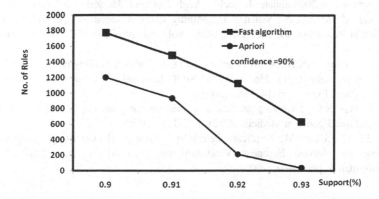

Fig. 4. Rule generation of algorithms on EMAGE dataset

5 Conclusion

In this paper, a novel method of mining frequent itemsets and strong association rules from the spatial gene expression data has been proposed. The proposed algorithm does not produce candidate itemsets, it spends less time for calculating k-supports of the itemsets with the Boolean matrix pruned with Bit AND,OR operations, and generating association rules with single antecedent with multiple consequents. The algorithm scans the database only once and it is very fast and memory efficient when compared with Aprioi-like algorithms.

References

1. Agrawal, R., Imielinski, T., Swami, A.: Mining Association rules between sets of items in large databases. In: ACM SIGMOD Intl Conf. on Management of Data (ACM SIGMOD 1993), Washington, USA, pp. 207–216 (1993)
2. Agrawal, R., Srikant, R.: Fast Algorithms for Mining Association Rules in large databases. In: 20th International Conference on Very Large Databases, Santiago, Chile, pp. 487–499 (1994)
3. Baldock, R.A., Bard, J.B., Burger, A., Burton, N., Christiansen, J., Feng, G., Hill, B., Houghton, D., Kaufman, M., Rao, J., et al.: EMAP and EMAGE: a framework for understanding spatially organized data. J. Neuroinformatics 1, 309–325 (2003)
4. Becquet, C., Blachon, S., Jeudy, B., Boulicaut, J., Gandrillon, O.: Strong association rule mining for large-scale gene-expression data analysis: a case study on human sage data. J. Genome Biology 3 (2002), research0067.1-0067.16
5. Creighton, C., Hanash, S.: Mining gene expression databases for association rules. J. Bioinformatics 19(1), 79–86 (2003)
6. EMAGE Spatial Gene Expression Data,
   http://genex.hgu.mrc.ac.uk/Emage/database
7. van Hemert, J., Baldock, R.: Mining Spatial Gene Expression Data for Association Rules. In: Hochreiter, S., Wagner, R. (eds.) BIRD 2007. LNCS (LNBI), vol. 4414, pp. 66–76. Springer, Heidelberg (2007)
8. Venkataraman, S., Stevenson, P., Yang, Y., Richardson, L., Burton, N., Perry, T.P., Smith, P., Baldock, R.A., Davidson, D.R., Christiansen, J.H.: Emage -Edinburgh mouse atlas of gene expression: 2008 update. J. Nucleic Acids Research 36, 860–865 (2008)
9. Deloado, M., Martin, N., Sanchez, D.: Mining fuzzy Association rules: an overview. In: Studies in Fuzziness and Soft Computing, vol. 164, pp. 351–373. Springer, Heidelberg (2005)
10. Cong, G., Tung, A.K.H., Xu, X., Pan, F., Yang, J.: Farmer: Finding interesting rule groups in microarray datasets. In: 23rd ACM SIGMOD International Conference on Management of Data, Paris, France, pp. 143–154 (2004)
11. He, Y., Hui, S.C.: Exploring ant-based algorithms for gene expression data analysis. J. Artificial Intelligence in Medicine 47(2), 105–119 (2009)
12. Koh, J.L.Y., Li Lee, M.: Duplicate Detection in Biological Data using Association Rule Mining. In: Second European Workshop on Data Mining and Text Mining in Bioinformatics, pp. 34–41 (2005)

Minimization of Lennard-Jones Potential Using Parallel Particle Swarm Optimization Algorithm

Kusum Deep and Madhuri Arya

Department of Mathematics,
Indian Institute of Technology Roorkee, 247667 Uttarakhand, India
kusumdeep@gmail.com, madhuriiitr@gmail.com

Abstract. Minimizing the Lennard-Jones potential, the most studied molecular conformation problem, is an unconstrained global optimization problem. Finding the global minimum of this function is very difficult because of the presence of a large number of local minima, which grows exponentially with molecule size. Attempts have been made to solve this problem using several optimization algorithms. In this paper a newly developed parallel particle swarm optimization (PPSO) algorithm is applied to solve this problem. Computational results for a cluster containing 10 atoms are obtained. The results obtained by PPSO show a significant performance in terms of speed-up without compromising the accuracy when compared to those obtained by sequential PSO. To the best of our knowledge this is the first attempt to solve Lennard-Jones 10 atoms problem using a PPSO.

Keywords: Lennard-Jones potential, Parallel Particle swarm optimization, Parallel Computing.

1 Introduction

The molecular conformation problem consists of finding a configuration of atoms in a cluster or molecule whose potential energy is minimum. Cluster sizes can range from a few atoms up to several hundred atoms. It is a central problem in the study of cluster statics, or the topography of a potential energy function in an internal configuration space. This problem is also important in the study of molecular dynamics, in which its solution is thought to provide the zero-temperature configuration or ground-state of the molecule. The solution of the molecular conformation problem is also of interest in the study of protein folding, in which the tertiary structure of the protein is sought. From the viewpoint of mathematical optimization, it is a difficult global optimization problem which does not yield easily either to discrete or to continuous optimization methods [2], [4].

In its simplest form, the potential energy of the molecule is modeled by the sum of the potential energies between pairs of atoms. In this form it is called Lennard-Jones problem. Even in this case, the problem of finding a global minimum of the energy can be extremely difficult due to the excessive number of non-global minima. In fact, it has been proved that the determination of the ground state structure of clusters,

S. Ranka et al. (Eds.): IC3 2010, Part I, CCIS 94, pp. 131–140, 2010.

which interact even under two-body central force, belongs to the class of NP-hard problems [8] for which no known algorithm is guaranteed to find the global minimum in polynomial time. Therefore traditional local optimization methods may not be useful for such problems.

One of the first, most efficient and successful approaches to L-J cluster optimization was introduced in [13] and further refined in [20]. This approach is based on the idea of starting local optimization from initial configurations built by randomly placing atoms in predefined points in space, according to lattice structures which are the most common ones found in nature. For the solution of these problems, simulated annealing (SA) has been widely employed [5], [19]. Population-based meta-heuristics called particle swarm optimization (PSO) and evolutionary algorithms (EA), such as genetic algorithms (GA) and the evolutionary programming (EP) have also become popular. There is, however, a cumbersome problem of temperature scheduling in SA. The generation of trial vector is also very problematical in SA. Although the GA is more powerful than the SA, it is usually augmented with traditional local optimization methods. The PSO [9] is a nature inspired general-purpose meta-heuristic which is free from the above-mentioned two defects of the SA and the GA.

Speed and accuracy are among the top most requirements while solving global optimization problems. Although PSO provides good solutions for L-J problem in most of the cases, it is often too time consuming. Parallelization is a possible way to speed up the search. Motivated by this observation a parallel approach has been used in this paper for the implementation of PSO on a cluster of workstations.

Our aim in this paper is to reproduce the lowest known structure of Lennard-Jones cluster containing 10 atoms, using recently developed parallel particle swarm optimization algorithm [6]. It uses a multi swarm approach to parallelize PSO and it has been proven to be more efficient than sequential PSO.

The paper is organized as follows. Section 2 gives a brief mathematical description of the Lennard-Jones potential energy function. In the third section the basic principles of PSO algorithm, on which the parallel implementation is based, is first described, followed by a brief literature survey of parallel PSO, and the parallelization strategy itself. Computational results and comparisons are presented in section 4. Finally we conclude the paper in section 5.

2 Lennard-Jones Problem

The Lennard-Jones problem assumes that the potential energy of a cluster of atoms is given by the sum of pairwise interactions between atoms, with these interactions being Vander Waals forces given by the Lennard-Jones 6-12 potential. The problem consists of determining the positions of an n atom cluster in such a way that the Lennard-Jones potential (LJP) given by equation (1), generated by atomic interactions is minimized.

$$V = \sum_{i=1}^{n-1} \sum_{j=i+1}^{n} \left(r_{ij}^{-12} - 2r_{ij}^{-6} \right). \tag{1}$$

Where r_{ij} is the Euclidean distance between the points t_i and t_j. Now, since each point corresponds to Cartesian coordinates in each of the x,y and z directions, the actual number of variables is three times the number of atoms in the given cluster. The problem is then to find the positions of each atom of the cluster that corresponds to the global minimum value of V, equation (1).

This problem has a long history [7], [12]. It has served as a test-bed for a wide variety of optimization algorithms, primarily due to the exponentially increasing number of local minima.

3 Parallel Particle Swarm Optimization (PPSO) Used for Solution

PSO is a relatively newer addition to the class of population based search techniques. Since its development in 1995, PSO has become one of the most promising optimization techniques for solving global optimization problems. But due to the complexity of Lennard-Jones problem it takes long solution time. So we implement a parallel version of PSO on a LINUX cluster to solve this problem in a reduced amount of time. The parallel algorithm is implemented using MPI (Message Passing Interface) [16]. This section presents the basic concept of PSO followed by a brief literature survey of parallel PSO, and the parallelization scheme implemented here.

3.1 Basic PSO

The concept of PSO is inspired by social and cooperative behavior displayed by various species like birds, fish etc. The PSO system consist of a population (swarm) of potential solutions called particles. Each particle has an associated fitness value. These particles move through search space with a specified velocity in search of optimal solution. Each particle maintains a memory which helps it in keeping the track of the best position it has achieved so far. This is called the particle's personal best position (pbest) and the best position the swarm has achieved so far is called global best position (gbest). PSO uses two primary operators: Velocity update and Position update. During each generation each particle is accelerated towards the gbest and its own pbest. At each iteration a new velocity value for each particle is calculated according to the following velocity update equation

$$v_{id} = \underbrace{wv_{id}}_{\substack{Inertia \\ component}} + \underbrace{c_1 r_1 (p_{id} - x_{id})}_{\substack{Cognitive \\ component}} + \underbrace{c_2 r_2 (p_{gd} - x_{id})}_{\substack{Social \\ component}}. \tag{2}$$

The new velocity value is then used to calculate the next position of the particle in the search space, according to the following position update equation:

$$x_{id} = x_{id} + v_{id}. \tag{3}$$

This process is then iterated until some stopping criterion is satisfied. Here $X_i=(x_{i1}, x_{i2}, ...x_{iD})$ represents the position of the ith particle in a D-dimensional search space, $P_{besti}=(p_{i1}, p_{i2}, ...p_{iD})$ is i^{th} particle's pbest position, $P_{gbest}=(p_{g1}, p_{g2}....p_{gD})$ is gbest position and $V_i=(v_{i1}, v_{i2}, ...v_{iD})$ is the velocity of ith particle. The inertia component serves as the memory of previous velocity, cognition component tells about the personal experience of the particle and the social component represents the cooperation among particles. Acceleration constants c_1, c_2 and inertia weight w are predefined by the user and r_1 and r_2 are uniformly generated random numbers in the range [0,1].

In the case of the Lennard-Jones problem each particle of the swarm is characterized by a set of 3n real numbers corresponding to the (x,y,z) positions of each atom. The fitness of a particle corresponds to the energy of the collection of n atoms, with the objective of making this energy as small as possible.

3.2 Literature on Parallel PSO

With the growing popularity of PSO the researches concerning its parallelization are also increasing. The strategies used in literature for the parallelization of PSO can be divided into two main categories. First are the master-slave parallelization strategies in which a processor (the master) distributes particles of a single swarm to many processors (slaves) for concurrent fitness evaluation. Master-slave approach is most suitable whenever the fitness evaluations are significantly computationally expensive. The second are the multi-swarm parallelization strategies which aim to partition the entire swarm into several sub swarms that are assigned to different processors and use some kind of information sharing among sub swarms.

A parallel version of PSO was first implemented by Schutte et al. [15]. They used a coarse grained master-slave parallelization approach. The implementation was based on a synchronous scheme. Venter and Sobieski [17] introduced a parallel asynchronous PSO (PAPSO) and compared it with a parallel synchronous PSO (PSPSO). Koh et al. [11] also proposed a PAPSO and compared it with PSPSO in homogeneous and heterogeneous computing environments. Chu and Pan [3] presented a parallel version of PSO (PPSO) together with three communication strategies that can be used according to independence of the data. Sahin et al. [14] implemented the PPSO algorithm on a computer cluster and studied the performance of the distributed PSO algorithm. Kim et al. [10] applied a parallel version of PSO based on coarse grained model for the solution of optimal power flow problem. Waintraub et al. [18] proposed three PPSO models inspired by traditional parallel GA models and applied them to two complex and time consuming nuclear engineering problems.

The most common observation in the above-mentioned real-world applications is the focus on speedup due to parallel processing, which is also the aim of our approach. Our approach is new and different from the approaches existing in the literature as it does not use the information sharing strategy among the swarms until some particular stage and after that stage too it uses a different idea as described in the next subsection of this paper.

3.3 Parallel PSO Used

The main idea behind the parallelization strategy used, is to first explore the search space in order to identify regions with high quality solutions and then to refine these high quality solutions. The algorithm decomposes the search process to work in two stages. In the first stage, called the parallel stage of the algorithm, the search space is explored by employing multiple independent swarms in parallel. In the second stage, called the sequential stage of the algorithm, the good solutions obtained at the parallel stage are refined by a single swarm.

The algorithm starts with multiple independent swarms with almost equal number of particles. There are as many processes as there are swarms, one process to perform calculations for each swarm. The data and calculations are independent on all processes. Each process runs a PSO with its own swarm without any communication with other swarms until termination, and then sends its best and second best particles with function values to the root process. Here the parallel stage of the algorithm ends and the sequential stage begins when the process root receives the best and the second best particles of all the swarms including itself. The received particles constitute the initial swarm for a new PSO which is now run on the process root. Then the best solution obtained by this process is the result of the algorithm.

Computational steps of parallel PSO are as follows:

(1) Set the number of processes (np) and assign each process its rank $(r=0,1,...,$ $np-1)$.
(2) For each process, initialize the set of parameters c_1, c_2, w, number of particles n_r, maximum number of iterations n_it, dimension of search space d and the range for each decision variable and then randomly initialize the positions and velocities for each particle $(i=1,2,....,n_r)$.
(3) For each process, run an independent sequential PSO until the stopping criterion is reached.
(4) For each process, find the second best particle of its own swarm.
(5) For each process send the best and second best particles along with their fitness values to the process 0.
(6) For the process 0, receive the best and second best particles along with their fitness values from all processes including itself. Taking the received particles as initial swarm run a PSO on process 0 until the termination condition is met.
(7) When the termination condition is satisfied, report results. The best particle found by the process 0 is the solution obtained by the algorithm.

4   Experiments and Discussions

This section focuses on the application of PPSO to the Lennard-Jones problem for 10 atoms cluster. The problem is to find the most stable conformation of the cluster with 10 atoms which has a predefined global minimum energy value of -28.422532 [7]. Cartesian coordinates of each atom are considered, the search space for all the atoms is $[-2, 2]^3$ as given in [7]. To avoid attributing the results to the choice of a particular initial population and to conduct fair comparisons, we have made 100 trials for each test, starting from various randomly selected points in the search space.

4.1   Experimental Setup

Both the sequential and the parallel implementations of PSO have been experimented on a multiuser LINUX cluster having 3 identical HP ProLiant DL140G2 nodes dedicated to computations. The configuration of each node is as follows:

- Processors 2 x Xeon 3.4 GHz (800 MHz FSB)
- 1024 KB L2 Cache
- 4 x 512 PC2-3200 DDR2 memory

- 2 x 146 GB ULTRA320 10k NHP
- Intel Chipset is E7520

Integrated Dual Broadcom 10/100/1000
Integrated 10/100 NIC dedicated for server management
Operating System-Red Hat Enterprise Linux Rel. 3.0
Application code is written in C using MPI library for parallelization.

4.2 Selection of Parameters

In case of many algorithms values of some parameters have to be provided by the user. PSO also has some parameters. In literature, different values of these parameters have been used. Here we use $w=0.5$, $c_1=c_2=2$. In order to make fair comparisons the size of the swarm has been kept equivalent in sequential and parallel PSO. For the sequential PSO the swarm size was 100 and stopping criterion was convergence to a solution within tolerance limit 0.000001 or exceeding maximum number of iterations 10000. For the PPSO, in the parallel stage the swarm sizes for initial swarms were taken according to the following formula:

$$n_r = floor((r+1)*100/np) - floor(r*100/np). \tag{4}$$

The stopping criteria used for parallel and sequential stage are same as for sequential PSO except that the maximum number of iterations are different for parallel and sequential stage. Experiments were performed for many different combinations of number of iterations at parallel and sequential stage. Finally we used the ones (5000 for parallel stage and 100 for sequential stage) that yielded the best results. All the other PSO parameters used in the parallel and sequential stages of the PPSO were the same as those used for sequential PSO.

4.3 Parallel Peformance Measures

In order to compare the performance of the parallel and sequential PSO, some performance measures have been borrowed from literature [1]. The definitions of these performance measures as given in literature are as follows:

Speedup. If T_k is the execution time of an algorithm using k processors. Then the speedup is the ratio between the mean execution time E $[T_1]$ on one processor and mean execution time $E[T_k]$ on k processors because of its nondeterministic nature. So the speedup s_k due to k processors is given by

$$s_k = \frac{E[T_1]}{E[T_k]}. \tag{5}$$

Efficiency. Efficiency is the normalized version of speedup. It normalizes the speedup value to a certain percentage and is defined as

$$e_k = \frac{s_k}{k} \times 100\%. \tag{6}$$

4.4 Computational Results

All the computational results obtained by sequential and parallel PSO are recorded in Table 1. The results shown for 1 processor are those obtained by the sequential PSO since we want to compare PPSO with sequential PSO. Also since the definition of the speedup requires that the sequential and parallel algorithms are compared by running them until the solution of same quality has been found. So in order to make fair comparisons the execution times shown in the table are mean execution times of successful runs (out of 100). A run is considered successful if the global minimum function value is reached within the tolerance limit.

Figure 1 and Figure 2 show the effect of increasing number of processors on execution time and success rate respectively. It is clear that as the number of processors increases, the execution time begins to decrease. This is because, for fixed problem size, as the number of processors employed in solving increases, the computation time

Table 1. Results obtained by sequential and parallel PSO

Number of processors	Execution Time (Sec.)	Speedup	Efficiency	Successful runs out of 100
1	23.017625			3
2	15.357099	1.498826	0.749413	5
3	12.569088	1.831288	0.610429	8
4	10.266054	2.242110	0.585247	9
5	9.832437	2.340988	0.448422	10
6	10.00395	2.300853	0.383475	12

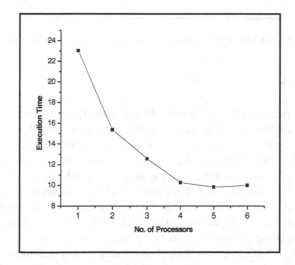

Fig. 1. This figure shows the behavior of *execution time* with the increase in *number of processors*

(work load) per processor decreases. And at some point, a processor's work load becomes comparable with its parallel overhead. From this point onwards, the execution time of problem starts increasing. It means that there is an optimal number of processors to be used. This is called the parallel balance point of the problem. In this problem the minimum execution time corresponds to 5 processes, so the parallel balance point of PPSO for this problem is 5.

In PPSO, we see that there are two causes for the increase in execution time after parallel balance point. One is the increased communication overhead with the increase in number of processors. The other is that as the number of processors increases the swarm size (on process 0) increases and so the processes other than the 0 process have to wait for longer, resulting in longer execution time. It is clear from Figure 2 that the success rate also increases with the number of processors which means that the reliability of the PPSO increases with the number of processors.

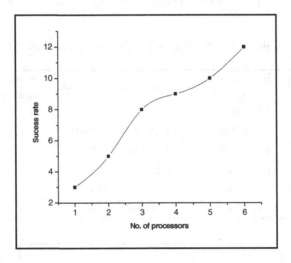

Fig. 2. This figure shows the increase in *success rate* with the *number of processors*

5 Conclusions

The Lennard-Jones potential of an atomic cluster with 10 atoms is minimized which is very useful in predicting the stable structure of the molecule which in turn dictates the majority of its properties. Computational results are obtained and presented for this case using parallel PSO (PPSO) and are compared with those obtained by sequential PSO and it is clearly seen (Table 1) that the solutions produced by PPSO are as good as those produced by the sequential PSO and that the algorithm achieves a substantial speedup. It is important to notice that this is for the first time that parallel PSO has been applied to the Lennard-Jones potential problem for 10 atoms cluster. However, it has earlier been applied for clusters containing 8 and 9 atoms [6].

The reason why PPSO used here takes less time is clearly that most of the search is completed in the parallel stage and afterwards the very good solutions obtained at the parallel stage are refined at the sequential stage in a few iterations, so the idle time of the processes (other than 0 process) at the sequential stage is very small. This is the main reason for better performance of PPSO as compared to sequential PSO.

Finally, PPSO has successfully obtained the global minimum of potential energy function in much less time. It can be concluded that PPSO is an efficient search algorithm and is it not limited to the case considered here but it can also be applied to some other and more complex cases.

Acknowledgments. This work is supported financially by Council of Scientific and Industrial Research, India. We are also thankful for the support provided for our work by the Institute Computer Center, Indian Institute of Technology Roorkee, India.

References

1. Alba, E.: Parallel evolutionary algorithms can achieve super-linear performance. Inform. Process. Lett. 82(1), 7–13 (2002)
2. Bernard, R.B., Bruccoleri, R.E., Olafson, B.D., States, D.J., Swaminathan, S., Karplus, M.: CHARMM: A program for macromolecular energy, minimization, and dynamics calculations. J. Comput. Chem. 4, 187–271 (1983)
3. Chu, S.C., Pan, J.S.: Intelligent parallel particle swarm optimization algorithms. Stud. Comp. Intell. 22, 159–175 (2006)
4. Colvin, M., Judson, R., Meza, J.: A genetic algorithm approach to molecular structure determination. In: International Conference on Industrial and Applied Mathematics, Washington DC (1991)
5. Corana, A., Marchesi, M., Martini, C., Ridella, S.: Minimizing multimodal functions of continuous variables with the "simulated annealing" algorithm. ACM T. Math. Software 13(3), 262–280 (1987)
6. Deep, K., Arya, M., Barak, S.: A New Multi-Swarm Particle Swarm Optimization and Its Application to Lennard-Jones Problem. Communicated to INFOCOMP Journal of Computer Science (March 5, 2010)
7. Hoare, M.R., Pal, P.: Adv. Phys. 20, 161 (1971); Nature (Physical Sciences) 230, 5 (1971); Nature (Physical Sciences) 236, 35 (1972)
8. Hoare, M.R.: Structure and Dynamics of Simple Microclusters. Adv. Chem. Phys. 40, 49–135 (1979)
9. Kennedy, J., Eberhart, R.C.: Particle swarm optimization. In: IEEE Conference on Neural Networks, Perth, pp. 1942–1948 (1995)
10. Kim, J.Y., Jeong, H.M., Lee, H.S., Park, J.H.: PC cluster based parallel PSO algorithm for optimal power flow. In: 14th International Conference on Intelligent System Applications to Power Systems, Kaohsiung, Taiwan (2007)
11. Koh, B., George, A.D., Haftka, R.T., Fregly, B.J.: Parallel Asynchronous Particle swarm optimization. Int. J. Numer. Methods Eng. 67, 578–595 (2006)
12. Leary, R.H., Doye, J.P.K.: Tetrahedral global minimum for the 98-atom Lennard-Jones cluster. Phys. Rev. E 60(R63), 20–22 (1999)
13. Northby, J.A.: Structure and binding of Lennard-Jones clusters: $13 \leq n \leq 147$. J. Chem. Phys. 87, 6166–6178 (1987)
14. Sahin, F., Yavuz, M.C., Arnavut, Z., Uluyo, O.: Fault diagnosis for airplane engines using Bayesian networks and distributed particle swarm optimization. Parallel Comput. 33, 124–143 (2007)

15. Schutte, J.F., Reinbolt, J.A., Fregly, B.J., Haftka, R.T., George, A.D.: Parallel global optimization with the particle swarm algorithm. Int. J. Numer. Methods Eng. 61(13), 2296–2315 (2004)
16. Snir, M., Otto, S., Huss-Lederman, S., Walker, D., Dongarra, J.: MPI: The Complete Reference. Massachusetts Institute of Technology, Cambridge (1996)
17. Venter, G., Sobieski, J.S.: A parallel Particle Swarm Optimization algorithm accelerated by asynchronous evaluations. J. Aerosp. Comput. Inform. Commun. 3(3), 123–137 (2005)
18. Waintraub, M., Schirru, R., Pereira, C.M.N.A.: Multiprocessor modeling of parallel Particle Swarm Optimization applied to nuclear engineering problems. Prog. Nucl. Energy 51, 680–688 (2009)
19. Wille, L.T.: Chem. Phys. Lett. 133(405) (1987)
20. Xue, G.L., Maier, R.S., Rosen, J.B.: Improvements on the Northby Algorithm for molecular conformation: Better solutions. J. Global. Optim. 4(4), 425–440 (1994)

An Artificial Bee Colony Algorithm for the 0–1 Multidimensional Knapsack Problem

Shyam Sundar[1], Alok Singh[1] and André Rossi[2]

[1] Department of Computer and Information Sciences
University of Hyderabad, Hyderabad 500046, India
{mc08pc17,alokcs}@uohyd.ernet.in
[2] Lab-STICC, Université de Bretagne-Sud, Centre de Recherche
BP 92116, 56321 Lorient Cedex, France
andre.rossi@univ-ubs.fr

Abstract. In this paper, we present an artificial bee colony (ABC) algorithm for the 0-1 Multidimensional Knapsack Problem (MKP_01). The objective of MKP_01 is to find a subset of a given set of n objects in such a way that the total profit of the objects included in the subset is maximized, while a set of knapsack constraints remains satisfied. The ABC algorithm is a new metaheuristic technique based on the intelligent foraging behavior of honey bee swarms. Heuristic-based repair operators and local search are incorporated into our ABC algorithm. Computational results demonstrate that our ABC algorithm not only produces better results but converges very rapidly in comparison with other swarm-based approaches.

Keywords: Artificial bee colony algorithm, combinatorial optimization, heuristic, multidimensional knapsack problem, swarm intelligence.

1 Introduction

The 0-1 Multidimensional knapsack Problem (MKP_01) is a well known $\mathcal{NP}$-Hard problem. In MKP_01, we are given a set J of n objects and a knapsack with m dimensions. Each object $j \in J$ has profit p_j and weight r_{ij} in dimension i ($1 \le i \le m$). Each dimension of the knapsack has a capacity b_i. The objective of MKP_01 is to find a subset of objects for inclusion into the knapsack in such a way that the total profit of the objects included is maximized, while the sum of the weights of the included objects in each dimension i should be less than or equal to b_i. By introducing binary variables x_j to indicate whether object j is included into the knapsack ($x_j = 1$) or not ($x_j = 0$), the MKP_01 can be formulated as:

$$\text{Maximize} \quad \sum_{j=1}^{n} p_j x_j$$

$$\text{Subject to} \quad \sum_{j=1}^{n} r_{ij} x_j \le b_i, i = 1, ..., m$$

$$x_j \in \{0, 1\}, j = 1, ..., n$$

S. Ranka et al. (Eds.): IC3 2010, Part I, CCIS 94, pp. 141–151, 2010.

The MKP_01 has many real applications like capital budgeting problem, cutting stock problem, cargo loading, allocating processors and databases in a distributed computer system.

In this paper, we propose a hybrid artificial bee colony algorithm ABC_MKP to solve MKP_01. The ABC algorithm is a new metaheuristic technique based on the intelligent foraging behaviour of honey bee swarms. This technique was proposed by Karaboga [6]. We have compared our hybrid ABC algorithm with other best performing swarm based approaches. Computational results show that our algorithm performs well in comparison to these approaches.

The rest of this paper is organized as follows: Section 2 provides a brief introduction to artificial bee colony algorithm. Section 3 describes in detail our hybrid approach for MKP_01. Computational results are presented in Section 4, whereas conclusions arc given in Section 5.

2   Artificial Bee Colony Algorithm

The artificial bee colony algorithm (ABC) is a new population-based metaheuristic technique based on the intelligent foraging behavior of honey bee swarm. It is proposed by Karaboga [6] and then extended by Karaboga & Basturk [6,7,8,9,10] and Singh [11]. On the basis of their foraging behavior, bees can be divided into three categories: employed, scouts and onlookers. Employed bees are those bees that are currently exploiting the food sources. All employed bees are responsible for bringing loads of nectar from their food sources to the hive sharing information about their food sources with onlookers. Onlookers are those bees which are waiting in the hive for employed bees to share information about their food sources. Scouts are those bees which are searching for a new food source in the vicinity of the hive. The employed bees share the information about their food sources with onlookers by dancing in a common area. The nature and duration of the dance of an employed bee depends on the quality of the food source currently being exploited by her. Onlookers watch numerous dances of employed bees before choosing a food source. The probability of choosing a food source is directly proportional to its quality. Therefore, the good food sources attract more onlookers than the poor ones. Whenever a bee, whether it is scout or onlooker, finds a food source it becomes employed. Whenever a food source is fully exploited, the associated employed bee abandons it and becomes scout. As soon as a scout searches a new food source in the vicinity of its hive, it again becomes employed. Thus, employed and onlooker bees can be seen as performing the job of exploitation, whereas scouts can be seen as performing the job of exploration.

The artificial bee colony algorithm (ABC) mimicking this intelligent foraging behavior of honey bee swarm was proposed by Karaboga [6]. Karaboga [6] also categorized the colony of artificial bees into same three groups: employed, onlookers and scouts. Employed bees are the first half of the colony, while onlookers are the latter half. In ABC algorithm, each food source represents a candidate solution to the problem and the nectar amount of a food source is an indicator of the quality (fitness) of the solution being represented by that food source.

Each employed bee is associated with a unique food source, i.e., the number of employed bees is same as the number of food sources. The employed bee becomes a scout when the food source associated with it is being fully exploited. As soon as, the scout finds a new food source, it again becomes employed.

The ABC algorithm is an iterative algorithm. The algorithm starts by associating each employed bee with a randomly generated food source. Then, during each iteration, each employed bee determines a new food source in the neighborhood of its currently associated food source and computes the nectar amount of this new food source. If the nectar amount of this new food source is higher than that of its currently associated food source, then this employed bee moves to the new food source abandoning the old one, otherwise it continues with the old one. After completion of this process by all employed bees, they start sharing information about their food sources with onlookers. Onlookers select the food sources probabilistically according to the nectar amount (fitness) of that food source. The probability p_i of selecting a food source i is computed as:

$$p_i = \frac{f_i}{\sum_{j=1}^{k} f_j}$$

where f_i is the fitness of the solution associated with the food source i and k is the total number of food sources. This selection method is known by the name "roulette wheel" in genetic algorithm community. According to this selection method, higher the fitness of a food source, the probability of its selection will be more. Therefore, richer nectar containing food sources attracts more onlookers than the poorer ones. Once all onlookers select their food sources in the aforementioned way, each of them determines a new food source in the neighborhood of its selected food source and computes the nectar amount of the new food source. Among all the neighboring food sources computed by onlookers associated with a particular food source i and food source i itself, richest food source will be the new location of food source i. If the solution represented by a food source i does not improve for a predetermined number of iterations (called *limit* parameter) then food source i is deemed to be completely exploited and its associated employed bee abandons it to become scout. This scout is again made employed by associating it with a new randomly generated food source. When the new locations of all food sources are determined, then the next iteration of ABC algorithm begins. This process is repeated until the termination criterion is satisfied.

The procedure for determining a food source in the neighborhood of a particular food source depends on the nature of the problem. Karaboga's original ABC algorithm was designed for continuous optimization. To determine a new food source in the neighborhood of a particular food source, his model changes the value of one randomly chosen solution parameter while keeping other parameters unchanged. This is done by adding to the current value of the chosen parameter the product of a uniform variate in [-1, 1] and the difference in values of this parameter for this food source and some other randomly chosen food source.

This method can not be applied for discrete optimization problems for which it produces at best a random effect. Later, Singh [11] presented a method that is applicable for subset selection problems. To generate a neighboring solution, in this method, an object is randomly removed from the solution and in its place another object, which is not already present in the solution is inserted. The object to be inserted is selected from another randomly chosen solution. If there are more than one candidate objects for insertion then ties are broken arbitrarily. This method is based on the idea that if an object is present in one good solution then it is highly likely that this object is present in many good solutions. Another advantage associated with this method is that it helps in restricting the number of duplicate solutions in the population. If the method fails to find an object in the randomly chosen solution different from the objects in the original solution then that means that the two solutions are identical. Such a situation was called "collision" and was resolved by making the employed bee associated with the original solution scout. This eliminates one duplicate solution.

3   ABC Algorithm for MKP_01

We have followed the ideas of ABC algorithm presented by Karaboga [6] and Singh [11]. We have integrated ABC algorithm with a problem specific heuristics of MKP_01 as well as local search. Our hybrid based ABC algorithm (ABC_MKP) for the MKP_01 is described below:

3.1   Initialization

A set of feasible solutions is generated randomly. The size (*pop_size*) of this set is same as number of employed bees and onlookers in our algorithm. Each solution is generated by following an iterative process. During each iteration, an object is selected randomly and added to the solution if it satisfies the knapsack constraints. This process is repeated until it is not possible to add any more objects to the knapsack without violating any of the constraints. Profit (fitness) is computed for each of these solutions. In our algorithm, each employed bee is initialized by associating it to one of these solutions.

3.2   Probability of Selecting a Food Source

In our ABC_MKP algorithm, we have used binary tournament selection method for selecting a food source for onlookers, instead of using roulette wheel selection method as described in section 2. In binary tournament selection method, two different food sources are selected randomly from the food sources associated with employed bees. With probability b_t, the food source containing richer nectar amount among the two food sources is selected otherwise poorer is selected. We have also experimented with roulette wheel selection method, but binary tournament selection method has been found to give better results always.

3.3 Determination of a New Food Source in the Neighborhood of a Food Source

Our method is derived from the method proposed in Singh [11]. Our method is based on the observation that if an object is present in one good solution, then the chances of this object being present in many other good solutions are more. To determine a food source in the neighborhood of a food source i, we randomly select another food source j (different from i), then we randomly select a maximum of two distinct objects (the value two is determined empirically) from j which are not present in i and add them to i which makes solution i infeasible. if this method fails to find even one object in j different from the objects of i, then it means that i and j are identical i.e., they represent the same solution. Such a situation was given the name collision in [11]. In case of an employed bee, if a collision occurs while determining a new neighboring food source, then employed bee abandons its associated food source to become scout and does not take place in further operations like repair operator and local search. This scout is again made employed by associating it with a new randomly generated food source. Thus, this collision helps in eliminating a duplicate solution. However, if a collision occurs while determining a new neighboring food source for an onlooker, then another food source j is selected randomly. This process is repeated until we find a food source j which is different from food source i. After that repair and local search takes place. It is very important to note that if a collision happens in case of an onlooker, it is worthless to generate a food source randomly for the onlooker because for survival this randomly generated food source has to compete with the original food source as well as with the food sources of all onlookers which are associated with the same original food source. Hence, it is highly likely that such a randomly generated solution seldom survive. This concept of collision was introduced in [11]. If there is no collision, then the process of making the infeasible solution feasible begins where, we have used a slightly modified version of repair operator proposed by Chu and Beasley [1] in our ABC_MKP algorithm. The repair operator consists of two phases. The first phase (DROP PHASE) drops objects in one of the two ways until the infeasible solution becomes feasible. With probability p_d, the objects of food source i are dropped in the increasing order of their pseudoutility ratios which will be described in the next paragraph, otherwise objects of the food source i are dropped randomly. In the second phase (ADD PHASE), objects which are not in the food source i are sorted in decreasing order on the basis of their pseudo-utility ratios. Each sorted unselected object is checked one by one whether it can be added to the food source i without violating the feasibility. If so, then it is added to the food source i. This process is repeated until all unselected objects are considered for inclusion.

Pseudo-utility ratio u_j for an object j is defined by the following expression

$$u_j = \frac{p_j}{\sum_{i=1}^{m} \omega_i r_{ij}}$$

and is a greedy heuristic information which helps in getting good solutions. Pseudo-utility ratios are calculated with the help of surrogate duality approach proposed by Pirkul [12]. Following the notational convention of [1], the surrogate relaxation problem of the MKP_01 is defined as:

$$\text{Maximize} \quad \sum_{j=1}^{n} p_j x_j$$

$$\text{subject to} \quad \sum_{j=1}^{n} \left(\sum_{i=1}^{m} \omega_i r_{ij} \right) x_j \leq \sum_{i=1}^{m} \omega_i b_i$$

$$x_j \in \{0, 1\}$$

where $\omega = \{\omega_1, ., ., \omega_m\}$ is a set of surrogate multipliers (or weights) of some positive real numbers. Pirkul suggested that linear Programming relaxation of the original MKP_01 should be solved and values of the dual variables should be used as the weights ω_i. The weight ω_i can be considered as the shadow price of the ith constraint in the Linear Programming relaxation of the original MKP_01.

Local search has been used in our algorithm to improve the solution quality of our ABC_MKP algorithm. This local search is derived from 1-1 exchange and 2-1 exchange used in complete/better fit heuristic described in [14]. Our local search tries to repeatedly exchange one or two selected objects with an unselected object if such an exchange can increase the total profit while maintaining the feasibility of the solution. In 1-1 exchange, we repeatedly exchange a selected object with the unselected object of highest profit that will keep the solution feasible after the exchange. The selected objects are tried for exchange in the order in which they appear in the knapsack. In 2-1 exchange, we exchange a pair of selected object with the first unselected object that will keep the solution feasible after the exchange and total profit will increase or remain same. In this local search, we first find a pair of minimum profit objects among selected objects, and then we exchange this pair of selected object with the first unselected object that will keep the solution feasible and that either increases the overall profit or keeps it same. If the exchange takes place, then the procedure is completed. If exchange does not take place, then we try to swap next minimum profit pair of selected objects. This procedure is repeated till a swapping move has been found or all pairs have been considered. As this local search is used repeatedly inside ABC algorithm, therefore, to keep its running time manageable, 1-1 exchange is applied maximum five times and 2-1 exchange is applied only once. These limits were chosen empirically. Moreover, 1-1 exchange and 2-1 exchange are used in a mutually exclusive manner, i.e., in a particular application of the local search, either 1-1 exchange is used or 2-1 exchange is used but not both. 1-1 exchange with maximum five applications is used as the local search with probability P_{ls}, otherwise a single 2-1 exchange is used as the local search.

3.4 Other Features

If a food source (solution) does not improve for a predetermined number of iterations *limit*, then employed bee associated with that food source abandons it and becomes a scout. This scout will generate a new food source randomly. After generating a food source, this scout again becomes employed. The parameter limit is an important control parameter of the ABC algorithm. As described in section 3.3, an employed bee can also become a scout through collision. Like [11], in our algorithm also, there is no upper limit on the number of scouts in a single iteration. In an iteration, there can be many scouts, if these two above conditions are met, or there can be no scouts, if these two above conditions are not met.

4 Computational Results

Our algorithm ABC_MKP has been implemented in C and executed on a Linux based 3.0 GHz Pentium 4 system with 512 MB RAM. Like [2], we have also used benchmark instances 5.100 and 10.100 from OR-Library of Chu and Beasley [1] for testing our algorithm. The benchmark set 5.100 has 30 instances with $m = 5$ constraints and $n = 100$ objects while benchmark set 10.100 has 30 instances with $m = 10$ constraints and $n = 100$ objects. Each set containing 30 instances is divided into 3 series with $\alpha = b_i / \sum_{j=1}^{n} r_{ij} = 1/4$, $\alpha = 1/2$ and $\alpha = 3/4$. Our algorithm ABC_MKP is executed 30 times on each instance with a different random seed. The ABC_MKP is executed for 5000 iterations on each instance of benchmark set 5.100 and 10000 iterations on each instance of benchmark set 10.100.

4.1 Parameter Settings

Since parameters of ABC_MKP algorithm play a crucial role in finding best as well as average results, therefore, we have chosen their values carefully after a large number of trials. We have five parameters, viz., *pop_size*, p_d, P_{1s}, *limit* and b_t. These parameters have been defined in the previous section. The values that we have tried for each parameter are as follows: [50, 100, 150] for *pop_size*, [0.2, 0.3, 0.4, 0.5, 0.6] for p_d, [0.98, 0.99, 1.0] for P_{1s}, [50, 100, 150, 200] for *limit* and [0.85, 0.90, 0.95] for b_t. During experimentation, the value of a single parameter is changed, while keeping the values of other parameters fixed. Based on extensive experimentation, we found that in most of the cases our ABC_MKP algorithm performs better in finding best as well as average results when *pop_size* = 100, p_d=0.3, P_{1s}=0.99, *limit*=100 and b_t=0.90.

4.2 Comparison with Other Swarm-Based Approaches

Since our ABC_MKP algorithm is a swarm-based approach, so we have compared our ABC_MKP algorithm with four other swarm_based approaches. The ABC_MKP is compared with ACO approaches of BAS_MKP of Min Kong *et al.*

Table 1. The results of ABC_MKP on 5.100 instances

No	Best known	L. & M. Best	L. & M. Avg.	Fidanova Best	Alaya et al. Best	Alaya et al. Avg.	BAS_MKP Best	BAS_MKP Avg.	BAS_MKP ATTB	ABC_MKP Best	ABC_MKP Avg.	ABC_MKP ATTB
00	24381	24381	24331	23984	24381	24342	24381	24381.00	1.52	24381	24381.00	0.18
01	24274	24274	24245	24145	24274	24247	24274	24274.00	22.63	24274	24274.00	0.18
02	23551	23551	23527	23523	23551	23529	23551	23551.00	82.40	23551	23547.10	11.96
03	23534	23527	23463	22874	23534	23462	23534	23534.00	141.45	23534	23534.00	0.29
04	23991	23991	23949	23751	23991	23946	23991	23991.00	12.87	23991	23988.50	14.50
05	24613	24613	24563	24601	24613	24587	24613	24613.00	3.20	24613	24613.00	0.36
06	25591	25591	25504	25293	25591	25512	25591	25591.00	0.25	25591	25591.00	0.14
07	23410	23410	23361	23204	23410	23371	23410	23410.00	0.95	23410	23410.00	0.11
08	24216	24204	24173	23762	24216	24172	24216	24216.00	135.60	24216	24216.00	0.79
09	24411	24411	24326	24255	24411	24356	24411	24411.00	11.50	24411	24411.00	0.42
10	42757	-	-	42705	42757	42704	42757	42757.00	38.96	42757	42757.00	0.13
11	42545	-	-	42445	42510	42456	42545	42541.20	203.08	42545	42545.00	0.73
12	41968	-	-	41581	41967	41934	41968	41967.90	173.23	41968	41968.00	11.51
13	45090	-	-	44911	45071	45056	45090	45090.00	74.74	45090	45090.00	0.34
14	42218	-	-	42025	42218	42194	42218	42218.00	4.18	42218	42218.00	0.15
15	42927	-	-	42671	42927	42911	42927	42927.00	1.63	42927	42927.00	0.25
16	42009	-	-	41776	42009	41977	42009	42009.00	1.28	42009	42009.00	0.10
17	45020	-	-	44671	45010	44971	45020	45020.00	14.26	45020	45020.00	0.27
18	43441	-	-	43122	43441	43356	43441	43441.00	60.58	43441	43441.00	0.31
19	44554	-	-	44471	44554	44506	44554	44554.00	11.22	44554	44554.00	1.46
20	59822	-	-	59798	59822	59821	59822	59822.00	6.61	59822	59822.00	0.22
21	62081	-	-	61821	62081	62010	62081	62060.33	139.41	62081	62081.00	0.11
22	59802	-	-	59694	59802	59759	59802	59800.73	113.73	59802	59802.00	1.78
23	60479	-	-	60479	60479	60428	60479	60479.00	69.74	60479	60479.00	0.31
24	61091	-	-	60954	61091	61072	61091	61091.00	59.42	61091	61091.00	0.87
25	58959	-	-	58695	58959	58945	58959	58959.00	3.77	58959	58959.00	0.54
26	61538	-	-	61406	61538	61514	61538	61538.00	35.20	61538	61538.00	0.95
27	61520	-	-	61520	61520	61492	61520	61520.00	52.15	61520	61520.00	0.06
28	59453	-	-	59121	59453	59436	59453	59453.00	2.03	59453	59453.00	0.17
29	59965	-	-	59864	59965	59958	59965	59965.00	50.87	59965	59965.00	1.75

[2], Alaya et al. [3], Fidanova [4] and Leguizamon and Michalewicz (L. & M.) [5]. Among these four approaches the BAS_MKP performs the best, therefore comparison of ABC_MKP with BAS_MKP is most important. Results are reported in tables 1 and 2. Table 1 reports the results of 30 instances of 5.100 benchmark set whereas Table 2 does the same for 10.100 benchmark set. Results of L. & M. are reported in [5] only for first 10 instances in each set whereas results of the approach of Fidanova are reported in [4] only for 5.100 set. In addition, no average solution quality is reported for this approach. For each instance, these tables report the best known solution from OR-library, the best and average solution found by aforementioned methods and ABC_MKP. In addition, average time to reach the best solution is reported for BAS_MKP and ABC_MKP. We have run our algorithm for 30 trials on each instance which is same as the number of trials used in BAS_MKP of Min Kong et al. [2].

Table 1 shows that our ABC_MKP algorithm finds best result for each instance of 5.100 benchmark set. Since BAS_MKP of Min Kong et al. [2] has also found best result for each instance while L. & M. [5], Fidanova [4] and Alaya et al.

Table 2. The results of ABC_MKP on 10.100 instances

No	Best known	L. & M. Best	Avg.	Alaya *et al.* Best	Avg.	BAS MKP Best	Avg.	ATTB	ABC MKP Best	Avg.	ATTB
00	23064	23057	22996	23064	23016	23064	23064.00	28.89	23064	23061.67	25.02
01	22801	22801	22672	22801	22714	22801	22801.00	38.85	22801	22801.00	3.77
02	22131	22131	21980	22131	22034	22131	22131.00	26.61	22131	22131.00	0.28
03	22772	22772	22631	22717	22634	22772	22771.70	5.90	22772	22772.00	12.89
04	22751	22654	22578	22654	22547	22751	22751.00	130.27	22751	22751.00	1.38
05	22777	22652	22565	22716	22602	22777	22771.93	247.77	22777	22770.53	38.49
06	21875	21875	21758	21875	21777	21875	21875.00	31.81	21875	21875.00	1.46
07	22635	22551	22519	22551	22453	22635	22635.00	14.63	22635	22635.00	22.18
08	22511	22418	22292	22511	22351	22511	22511.00	91.87	22511	22511.00	5.46
09	22702	22702	22588	22702	22591	22702	22702.00	0.87	22702	22702.00	0.28
10	41395	-	-	41395	41329	41395	41388.70	38.53	41395	41395.00	7.99
11	42344	-	-	42344	42214	42344	42344.00	163.70	42344	42344.00	2.18
12	42401	-	-	42401	42300	42401	42401.00	57.83	42401	42353.30	28.96
13	45624	-	-	45624	45461	45624	45606.67	186.84	45598	45598.00	4.56
14	41884	-	-	41884	41739	41884	41881.00	359.18	41884	41884.00	7.17
15	42995	-	-	42995	42909	42995	42995.00	18.62	42995	42995.00	0.17
16	43559	-	-	43553	43464	43574	43561.00	67.44	43574	43557.70	22.36
17	42970	-	-	42970	42903	42970	42970.00	18.62	42970	42970.00	23.96
18	42212	-	-	42212	42146	42212	42212.00	0.58	42212	42212.00	0.35
19	41207	-	-	41207	41067	41207	41198.60	218.88	41207	41172.00	14.76
20	57375	-	-	57375	57318	57375	57375.00	25.59	57375	57375.00	0.12
21	58978	-	-	58978	58889	58978	58978.00	83.20	58978	58978.00	0.09
22	58391	-	-	58391	58333	58391	58391.00	34.22	58391	58391.00	0.76
23	61966	-	-	61966	61885	61966	61919.20	141.42	61966	61966.00	0.51
24	60803	-	-	60803	60798	60803	60803.00	3.24	60803	60803.00	0.11
25	61437	-	-	61437	61293	61437	61418.60	227.48	61437	61437.00	16.98
26	56377	-	-	56377	56324	56353	56353.00	133.99	56377	56376.20	22.75
27	59391	-	-	59391	59339	59391	59391.00	5.26	59391	59391.00	0.34
28	60205	-	-	60205	60146	60205	60199.80	194.22	60205	60205.00	0.65
29	60633	-	-	60633	60605	60633	60633.00	10.18	60633	60633.00	0.09

[3] have not obtained best result for each instance. In case of average results, ABC_MKP performs better than BAS_MKP of Min Kong et al. [2], L. & M. [5] and Alaya *et al.* [3]. ABC_MKP finds 28 out of 30 instances in which average results are equal to best results while BAS_MKP of Min Kong *et al.* [2] has found 26 out of 30 instances.

Table 2 shows that our ABC_MKP algorithm finds 29 best results out of 30 instances of 10.100 benchmark set which are better than L. & M. [5] and Alaya *et al.* [3]. BAS_MKP of Min Kong *et al.* [2] has also found 29 best results out of 30 instances. ABC_MKP is unable to find best known result of 10.100.13 instance. ABC_MKP also finds best result of 10.100.16 instance as BAS_MKP of Min Kong *et al.* [2] has found which is not given in OR-library. In case of average results, ABC_MKP is better than BAS_MKP of Min Kong *et al.* [2], L. & M. [5] and Alaya *et al.* [3]. ABC_MKP finds average solutions in 23 out of 30 instances equal to best results while BAS_MKP has found the same in 19 out of 30 instances.

In terms of average time to reach the best solution, ABC_MKP is much faster in comparison to BAS_MKP of Min Kong *et al.* [2] on most of the instances. The BAS_MKP takes maximum time of 203.08 and 359.18 seconds on average to reach the best solution respectively on 5.100 and 10.100 benchmark sets whereas ABC_MKP takes a maximum of 14.50 and 38.49 seconds on average to reach the best solution.

Tables 1 and 2 clearly show the superiority of ABC_MKP over BAS_MKP of Min Kong *et al.* [2] in terms of solution quality as well as average time to reach the best solution.

5   Conclusions

In this paper we have proposed an artificial bee colony based approach ABC_MKP for the 0-1 Multidimensional Knapsack Problem. The ABC_MKP has been compared with four other swarm based approaches. Computational results demonstrate the superiority of the ABC_MKP over other approaches. As a future work we intend to extend our approach to multiple knapsack problem.

References

1. Chu, P.C., Beasley, J.E.: A Genetic Algorithm for the Multidimentional Knapsack Problem. Journal of Heuristic 4, 63–86 (1998)
2. Kong, M., Tian, P., Kao, Y.: A New Ant Colony Optimization Algorithm for the Multidimensional Knapsack Problem. Computers and Operations Research 35, 2672–2683 (2008)
3. Alaya, I., Solnon, C., Ghéira, K.: Ant Algorithm for the Multi-Dimensional Knapsack Problem. In: International Conference on Bio-Inspired Optimization Methods and Their Applications (BIOMA 2004), pp. 63–72 (2004)
4. Fidanova, S.: Evolutionary Algorithm for Multidimensional Knapsack Problem. In: PPSN VII Workshop (2002)
5. Leguizamon, G., Michalewicz, Z.: A New Version of Ant System for Subset Problem. In: Congress on Evolutionary Computation, pp. 1459–1464 (1999)
6. Karaboga, D.: An Idea Based on Honey Bee Swarm for Numerical Optimization. Technical Report TR06, Computer Engineering Department, Erciyes University, Turkey (2005)
7. Basturk, B., Karaboga, D.: An Artificial Bee Colony (ABC) Algorithm for Numeric Function Optimization. In: Proceedings of the IEEE Swarm Intelligence Symposium, Indianapolis, USA, May 12-14 (2006)
8. Basturk, B., Karaboga, D.: A Powerful and Efficient Algorithm for Numeric Function Optimization: Artificial Bee Colony (ABC) algorithm. Journal of Global Optimization 39, 459–471 (2007)
9. Basturk, B., Karaboga, D.: Artificial Bee Colony (ABC) Optimization Algorithm for Solving Constrained Optimization Problems. In: Melin, P., Castillo, O., Aguilar, L.T., Kacprzyk, J., Pedrycz, W. (eds.) IFSA 2007. LNCS (LNAI), vol. 4529, pp. 789–798. Springer, Heidelberg (2007)

10. Karaboga, D., Basturk, B.: On the Performance of Artificial Bee Colony (ABC) Algorithm. Applied Soft Computing 8, 687–697 (2008)
11. Singh, A.: An Artificial Bee Colony (ABC) Algorithm for the Leaf-Constrained Minimum Spanning Tree Problem. Applied Soft Computing 9, 625–631 (2009)
12. Pirkul, H.: A Heuristic Solution Procedure for the Multiconstraint Zero–One Knapsack Problem. Naval Research Logistics 34, 61–72 (1987)
13. Martello, S., Toth, P.: Knapsack Problems: Algorithms and Computer Implementations. Wiley, Chichester (1990)
14. Singh, A., Gupta, A.K.: Two Heuristics for the One-Dimensional Bin-Packing Problem. OR Spectrum 29, 765–781 (2007)

Automatic Summary Generation from Single Document Using Information Gain

Chandra Prakash and Anupam Shukla

Indian Institute of Information Technology and Management Gwalior,
Madhya Pradesh – 474010, India
cpiiitm2010@gmail.com, dranupamshukla@gmail.com

Abstract. With tons of information pouring in every day over Internet, it is not easy to read each and every document. The information retrieval from search engine is still far greater than that a user can handle and manage. So there is need of presenting the information in a summarized way. In this paper, an automatic abstractive summarization technique from single document is proposed. The sentences in the text are identified first. Then from those sentences segments, unique terms are identified. A Term-Sentence matrix is generated, where the column represents the sentences and the row represents the terms. The entries in the matrix are weight from information gain. Column with a maximum cosine similarity is selected as first sentence of the summary sentence and likewise. Results over documents indicate that the performance of the proposed approach compares very favorably with other approaches.

Keywords: text summarization, information gain, single document, data mining, abstractive summarization technique.

1 Introduction

With the coming of the information revolution, electronic documents are becoming a principle media of business and academic information. Thousands of electronic documents are produced and made available on the internet each day. But it is not easy to read each and every document. So there is need of presenting the information as a summarization so that there is no need to read the whole document. The summary should present an abstract of the document. Huge amount of data is available on net, but retrieving the correct and relevant data is not possible. Search engines such as Google, Yahoo etc. tries to serves as an information access agent[1]. They retrieve and rank information as per the user's request. But because of the lack of deep understanding of natural language and human intelligence, they only perform shallow string information (shallow parsing [2]). The information retrieval is still far greater than that a user can handle and manage. The user has to analyze the searched result one by one until satisfactory information is acquired. This is time consuming and inefficient.

If the document can be representing in lesser words with main important words, then this make our life easier. Automatic Text summarization is an active research area where a computer automatically summarizes text from both single and multi

S. Ranka et al. (Eds.): IC3 2010, Part I, CCIS 94, pp. 152–159, 2010.

documents. Text Summarization is possible because of the naturally occurring redundancy in text and because important or salient information is spread unevenly in textual documents. The main challenge is to identifying the redundancy.

The summarization helps in making abstracts for Scientific and other articles. This will also helps in news summarization. It's also facilities classification of articles and other written data. This will improve Search engines indexing efficiency of web pages and thus assists in storing the text in much lesser space. This also enables Cell phones to access the Web information. The indirect functions of summary are classification, indexing and keyword extraction from a given text.

Generating a good automated summary is not an easy task, there are various obstacles. The first major challenge is the extent to which one can "understand" the chosen text. It is very complicated to understand a document without processing the whole text. However, detailed parsing is tedious and not even guarantee to give a good summary.

2 Previous Approaches

Test summarization is not a new idea. Text summarization has been developed since 1958 [3],[4]and[5]. Several researchers continued investigating various approaches to this problem was proposed in seventies and eighties. Most methods still rely on 50'-70' algorithms. Many innovative approaches began to explore such as statistical and information-centric approach, linguistic approaches and the combination of them. Statistical techniques include dropping unimportant words such as stopping words, determiners and adverbs. Then the sentences with more important terms are extracted in higher priories. Common ways to determine term importance is Term Frequency/ Inverse-documents-frequency (TF-IDF) [6,7] Weighting scheme, entropy, mutual information etc. Linguistic techniques looks for text semantics, which yield better results. Linguistic techniques extract sentence by means of natural language processing (NLP). In order to find the key terms, parsing and part of speech tagging is among the starting steps.

With the introduction of machine learning techniques in NLP, a sequence of publications were appeared for text summarization in 1990's. These approaches were based on statistical techniques. Initially most systems that were produced for text summarization were based on naive-Bayes methods[8] and assumed to be feature independence. Hidden Markov model[9] and log-linear models are some of the other significant approaches suggested to improve extractive summarization. Recently neural networks and query based search third party feature Text summarization approaches are also suggested to improve purely extractive single document summarization.

In the proposed approach, we do not claim to generate a summary by using abstraction method after understanding the whole text, but rather, by we implement extract meaning to extort key segments (terms) out of the text. This summarization by extract will be good enough for a reader to understand the main idea of a document, though the understand ability might not be as good as a summary by abstract.

Details of this system are described in the remainder of this paper. The paper is organized as follows: Section 3 covers the methodology of the system, section 4 covers experimental results of evaluating the developed techniques are presented. Finally, conclusions and future scope are discussed in section 5.

3 Methodology of the System

The methodology of text summarization involves four steps: Term Selection using pre-processing, Term weighting, sentence scoring using information gain and sentence selection using cosine similarity. Figure 1 presents the model of text summarization using Information Gain Method.

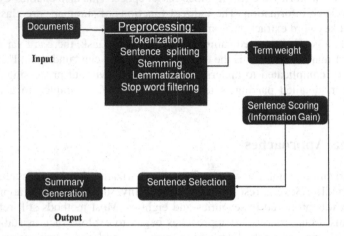

Fig. 1. Model for text summarization using Information Gain Method

3.1 Preprocessing

In the preprocessing step a structured representation of original test is obtained. The sentences in the text are identified first using word-boundary markers [10]. Besides isolation, other forms of pre-processing (Tokenization or segmentation, stopword filtering, stemming or lemmatization) are done.

3.2 Term Weighting

Estimating the individual terms is known as term weighting. One of the ways to estimate the usefulness of a sentence is to sum up usefulness weights of individual terms of which the sentence consists. Sentence can be considered as vectors consisting of the terms that occur within the document, with weights attached to each term denoting its importance for the sentence.

$$S_i = [T_1, T_2, T_3, \ldots\ldots T_N], \tag{1}$$

where S_i is the ith sentence , T_1 is the 1st term , T_2 is 2nd term and T_N is the Nth term in the document.

Term Frequency, Inverse Document Frequency (*IDF*) and *TF-IDF* are some of the methods for assigning weight to a term in a document[11]. As the proposed approach is for single document summarization, for applying these term weights we can consider the document as a collection of sentences instead of a collection of documents.

Binary weighting. The simplest way to assign weight to a term on the basis of presence or absence of a term in the sentence, defined as:

$$W_i(T_j) = \begin{cases} 1 & \text{if the term } T_j \text{ appears in sentence i} \\ 0 & \text{other wise} \end{cases} \tag{2}$$

Term Frequency (TF). It shows the number of times the term appears in the sentences. The approach of Term Frequency for documents was proposed by Luhn [2].

$$W_i(T_j) = f_{ij} \tag{3}$$

where f_{ij} is the frequency of jth term in sentence i.

Inverse Sentence Frequency (ISF). Salton proposed Inverse Document Frequency (*IDF*) to overcome the problem of appearing a term in almost all the documents in the collection as per Term Frequency [7]. Here we are dealing with single document summary so we have Sentence instead of document. *ISF* is defined as:

$$W_i(T_j) = \log\left(\frac{N}{n_j}\right) \tag{4}$$

where $W_i(T_j)$ is the weight of jth term, N is the number of sentences in the collection and n_j is the number of sentence where the term j appears.

3.3 Sentence Scoring

Sentence Signature are those sentences that indicate key concepts in a document. The sentence with more terms in it has a greater probability to be selected in summary. A Term-Sentence matrix is generated. The entries in the matrix are weight from information gain.

Term sentence matrix. Term-Sentence matrix (*TSM*) shown below, where the column represents the sentences and the row represents a specific term existing in any of the sentences.

$$TSM = \begin{bmatrix} W_{11} & W_{12} & \cdots & W_{1N} \\ W_{21} & W_{22} & \cdots & W_{2N} \\ \cdots & \cdots & \cdots & \cdots \\ W_{M1} & W_{M2} & \cdots & W_{MN} \end{bmatrix} \tag{5}$$

Sentence vectors are considered to be the projections in a multidimensional space, where the dimensionality is given by the M number of sentences and N number of index terms. The entries in the matrix are weight from information gain. Lexical similarity between two sentences can be found out by calculating the Euclidean distance between these vectors in space.

Information Gain. Information Gain is the indicator of the importance of a term in a document. It is combination of Term frequency weight Score, Inverse Sentence Frequency score, normalized sentence length score, sentence position score.

- **Term Frequency Weight Score.** Assume that there are n distinct terms in a sentence and term j occurs W_j times. i.e. W_j is the frequency of the term j. Then the Term Frequency Weight Score of sentence i defined as:

$$\text{TFW}_i = \sum_{j=1}^{n} (\emptyset(i, j)) wj \qquad (6)$$

where $\emptyset(i, j) = 1$ if j^{th} term exists in sentence i; otherwise 0.

- **Inverse Sentence Frequency score:**

$$\text{ISFS(T}_j) = \log\left(\frac{N}{nj}\right) \qquad (7)$$

where N is the number of sentences in the collection and n_j is the number of sentence where the term j appears.

- **Normalized Sentence length score:** This feature is employed to penalize sentences that are too short. The Normalized sentence length score defines as:

$$\text{NSL}_i = \frac{\text{No of Words occuring in the sentences}}{\text{No of words occuring in the longest sentence in the document}} \qquad (8)$$

- **Sentence position score:** If n denotes the number of sentences in the document, position weight of ith sentence in the document is:

$$\text{SPS}_i = \frac{n - i + 1}{n} \qquad (9)$$

- **Numerical Data Score:** Generally the sentence that contains numerical data is an important one. The Numerical data score is calculated as:

$$\text{NDS}_i = \frac{\text{No of numerical data in the sentences}}{\text{Length of the sentence}} \qquad (10)$$

- **Proper Noun Score:** The idea behind this feature is that the occurrence of proper names, referring to people and places, are clues that a sentence is relevant for the summary. Proper names were detected by a part-of speech tagger. The Proper noun score is calculated as:

$$\text{PNS}_i = \frac{\text{No of Proper Noun in the sentences}}{\text{Length of the sentence}} \qquad (11)$$

Information Gain is calculated as the scalar sum of the above factors.

$$\text{Information Gain} = \text{TFW}_i + \text{ISFS(T}_j) + \text{NSL}_i + \text{SPS}_i + \text{NDS}_i + \text{PNS}_i \qquad (12)$$

Information gain tells the importance of the term in the documents. Then the final Term-Sentence matrix will be:

$$(TSM) = \begin{bmatrix} IG(W_{11}) & IG(W_{12}) & \cdots & IG(W_{1N}) \\ IG(W_{21}) & IG(W_{22}) & \cdots & IG(W_{2N}) \\ \cdots & \cdots & \cdots & \cdots \\ IG(W_{M1}) & IG(W_{M2}) & \cdots & IG(W_{MN}) \end{bmatrix} \qquad (13)$$

3.4 Summary Generation

In the summary generation step, The cosine similarity of each column (sentence) is determined. The sentence corresponding to the column having maximum similarity is selected as summary sentence. Thus the summary generated will be good enough for a reader to understand the main idea of a document.

Cosine similarity is a method to measure similarity between two vectors with dimensions n. The cosine angle between the vector is often used to compare documents in text mining. The Cosine Similarity(Φ), between two vectors with attributes, A and B, is represented using a scalar product and magnitude as

$$\text{Cosine Similarity} = \cos(\Phi) = \frac{A \cdot B}{\|A\| \cdot \|B\|} \tag{14}$$

Therefore maximum similarity corresponds to $cos\ \Phi = 1$, whereas $cos\ \Phi = 0$ indicates total discrepancy between the text elements.

4 Experimental Results

The proposed Text Summarization Method, implemented on an article taken from website of *The Hindu* [12].

The measure of the system's quality is the usual notion of the information-retrieval criteria. In the field of information retrieval, precision [13] is the fraction of retrieved documents that are relevant to the search:

$$\text{Precision (P)} = \frac{100 \times r}{K_m} \tag{15}$$

where, r is no of common sentence, K_m is length of machine generated summary.

Recall in another form of Information Retrieval. It is the fraction of the documents that are relevant to the query that are successfully retrieved.

$$\text{Recall (R)} = \frac{100 \times r}{K_h} \tag{16}$$

where, r is no of common sentence, K_h is length of human generated summary. A measure that combines *Precision* and *Recall* is the weighted harmonic mean of precision and recall, the traditional F-measure or balanced *F-score*:

$$F - score = \frac{2 \times P \times R}{P + R} = \frac{100 \times 2r}{K_h + K_m} \tag{17}$$

This is also known as the F_1 measure, because recall and precision are evenly weighted.

Summary is generated for an article from *The Hindu* [11] using information gain approach. Then summary is generated using some available automated text summarizers such as *Open Text summarizer (OTS), Pertinence Summarizer (PS),* and *Extractor Test Summarizer Software (ETSS)*. The compression ratio is 30% of the original text. Table 1 shows the comparison of generated text summary.

Table 1. Comparison of generated text summary

Methods	Precision value (P)	Recall Value(R)	F-score
IG summary	75	65	70.57
OTS	75	60	66.66
PS	75	60	66.66
ETSS	75	60	66.66

5   Conclusion and Future Scope

A novel approach for automatic text summarization by sentence extraction using information gain from single document is proposed in this paper. Its involves term selection, term weighting, sentence scoring using information gain and sentence selection steps. A set of features (e.g. term frequency weight, Normalized sentence length, sentence position and inverse sentence frequency score) is defined for each sentence segment. Then the extracted summary is compared with some of the available automated text summarizer (*Open Text summarizer (OTS), Pertinence Summarizer (PS),* and *Extractor Test Summarizer Software (ETSS)*). Figure 2 shows the comparison of recall, precision and F-score of generated summary. The text summary generated using Information gain is better than summary generated by other summarizer.

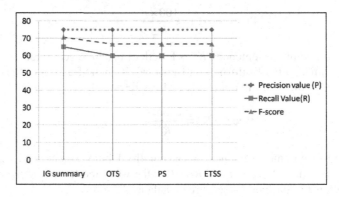

Fig. 2. Comparison of Recall, Precision Value and F-score

The proposed approach is single document text summarization based on extraction method. "Shallow parsing" is performed to determine the sentence silent segments. Extract meaning is implement to extort key segments out of the text. This summarization by extract will be good enough for a reader to understand the main idea of a document, though the understand ability might not be as good as a summary by abstract. Another limitation is that the result is based on a article from "the Hindu", so we can't generalize the result, so there is a need of analysis of the result over a larger text corpus database.

As a future work this approach can be exacted for multi-document summary document extraction using machine learning. Machine Learning Techniques such as Reinforcement Learning will help in finding the more accurate term-sentence matrix. we can introduce the concept of multi agent into the system. This will increase its speed as well make the summary or abstract more generic.

References

1. Verma, R., Chen, P.: Integrating Ontology Knowledge into a Query-based Information Summarization System. In: DUC 2007, Rochester, NY (2007)
2. Zhong, M.-S., Liu, L., Lu, R.-Z.: Shallow Parsing Based on Maximum Matching Method and Scoring Model
3. Lunh, H.P.: The automatic creation of literature abstracts. IBM Journal of Research and Development 2, 159–165 (1958)
4. Edmundson, H.P.: New Methods in Automatic Extracting. Journal of the ACM (JACM) 16(2), 264–285 (1969)
5. Salton, G., Buckley, C.: Term-Weighting Approaches in Automatic Text Retrieval Information Processing & Management 24, 513–523 (1988)
6. Luhn, H.P.: A Statical Approach to Mechanical Encoding and Searching of Literary Information. IBM Journal of Research and Development, 309–317 (1975)
7. Salton, G., Buckley, C.: Term-Weighting Approaches in Automatic Text Retrieval. Information Processing & Management 24, 513–523 (1988)
8. Kupiec, J., Pedersen, J., Chen, F.: A trainable document summarizer. In: Proceedings of SIGIR (1995)
9. Conroy, J.M., O'leary, D.P.: Text summarization via hidden markov model. In: Proceedings of SIGIR 2001, New York, NY, USA, pp. 406–407 (2001)
10. Agarwal, N., Ford, K.H., Shneider, M.: Sentence Boundary Detection using a MaxEnt Classifer
11. García-Hernández, R.A., Ledeneva, Y.: Word Sequence Models for Single Text Summarization. In: 2009 Second International Conferences on Advances in Computer-Human Interactions, pp. 44–48 (2009)
12. The Hindu, http://www.hinduonnet.com/ (accessed on June 23, 2009)
13. Van Rijsbergen, C.J.: Information Retrieval, 2nd edn. Dept. of Computer Science, University of Glasgow (1979)

An Alternate Approach to Compute the Reliability of a Computer Communication Network Using Binary Decision Diagrams

Manoj Singhal[1], R.K. Chauhan[2], and Girish Sharma[3]

[1] Asso. Prof., Deptt. of MCA, Academy of Business and Engineering Sciences,
19th K.M. stone, Delhi-Hapur by pass Road, NH-24, Vijay Nagar, Ghaziabad, (U.P.), India
manoj_singhal@rediffmail.com
[2] Prof. & Chairman, Deptt. of Computer Science and Applications,
Kurukshetra University, Kurukshetra (Haryana), India
rkc.dcsa@gmail.com
[3] Asstt. Prof., Deptt. of MCA, Bhai Parmanand Institute Of Business Studies, Delhi, India
gkps123@gmail.com

Abstract. In this paper we adopted an efficient approach for generating the binary decision diagram of a computer communication network represented in the form of a directed graph for calculating the reliability of the computer communication network. We have shown that this binary decision diagram is of the minimum size. We have also generated modified binary decision diagrams of the given graph when a particular edge of this graph is down and these modified binary decision diagrams are of minimum size. Conclusively, we can say that if all min-paths of a network are disjoint, then more than one optimal ordering may be possible for finding the reliability of a computer communication network.

Keywords: Binary Decision Diagrams (BDD), Directed Acyclic Graph (DAG), Computer Communication Network (CCN), Modified Binary Decision Diagrams (MBDD).

1 Introduction

Network reliability analysis receives considerable attention for the design, validation, and maintenance of many real world systems, such as computer, communication, or power networks. The components of a network are subject to random failures, as more and more enterprises become dependent upon CCN or networked computing applications. Failure of a single component may directly affect the functioning of a network. So the probability of each component of a CCN is a crucial consideration while considering the reliability of a network. Hence the reliability consideration is an important factor in CCN. The IEEE 90 standard defines the reliability as *"the ability of a system or component to perform its required functions under stated conditions for a specified period of time."* There are so many exact methods for computation of

S. Ranka et al. (Eds.): IC3 2010, Part I, CCIS 94, pp. 160–170, 2010.
© Springer-Verlag Berlin Heidelberg 2010

network reliability [6]. The network model is a directed stochastic graph G = (V, E), where V is the vertex set, and E is the set of directed edges. An incidence relation which associates with each edge of G a pair of nodes of G, called its end vertices. The edges represent components that can fail with known probability. In real problems, these probabilities are usually computed from statistical data.

The problem related with connection function is NP-hard [13]. The same thing is observed for planar graphs [12]. In the exact method there are two classes for the computation of the network reliability. The first class deals with the enumeration of all the minimum paths or cuts. A path is a subset of components (edges and/or verti-ces), that guarantees the source and the sink to be connected if all the components of this subset are functioning. A path is a minimal if a subset of elements in the path does not exist that is also a path. A cut is a subset of components (edges and/or verti-ces), whose failure disconnect the source and sink. A cut is a minimal if the subset of elements in the cut does not exist that is also a cut. The probabilistic evaluation uses the inclusion-exclusion, or sum of disjoint products methods because this enumeration provides non-disjoint events. Numerous works about this kind of methods have been presented in literature [14, 23, 24].

In the second class, the algorithms are based on graph topology. In the first process we reduce the size of the graph by removing some structures. These structures as polygon-to-chain [15] and delta-to-star reductions [11]. By this we will be able to compute the reliability in linear time and the reduction will result in a single edge. The idea is to decompose the problem in to one failed and another functioning. The same was confirmed by Theologou & Carlier [20] for dense networks. Satyanarayana & Chang [4] and Wood [22] have shown that the factoring algorithms with reductions are more efficient at solving this problem than the classical path or cut enumeration methods.

2 Binary Decision Diagrams

Akers [5] first introduced BDD to represent Boolean functions i.e. a BDD is a data structure used to represent a Boolean Function. Bryant [21] popularized the use of BDD by introducing a set of algorithms for efficient construction and manipulation of BDD structure. The BDD structure provides compact representations of Boolean expressions. A BDD is a directed acyclic graph (DAG) based on the Shannon decomposition. The Shannon decomposition for a Boolean function is defined as follows:

$$F = x. F_{x=1} + \overline{x}. F_{x=0}$$

where x is one of the decision variables, and F is the Boolean function evaluated at x = i. By using Shannon's decomposition, any Boolean expression can be transformed in to binary tree. BDD are used to work out the terminal reliability of the links. Madre and coudert [19] found BDD usefulness in reliability analysis which was fur-ther extended by Rauzy [2, 3]. They are specially used to assess fault trees in system

162   M. Singhal, R.K. Chauhan, and G. Sharma

analysis. In the network reliability framework, Sekine & Imai [9], and Trivedi [28] have shown how to functionally construct the corresponding BDD.

Figure 1 shows the truth table of a Boolean function F and its corresponding Shannon tree.

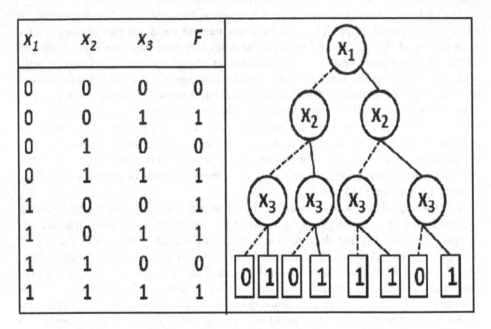

X_1	X_2	X_3	F
0	0	0	0
0	0	1	1
0	1	0	0
0	1	1	1
1	0	0	1
1	0	1	1
1	1	0	0
1	1	1	1

Fig. 1. Truth table of a Boolean Function F and its corresponding Shannon tree

Sink nodes are labelled either with 0, or with 1, representing the two corresponding constant expressions. Each internal node u is labelled with a Boolean variable var(u), and has two out-edges called 0-edge, and 1-edge. The node linked by the 1-edge represents the Boolean expression when $x_i = 1$, i.e. $F_{xi=1}$; while the node linked by the 0-edge represents the Boolean expression when $x_i = 0$, i.e. Fxi=0. The two outgoing edges are given by two functions low(u) and high(u).

Indeed, such representation is space consuming. It is possible to shrink by using following three postulates.

(i) **Remove Duplicate Terminals:** Delete all but one terminal vertex with a given label, and redirect all arcs into the deleted vertices to the remaining one.
(ii) **Delete Redundant Non Terminals:** If non terminal vertices u, and v have var(u) = var(v), low(u) = low(v), and high(u) = high(v), then delete one of the two vertices, and redirect all incoming arcs to the other vertex.
(iii) **Delete Duplicate tests:** If non terminal vertex v has low(v) = high(v), then delete v, and redirect all incoming arcs to low(v).

If we apply all these three rules then the above decision tree can be reduced in to the diagrams given below in figure 2.

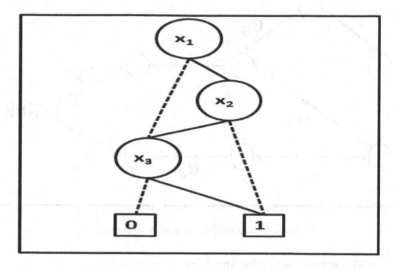

Fig. 2. Reduced BDD of the above decision Tree

3 Network Reliability

The reliability of a network G is the probability that G supports a given operation. We distinguish three kinds of operation and hence three kind of reliability [1, 10].

(i)   **Two Terminal Reliability:** It is the probability that two given vertices, called the source and the sink, can communicate. It is also called the terminal-pair reliability [27].

(ii) **K Terminal reliability:** When the operation requires only a few vertices, a subset k of N(G), to communicate each other, this is K terminal reliability [7].

(iii) **All Terminal Reliability:** When the operation requires that each pair of vertices is able to communicate via at least one operational path, this is all terminal reliability. We can see that 2-terminal terminal reliability and all terminal reliability are the particular cases of K-terminal reliability [8].

Let us take an example of a directed network which is represented in the form of a directed graph G (V, E) with single source and single sink shown below in figure 3.

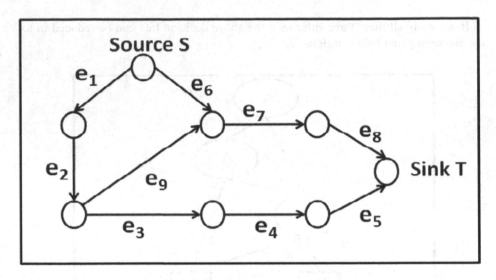

Fig. 3. A Directed Network of Nine Edges

The network has three min-paths. These are

$$H_1= \{e_1, e_2, e_3, e_4, e_5\} \quad H_2= \{e_6, e_7, e_8\}, \quad H_3= \{e_1, e_2, e_9, e_7, e_8\}.$$

Let H_1, H_2,-----H_n be the n min-paths from source to sink in a network then the network connectivity function C can be represented as a logical OR of its min-paths.

$$C = H_1 U H_2 ---- U H_i ----- U H_n$$

So the point to point reliability is:

$$R_s = Pr\{C\} = Pr \{ H_1 U H_2 ---- U H_i ----- U H_n\} \tag{1}$$

So the network connectivity of our network can be expressed as

$$C_{1-4} = e_1 e_2 e_3 e_4 e_5 U e_6 e_7 e_8 U e_1 e_2 e_9 e_7 e_8 \tag{2}$$

The probability of the union of non-disjoint events, as in Formula(1), can be computed by several techniques (Exact Methods) [6]. Here we apply the inclusion-exclusion method.

Inclusion-exclusion Method: One method of transforming a Boolean expression $\Phi(G)$ into a probability expression is to use Poincare's theorem, also called inclusion-exclusion method [6]. The inclusion-exclusion formula for two minimal paths H_1 and H_2 is express as follows:

$$E(H_1 + H_2) = E(H_1) + E(H_2) - E(H_1 . H_2)$$

Let P_i denote the probability of edge e_i of being working, by applying the Classical inclusion-exclusion formula for calculating the probability of given network (figure 3), we get

$Pr = p_1p_2p_3p_4p_5 + p_6p_7p_8 + p_1p_2p_9p_7p_8 - p_1p_2p_3p_4p_5\ p_6p_7p_8 - p_1p_2p_3p_4p_5\ p_7p_8p_9 -$
$p_1p_2p_6p_7p_8p_9 + p_1p_2p_3p_4p_5\ p_6p_7p_8p_9$

4 Generation of BDD

A particular sequence of variable ordering is known as variable ordering. It has been observed that the size of the BDD strongly depends on the ordering of variables. An ordering is said to be optimal if it generates the minimum size BDD [18, 25, 26]. Here we find an optimal ordering to generate the BDD of the given network by applying a heuristic approach. The optimal ordering of the given graph is

$$e_1 < e_2 < e_3 < e_4 < e_5 < e_9 < e_6 < e_7 < e_8$$

The BDD of the given network and probability computation is shown below in figure 4.

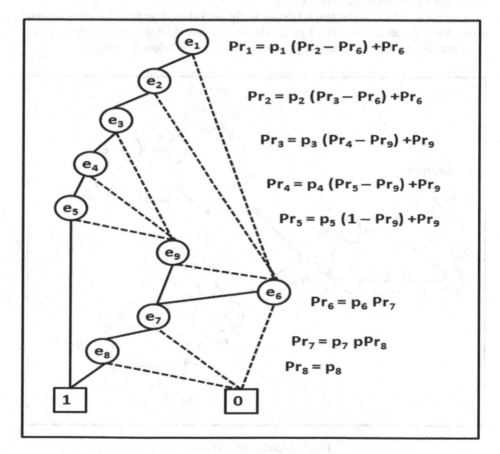

$$Pr_1 = p_1\ (Pr_2 - Pr_6) + Pr_6$$

$$Pr_2 = p_2\ (Pr_3 - Pr_6) + Pr_6$$

$$Pr_3 = p_3\ (Pr_4 - Pr_9) + Pr_9$$

$$Pr_4 = p_4\ (Pr_5 - Pr_9) + Pr_9$$

$$Pr_5 = p_5\ (1 - Pr_9) + Pr_9$$

$$Pr_6 = p_6\ Pr_7$$

$$Pr_7 = p_7\ pPr_8$$

$$Pr_8 = p_8$$

Fig. 4. Binary Decision Diagram of the given Network in figure 3

The computation of the probability of the BDD can be calculated recursively by resorting to the Shannon decomposition.

$$Pr\{F\} = p_1 Pr\{Fx_1 = 1\} + (1 - p1)Pr\{Fx_1 = 0\}$$
$$= Pr\{Fx_1 = 0\} + p_1(Pr\{Fx_1 = 1\} - Pr\{Fx_1 = 0\})$$

where p_1 is the probability of the Boolean variable x_1 to be true and $(1 - p_1)$ is the probability of the Boolean variable x_1 to be false.

Here we found that the reliability obtained by BDD is equal to the reliability obtained by inclusion-exclusion formula. There are several variables ordering are possible for constructing the different BDDs of the given CCN (figure 3) but the size is minimum only in one case. We have constructed only optimal BDD of the given CCN and compute the reliability of the given CCN by using the BDD.

The size of the BDD is the number of non-terminal nodes and number of nodes in a particular level. If a graph has n directed edges then its minimum size BDD must contain at least n non-terminal vertices [17].

If we factorize the given graph (shown in figure 3) based on the edge e_9 is up and down, then we get the factorized graph shown in figure 5. If we remove the edge e_9 from our directed network then we get the network shown below in figure 6.

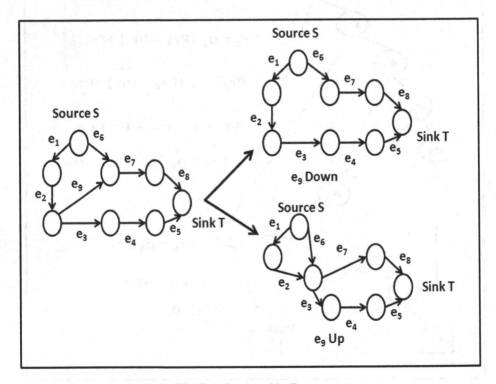

Fig. 5. A Graph and its Factors

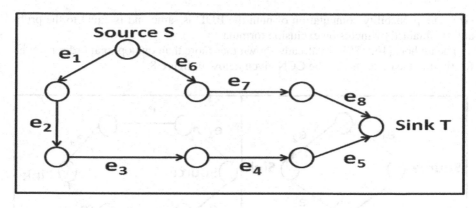

Fig. 6. When edge e_9 is Down

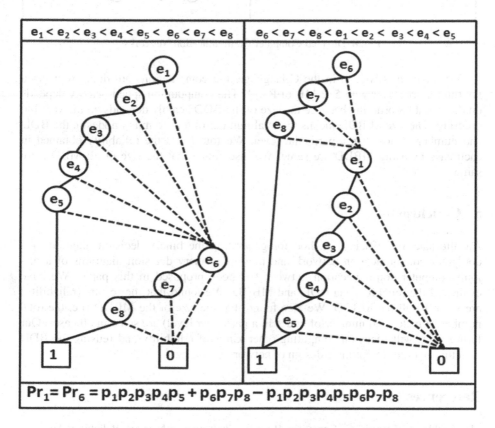

Fig. 7. BDD of figure 6

Here we have found two different optimal variable ordering. These are $e_1 < e_2 < e_3 < e_4 < e_5 < e_6 < e_7 < e_8$ and $e_6 < e_7 < e_8 < e_1 < e_2 < e_3 < e_4 < e_5$. The BDDs are shown below in figure 7. The BDDs shown in figure 7 are called modified binary decision diagrams (MBDD) [16, 17, 18] because they are of same size and both have minimum size. The probability computation of both the BDD is same and is equal to the probability obtained by inclusion exclusion formula.

The authors [16, 17] have already shown that more than one optimal ordering exist for finding the reliability of the CCN given below in figure 8.

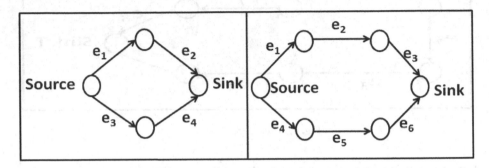

Fig. 8. Directed Computer Communication Networks

Our program is written in the C language and computations are done by using a Pentium 4 processor with 512 MB of RAM. The computation speed heavily depends on the variables ordering because the size of the BDD heavily depends on the variable ordering. The size of BDD means the total number of non-terminal nodes in the BDD and number of nodes in a particular level. We found that the reliability obtained in each case by using MBDD are same. We also found that the size of all MBDD are same.

5 Conclusions

An alternate and efficient method for generating the binary decision diagram of a computer communication network and modified binary decision diagrams of a disjoint computer communication network has been proposed in this paper. We have evaluated the reliability via BDD and MBDD. We found that the results (reliability) are same by all the MBDD. We also found that the size of the MBDD (i.e. the total number of nodes and number of nodes in a particular level) are same in all cases. Our future work will focus on computing other kinds of reliability and reusing the BDD structure in order to optimize design of network topology.

References

1. Bobbio, A., Ferraris, C., Terruggia, R.: New Challenges in Network Reliability Analysis. Technical Report, TR-INF-UNIPMN, pp. 1–8 (2006)
2. Rauzy, A.: New algorithms for fault tolerant trees analysis. Reliability Engineering and System Safety 5(59), 203–211 (1993)
3. Rauzy, A.: A new methodology to handle Boolean models with loops. IEEE Trans. Reliability R-52(1), 96–105 (2003)

4. Satyanarayana, A., Chang, M.K.: Network reliability and the factoring theorem. Networks 13, 107–120 (1983)
5. Akers, B.: Binary decision diagrams. IEEE Trans. Computers C-27, 509–516 (1978)
6. Lucet, C., Manouvrier, J.-F.: Exact methods to compute network reliability. In: Ionescu, D.C., Limnios, N. (eds.) Statistical and Probabilistic Models in Reliability, pp. 279–294. Birkhauser, Boston (1999)
7. Yeh, F., Lu, S., Kuo, S.: OBDD-based evaluation of k-terminal network reliability. IEEE Trans. Reliability R-51(4), 443–451 (2002)
8. Hardy, G., Lucet, C., Limnios, N.: Computing all-terminal reliability of stochastic networks with binary decision diagrams. In: Proc.11th International Symposium on Applied Stochastic Models and Data Analysi., pp. 1468–1473 (2005)
9. Imai, H., Sekine, K., Imai, K.: Computational investigations of all terminal network reliability via BDDs. IEICE Transactions on Fundamentals E82-A(5), 714–721 (1999)
10. Carlier, J., Lucet, C.: A decomposition algorithm for network reliability evaluation. Discrete Applied Mathematics 65, 141–156 (1996)
11. Gadani, J.P.: System effectiveness evaluation using star and delta transformations. IEEE Trans. Reliability R-30(1), 43–47 (1981)
12. Provan, J.S.: The complexity of reliability computations on planar and acyclic graphs. SIAM J. Computing 15(3), 694–702 (1986)
13. Ball, M.O.: Computational complexity of network reliability analysis An overview. IEEE Trans. Reliability R-35(3), 230–239 (1986)
14. Locks, M.O.: A minimizing algorithm for sum of disjoint products. IEEE Trans. Reliability R-36(4), 436–445 (1987)
15. Choi, M.S., Jun, C.H.: Some variant of polygon-to-chain reductions in evaluating reliability of undirected network. Microelectron Reliability 35(1), 1–11 (1985)
16. Singhal, M., Chauhan, R.K., Sharma, G.: Use of Modified Binary Decision Diagrams in Reliability Evaluation of a Directed Computer Communication Network. The Icfai University Journal of Computer Sciences III(3), 22–30 (2009)
17. Singhal, M., Chauhan, R.K., Sharma, G.: A New Optimal Approach for evaluating the size of BDD (Binary Decision Diagram) for calculating the Reliability of a CCN (Computer Communication Network). International Journal of Advanced Networking and Applications 1(4), 230–235 (2010)
18. Singhal, M., Chauhan, R.K., Sharma, G.: Effects of Variable Ordering on Binary Decision Diagrams for Computation of Reliability of a Computer Communication Network. Journal of Computer Science (accepted 2010)
19. Coudert, O., Madre, J.C.: Implicit and incremental computation of primes and essential primes of Boolean functions. In: Proc. of the 29th ACM/IEEE Design Automation Conference, pp. 36–39 (1992)
20. Theologou, O., Carlier, J.: Factoring and reductions for networks with imperfect vertices. IEEE Trans. Reliability R-40, 210–217 (1991)
21. Bryant, R.E.: Symbolic Boolean manipulation with ordered binary-decision diagrams. ACM Computing Surveys 24(3), 293–318 (1992)
22. Wood, R.K.: A factoring algorithm using polygon-to-chain reductions for computing K-terminal network reliability. Networks 15, 173–190 (1985)
23. Hariri, S., Raghavendra, C.S.: SYREL- A symbolic reliability algorithm based on path and cut set methods. IEEE Trans. Computers C-36(10), 1224–1232 (1987)
24. Ahmad, S.H.: Simple enumeration of minimal cut sets of acyclic directed graph. IEEE Trans. Reliability R-27(5), 484–487 (1988)

25. Friedman, S.J., Supowit, K.J.: Finding the optimal variable ordering for binary decision diagrams. In: Proc. 24th ACM/IEEE Conference on Design Automation, pp. 348–356 (1987)
26. Friedman, S.J., Supowit, K.J.: Finding an optimal variable ordering for binary decision diagrams. IEEE Trans. Computers C-39(5), 710–713 (1990)
27. Kuo, S., Yeh, S., Lu, Y.F.: Determining terminal pair reliability based on edge expansion diagrams using OBDD. IEEE Trans. Reliability 48(3), 234–246 (1999)
28. Zang, X., Sun, H., Trivedi, K.S.: A BDD-based algorithm for reliability Graph Analysis. Technical Report,
    http://www.ee.duke.edu/~hairong/workinduke/relgrap

A Multi-Level Blocks Scrambling Based Chaotic Image Cipher

Musheer Ahmad and Omar Farooq

Department of Computer Engineering,
ZH College of Engineering and Technology
A. M. U., Aligarh-202 002, India
Department of Electronics Engineering,
ZH College of Engineering and Technology
A. M. U., Aligarh-202 002, India

Abstract. In this paper, an image encryption scheme based on multi-level blocks scrambling is proposed. The image is first decomposed into non-overlapping blocks and scrambling of these blocks is done by using 2D Cat transform. Multi-level blocks scrambling (*MLBS*) is implemented by starting with a large block size and the size of blocks gets reduced iteratively at each level. The scrambling of blocks is performed at multiple levels to get cummulative effect. At each level, the control parameters of scrambling are randomly generated through 2D coupled Logistic map to make the process of scrambling key dependent. The scrambled image obtained after carrying out *MLBS* scrambling is encrypted using chaotic sequence generated by one-dimensional Logistic map. The experimental results show that the proposed encryption scheme can successfully encrypts/decrypts the images with same secret keys. The algorithm has large key space and high sensitivity to a small change in secret keys. The simulation analysis also demonstrates that the ciphered images have high information entropy, very low correlation coefficients and uniform gray level distribution.

Keywords: Information security, image encryption, image scrambling, logistic map, information entropy.

1   Introduction

In recent years, the chaos based cryptographic algorithms have suggested some new and efficient ways to develop secure image encryption techniques in order to meet the demand for real-time image transmission over the communication channels. Chaotic systems are considered good for practical image encryption and transmission because they have important characteristics such as sensitivity to initial conditions and system parameters, pseudo-random property and non-periodicity as the chaotic signals usually noise-like, etc. The characteristics of chaotic signals make image cryptosystems excellent and robust against any statistical attacks. Therefore, chaos based image encryption is given much attention in the research of information security. A lot of image encryption algorithms

S. Ranka et al. (Eds.): IC3 2010, Part I, CCIS 94, pp. 171–182, 2010.

based on chaotic systems have been proposed [1,2,3,4,5,6,7,8,9,10,11,12,13]. These image encryptions algorithms are based on chaotic maps like the Logistic map [5,6,7], the Standard map [8], the Baker map [9,10], the Piecewise nonlinear chaotic map [11] the Cat map [12,13], the Chen map [6,13] etc.

The most widely used methodology to encrypt an image is to use the concept of scrambling the positions of pixels in the plain-image and changing the gray values of pixels in the scrambled image. The purpose of image scrambling is to transform a meaningful image into a meaningless or distorted image to enhance the security [14]. This can be done by permuting the coordinates of image pixels to achieve the visual effect of disorder [15]. A good scrambled image prevents human visual or computer vision system from understanding the real meaning of the original image. In the past decade, many scrambling schemes have been proposed; these schemes are based on Cat transform [12,13,16,17,18,19], Lorenz system [20,21], Logistic map [6,7], Chebyshev map in DCT domain [22] etc. In these scrambling schemes, all the pixels of an image are permuted to achieve image scrambling. The application of single iteration of these methods needs to perform a lot of computations.

In this paper, an image encryption scheme is proposed which is based on novel concept of multi-level blocks scrambling (*MLBS*). *MLBS* scrambling is performed by scrambling the blocks of image at multiple levels rather than scrambling all pixels. *MLBS* scrambling scheme reduces the number of computations required to achieve good scrambling effect as compared to the conventional pixels scrambling. Two chaotic maps are used to perform *MLBS* scrambling: one map is employed to carry out scrambling of blocks while the control parameters of scrambling are randomly generated by other map. To enforce the security of the proposed scheme, the encryption of scrambled image obtained after *MLBS* phase is performed using a third chaotic map.

The paper is organized as follows: Section 2 describes the different chaotic maps used. Section 3 discusses the proposed *MLBS* scrambling based image encryption algorithm in detail. The experimental results are discussed in Section 4 followed by conclusions in Section 5.

2   Chaotic Maps

According to the chaos theory, chaotic maps are the nonlinear dynamical systems whose state evolves with time and are highly sensitive to initial conditions. The future dynamics of these systems are fully defined by their initial conditions. As a result, the behavior of these systems appears random. In the proposed *MLBS* based image encryption algorithm, the following three distinct chaotic maps are used:

2.1   Two-Dimensional Coupled Logistic Map

The two-dimensional coupled Logistic map [23] is described as follows:

$$\left. \begin{array}{l} x_{n+1} = \mu_1 x_n (1 - x_n) + \gamma_1 y_n^2 \\ y_{n+1} = \mu_2 y_n (1 - y_n) + \gamma_2 (x_n^2 + x_n y_n) \end{array} \right\} \qquad (1)$$

Three quadratic coupling terms introduce strength to the complexity of 2D Logistic map. This map is chaotic when $2.75 < \mu_1 \leq 3.4$, $2.7 < \mu_2 \leq 3.45$, $0.15 < \gamma_1 \leq 0.21$, $0.13 < \gamma_2 \leq 0.15$ and generate chaotic sequences $x, y \in (0, 1)$. To examine the statistical performance, the map is iterated for 16000 times with initial conditions/parameters as: $x_0 = 0.0215$, $y_0 = 0.5734$, $\mu_1 = 2.93$, $\mu_2 = 3.17$, $\gamma_1 = 0.197$ and $\gamma_2 = 0.139$. The statistical analysis of x and y sequences shows that they have poor balance, autocorrelation and cross-correlation properties. The mean values of the sequences x and y are 0.6456 and 0.6590 respectively. To improve these statistical properties of the sequences generated by 2D map, the following pretreatment is done.

$$x_i = 10^6 x_i - floor(10^6 x_i) \atop y_i = 10^6 y_i - floor(10^6 y_i) \Big\} \tag{2}$$

The mean values after preprocessing of the sequences x and y are 0.5004 and 0.4984 respectively, which are closer to the ideal value 0.5. Now, the preprocessed sequences have better balance distribution, auto as well as cross correlation properties and they can be utilized in a cryptographic process.

2.2 2D Cat Transform

A 2D Cat map is first presented by V. I. Arnold in the research of ergodic theory. Let the coordinates of positions of pixels in an image are P = {(x, y) | x, y = 1, 2, 3, . . ., N}. A 2D Cat map with two control parameters [12] is as follows:

$$x\prime = (x + ay)mod(N) \atop y\prime = (bx + (ab + 1)y)mod(N) \Big\} \tag{3}$$

Where, a, b are control parameters which are positive integers. The Cat map translates the pixel position (x, y) of plain-image of size N × N to a new position $(x\prime, y\prime)$ when applied once to plain-image. Cat transform permutes the organization of pixels of plain-image by replacing the position of the image pixel points with new coordinate. After several iterations, the correlation among the adjacent pixels is disturbed completely and the image appears distorted and meaningless. Due to the periodicity of the Cat transform it is possible to recover the original image after iterating Cat transform many times [13]. To deal with this problem of Cat transform, a block based image scrambling is performed at multiple levels in which the control parameters a, b of transform are randomly generated by 2D coupled Logistic map at each level of *MLBS* scrambling.

2.3 One-Dimensional Logistic Map

The one-dimensional Logistic map proposed by May [24] is one of the simplest nonlinear chaotic discrete systems that exhibit chaotic behavior and is defined by the following equation:

$$z_{n+1} = \lambda z_n(1 - z_n), n \geq 0 \tag{4}$$

where z_o is initial condition, λ is the system parameter and n is the number of iterations. The research shows that the map is chaotic for $3.57 < \lambda < 4$ and $z_{n+1} \in (0, 1)$ for all n. The sequence generated from Eq. 4 does not require any pretreatment as the sequence has random-like behavior. The sequence generated by Logistic map is used to improve the statistical properties of the scrambled image obtained after $MLBS$ scrambling phase.

3 Proposed Image Encryption Algorithm

Statistical analysis of images shows that the image data have strong correlations among adjacent pixels. For image security and secrecy, one has to disturb this correlation. In the proposed algorithm, the average correlation among the adjacent pixels of plain-image is reduced by first scrambling larger image blocks and then iteratively reduces the block size at each level to achieve the desired scrambling result. At level-k, the blocks of size $2^{L-k+1} \times 2^{L-k+1}$ of image obtained after applying previous level scrambling are scrambled to get cumulative effect, where $L = log_2(N)$ - 1 for a plain-image of size N $\times$ N and k varies from 1 to L. The multi-level blocks scrambling ($MLBS$) scheme makes use of 2D Cat transform in which the control parameters are randomly generated through two key dependent sequences obtained from 2D coupled Logistic map. The control parameters of Cat transform are the control parameters of scrambling in $MLBS$ phase. The sequences obtained from 2D Logistic map are first preprocessed through Eq. 5 and then the control parameters a, b are evaluated. The process of random generation of control parameters is as follows:

First the map given in Eq. 1 is iterated $t = 500$ times with initial conditions: $x_0 = 0.0215$, $y_0 = 0.5734$, $\mu_1 = 2.93$, $\mu_2 = 3.17$, $\gamma_1 = 0.197$ and $\gamma_2 = 0.139$, these 500 values of x and y are discarded. The map is again iterated to produce next x_i and y_i values, where $i = 1, 2, \ldots, L$. The control parameters a_i and b_i of $MLBS$ scrambling from x_i and y_i are calculated as:

$$\left.\begin{aligned} \Psi(x_i) &= 10^{14}(10^6 x_i - floor(10^6 x_i)) \\ \Psi(y_i) &= 10^{14}(10^6 y_i - floor(10^6 y_i)) \\[6pt] \phi(x_i) &= (\Psi(x_i)mod(83)) + 17 \\ \phi(y_i) &= (\Psi(y_i)mod(107)) + 19 \\[6pt] a_i &= (\Psi(x_i)mod(\phi(y_i))) + 1 \\ b_i &= (\Psi(y_i)mod(\phi(x_i))) + 1 \end{aligned}\right\} \tag{5}$$

The control parameters a_i, b_i of scrambling are made sensitive to secret keys of 2D Logistic map. As a result, the $MLBS$ scheme becomes sensitive to a small change in secret keys. Thus, the attacker cannot make use of Cat transform's periodicity to obtain the plain-image without secret keys. Moreover, the statistical properties like gray value distribution, mean value of gray values, information entropy etc of an image do not change after scrambling. The attacker can make use of these properties of scrambled image to recover the plain-image. To further improve the security provided by the algorithm, these statistical properties of scrambled image needs to be improved. The statistical properties are improved by encrypting the scrambled image using chaotic key sequence generated from 1D Logistic map. The complete procedure of proposed image encryption scheme is as follows:

$P(x, y)$: Plain-image of size N × N, where $x, y = 1, 2, 3, \ldots,$ N.
x_0, y_0, z_0 : Secret keys of algorithm.
$\mu_1, \mu_2, \gamma_1, \gamma_2, \lambda$: Initial parameters of chaotic maps.
$C(x, y)$: Ciphered image of size N x N obtained as output of algorithm.

Step 1. [Initialization]: Set $I(x, y) = P(x, y)$, $k = 1$, $L = log_2(N)$ - 1, $m = L$.
Step 2. Repeat Steps 3 to 6 while $k \leq L$.
Step 3. [Decomposition]: Decompose the whole image $I(x, y)$ into $2^m \times 2^m$ size blocks.
Step 4. [Control Parameter]: Generate control parameters a_k and b_k for level-k scrambling using 2D coupled logistic map and Eq. 5.
Step 5. [Level-k Scrambling]: Apply Cat transform to scramble the blocks of size $2^m \times 2^m$ within the image $I(x, y)$ using control parameters a_k and b_k. We get $S_k(x, y)$ scrambled image as output of level-k scrambling process.
Step 6. Set $I(x, y) = S_k(x, y)$, $k = k + 1$ and $m = m$ - 1.
Step 7. [Encryption Variable]: Iterate 1D logistic map to get discrete variable z_i and evaluate key $K(i)$ as:

$$K(i) = (10^{14} z_i) mod(256)$$

Step 8. [Binary Conversion]: Convert the decimal gray values (0 to 255) of scrambled image $S_L(x, y)$ and key $K(i)$ to equivalent 8-bit binary numbers as:

$SB(x, y) = DecimalToBinary(S_L(x, y))$.
$KB(i) = DecimalToBinary(K(i))$.

The function $DecimalToBinary(x)$ converts the decimal number x to 8-bit binary number and $(x)mod(y)$ returns the remainder whenever x is divided by y.
Step 9. [Encryption]: Encrypt the scrambled image $S_L(x, y)$ using the key $K(i)$ as:

$$CB(x, y) = SB(x, y) \oplus KB(i) .$$

Where $i = N \times (x - 1) + y$; and $x, y = 1, 2, 3, \ldots,$ N. The $CB(x, y)$ is the 8-bit binary equivalent of gray value of the ciphered image $C(x, y)$ with pixel coordinate (x, y). The symbol $\oplus$ represents the exclusive-OR operation bit by bit.
Step 10. [Repeat]: Steps 7 to 9 are repeated for N x N times to encrypt all the pixels of the scrambled image.

Step 11. [Decimal Conversion]: Convert all the binary numbers $CB(x, y)$ to decimal numbers to get resultant Ciphered image $C(x, y)$ as:

$$C(x, y) = BinaryToDecimal(CB(x, y))$$

The function $BinaryToDecimal(x)$ converts an 8-bit binary number x to its equivalent decimal number.

The plain-image can be recovered successfully by applying the proposed algorithm in reverse order. The block diagram of the proposed image encryption algorithm is shown in Fig. 1.

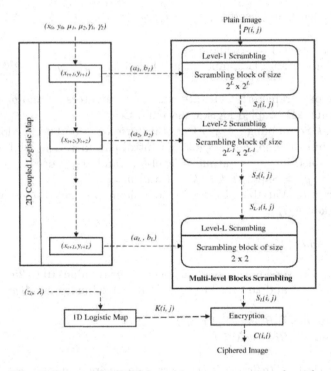

Fig. 1. Proposed *MLBS* based image encryption algorithm

4   Experimental Results

The proposed encryption scheme is applied to various plain-images like *Lena*, *Baboon*, *Peppers*, *Cameraman*, *Barbara*, *Boat* and *Airplane* of 256×256 size. Among them, the plain-images of *Lena*, *Baboon*, *Cameraman*, *Boat* and their respective histograms are shown in Fig. 2. As can be seen in this figure that the gray value distributions of plain-images are not uniform. The initial conditions and system parameters taken for experimentation are: $x_0 = 0.0215$, $y_0 = 0.5734$, $z_0 = 0.3915$, $\mu_1 = 2.93$, $\mu_2 = 3.17$, $\gamma_1 = 0.197$, $\gamma_2 = 0.139$ and $\lambda = 3.9985$. The results of multi-level blocks scrambling (*MLBS*) scheme are shown in Fig. 3.

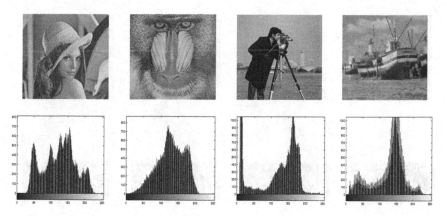

Fig. 2. Plain-images of *Lena, Baboon, Cameraman, Boat* and their histograms

The ciphered images of *Lena, Baboon, Cameraman* and *Boat* using proposed encryption algorithm and their histograms are shown in Fig. 4 respectively. It is clear from the Fig. 4 that the ciphered images are very much indistinguishable and appears like a noise. Moreover, as seen in Fig. 4 that the distribution of gray values of the ciphered images is fairly uniform and much different from the histograms of the plain-images shown in Fig. 2. The statistical property of the plain-images is changed absolutely in ciphered images in such a manner that ciphered images have good balance property. To quantify the balance property of the ciphered images, the mean value of gray values of plain-images and ciphered images are evaluated and listed in Table 1. It is evident from the mean values obtained that no matter how gray values of plain-images distributed, the mean value of ciphered images comes out to about 127. This shows that the ciphered image doesn't provide any information regarding the distribution of gray values to the attacker. Hence, the proposed algorithm can resist any type of histogram based attacks and strengthen the security of ciphered images significantly.

4.1 Key Space of Cipher

Key space is the total number of different keys that can be used in the cryptographic system. A cryptographic system should be sensitive to all secret keys. There are total eight initial conditions of chaotic map used in the algorithm. The initial conditions for x_0, y_0, and z_0 used as secret keys of encryption and

Fig. 3. Scrambled images of *Lena, Baboon, Cameraman* and *Boat* using *MLBS* scheme

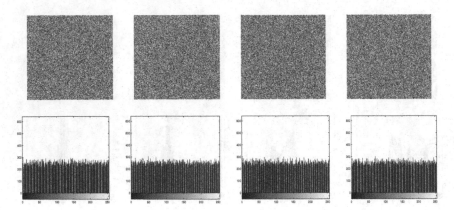

Fig. 4. Ciphered images of *Lena*, *Baboon*, *Cameraman*, *Boat* using proposed scheme and their histograms

decryption. In the proposed cryptosystem, all the variables are declared as type *double* which has a 15-digit precision, the decimal fractions of the variables are multiplied by 10^{14}, therefore the key space of proposed image cipher is $(10^{14})^3$ i.e. $10^{42} \approx 2^{140}$. The initial conditions to parameters μ_1, μ_2, γ_1, γ_2 and λ also increase the size of key space. Thus, the key space of the cipher is extensively large enough to resist the exhaustive attack.

4.2   Sensitivity to Keys

A good cryptosystem should be sensitive to a small change in secret keys i.e. a small change in secret keys during decryption process results into a completely different decrypted image. Proposed encryption algorithm is sensitive to a tiny change in the secret keys. Any change in the initial conditions: even of the order of (10^{-14}), a decrypted image is totally different from plain-image. As an example, consider the ciphered image *Lena* shown in Fig. 4, if one of the initial conditions, say x_0, y_0 and z_0 is changed a little (10^{-14}) then the respective decrypted images obtained are shown in Fig. 5. The images shown in Fig. 5 are totally different from the plain-image shown in Fig. 2. Further, the decrypted images appear like

Table 1. Mean values of Original and Ciphered Images

Test Images	Original	Ciphered
Lena	124.09	127.48
Baboon	129.41	127.14
Peppers	123.10	127.56
Cameraman	128.72	127.01
Barbara	127.39	127.42
Boat	129.71	127.28
Airplane	129.17	127.59

Fig. 5. Key sensitivity: decrypted image with $x_0 = 0.02150000000001$; decrypted image with $y_0 = 0.57340000000001$ and decrypted image with $z_o = 0.39150000000001$

a noise. Similar sensitivity is noticed for the case of wrong μ_1, μ_2, γ_1, γ_2 and λ. Hence, the proposed encryption scheme can be said to be highly sensitive to a small change in secret keys.

4.3   Computational Analysis

Image scrambling is carried out by re-locating the pixels of the image from one position to another. In most of the existing image scrambling algorithms [6,7,12,13,16,17,18,19,20,21,22], many iterations of these algorithms are applied to get good scrambling effect. In order to evaluate computation required to scramble an image using Cat transform, we calculate the number of times the Cat transform given in Eq. 3 is executed. If only single iteration of Cat transform is applied to scramble all the pixels of an image of size 256×256, it needs to perform 65536 computations of Cat transform. However, only $2 \times 2 + 4 \times 4 + 8 \times 8 + 16 \times 16 + 32 \times 32 + 64 \times 64 + 128 \times 128 = 21844$ computations of Cat transform are required to scramble the image of same size using proposed *MLBS* scheme. This results in a saving of about 66.6% computations required to scramble an image using the proposed scrambling scheme as compared to the pixel level scrambling used in [12,13,16,17,18,19].

4.4   Correlation Coefficient Analysis

In order to evaluate the encryption quality of the proposed encryption algorithm, the correlation coefficient is used. The correlation coefficients between two vertically, horizontally and diagonally adjacent pixels of a ciphered image is calculated as [9].

$$\rho = \frac{N \sum_{i=1}^{N}(x_i \times y_i) - \sum_{i=1}^{N} x_i \times \sum_{i=1}^{N} y_i}{\sqrt{(N \sum_{i=1}^{N} x_i^2 - (\sum_{i=1}^{N} x_i)^2) \times (N \sum_{i=1}^{N} y_i^2 - (\sum_{i=1}^{N} y_i)^2)}} \qquad (6)$$

Where x and y are gray values of two adjacent pixels in an image. Correlation coefficients of 1000 pairs of vertically, horizontally and diagonally adjacent randomly selected pixels are evaluated. The average of 50 such correlation coefficients of adjacent pixels in plain and ciphered images in three directions are listed in Table 2 and Table 3 respectively. The values of correlation coefficients show that the two adjacent pixels in the plain-images are highly correlated to

Table 2. Correlation Coefficient of two adjacent pixels in Original images

Test Images	Vertical	Horizontal	Diagonal
Lena	0.95967	0.92479	0.90236
Baboon	0.79835	0.84413	0.75661
Peppers	0.95807	0.95513	0.91878
Cameraman	0.95899	0.93702	0.91097
Barbara	0.95012	0.92208	0.91518
Boat	0.94182	0.91856	0.87697
Airplane	0.92944	0.93696	0.88629

Table 3. Correlation Coefficient of two adjacent pixels in Ciphered images

Test Images	Vertical	Horizontal	Diagonal
Lena	0.00095	0.00205	0.00188
Baboon	0.00088	0.00170	0.00129
Peppers	0.00118	0.00191	0.00031
Cameraman	0.00133	0.00046	0.00182
Barbara	0.00077	0.00085	0.00173
Boat	0.00026	0.00032	0.00115
Airplane	0.00372	0.00081	0.00324

each other and correlation coefficients are close to 1, whereas the values obtained for the ciphered images are close to 0. This means that the proposed algorithm highly de-correlate the adjacent pixels in the ciphered images.

4.5   Information Entropy Analysis

The entropy H of a symbol source S can be calculated by following equation [25].

$$H(S) = - \sum_{i=0}^{255} p(s_i) log_2(p(s_i)) \tag{7}$$

Where $p(s_i)$ represents the probability of symbol s_i and the entropy is expressed in bits. If the source S emits 2^8 symbols with equal probability, i.e. $S = \{ s_0, s_1, \ldots, s_{255}\}$, then the result of entropy is $H(S) = 8$, which corresponds to a true random source and represents the ideal value of entropy for message source S. Information entropy of a ciphered image can show the distribution of gray value. The more the distribution of gray value is uniform, the greater the information entropy. If the information entropy of a ciphered image is significantly less than the ideal value 8, then, there would be a possibility of predictability which threatens the image security. The values of information entropy obtained for plain-images and ciphered images are given in Table 4. The values obtained for ciphered images are close to the ideal value 8. This implies that the information leakage in the proposed encryption process is negligible and the image encryption system is secure against the entropy attack.

Table 4. Information Entropy of Original and Ciphered Images

Test Images	Original	Ciphered
Lena	7.4439	7.9969
Baboon	7.2649	7.9976
Peppers	7.5327	7.9973
Cameraman	7.0097	7.9969
Barbara	7.5482	7.9974
Boat	7.1124	7.9969
Airplane	6.7074	7.9975

5 Conclusion

In this paper, a new algorithm of encryption and decryption of images is presented. The algorithm is based on the concept of scrambling the pixel's positions and changing the gray values of the image pixels. To perform the scrambling of the plain-image's pixels, a multi-level blocks based scrambling scheme is suggested. At each level, the image is first decomposed into blocks whose size depends on the level and then the blocks are scrambled through 2D Cat transform. The control parameters of scrambling are randomly generated using a 2D coupled Logistic map to enforce the secrecy of the images. The encryption of the scrambled image is done using chaotic sequence generated through 1D Logistic map. All the simulation and experimental analysis show that the proposed image encryption system has very large key space, high sensitivity to secret keys, better diffusion of information in the ciphered images and low correlation coefficients. Hence, the proposed image encryption algorithm has high level of security with less computation and is more robust towards cryptanalysis.

References

1. Fridrich, J.: Symmetric Ciphers based on two-dimensional Chaotic maps. International Journal of Bifurcation and Chaos 8(6), 1259–1284 (1998)
2. Yen, J.C., Guo, J.I.: A New Image Encryption Algorithm and Its VLSI Architecture. In: IEEE Workshop on Signal Processing Systems, pp. 430–437 (1999)
3. Yen, J.C., Guo, J.I.: A New Chaotic Key-based Design for Image Encryption and Decryption. In: IEEE International Symposium on Circuits and Systems, vol. 4, pp. 49–52 (2000)
4. Zhang, L., Liao, X., Wang, X.: An Image Encryption Approach based on Chaotic maps. Chaos, Solitons and Fractals 24(3), 759–765 (2005)
5. Pisarchik, A.N., Flores-Carmona, N.J., Carpio-Valadez, M.: Encryption and Decryption of Images with Chaotic map lattices. CHAOS Journal, American Institute of Physics 16(3), 033118-033118-6 (2006)
6. Dongming, C., Zhiliang, Z., Guangming, Y.: An Improved Image Encryption Algorithm Based on Chaos. In: IEEE International Conference for Young Computer Scientists, pp. 2792–2796 (2008)
7. Pareek, N.K., Patidar, V., Sud, K.K.: Image Encryption using Chaotic Logistic map. Image and Vision Computing 24(9), 926–934 (2006)

8. Lian, S., Sun, J., Wang, Z.: A Block Cipher based on a Suitable use of Chaotic Standard map. Chaos Solitons and Fractals 26(1), 117–129 (2005)
9. Mao, Y., Lian, S., Chen, G.: A Novel Fast Image Encryption Scheme based on 3D Chaotic Baker maps. International Journal of Bifurcation and Chaos 14(10), 3616–3624 (2004)
10. Salleh, M., Ibrahim, S., Isnin, I.F.: Enhanced Chaotic Image Encryption Algorithm based on Baker's map. In: IEEE International Conference on Circuits and Systems, vol. 2, pp. 508–511 (2003)
11. Behnia, S., Akhshani, A., Ahadpour, S., Mahmodi, H., Akhavand, A.: A Fast Chaotic Encryption Scheme based on Piece-wise Nonlinear Chaotic maps. Physics Letter A 366(4-5), 391–396 (2007)
12. Chen, G.Y., Mao, Y.B., Chui, C.K.: A Symmetric Image Encryption Scheme based on 3D Chaotic Cat maps. Chaos Solitons and Fractals 21(3), 749–761 (2004)
13. Guan, Z.H., Huang, F., Guan, W.: Chaos-based Image Encryption Algorithm. Physics Letters A 346(1-3), 153–157 (2005)
14. Hsu, C.T., Wu, J.L.: Hidden Digital watermarks in Image. IEEE Transactions on Image Processing 8(1), 58–68 (1999)
15. Yang, Y.L., Cai, N., Ni, G.Q.: Digital Image Scrambling Technology Based on the Symmetry of Arnold Transformation. Journal of Beijing Institute of Technology 15(2), 216–220 (2006)
16. Liu, H., Zhu, Z., Jiang, H., Wang, B.: A Novel Image Encryption Algorithm Based on Improved 3D Chaotic Cat Map. In: 9th IEEE International Conference for Young Computer Scientists, pp. 3016–3021 (2008)
17. Shang, Z., Ren, H., Zhang, J.: A Block Location Scrambling Algorithm of Digital Image Based on Arnold Transformation. In: 9th IEEE International Conference for Young Computer Scientists, pp. 2942–2947 (2008)
18. Liehuang, Z., Wenzhou, L., Lejian, L., Hong, L.: A Novel Image Scrambling Algorithm for Digital Watermarking Based on Chaotic Sequences. International Journal of Computer Science and Network Security 6(8B), 125–130 (2006)
19. Fu-Yan, S., Shu-Tang, L., Zong-Wang, L.: Image Encryption using high-dimensional Chaotic System. Chinese Physics 16(12), 3616–3623 (2007)
20. Jian-Liang, M., Hui-jing, P., Wang-qing, G.: New Color Image Encryption Algorithm based on Chaotic Sequence Ranking. In: IEEE International Conference on Intelligent Information Hiding and Multimedia Signal Processing, pp. 1348–1351 (2008)
21. Fu, C., Zhang, Z., Cao, Y.: An Improved Encryption Algorithm Based on Chaotic Maps. In: Third IEEE International Conference on Natural Computation, pp. 189–193 (2007)
22. Li, T., Zhou, S., Zeng, Z., Ou, Q.: A New Scrambling Method Based on Semi-frequency Domain and Chaotic System. In: IEEE International Conference on Natural Computation, pp. 607–610 (2005)
23. Wang, X.Y., Shi, Q.J.: New Type Crisis, Hysteresis and Fractal in Coupled Logistic Map. Chinese Journal of Applied Mechanics, 501–506 (2005)
24. May, R.M.: Simple Mathematical Model with very Complicated Dynamics. Nature 261, 459–467 (1976)
25. Tao, X., Liao, X.F., Tang, G.P.: A Novel Block Cryptosystem based on Iterating a Chaotic map. Physics Letter A 349(1-4), 109–115 (2006)

Maxillofacial Surgery Using X-Ray Based Face Recognition by Elastic Bunch Graph Matching

Manish Madhav Tripathi, Mohd Haroon, Minsa Jafar, and Mansi Jain

Integral University, Lucknow, India

Abstract. Oral and maxillofacial surgery is a surgery to correct a wide spectrum of diseases, injuries and defects in the head, neck, face, jaws and the hard soft tissues of maxillofacial region. Our aim is to efficiently reconstruct a damaged human face by matching the deformed skull structure along with the patient's image with our existing images in the database and then selecting the image and pose that best matches the face that needs to be reconstructed. A similar kind of facial structure can then be constructed for the damaged face. Following a sequence of five steps including, face detection, feature detection, replacement, shifting and blending a final conclusion is drawn.

Keywords: Elastic Bunch graphs, Gabor wavelet, feature detection, replacement, blending and shifting.

1 Introduction

Maxillofacial plastic surgeries have increased dramatically in the past few decades. More recently, advances in computer modeling have allowed pre-surgical observation and simulation of the effects of such operations, thus reducing the risk of unwanted result. Craniofacial surgery is a surgical subspecialty of oral and Maxillofacial surgery, plastic surgery, and ENT that deals with congenital and acquired deformities of the skull, face, and jaws. Although craniofacial treatment often involves manipulation of bone, craniofacial surgery is not tissue-specific, i.e., craniofacial surgeons deal with bone, skin, muscle, teeth, etc. The work presented in this paper attempts to leverage content on both maxillofacial and craniofacial surgeries using simple but accurate face detection scheme. In addition to the classical problems of face finding and feature detection, our system addresses and solves the problem of fusing a face with facial features belonging to another individual possibly of different color. This is required in order to achieve a natural looking result.

S. Ranka et al. (Eds.): IC3 2010, Part I, CCIS 94, pp. 183–193, 2010.

2 The System

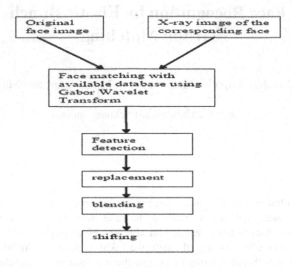

Fig. 1.

2.1 Face Matching

According to Richa Singh et al.[1] facial matching after plastic surgery using present algorithms will be a difficult issue in future as plastic surgery will be common. So we have added X-Ray based image recognition to Elastic Bunch Graph matching used by Laurenz Wiskottlz [2]. They have used Gabor Wavelets on all the pixels positions with a localized pixel function jet.

Jet is defined for pixel x = (x,y) as:

$$J_i(x) = \int I(x)\psi_i(x-x')d^2x.... \tag{1}$$

Where Gabor kernel is :

$$\psi_i(x) = (k^2_i/\sigma^2) \exp (k^2_i x^2/\sigma^2) [\exp (ik_i x) - \exp (- \sigma^2/2)] \tag{2}$$

Ki is a wave vector restricted by a Gaussian envelope function (Daugnan, 1988). Jets are themselves set of coefficients obtained for one image point.A sparse collection of such jets together with some information about their relative location constitutes an image graph, used to represent an object, such as a face. We employ a discrete set of 5 different frequencies and 10 orientatios to compute 50 coefficients each representing a jet. Gabor Wavelets have strong robustness as a data format. Their DC free nature provides freedom from varying brightness in the image. And normalizing the jets can solve the problem of varying contract in the image.

2.1.1 Phase Rotation Issues in Jets
Jets taken from points at close proximity have very different coefficients due to phase rotation even if they represent he same local feature. To solve this problem we there-fore either ignore the phase or compensate for its variation explicitly as stated by Lauranz Wiskootlz[2].

2.1.2 Face Representation

Face representation is done in two ways: presenting individual faces and presenting group of faces.

2.1.2.1 Individual Faces. Each face is defined by a set of fiducial points, e.g. the eyes, the jaw bones, the nose pinna and ear lobes etc. A labeled graph G representing a face consists of M nodes on these fiducial points at positions $x(m)$; $m = 1......M$ and E edges between them. The nodes are labeled with jets J_m. The edges are labeled with distances $\Delta x(e) = x_m - x_{m'}$; $e = 1......E$, where edge e connects node m' with m. Hence the edge labels are two- dimensional vectors. (When referring to the geometrical structure of a graph, unlabeled by jets, we call it a grid.) . Graphs for different head pose differ in geometry and local features. Although the fiducial points refer to corresponding object locations, some may be occluded, and jets as well as distances vary due to rotation in depth. Manual pointers are defined to associate corresponding nosed in the different graphs for their comparison.

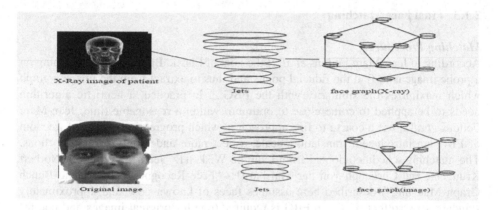

Fig. 2. Face Graphs are constructed for both x ray image and original image of the patient the Gabor wavelet transform, a convolution with a set of wavelet kernels.

There is a need for a general representation rather than a model of individual faces. Such representation should cover wide range of possible changes in appearances of faces.

2.1.2.2 Group of Faces. Thus individual model graphs are combined into a stack like structure called face bunch graph, see fig 3. Nodes in FBG refer to identical fiducial points. A set of jets referring to one fiducial point is called a bunch. A nose bunch, for instance, may include jets from flat, clipped, chiseled, female, and male nose, etc., to cover these local variations. Thus, the full combination of jets in the bunch graph is available, covering a much larger range of facial variation than represented in the constituting model graphs themselves. A similar data structure based on templates has been developed independently by Beymer (1994).

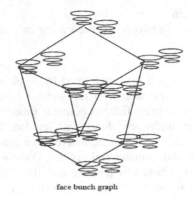

face bunch graph

Fig. 3. The Face Bunch Graph (FBG) serves as a representation of faces in general. It is designed to cover all possible variations in the appearance of faces.

2.1.3 Final Face Matching

Matching Procedure
According to Jean-Marc Fellous *et al*[2] the goal of Elastic Bunch Graph Matching on a probe image is to find the fiducial points and thus to extract from the image a graph which maximizes the similarity with the FBG . In practice, a heuristic algorithm needs to be applied to come close to optimum within a reasonable time. Jean-Marc Fellous *et al*[2] use a coarse to fine approach in which progressive degree of freedom of FBG are introduced: translation, scale, aspect ratio, and finally local distortions. The matching schedule(adopted from Laurenz Wiskott1z, Jean-Marc Fellous,Norbert Kruuger1, and Christoph von der Malsburg1; "Face Recognition by Elastic Bunch Graph Matching") described here assumes faces of known pose and approximately standard size, so that only two FBG is required.(one for original images and one for X-ray images)

Step 1: Find approximate face position. Condense the FGB into an average graph by taking the average magnitudes of the jets in each bunch of the FBG (or, alternatively, select one arbitrary graph as a representative).

Step 2: Refine position and size. Now the FBG is used without averaging, varying it in position and size.

Step 3: Refine size and find aspect ratio. A similar relaxation process as described for Step 2 is applied,

Step 4: Local distortion. In a pseudo-random sequence the position of each individual image node is varied to further increase the similarity to the FBG.

The resulting graph is called the image graph and is stored as a representation of the individual face of the image.

2.1.4 Data Base Structure for Face Matching

As per our requirements our database must have a collection of images of different people along with their X-ray images so that two major face bunch graphs can be constructed one for original image and one for x-ray images. At the time of face recognition both x-ray image face graph and original image face graph is compared with their respective face bunch graphs to find a similar looking face, where feature replacement is possible for the deformed facial structure. The background is always a homogeneous light or grey, except for smoothly varying shadows. The size of the faces varies by about a factor of three (but is constant for each individual,). The format of the original images is 256*384 pixels

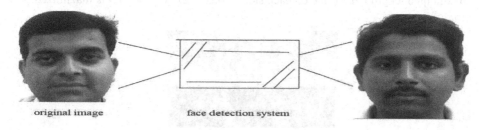

original image   face detection system

Fig. 4.

2.2 Feature Detection

Due to the general similarities between the human faces, it is possible to find specific rectangular regions around the fiducial points. However, these rectangular regions are quite large. The feature detection algorithms helps in highlighting the exact positions with more accuracy so that smoothing and blending of features can be obtained as per our requirement.

Fig. 5. Rectangular regions around eyes and lips have been drawn to highlight the features that have to be exchanged

Procedure

It starts with detection of eyes and the lips in the image. Considering eyes first, an eye box of size Len y X Len x (named as eye box E) that contains both the eyes. Our need is to find two smaller boxes of size len y X len x that contains the pupil of each eye to capture its important features. It will eliminate the unnecessary regions. This task is done by performing the Prewitt edge detection algorithm.

Sum of edges in each column along the length of E is found by the formula :

$$S(a)= \sum_{b=1}^{Len\ y} Ed(a,b) \tag{3}$$

where $1 < a < Len\ x$, and Ed is the image representing the edges in the eye box of size Len y x Len x.

Since majority of edges occur around eyes, hence as we approach the eyes more edges become visible. These edges include the outline of the eyes themselves, the eyelids and the eyebrows .The horizontal edges are calculated by finding two intervals of equal length len x (one on each side of the face), for which S is mazimized.

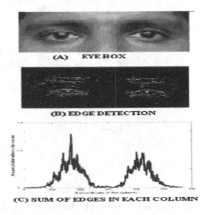

(A)   EYE BOX

(B) EDGE DETECTION

(C) SUM OF EDGES IN EACH COLUMN

Fig. 6. The result of performing the Prewitt edge detection algorithm on the eye box

$$h = \arg\max \sum_{a=h}^{h+len\ x} S(a) \tag{4}$$

where $h < a < h + 11$ is the horizontal edge of the left eye box or the right eye box, depending on whether the algorithm was performed on the left or right side of the face. The same algorithm is performed in vertical direction but this time we find sum of rows. This yields vertical edges of the eye boxes.

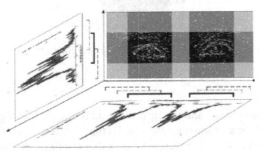

Fig. 7. The horizontal and vertical projections of edges in the eye box

Notice the presence of spikes on the either ends of the graph of S, which occurred due the presence of regions outside the face contained in eye box E. These spikes could cause problem in feature detection algorithm. According to S.A.Rabi *et al*[3] multiplying S by a double Gaussian with means around the expected location of the eyes and standard deviations of len x will eliminate this problem. Using the same algorithm, we can detect the exact location of the lips.

2.3 Replacement

Once the rectangular boxes containing the eyes and lips have been identified in both the images we can now proceed with replacing the features of h the ultimate goal of replacing the current features of the original face with the desired features of the model face (i.e. the face selected from the database). We start with adjusting the size of boxes in model face with the size appropriate for the original face, and then superimpose it on the original face. However as visible from picture below this superimposition does not produces natural looking results due to difference in skin tone of two people. Hence in the coming section we introduce the method of blending which helps in smudging of sharp differences in skin tones there by producing realistic effects.

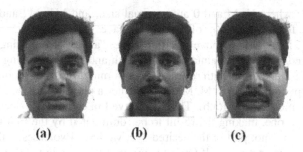

(a)   (b)   (c)

Fig. 8. (a) and (b) are the original face and model face, respectively. (c) represents the final face.

2.4 Blending

From fig 8 (c) we can see the difference between colors of original part and replaced parts. So blending is required for the faces belonging to two different individuals, so that the final image looks realistic, natural and smooth. It has been already demonstrated in the previous section that mere replacement is not sufficient, thus additional processing is required to make the result look more natural.. According to S.A.Rabi *et al*[3] the method of blending that is proposed for eyes can also be used for lips. Suppose P(xa, xb) is the probability that pixel(xa, xb)belong to eyes in the original image. Similarly, P(x'a, x'b) is the probability that pixel (x'a, x'b)belongs to model face. We assume that we know the probability distribution functions (pdf) P(xa, xb) and P(x'a, x'b). Consider the new eye box, N, constructed from the original eye box, 0, and the desired eye box, M, using the following formula:

$$N(a, b, h)= P(x'a , x'b) M(a , b, h) + (1- P(x'a, x'b)) (1-P(xa , xb)) O(a, b, h) = (1-P(X'a , X'b)) P(Xa, Xb) Mh$$

(5)

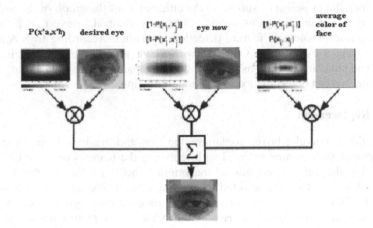

Fig. 9. The result of replacing the left eye in the original face with the left eye of the model face. Together,the shifting and blending modules achieve a smooth, natural-looking result.

For h = 1, 2, 3; where N, M and 0 are of equal size, and M1, M2 and M3 are the mean RGB values for the skin color of the original face.

S.A.Rabi *et al*[3] argue that above equation gives a way of replacing the original eye with the desired eye, while maintaining a smooth and natural looking face. To see this, let us consider a pixel in the ath row and bth column of the newly constructed eye box, N. the corresponding pixel in M, M(a,b), is either a part of the desired eye, or it is not. If it is, N(a,b) must equal M(a,b). This is achieved in equation 5, since in this case P(xa, xb) is close to one, making the result to be dominated by the first term. On the other hand, if M(a,b) is not part of the desired eye, we have two cases: either O(a,b) is part of the original eye or it is not. If O(a,b) is not part of the original eye, N(a,b) must equal O(a,b); effectively this ensures that the skin color and texture of the original face is preserved, which would achieve a smooth and natural blending. On the other hand, in the second case where neither O(a,b) nor M(a,b) are eye pixels,   we need to find N(a,b) with the "skin" of the original face. Close examination of equation 5 reveals that in all of the possible cases, the correct result is obtained. So we need to obtain the probability distribution functions (pdf) P(xa, xb) and P(x'a, x'b). Define P(xa) to be the probability that the pixels in the ath row of the original eye box, 0, are eye pixels. Similarly, let P(xb) to be the probability that the pixels in the bth column of the original eye box, 0, are eye pixels.P(x'a) and P(x'b) are the corresponding pdf's for the desired eye box, M. We can write P(xa, xb) in terms of P(xa) and P(xb) as follows:

$$P(xa, xb) = P(xa \cap xb) \qquad (6)$$
$$= P(xa)\, P(xb)$$

We assume independence of random variables xa and xb. Similarly, for P(x'a, x'b) we can write:

$$P(x'a, x'b) = P(x'a \cap x'b) \qquad (7)$$
$$= P(x'a)P(x'b)$$

We calculate P(xb) by summing the edges in the bth column of the original face's eye box. According to S.A.Rabi *et al*[3] the pdf's derived as P(xa), P(xb), P(x'a), and P(x'b), suffer from one major shortcoming: rather than being a continious function of positions,they consisit of discontinuous sharp peaks and deep valleys between the peaks. This problem has been addressed by convolving the pdf's by the sinc function. Till this point, we have not mentioned anything about the relative position of the eyes in the original eye box, 0, and the desired eye box, M. For instance, it is possible for the eye to be located in the upper left corner of 0 and the desired eye to be in the lower right corner of M. In this case, equation 5 will construct a new eye box, N, in which the upper left corner is covered by the "skin" of the original face, and the lower right corner is occupied by the desired eye. It can be predicted that in this case, the constructed eye box, N, will not look as natural as desired. This is because the average skin color Mh in equation 5 is an average for the entire face, which might not be a good representative of the skin color in the region of interest, i.e. around the eyes. Solution to the above problem is shifting the desired eye box, M, such that the desired eye in M is located at around the same relative position that the original eye is located in 0. If such shifting is performed prior to using equation 5, the discussed problem is effectively eliminated, since there are a few pixels that need to be covered by "skin". This is achieved using the shifting module.

2.5 Shifting

According to S.A.Rabi *et al*[3] we too have used the concept of location of the center of mass of P(xa, xb)and P(x'a, x'b) to determine where the eyes are located within the original eye box and the desired eye box, respectively. The x and y coordinates of the center of mass ,COMx and COMy for a given pdf P(xa,xb) could be found using the following formulae:

$$COMx = \sum_{b=1}^{n} P(xa, xb) \tag{8}$$

$$COMy = \sum_{a=1}^{m} P(xa, xb) \tag{9}$$

In figure 10(a) i and ii show the center mass of the original eye box and the desired eye box. In iii we have superimposed the two images and indicated the translation under which the eye in the desired eye box will be transferred to a location same as the location of the eye in the original eye box. Figure 10(b)shows an alternative approach where instead of moving the eye using this translation vector, we can move the eye box using the inverse of the translation both the desired eye and the original eye will be located at approximately the same relative position within their corresponding eye boxes. The same shifting operation is performed on the lip boxes. The face resulting from the replacement of features of the face in figure 8(b) with the corresponding features of the face in figure 8(a), followed by shifting and blending, is shown in 11. Comparing this picture with the one shown in 8(c), shows the importance of the shifting and blending modules in obtaining a smooth and natural-looking result.

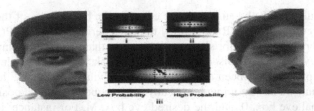

(a) i and ii are the eye boxes for the faces shown center of mass in each figure. In iii, i and ii are superimposed to find the translation vector under which the eyes will have the same location.

(b) i and ii are the eye boxes for the faces shown on the left and right, respectively, after the eye box in figure 11(a) i was shifted.

Fig. 10. Shifting the eye box, so that the eyes are in the same general location

Fig. 11. The face resulting from the replacement of features of the face in figure 8(b) with the corresponding features of the face in figure 8(a), followed by shifting and blending. Comparison with figure 8(c) shows the improvement gained as a result of performing the shifting and blending algorithms described above.

3 Conclusion

Maxillofacial Surgery, which can either be Cosmetic or Reconstructive, gives a new structure to the jaw bone, head, face and other such injuries. In other words, your body structure can be rectified to a great extent by this procedure. However, the treatment is only given after a proper study of the patient's condition. Needless to say, Maxillofacial Surgery is a very complex procedure. So areas like the face, head, and neck can be rectified to a great extent by this surgical process. Our attempt is to give patient an idea regarding the outcome of such a surgical procedures using approximations and face matching. This paper thus focuses on how surgeons can select the best possible facial feature before actually performing the surgery on patient's face.

4 Future Scope

Variations in pose, expression, Illumination, aging and disguise are considered as major challenges in face recognition and several techniques have been proposed to address these challenges. Plastic surgery, on the other hand, is considered as an arduous research issue; however, it has not yet been studied either theoretically or experimentally. The experimental results indicate that existing face recognition or matching algorithms perform poorly when matching pre and post surgery face images. The results also suggest that it is imperative for future face recognition systems to be able to address this important issue and hence there is a need for more research in this important area. Also the intensity based Gabor Wavelet scheme is prone to errors in case the background lighting and X-ray machine specifications changes while taking the patient's image.

References

1. Singh, R., Vatsa, M., Noore, A.: Effect of Plastic Surgery on Face Recognition: A Preliminary Study. IEEE publications 978-1-4244-3993-5/09/ (2009)
2. Wiskottz, L., Fellous, J.-M., Kruuger, N., von der Malsburg, C.: Face Recognition by Elastic Bunch Graph Matching. In: Jain, L.C., et al. (eds.) Intelligent Biometric Techniques in Fingerprint and Face Recognition, ch. 11, pp. 355–396. CRC Press, Boca Raton (1999)
3. Rabi, S.A., Aarabi, P.: Edward S. Rogers Sr. Department of Electrical and Computer Engineering Face Fusion: An Automatic Method For Virtual Plastic Surgery
4. Goin, M.K., Rees, T.D.: A prospective study of patients' psychological reactions to rhinoplasty. Annals of Plast Surgery 27(3), 210–215 (1991)
5. Hjelmas, E.: Face Detection: A Survey. Computer Vision and Image Understanding 83(3), 236–274 (2001)
6. Atick, J.J., Griffin, P., Redlich, A.N.: Face-recognition from live video for real-world applications now. Advanced Imaging (1995)
7. Blanz, V., Romdhami, S., Vetter, T.: Face identification across different poses and illuminations with a 3d morphable model. In: Proceedings of International Conference on Automatic Face and Gesture Recognition, pp. 202–207 (2002)

A Phenomic Approach to Genetic Algorithms for Reconstruction of Gene Networks

Rio G.L. D'Souza[1], K. Chandra Sekaran[2], and A. Kandasamy[2]

[1] St Joseph Engineering College, Vamanjoor Post, Mangalore 575028, India
[2] National Institute of Technology Karnataka, Surathkal, Mangalore 575 025, India
`rio@ieee.org`, `kchnitk@ieee.org`, `kandy@nitk.ac.in`

Abstract. Genetic algorithms require a fitness function to evaluate individuals in a population. The fitness function essentially captures the dependence of the phenotype on the genotype. In the Phenomic approach we represent the phenotype of each individual in a simulated environment where phenotypic interactions are enforced. In reconstruction type of problems, the model is reconstructed from the data that maps the input to the output. In the phenomic algorithm, we use this data to replace the fitness function. Thus we achieve survival-of-the-fittest without the need for a fitness function. Though limited to reconstruction type problems where such mapping data is available, this novel approach nonetheless overcomes the daunting task of providing the elusive fitness function, which has been a stumbling block so far to the widespread use of genetic algorithms. We present an algorithm called Integrated Pheneto-Genetic Algorithm (IPGA), wherein the genetic algorithm is used to process genotypic information and the phenomic algorithm is used to process phenotypic information, thereby providing a holistic approach which completes the evolutionary cycle. We apply this novel evolutionary algorithm to the problem of elucidation of gene networks from microarray data. The algorithm performs well and provides stable and accurate results when compared to some other existing algorithms.

Keywords: Genetic algorithms, Phenomic algorithms, Reconstruction, Fitness function, Multiobjective evolutionary algorithms, Gene networks.

1 Introduction

Genetic Algorithms have been used to solve a wide range of search and optimization problems ever since their introduction by Goldberg [1]. The robust and multimodal nature of these algorithms makes them ideally suited for many applications. However, genetic algorithms impose a few pre-requisites which need to be satisfied before applying them to solve a problem. Encoding of the solution into genetic information, development of a fitness function, or objective function, which evaluates each solution, selection of appropriate mechanisms for crossover and mutation, are some of these pre-requisites. Among these, the need for a fitness function is the major hurdle which prevents the potential application of genetic algorithms to many problems.

S. Ranka et al. (Eds.): IC3 2010, Part I, CCIS 94, pp. 194–205, 2010.

Reconstruction problems are encountered in reverse engineering scenarios where the model of the system is unknown and needs to be recreated solely from the interactions of the system with the outside world. Generally, a series of stimuli are applied to the system and the response is recorded. The stimulus-response pairs are then utilized to reconstruct the system model. For example, a series of input signals can be applied to an electronic device and the response waveform can then be analyzed to understand the internal make-up of the device.

When applying genetic algorithms to reconstruction problems, the ready availability of stimuli-response pairs can be exploited to avoid the need to develop the fitness function. Each individual of the population can embed one of the stimuli-response pairs, thereby avoiding the need to explicitly evaluate the individual using a fitness function. This novel idea has motivated us into developing a Phenomic approach to the survival-of-fittest phase in a typical genetic algorithm. We call it the phenomic approach since the emphasis is on the phenotype, rather than the genotype. The phenotype is the key player in the environment where survival-of-the-fittest determines which individuals are selected for propagating their genes into the next generation.

We have developed the phenomic approach which simulates an environment where individuals meet and interact. The interactions are modeled to represent the survival-of-the-fittest as it occurs in nature. Since each individual has its response embedded within itself, the selection of some individuals over the others will depend on this response. Thus there is no need to explicitly evaluate each individual using a fitness function. The rest of the genetic algorithm proceeds as usual, with crossover and mutation being used to create a new offspring population, which then becomes the basis for the next generation.

We have implemented the phenomic approach in a genetic algorithm that elucidates gene networks from microarray data. This is a typical reverse engineering problem which seeks to determine the causal gene network that can best account for observed measurements of RNA concentrations made under either different experimental conditions, or at different points of time.

The rest of the paper is organized as follows: in section 2, we review related work done by others in the area of genetic algorithms, especially when applied to reconstruction problems and reverse engineering of gene networks. In section 3, we present details of our approach followed by application of the novel approach to the problem of reconstructing gene networks from microarray data. We then present the results of our experiments, in section 4, and a discussion of its relative strengths and weaknesses. Finally, in section 5, we conclude the paper, with suggestions for possible future directions of research in this area.

2 Related Work

Genetic Algorithms have come a long way in the field of search and optimization. In the following sub-sections, we discuss only those works that are directly related to our work. We discuss work done by others on reconstruction problems, specifically with reference to reverse engineering of gene networks from microarray data, since our work is also of the same nature.

2.1 Genetic Algorithms

Ever since their introduction by Goldberg [1], genetic algorithms have undergone continuous development. Most early attempts were focused on formation of better encoding techniques, or better fitness functions. Some researchers tried to modify the structure of the basic algorithm itself. But most of the work has been focused on making the genetic algorithm more powerful by improving its basic mechanisms, such as crossover and mutation. Also there has been considerable work done in extending the basic algorithm to solve a wider variety of problems than initially possible. Among various approaches that emulate evolution as a problem-solver, genetic algorithms are more widely used. Also, several extensions of the basic algorithm are used for multiobjective optimization, and other contemporary applications. Notable among these algorithms is the non-dominated sorting genetic algorithm (NSGA) and its variations which have been applied to the problem of classification of cancer based on gene expression data [2].

2.2 Application of GAs to Reconstruction Problems

The application of genetic algorithms to reverse engineering problems involving reconstruction has seen remarkable success in the field of medical diagnostics. Lewis and Mosher [3] have developed a procedure wherein the currents in the brain are reconstructed by analyzing the external magnetic signals that result from such currents. Such methods have been surveyed by Munshi [4] and Kodali et al [5]. In a related work, Mou et al. [6] have applied genetic algorithms to reconstruct images obtained through electrical capacitance tomography.

Reconstruction using genetic algorithms has been reported in other fields, such as in the study of surface morphology by Li et al. [7] and in image reconstruction for immersed conductors by Huang et al [8]. Shape reconstruction is another potential field from which results have been reported by Xiyu et al. [9] and Fayolle et al [10].

2.3 Reconstruction of Gene Networks

Recently interest has developed in reverse engineering a gene network from its activity profiles. In a first attempt, a simple method was introduced that showed that reverse engineering is possible in principle [11]. A more systematic and general algorithm was developed by Liang et al. [12], using mutual information to identify a minimal set of inputs that uniquely define the output for each gene at the next time step. Akutsu et al. [13], [14] proposed simplified reverse engineering algorithms and rigorously examined the input data requirements. In an early work, D'haeseleer et al. [15] have reverse engineered Boolean gene networks from microarray data.

The S-system proposed by Savageau [16] has been used by some researchers [17], [18] in order to formulate an objective function for the evolutionary algorithm that they use to reverse engineer gene networks. Lubovac and Olsson [19] have suggested bringing in additional information resources into the evolutionary algo-rithms, so that more relevant relationships between genes can be derived. It is pos-sible to develop better evolutionary algorithms by finding better objective functions since the critical dependency between the genotype and phenotype is characterized by them [20], [21].

The Phenomic Algorithm, introduced in [22], presents an approach based on popu-lation dynamics. It is based on phenotypic interactions rather than genotypic mecha-nisms which are used in traditional genetic algorithms. Here the aim is to model the gene expression record of each gene as an individual and then to let these individuals interact in an environment that simulates the survival-of-the-fittest. Thus the need for an explicit objective function is avoided. In this paper, we use the multiobjective version of the phenomic algorithm to process the phenotypic information. We also use the conventional genetic algorithm to process the genotypic information and hence we have called the combined algorithm as the Integrated Pheneto-Genetic Algorithm (IPGA).

3   The Integrated Pheneto-Genetic Algorithm

First, we discuss the basic phenomic algorithm as given in [22]. Thereafter, we dis-cuss the multiobjective version of the phenomic algorithm, as given in [23]. Finally, we present the IPGA, wherein we integrate the features of the multiobjective phenomic algorithm into a genetic algorithm and thus create a holistic evolutionary algorithm.

3.1   The Basic Phenomic Algorithm

The basic phenomic algorithm, like most evolutionary algorithms, starts with a popu-lation of individuals. Each individual has genetic information embedded within it. It is the basic dogma of molecular biology that the phenotype of an individual is depend-ent on its genotype. Genotypic information manifests as the phenotype in the envi-ronment. An objective function is generally used in evolutionary algorithms to char-acterize this dependence. In the phenomic algorithm, we embed the expression of a gene within the individual. Thus we have a ready reference for determining fitness and do not need an objective function.

The presence of a strong correlation between expression patterns of two genes suggests co-regulation of these genes. Co-expressed genes in the same cluster are very likely to be involved in the same cellular processes. This can lead to an elucidation of regulatory networks. When constructing gene networks, we study the relationship between genes. If g_i and g_j are objects representing two such genes, their expression patterns across m samples may be written as $g_i = \{w_{ik} | 1 \le k \le m\}$ and $g_j = \{w_{jk} | 1 \le k \le m\}$. The basic phenomic algorithm is given below. It has a structure similar to a typical genetic algorithm with an evolutionary cycle.

The basic phenomic algorithm and its main functions.

```
basic_phenomic_algorithm( )
{
divide gene expression data into segments;
initialize population with first segment replicated;
set segment count to 0;
while population has not reduced to size of single
segment and there are more segments to process
    {
    interact_population;
    consolidate_population;
    replicate and add next segment;
    increment segment count;
    }
read gene-links stored in the final population;
display gene networks constructed from links;
}


interact_population( )
{
for a preset number of iterations
    {
    select two individuals from current population;
    apply interaction criteria in Eqns. (2) to (5);
    update gene-links of both individuals;
    }
}

consolidate_population( )
{
for a preset number of iterations
    {
    select two individuals from current population;
    if the indices of both individuals are same
            eliminate one of them after copying its links;
    }
}
```

The proximity between genes can be expressed in terms of a correlation coefficient, where w_{ij} is the expression level of the ith gene in the jth sample and μ_{gi} is the average of expression levels of the ith gene over all the samples. This proximity measure, shown in Eqn. (1), is called Pearson correlation coefficient.

$$Pear(g_i, g_j) = \frac{\sum_{k=1}^{m}\left(w_{ik} - \mu_{g_i}\right)\left(w_{jk} - \mu_{g_j}\right)}{\sqrt{\sum_{k=1}^{m}\left(w_{ik} - \mu_{g_i}\right)^2}\sqrt{\sum_{k=1}^{m}\left(w_{jk} - \mu_{g_j}\right)^2}} . \tag{1}$$

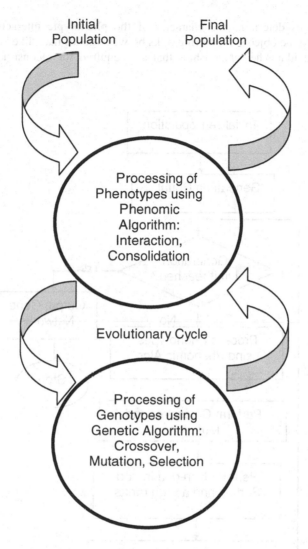

Fig. 1. Diagrammatic representation of the cycle of phenotypic and genotypic processing

Once the proximity measure for the genes is defined, the gene interactions such as "meet", "know", "like", "dislike" can be defined as operations on genes g_i and g_j, as shown in Eqns. (2) to (5).

$$meet(g_i, g_j) \: returns \: TRUE \;\; iff \;\; g_i \; and \; g_j \; were \; partners, at \; least \; once \; . \tag{2}$$

$$know(g_i, g_j) \: returns \: TRUE \;\; iff \;\; the \; proximity \; measure \; for \; g_i \; and \; g_j \; is \; known \; \cdot \tag{3}$$

$$like(g_i, g_j) \: returns \: TRUE \;\; iff \;\; Pear(g_i, g_j) \le D \cdot \tag{4}$$

$$dislike(g_i, g_j) \: returns \: TRUE \;\; iff \;\; Pear(g_i, g_j) > D \cdot \tag{5}$$

These operations determine the character of the phenotypic interactions that take place between gene objects. By storing links between genes that "like" each other it is possible to elucidate the relationships that are required for reconstructing the gene network.

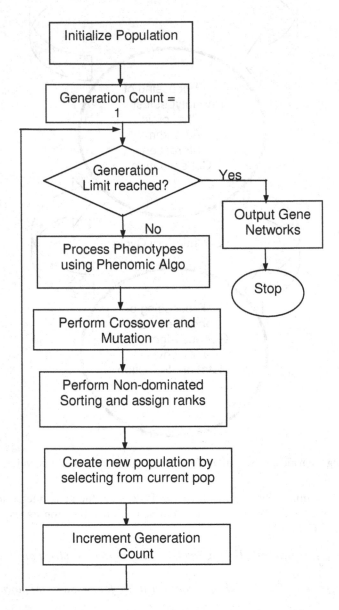

Fig. 2. Flowchart of the integrated pheneto-genetic algorithm

Other evolutionary methods which are used in the analysis of microarray datasets ignore the inherent advantages due to the ready availability of the expression of genes. An approach based on phenotypic features which exploits these inherent advantages is the basis for developing the phenomic evolutionary algorithm [22]. We present a description of the main functions of this algorithm below:

1.   Modeling genes as individuals: While modeling the genes as individuals, we embed the expression profile of the gene within the object itself. Also we store the relationships with other genes, which are discovered during the interaction phase, within the individual itself. We ensure sufficient density of individuals by replicating them as required.

2.   Simulating gene interaction: We set the stage for the survival-of-the-fittest by letting individuals to meet randomly. Eqns. (2) to (5) define the nature of these interactions between partners that meet. Partners would meet, know, like, or dislike each other depending upon the closeness of their expression profiles and whether they have met already.

3.   Enforcing natural processes: From time to time we consolidate the population by eliminating individuals which are replicates and have not acquired any links with other individuals. Thereafter we bring in the remaining segments of the data, one by one, till all segments have been considered. At the end of the process, the links between the genes, which are stored in the individuals, are used to construct the gene networks.

3.2 The Multiobjective Phenomic Algorithm

Gene networks discovered by the basic phenomic algorithm are based on correlation between expression profiles of the genes. When the correlation distance is set very low (< 0.05) only very few links are recovered. However when the correlation distance is set high (> 0.25) the links are too numerous and obviously implausible. The optimal setting lies in between these two extreme cases.

It is well known that most biological networks display the small-world network property that predicates sparseness between key nodes and dense local connections around each key node [17]. We use the similarity of the target network to small-world networks as an objective in order to determine the network that has the optimal number of links.

At the consolidation phase in the basic phenomic algorithm, we introduce selection of individuals after non-dominated sorting [2] based upon the two objectives: number of links (NOL) and small-world similarity factor (SWSF) [17], which are shown in Eqn. (6) and Eqn. (7).

$$NOL = \sum_{i=1}^{N} l_{ij} \,. \tag{6}$$

$$SWSF = \sum_{i=1}^{N} \sum_{j=1}^{N} l_{ij} \,. \tag{7}$$

Where, $l_{ij} = 1$ if gene g_i is linked to gene g_j, else $l_{ij} = 0$ and N is the total number of genes in the target network. We maximize objective NOL, while we minimize objective SWSF. Thus we perform multiobjective optimization within the phenomic algorithm.

3.3 The Integrated Algorithm, IPGA

We have integrated the techniques described in the previous sub-sections such that we have a holistic algorithm which represents the evolutionary cycle with both genotypic and phenotypic processing. In this integrated algorithm, the genotypic information is processed as in a genetic algorithm (using crossover, mutation and selection) and the phenotypic information is processed as in the phenomic algorithm (using segmentation, interaction and consolidation). We represent this process diagrammatically in Fig. 1.

The IPGA is shown in Fig. 2 and a brief discussion on the mechanisms adopted in this algorithm follows:

1. Initialization of population: We create an initial population of solutions wherein each solution is represented by one gene expression record from the microarray data. This gene could become the focal point of a gene network, as the evolutionary algorithm proceeds.

2. Processing of phenotypes using phenomic algorithm: We allow solutions in the current population to interact using equations that were described earlier. We also consolidate the population such that replicated solutions are removed.

3. Mutation and crossover: After processing of phenotypes, we perform crossover and mutation on all solutions subject to preset probabilities.

4. Non-dominated sorting and assigning ranks: We use the fast procedure for non-dominated sorting as explained in [23]. We assign ranks in ascending order based on the sorted sequence of solution.

5. Selection of new population: We use the assigned ranks to select a subset of the current population to form the new population.

The above mentioned steps are repeated until a preset number of generations have completed. This preset number is determined by trial and error. At the end of the preset number of generations, the current population will have solutions which are the gene networks elucidated by the algorithm.

4   Results and Validation

In this study, we used expression data from a study by Chu et al [24]. Saccharomyces cerevisiae (common yeast) was synchronized by transferring to a sporulation medium at time t=0 to maximize the synchrony of sporulation. RNA was harvested at time t=0, 0.5, 2, 5, 7, 9 and 11.5 hours after transfer to sporulation medium. Each gene's mRNA expression level just before transfer was used as control.

Expression profiles of about 6100 genes are included in this dataset. Using them, we followed the same method as Chu et al. [24] to extract the genes that showed significant increase of mRNA levels during sporulation. Among them, we selected 45 genes, whose functions are biologically characterized by Kupiec et al [25].

Table 1. Validation results obtained by 10-fold LOOCV using Yeast sporulation dataset

Validation Metric	Basic phenomic algorithm	Multiobjective phenomic algorithm	Integrated Pheneto-Genetic Algorithm
Stability Factor, SF	0.68	0.82	0.96
Accuracy Factor, AF	0.74	0.92	0.99

We validate these results by performing 10-fold leave-one-out-crossover validation (LOOCV). We make ten runs of each algorithm and compare the result of each run taken separately against the consensus results of the other nine runs. The average number of correctly identified edges resulting from all the ten comparisons indicates the stability of the algorithm. The average number of incorrectly identified edges resulting from all the ten comparisons indicates the accuracy of the algorithm. We formally define these metrics as Stability Factor (SF) and Accuracy Factor (AF) in Eqn. (8) and Eqn. (9).

$$SF = \frac{1}{n}\sum_{i=1}^{n}\frac{CE_i}{E_i}. \tag{8}$$

$$AF = 1 - \frac{1}{n}\sum_{i=1}^{n}\frac{IE_i}{E_i}. \tag{9}$$

where CE_i is the number of correctly identified edges in the ith comparison, IE_i is the number of incorrectly identified edges in the ith comparison, n is the total number of comparisons, which is ten in our case, and E_i is the total number of edges in each consensus network.

5   Conclusion

We have presented the reconstruction of gene networks using IPGA and validated the results for stability and accuracy. The phenomic nature of the algorithm is manifested in its focus on the phenotypic, rather than genetic, features of an individual. Due to the implicit survival-of-the-fittest mechanisms the need for an explicit objective function was avoided. The algorithm was applied to yeast sporulation data and the resulting gene networks are found to be biologically relevant.

The multiobjective variant of the phenomic algorithm performs better on the validation metrics, but this comes at a higher computational cost. This is because there is no robust means to search the space for possible combinations of solutions that might be better than those found in a particular generation. This problem is overcome by integrating the multiobjective phenomic algorithm with the genetic algorithm. The integrated algorithm is found to be more stable than its predecessors and also provides more accurate results. Hence it can become a plausible alternative to other methods which are used for reconstruction of gene networks.

References

1. Goldberg, D.E.: Genetic Algorithms for Search, Optimization, and Machine Learning. Addison-Wesley, Reading (1989)
2. Deb, K.: Multi-objective Optimization using Evolutionary Algorithms. Wiley, Chichester (2001)
3. Lewis, P.S., Mosher, J.C.: Genetic algorithms for neuromagnetic source reconstruction. In: 1994 IEEE International Conference on Acoustics, Speech, and Signal Processing, ICASSP 1994, Adelaide, vol. 5, pp. 293–296 (1994)
4. Munshi, P.: X-ray and ultrasonic tomography. Insight - Non-Destructive Testing and Condition Monitoring 45(1), 47–50 (2003)
5. Kodali, S.P., Bandaru, S., Deb, K., Munshi, P., Kishore, N.N.: Applicability of genetic algorithms to reconstruction of projected data from ultrasonic tomography. In: Proceedings of the 10th Annual Conference on Genetic and Evolutionary Computation, Atlanta, pp. 1705–1706 (2008)
6. Mou, C., Peng, L., Yao, D., Xiao, D.: Image Reconstruction Using a Genetic Algorithm for Electrical Capacitance Tomography. Tsinghua Science & Technology, Science Direct 10(5), 587–592 (2005)
7. Li, X., Kodama, T., Uchikawa, Y.: A reconstruction method of surface morphology with genetic algorithms in the scanning electron microscope. J. Electron Microscopy (Tokyo) 49(5), 599–606 (2000)
8. Huang, C.-H., Lu, H.-C., Chiu, C.-C., Wysocki, T.A., Wysocki, B.J.: Image reconstruction of buried multiple conductors by genetic algorithms. International Journal of Imaging Systems and Technology 18(4), 276–281 (2008)
9. Xiyu, L., Mingxi, T., Frazer, J.H.: Shape reconstruction by genetic algorithms and artificial neural networks. Engineering Computations 20(2), 129–151 (2003)
10. Fayolle, P.-A., Rosenberger, C., Toinard, C.: 3D Shape Reconstruction of Template Models Using Genetic Algorithms. In: 17th International Conference on Pattern Recognition (ICPR 2004), vol. 2, pp. 269–272 (2004)
11. Somogyi, R., Fuhrman, S., Askenazi, M., Wuensche, A.: The gene expression matrix: towards the extraction of genetic network architectures. In: Proc. of Second World Cong. of Nonlinear Analysts (WCNA 1996), vol. 30(3), pp. 1815–1824 (1996)
12. Liang, S., Fuhrman, S., Somogyi, R.: REVEAL, a general reverse engineering algorithm for inference of genetic network architectures. In: Pacific Symp. on Biocomputing, vol. 3, pp. 18–29 (1998)
13. Akutsu, T., Miyano, S., Kuhara, S.: Identification of genetic networks from a small number of gene expression patterns under the boolean network model. In: Pacific Symp. on Biocomputing, vol. 4, pp. 17–28 (1999)
14. Akutsu, T., Miyano, S., Kuhara, S.: Algorithms for inferring qualitative models of biological networks. In: Pacific Symp. on Biocomputing (2000)
15. D'haeseleer, P., Liang, S., Somogyi, R.: Genetic network inference: from co-expression clustering to reverse engineering. Bioinformatics 16(8), 707–726 (2000)
16. Savageau, M.A.: Power-law formalism: a canonical nonlinear approach to modeling and analysis. In: Proceedings of the World Congress of Nonlinear Analysts 1992, pp. 3323–3334 (1992)
17. Spieth, C., Streichert, F., Speer, N., Zell, A.: Optimizing Topology and Parameters of Gene Regulatory Network Models from Time Series Experiments. In: Deb, K., et al. (eds.) GECCO 2004. LNCS, vol. 3102, pp. 461–470. Springer, Heidelberg (2004)

18. Noman, N., Iba, H.: Reverse engineering genetic networks using evolutionary computation. Genome Informatics 16(2), 205–214 (2005)
19. Lubovac, Z., Olsson, B..: Towards reverse engineering of genetic regulatory networks. Technical Report No. HS-IDA-TR-03-003, University of Skovde, Sweden (2003)
20. Kampis, G.: A Causal Model of Evolution. In: Proc. of 4th Asia-Pacific Conf. on Simulated Evol. and Learning (SEAL 2002), pp. 836–840 (2002)
21. Dawkins, R.: The blind watchmaker. Penguin Books (1988)
22. D'Souza, R.G.L., Chandra Sekaran, K., Kandasamy, A.: A Phenomic Algorithm for Reconstruction of Gene Networks. In: IV International Conference on Computational Intelligence and Cognitive Informatics, Venice, CICI 2007, WASET, pp. 53–58 (2007)
23. D'Souza, R.G.L., Chandra Sekaran, K., Kandasamy, A.: Reconstruction of Gene Networks Using Phenomic Algorithms. International Journal of Artificial Intelligence and Applications (IJAIA) 1(2) (2010)
24. Chu, S., DeRisi, J., Eisen, M., et al.: The transcriptional program of sporulation in budding yeast. Science 282, 699–705 (1998)
25. Kupiec, M., Ayers, B., Esposito, R.E., Mitchell, A.P.: The molecular and cellular biology of the yeast Saccaromyces. Cold Spring Harbor, 889–1036 (1997)

An Algorithm to Determine Minimum Velocity-Based Stable Connected Dominating Sets for Ad Hoc Networks

Natarajan Meghanathan

Jackson State University
Jackson, MS 39217, USA
natarajan.meghanathan@jsums.edu

Abstract. The high-level contribution of this paper is an algorithm to determine a stable connected dominating set (CDS), based on node velocities, for mobile ad hoc networks (MANETs). The algorithm, referred as MinV-CDS, includes in the CDS, nodes that are slow-moving with lower velocity, rather than the usual approach of preferring nodes with a larger density, i.e., a larger number of uncovered neighbors, referred as MaxD-CDS. If a node has lower velocity and is the next candidate node to be considered for inclusion in the CDS, it is added to the CDS if it has at least one neighbor that is yet to be covered. Simulation results illustrate that MinV-CDS has a significantly longer lifetime than MaxD-CDS; MinV-CDS also has a larger number of nodes and edges compared to MaxD-CDS and this helps to reduce the hop count as well as the end-to-end delay and improves the fairness of node usage.

Keywords: Connected Dominating Set, Mobile Ad hoc Network, Node Velocity, Density, Algorithm.

1 Introduction

A mobile Ad hoc network (MANET) is a dynamic distributed system of arbitrarily moving wireless nodes that operate on a limited battery charge. The network operates on a limited bandwidth and the transmission range of each node is limited. As a result, multi-hop communication is very common in MANETs. Route discovery in MANETs has been traditionally accomplished through a flooding-based Route-Request-Reply cycle in which all the wireless nodes are responsible for forwarding the Route-Request (RREQ) messages from the source towards the destination and propagating the Route-Reply (RREP) messages on the discovered path from the destination to the source. Recent studies (e.g., [1][2][3][4][5]) have demonstrated the use of connected dominating set (CDS)-based virtual backbones to propagate the RREQ and RREP messages. With such a backbone approach, routing control messages are exchanged only among the nodes that are part of the CDS instead of being broadcast by all the nodes in the network, thus reducing the number of unnecessary retransmissions.

Ad hoc networks are often represented as a unit disk graph [6], in which vertices represent wireless nodes and a bi-directional edge exists between two vertices if the

S. Ranka et al. (Eds.): IC3 2010, Part I, CCIS 94, pp. 206–217, 2010.
© Springer-Verlag Berlin Heidelberg 2010

corresponding nodes are within the transmission range of each other. A connected dominating set (CDS) is a sub graph of the undirected graph such that all nodes in the graph are included in the CDS or directly attached to a node (i.e., covered by the node) in the CDS. A minimum connected dominating set (MCDS) is the smallest CDS (in terms of number of nodes in the CDS) for the entire graph. For a virtual backbone-based route discovery, the smaller the size of the CDS, the smaller is the number of unnecessary retransmissions. If the RREQ packets are forwarded only by the nodes in the MCDS, we will have the minimum number of retransmissions. Unfortunately, the problem of determining the MCDS in an undirected graph like that of the unit disk graph is NP-complete. Efficient heuristics (e.g., [7][8][9]) have been proposed to approximate the MCDS in wireless ad hoc networks. A common thread among these heuristics is to give preference to nodes that have high neighborhood density (i.e., a larger number of uncovered neighbors) for inclusion in the MCDS. The MaxD-CDS algorithm [10] studied in this paper is one such density-based heuristic earlier proposed by us.

In this paper, we show that aiming for the minimum number of nodes for the CDS in MANETs, results in CDSs that are highly unstable. The CDS itself has to be frequently rediscovered and this adds considerable overhead to the resource-constrained network. Our contribution in this paper is a minimum-velocity based CDS construction algorithm that gives preference to include slow-moving nodes (i.e., nodes with lower velocity) in the CDS rather than nodes that have high neighborhood density. The proposed algorithm, referred to as MinV-CDS, starts with the inclusion of the node having the lowest velocity, into the CDS. Once a node is added to the CDS, all its neighbors are said to be covered. The covered nodes are considered in the increasing order of their velocity, for inclusion in the CDS. If a node has lower velocity and is the next candidate node to be considered for inclusion in the CDS, it is added to the CDS if it has at least one neighbor that is yet to be covered. This procedure is repeated until all the nodes in the network are covered. The overall time complexity of the MinV-CDS algorithm is $O(|E| + |V|\log|V|)$ where $|V|$ and $|E|$ are the number of nodes and edges in the underlying ad hoc network graph, which could be a snapshot of the network at a particular time instant. A CDS is used as long as it exists. We outline an $O(|CDS\text{-}Node\text{-}List|^2 + |V|)$ algorithm to check the existence of a CDS at any particular time instant, where $|CDS\text{-}Node\text{-}List|$ and $|V|$ are the number of nodes part of the CDS and the underlying network graph respectively. Upon failure of the existing CDS, we again initiate the MinV-CDS algorithm to determine a new CDS.

We compare the performance of MinV-CDS with a maximum-density based algorithm (referred as MaxD-CDS) that gives preference to nodes that have a larger number of uncovered neighbors for inclusion in the CDS. Simulation results illustrate that the minimum-velocity based CDSs have a significantly longer lifetime than the density-based CDSs. The tradeoff is an increase in the number of nodes and number of edges that are part of the MinV-CDS vis-à-vis MaxD-CDS. However, this helps the MinV-CDS to support a relatively lower hop count per source-destination path, rather than that obtained through MaxD-CDS.

The rest of the paper is organized as follows: Section 2 reviews related work in the literature on stable connected dominating sets. Section 3 describes our MinV-CDS algorithm and also the MaxD-CDS algorithm with which the former is compared to.

In addition, we outline an algorithm to check the existence of a CDS at any time instant. Section 4 presents the simulation environment and describes the simulation results comparing the performance of MinV-CDS with that of MaxD-CDS. Section 5 concludes the paper and discusses future work. Throughout the paper, the terms 'node' and 'vertex'; 'link' and 'edge' are used interchangeably. They mean the same.

2 Related Work

Very few algorithms have been proposed in the literature to determine a stable connected dominating set for MANETs. In [2], the authors propose a localized algorithm, called maximal independent set with multiple initiators (MCMIS), to construct stable virtual backbones. MCMIS consists of two phases: In the first phase, a forest consisting of multiple dominating trees rooted at multiple initiators is constructed. A dominating tree, rooted at an initiator node, comprises of a subset of the nodes in the network topology. Multiple dominating trees, each started by its initiator, are constructed in parallel. In the second phase, dominating trees, with overlapping branches are interconnected to form a complete virtual backbone. Nodes are ranked according to the tuple (stability, effective degree, ID) and are considered as candidate nodes to be initiators, in decreasing order of importance.

A novel mobility handling algorithm proposed in [3] shortens the recovery time of CDS (i.e., changes in the CDS) in the presence of node mobility as well as maintains the CDS size as small as possible. In [4], the authors describe an algorithm to calculate stable CDS based on MANET link-stability. According to this algorithm, a link is said to be non-weak if the strength of the beacon signals received on that link is above a threshold. For inclusion in the stable CDS, nodes are considered in the decreasing order of the number of non-weak links associated with a node.

In [5], the authors propose a distributed topology management algorithm that constructs and maintains a minimal dominating set (MDS) of the network and the members of the MDS are connected to form a CDS that is used as the backbone infrastructure for network communication. Each node self-decides the membership of itself and its neighbors in the MDS based on the two-hop neighborhood information disseminated among neighboring nodes.

In [10], we had earlier proposed a centralized algorithm, referred to as *OptCD-STrans*, to determine a sequence of stable static connected dominating sets called the Stable Mobile Connected Dominating Set for MANETs. Algorithm *OptCDSTrans* operates according to a simple greedy principle, described as follows: whenever a new CDS is required at time instant t, we choose the longest-living CDS from time t. The above strategy when repeated over the duration of the simulation session yields a sequence of long-living stable static connected dominating sets such that the number of CDS transitions (changes from one CDS to another) is the global minimum. Some of the distinguishing characteristics of *OptCDSTrans* are that the optimal number of CDS transitions does not depend on the underlying algorithm or heuristic used to determine the static CDSs and the greedy principle behind *OptCDSTrans* is very generic such that it can be applied to determine the stable sequence of any communication structure (for example, paths or trees) as long as there is a heuristic or algorithm to determine that particular communication structure in a given network graph [11].

3 Algorithms to Determine MinV-CDS and MaxD-CDS

3.1 Data Structures

We maintain four principal data structures:

(i) *MinV-CDS-Node-List* – includes all the nodes that are part of the minimum-velocity based CDS.

(ii) *Covered-Nodes-List* – includes nodes that either in the *MinV-CDS-Node-List* or covered by a node in the *MinV-CDS-Node-List*

(iii) *Uncovered-Nodes-List* – includes all the nodes that are not covered by a node in the *MinV-CDS-Node-List*

(iv) *Priority-Queue* – includes nodes that are in the *Covered-Nodes-List* and are probable candidates for addition to the *MinV-CDS-Node-List*. This list is sorted in the decreasing order of the velocity of the nodes. A dequeue operation returns the node with the lowest velocity among the nodes in the queue.

3.2 Algorithm to Determine the Minimum Velocity-Based Connected Dominating Set (MinV-CDS)

The MinV-CDS (pseudo code in Figure 1) is primarily constructed as follows: The *Start Node* is the first node to be added to the *MinV-CDS-Node-List*. As a result of this, all the neighbors of the *Start Node* are said to be covered: removed from the *Uncovered-Nodes-List* and added to the *Covered-Nodes-List* and to the *Priority-Queue*. If both the *Uncovered-Nodes-List* and the *Priority-Queue* are not empty, we dequeue the *Priority-Queue* to extract a node *s* that has the lowest velocity and is not yet in the *MinV-CDS-Node-List*. If there is at least one neighbor node *u* of node *s* that is yet to be covered, all such nodes *u* are removed from the *Uncovered-Nodes-List* and added to the *Covered-Nodes-List* and to the *Priority-Queue*; node *s* is also added to the *MinV-CDS-Node-List*. If all neighbors of node *s* are already covered, then node *s* is not added to the *MinV-CDS-Node-List*. The above procedure is repeated until the *Uncovered-Nodes-List* becomes empty or the *Priority-Queue* becomes empty. If the *Uncovered-Nodes-List* becomes empty, then all the nodes in the network are covered. If the *Priority-Queue* becomes empty and the *Uncovered-Nodes-List* has at least one node, then the underlying network is considered to be disconnected. During a dequeue operation, if two or more nodes have the same lowest velocity, we choose the node with the larger number of uncovered neighbors. If the tie cannot be still broken, we randomly choose to dequeue one of these candidate nodes.

Input: Snapshot of the Network Graph G = (V, E), where V is the set of vertices and E is the set of edges

Auxiliary Variables and Functions:
MinV-CDS-Node-List, Covered-Nodes-List, Uncovered-Nodes-List, Priority-Queue minVelocity

Dequeue(*Priority-Queue*) – Extracts the node with the minimum velocity from the queue – if two or more nodes have the same minimum velocity, then a node is randomly chosen and extracted from the queue.
Neighbors(s) – List of neighbors of node *s* in graph *G*
velocity(u) – the velocity (in m/s) of node *u*
startNode – the first node to be added to *MinV-CDS-Node-List*

Output: *MinV-CDS-Node-List* // contains the list of nodes part of the minimum
                                 // velocity – based CDS.

Initialization:
MinV-CDS-Node-List = Φ; *Covered-Nodes-List* = Φ; *Priority-Queue* = Φ;
Uncovered-Nodes-List = V

Begin Construction of MinV-CDS

// To Determine the *Start Node*
  minVelocity = ∞

  for every vertex *u*∈ V **do**   // the loop runs in O(|V|) time
    if (*minVelocity* > *velocity(u)*) **then**
      minVelocity = *velocity(u)*
      startNode = *u*
    end if
  end for

// Initializing the data structures
  MinV-CDS-Node-List = {*startNode*}
  Priority-Queue = {*startNode*}
  Covered-Nodes-List = {*startNode*}
  Uncovered-Nodes-List = *Uncovered-Nodes-List* – {*startNode*}

// Constructing the MinV-CDS-Node-List
  while (*Uncovered-Nodes-List* ≠ Φ and *Priority-Queue* ≠ Φ) **do**   // the loop runs
                                                       in O(|E|+|V|log|V|) time
      node *s* = Dequeue(*Priority-Queue*)
      // removes, from the *Priority-Queue*, the node with the minimum velocity
      // each Dequeue operation takes O(|V|) time for arrays or O(log|V|) time for
      // binary heap, depending on the implementation

      alreadyCovered = true // to test whether all neighbors of node *s* have already
                               // been covered or not

        for all node *u*∈ Neighbors(*s*) **do**
          if (*u* ∈ *Uncovered-Nodes-List*) **then**
            alreadyCovered = false
            Uncovered-Nodes-List = *Uncovered-Nodes-List* – {*u*}
            Covered-Nodes-List = *Covered-Nodes-List* U {*u*}

          Priority-Queue = *Priority-Queue* U {*u*}
        end if
        end for

    end if

  end while

  return *MinV-CDS-Node-List*

End Construction of MinV-CDS

Fig. 1. Pseudo Code for the MinV-CDS Construction Algorithm

3.3 Algorithm to Determine the Maximum Density-Based Connected Dominating Set (MaxD-CDS)

The MaxD-CDS algorithm works similar to that of the MinV-CDS algorithm. The major difference is that the criterion for including nodes in the CDS is the number of uncovered neighbors and not the node velocity. The *Start Node* is the node with the maximum number of uncovered neighbors. In subsequent iterations, we dequeue the node with the maximum number of uncovered neighbors from the *Priority-Queue*. Ties are broken arbitrarily. The procedures to update the *Covered-Nodes-List* and the *Uncovered-Nodes-List* are the same as in MinV-CDS.

3.4 Time Complexity of MinV-CDS and MaxD-CDS

If we use a binary heap for maintaining the *Priority-Queue* of $|V|$ nodes, each dequeue and enqueue operation can be completed in $O(\log|V|)$ time; otherwise if the *Priority-Queue* is simply maintained as an array, each dequeue and enqueue operation takes $O(|V|)$ time. Overall, all the $|V|$ nodes and their associated $|E|$ edges in the underlying network have to be explored for inclusion in the CDS. Assuming the *Priority-Queue* is implemented as a binary heap (as in our simulations), the overall time complexity of both the MinV-CDS and MaxD-CDS algorithms is $O(|E| + |V|*\log |V|)$.

3.5 Algorithm to Check the Existence of a CDS at Any Time Instant

The algorithm to check the existence of a CDS (applicable for both MinV-CDS and MaxD-CDS) at a particular time instant t works as follows: Given the currently known list of nodes in the CDS (referred to as *CDS-Node-List*), we first construct the list of edges (referred to as *CDS-Edge-List*) that may exist at time instant t between any pair of nodes in the *CDS-Node-List*. An edge exists between any two nodes if and only if the Euclidean distance between the co-ordinates of these two nodes is less than or equal to the transmission range per node. We run the well-known Breadth First Search (BFS) algorithm [12] on the *CDS-Node-List* and *CDS-Edge-List* and examine whether the underlying CDS is connected or not. If the CDS is not connected, the algorithm returns false and a new run of the CDS construction algorithm is initiated. If the CDS is found to be connected, we then test whether every non-CDS node in the network is a neighbor of at least one CDS node. If there exists at least one non-CDS node that is not a neighbor of any CDS node at time t, the algorithm returns false – necessitating the instantiation of the appropriate CDS construction algorithm. If every non-CDS node has at least one CDS node as neighbor, the algorithm returns true – the current CDS covers the entire network and there is no need to determine a new CDS.

4   Simulation Conditions and Results

All of the simulations are conducted in a discrete-event simulator developed by the author in Java. This simulator has also been successfully used in recent studies (e.g., [13][14][15]). The network topology is of dimensions 1000m x 1000m. The network density is represented as a measure of the average neighborhood size, which is calcu-lated as follows: $N*\pi R^2/A$, where N is the number of nodes in the network, R is the transmission range of a node and A is the network area. The transmission range per node used in all of our simulations is 250 m. With a fixed transmission range and network area, the network density is varied from low to moderate and high by altering the number of nodes. We employ 50, 100 and 150 nodes to represent networks of low (average of 9.8 neighbors per node), moderate (average of 19.6 neighbors per node) and high (average of 29.4 neighbors per node) respectively.

We use the Random Waypoint mobility model [16], one of the most widely used models for simulating mobility in MANETs. According to this model, each node starts moving from an arbitrary location to a randomly selected destination with a randomly chosen speed in the range $[v_{min} .. v_{max}]$. Once the destination is reached, the node stays there for a pause time and then continues to move to another randomly selected destination with a different speed. We use $v_{min} = 0$ and pause time of a node is also set to 0. The values of v_{max} used are 5 and 50 m/s representing low and high mobility levels respectively.

We obtain a centralized view of the network topology by generating mobility trace files for a simulation time of 1000 seconds under each of the above simulation conditions. We sample the network topology for every 0.25 seconds. Note that, two nodes a and b are assumed to have a bi-directional link at time t, if the Euclidean distance between them at time t (derived using the locations of the nodes from the mobility trace file) is less than or equal to the wireless transmission range of the nodes. If a CDS does not exist for a particular time instant, we take a snapshot of the network topology at that time instant and run the appropriate CDS algorithm.

We measure the following performance metrics. Each data point in Figures 2 – 5 is an average computed over 10 mobility trace files and 15 s-d pairs from each of the mobility trace files. The starting time for each s-d session is uniformly distributed between 1 to 20 seconds.

- *CDS Node Size*: This is a time-averaged value of the number of nodes that are part of the CDS, determined by the MaxD-CDS and MinV-CDS algorithms. For example, if there exists a CDS of size 20 nodes, 23 nodes and 18 nodes in the network for 5, 10 and 5 seconds respectively, then the average CDS Node Size is $(20*5 + 23*10 + 18*5)/(5 + 10 + 5) = 21.0$ and not $(20 + 23 + 18)/3 = 20.3$.
- *CDS Edge Size*: This is a time-averaged value of the number of edges connecting the nodes that are part of the CDS, determined by the MaxD-CDS and MinV-CDS algorithms.
- *CDS Lifetime*: This is the time elapsed between the discovery of a CDS and its disconnection, averaged over the entire duration of the simulation.
- *Hop Count per Path*: This is the time-averaged hop count of individual source-destination (s-d) paths involving the CDS nodes as source, intermediate and destination nodes, averaged for all the s-d paths over the entire simulation time.

4.1 CDS Node Size

The MinV-CDS, based on node velocity, includes more nodes (refer Figure 2) compared to the MaxD-CDS, based on node density. The maximum density-based CDS attempts to minimize the number of nodes that are part of the CDS as it gives preference to nodes that have a larger number of uncovered neighbors over nodes that have a smaller number of uncovered neighbors. On the other hand, the minimum velocity-based CDS does not give much importance to the number of uncovered neighbors of a node before including the node in the *CDS-Node-List*. If a node has a lower velocity and is the next candidate node to be considered for inclusion (when the already covered nodes are considered in the increasing order of their velocity) in the *CDS-Node-List*, the low velocity node is added to the *CDS-Node-List* if it has at least one neighbor that is yet to be covered. As a result, the number of nodes in the *CDS-Node-List* is relatively high for the CDS based on minimum velocity.

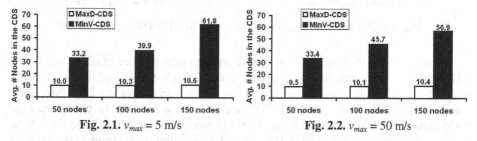

Fig. 2.1. $v_{max} = 5$ m/s   Fig. 2.2. $v_{max} = 50$ m/s

Fig. 2. CDS Node Size – Number of Nodes per MaxD-CDS and MinV-CDS

With respect to the magnitude of the difference in the number of nodes in the *CDS-Node-List*, we observe that the Node Size for a MinV-CDS is 3.3 (low network density) to 5.8 (high network density) times larger than that of the Node Size for a MaxD-CDS. In the case of a MaxD-CDS, for fixed node mobility, as we increase node density from low to high, there is only at most a 10% increase in the Node Size. On the other hand, for the MinV-CDS, for fixed node mobility, as we increase the node density from low to high, the Node Size can increase as large as by 190%. This can be attributed to the relative insensitivity of the MinV-CDS based algorithm to consider the number of uncovered neighbors of a node before including the node in the CDS. A long-living stable CDS is eventually formed by including more nodes to be part of the CDS. While, even if the network density is tripled, the MaxD-CDS algorithm manages to cover all the nodes in the high-density network by incurring only at most a 10% increase in the CDS Node Size, compared to that for a low-density network. For a given node density, as we increase the node mobility from low to high, the Node Size for a MaxD-CDS does not change appreciably, whereas the Node Size for a MinV-CDS changes by at most 15%.

4.2 CDS Edge Size

The MaxD-CDS algorithm, in its attempt to minimize the CDS Node Size, chooses CDS nodes that are far away from each other such that each node covers as many uncovered neighbors as possible. As the CDS nodes are more likely to be away from each other, spanning the entire network, the number of edges between the MaxD-CDS nodes is very low. On the other hand, since the MinV-CDS algorithm incurs a larger Node Size because of its relative insensitivity to the number of uncovered neighbors of a node, there is a corresponding increase in the number of edges (refer Figure 3) between these CDS nodes.

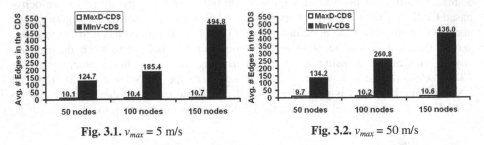

Fig. 3.1. v_{max} = 5 m/s　　　　　　　　　　Fig. 3.2. v_{max} = 50 m/s

Fig. 3. CDS Edge Size – Number of Edges per MaxD-CDS and MinV-CDS

With respect to the magnitude of the difference in the number of edges among the CDS nodes, we observe that the Edge Size for a MinV-CDS is 12.4 (low network density) to 46.0 (high network density) times larger than that of the Edge Size for a MaxD-CDS. In the case of a MaxD-CDS, for fixed node mobility, as we increase the node density from low to high, there is only at most a 7% increase in the Edge Size. On the other hand, for the MinV-CDS, at fixed node mobility, as we increase the node density from low to high, the Edge Size increases as large as by 400%. This can be attributed to the huge increase (as large as by 190%) in the MinV-CDS Node Size, with increase in network density. The increase in the number of edges and nodes significantly contribute to the increase in the MinV-CDS lifetime (refer Section 4.3) as the network density is increased. For a given node density, as we increase the node mobility from low to high, the Edge Size for a MaxD-CDS does not change appreciably, whereas the Edge Size for a MinV-CDS changes by at most 40%.

4.3 CDS Lifetime

In the case of MinV-CDS, the relatively larger CDS Node Size and Edge Size significantly contribute to the lifetime of the CDS (refer Figure 4). As the constituent nodes of the MinV-CDS are chosen based on the minimum velocity metric, the edges between the CDS nodes are bound to exist for a relatively longer time and the connectivity of the nodes that are part of the MinV-CDS is likely to be maintained for a longer time. On the other hand, the MaxD-CDS algorithm chooses nodes that are far away from each other (but still maintain an edge between them) as part of the CDS. The edges between such nodes are likely to fail sooner, leading to loss of connectivity between the nodes that are part of the MaxD-CDS. We thus observe a tradeoff between the CDS Node Size and the CDS Lifetime. If we meticulously choose slow-moving nodes to be part of the CDS, the lifetime of the CDS could be significantly improved, at the expense of the Node Size. On the other hand, if we aim to select a CDS with the minimum number of nodes required to cover all the nodes in the network, the lifetime of the CDS would be significantly lower.

With respect to the magnitude, the lifetime per MinV-CDS is 6 (low network density) to 25 (high network density) times more than that of the MaxD-CDS. The relatively high stability of MinV-CDS at high network density can be attributed to the inclusion of a significantly larger number of slow-moving nodes and their associated

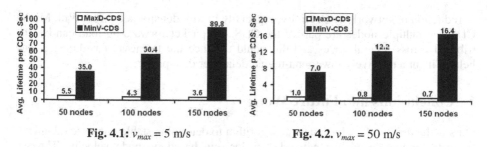

Fig. 4.1: $v_{max} = 5$ m/s   **Fig. 4.2.** $v_{max} = 50$ m/s

Fig. 4. Average Lifetime per MaxD-CDS and MinV-CDS

edges as part of the CDS. The relatively poor stability of MaxD-CDS at high network density can be attributed to the need to cover a larger number of nodes in the network without any significant increase in the number of nodes that are part of the CDS. For both MaxD-CDS and MinV-CDS, for a fixed network density, as we increase node mobility from low to high, the lifetime per CDS decreases by a factor of 5.3.

4.4 Hop Count Per Path

The average hop count per path (refer Figure 5) between an s-d pair through the nodes that are part of the MaxD-CDS is 1.06 (at low network density) to 1.15 (at moderate and high network density) more than that incurred with MinV-CDS. The relatively lower hop count per s-d path, in the case of a MinV-CDS, can be attributed to the larger CDS Node Size and the presence of a larger number of edges connecting the CDS nodes. Hence, the MinV-CDS can support several s-d paths between any two nodes s and d in the network and we choose the minimum hop s-d path among them while computing the average hop count per path. On the other hand, with fewer edges in the MaxD-CDS, the paths between any two nodes through the nodes of the MaxD-CDS will have a relatively larger hop count.

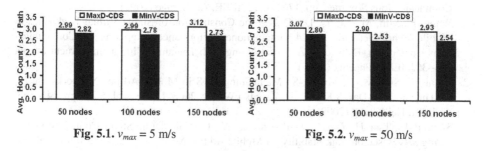

Fig. 5.1. $v_{max} = 5$ m/s   **Fig. 5.2.** $v_{max} = 50$ m/s

Fig. 5. Average Hop Count per Path in a MaxD-CDS and MinV-CDS

The consequences of having larger hop count per path with a fewer number of nodes per MaxD-CDS are a larger end-to-end delay per data packet and unfairness of node usage. Nodes that are path of the MaxD-CDS could be relatively heavily used compared to the nodes that are not part of the MaxD-CDS. This could lead to premature failure of critical nodes, mainly nodes lying in the center of the network, resulting in reduction in network connectivity, especially in low-density networks. With MinV-CDS, as multiple nodes are part of the CDS, the packet forwarding load can be distributed across several nodes and this could enhance the fairness of node usage and help to incur a relatively lower end-to-end delay per data packet.

5 Conclusions and Future Work

Ours is the first work to formulate an algorithm to determine stable connected dominating sets for mobile ad hoc networks, exclusively based on node velocity. Through extensive simulations, we demonstrate that the proposed algorithm, MinV-CDS, can determine connected dominating sets that have a significantly longer lifetime compared to that of the maximum density-based MaxD-CDS algorithm. The MinV-CDS also has a relatively larger number of constituent nodes and edges and this helps to reduce the hop count per path as well as the end-to-end delay and improves the fairness of node usage. We thus observe a tradeoff between the CDS Node Size and the CDS Lifetime. If we meticulously choose slow-moving nodes to be part of the CDS, the lifetime of the CDS could be significantly improved, at the expense of the Node Size. On the other hand, if we aim to choose a CDS with the minimum number of nodes required to cover all the nodes in the network, the lifetime of the CDS would be significantly lower.

As future work, we will study the performance of MinV-CDS along with that of the theoretically optimal *OptCDSTrans* algorithm and compare the lifetimes of the minimum velocity-based connected dominating sets and the stable mobile connected dominating sets. Future work would also involve developing a distributed implementation of the MinV-CDS algorithm and explore its use as a virtual backbone for unicast, multicast and broadcast communication in MANETs.

References

1. Sinha, P., Sivakumar, R., Bhargavan, V.: Enhancing Ad hoc Routing with Dynamic Virtual Infrastructures. In: 20th Annual Joint International Conference of the Computer and Communications Societies, pp. 1763–1772. IEEE, Anchorage (2001)
2. Wang, F., Min, M., Li, Y., Du, D.: On the Construction of Stable Virtual Backbones in Mobile Ad hoc Networks. In: 24th International Performance Computing and Communications Conference, Enhancing Ad hoc Routing with Dynamic Virtual Infrastructures, pp. 355–362. IEEE, Phoenix (2005)
3. Sakai, K., Sun, M.-T., Ku, W.-S.: Maintaining CDS in Mobile Ad hoc Networks. In: Li, Y., Huynh, D.T., Das, S.K., Du, D.-Z. (eds.) WASA 2008. LNCS, vol. 5258, pp. 141–153. Springer, Heidelberg (2008)
4. Sheu, P.-R., Tsai, H.-Y., Lee, Y.-P., Cheng, J.Y.: On Calculating Stable Connected Dominating Sets Based on Link Stability for Mobile Ad hoc Networks. Tamkang Journal of Science and Engineering 12(4), 417–428 (2009)
5. Bao, L., Garcia-Luna-Aceves, J.J.: Stable Energy-aware Topology Management in Ad hoc Networks. Ad hoc Networks 8(3), 313–327 (2010)
6. Kuhn, F., Moscibroda, T., Wattenhofer, R.: Unit Disk Graph Approximation. In: Joint Workshop on the Foundations of Mobile Computing, pp. 17–23. ACM, Philadelphia (2004)

7. Alzoubi, K.M., Wan, P.-J., Frieder, O.: Distributed Heuristics for Connected Dominating Set in Wireless Ad hoc Networks. IEEE/KICS Journal on Communication Networks 4(1), 22–29 (2002)
8. Butenko, S., Cheng, X., Du, D.-Z., Paradlos, P.M.: On the Construction of Virtual Backbone for Ad hoc Wireless Networks. In: Cooperative Control: Models, Applications and Algorithms, pp. 43–54 (2002)
9. Butenko, S., Cheng, X., Oliviera, C., Paradlos, P.M.: A New Heuristic for the Minimum Connected Dominating Set Problem on Ad hoc Wireless Networks. In: Recent Developments in Co-operative Control and Optimization, pp. 61–73 (2004)
10. Meghanathan, N.: An Algorithm to Determine the Sequence of Stable Connected Dominating Sets in Mobile Ad hoc Networks. In: 2nd Advanced International Conference on Telecommunications, Guadeloupe, French Caribbean (2006)
11. Meghanathan, N., Farago, A.: On the Stability of Paths, Steiner Trees and Connected Dominating Sets in Mobile Ad hoc Networks. Ad hoc Networks 6(5), 744–769 (2008)
12. Cormen, T.H., Leiserson, C.E., Rivest, R.L., Stein, C.: Introduction to Algorithms, 2nd edn. MIT Press/ McGraw Hill, New York (2001)
13. Meghanathan, N., Sugumar, M.: A Beaconless Minimum Interference Based Routing Protocol to Minimize End-to-End Delay per Packet for Mobile Ad hoc Networks. International Journal of Interdisciplinary Telecommunications and Networking 2(1), 12–26 (2010)
14. Meghanathan, N., Odunsi, A.: Investigating the Scalability of the Fish-eye State Routing Protocol for Ad hoc Networks. Journal of Theoretical and Applied Information Technology 12(1), 60–70 (2010)
15. Meghanathan, N.: Multicast Extensions to the Location-Prediction Based Routing Protocol for Mobile Ad hoc Networks. In: Liu, B., Bestavros, A., Du, D.-Z., Wang, J. (eds.) Wireless Algorithms, Systems, and Applications. LNCS, vol. 5682, pp. 190–199. Springer, Heidelberg (2009)
16. Bettstetter, C., Hartenstein, H., Perez-Costa, X.: Stochastic Properties of the Random-Way Point Mobility Model. Wireless Networks 10(5), 555–567 (2004)

An Efficient Intrusion Detection System Using Clustering Combined with Fuzzy Logic

Ajanta Konar and R.C. Joshi

Department of Electronics and Computer Engineering,
Indian Institute of Technology Roorkee
Roorkee, India 247667
Ajanta.konar@gmail.com, rcjosfec@iitr.ernet.in

Abstract. In dynamic network environment, where the traffic patterns are always changing and huge amount of data are coming every second, it is a real difficult job to process the huge data to detect intrusion and at the same time adapting with the change in the traffic pattern to be able to detect novel attack. Our approach uses unsupervised learning with the help of Self-Organizing Map to be able to isolate unseen patterns and predict its suspicious nature from neighboring map units. To have a finer classification of the group of data corresponding to a map unit, we have built a small fuzzy model for every map unit. The small fuzzy rule-base corresponding to the selected map unit will be updated if new attack occurs, rather than the entire model, thus avoiding processing overhead to a great extent. It gives high detection rate in KDD 99 cup dataset with very low false positive rate.

Keywords: Self-organizing map, fuzzy logic, network security.

1 Introduction

With the rapid growth of computer networks and heavy reliance on Internet, network attacks have been increasing in frequency and severity. The new automated hacking tools appearing everyday on web along with various system vulnerability information are responsible for this growing intrusion rate. Intrusion detection systems (IDS) have been developed in order to defend computer networks against continuous evolution of various types of attacks. Their role in general computer network security is illustrated in Fig. 1. It is intended to fulfill the limitations of the existing firewall, access control module, vulnerability scanning system as shown in the fig. 1. It has been a very important subject of research for many years. Data mining and machine learning approach [1, 2, 3, 4, 6, 7, 8] have drawn the most attention of researchers in this field.

There are two broad approaches of intrusion detection. One is anomaly based approach, which first builds the normal profile that contains metrics derived from the system operation. While monitoring the system, current observation is compared with the normal profile in order to detect changes in the patterns of behavior of the system. There are many existing anomaly detection IDS [6]. Another is misuse detection system, which relies on patterns of known intrusions to match and identify intrusions. In this case, the intrusion detection problem is a classification problem. The patterns of

S. Ranka et al. (Eds.): IC3 2010, Part I, CCIS 94, pp. 218–228, 2010.

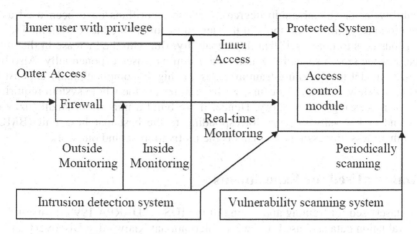

Fig. 1. Role of IDS in general computer security

known attack types are stored as rules, for e.g., if then else rules. Problem with supervised classification technique is that it cannot accommodate new intrusion patterns. Hence, unsupervised learning techniques are more appropriate for detecting anomalous behaviors and new attacks in a dynamic intrusion detection environment. Unsupervised learning or clustering algorithms have been recently refocused on research areas [7, 8]. Clustering algorithms can group new data instances into coherent groups which can be used to increase the performance of existing classifiers. In this paper, we have taken a novel approach of using self-organizing map (SOM) [7] neural network as a clustering tool and then modeling a fuzzy rule-base for every output neuron of the feature map. For fuzzy rule learning, we have modified the classic WM's algorithm [11]. It has proven to achieve higher performance with no significant cost added to it.

We describe our motivation for the work in section 2, our intrusion detection system in section 3, our experimental results and observations in section 4 and the future work in section 5.

2 Related Work

Our work was motivated by Hayoung et. All, who used SOM to produce the feature map of historical traffic data and then labeled the map units using correlation of features to detect mainly DoS and probing attacks [7]. But labeling a map unit can limit the detection accuracy as a map unit corresponds to a group of similar data, which may contain both attack and normal data as some attack may be more similar to normal in behavior. Also the number of map units influences the detection accuracy. Therefore it needs a finer examination of the dataset corresponding to a map unit. In this paper, we have built a separate fuzzy rule-base corresponding to every map unit, which fulfils the need of separating different data in a group.

Attackers try to behave in normal way to prevent being caught up. Therefore, fuzzy rules using linguistic terms are more suitable to detect such attacks in terms of probability factor (membership degree). Genetic algorithms have been used as rule generation and optimization tools in the design of fuzzy rule-based systems [3, 4] for their robustness to noise, self-learning capability. But with the increase in the number of features the search space for genetic algorithm increases exponentially. Also building fuzzy model for the entire training dataset is highly computationally expensive. If some completely new attack occurs, we have to retrain the whole system requiring so much of processing and memory. Hence, if we build a number of small fuzzy rule-bases and update only the one corresponding to the best matching unit (BMU), it would incur less processing cost. That is the motivation behind our work.

3 Dataset Used for Experiments

The dataset used for training and testing of the IDS is "DARPA 1998 Intrusion Detection Evaluation data set" used in the 3rd International Knowledge Discovery and Data Mining Tools Competition in 1999 (KDD Cup 1999) [5]. It is TCPdump data generated over nine weeks of simulated network traffic in a hypothetical military local area network. It includes some 7 million TCP connection records. DARPA 1998 Intrusion Detection Evaluation data set consists of the labeled training data with about 5 million connections and the test data with 2 million connections. Each connection is detailed in terms of 41 features, categorized as follows: Basic TCP features, Content features, and Time- and Host-based Traffic features [5].The dataset simulates 24 types of attacks in the training data and an additional 14 types in the test data. The attacks include the four most common categories of attack, which are the following.

- **Denial of Service Attack (DoS)** is an attack in which the attacker makes some computing or memory resource too busy or too full to handle legitimate requests, or denies legitimate users access to a machine.
- **User to Root Attack (U2R)** is a class of exploit in which the attacker starts out with access to a normal user account on the system (perhaps gained by sniffing passwords, a dictionary attack, or social engineering) and is able to exploit some vulnerability to gain root access to the system.
- **Remote to Local Attack (R2L)** occurs when an attacker who has the ability to send packets to a machine over a network but who does not have an account on that machine exploits some vulnerability to gain local access as a user of that machine.
- **Probing Attack:** is an attempt to gather information about a network of computers for the apparent purpose of circumventing its security controls.

The subsets of KDD99 cup dataset, which we have chosen for our training and testing experiments are following:

- ➢ For training KDD_TNG: 10% of KDD 99 Cup dataset
- ➢ For testing three datasets each containing 50,000 records, namely KDD_TST1, KDD_TST2 and KDD_TST3. First two datasets are randomly taken from the full training dataset and the third one is taken from corrected test dataset of KDD99 cup dataset.

4 The Proposed Approach for Intrusion Detection

The proposed approach for training and testing of the IDS is shown in Fig. 2.

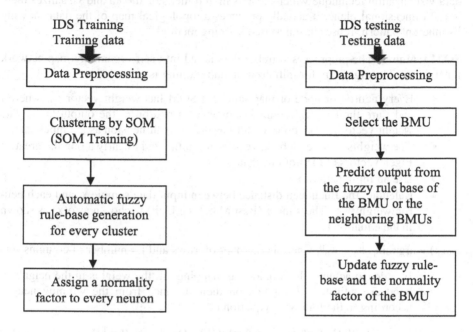

Fig. 2. Flow chart of training and testing process

4.1 Data Preprocessing

We first eliminate the features not having numerical values, which are protocol_type, service and flag as numerical data is required for further processing. Then every feature's value is normalized in [0 1] range so that a feature with originally higher range cannot dominate others. Now for dimension reduction, we have used Principal component analysis method [9].

4.1.1 PCA for Feature Reduction

To reduce time and space complexity and to achieve high detection accuracy, the redundant features have to be eliminated. Principal Component Analysis [9] reduces the dimensionality of data by restricting attention to those directions in the feature space in which the variance is greatest. In PCA, the proportion of the total variance accounted for by a feature is proportional to its Eigen value. If we sort the Eigen values according to descending order, first 23 Eigen values add up to 99.97% of the total sum of Eigen values. Increasing the number from 23 to any larger value does not increase the accuracy significantly. Therefore the rest (38 – 23) or 15 principal components are ignored as they are not contributing much in the total variance.

4.2   Clustering by Self-Organizing Map (SOM)

SOM neural network, invented by Professor Teuvo Kohonen, are basically used as a data visualization technique which clusters high dimensional data and visualizes them in a 2 dimensional plane. It actually produces a topological map of the data showing its inherent pattern. It uses unsupervised learning method.

SOM training: The preprocessed traffic data is fed into self-organizing map network for training. The algorithm for initialization and training is given below:

- Every neuron or node or map unit of a SOM has weight vector w_{ij}, where i and j are the row and column number of a neuron in the output layer. The weight vector or codebook vector has the same dimension as the input data.
- The weights w_{ij} or codebook vectors are initialized linearly along the greatest Eigen vectors of the training data.
- Use an input pattern x
- Calculate the Euclidean distance between input data sample x, and each neuron weight w_{ij}. The winner (Best Matching Unit) is chosen as o(x) as shown in the equation (1):

$$o(x) = \arg \min_{i,j} \|x - w_{ij}\|, \text{ where } i = \text{number of rows and } j = \text{number of columns} \quad (1)$$

- In order to achieve the topological mapping, all the weights in the neighborhood are adjusted, depending on their distance from the winning neuron according to the following equation (2):

$$\forall j : w_{ij}(t) = w_{ij}(t-1) + \alpha(t)\,\eta(t') \cdot (x_i(t) - w_{ij}(t-1)) \quad (2)$$

Where α is the learning rate and η the neighborhood function and t', the time that was spent in the current context and t is the current time. The neighborhood function η decreases as t' increases.

- Present the next input. Reduce the neighborhood according to the neighborhood function. Repeat steps 3, 4 and 5 until convergence is achieved.

The choice of the number of neurons, number of training epochs, learning rate, neighborhood function etc. has great effect on the speed of convergence and accuracy of produced feature map. So, we have chosen the parameters by experimenting many times with different parameter values and selecting the one giving the best result.

4.3   Automatic Fuzzy Rule-BASE Generation for Every Cluster

4.3.1   Modified WM's method: The fuzzy modeling of the dataset associated with a single neuron of the SOM can be done using the modified Wang and Mendel [11] method. We have proposed a modification on the way of eliminating contradictory rules.

- **Dividing the input and output space into fuzzy regions:** Given a set of training data with say, m number of features and one output label (0 for normal or 1 for attack) $(x_j^{k} ; y_j^{k})$ where j=1,2 ,.. up to m, we define the universe of discourse for every feature $[x_j^{-} ; x_j^{+}]$ where x_j^{-} and x_j^{+} are the minimum and maximum value of that feature in a particular dataset corresponding to a cluster. Then we divide each universe of discourse into equal four regions and the shape of membership function associated with each region is triangular as shown in Fig. 3. The fuzzy linguistic terms (or membership function) associated with each feature are VS (Very Small), S (Small), M (Medium), B (Big) and VB (Very big). Similarly the output space [0; 1] is also divided into three regions corresponding to the fuzzy terms N (Certainly normal), NA (Can be normal or attack, not sure), A (Certainly attack) as shown in Fig. 4.

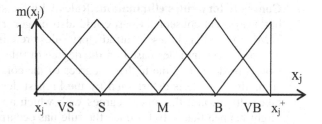

Fig. 3. Division of input space into fuzzy regions

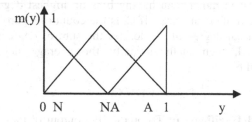

Fig. 4. Division of output space into fuzzy regions

- **Generate fuzzy rules from given training data:** First, determine the membership degrees of each example belonging to each fuzzy term defined for each region, variable-by-variable. Membership degree is the degree of association to a particular fuzzy set. Secondly, associate each example with the term having the highest membership degree variable by variable, denoted as md_j. Finally, obtain one rule for each example, using the term selected in the previous step. The rules so generated are "and" rules i.e. the antecedents of the IF part of each rule must be met simultaneously in order for the consequent of the rule to occur. Letting Tx_j be a term selected for variable x_j of an example, a rule could be like:

IF x_1 is Tx_1 (with md_1) and x_2 is Tx_2 (with md_2) and.. THEN y is Ty (with md_y)

- **Assign a degree to each rule:** The rule degree is computed as the product of the membership degree (md_j) of all fields. The degree of a rule generated by an example indicates how strong the rule is. Let D^k be the degree of the rule generated by example k. Mathematically,

$$D^k = \Pi_{j=1, 2. 3..m} md_j^k \qquad (3)$$

- **Assign an occurrence count to each rule:** Occurrence count is the number of times a particular rule is triggered. We have used this count in contradictory fuzzy rule elimination.
- **Create a combined fuzzy rule-base:** Redundant and contradictory rules must be eliminated to maintain the integrity of the rule-base.
  - **Redundant rules elimination:** When the number of examples is high, it is possible that the same rule could be generated for more than one example. These redundant rules can be removed based on the degree of the rule. Only the highest degree rule is kept and others are eliminated.
  - **Contradictory rules elimination:** Rules with the same antecedent part but a different consequent part could also be generated. In the original WM's method [11] these contradictory rules are eliminated in the same way as redundant rules based on the degree of rules. There the comparison is made among the highest degrees of the contradictory rules. The strength of a rule is determined by the highest degree. But it does not take into account the other degrees with which a rule has occurred. It might happen that only for once the rule has occurred with high degree and for the rest of the times with very less degree. So, our modification is to take the average degree of every rule in order to have an unbiased comparison rather than having bias on highest degree and no bias on the count of occurrences. If C^k is the count of a particular rule and $\Sigma\, D^k$ is the total degree of a rule, i.e. the sum of degrees for which it was triggered, then mathematically the average degree of a rule is defined by

$$D_{Avg} = \Sigma\, D^k / C^k \qquad (4)$$

- **Centroid defuzzification:** To predict the output of the test data denoted as x_j, the centroid defuzzification formula is used. Accordingly, the predicted output, y, is computed as

$$y = \left(\textstyle\sum_{r=1}^{R} amd^r \times c^r\right) \div \sum_{r=1}^{R} amd^r \qquad (5)$$

Where $amd^r = \Pi_{j=1, 2, R}\ md_j^r$ and c^r is the center value of the consequent term of rule r; and R denotes the total number of combined rules.

4.4 Normality Factor for Every Neuron

After completion of the fuzzy rule-base creation, we assign a normality factor to every neuron implying the possibility of the neuron being selected for a normal traffic. Mathematically it is calculated as:

$$NF = (N + 0.5*NA) / T \qquad (6)$$

Where N = No. of times the neuron was selected for certainly normal traffic, NA = No. of times it was selected for suspicious traffic, which may or may not be normal and T = Total number of times, the neuron was selected as a BMU. If a new type of traffic occurs, we will predict the expected output type of the traffic by consulting its neighboring neurons' normality factor. Neighborhood distance is measured by the Euclidean distance of the codebook vectors of two neighboring neurons. If NF_i is the normality factor of the ith nearest neighbor, then the expected output of the test traffic Y is calculated as

$$Y = (k * NF_1 + (k\text{-}1) * NF_2 + \dots\dots + 1 * NF_k) / \sum_{i=1}^{k} NF_i, \text{ Where k is the} \tag{7}$$
number of neighbors to be examined.

5   Experimental Results and Observations

We have implemented the IDS in Matlab R2006a. For SOM clustering, we have used the SOM toolbox version 2 [5]. As described in section 3.1, KDD_TNG is used for training, which is 10% subset of KDD 99 entire training dataset and KDD_TST1, KDD_TST2 and KDD_TST3 are used for testing. As mentioned in section 3.2, we have performed PCA on the dataset. We obtained the first 23 Eigen values having 99.97% variance in the total sum of variances. So, we have considered 23 principal components or Eigen vectors for our further clustering and fuzzy modeling.

The number of map units taken affects our system performance. To make it real-time IDS, we have to consider least detection time as well as modeling time. We have experimented the system using varying number of map units and compared their results with respect to detection time as shown in Fig. 5 and modeling time as shown in Fig. 6. From the two graphs, we take the number of units parameter as 500 as it gives the best result for both.

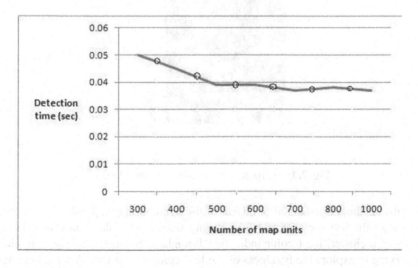

Fig. 5. Comparison of detection time with different number of map units

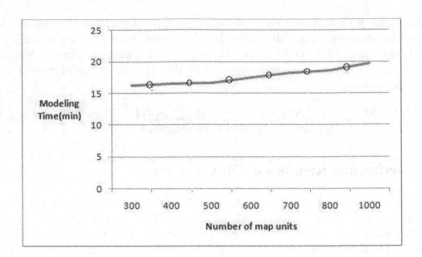

Fig. 6. Comparison of modeling time with different number of map units.Modelingtime = clustering time + fuzzy rule-base creation time

The u-matrix obtained from the SOM clustering is shown in fig. 7.

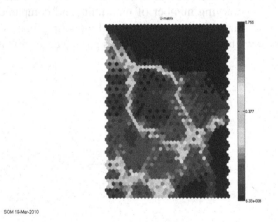

SOM 19-Mar-2010

Fig. 7. U-matrix representation of produced map

U-matrix is the unified distance matrix of the neighboring map units. The representation shows the broad clusters in the training data. Dark colour indicates the compactness of a cluster, light colur indicating boundary. Basically by fuzzy modeling, we are trying to explore the fuzziness of the less compact clusters. After fuzzy modeling, we now compare its performance with a system doing only clustering and labeling its map units by the category of the majority as shown in Table1.

Table 1. Comparison of detection accuracy between two systems (One using only SOM clustering and the other using both SOM clustering and fuzzy rule-base for each cluster)

Test dataset	Performance measure	Only SOM, no fuzzy rule-base	SOM with fuzzy rule-base for each neuron
KDD_TST1	Detection rate	88.09	99.58
	False Positive rate	0.23	0.34
KDD_TST2	Detection rate	97	97.62
	False Positive rate	4.19	0
KDD_TST3	Detection rate	98.16	99.08
	False Positive rate	0.74	0.08

Due to the presence of teardrop attack with similar features like normal in KDD_TST1, only SOM is giving poor result whereas our system performs excellently. KDD_TST3 contains apache2 DoS attack, which was not in KDD_TNG. Our system successfully detected the new attack.

Table 2. Comparison of cost between two systems (single or multiple rule-base)

Fuzzy Model type	Modeling Time	Detection Time	Update Time
For the entire dataset single fuzzy rule-base	~30 mins	0.67 sec	~0.7 sec
For every small cluster fuzzy rule-base + SOM clustering	16.63 mins	0.037 sec	~0.04 sec

The reason of high modeling and update time for single fuzzy rule-base method is that single rule-base for the entire dataset is comparatively huge than the rule-base of a single cluster.

6 Conclusions and Future Work

Our system is capable of detecting attacks with unclear characteristics with the help of fuzzy rules. False positive rate is also low.

The IDS has been trained and tested with historical KDD 99 cup data. However, this technique can also be applied on a new dataset. As KDD 99 is the only exhaustive dataset available freely on internet and all the past research work has been done on it, we chose this dataset for our experiment. A possible future course of work can be to run our IDS on live network and examine its detection accuracy. The accuracy of fuzzy modeling by our modified WM's method can be tested by comparing with genetic algorithms. The attacks can also be classified by defining a fuzzy region for each type.

References

1. Lee, W., Stolfo, S.J.: Data mining approaches for intrusion detection. Columbia Univ. New York Dept. of Computer Science (2000)
2. Abraham, A., Jain, R., Thomas, J., Han, S.Y.: D-SCIDS, Distributed Soft Computing Intrusion Detection System. J. Network and Computer Applications 30(1), 81–98 (2007)
3. Fries, T.P.: A fuzzy-genetic approach to network intrusion detection, pp. 2141–2146 (2008)
4. Abadeh, M.S., Habibi, J., Lucas, C.: Intrusion Detection Using a Fuzzy Genetics-Based Learning Algorithm. J. Network and Computer Applications 30(1), 414–428 (2007)
5. KDD Cup 1999 Data (1999),
   http://kdd.ics.uci.edu/databases/kddcup99/kddcup99.html
6. Shon, T., Moon, J.: A Hybrid Machine Learning Approach to Network Anomaly Detection. Information Sciences 177(18), 3799–3821 (2007)
7. Hayoung Oh, K.C.: Real-time Intrusion Detection System based on Self-Organized Maps and Feature Correlations. In: Third 2008 International Conference on Convergence and Hybrid Information Technology (2008)
8. Gonzalez, F., Dasgupta, D.: Neuro-Immune and Self-Organizing Map Approaches to Anomaly Detection: A comparison. In: ICARIS (2002)
9. Kuchimanchi, G.K., Phoha, V.V., Balagami, K.S., Gaddam, S.R.: Dimension Reduction Using Feature Extraction Methods for Real-time Misuse Detection Systems. In: Proceedings of the 2004 IEEE Workshop on Information Assurance and Security, pp. 195–202 (2004)
10. SOM Toolbox for Matlab, http://www.cis.hut.fi/projects/somtoolbox
11. Wang, L.-X., Mendel, J.M.: Generating fuzzy rules by learning from examples. IEEE Trans. Syst. Man Cybern. 22(6), 1414–1427 (1992)

Assessing the Performance of Bi-objective MST for Euclidean and Non-Euclidean Instances

Soma Saha, Mohammad Aslam, and Rajeev Kumar

Dept. of Computer Science & Engineering
Indian Institute of Technology Kharagpur
Kharagpur, WB 721302, India
{somasaha,maslam,rkumar}@cse.iitkgp.ernet.in

Abstract. The Bounded Diameter (a.k.a Diameter Constraint) Minimum Spanning Tree (BDMST/DCMST) is a well-studied combinatorial optimization problem. Several well-known deterministic heuristics and evolutionary approaches exist to solve the problem for a particular diameter. In this paper, we recast the BDMST problem as a Bi-Objective Minimum Spanning Tree (BOMST) problem and study the Pareto fronts. Instead of assessing performance of a single value obtained from BDMST algorithms, we assess the performance of the different heuristics over a Pareto front drawn across the diameter range. The advantege of this work is to give a provision to choose the better heuristics depending on particular diameter range for concerned real-life problem by observing the Pareto front.

Keywords: combinatorial optimization, multiobjective optimization, heuristics, BDMST problem, Pareto front.

1 Introduction

Minimum Spanning Tree (MST) has many applications, particularly in electrical, communication and transport networks, as well as in distributed mutual exclusion algorithms and in data compression. Much research has been performed on MST problem with a particular diameter constraint, which is a well-known BDMST problem. In the process researchers have shown the performance of various heuristics for different values for the constraint diameter. With on bi-objective aspects, one can choose a particular existing heuristics for BDMST problem to obtain better solutions for a given real-life problem on a known diameter range by easily visualizing only Pareto front solutions.

Deterministic polynomial time algorithm exists for BDMST problem having diameter bound atmost 3. But, it is an NP-hard problem within diameter range $4 \leq diameter, D < |V| - 1$ [1]. Existing well-known deterministic heuristics for BDMST problem are: one time tree construction (OTTC) and iterative refinement (IR) proposed by Deo and Abdalla [2], center based tree construction (CBTC) proposed by Julstrom [3], randomized greedy heuristics (RGH) by Raidl and Julstrom [4] or randomized tree construction (RTC) by Julstrom [3], and center based recursive clustering (CBRC) by Nghia and Binh [5].

S. Ranka et al. (Eds.): IC3 2010, Part I, CCIS 94, pp. 229–240, 2010.
© Springer-Verlag Berlin Heidelberg 2010

There are well-known stochastic methods that includes evolutionary algorithms (EA), like edge-set encoding EA (JR-ESEA) [4], permutation-coded EA
(PEA) [6] and among other well-known approaches are variable neighbourhood
search (VNS) [7], modified hybrid genetic algorithm (MHGA) [8]. Singh and
Gupta [9] suggested two improvements over CBTC and RGH and PEA, named
as CBTC-I, RGH-I and PEA-I, to get better solutions for BDMST problem.
Some work has also been done using evolutionary programming (EP) by Kumar
et al. [10]. Quality performance of different heuristics and EA for bi-objective
MST problem has been done by Kumar and Singh [11].

In our work, we have adapted the BDMST deterministic heuristics for
bi-objective MST formulation and then obtained a Patero-front. We have considered IR, OTTC, RGH and CBRC for both Euclidean and non-Euclidean instances and show the Pareto front to assess the performance of those heuristics.

The paper is organized as follows, in Section 2, we include the basic definitions
and outline problem formulation. Next, Section 3 contains the overview of those
heuristics which we deal in this work. The results are contained in Section 4. We
conclude with short discussion and furture work in Section 5.

2   Basic Definitions and Problem Formulation

Definition 1. Multiobjective Optimization Problem (MOP).
An m-objective optimization problem includes a set of n decision variables
$\mathbf{X} = (x_1, x_2, \ldots, x_n)$, a set of m objective functions $F = \{f_1, f_2, \ldots, f_m\}$ and a
set of k constraints $C = \{c_1, c_2, \ldots, c_k\}$. The objectives and the constraints are
functions of the decision variables. The goal is to:

Maximize/Minimize : $F(\mathbf{X}) = \{f_1(\mathbf{X}), f_2(\mathbf{X}), \ldots, f_m(\mathbf{X})\}$
subject to satisfaction of the constraints:
$C(\mathbf{X}) = \{c_1(\mathbf{X}), c_2(\mathbf{X}), \ldots, c_k(\mathbf{X})\} \leq (0, \ldots, 0)$

The collection of decision variables constitutes a *decision space* and a set of
objective values forms an *objective space*. In some problem definitions the constraints are treated as objective functions. The objectives may also be treated
as constraints to reduce the dimensionality of the objective-space.

Definition 2. Pareto-optimal set.
Without loss of generality we assume an m-objective minimization problem. We
say that a vector of decision variables $x \in X'$ includes in Pareto-optimal set as
a Pareto-optimal point if another x^* does not exist such that $f_i(x^*) \leq f_j(x)$ for
all $i = 1, 2, 3, \ldots, m$ and $f_i(x^*) < f_j(x)$ for atleast one j. Here, X' denotes the
feasible region of the problem (i.e. where the constraints are satisfied).

Definition 3. Bi-Objective MST Problem (BOMST).
A connected, undirected, weighted graph $G = (V, E)$ is given; a minimum spanning tree (MST) or minimum-weight spanning tree is a spanning tree T with

weight less than or equal to the weight of every other spanning tree. The single-objective MST problem can be formally stated as:

$Minimizes, Wt(T) = \sum_{e \epsilon T} wt(e)$

The diameter of a tree is the maximum eccentricity of its vertices, the maximum longest path exists between two vertices. The BDMST problem is formulated as:

$Minimizes, Wt(T) = \sum_{e \epsilon T} wt(e)$
with constraint, diameter of $T \leq D$, where D, the diameter bound, is given.

We recast this single-objective MST problem with a constraint on diameter to a bi-objective MST problem with two conflicting objectives (minimizing weights and minimizing diameters) and generate Pareto front for entire range of diameter 2 to $|V| - 1$. Now, we can easily say that BDMST problem is a subset of our bi-objective MST problem. In our work, through Pareto front, we can also visualize that no single existing heuristics for BDMST problem is better for whole range of diameter, one heuristics may be good for a small range, other may be good for higher range. For example, in Fig.1, RGH is better for diameter range upto 10 and IR gives superior results for larger values of diameter for 50 node Euclidean instances. Similar phenomenon can be observed for Fig. 2 which depicts Pareto front for 100 node Euclidean instances. As the diameter bound changes from D to D+1, the heuristics generates a different set of MSTs (few MSTs may overlap) with different diameter. Therefore, we have drawn Pareto curve taking lower-cost MST among a set of MSTs at a constraint diameter. It is possible to get an MST with lower-cost in lower diameter than current diameter constraint due to the change of diameter bound and different MST with different diameter are generated.

3   Adaptation of Deterministic Heuristics

In the bi-objective MST problem, we consider four heuristics OTTC, IR, RGH or RTC and CBRC known for BDMST problem. We have adapted the BDMST algorithms to yeild the Pareto front. This way we have recasted the BDMST problem to bi-objective MST problem.

3.1   One Time Tree Construction

Deo and Abdalla [2] presented *One Time Tree Construction (OTTC)*, based on *Prim*'s algorithm, grows a spanning tree, from each node and connecting the nearest neighbour that does not violate the diameter constraint. The complexity of this algorithm is $O(n^3)$, where n is the number of vertices in the graph. There are number of research papers for BDMST problem using OTTC for both Euclidean and non-Euclidean instances [2,3,4,5,8,9]; these works generalize MST problem with particular diameter constraint. But, for bi-objective MST problem

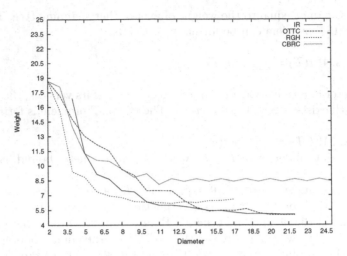

Fig. 1. Pareto front obtained from OTTC, IR, RGH and CBRC heuristics for 50 node Euclidean instance

using OTTC heuristics very little work has been done [10]. So, naturally OTTC is considered in our work.

3.2 Iterative Refinement

Second heuristics proposed again by Deo and Abdalla [2] is an *Iterative Refinem-ent* (*IR*); initially, an unconstrained minimum spanning tree (*MST*) for the input graph is computed using the *Prim*'s algorithm, then in each iteration one edge is removed that breaks the longest path in the spanning tree and replaced it by a non-tree edge without increasing the diameter. This process continues until diameter constraint is satisfied or the algorithm fails. The complexity of this algorithm is $O(n^3)$.

Because of slow characteristics, not much work has been done on BDMST problem taking IR into consideration. But, in real-life, variety of problem domain exists, somewhere this charctertistics may be ignorable and this is a reason behind to consider IR in our work. We have seen in our obtained Pareto front that for a particular range of diameter, IR works better than other few heuristics for Euclidean instances and it supports that IR works better for large diameter.

3.3 Randomized Greedy Heuristics or Randomized Tree Construction

Raidl and Julstrom [4] proposed this heuristics, providing randomness by choosing the start vertex and all subsequent vertices at random from those not yet in the spanning tree. But the connection of new vertex to the tree is yet greedy; it always connects lowest-weight edge between new vertex and tree-eligible vetex

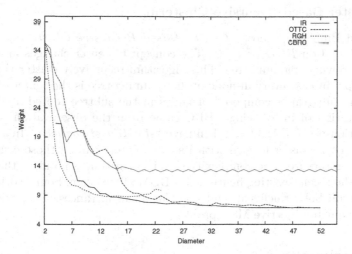

Fig. 2. Pareto front obtained from OTTC, IR, RGH and CBRC heuristics for 100 node Euclidean instance

whose depth is less than $D/2$. This heuristic is named as *Randomized Tree Construction (RTC)* in [3] and as *Randomized Greedy Heuristics* in [4]. *RTC* has the complexity of $O(n^3)$. RGH is a well-known heuristics for generating better solutions (i.e. MSTs) for low-range diameter on Euclidean instances for BDMST problem. We consider RGH for both Euclidean and non-Euclidean instances for our bi-objective MST problem to easily visualize the solution characteristics over different diameter range through obtained Pareto front.

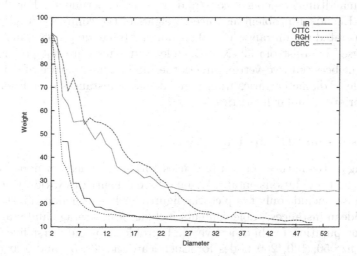

Fig. 3. Pareto front obtained from OTTC, IR, RGH and CBRC heuristics for 250 node Euclidean instance

3.4   Center Based Recursive Clustering

Nghia and Binh [5] proposed *Center Based Recursive Clustering* (*CBRC*) heuristic based on *RGH* or *RTC*. The concept of center changes in each level with the growing spanning tree. This algorithm recursively cluster the vertices of the graph, in that every in-node of the spanning tree is the center of the sub-graph; this sub-graphs composed of nodes in the subtree rooted at this node. The inspiration of introducing CBRC came from the obseravation [4,12] that good solutions for *BDMST* problem have *"star-like structures"*. In a *star-like structure*, each cluster formed with its own center, joining those centers form a complete structure. The complexity of this algorithm is no more than $O(n^3)$. CBRC is the recent existing heuristic for BDMST problem. Some work [5,8] has been done on both Euclidean and non-Euclidean instances. Thus we consider CBRC for our bi-objective MST problem.

4   Experiments

4.1   Problem Instances

In this paper, we consider complete Euclidean and complete Non-Euclidean graphs. In case of a Euclidean graph, a point in 2D plane, i.e. having x and y co-ordinate values represents a vertex and the straight-line connecting two such points represents an edge. The Euclidean distance is considered as weight of that edge. Here, we consider all points of the Eulidean graphs fall in unit square range. In case of Non-Euclidean graphs, a vertex is represented by positive numbers and the weight of an edge connecting two vertex is considered as a random weight.

We have used the benchmark Euclidean problem instances, downloadable from http://tomandtun.googlepages.com/phd, for our experiments. For 20 and 50 node non-Euclidean problem instances, weights of the complete graphs are randomly generated within range [0.01,0.99] and for 100 node problem instances are same as used by Julstrom [3]. Non-Euclidean instances are not position-based, only weight between two vertex directs the MST. Thus, nature of solutions on wide range of diameter varies from non-Euclidean instances over Euclidean instances for even similar heuristics.

4.2   Results and Discussion

Depending on the nature of input instances (either Euclidean or non-Euclidean), the nature of the solutions obtained from different heuristics varies. Due to space limilation, we include only few pictorial figures for both Euclidean instances and non-Euclidean instances; table contents include best, average and standard deviation computation for bi-objective MST problem for only first five instances of input size 50, 100, 250 nodes for Euclidean and 20, 50 and 100 nodes for non-Euclidean complete graphs. The best, average and standard deviation are taken accross the diameter range instead for a single diameter value. As the

Table 1. Results of OTTC, IR, RGH, CBRC on 5 Euclidean instances of bi-objective minimum spanning tree problem of size 50, 100 and 250 [The subscript over the size indicates a different instance]

Instance	OTTC			IR			RGH			CBRC		
$Size_{Instance}$	Best	Avg	SD	Best	Avg	SD	Best	Avg	SD	Best	Avg	SD
50_1	5.0	9.2	4.4	5.0	6.8	2.0	6.3	8.5	3.9	8.6	9.8	2.6
50_2	5.1	8.2	3.9	5.2	7.2	3.1	6.3	8.3	3.5	9.1	10.0	1.9
50_3	4.4	8.0	3.8	5.0	6.6	2.0	6.1	8.2	3.6	7.8	8.7	2.2
50_4	4.6	8.3	3.8	4.6	6.5	2.2	5.8	7.54	3.0	7.9	8.5	1.9
50_5	5.0	8.7	4.1	5.1	7.0	2.9	6.2	8.18	3.5	8.1	9.2	2.1
100_1	6.6	12.9	8.9	6.7	10.2	7.5	8.4	12.1	7.1	14.1	15.2	3.8
100_2	6.8	11.7	7.3	6.9	9.1	3.5	8.8	12.0	6.4	13.0	14.3	3.5
100_3	6.8	14.6	9.1	6.8	9.9	5.4	8.8	12.6	7.4	13.6	15.2	4.3
100_4	6.8	13.6	8.4	6.8	10.4	6.1	8.9	12.3	7.0	12.9	14.2	3.8
100_5	6.9	13.1	8.4	6.9	10.0	5.2	8.9	12.7	7.3	12.6	14.1	4.0
250_1	11.7	39.9	24.3	10.6	16.2	10.8	14.9	35.4	25.7	27.1	33.0	12.7
250_2	12.6	43.5	24.4	10.4	15.7	9.8	15.0	34.6	25.7	25.9	30.4	12.4
250_3	11.9	41.6	23.0	10.4	14.1	6.9	14.7	33.4	24.8	25.4	30.4	12.5
250_4	13.9	42.1	24.3	10.8	15.2	9.5	15.0	35.3	26.5	25.7	30.7	13.0
250_5	12.8	39.8	24.3	10.6	16.0	13.3	14.9	32.7	24.4	27.7	32.4	11.6

diameter bound changes from D to D+1, the heuristics generates a different set of MSTs (few MSTs may overlap) with different diameter. Therefore, we have drawn Pareto curve taking lower-cost MST among a set of MSTs at a constraint diameter. It is possible to get an MST with lower-cost in lower diameter than current diameter constraint due to the change of diameter bound and different MST with different diameter are generated. This procces leads to the non-smoother Pareto curves. In this way, we can assess performance of different heuristics over wide range of diameter bound.

Performance on Euclidean instances. We plot the Pareto front generated by OTTC, IR, RGH and CBRC for 50, 100 and 250 node Euclidean instances in Fig.1, Fig.2 and Fig.3 respectively. Depending on real-life problem domain and real-life constraints, categorization of the diameter range is necessary that will help to choose a particular heuristic from a list of existing ones for a particular problem on demand and provide better solutions. Our experiments over a wide range of instances for each 50, 100 and 250 node Euclidean instance demonstrate that optimal-weight MST can be found within maximum diameter range $(total\ nodes)/2$ to $((total\ nodes)/2) + 5$. Therefore, above this diameter range, expecting a superior low-weight MSTs is meaningless.

In case of diameter = 2, a simple star-like MST is the only possiblity and this leads to equal or near-equal (due to randomness of RGH) weight MSTs obtained from OTTC and RGH heuristics. In this type of cases, heuristics should be chosen by considering the complexity only. Visualizing the Pareto fronts in Figures 1, 2 and 3 chosen randomly among varity of scattered and non-scattered 50, 100

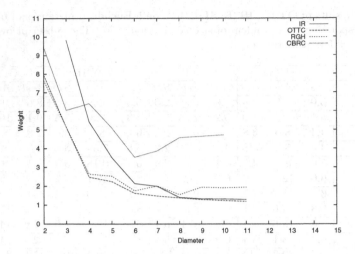

Fig. 4. Pareto front obtained from OTTC, IR, RGH and CBRC heuristics for 20 node non-Euclidean instance

and 250 node Euclidean instances, respectively, it is realizable that for low-range diameter, RGH gives better solutions than IR and OTTC. OTTC and IR, both are greedy heuristics. OTTC is generally based on *Prim*'s minimum spanning tree (*MST*) approach and grow as diameter-restricted tree from a chosen center at initial point. *IR* gives slightly better results than *OTTC* for small diameter for Euclidean instances.

In OTTC, the backbone of the *MST* is constructed using lowest-weight edges near the center. So,the majority of nodes connected to the backbone with large-weight edges (a.k.a longer edges). This nature generates large-diameter spanning trees than shorter for Euclidean instances. The solution of this problem can be considered by including few longer edges to construct the backbone so that it spans the whole area of the graph and majority of nodes connected as leaves with smaller or cheaper edges [13]. With any greedy heuristics, this solution cannot be achieved. *RGH* or *RTC*, the random heuristics has the probability to add few longer edges to the backbone of *MST*. Therefore, *RTC* or *RGH* gives better results than *OTTC* for smaller diameter bound on Euclidean instances. It has been seen that for both scaterred and non-scaterred Euclidean instances, Pareto front obtained by RGH is good for diameter range 3 to $\sqrt{total\ nodes}$. Due to its randomness, above this diameter range upto a few diameter RGH Pareto front tends to show little bit poor results than IR and later it does not generates spanning trees for higher range diameter as mentioned above where optimal MST can be found. Diameter range starts after $\sqrt{total\ nodes}$ to optimal valid diameter range IR and OTTC shows nearequal MSTs. Mostly in this range, MSTs obtained using IR heuristics are slightly low-weight than MSTs generated by OTTC.

CBRC is the recently proposed heuristics [5] to provide solutions to the BDMST problems. Its performance varies depending on the size of the

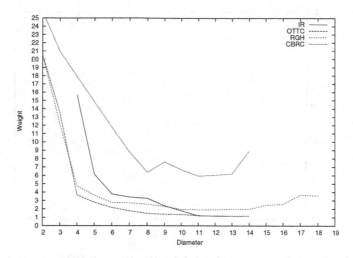

Fig. 5. Pareto front obtained from OTTC, IR, RGH and CBRC heuristics for 50 node non-Euclidean instance

tournament pool which is h% chosen intially to select the center during the algorithm run for growing the MST. As we are recasting the BDMST problem to bi-objective MST problem and providing solution in the pictorial form of Pareto front over wide range of diameter no biasing is considered; we choose h% as zero value i.e. first minimum-distance vertex is chosen for upgrowing MST during a single run. The nature of clustering tends to add minimum distance edges first when h% equals zero value. It gives better solutions than OTTC from starting possible diameter range to middle of the our mentioned valid diameter range for Euclidean instances. After that range it tends to stick with its last better result. When h% taken as zero value, CBRC generates poor solutions than RGH and IR.

The best, average value and standard deviation is shown in Table 1 for first five Euclidean instances of size 50, 100 and 250. Standard deviation is computed considering bi-objective MSTs i.e. MSTs over entire range of diameter where minimum MSTs are found is considered and this causes high value for standard deviation for all heuristics. Best valued MSTs are from OTTC for smaller size instances whereas higher size of instances, IR generated best-valued MSTs. Average and standard deviation are always better for IR than OTTC, RGH and CBRC (h% = zero).

Performance on Non-Euclidean instances. The pictorial figure of solutions i.e. the Pareto front over one 20 node, 50 node and 100 node non-Euclidean instance are drawn in Fig.4, Fig.5 and Fig.6 respectively. In small-diameter range, OTTC and RGH generates almost similar results; IR gives a little poorer result. But, as the diameter range increases, OTTC and IR tend to show better results than RGH. Considering the entire possible diameter range, OTTC shows better result than IR, RGH and obviously CBRC. The tendency to form

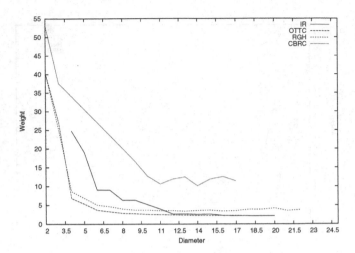

Fig. 6. Pareto front obtained from OTTC, IR, RGH and CBRC heuristics for 100 node non-Euclidean instance

greedy-backbone when adding new vertex into growing MST helps OTTC to provide better solutions for non-Euclidean instances through its Pareto front than randomized RGH.

The best, average value and standard deviation are shown in Table 2 for first five non-Euclidean instances of size 20, 50 and 100. Standard deviation is

Table 2. Results of OTTC, IR, RGH, CBRC on 5 Non-Euclidean instances of bi-objective minimum spanning tree problem of size 20, 50 and 100 [The subscript over the size indicates a different instance]

Instance	OTTC			IR			RGH			CBRC		
$Size_{Instance}$	$Best$	Avg	SD	$Best$	Avg	SD	$Best$	Avg	SD	$Best$	Avg	SD
20_1	1.4	3.0	2.55	1.6	2.9	1.4	1.7	3.1	2.1	3.5	5.3	2.2
20_2	1.8	3.2	2.0	2.5	4.0	1.6	2.0	3.4	1.8	3.7	5.8	3.1
20_3	1.2	2.6	2.1	1.3	3.1	2.7	1.6	2.9	1.9	3.5	5.7	2.0
20_4	1.3	2.9	2.2	1.6	2.5	1.2	1.5	2.9	1.9	3.4	6.1	3.1
20_5	1.1	2.2	2.0	1.1	2.5	1.8	1.4	2.7	1.8	2.3	5.8	3.2
50_1	1.2	4.1	5.7	1.3	4.1	3.5	2.2	4.7	4.9	9.4	14.3	4.8
50_2	1.1	3.7	5.4	1.2	4.2	3.0	1.8	4.2	4.8	7.5	14.2	5.8
50_3	1.1	4.1	5.7	1.2	4.0	4.2	1.7	4.3	4.7	5.9	10.5	6.4
50_4	1.1	3.4	4.5	1.2	3.6	3.9	2.0	4.4	4.5	6.9	15.2	6.1
50_5	1.2	3.7	4.9	1.2	3.3	2.8	1.9	4.4	4.6	5.5	11.8	5.7
100_1	2.2	6.2	10.3	2.2	6.2	10.3	3.6	7.6	9.7	10.7	18.0	13.0
100_2	2.2	6.2	9.70	2.2	6.2	9.7	3.4	7.0	8.7	10.1	18.3	13.3
100_3	2.2	6.3	10.0	2.2	6.3	10.0	3.4	7.3	9.3	9.5	17.4	11.7
100_4	2.0	5.0	8.8	2.0	5.0	8.8	2.9	7.2	9.2	9.7	17.8	13.1
100_5	2.0	5.0	8.6	2.0	5.0	8.6	3.4	7.3	9.2	10.8	20.3	13.4

computed considering bi-objective MSTs i.e. MSTs over entire range of diameter where minimum MSTs are found, are considered and this causes a little bit high value for standard deviation for all heuristics. Consistent best valued MSTs are obtained from OTTC for all instances of different size complete non-euclidean graphs; IR generated best-valued MSTs in few instance but, the diffrence is negligible. Average and standard deviation are better for RGH than OTTC, IR and CBRC (h% = zero) for non-Euclidean instances with smaller node size (say for 20 and 50) because RGH generated a number of MSTs with different variety of lower weights than others throughout the entire diameter range.

5   Conclusions and Future Work

We assess the performance of various heuristics with obtained Pareto front over wide-diameter range instead of assessing the performance of those algorithms for a single diameter as the BDMST problem does. We have drawn Pareto front for both Euclidean instances and non-Euclidean instances. It is easy to visualize which heuristics performs better than other or near-equal to other in a particular range of diamter. Moreover, the best value MST in tables is showing which heuristics can generate best MST over entire range of diameter; average and standard deviation compares the performance of different heuristics over entire range of diameter.

In future, we will include other existing deterministic heuristics and evolutionary approaches in our final work to extend our bi-objective approach and find concrete proposal across the diameter ranges so that in real-life problems where diameter-range is expectedly known, we can use specific heuristics or evolutionary approaches and definitly obtain better solutions.

References

1. Garey, M.R., Johnson, D.S.: Computers and Interactibility: A guide to the theory of NP-Completeness. W. H. Freeman, New York (1979)
2. Deo, N., Abdalla, A.: Computing a diameter-constrained minimum spanning tree in parallel. In: Bongiovanni, G., Petreschi, R., Gambosi, G. (eds.) CIAC 2000. LNCS, vol. 1767, pp. 17–31. Springer, Heidelberg (2000)
3. Julstrom, B.A.: Greedy heuristics for the bounded diameter minimum spanning tree problem. Journal of Experimental Algorithmics (JEA) 14, 1.1:1–1.1:14 (2009)
4. Raidl, G.R., Julstrom, B.A.: Greedy heuristics and an evolutionary algorithm for the bounded diameter minimum spanning tree problem. In: 18th ACM Symposium on Applied Computing (SAC 2003), pp. 747–752 (2003)
5. Nghia, N.D., Binh, H.T.T.: Heuristic algorithms for solving bounded diameter minimum spanning tree problem and its application to genetic algorithm development. Advances in Greedy Algorithms, 586 (November 2008)
6. Julstrom, B.A., Raidl, G.R.: A permutation coded evolutionary for the bounded diameter minimum spanning tree problem. In: Cantú-Paz, E., Foster, J.A., Deb, K., Davis, L., Roy, R., O'Reilly, U.-M., Beyer, H.-G., Kendall, G., Wilson, S.W., Harman, M., Wegener, J., Dasgupta, D., Potter, M.A., Schultz, A., Dowsland, K.A., Jonoska, N., Miller, J., Standish, R.K. (eds.) GECCO 2003. LNCS, vol. 2724, pp. 2–7. Springer, Heidelberg (2003)

7. Gruber, M., Hemert, J.V., Raidl, G.R.: Neighbourhood searches for the bounded diameter minimum spanning tree problem embedded in a vns, ea, and aco. In: GECCO 2006 (July 2006)
8. Binh, H.T.T., Hoai, N.X., Mckay, R.I., Nghia, N.D.: New heuristic and hybrid genetic algorithm for solving the bounded diameter minimum spanning tree problem. ACM, New York (2009)
9. Singh, A., Gupta, A.K.: Impoved heuristics for the bounded diameter minimum spanning tree problem. Journal Soft Computing 11, 911–921 (July 2007)
10. Kumar, R., Bal, B.K., Rockett, P.I.: Multiobjective genetic programming approach to evolving heuristics for the bounded diameter minimum spanning tree problem. In: GECCO 2009 (2009)
11. Kumar, R., Singh, P.K.: On quality performance of heuristic and evolutionary algorithms for biobjective minimum spanning trees. In: GECCO 2007: Proceedings of the 9th Annual Conference on Genetic and Evolutionary Computation, p. 2259. ACM Press, New York (2007)
12. Abdalla, A.: Computing a Diameter-constraint Minimum Spanning Tree. PhD thesis, The School of Electrical Engineering and Computer Science, University of Central Florida, Florida (2001)
13. Gruber, M., Raidl, G.R.: Solving the euclidean bounded diameter minimum spanning tree problem by clustering based (meta) heuristics. In: Moreno-Díaz, R., Pichler, F., Quesada-Arencibia, A. (eds.) Computer Aided Systems Theory - EUROCAST 2009. LNCS, vol. 5717, pp. 665–672. Springer, Heidelberg (2009)

PSO - SVM Based Classifiers: A Comparative Approach

Yamuna Prasad and K.K. Biswas

Department of Computer Science and Engineering, Indian Institute of Technology, Delhi, India
yprasad@cse.iitd.ernet.in, kkb@cse.iitd.ernet.in

Abstract. Evolutionary and natural computing techniques have been drawn considerable interest for analyzing large datasets with large number of features. Various flavors of Particle Swarm Optimization (PSO) have been applied in the various research applications like Control and Automation, Function Optimization, Dimensionality Reduction, classification. In the present work, we have applied the SVM based classifier along with Novel PSO and Binary PSO on Huesken dataset of siRNA features as well as on nine other benchmark dataset and achieved results are quite satisfactory. The results of our study have been compared with other results available in the literature.

Keywords: siRNA, PSO, ACO, GA, LibSVM, RBF.

1 Introduction

Recently, there has been a lot of interest in evolutionary computation for the purpose of data classification. There are large numbers of datasets publically available [6] for the model validation purpose. Ant Colony Optimization (ACO), Genetic Algorithm (GA) and Particle Swarm Optimization (PSO) are well documented in literature for the purpose of combinatorial optimization, routing, scheduling and classification etc. [12-20]. The complexity of ACO is higher than the complexity of GA and PSO whereas the complexity of GA is greater than the complexity of PSO [10, 11, 19], which motivated the researchers to come up with new flavor of PSO algorithm. Khanesar et. al. [17] reported a novel binary PSO algorithm for the purpose of function optimization and presented comparable results with the standard Binary PSO (BPSO) method. He also claims the stability of the novel PSO (NPSO) algorithm for function optimization.

Classification accuracy is majorly dependent upon the goodness of the features. Some of the features may degrade the performance as well. Feature selection is also complex process [4, 10, 18, 19, 20]. Decision about the goodness of features plays vital role in the classification. The problem of deciding the goodness of features has been modeled as feature selection problem.

The problem of feature selection in classification can be defined as "finding minimal feature subset 's' of features from the complete feature set 'S' to achieve maximal classification accuracy. Searching for the minimal subset which maximizes the classification is hard as it requires the computation time of exponential order

S. Ranka et al. (Eds.): IC3 2010, Part I, CCIS 94, pp. 241–252, 2010.

(O $(2^{|S|})$). For feature selection problem, researchers have applied widely known evolutionary and natural computing heuristics like GA, ACO, and PSO etc., [10, 11, 15, 19, 20] for better classification and reported their suitability for the problems associated with large class of research domains like network simulation, anomaly detection, security and vigilance, image classification and Bioinformatics [9,10].

Our work is directed towards the comparative study of the Binary PSO and Novel PSO approaches for the identification of optimal features for the siRNA dataset [2] and nine other benchmark dataset [6]. Since the availability of the siRNA dataset [2], number of research workers has been analyzing this data for better siRNA efficacy prediction [3, 4, 5, 19]. In [5] a SVM classifier has been used on Huesken dataset [2] and presents 77% classification accuracy with certain filtering criteria. This work uses 200 most potent and 200 least potent siRNAs for designing purpose. In the siRNA designing, while sequence based features play significant role to determine the efficacy comparatively [1], the thermodynamic features also play an important role in effective designing [5, 19]. Xiaowei et. al. [5] also brings out the need for feature selection process modeling.

In this work, we have applied NPSO approach [17] for the feature selection along-with SVM classifier unlike the conventional function optimization [17]. We have also shown that SVM classifier for siRNA efficacy prediction coupled with evolutionary computing heuristic significantly improves the prediction results. We are using these to obtain the most appropriate set of features for siRNA efficacy prediction and nine other dataset [6] classifications. We have used RBF kernel for the SVM classifier. We present results for PSO-SVM, NPSO-SVM for ten benchmark datasets. We also compare our results with the published results on the four data sets [5, 15, 19, 20]. A study also has been carried out for the stability prediction of both the models.

2 Methodology

Nature inspired optimization methods like ant colony optimization, genetic algorithm and particle swarm optimization, often based on local neighborhood searches, are rather sensitive to starting point conditions and tend to get trapped in local minima. Conversely, in order to avoid these types of problems Ant Colony Optimization, Genetic Algorithms and Particle Swarm optimization randomizes the search space stochastically and also use the information of previous generation to explore the search space [9, 10, 11, 12, 13, 16, 17] which provides global optima with proper tuning of the parameters. These optimization approaches have been widely used for large class of challenging problems of various domains. We have used binary particle swarm optimization and novel particle swarm optimization (NPSO) for the feature selection. The goodness of the particles in both of the approaches is computed by SVM classifier. The detail descriptions of both of the approaches for optimal feature selection have been described in the subsections below.

2.1 Binary PSO

Particle swarm optimization (PSO) was developed for the solution of optimization problems using social and cognitive behavior of swarm [17]. In PSO each particle has some velocity according to which it moves in the multi-dimensional solution space; and memory to keep information of its previous visited space. Hence, its movement is influenced by two factors: the local best solution due to itself and the global best solution due to all particles participating in the solution space. The algorithm is guided by two factors: the movement of particles in the global neighborhood and the movement in the local neighborhood. In the global neighborhood each particle searches for the best position (solution) and towards the best particle in the whole swarm while in the local neighborhood, each particle moves towards the best position (solution) towards the best particle in the restricted neighborhood (swarm). During an iteration of the algorithm, the local best position and the global best position are updated if better solution is found and the process is repeated till the desired results are achieved or specified number of iterations are exhausted .

Let us consider an N-dimensional solution space. The ith particle can be represented as an N- dimensional vector, $X_i = (x_{i1}, x_{i2}, x_{i3}, \ldots \ldots, x_{iN})$ where the first subscript denotes the particle number and the second subscript denotes the dimension. The velocity of the particle is denoted by a N-dimensional vector $V_i = (v_{i1}, v_{i2}, v_{i3}, \ldots \ldots, v_{iN})$. The memory of the previous best position of the particle is represented by an N- dimensional vector $Pos_i = (p_{i1}, p_{i2}, p_{i3}, \ldots \ldots, p_{iN})$ and the global best position (considering the whole population as topological neighbor) by$Pos_g = (p_{g1}, p_{g2}, p_{g3}, \ldots \ldots, p_{gN})$. Initially particles are distributed randomly over the search space. In the succeeding iterations, each particle is updated by Pos_i and Pos_g values. Each particle keeps track of its co-ordinates in the problem space, which are associated with the best solution (goodness) the particle has achieved so far using Pos_i. The movement of particle is affected by its own best position and global best position. The velocity of the particle X_i at $(k+1)^{th}$ iteration d^{th} dimension is updated by:

$$v_{id}^{k+1} = \omega * v_{id}^{k} + r_1 * \alpha * (Pos_{id} - x_{id}^{k}) + r_2 * \beta * (Pos_{gd} - x_{id}^{k}) \qquad (1)$$

The corresponding position of the particle is updated by:

$$x_{id}^{k+1} = x_{id}^{k} + v_{id}^{k} \qquad (2)$$

Where, i = 1, 2, 3, ...m; m being the number of particles and d = 1, 2, 3, ...N is the dimension of a particle; α and β are the positive constants, called cognitive parameter and social parameter respectively which indicates the relative influence of the local and global positions; r1 and r2 are the random numbers distributed uniformly in [0, 1]; and k = 1, 2, 3, ...Max_iteration is the iteration or generation step; ω is called inertia weight [17].

For the problem of feature selection, in binary PSO the particles are represented by a vector of binary values '1' or '0' which suggests the selection and removal of particular feature in the feature vector represented by the particles. The velocity and particle updating for binary PSO are the same as in the case of continuous one. However, the final decisions are made in terms of the output generated by Sigmoid function [16, 17] based on the probabilistic decision induced by the velocity vector.

$$S(v_{id}^{k+1}) = \frac{1}{1 + e^{-v_{id}^{k+1}}} \qquad (3)$$

The particles select the feature according to the value obtained by the equation (3) from 0 to 1 as follows:

$$x_{id}^{k+1} = \begin{cases} 1 & if\ r < S(v_{id}^{k+1}) \\ 0 & oteherwise \end{cases} \tag{4}$$

Where, 'r' is the random number generated in the range [0, 1]; $S(v_{id}^{k+1})$ is the sigmoid value generated using velocity component of the particle for each dimension. If $S(v_{id}^{k+1})$ is larger than a randomly produced disorder number that is within [0, 1] in the particular dimension, then the corresponding feature is selected otherwise it is dropped. Details can be found in [15].

2.2 Novel PSO

In the NPSO (a modified BPSO) approach for the function optimization, Khanesar et. al. [17] suggested the different interpretation of swarm velocity. The velocity of a particle is its probability to change its state from its previous state to its complement value, unlike the probability of change to 1. Two velocity vectors $V_i^0 = (v_{i1}^0, v_{i2}^0, v_{i3}^0, \ldots \ldots \ldots v_{iN}^0)$ and $V_i^1 = (v_{i1}^1, v_{i2}^1, v_{i3}^1, \ldots \ldots \ldots v_{iN}^1)$ for each ith particle are introduced. V_i^0 is the probability of the bits of ith particle to change to zero while V_i^1 represents the probability that bits of ith particle change to one. The probability of change in d^{th} bit of ith particle at $(k+1)^{th}$ iteration is simply defined as follows:

$$v_{id}^{f,k+1} = \begin{cases} v_{id}^{1,k+1}, & if\ x_{id}^k = 0 \\ v_{id}^{0,k+1}, & if\ x_{id}^k = 1 \end{cases} \tag{5}$$

Consider that the dth bit of ith best particle (Pos_{id}) is one. So to guide the dth bit of ith particle to its best position, the velocity of change to one (V_i^1) for that particle 'i' increases and the velocity of change to zero (V_i^0) is decreases. Using this concept following rules for the purpose of velocity update of V_i^0 and V_i^1, has been extracted:

$$if\ Pos_{id} = 1\ then\ D_{id,1}^1 = \alpha * r_1\ and\ D_{id,1}^0 = -\alpha * r_1$$
$$if\ Pos_{id} = 0\ then\ D_{id,1}^0 = \alpha * r_1\ and\ D_{id,1}^1 = -\alpha * r_1$$
$$if\ Pos_{gd} = 1\ then\ D_{id,2}^1 = \beta * r_2\ and\ D_{id,2}^0 = -\beta * r_2$$
$$if\ Pos_{gd} = 0\ then\ D_{id,2}^0 = \beta * r_2\ and\ D_{id,2}^1 = -\beta * r_2$$

Where D_{id}^1 and D_{id}^0 are two temporary values and all the other parameters has the same interpretation as in the BPSO approach. The velocities V_i^0 and V_i^1 are computed as follows:

$$v_{id}^{1,k+1} = \omega * v_{id}^{1,k} + D_{id,1}^1 + D_{id,2}^1 \tag{6}$$

$$v_{id}^{0,k+1} = \omega * v_{id}^{0,k} + D_{id,1}^0 + D_{id,2}^0 \tag{7}$$

In fact, in this approach if the dth bit in the global best variable (Pos_{gd}) is zero or if the dth bit in the corresponding personal best variable (Pos_{id}) is zero the velocity (v_{id}^0) is increased. And the probability of changing to one is also decreases with the same rate and if the dth bit in the global best variable (Pos_{gd}) is one v_{id}^1 is increased and v_{id}^0

decreases. In this approach previously found direction of change to one or change to zero for a bit is maintained and used so particles make use of previously found direction. After updating velocities of particles, V_i^0 and V_i^1, the final velocity $V_i^f = (v_{i1}^f, v_{i2}^f, v_{i3}^f, \dots\dots v_{iN}^f)$ is obtained as in (5). For the purpose of feature selection, we normalize the final velocity V_i^f unlike the velocity in BPSO, using sigmoid function as in equation 3. The particles select the feature according to equation (8) as below.

$$x_{id}^{k+1} = \begin{cases} \tilde{x}_{id}^k & if \ r < v_{id}^f \\ x_{id}^k & otehrwise \end{cases} \tag{8}$$

Where, $\tilde{x}_{id}$ is the 2's complement of x_{id} and r is uniform random number between 0 and 1.

The inertia term 'ω' used maintains the previous direction of bits of particle to the personal best bit or global best bit whether it is 1 or 0 [17]. The Pos_i and Pos_g are updated according to the BPSO. The interpretation of velocity in NPSO approach is same as in the continuous PSO which is the rate of change in particle's position as in continuous PSO if the maximum velocity value considered is large, random search will happen. Small values for maximum velocity cause the particle to move less [17]. In NPSO approach, the previous states of the bits (feature) of the particles are also taking into account. Using the equation (6) and equation (7) the previous value of the particle is taken into account, while in BPSO just velocity decides that which feature should be include and which should not. The validity and suitability of the NPSO approach for feature selection is carried out through the experiments which are explained in the section representing implementation and results.

2.3 SVM

Generally machine learning methods are used to identify the pattern in the input dataset. SVM, Support vector machines (SVM), developed by Vapnik 1963, are a group of supervised learning methods that can be applied to classification or regression [8]. SVMs classify the input dataset as a vector in the multidimensional space with the construction of maximal-margin in hyper-planes between the two datasets. This provides better classification, as an assumption that the maximum distance between the data margin leads less generalization error, thus improves the classification accuracy. LibSVM [7] is an integrated software for support vector classification, (C-SVC, nu-SVC), regression (epsilon-SVR, nu-SVR) and distribution estimation (one-class SVM).

In this work, we have applied the SVM classifier for evaluating the goodness in both of the methodology described earlier. We have pipelined the SVM classifier of LibSVM library with the feature selection methodologies presented earlier.

2.4 Proposed Hybrid Model

We have proposed two models BPSO-SVM and NPSO-SVM for classification.

The goodness of the feature subset is evaluated by SVM classifier using radial basis function kernel and 10-fold cross-validation. In both the approaches initially a population of particles is generated randomly using uniform random number generator. Then goodness of each particle is evaluated as the testing accuracy obtained through SVM classifier using the radial basis function kernel and 10-fold cross-validation. Further, the local best and global best population is computed using the fallowing rule:

"If goodness is same for two feature subsets then the subset of minimal size is returned, but if goodness and size of the subsets are same then subset with maximal cross validation accuracy is returned."

The new velocity for each particle in the population is evaluated and the particles for next generation are updated. The process is repeated until the convergence/ stopping criteria (number of iterations) is achieved. Finally, the subset which achieves higher accuracy is returned as the optimal feature subset. Figure1 illustrates the working of proposed models.

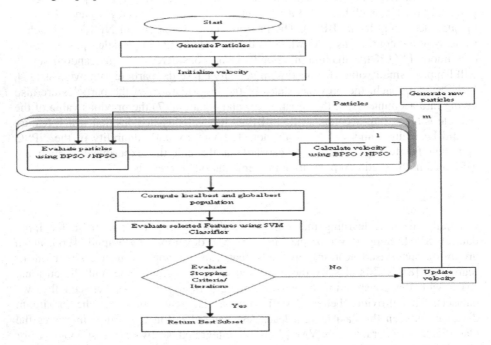

Fig. 1. BPSO/ NPSO –SVM hybrid model ('m' represents the size of population in the figure)

3 Implementation and Results

3.1 Dataset

In our experiment, we have used 10 benchmark datasets [2, 6] namely, the siRNA dataset, wine dataset, breast cancer gene wdbc dataset, heart disease spect dataset, perkinson dataset, ecoli dataset, forest dataset, zoo dataset, glass dataset and iris dataset [6], which have been divided into four groups from group-1 to group -4 according to the number of features described in table 1 below.

Table 1. Description of dataset

Dataset	Number of Samples	Number of Features	Number of Classes	Group Number
Iris	150	4	3	1
Ecoli	336	7	8	2
Glass	214	9	7	2
Forest	517	12	6	3
Wine	178	13	3	3
Zoo	101	16	7	3
Perkinson	195	22	2	4
Spect	267	22	2	4
Wdbc	569	30	2	4
Heuskin	400	110	2	4

3.2 Experiments

The experiments have been conducted in C on Linux platform with gcc compiler. Table 2- table 5 illustrates the values of the parameters tuned for the experiments for BPSO-SVM and NPSO-SVM. For the purpose of the experiment all the parameters of the models have been set according to the table 2 – table 5. The datasets have been randomly divided into two groups, with 70% samples for training and 30% samples for testing. The proposed model computes more stable results as dataset (according to the feature subset) is randomly partitioned into 10 groups, nine of which are used for training and remaining one is used for testing, 10 times and then classification is performed each time then average(10 –fold) is taken as the goodness of the feature subset. Finally the 5 runs of each algorithm are carried out and average result is presented in table 6. The maximum achieved optimal results are illustrated in the table 7.

Table 2. Parameter values of models for Group - 1 dataset

Models	α	β	ω	v (initial velocity)	Pop-size	Max-iteration
PSO -SVM	2.0	2.0	1.0	0.0	5	5
MPSO - SVM	2.0	2.0	1.0	0.0	5	5

Table 3. Parameter values of models for Group - 2 dataset

Models	α	β	ω	v (initial velocity)	Pop-size	Max-iteration
PSO -SVM	2.0	2.0	1.0	0.0	10	10
MPSO - SVM	2.0	2.0	1.0	0.0	10	10

Table 4. Parameter values of models for Group - 3 dataset

Models	α	β	ω	v (initial velocity)	Pop-size	Max-iteration
PSO -SVM	2.0	2.0	1.0	0.0	10	20
MPSO - SVM	2.0	2.0	1.0	0.0	10	20

Table 5. Parameter values of models for Group - 4 dataset

Models	α	β	ω	v (initial velocity)	Pop-size	Max-iteration
PSO -SVM	2.0	2.0	1.0	0.0	20	30
MPSO - SVM	2.0	2.0	1.0	0.0	20	30

The two parameters C and r of SVM classifier has been set to initial value 2^{12} and 16 for the datasets. SVM – classifier tool available in LibSVM package [10] optimizes the parameter value. These values are obtained by carrying out the experiments number of times on small artificially generated data sets.

3.3 Results and Discussions

We have implemented proposed models with radial basis function (RBF) kernel for the SVM- classifier. From the results it can be seen that both of the approaches for classification produces the better results than the conventional hybrid SVM approaches [15, 19, 20]. In the following tables NF stands for number of features, CVA stands for cross validation accuracy and TA stands for test accuracy.

Table 6. Average results of 5 iterations using RBF SVM-classifier

Dataset	BPSO-SVM			NPSO-SVM		
	CVA	TA	NF	CVA	TA	NF
Ecoli	87.667	84.345	5.000	86.467	82.738	4.200
Heuskin	94.667	92.100	56.400	93.778	91.700	55.600
Forest	87.097	83.172	4.000	87.312	82.979	6.000
Glass	71.875	64.953	6.200	72.187	67.103	5.000
Iris	98.519	96.000	2.000	98.371	95.733	3.000
Perkinson	94.023	88.308	10.200	93.908	88.718	10.800
Spect	86.667	81.498	8.600	86.333	81.423	11.600
Wdbc	99.138	97.856	17.000	98.902	97.645	16.000
Wine	100.000	98.876	9.000	99.371	95.955	8.000
Zoo	100.000	97.624	7.200	100.000	99.604	4.600

Table 6 shows that average number of features (NF) computed in five iterations, selected by NPSO-SVM approach for ecoli, heuskin, glass, wdbc, wine, and zoo datasets is better than the average number of features selected by BPSO-SVM approach. The average accuracy of NPSO-SVM approach for ecoli and zoo dataset is higher than BPSO-SVM model whereas for the heuskin, forest, glass, iris, perkinson, spect, wdbc and wine datasets average accuracy achieved by NPSO-SVM in 5 iterations is comparable to BPSO-SVM approach.

The maximum accuracy with reduced size of features achieved by NPSO-SVM is comparable to BPSO-SVM which can be seen in table 7. During the experiments, it has also been observed that the time taken by both of the NPSO-SVM and BPSO-SVM is approximately same.

Table 7. Maximum Accuracy results using RBF SVM-classifier

Dataset	BPSO-SVM			NPSO-SVM		
	CVA	TA	NF	CVA	TA	NF
Ecoli	88.000	86.012	6	87.667	84.524	5
Heuskin	94.722	93.750	58	92.778	92.500	61
Forest	87.097	83.172	4	87.312	82.979	6
Glass	72.396	66.355	5	75.000	68.224	4
Iris	99.259	96.000	1	99.259	96.000	3
Perkinson	93.678	89.231	12	94.253	90.769	12
Spect	87.500	84.644	9	86.667	83.521	10
Wdbc	99.412	98.418	18	99.020	97.891	14
Wine	100.000	98.876	9	99.371	97.753	10
Zoo	100.000	99.010	6	100.000	100.000	4

The observed results have been compared with the results reported by the various researchers. The comparison of proposed model for wine, wdbc and glass datasets is reported in the table 8. The comparison results for the heuskin dataset are presented in the table 9.

Table 8. Comparison of proposed models with previous PSO-SVM models

Dataset	Chung-Jui et. al. [15]	Wen et. al. [20]	Proposed BPSO-SVM	Proposed NPSO-SVM
Wine	100	91.803	98.876	95.955
Wdbc	95.61	97.856	97.856	97.645
Glass	-------	68.056	64.953	67.103

Table 9. Comparison of proposed models with previous SVM model for siRNAa data

Dataset	Xiaowei et. al. [5]	Jain et. al. [19]	Proposed BPSO-SVM	Proposed NPSO-SVM
Heuskin	77.00	71.10	92.100	91.700

From the table 8, it is obvious that the results proposed by our models with the parameters described in table 2- table 5, yield higher accuracy than that reported by Chung-Jui et.al [15] and Wen et. al. [20]. Table 9 shows that the observed results after feature selection have outperformed the results reported by Xiaowei et. al. [5] and Jain et. al. [19].

Further, a study has been carried out for the stability of both models by computing the population goodness during the iterations. Figure 2a and figure 2b represent the stability of both of the proposed models for spect and perkinson datasets, respectively.

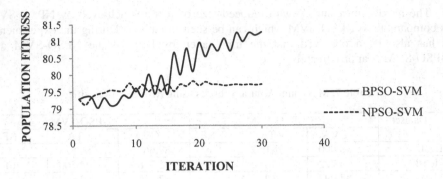

Fig. 2a. Population goodness for SPECT dataset

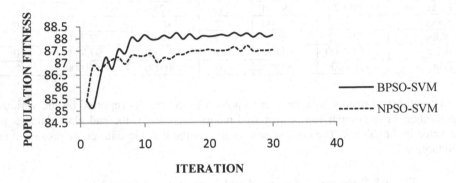

Fig. 2b. Population goodness for Perkinson dataset

From the figure 2a and figure 2b it is obvious that NPSO-SVM model is more stable than the BPSO-SVM model for spect dataset and has comparable stability for perkinson dataset in terms of population goodness. Similar stability pattern of NPSO-SVM over BPSO-SVM model have been observed for the remaining datasets. The results obtained show the higher accuracy than that of the previously reported one. NPSO-SVM and BPSO-SVM both achieve the optimality.

4   Conclusion

In this paper, we have conducted experiment to present the suitability of NPSO for feature selection unlike function optimization [17] along with the SVM classifier and compared the results with the BPSO-SVM model. We have observed that both BPSO and NPSO methods supported by a SVM classifier yield better siRNA efficacy predictions than the previously reported [5, 19]. The accuracy of proposed models is better than Wen et. al.[20] and comparable to Chung-jui et. al.[15] for wine dataset, wdbc dataset and glass dataset. It also shows that appropriate feature selection is carried out for all the data sets. Further, the paper demonstrates the suitability of NPSO algorithm for feature subset optimization. The stability of the NPSO is comparable to BPSO. The obtained results using our proposed models BPSO-SVM and NPSO-SVM describes the significance of both sequence and thermodynamic features [2, 19] in siRNA dataset generated by Hcuskin et. al.[2].

References

1. Saetrom, P., Snove, O.: A comparison of siRNA efficacy predictors. Biochem. Biophys. Re. Commun. 321(1), 247–253 (2004)
2. Huesken, D., Lange, J., Mickanin, C., Weiler, J., Asselbergs, F., Warner, J., Meloon, B., Engel, S., Rosenberg, A., Cohen, D., Labow, M., Reinhardt, M., Natt, F., Hall, J.: Design of a genome-wide siRNA library using an artificial neural network. Nat. Biotechnology 23, 995–1001 (2005)
3. Vert, J.P., Foveau, N., Lajaunie, C., Vandenbrouck, Y.: An accurate and interpretable model for siRNA efficacy prediction. BMC Bioinformatics 7, 520 (2006)
4. Matveeva, O., Nechipurenko, Y., Rossi, L., Moore, B., Sætrom, P., Ogurtsov, A.Y., Atkins, J.F., Shabalina, S.A.: Comparison of approaches for rational siRNA design leading to a new efficient and transparent method. Nucleic Acids Res. 35, e63 (2007)
5. Xiaowei, W., Xiaohui, W., Verma, R.K., Beauchamp, L., Maghdaleno, S., Surendra, T.J.: Selection of Hyperfunctional siRNAs with improved potency and specificity. Nucleic Acids Research 37(22), e152 (2009)
6. Asuncion, A., Newman, D.J.: UCI Machine Learning Repository. University of California, School of Information and Computer Science, Irvine (2007),
   http://www.ics.uci.edu/~mlearn/MLRepository.html
7. Chih-Chung, C., Chih-Jen, L.: LIBSVM: a library for support vector machines (2001),
   http://www.csie.ntu.edu.tw/~cjlin/libsvm
8. Drucker, H., Burges, C.J.C., Kaufman, L., Smola, A., Vapnik, V.: Support Vector Regression Machines. Advances in Neural Information Processing Systems, NIPS 9, 155–161 (1997)
9. Tsang, C.H.: Ant Colony Clustering and Feature Extraction for Anomaly Intrusion Detection. In: Swarm Intelligence in Data Mining, pp. 101–123. Springer, Heidelberg (2007)
10. Nemati, S., Basiri, M.E., Ghasem-Aghaee, N., Aghdam, M.H.: A novel ACO–GA hybrid algorithm for feature selection in protein function prediction. Expert Systems with Applications 36, 12086–12094 (2009)
11. Aghdam, M.H., Ghasem-Aghaee, N., Basiri, M.E.: Text feature selection using ant colony optimization. Expert Systems with Applications 36, 6843–6853 (2009)
12. Yang, J., Honavar, V.: Feature subset selection using a genetic algorithm. IEEE Intelligent Systems 13(2), 44–49 (1998)
13. Zhao, X., Huang, D., Cheung, Y., Wang, H., Huang, X.: A Novel Hybrid GA/SVM System for Protein Sequences Classification. In: Yang, Z.R., Yin, H., Everson, R.M. (eds.) IDEAL 2004. LNCS, vol. 3177, pp. 11–16. Springer, Heidelberg (2004)
14. Raymer, M., Punch, W., Goodman, E., Kuhn, L., Jain, A.K.: Dimensionality reduction using genetic algorithms. IEEE Transactions on Evolutionary Computing 4, 164–171 (2000)
15. Chung-Jui, T., Li-Yeh, C., Jun-Yang, C., Cheng-Hong, Y.: Feature Selection using PSO-SVM. IAENG International Journal of Computer Science 33(1), IJCS_33_1_18 (2007)
16. Liu, Y., Qin, Z., Xu, Z., He, H.: Feature selection with particle swarms. In: Zhang, J., He, J.-H., Fu, Y. (eds.) CIS 2004. LNCS, vol. 3314, pp. 425–430. Springer, Heidelberg (2004)

17. Khanesar, M.A., Teshnehlab, M., Soorehdeli, M.A.: A Novel Binary Particle Swarm Optimization. In: Proc. 15th Mediterranean Conference on Control and Automation (2007)
18. Correa, S., Freitas, A.A., Johnson, C.G.: Particle Swarm and Bayesian networks applied to attribute selection for protein functional classification. In: Proc. of the GECCO 2007 Workshop on Particle Swarms, The Second Decade, pp. 2651–2658 (2007)
19. Jain, C.K., Prasad, Y.: Feature selection for siRNA efficacy prediction using natural computation. In: World Congress on Nature & Biologically Inspired Computing (NaBIC 2009), pp. 1759–1764. IEEE Press, Los Alamitos (2009)
20. Wen, X., Cong, W.: Feature Selection: A hybrid approach based on self adaptive Ant Colony and Support Vector Machine. In: International Conference on Computer Science and Software Engineering (CSSE 2008), pp. 751–754. IEEE Press, Los Alamitos (2008)

Efficient Job Division for Grids Running SIMD Algorithms

Ashish Kurmi[*] and Srinivasan Iyer

Vivekanand Education Society's Institute of Technology,
Sindhi Society, Chembur, Mumbai-71, India
{kurmiashish,srinivasaniyer88}@gmail.com

Abstract. This paper describes two efficient algorithms, namely, the Redistribution algorithm and the Dynamic Grain Size algorithm, to divide large SIMD jobs among the various nodes of a Grid. An implementation (SHA1 hash reversing) of the algorithms on an 8 machine Grid is then discussed. The total time taken for execution is calculated under several scenarios and a detailed analysis and comparison is then provided. The results show that the Redistribution algorithm performs performs almost optimally. However, the requirements of the Redistribution algorithm may be too strict in practical scenarios and in such situations, the Dynamic Grain Size algorithm comes to the rescue and is only slightly more time consuming (with some exceptional cases).

1 Introduction

A large class of optimization problems[1] require the enumeration and verification of all possible solutions to find the optimal solution. These are easily expressed as parallel algorithms for the SIMD[2] Grid. The job is divided into grains and passed on to individual machines. We thus define a grain to be a packet of possible solutions to the optimization problem, which need to be verified.

The machines used in a Grid are usually not dedicated and their speeds of execution vary with time. This causes several problems, one of them being that it does not allow a one time job distribution. This paper explores several ways of handling these problems.

Most of the research in this area has been diverted towards the efficient scheduling of jobs among the various machines of a Grid, but very few focus on the processing of an individual job by splitting it into subjobs, as we have done. [3] suggests techniques for determining resource imbalances and then migrating jobs by identifying potential job senders and job receivers. We have used a technique similar to this one for our Redistribution algorithm. We have adapted a combination of several techniques employed for Global Grid Scheduling[3] to the scheduling of sub-jobs of a single job.

---

[*] In no particular order.
[1] Especially NP-Complete problems.
[2] Single Instruction Multiple Data.
[3] refer to [3].

S. Ranka et al. (Eds.): IC3 2010, Part I, CCIS 94, pp. 253–264, 2010.

The algorithms presented here are for Compute-Intensive jobs which are themselves very huge and usually require many days for computation. These jobs can be split into many subjobs, unlike the usual variety of jobs whose scheduling is discussed in the papers cited above, thus, giving us better control over the total time taken. There are several other parameters which researchers have taken into account such as job resource requirements and payoff as in [4] and fairness as in [5]. Since all subjobs are equal, these parameters do not apply to our algorithms.

Section 2 describes two solutions to the problem, presents an example to understand the intricacies of the solutions,gives formal algorithms for their implementation and also provides a comparison. Section 3 describes an implementation of the two solutions and the results so obtained are discussed in Section 3.2. An efficient job division algorithm can save a lot of time (in days) when large problems are being solved and this is what gives importance to this study.

2   The Problem and Its Solutions

2.1   Formal Statement

Consider a Grid of N machines, one of them being the Grid Controller and let d be the average network delay to submit a job to a machine. Problem X of input size n has to be solved using this Grid and algorithm A can be used to verify a solution to this problem. Let $H(n)$ be the number of possible solutions to the problem. We have speed profiling functions, $S_i(t) : 1 \leq i \leq N - 1$ which give the number of solutions that can be tested per second at time t by machine i, using Algorithm A. However, these functions are not known to the Grid Controller. The Grid Controller has to allot the $H(n)$ solutions to the machines in such a way that the overall time required to test and verify all the solutions is minimized.

2.2   Description of a Problem Instance

Consider a Grid with 3 nodes and one Grid Controller ($N = 4$). Let there be an average job submission delay of 2 seconds ($d = 2$). The problem requires us to test 120000 solutions ($H(n) = 120000$). These solutions are to be allotted to the 3 machines in such a manner that the overall execution time is minimized. The speed profiles of all the machines are shown in Figure 1. These speeds are measured in *solutions/sec* and are specific to problem X solutions tested using Algorithm A. We assume that all solutions are of the same length and thus, take the same time to be executed.

Sudden changes in machine speeds often occur in practice owing to certain CPU intensive programs being started and it also simplifies[4] the discussion, hence this assumption.

---

[4] But is not a limitation to the algorithms.

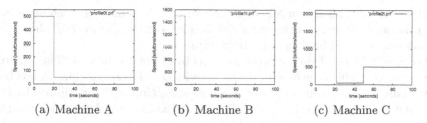

(a) Machine A   (b) Machine B   (c) Machine C

Fig. 1. Speed Profiles

2.3   The Optimal Allotment

The optimal job division algorithm serves as a means of measuring the effectiveness of other job division algorithms. It requires the Grid Controller to be omniscient and thus, know the $S_i : 1 \leq i \leq N - 1$ series of functions.

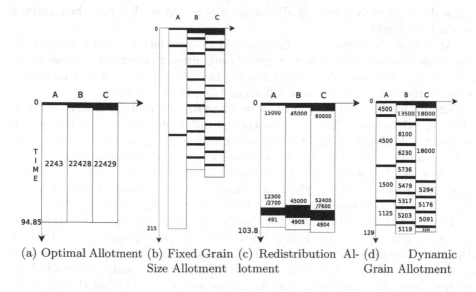

(a) Optimal Allotment (b) Fixed Grain (c) Redistribution Al- (d)   Dynamic
Size Allotment   lotment   Grain Allotment

Fig. 2. The Allotment Strategies

As shown in Figure 2(a), the Grid Controller makes an exact calculation and allots, 2243, 22428 and 22429 solutions to Machines A,B and C respectively. There is a delay of 2 seconds for each job submission. No Algorithm can perform better than this and this is the benchmark for which other algorithms strive. The total time taken is 94.85 seconds.

2.4   Fixed Packet Allocation

This algorithm is discussed in [1] in detail and therefore, its formal algorithm will not be discussed. A suitable grain size is chosen and grains of this size are alloted to the machines in a round robin fashion[5]. As soon as a machine finishes its grain, another grain of the same size is alloted to it. Figure 2(b) shows how the allotment would be done for our example.

Every box in the figure represents a grain of 5000 solutions. The inherent disadvantage of this type of assignment is evident. Though Machine A has been performing badly, as compared to the others since $time = 20$, it still receives the same share of solutions as the rest and owing to that, the total execution time has been stretched to 215 seconds. Machines B and C are idle for a long time while machine A executes slowly. It is to be noted that changing the grain size does have a significant impact on the execution time, however, the Grid Controller, when fixing the grain size, would have no clue as to how each machine is going to perform.

2.5   Grain Redistribution Algorithm

This algorithm strives to keep all machines occupied at all times, thus working towards optimality.

We assume that a one to one mapping exists from the set of whole numbers to the set of solutions to be tested. A grain is submitted to a machine as a sequence of $(Start, Span)$ pairs where $Start$ denotes the solution to begin with and $Span$ denotes the number of solutions following $Start$ to be processed.

The algorithm relies on a probing mechanism, with which, at any point in time, the Grid Controller may stop the operation of a node and request it to return the number and extent of the solutions remaining, and its current speed. Based on this information, the Controller will perform a redistribution.

The style of presenting the algorithm is similar to the one used in [6]. When a probe is executed on a machine, any current grain processing is stopped. The current speed is determined, perhaps, by executing a small test grain[6].

The entire grain is then iterated through, to determine the parts which are yet remaining to be done. This is represented as the sequences St and Sp. A threshold parameter is included so that, in the event of the machine about to complete the grain in t seconds, its grain is not divided and redistributed. In such a case, processing continues. An important thing to be noted is that the time to complete can only be extrapolated using the current speed at this stage. This scenario will be discussed later, alongwith the main algorithm.

The Job Division Algorithm, Algorithm 2 takes a problem instance X and an Algorithm A to verify its solutions, the total number of solutions $total$ and the threshold time t and it determines how the job allocation is to be done. It can be seen as two sections: the Initial Allotment section and the Redistribution Section.

Every machine has $Start$ and $Span$ sequences, which describe the current grain held by the machine. $done$ on every machine holds the number of solutions

---

[5] Other orderings such as fastest machine first may be used to achieve small reductions in time.

[6] This can be done periodically in the background so as to reduce delay.

Algorithm 1. Procedure to probe machines

---
procedure $Probe(Start, Span, done, t)$

Model: Interconnection Network
Input:
t (time threshold)
Start (List of Start indices) range: $P_i, 1 \leq i \leq 7$
Span (List of Spans) range: $P_i, 1 \leq i \leq 7$
done (Solutions already tested) range: $P_i, 1 \leq i \leq 7$

Output:
S (Current Speed)
H (number of solutions remaining)
St (List of Start indices of solutions remaining
Sp (List of Spans for each Start index)

```
 1: StopProcessing()
 2: S ← GetSpeed()
 3: k ← 0
 4: H ← 0
 5: for 1 ≤ i ≤ size(Start) do
 6:     for  Start[i] ≤ j ≤ Start[i] + Span[i] − 1 do
 7:         k ← k + 1
 8:         if k > done then
 9:             Add(St, j)
10:             Add(Sp, Start[i] + Span[i] − j)
11:             H ← H + Start[i] + Span[i] − j
12:             break
13:         end if
14:     end for
15: end for
16: esttime ← H/S
17: if esttime ≤ t then
18:     H ← 0
19:     St ← Sp ← NULL
20:     ContinueProcessing()
21: end if
end Probe
```

Algorithm 2. Procedure for Redistribution of grains

---

function $PacketRedistribute(X, A, total, t, Start, Span, done, running)$

Model: Interconnection Network
Input:
front end variables: X (A problem instance to be Solved), A (Solution verification algorithm) , total (the total number of solutions) ,t (time threshold)
Start (List of Start indices) range: $P_i, 1 \leq i \leq 7$
Span (List of Spans) range: $P_i, 1 \leq i \leq 7$
done (Number of solutions done) range: $P_i, 1 \leq i \leq 7$
running (Grain is being processed) range: $P_i, 1 \leq i \leq 7$

1: **for** $P_i, 1 \leq i \leq 7$ **do**
2:     $S[i] \leftarrow GetSpeed()$
3:     $speedsum \leftarrow speedsum + S[i]$
4: **end for**
5: $sstart \leftarrow 0$
6: $ttotal \leftarrow total$
7: **for** $P_i, 1 \leq i \leq 7$ **do**
8:     $sstart \leftarrow tstart \leftarrow tspan \leftarrow NULL$
9:     $gsize \leftarrow \lceil S[i] * total/speedsum \rceil$
10:    $Add(tstart, sstart)$
11:    $gsize \leftarrow GetGrainSize(gsize, ttotal, sstart)$
12:    $Add(tspan, gsize)$
13:    $ProcessGrain(X, A, P_i : Start, P_i : Span, tstart, tspan, P_i : done, P_i : running)$
14: **end for**
15: **while** $true$ **do**
16:    **if** P_i not in use **then**
17:        $speedsum \leftarrow hashsum \leftarrow 0$
18:        $tStart \leftarrow tSpan \leftarrow NULL$
19:        **for** $P_i, 1 \leq i \leq 7$ **do**
20:            $(S[i], H[i], St, Sp) \leftarrow Probe(P_i : Start, P_i : Span, P_i : done, t)$
21:            $speedsum \leftarrow speedsum + S[i]$
22:            $hashsum \leftarrow hashsum + H[i]$
23:            $Add(tStart, St)$
24:            $Add(tSpan, Sp)$
25:        **end for**
26:        **if** $hashsum = 0$ **then**
27:            $break$
28:        **end if**
29:        $thashsum \leftarrow hashsum$
30:        **for** $1 \leq i \leq 7$ **do**
31:            $tstart \leftarrow tspan \leftarrow NULL$
32:            $gsize \leftarrow \lceil S[i] * hashsum/speedsum \rceil$
33:            $gsize \leftarrow GetGrainSize(gsize, thashsum, sstart)$
34:            $(tstart, tspan) = GetStartSpan(tStart, tSpan, sstart, gsize)$
35:            $ProcessGrain(X, A, P_i : Start, P_i : Span, tstart, tspan, P_i : done, P_i : running)$
36:        **end for**
37:    **end if**
38: **end while**

---

end $PacketRedistribute$

---

tested in the current grain and *running* is true if solutions are currently being processed by the machine.

The Initial Allotment section first sends a tiny test grain to every machine to determine its speed. For every machine i, the grain size *gsize* is calculated using the simple ratio method. *tstart* and *tspan* are temporary collectors for the grain sequences and are used because, when a job is started on the remote machine using **ProcessGrain**, a former job may already be running and thus, the new grain must be attached to the previous grain and cannot overwrite the previous grain. *GetGrainSize()* is used to handle the boundary cases, where *gsize* may not be available to allot. It modifies the *start* and *hashremaining* inputs accordingly. Ultimately, the **ProcessGrain** function is called to start the job on the Grid node.

In the Redistribution Section, a machine which has finished its grain is picked up. A probe request is then sent to every other machine. The grain sequences returned by them are collected in tStart and tSpan. Note that if a machine claims that it will finish before the threshold, it does not return any grain sequences, however, it will be a candidate for the redistribution. The grain sequences so obtained are now redistributed in a fashion similar to the initial allotment, however, since we now have a non-contiguous sequence of solutions to be alloted, we require a function **GetStartSpan** to handle the case.

When none of the probes return any grain sequences, all machines claims that they will finish before the threshold, and the Grid Controller has finished its job. It may be necesary to continue to probe every t seconds till all machines truly finish.

And now, for sake of completeness, we discuss the **ProcessGrain** routine.

The procedure accepts a problem instance X and a verification algorithm A and using it, verifies the solutions represented by the $(Start, Span)$ sequence. The main section is the double for loop, where it loops through the whole numbers representing the solutions, runs A on them and checks if the solution is correct. If yes, it is added to the list of solutions, C. The *done* counter is appropriately incremented.

The initial portion of the routine is interesting. Since the **ProcessGrain** routine may be called on a machine even when a prior call is active, the *running* flag will cause the new call to add the new grain to the previous grain and exit.

Considering the same example that we have been using and setting a threshold of 15 seconds, this results in an allotment pattern as shown in Figure 2(c)

From a peek at the initial speeds, the machines A, B and C are alloted 15000, 45000 and 60000 size grains respectively. Machine B is the first to finish its grain. 2700 solutions from A and 7600 solutions from C are redistributed and the three machines are now alloted 491, 4905 and 4904 size grains respectively. Again, machine A finishes first, however, this time, there is no redistribution since machines B and C promise to finish within 15 seconds. One must appreciate the inclusion of the threshold parameter, without which, a redistribution would have occurred after machine A finished its 491, which, clearly would have been wasteful[7].

---

[7] Owing to network delays.

Algorithm 3. Procedure for the processing of grains

---

procedure $ProcessGrain(X, A, Start, Span, tst, tsp, done, running)$

Model: Interconnection Network
Input:
X (The problem instance to be solved)
A (Solution verification algorithm)
Start (List of Start indices) range: $P_i, 1 \leq i \leq 7$
Span (List of Spans) range: $P_i, 1 \leq i \leq 7$
tst (New List of Start indices)
tsp (New List of Spans)
done (Number of solutions done) range: $P_i, 1 \leq i \leq 7$
running (One instance is already running) range: $P_i, 1 \leq i \leq 7$

Output:
C (a list of solutions)

1: **if** $running = true$ **then**
2:      $Add(Start, tst)$
3:      $Add(Span, tsp)$
4:      $exit()$
5: **else**
6:      $Start \leftarrow tst$
7:      $Span \leftarrow tsp$
8: **end if**
9: $running \leftarrow true$
10: $cindex \leftarrow done \leftarrow 0$
11: **for** $1 \leq i \leq size(Start)$ **do**
12:     **for** $Start[i] \leq j \leq Start[i] + Span[i] - 1$ **do**
13:         **if** $A(X, j) = true$ **then**
14:             $C[cindex] \leftarrow j$
15:             $cindex \leftarrow cindex + 1$
16:         **end if**
17:         $done \leftarrow done + 1$
18:     **end for**
19: **end for**
20: $running \leftarrow false$

---

end $ProcessGrain$

The overall time taken is very close to the optimal time of 94.85 seconds, and differs mainly owing to network delays. This would be true even for large solution spaces. Technically, if network delays are ommitted and if probes could be done instantaneously, this algorithm would perform optimally.

2.6 Dynamic Grain Size Algorithm

The Redistribution algorithm , though very efficient, cannot be implemented under several scenarios. Owing to various network related problems, such as

firewalls and NAT schemes, it is not always possible for the Grid Controller
to probe machines. Sometimes, the client nodes request for a job and the Grid
Controller replies with a job. The Controller is unable to initiate any connection
by itself. To handle such schemes without compromising much on the efficiency,
we tweak the Fixed Grain Size Algorithm, and adjust the grain size after every
reply(on finishing a grain) from the nodes.

We observe in Figure 2(b) that machine A's speed has been $50 soln/sec$ since
time 20 and it still get a large grain. This scenario is avoided in the Dynamic
Grain Size Algorithm whose pseudo code is presented in Figure 2(d).

The variables $X, A, Start, Span, total$ and $done$ have the same meanings as
before and the initial node speeds are determined on the first allotment. The
machines are allotted as many solutions as they can solve in time $basetime$.
This is done, so that, after a certain fixed interval, the machine's new speed is

---

Algorithm 4. Procedure for the distribution of grains

function $DynamicPacket(X, A, total, basetime, Start, Span, done)$

Model: Interconnection Network
Input:
X (A problem instance to be Solved) front end variable
A (Solution verification algorithm) front end variable
Start (List of Start indices) range: $P_i, 1 \leq i \leq 7$
Span (List of Spans) range: $P_i, 1 \leq i \leq 7$
done (Number of solutions done) range: $P_i, 1 \leq i \leq 7$
total (the total number of solutions) front end variable
basetime (the size of the time quantum) front end variable

```
 1: starttime ← CurrentTime()
 2: sstart ← 0
 3: while true do
 4:    if total = 0 then
 5:       break
 6:    end if
 7:    if Pᵢ not in use then
 8:       if first allotment to Pᵢ then
 9:          avgspeed = GetSpeed()
10:       else
11:          avgspeed = Pᵢ : done/(CurrentTime() − starttime)
12:       end if
13:       gsize ← avgspeed * basetime
14:       gsize ← GetGrainSize(gsize, total, sstart)
15:       Pᵢ : Start ← sstart
16:       Pᵢ : Span ← gsize
17:       ProcessGrain(X, A, Pᵢ : Start, Pᵢ : Span, Pᵢ : done)
18:    end if
19: end while
end DynamicPacket
```

noted and its grain size is adjusted. When a machine finishes its grain, it notifies the Controller, the algorithm in this case. The machine's average speed is then calculated using the *done* variable of the node.

The grain size is then calculated as the number of solutions that the machine is expected to solve in time *basetime*. The machine is then alloted the grain by calling the **ProcessGrain** function. Note that this **ProcessGrain** function is much simpler than the previous version as only one instance will run at any time on a particular node.

Using this algorithm on our example, the results are as shown in Figure 2(d). All three machines are being utilized more or less equally, except at the end. It can be seen that machine A's grain size is being reduced continuously. If a machine's average speed remains constant in the last grain allotment, and there is no network delay, the completion time would differ from the optimum by a maximum of $base_timeseconds$. It takes longer than the Redistribute algorithm mainly owing to the increased number of grains, thus increasing the network delay, and the possible delay because of the last allotment.

3   An Implementation

This section describes an implementation of the Redistribution algorithm and the Dynamic Grain Size Algorithm. A Grid test bed of 8 machines (7 nodes and one Grid Controller) was used to test the algorithms. Details of setup can be found in [2]. The machines had been so chosen as to represent processing elements with a variety of speeds. We have executed certain CPU intensive programs at particular moments for speed changes. Though there would have been small variations of the speed profile on successive runs, the difference is trivial enough to be neglected.

3.1   The Test Algorithm

The basic problem of SHA1 hash reversing was used as the test algorithm. The objective of the program was to reverse 10000 SHA1 hashes. The character set c for passwords for our implementation was chosen as 'a-zA-Z' and the password length w was set at 4. Thus, the solution space comprises all strings of length 4, formed using characters 'a-zA-Z.' The number of solutions to be tested are 52*52*52*52=7311616. Its implementation is extremely straightforward and will not be discussed.

3.2   Results

The Fixed Grain Size algorithm was run for different grain sizes and the dynamic grain size algorithm for different values of base time. The Redistribution algorithm was run with a threshold of 15 seconds[8]. We have also empirically determined the optimal time required.

---

[8] Varying this makes very little difference in time.

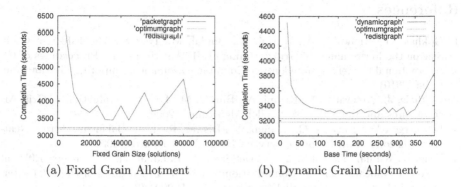

(a) Fixed Grain Allotment   (b) Dynamic Grain Allotment

Fig. 3. Performance Graphs

The results are summarized in Figure 3.

Firstly, we can see that the Redistribution Algorithm (blue) takes a time of 3226 seconds, only 43 seconds more than the optimal value, ie, 3183(green). Thus, this algorithm is extremely effective in solving the job distribution problem.

On Comparing the graphs of the Fixed Grain Size and the Dynamic Grain Size schemes, the dynamic Grain Size scheme proves to be superior. The Fixed Grain Size scheme's completion time varies a lot with the Grain Size. The Grid Controller cannot know what grain size to use. If it chose a grain size of 80000, the completion time would be 4648 seconds, ie. approximately 24 minutes more than optimal.

On the other hand, the Dynamic Grain Size scheme needs us to choose an appropriate base time. However, one can observe that for most of the values of base time, the completion times remains within [3200, 3400]. When the base time is too low, the number of grains are too high and therefore, network delays pull up the completion time. When the base time becomes high grains span a larger time period and thus the probability of the speeds changing within the last allotment becomes higher. With a base time as high as 350, machine A could only get one grain and thus, stretched the completion time. However, under normal circumstances, it is extremely easy to get a base time between these two extremes in a single guess. In this case, considering a completion time of 3400, we are still only 3.6 minutes away from the optimum, as compared to 24 minutes of the Fixed Allocation Scheme.

4 Conclusions

The Redistribution method is an extremely effective technique to solve the Job Distribution Problem and in cases where it cannot be used, the Dynamic Grain Size Algorithm serves as an effective replacement. These algorithms may be used as stepping stones by Intelligent Grid Controllers to obtain maximum utilization of the Grid nodes.

References

1. Gokhale, J., Arsiwalla, A., Kurmi, A., Bindal, M., Iyer, S.: The Effect of Grain Size on the Performance of Grids running SIMD Algorithms. In: Proceedings of the International Conference on Control, Communication and Computing, Trivandrum, India (2010)
2. Gokhale, J., Arsiwalla, A., Kurmi, A., Bindal, M., Iyer, S.: Evaluation of Grid Architectures and the Study of Parallel Algorithms (2009)
3. Leinberger, W., Karypis, G., Kumar, V., Biswas, R.: Load Balancing Across Near-Homogeneous Multi-Resource Servers. IEEE, Los Alamitos (2000)
4. Kale, L., Kumar, S., Potnuru, M., DeSouza, J., Bandhakavi, S.: Faucets: Efficient Resource Allocation on the Computational Grid. In: Proceedings of the 2004 International Conference on Parallel Processing, ICPP 2004 (2004)
5. Karatza, H., Hilzer, R.: Performance Analysis of Parallel Job Scheduling in Distributed Systems. In: The 36th Annual Simulation Symposium (2003)
6. Kenneth, B., Jerome, P.: Sequential and Parallel Algorithms. Thomson, Brooks/ Cole, Singapore (2003)

A Novel Algorithm for Achieving a Light-Weight Tracking System

Sanketh Datla[1], Abhinav Agarwal[2], and Rajdeep Niyogi[3]

[1,3] Department of Electronics and Computer Engineering,
[2] Department of Electrical Engineering
Indian Institute of Technology, Roorkee
{sankipec,abhiapee,rajdpfec}@iitr.ernet.in

Abstract. Object tracking is fundamental to automated video surveillance, activity analysis and event recognition. Only a small percentage of the system resources can be allocated for tracking in real time applications, the rest being required for high-level tasks such as recognition, trajectory interpretation, and reasoning. There is a desperate need to carefully optimize the tracking algorithm to keep the computational complexity of a tracker as low as possible yet maintaining its robustness and accuracy. This paper proposes a novel algorithm which attempts to attain a light weight tracking system by reducing undesirable and redundant computations. The frames of the video are passed through a preprocessing stage which transmits only motion detected blocks to the tracking algorithm. Further frames containing little motion in the search area of the target object are detected in preprocessing stage itself and are blocked from further processing. Our experimental results demonstrate that the throughput of the new proposed tracking system is exceptionally higher than the traditional one.

Keywords: Video Surveillance, Object Tracking, Appearance models, Block Cluster, Performance.

1 Introduction

The increasing availability of video sensors and high performance video processing hardware opens up exciting potential for tackling many video surveillance problems. It is important to develop robust video surveillance techniques which can process large amounts of data in real time. As an active research topic in computer vision, visual surveillance in dynamic scenes attempts to detect, recognize and track certain objects from image sequences, and more generally to understand and describe object behaviors. The aim is to develop intelligent visual surveillance to replace the traditional passive video surveillance that is proving ineffective as the number of cameras exceeds the capability of human operators to monitor them. In short, the goal of visual surveillance is not only to put cameras in the place of human eyes, but also to accomplish expressways, detection of military targets. A survey on visual surveillance of object motion and behaviors is given in [1] . Real-time object tracking is the critical task in many computer vision applications such as surveillance [2, 3], augmented reality [4], object-based video compression [5], and driver assistance. In its simplest

S. Ranka et al. (Eds.): IC3 2010, Part I, CCIS 94, pp. 265–276, 2010.

form, tracking can be defined as the problem of estimating the trajectory of an object in the image plane as it moves around a scene [6,17]. In other words, a tracker assigns consistent labels to the tracked objects in different frames of a video. Additionally, depending on the tracking domain, a tracker can also provide object-centric information, such as orientation, area, or shape of an object. In the recent decade, different techniques on object tracking are proposed [7,8,9]. Perhaps, the most extensive coverage of different object tracking techniques is covered in [6].

Object tracking is highly computationally intensive task. In real-time applications, only a small percentage of the system resources can be allocated for tracking, the rest being required for the preprocessing stages or to high-level tasks such as recognition, trajectory interpretation, and reasoning. Therefore, it is desirable to keep the computational complexity of a tracker as low as possible. There is a need to optimize tracking algorithms for its real time applications to be feasible. In this paper, we propose a novel framework for object tracking systems that aims at achieving a light weight, computationally inexpensive tracking system. As against traditional tracking systems, the proposed system works in two phases namely, preprocessing phase and iterative tracking phase.

The reminder of this paper is organized as follows. Section 2 describes the general framework of traditional and proposed tracking systems and outlines the differences between them. In Section 3, the first stage of our proposed framework, the Preprocessing phase is described. In section 4, the second phase called Iterative tracking phase is described. Section 5 shows the experimental results demonstrating the superiority of our system over the existing one and section 6 concludes the paper.

2   Traditional vs. Proposed Algorithms

We first describe the traditional framework of tracking systems briefly and then illustrate our proposed framework of tracking systems. We clearly outline the differences and advantages of the proposed technique over the existing one.

2.1   Traditional Algorithm Used for General Tracking Systems

The general framework of a typical automatic VS system is shown in Figure 1. The main video processing stages include background modeling, object segmentation, object tracking, behaviors analysis. Every video surveillance system starts with Motion detection. It aims at segmenting the moving objects from the rest of the image. The process of Motion detection involves Environment modeling, Motion segmentation and object classification. Subsequent processes like tracking and behavior analysis are dependent on it. In [1,10], a good description of video processing in surveillance framework is presented. A brief review of these stages is given below:

Background Modeling. The continuous construction and updating of background models are indispensable to any video surveillances system. The main problem in background modeling is to automatically recover and update background from a dynamically changing video sequence. Changes in the scene such as moved objects, parked vehicle etc. need to be carefully handled so that interesting foreground targets are detected. In paper [11], a framework is presented for recovering and updating background images based on a process in which a mixed Gaussian model is used for each pixel value. An online estimation is used to update background images in order to adapt to illumination variance and disturbance in backgrounds. Paper [12] proposes a simple layered modeling technique to update a background model. In addition, important issues related to background updating for visual surveillance are discussed.

Motion Segmentation. Motion Segmentation in video aims at detecting regions corresponding to moving objects such as humans and vehicles. Most of the segmentation methods use either spatial or temporal information in the image sequence. Some of the commonly employed approaches for motion segmentation are background subtraction, temporal differencing and optical flow.

Background Subtraction is the most popularly used method for motion segmentation, especially in a relatively static background. It detects moving regions in a video by taking the difference between the current frame and the reference background frame. It is simple in approach but is highly sensitive to background illumination changes. In Temporal differencing, the pixel-wise differences between two or more consecutive frames in an image sequence are used to extract moving regions. The temporal difference technique is very adaptive to changes in dynamic environment and another advantage is that it does not make assumptions about the scene. Paper [13] detects moving objects in real video streams using temporal differencing. Here instead of consecutive frames, the video frames separated by a constant time δt are compared to find regions which have changed. In Optical flow methods, the characteristics of flow vectors of moving objects over time are used to detect moving regions in an image sequence. Optical flow based methods can be used to detect independently moving objects even in the presence of camera motion.

Object Classification. The moving regions which are identified in the above steps may correspond to different targets. For example, the surveillance of road traffic scenes include humans, vehicles and other moving objects like flying birds and moving clouds, etc. To further track objects, object classification is essential. Object classification is purely a pattern recognition issue. There are two main approaches for object classification namely shape based classification and motion based classification.

In Shape-based classification, Different descriptions of shape information of motion regions such as points, boxes, silhouettes and blobs are available for classifying moving objects. For example, in paper [13], the area of image blobs is used as classification metric to classify all moving-object blobs into humans, vehicles and clutter. In Motion based classification, Human motion shows a periodic property, so this can be used as strong cue for classification of moving objects. Paper [14] presents a similarity based technique to detect and analyze periodic motion. Here the self-similarity of a moving object is computed, as it evolves over time. For periodic motion, the self-similarity measure is also periodic. The tracking and classification of moving objects are implemented using periodicity.

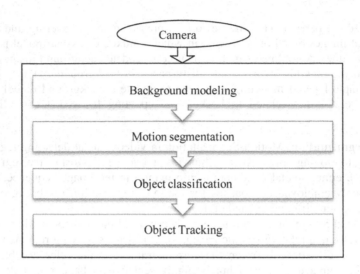

Fig. 1. Traditional Algorithm for Object Tracking

Object Tracking. In a tracking scenario, an object can be defined as anything that is of interest for further analysis. The aim of an object tracker is to generate the trajectory of an object over time by locating its position in every frame of the video.

For at least two decades, the scientific community has been involved in experimenting with Video Surveillance data to improve image processing tasks by generating more accurate and robust algorithms in object detection and tracking [15, 18, and 19] and tracking performance evaluation tools [16]. The tasks of detecting the object and establishing correspondence between the object instances across the frames can either be performed separately or jointly. In the first case, possible object regions in every frame are obtained by means of an object detection algorithm, and then the tracker corresponds to the objects across frames. In the latter case, the object region and the correspondence is jointly estimated by iteratively updating object location and region information obtained from previous frames. Tracking methods are divided into four major categories: region-based tracking, active-contour-based tracking, feature based tracking, and model-based tracking [1].

Region-based tracking algorithms track objects according to variations of the image regions corresponding to the moving objects. For these algorithms, the background image is maintained dynamically and motion regions are usually detected by subtracting the background from the current image. Active contour-based tracking algorithms track objects by representing their outlines as bounding contours and updating these contours dynamically in successive frames. These algorithms aim at directly extracting shapes of subjects and provide more effective descriptions of objects than region-based algorithms. Feature-based tracking algorithms perform recognition and tracking of objects by extracting elements, clustering them into higher level features and then matching the features between images. Model-based tracking algorithms track objects by matching projected object models, produced with prior knowledge, to image data. The models are usually constructed off-line with manual measurement or computer vision techniques. After successfully tracking the moving objects from one frame to another in an image sequence, behavior analysis is done. It involves the analysis and recognition of motion patterns, and the production of high-level description of actions and interactions.

2.2 Proposed Algorithm for Object Tracking

Here Tracking is implemented in two phases namely Preprocessing stage (Phase I) and Iterative tracking stage (phase II). The frames are first passed to a preprocessing stage called Block Motion Detection phase, where motion in the frames are detected in block wise sense and the static blocks (i.e. the blocks containing no motion with respect to corresponding blocks in the previous frame) are removed from the frames for further processing and then passed to Iterative tracking phase. Further, if the search region in the frame (i.e. the region surrounding the object in the previous frame) contains all the static blocks, then the entire frame is removed for further processing and is blocked from passing to the second phase. The steps in the pre-processing phase are broadly divide into Frame Partitioning, Block-wise similarity

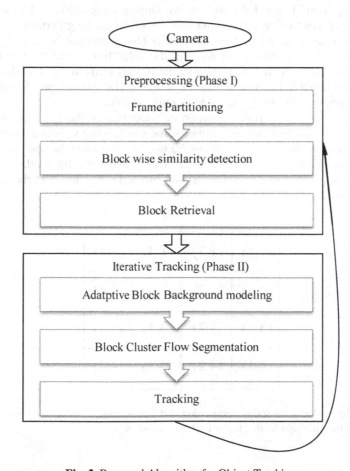

Fig. 2. Proposed Algorithm for Object Tracking

detection and Block retrieval phase. These are shown in Fig. 2. These steps are elaborated in the next section. The second phase is called Iterative tracking phase which operates only on the motion detected blocks that are passed on to it by the above preprocessing stage . It is so named because the object tracker first moves to the centre of every received block in search region and searches for the appearance similarity of the object tracked in the previous frame. If the appearance similarity is greater than a certain threshold in a block, then that object tracker iteratively updates the object position. The object position update is done in a direction such that the appearance similarity is increased. The stages in this Iterative tracking phase are logically similar to the stages in the traditional tracking system but differ in some aspects which will be explained later in the next section.

3 Preprocessing Stage (Phase I)

3.1 Frame Partitioning

The incoming frame is divided into non-overlapping image blocks. The size of the block is an important characteristic and will affect the tracking performance. Bigger blocks are less sensitive to noise, while smaller blocks produce better contours. The next two factors are the amount of noise in the video frames and the texture of the objects and the background. The texture of the objects leads to the so called aperture problem (also found in block matching algorithms). The aperture problem appears in situations where the objects of interest have uniform color.

When the uniform color regions consist of fewer blocks, there is a greater chance that their motion will be detected because some overlapping with non-uniform color regions is likely. A bigger block size can be used to overcome the aperture problem. Once the decision on the block size is made, the frame is logically divided into blocks and each block is assigned a two-dimensional block ID. Any block in the subsequent stages is referred by this block ID.

(1,1)	(1,2)	(1,3)	(1,4)
(2,1)	(2,2)	(2,3)	(2,4)
(3,1)	(3,2)	(3,3)	(3,4)
(4,1)	(4,2)	(4,3)	(4,4)

Fig. 3. The figure shows the frame partitioning and corresponding two dimensional block ID's of a frame (if the no of blocks in a frame is chosen to be 16)

3.2 Block Wise Similarity Detection (Scope for Parallelization)

The similarity between the corresponding blocks in the successive frames is computed. Some of the similarity measures that can be used here are Sum of absolute difference (SAD), Mean Absolute Difference (MAD) and Normalized cross correlation (NCC). We have used Normalized cross correlation in our experiments. The correlation between two blocks is computed in MATLAB using the following code.

```
a = a - mean(a)
b = b - mean(b)
c = sum(sum(a.*b))/sqrt(sum(sum(a.*a))*sum(sum(b.*b)))
```

The function mean calculates the mean of the input matrix. The function sum calculates sum of all elements of the input vector. Here 'a' is the matrix representing the pixel intensities of the block in the present frame and 'b' the matrix representing the pixel intensities of corresponding block in the previous frame. 'c' gives the correlation between the two blocks 'a' and 'b'. The correlation is computed between all the blocks in the present frame and corresponding blocks in the previous frame (as shown in the Fig. 4). This step can be done in parallel. Several parallel programming models like OpenMP, MPI on clusters and Nvidia CUDA on Graphics processing unit (GPU) can be used for parallelization.

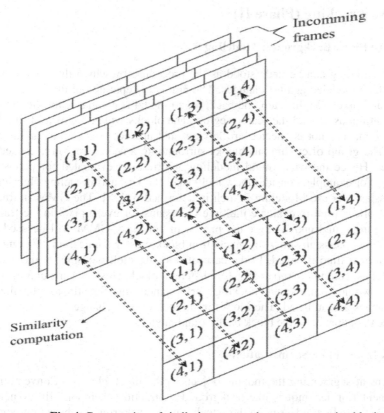

Fig. 4. Computation of similarity measure between successive blocks

3.3 Block Retrieval

The above process produces N (N is equal to the number of blocks in the image) values ranging from 0 to 1 depending on the absolute difference of the two correlated images. A minimum value of correlation called motion threshold is defined to detect motion. In normal cases, motion can easily be detected when the measured minimum cross correlation value of all the N values is used to set the threshold. However, detection fails when images contain global illumination variations or during camera movement. If the correlation of a block with respect to corresponding block in the previous frame is more than the motion threshold, then the block is considered to be static (i.e. motion less) and is removed from the image for further computations. If all the blocks in the search region around the object to be tracked are detected as static, then the corresponding frame is removed and is not passed to the tracking phase. This saves a lot of redundant computation in the tracking phase and facilitates real-time tracking. Thus, only a subset of frames that too containing only a subset of blocks (i.e. the motion detected blocks) are passed to the tracking phase. These subset of blocks in a frame typically consists of the blocks containing the object and blocks containing the holes left by the object movement and other blocks affected by the illumination changes.

4 Iterative Tracking (Phase II)

4.1 Adaptive Block Background Modeling

Background modeling can be understood as the procedure by which the background of a video file is modeled against changes. The aim is to separate out the foreground and background pixels. In this step, the background model is estimated for the blocks which are continuous around the search region. The blocks which are away from the search region and are not connected are left out and are not considered for further processing. The group of continuous blocks surrounding a search region is named a Block cluster. Hence the background modeling algorithm is evaluated for pixels in block cluster. For example, consider the widely used Background modeling algorithm GMM (Gaussian Mixture Modeling) which is described in [28]. The GMM in traditional framework is used to evaluate multiple Gaussians for every pixel in the frame to segregate foreground and background pixels. In our case, GMM will be used to evaluate multiple Gaussians only for pixels in a block cluster. Hence, lot of memory and computational time is saved. In the case of tracking multiple objects, the background model is computed separately for different block clusters surrounding the objects. This would improve the tracking performance significantly as globalized lightning changes are nullified. The blocks in a block cluster changes from frame to frame. Hence the name adaptive block background modeling.

4.2 Block Cluster Flow Segmentation

This step aims at segmenting the moving objects in the block clusters. Conventional motion segmentation techniques like background subtraction, Temporal differencing and optical flow can be used. Among these techniques, Background subtraction works very well . The background model calculated in the previous step is subtracted from the corresponding group of blocks. The image obtained after subtraction is used as a reference image for tracking in the next frame. Several other conventional motion segmentation approaches like temporal differencing may not give satisfactory results because the block clusters around the target object may change from frame to frame.

4.3 Tracking

The position of the reference image obtained from the above segmentation phase is updated over time for every incoming frame. The object tracker moves to every block in the cluster and a similarity measure is computed. If the similarity in a block is less than a certain threshold, then the tracker moves on to the next block in the cluster. If the similarity is greater than the threshold, then the object tracker maximizes the similarity iteratively by comparing the appearance similarity of the object detected in the previous block cluster and the appearance in the window of the present block. At each iteration, the similarity is computed such that the appearance similarity is increased. This process is repeated until convergence is achieved, which usually takes four to five iterations. After the convergence is attained, the block number corresponding to the tracked object location is passed on to the preprocessing stage which will be used to evaluate motion in the new search region for the next frame. The actual position of the object with respect to the entire image is calculated based using the two dimensional block ID (B_x, B_y) , the centroid (C_x, C_y) and the block size (s_1, s_2) as per the below equations.

$$\text{X-coordinate of the object detected} = (B_x - 1) \times s_1 + C_x . \tag{1}$$

$$\text{Y-coordinate of the object detected} = (B_y - 1) \times s_2 + C_y . \tag{2}$$

5 Results

The visual tracker implemented according to the proposed framework was applied to many sequences and for several applications. Here we just present some representative results. We performed experiments both using the proposed tracking framework and the traditional framework for evaluating their relative performances. Compared to the traditional implementation, this new system performed significantly well in terms of throughput. For example, for the simple image sequences with a relatively static background as shown in this Fig. 5, the new system could track well up to 25

Fig. 5. The original frames of the video

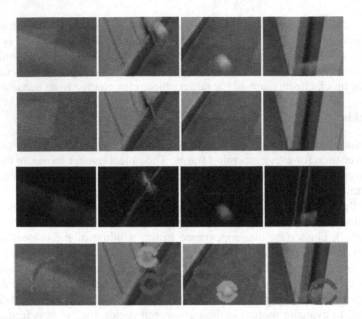

Fig. 6. The frames 5,12, 15, 21 and 32 are shown. First row shows the blocks extracted from the original frames corresponding to minimum correlation. Images in row 2 shows the background extracted, Row 3 images show the difference images and Finally row 4 shows the kalman tracking using our proposed algorithm.

Fig. 7. Multiple object tracker using traditional algorithm

frames/second, whereas the traditional system could track the same sequence only until 15 frames/second on a low end system. The object tracker used in this image sequence is kalman filter which is composed of two steps, prediction and correction step. The prediction predicts the approximate location of the object. The correction step computes the exact location of the object. The prediction and correction steps are shown by the red and green circles in the Fig.6 (row 4) respectively. Fig. 7 shows the tracking of two persons moving in an outdoor environment using the traditional multiple tracker using mean shift iterations. Fig. 8 shows the tracking of same sequence using our proposed framework. The object clusters used for tracking can also be observed.

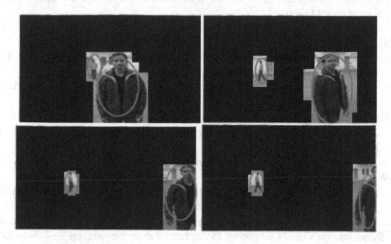

Fig. 8. Multiple object tracker using our proposed algorithm. Block clusters for different objects are shown in each frame.

6 Conclusion

This paper presents a novel generalized algorithm for realising a light weight tracking which greatly reduces the computational complexity and facilitates real time tracking. The system described here ran successfully using several different object trackers. However, though the system performed very well for many conventional trackers, it has certain limitations. All prevailing techniques used for different stages like Environment modeling, Motion segmentation and tracking may not give satisfactory results. For example, Motion segmentation techniques like temporal differencing and optical flow methods may not give satisfactory results because of the block clusters dynamically change in position and shape in every frame.

References

1. Hu, W., Wang, L.T., Maybank, S.: A Survey on visual surveillance on object motion and behaviours. IEEE Transactions on systems, man and cybernatics 34(3), 334–352 (2004)
2. Greiffenhagen, M., Commaniciu, D., Niemann, H., Ramesh, V.: Design, Analysis and Engineering of Video Monitoring Systems: An approach and a case study. Proc. IEEE, 1498–1517 (2001)
3. Collins, R., Lipton, A., Fujiyoshi, H., Kanade, T.: Algorithms for Cooperative Multisensor Surveillance. Proc. IEEE 89(10), 1456–1477 (2001)

4. Ferrari, V., Tuytelaars, T., Gool, L.V.: Real-Time Affine Regiion Tracking and Coplanar Grouping. In: Proc. IEEE Conference Computer Vision and Pattern Recognition, vol. 2, pp. 226–233 (2001)
5. Bue, A.D., Commaniciu, D., Ramesh, V., Regazzoni, C.: Smart Cameras with Real-Time Video Object Generation. In: Proc. of International Conference on Image Processing, vol. 3, pp. 429–432 (2002)
6. Yilmaz, A., Javed, O., Shah, M.: Object tracking- a survey. ACM Computer Surveys 38(4), 1–45 (2006)
7. Commaniciu, D., Ramesh, V., Meer, P.: Kernel Based Object Tracking. IEEE Trans. on Pattern Anal. and Machine Intell. 22, 781–796 (2000)
8. Han, S.A., Hua, W., Gong, Y.: A Detection Based multiple Object Tracking Method. In: Proc. IEEE International Conference on Image Processing (2004)
9. McKenna, S.J., Jabri, S., Duric, Z., Wechsler, H.: Tracking Interacting people. In: Proc. of the International Conf. on Automatic Face and Gesture Recognition, Grenoble, France, March 28-30, pp. 348–353 (2000)
10. Dick, A.R., Brooks, M.J.: Issues in automated visual surveillance. In: DICTA, Sydney, NSW, Australia, pp. 195–204 (2003)
11. Stauffer, C., Grimson, W.: Adaptive background mixture models for real-time tracking. In: Proc. IEEE Conf. Computer Vision and Pattern Recog., vol. 2, pp. 246–252 (1999)
12. Kim, K., Harwood, D., Davis, L.S.: Background updating for visual surveillance. In: First Int. Symosium on Visual Computing, ISVC, Lake Tahoe, Nevada, pp. 337–346 (2005)
13. Lipton, A.J., Fujiyoshi, H., Patil, R.S.: Moving Target classification and tracking from a real-time video. In: Proc. IEEE Workshop Applications of Computer Vision, pp. 8–14 (1998)
14. Cutler, R., Davis, L.S.: Robust real-time periodic motion detection, analysis and applications. IEEE Transactions on Pattern Analysis and Machine Intelligence 22, 781–796 (2000)
15. Tao, H., Sawhney, H.S., Kumar, R.: Object Tracking with Bayesian Estimation of Dynamic Layer Representations. IEEE Trans. Pattern Anal. Mach. Intell. 24(1), 75–89 (2002)
16. Black, J., Ellis, T., Rosin, P.: A novel method for video tracking performance evaluation. In: Joint IEEE Int. Workshop on Visual Surveillance and Performance Evaluation of Tracking and Surveillance (VS-PETS), pp. 125–132 (2003)
17. Moeslund, T., Franum, E.: A survey of computer vision-based human motion capture. Comput. Vision Image Understand 81(3), 231–268 (2001)
18. Mittal, A., Davis, L.: M2 tracker: A multiview approach to segmenting and tracking people in a cluttered scene. Int. J. Comput. Vision 51(3), 189–203 (2003)
19. Maddalena, L., Petrosino, A.: Self-Organizing Approach to Background Subtraction for Visual Surveillance Applications. IEEE Transactions on Image Processing 17(7), 1168–1177 (2008)

Computer Simulation Studies of Drug-DNA Interactions: Neothramycin B

Rajeshwer Shukla and Sugriva Nath Tiwari

Department of Physics
D.D.U. Gorakhpur University,
Gorakhpur-274 009, India
rajshukla_biop@rediffmail.com, sntiwari123@rediffmail.com

Abstract. Neothramycin B is a potential antibiotic drug. It is reported to bind to DNA and thereby inhibits the functions of DNA. In view of this fact, stacking interactions between neothramycin B and DNA base pairs have been evaluated using quantum mechanical methods. Binding patterns, relative stability of various drug-base pair complexes and preferred binding sites of the drug have been presented. An attempt has been made to elucidate the pharmacological properties of the drug.

Keywords: Intermolecular interactions, CNDO, Multicentred-multipole, Nucleic acids, Antibiotic and Computer Simulation.

1 Introduction

DNA is a well-characterized intracellular target but its large size and sequential nature makes it an elusive target for selective drug action. The biological activity of certain low molecular weight antitumour compounds appears to be related to their mode and specificity of interaction with particular DNA sequences. Such small molecules are of considerable interest in chemistry, biology and medicine. Many of the anticancer drugs employed clinically also exert their antitumour effect by inhibiting nucleic acid (DNA or RNA) or protein synthesis. Binding of low molecular weight ligands to DNA causes a wide variety of potential biological responses. [1-4].

Neothramycin B (NB) is a member of the pyrrolo [1,4]–benzodiazepine family. It is an antibiotic drug with potent antitumour, antimicrobial, amebicidal and chemosterilant activities. By virtue of its ability to form complexes with DNA, it inhibits the activity of DNA-dependent RNA polymerase and certain DNA nucleases [5]. With an aim to gain a deeper insight into the molecular basis of drug-DNA interactions,considerable efforts have been made in our laboratory [6-11]. In continuation, the present paper deals with the binding mechanism of neothramycin B with nucleic acid base pairs with an emphasis on the site, mode and structural specificity of the binding patterns.

2 Method of Calculation

The Modified Rayleigh-Schrodinger second order perturbation theory along with multicentred-multipole expansion technique as developed by Claverie and coworkers

S. Ranka et al. (Eds.): IC3 2010, Part I, CCIS 94, pp. 277–283, 2010.
© Springer-Verlag Berlin Heidelberg 2010

has been used to calculate interaction energy between drug molecule and DNA base pairs. According to this, the total interaction energy (E_{TOT}) between two molecules is expressed as:

$$E_{TOT} = E_{EL}+E_{POL}+E_{DISP}+E_{REP}$$

where E_{EL}, E_{POL}, E_{DISP} and E_{REP} represent electrostatic, polarization, dispersion and repulsion energy components respectively [12].

The electrostatic energy term is expressed as:

$$E_{EL} = E_{QQ}+E_{QMI}+E_{MIMI} +\ldots\ldots\ldots$$

where E_{QQ}, E_{QMI} and E_{MIMI} etc. represent monopole-monopole, monopole-dipole, dipole-dipole and interaction energy terms consisting of multipoles of higher orders respectively. However, consideration upto the first three terms has been found to be sufficient for most of the molecular interaction problems [13].

The molecular geometry of neothramycin B has been constructed using the crystallographic data from literature and standard values of bond lengths and bond angles [14]. Net atomic charge and corresponding dipole moment components at each of the atomic centres of the molecule have been computed by CNDO/2 method [15]. During energy minimization, base pairs are kept fixed throughout the process while both lateral and angular variations are introduced in the neothamycin B molecule in all respects relative to the fixed one and vice versa. Accuracies up to 0.1Å in sliding (translation) and 1^0 in rotation have been achieved. The details of the mathematical formalism and optimization process may be found in literature [12,15].

3 Results and Discussion

The molecular geometry of neothramycin B as used for CNDO/2 studies is shown in Fig. 1. The molecular charge distribution is listed in Table 1.

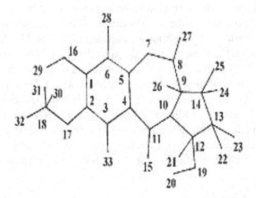

Fig. 1. Molecular geometry of neothramycin B with various atomic index numbers

Table 1. Molecular charge distribution of the neothramycin B molecule

Atom No.	Atom Symbol	Charge (e.u.)	Atomic dipole components (debye)		
			X	Y	Z
1	C	0.145	-0.011	-0.079	-0.024
2	C	0.133	0.094	-0.065	0.052
3	C	-0.011	-0.173	0.002	0.005
4	C	-0.077	0.006	-0.145	-0.078
5	C	0.123	-0.093	0.017	-0.044
6	C	-0.050	0.140	-0.076	0.067
7	N	-0.146	1.526	0.384	0.376
8	C	0.036	-0.112	-0.261	0.408
9	C	0.110	0.162	-0.001	-0.110
10	N	-0.216	-0.001	0.090	0.079
11	C	0.350	-0.043	0.209	0.078
12	C	0.288	-0.010	-0.176	0.140
13	C	-0.012	-0.070	-0.129	-0.014
14	C	0.001	0.117	-0.093	-0.114
15	O	-0.341	-1.299	0.174	0.487
16	O	-0.256	-0.642	1.098	-0.076
17	O	-0.214	0.556	1.211	-0.083
18	C	0.133	-0.329	0.007	0.004
19	O	-0.290	-0.898	-0.891	-0.042
20	H	0.149	0.000	0.000	0.000
21	H	-0.043	0.000	0.000	0.000
22	H	0.020	0.000	0.000	0.000
23	H	0.002	0.000	0.000	0.000
24	H	0.001	0.000	0.000	0.000
25	H	0.003	0.000	0.000	0.000
26	H	-0.010	0.000	0.000	0.000
27	H	0.022	0.000	0.000	0.000
28	H	0.018	0.000	0.000	0.000
29	H	0.132	0.000	0.000	0.000
30	H	-0.009	0.000	0.000	0.000
31	H	-0.012	0.000	0.000	0.000
32	H	0.001	0.000	0.000	0.000
33	H	0.024	0.000	0.000	0.000

(Total energy = -200.26 a.u., Binding energy = -16.69 a.u., Total dipole moment = 3.52 debyes).

As expected, Table 1 shows that atoms such as nitrogen and oxygen always bear electronegative charges while carbon atoms adjust their charges according to their position.

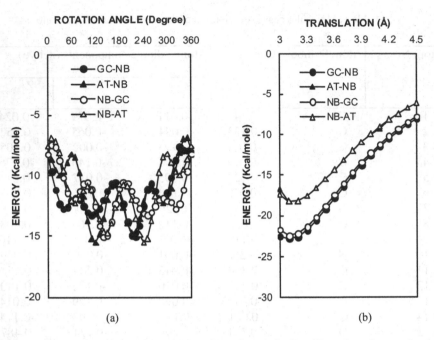

Fig. 2. Variation of total stacking energy of neothramycin B with various base pairs as a function of (a) angular rotation and (b) interplanar separation.

Table 2. Stacking energy of various complexes formed between neothramycin B and DNA base-pairs.

Energy Terms (Kcal/mole)	Stacked Complexes			
	GC-NB (I)	AT-NB (II)	NB-GC (III)	NB-AT (IV)
E_{QQ}	-2.14	-0.56	-2.20	-0.56
E_{QMI}	-3.62	-2.51	-3.45	-2.44
E_{MIMI}	-0.83	-1.92	-0.44	-1.78
E_{EL}	-6.58	-4.99	-6.08	-4.78
E_{POL}	-3.56	-1.76	-3.65	-1.81
E_{DISP}	-27.19	-24.11	-27.68	-24.58
E_{REP}	13.72	12.43	14.16	12.73
E_{TOT}	**-23.61**	**-18.42**	**-23.25**	**-18.48**
Inter-planar separation (Å)	3.1	3.1	3.1	3.1

*drug-base pair inter-planar separation (Å).

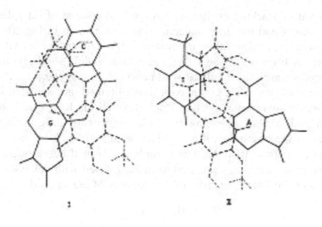

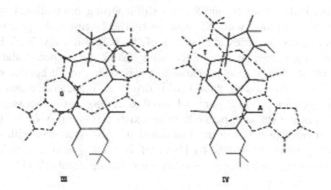

Fig. 3. Stacked minimum energy configurations of neothramycin B with DNA base pairs. The geometry shown by dotted lines represents the upper molecule in each case.

The variation of stacking energy with respect to change of orientation of drug molecule keeping base pairs fixed and vice versa, is shown in Fig.2(a). As evident from this figure, two minima are located for GC-NB complex having energy values -12.78 kcal/mole at 40^0 and -15.09 kcal/mole at 220^0. In case of AT-NB stacking, two minima one at 120^0 with energy -15.52 kcal/mole and the other at 220^0 with energy -14.63 kcal/mole are obtained. Similarly, two minima are located for NB-GC complex having energy values -15.09 kcal/mole at 140^0 and -12.78 kcal/mole at 320^0. In case of NB-AT complex, again two minima are located- one at 150^0 with energy -14.73 kcal/mole and the other at 240^0 with energy -15.52 kcal/mole. Although two minima are located by each curve, these minima are separated nearly by a difference of 3.0 kcal/mole in case of GC base pairs while in case AT base pairs the energy difference between the minimum positions is reduced to approximately 1.0 kcal/mole. The minima having lower energy values have been chosen for further refined calculations.

The variation of stacking energy with respect to change of interplanar separation between base pairs and the drug molecule has been shown in Fig.2(b) which shows that all the complexes exhibit their minima at 3.1Å. The energy for GC-NB and NB–GC complexes is found to be the same (–22.8 kcal/mole). Similarly, the AT-NB and NB-AT complexes are also stabilized with nearly the same energy, –18.22 kcal/mole. The minimum energy stacked complexes, thus obtained, are depicted in Fig.3 which shows that neothramycin B molecules stack through the hydrogen bonded region of base pairs in all the cases. The long molecular axis of the drug molecule lies nearly perpendicular to the base pair tilt axis. The details of stacking energy are listed in Table 2. It is clear from the table that complexes formed between the drug and GC base pairs are more stable as compared to those formed with AT base pairs. Further, Table 2 indicates the following order of the stability of the stacked complexes:

$$ I \geq III > IV \geq II $$

It seems worthwhile to mention that the dispersion component plays a dominant role in stabilizing all the complexes and electrostatic energy is largest (-6.58 kcal/mole) in case of GC-NB complex. These results suggest that complexes formed with GC base pair are energetically more favoured and exhibit strong orientational specificity as compared to those formed with AT base pair. The largest stability contribution is derived from dispersion forces irrespective of the base pairs involved. Further, it is observed that long molecular axis of the drug lies nearly perpendicular to the base pair tilt axis and stacking occurs primarily through the hydrogen-bonded region of the base pairs. Thus binding of neothramycin B drug in a dinucleotide unit having guanine and cytosine bases will be more stabilized as compared to other sequences. Also as observed from the stacking patterns, there exists a possibility of the bond formation/ due to interaction between the functional groups associated with the chromophore of the drug molecule and the backbone of the nucleic acid helices. These results are similar to those obtained in case of other intercalating agents [6-11].

4 Conclusion

The present study reveals that binding of neothramycin B (NB) to GC rich region of nucleic acid helices is more preferred and the mode of binding is similar to other intercalating agents such as ellipticines etc. The largest stability contribution is derived from dispersion forces irrespective of the base pairs involved. Also as observed from the stacking patterns, there exists a possibility of the bond formation/ interaction between the functional groups associated with the chromophore of the drug molecule and the backbone of the nucleic acid helices. Therefore, intercalative binding may be held responsible for the pharmacological properties of the drug.

Acknowledgments

SNT and RS are thankful to the Department of Science and Technology, New Delhi for financial support in the form of a research project (Reference No. SP/SO/D-12/95).

References

1. Saenger, W.: Principles of Nucleic Acid Structure. Springer, New York (1984)
2. Maiti, M.: Perspectives in Structural Biology, p. 583. Universities Press, India (1999)
3. Haq, I., Ladbury, J.: J. Mol. Recognit. 13, 188 (2000)
4. Kumar, R., Lown, J.W.: Org. Biolmol. Chem. 1, 3327 (2003)
5. Horwitz, S.B.: Progress in Molecular & Subcellular Biology, vol. 2, p. 39. Springer, New York (1971)
6. Sanyal, N.K., Roychoudhury, M., Tiwari, S.N., Ruhela, K.R.: Indian J. Biochem. Biophys. 27(213), 27(222) (1990)
7. Tiwari, S.N., Ruhela, K.R., Roychoudhury, M., Sanyal, N.K.: Indian J. Phys. 65B, 495 (1991)
8. Sanyal, N.K., Tiwari, S.N.: J. Biosci. 24(S-1), 91 (1999)
9. Tiwari, S.N., Sanyal, N.K.: J. Biosci. 24(S-1), 92 (1999)
10. Shukla, R., Mishra, M., Tiwari, S.N.: Progress in Crystal Growth and Characterization of Materials, USA 52, 107–112 (2006)
11. Shukla, R., Tiwari, S.N.: International Conference on Contemporary Computing. LNCS, vol. 40, pp. 454–460. Springer, Berlin (2009)
12. Claverie, P.: Intermolecular Interactions: From Diatomics to Biopolymers, p. 69. John Wiely, New York (1978)
13. Rein, R.: Intermolecular Interactions: From Diatomics to Biopolymers, p. 307. John Wiely, New York (1978)
14. Arora, S.K.: Acta Cryst B35, 2945 (1979)
15. Pople, J.A., Beveridge, D.L.: Approximate Molecular Orbital Theory. Mc-Graw Hill Pub. Co., New York (1970)

Effect of Speech Coding on Recognition of Consonant-Vowel (CV) Units

Anil Kumar Vuppala[1], Saswat Chakrabarti[1], and K. Sreenivasa Rao[2]

[1] G. S. Sanyal School of Telecommunications
[2] School of Information Technology
Indian Institute of Technology Kharagpur
Kharagpur - 721302, West Bengal, India
anil.vuppala@gmail.com, saswat@ece.iitkgp.ernet.in, ksrao@iitkgp.ac.in

Abstract. The rapid growth of mobile users is creating great deal of interest in the development of robust speech systems in wireless environment. The major challenges involved in adapting the present speech processing technology to mobile wireless systems are: (1) Effect of varying background conditions in mobile environment. (2) Degradations introduced by the speech coders. (3) Errors introduced due to wireless radio channels. In this paper we analyzed the effect of different low bit rate speech coders on the recognition of Consonant-Vowel (CV) units in Indian languages using monolithic SVM and hybrid HMM-SVM models. Speech coders considered in this work are GSM full rate (ETSI 06.10), CELP (FS-1016), and MELP (TI 2.4kbps). From the results, it is observed that there is a significant effect of coding on the recognition of CV units.

Keywords: Speech coding, Consonant-Vowel (CV) units, GSM full rate (ETSI 06.10), CELP (FS-1016), and MELP (TI 2.4kbps).

1 Introduction

The main goal of this paper is to study the effect of speech coding on the recognition of Consonant-Vowel (CV) units in the context of Indian languages. This study is motivated by the rapid growth of mobile users. There are three major challenges involved in adapting the present speech processing technology to mobile wireless systems: (1) Effect of varying background conditions in mobile environment. (2) Degradations introduced by the speech coders. (3) Errors introduced due to wireless radio channels. Whilst the first one has already received a lot of attention [1,2], the last two deserve further investigation.

Speech coder represents the sequence of speech samples into a set of compact parameters and then these parameters are encoded into bit sequence. Encoded bits are transmitted to the receiver where the parameters are decoded, and speech signal is resynthesized. Features extracted from the resynthesized speech will be given as input to the recognizer. Due to the low bit-rate coding of speech, information present in speech signal (message, speaker and language

S. Ranka et al. (Eds.): IC3 2010, Part I, CCIS 94, pp. 284–294, 2010.

information) will be degraded. Coding will effect more when back ground noise is present in the speech, because most of the speech coding techniques exploit the production and perception aspects of speech in clean environments.

The effect of speech coders such as GSM and CELP coders on digit recognition performance by using HMM models has been discussed in [3,4]. Juan Huerta (2000) proposed weighted acoustic models to reduce the effect of GSM full rate coder on the speech recognition performance in his Ph.D thesis work [5]. From his study it is evident that not all phonemes in a GSM coded corpus are not distorted to the same extent due to coding.

In this work we analyzed the effect of different low bit-rate speech coders on the recognition performance of Consonant-Vowel (CV) units. Phonemes are widely used subword units of speech for speech recognition, but recent studies reveal that syllables (combinations of phonemes) are the suitable subword units for recognition [6,7]. Context-dependent units such as syllables capture significant co-articulation effects and pronunciation variation compared to phonemes. In general, the syllable-like units are of type $C^m V C^n$, where C refers to consonant, V refers to a vowel, m and n refers to the number of consonants preceding and following in a syllable. Among these units, the CV units are the most frequently (around 90% in Indian languages) occurring basic units [6], and hence CV units are considered to carry out this study.

Speech coders considered in this work are GSM full rate (ETSI 06.10), CELP (FS-1016), and MELP (TI 2.4kbps). GSM full rate coder provides 13 kbps bit rate using regular pulse excitation and long term prediction (RPE-LTP) techniques. This coder is used in GSM standard mobile communications. CELP coder provides 4.8 kbps bit rate using code excited linear prediction technique. CELP is widely used speech coding algorithm, and one of the practical application of it is in Selective Mode Vocoder (SMV) for CDMA. MELP coder provides 2.4 kbps bit rate using mixed excitation linear prediction technique. MELP based coders provides very low bit rates from 2.4 kbps to 600 bps. MELP is used in military, satellite, and secure voice applications.

This paper is organized as follows. Issues involved in recognition of CV units, and experimental setup used for the recognition of CV units are presented in section II. Experimental results for recognition of CV units using different models, and the effect of different speech coders on recognition performance of CV units are discussed in section III. Summary and conclusions of the present work and scope for the future work are mentioned in Section IV.

2   CV Recognition

Large number of CV classes and high similarity among several CV units are the major issues involved in the recognition of CV units. In literature Hidden Markov Models (HMM), Support Vector Machines (SVM), and Multi Layer FeedForward Neural Network (MLFFNN) are used for recognition of CV units in Indian languages [6,7,8]. From their studies it is evident that MLFFNN models and SVM models are working better for recognition of CV units compared to

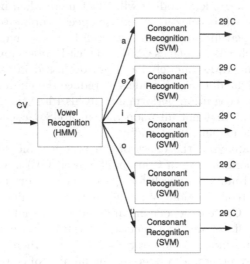

Fig. 1. CV recognition system using HMM and SVM

commonly used HMM models. As the number of CV classes are more, multi level acoustic models or hybrid acoustic models may perform better compared to monolithic acoustic models. To verify the above hypothesis, hybrid HMM and SVM based approach for acoustic modeling of CV units is proposed. Performance of proposed approach is compared with monolithic HMM, SVM, and other two level HMM and SVM based approaches.

Proposed model for CV recognition is shown in Fig 1. Among different syllable units present in the database we considered 145 most frequently occurred CV units for this study. In hybrid HMM and SVM based approach 145 CV units are divided into five subclasses based on vowel to reduce the influence of vowel on recognition of CV units. Each vowel subclass contains 29 consonants. In the first level of hybrid CV recognition, vowel will be recognized using HMM models and at the second level consonant will be recognized using SVM models. Vowel recognition models are trained using features extracted from vowel onset point (VOP) to end of CV segment and consonant models are trained using features extracted from start of CV segment to transition region.

For analyzing the duration of transition region 20 ms, 40 ms, and 60 ms to the right of VOP are experimented on /i/ subclass recognition, and results are shown in Table 1. Additional 20 ms from VOP is not giving good performance,

Table 1. Recognition performance of consonants in /i/ subclass for different segment lengths

/i/ subclass	VOP+20	VOP+40	VOP+60
performance (%)	42.24	49.26	47.16

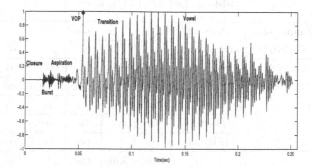

Fig. 2. Regions of significant events in the production of the CV unit /ka/

because it may not sufficient to capture co-articulation effects. Additional 60 ms from VOP is influenced by vowel, so performance is poor. Additional 40 ms from VOP is giving better performance among different segment lengths for consonant recognition. So we considered additional 40ms from VOP in this study. Different regions of significant events in the production of the CV unit /ka/ is shown in Fig. 2.

2.1 Experimental Setup Used for CV Recognition

Isolated Indian languages syllable database collected by International Institute of Information Technology, Hyderabad, India is used to carryout this study. Among different syllable units present in the database we considered 145 most frequently occurred CV units for this study, and they are shown in Table 2. Syllable database contains utterances of 25 male and 25 female speakers from different parts of India, in four different sessions. Three sessions are considered for training and one session for testing. Syllable database is collected at 16000 Hz sampling rate, and it is down sampled to 8000 Hz for this study. For building HMM based acoustic models HTK software developed by Carnegie Mellon University (CMU) [13] is used, and for SVM based models SVMTORCH [14] is used. HMM models are trained using maximum likelihood approach, and SVM models are trained using one against the rest approach.

Mel-frequency cepstral coefficients (MFCC) [15] extracted from every 25 ms of CV segment with 5 ms frame shift are used for training and testing the acoustic models. For building SVM models fixed dimension MFCC feature vectors are extracted using the formula

$$s = (p * SL)/PL, \quad p = 0, 1, ..., PL - 1, and$$
$$s = 0, 1, ..., SL - 1. \tag{1}$$

Where PL is pattern length, and SL is segment length. If segment length SL is greater than PL, a few frames of the segment are omitted. If the segment length SL is smaller than PL, a few frames of the segment are repeated. Pattern

Table 2. List of 145 CV units

Manner of articulation	Place of articulation	Vowel				
		/a/	/i/	/u/	/e/	/o/
Unvoiced Unaspirated (UVUA)	Velar	ka	ki	ku	ke	ko
	Palatal	cha	chi	chu	che	cho
	Alveolar	Ta	Ti	Tu	Te	To
	Dental	ta	ti	tu	te	to
	Bilabial	pa	pi	pu	pe	po
Unvoiced aspirated (UVA)	Velar	kha	khi	khu	khe	kho
	Palatal	Cha	Chi	Chu	Che	Cho
	Alveolar	Tha	Thi	Thu	The	Tho
	Dental	tha	thi	thu	the	tho
	Bilabial	pha	phi	phu	phe	pho
voiced Unaspirated (VUA)	Velar	ga	gi	gu	ge	go
	Palatal	ja	ji	ju	je	jo
	Alveolar	Da	Di	Du	De	Do
	Dental	da	di	du	de	do
	Bilabial	ba	bi	bu	be	bo
voiced aspirated (VA)	Velar	gha	ghi	ghu	ghe	gho
	Palatal	jha	jhi	jhu	jhe	jho
	Alveolar	Dha	Dhi	Dhu	Dhe	Dho
	Dental	dha	dhi	dhu	dhe	dho
	Bilabial	bha	bhi	bhu	bhe	bho
Nasals	Dental	na	ni	nu	ne	no
	Bilabial	ma	mi	mu	me	mo
Semivowels	Palatal	ya	yi	yu	ye	yo
	Alveolar	ra	ri	ru	re	ro
	Dental	la	li	lu	le	lo
	Bilabial	va	vi	vu	ve	vo
Fricatives	Velar	ha	hi	hu	he	ho
	Alveolar	sha	shi	shu	she	sho
	Dental	sa	si	su	se	so

lengths of 8, 10, and 14 are tried for developing the consonant models. Over all consonant recognition performance for pattern lengths of 8, 10, and 14 are shown in Table 3. There is a significant improvement in recognition performance from pattern length 8 to 10, compared to 10 to 14. To reduce computational complexity, pattern length of 10 is preferred over 14 for this study.

Table 3. Recognition performance of consonant in CV units for different pattern lengths

Pattern Lengths	PL=8	PL=10	PL=14
Recognition Performance (%)	53.93	57.03	57.23

Vowel onset point algorithm presented in [9] is used for detecting the VOP in this study. This VOP algorithm uses combined evidences from excitation source, spectral peaks, and modulation spectrum energies. The Hilbert envelope (HE) of the linear prediction (LP) residual represents the excitation source information. The sum of ten largest peaks in the discrete Fourier transform (DFT) spectrum represents the vocal tract shape. The modulation spectrum represents the slowly varying temporal envelope. Thus, each of these three features represents a different aspects of speech production, it may be possible that they contain complementary information about the VOP. The individual evidences are therefore combined for detecting the final VOPs. Location of maximum value in the combined VOP evidence plot of CV unit is considered as final VOP. This Combined VOP algorithm works better compared to individual evidences collected from source, spectral peaks, and modulation spectrum energies [9,10,11,12]. VOP detection using individual and combination of all three evidences for speech signal of /ni/ is shown in Fig 3. Combined VOP evidence plot in Fig 3 is showing the elimination of the wrong prediction of VOP by modulation spectrum.

3   Results and Discussion

Recognition performance of CV units using monolithic and hybrid HMM-SVM models are shown in Tables 4 and 5. As shown in Table 5 Among different hybrid HMM and SVM models, HMM for vowel recognition followed by SVM for consonant recognition is giving optimal performance. From the results it is evident that hybrid HMM and SVM acoustic modeling approach for CV recognition is giving 7.62% improvement in performance compared to monolithic SVM models.

Further, the effect of coding on the recognition performance of CV units is analyzed by giving features extracted from the coded speech as input to monolithic SVM and proposed hybrid HMM-SVM models. Initially coding effect is analyzed by using CV recognition models trained with clean speech (PCM speech) and tested with coded speech. Later to improve the recognition performance under coded condition, training and testing are done with the corresponding coded speech (i.e matched condition).

First, recognition performance of CV units under coded conditions using monolithic SVM models is shown in Table 6. Degradation of around 12 %, 20 %, and 17 % is observed in CV recognition performance due to GSM full rate, CELP, and MELP coders, respectively. Later the effect of coding on recognition performance of CV units is analyzed using two-level SVM-HMM CV recognition models. Vowel part of CV recognition performance with coded speech using

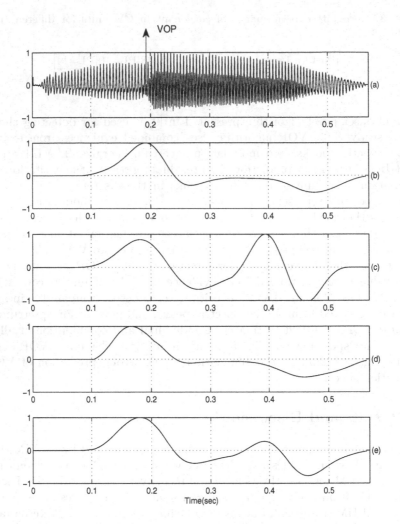

Fig. 3. VOP detection using combination of all three evidences. (a) Speech signal of *ni*. VOP evidence plot for (b) excitation source. (c) Modulation spectrum. (d) Spectral peaks. (e) Combined VOP evidence plot.

HMM and SVM models is shown in Tables 7 and 8, respectively. Form the results it is observed that for vowel recognition, HMM models are working better compared to SVM (see Tables7 and 8) . Degradation of around 3 %, 8 %, and 4 % is observed in vowel recognition performance using HMM models under GSM full rate, CELP, and MELP coders, respectively. From the results it is evident that, vowel recognition performance under coding is improved by using matched condition training.

Consonant part of CV recognition performance with coded speech using HMM and SVM models is shown in Tables 9 and 10. From the results it is observed

Table 4. Overall Performance of CV recognition system

Models	Overall CV recognition (%)
HMM	29.84
SVM	46.19
HMM-HMM	45.32
SVM-SVM	50.31
SVM-HMM	42.37
HMM-SVM	53.81

Table 5. Recognition performance of vowel and consonant from CV units using SVM and HMM

	Recognition performance (%)			
	Vowel from CV		Consonant from CV	
subclass	HMM	SVM	HMM	SVM
a	97.33	94	56.54	64.68
i	94.83	89.88	44.52	49.26
u	91.75	81.95	45.35	54.32
e	96.45	92.70	42.21	55.81
o	91.45	82.58	51.54	61.08
overall	94.36	88.23	48.03	57.03

that for consonant recognition, SVM models are working better compared to HMM, due to the discriminative learning used in SVM models (see Tables 9 and 10). Degradation of around 10 %, 15 %, and 17 % is observed in consonant recognition performance using SVM models under GSM full rate, CELP, and MELP coders respectively. Recognition performance is improved by using matched condition training. From the results it is evident that, even under matched condition consonant recognition performance is poor. Overall CV recognition performance with coded speech using two levels SVM-HMM models is shown in Table 11.

Recognition performance of CV units is decreasing as coding rate decreases. Degradation in case of monolithic models is more compared to two level models (see tables 6 and 11) . As shown in Tables 7, 8, 9, and 10 consonant recognition performance is much degraded compared to vowel recognition performance due to coding. For example, in case of vowel recognition performance of CELP coded speech using HMM or SVM models is degraded approximately by 8 %,

Table 6. Recognition performance of CV units with coded speech using monolithic SVM models

Coders	PCM	GSM	CELP	MELP
CV recognition (%)	46.19	34.92	26.54	29.06

Table 7. Recognition performance of vowel from CV units using HMM models under different coders

Training	Recognition performance (%)						
	PCM training				Matched training		
Testing	PCM	GSM	CELP	MELP	GSM	CELP	MELP
a	97.33	96.63	89.45	97.33	97.38	95.33	96.70
i	94.83	91.66	95.79	86.83	90.16	91.75	87.91
u	91.75	81.92	86.08	84.95	86.66	86.20	80.29
e	96.45	96.45	81.95	95.08	96.04	92.08	94.66
o	91.45	92.88	88.08	88.38	92.33	85.75	91.54
overall	94.36	91.9	86.68	90.52	92.52	90.22	90.22

Table 8. Recognition performance of vowel from CV units using SVM models under different coders

Training	Recognition performance (%)						
	PCM training				Matched training		
Testing	PCM	GSM	CELP	MELP	GSM	CELP	MELP
a	94	92.91	87.33	93.20	93.04	95.45	93.04
i	89.88	62.08	86.58	73.91	86.08	86	86.5
u	81.95	88.04	75.87	83.87	83.75	81.46	82.71
e	92.7	90.41	85.29	87.29	93.88	91.29	93.54
o	82.58	78.41	82.20	67.45	84.25	79.63	78.33
overall	88.22	82.38	83.45	81.15	88.2	86.77	86.83

Table 9. Recognition performance of consonant from CV units using HMM models under different coders

Training	Recognition performance (%)						
	PCM training				Matched training		
Testing	PCM	GSM	CELP	MELP	GSM	CELP	MELP
a	56.54	51.14	41.9	35.27	57.38	44.16	46.37
i	44.52	39.57	32.63	25.11	40.85	33.69	27.86
u	45.35	38.5	31.8	24	39.44	33.67	30.32
e	42.21	37.09	25.68	24.18	42.75	28.47	28.29
o	51.14	44.96	34.74	26.74	45.67	35.67	33.81
overall	48.03	42.252	33.35	27.06	45.22	35.13	33.33

but for consonant recognition performance for CELP coded speech using HMM or SVM models is degraded approximately by 15 %. Reason for this is, speech coders fail to parameterize accurately the unvoiced region of consonant. Matched condition training is working well for vowel recognition compared to consonant recognition. Matched condition (training and testing with same coded speech) is increasing the recognition performance significantly for GSM fullrate coder, but for CELP and MELP coders even under matched condition recognition

Table 10. Recognition performance of consonant from CV units using SVM models under different coders

Training	Recognition performance (%)						
Training	PCM training				Matched training		
Testing	PCM	GSM	CELP	MELP	GSM	CELP	MELP
a	64.68	57.27	46.42	42.4	61.18	51.11	54.81
i	49.26	37.41	20.88	20	43.48	29.29	31.78
u	54.32	46.32	29	25	51.4	35.46	35.88
e	55.81	44.15	27.85	30.46	49.28	34.17	، 40
o	61.08	51.96	36.72	33	56.1	40.58	43.56
overall	57.03	47.42	32.17	30.17	52.88	38.12	41.21

Table 11. Overall recognition performance of CV units using two level acoustic models under different coders

Training	Recognition performance (%)						
Training	PCM training				Matched training		
Testing	PCM	GSM	CELP	MELP	GSM	CELP	MELP
HMM-HMM	45.32	38.82	28.9	24.49	41.84	31.69	30.07
SVM-SVM	50.31	39.06	26.85	24.48	46.64	33.08	35.78
SVM-HMM	42.37	34.8	27.83	21.96	39.88	30.48	28.94
HMM-SVM	53.81	43.58	27.88	27.31	48.92	34.39	37.18

performance is not upto the mark. Under matched condition compared to CELP coded, MELP coded units are giving better performance. It is due to the approximation technique used to compress the excitation signal in CELP coder compared to MELP coder, to reduce computational complexity.

4   Summary and Conclusions

In this paper, we have studied the performance of different monolithic and two-level acoustic models for recognition of CV units in Indian languages under low bit rate speech coders. Among different models used for recognition of CV units, HMM for vowel recognition followed by SVM for consonant recognition is giving optimal performance. From the results it is evident that recognition performance of CV units is decreasing as coding rate decreases. Due to coding, consonant recognition performance is much degraded compared to vowel recognition performance. Matched condition (training and testing with same coded speech) is slightly increasing the recognition performance.

Further, two level HMM and SVM based approach can be extended to recognition of CV units in continuous speech. Effect of ultra low bit rate coders (bit rates like 600 bps) on speech recognition performance can be studied in future. Speech coding will give more effect when background noise is present in speech, so present study can be extended to coded noisy condition.

Acknowledgment

Authors thank Prof. Suryakanth V. Gangashetty and Ms. Chetana, International Institute of Information Technology, Hyderabad, India for making the Indian languages syllable data available for our studies.

References

1. Vicente-Pena, J., Gallardo-Antoln, A., Pelaez-Moreno, C., Daz-de-Mara, F.: Bandpass filtering of the time sequences of spectral parameters for robust wireless speech recognition. Speech Communication 48(10), 1379–1398 (2006)
2. Zaykovskiy, D.: Survey of the speech recognition techniques for mobile devices. In: Proceedings of DS Publications (2006)
3. Euler, S., Zinke, J.: The influence of speech coding algorithms on automatic speech recognition. In: Proceedings of ICASSP, pp. 621–624 (1994)
4. Lilly, B.T., Paliwal: Effect of speech coders on speech recognition performance. In: Proceedings of ICSLP, pp. 2344–2347 (1996)
5. Huerta, J.M.: Speech recognition in mobile environments. PhD thesis, CMU (April 2000)
6. Gangashetty, S.V.: Neural network models for recognition of consonant-vowel units of speech in Multiple Languages. PhD thesis, IIT Madras (October 2004)
7. Chandra Sekhar, C.: Neural Network models for recognition of stop consonant-vowel (SCV) segments in continuous speech. PhD thesis, IIT Madras (1996)
8. Chandra Sekhar, C., Lee, W.F., Takeda, K., Itakura, F.: Acoustic modeling of subword units using support vector machines. In: WSLP (2003)
9. Mahadeva Prasanna, S.R., Sandeep Reddy, B.V., Krishnamoorthy, P.: Vowel onset point detection using source, spectral peaks, and modulation spectrum energies. IEEE Transactions on Audio, Speech, and Language Processing 17(4), 556–565 (2009)
10. Hermes, D.J.: Vowel onset detection. J. Acoust. Soc. Amer. 87, 866–873 (1990)
11. Mahadeva Prasanna, S.R.: Event-Based analysis of speech. PhD thesis, IIT Madras (March 2004)
12. Mahadeva Prasanna, S.R., Yegnanarayana, B.: Detection of vowel onset point events using excitation source information. Interspeech, 1133–1136 (September 2005)
13. Young, S., Kershaw, D., Odell, J., Ollason, D., Valtchev, V., Woodland, P.: The HTK Book Version 3.0. Cambridge University Press, Cambridge (2000)
14. Collobert, R., Bengio, S.: SVMTorch, support vector machines for large-scale regression problems. J. Mach. Learn. Res. 1, 143–160 (2001)
15. Picone, J.W.: Signal modeling techniques in speech recognition. Proceedings of the IEEE 81, 1215–1247 (1993)

Cloudbank: A Secure Anonymous Banking Cloud

Ridhi Sood and Meenakshi Kalia

Shobhit Institute of Engineering and Technology,
UPTU Meerut-Uttar Pradesh, India
ridsood90@gmail.com, meenameets@gmail.com

Abstract. In this paper a novel banking framework residing over the cloud storage architecture for electronic payment which takes place over the Internet is presented. It implements electronic cash-based transactions, between customers and merchants through the CloudBank. It is based on a bank account, though it can be easily extended and can be readily applied to other account payment models like debit cards. The proposed architecture is designed using Millicent's main concept (scrip) technique. In this architecture, financial institutions become partners in the e-commerce transaction, conducted by their customers over the Internet. The innovation of the proposed framework is the removal of the involvement of the financial institutions to ancillary support services like helping on establishing trust between the parties payment transaction. Moreover, the proposed system can be characterized as distributed virtual banking environment provided to users (customers/merchants) authorizing all payments taking place between them. Finally, in this architecture e-cash once used is never used again so all the e-transactions are secure.

Keywords: Cloud Computing, cryptography, Millicent, scrip, CloudBank.

1 Introduction

Electronic commerce [6] is a modern business methodology that addresses the needs of organizations, merchants, and consumers to cut costs while improving the quality of goods and services and increasing the speed of service delivery. It provides a business environment that allows the transfer of electronic payments as well as transactional information via Internet. The effects of e-commerce are already appearing in all areas of business from customer service to new product design and it flourishes as global success because of the openness, speed, anonymity, digitization and worldwide accessibility of the Internet.

At the turn of the century over 70 million computers were connected to the Internet [1]. This was certainly the untapped source for many companies who were looking outside their organizations as well as within when shaping their business strategies. Their activities included establishing private electronic connections with their customers, suppliers, and partners etc so as to improve the business communication. Electronic commerce is viewed even today by many companies with mix of eagerness, fear, and confusion. But the success of business sites like Amazon.com [2], or eBay [3] and retail sites like Wal-Mart [4] has paved the path for new business

S. Ranka et al. (Eds.): IC3 2010, Part I, CCIS 94, pp. 295–304, 2010.

models. People now, can buy and sell goods using their web browsers. These business sites provide a centralized trading platform, which offers a certain degree of security to its customers. Rules can be easily forced in these centralized architecture but high infrastructure requirements of these systems make them too difficult to maintain.

Furthermore, this kind of architecture is not suitable for small companies or small merchants that can't afford a high infrastructure. This is where the cloud computing [7] architecture comes to give the solution. The cloud computing paradigm is increasingly receiving attention as a new distributed computing scheme because of its potential of optimum utilization of computation resources. Basically cloud is a metaphor for internet and is an abstraction for the complex infrastructure it conceals. The main idea is to use the existing infrastructure in order to bring all feasible services to the cloud and make it possible to access those services regardless of time and location.

This new cloud architecture offers new possibilities for electronic commerce. The most important aspect of this architecture is the reduction of the competence of the financial institutions. Also people over electronic market can both act as merchants by selling their second-hand products as well as customers by buying goods online from other merchants; this architecture easily deals with such situation very easily. These people also refer as peers. They can exploit the benefits of electronic market without any worry of security related problems often associated with online shopping marketplace with the help of proposed architecture and can do business with his/her PC.

Our new architecture provides a completely anonymous, secure and practical framework, in which each peer can act both as a merchant and a customer. Further, it also provides a full and secure mechanism where personal information and order information cannot be exposed to unauthorized third parties. This architecture uses the scrip of Millicent [5].

Millicent offers anonymity, privacy and authenticity [8].Even the scrip of Millicent cannot be spent twice because of its serial number. It's "Certificate" prevents tampering and counterfeiting. It can only spend by its owner and it has a value only for a specific merchant. And finally it can be produced "on the fly", so there is no need to create it and save it in a big database.

Many companies today are also using the P2P characteristics with e commerce. They support P2P commerce by using emails or SSL (Secure Socket Layer) [9] for the purchase transaction. SSL is the de facto standard for the secure communication on the web. It was proposed by Netscape Communications for providing data security layered between high-level applications and TCP/IP. It provides data encryption, server authentication, message integrity, and optional client authentication for a TCP/IP connection. Today SSL is integrated in almost all web browsers and servers. SSL uses asymmetric encryption. Encrypting bank account data with SSL is certainly better than sending them in a clear, but the gain in security is very limited.

a) SSL doesn't hide bank account numbers or any other information from the merchant.
b) Also there is no guarantee that a customer can verify the merchant's public key.
c) Merchants and brokers also need additional information (beyond SSL) to transmit bank account data and authorization information.

Additionally, other electronic payment systems are basically based on cryptographic systems like "digital signatures" [10]. Cryptographic systems provide the strong framework for providing security to the transaction and communication taking place over the Internet but time taken to encrypt the data is very high i.e. encryption and decryption slows the process of communication. But the payment systems present today use encryption/decryption process for all the communication taking place between different parties (between customer and broker or broker and merchants etc). hence most of the time of the payment system is consumed in encrypting and decrypting the messages exchanged between these parties.

Hence in this paper we propose an architecture which reduces this unnecessary communication taking place between these parties and slowing the performance of the overall payment system.

2 E-Cash

E-cash is scrip that generated by the cloud bank
The main properties of scrip are:

a) It has value at a specific vendor.
b) It can be spent only once.
c) It is tamper resistant and hard to counterfeit.
d) It can be spent only by its rightful owner.
e) It can be efficiently produced and validated.
f) The text of the scrip gives its value and identifies the vendor.
g) The scrip has a serial number to prevent double spending.
h) There is a digital signature to prevent tampering and counterfeiting.
i) The customer signs each use of scrip with a secret that is associated with the scrip.
j) The signatures can be efficiently created and checked using a fast one-way hash function (like MD5 [12] or SHA [13]).

2.1 Definitions

Following terms are used in description of the account, customer and e-cash.

BankSecret: is the combination of two secrets: The secret of the bank and the secret of the Customer/Merchant. Both the bank and the customer/merchant have this combination.

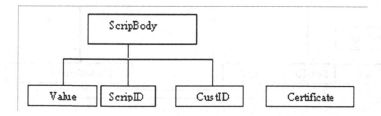

Fig. 1. Scrip

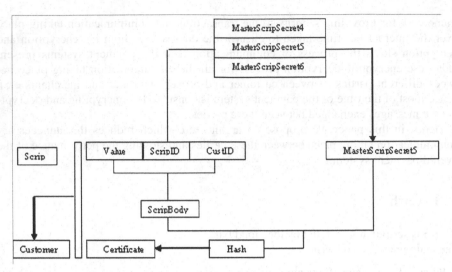

Fig. 2. Certificate creation and Scrip's structure completion

ID: is a unique identifier for the customer/merchant and it can certify his/her identity. It is the digest: Hash (BankSecret|Hash (BankSecret)| bank account number)

UserID: is a unique identifier for each user and it does not provide any information about the identity of the user.

ScripBody: consists of the following fields (Figure 1):

a) Value: is the amount of the scrip.
b) ScripID: is an identifier of the Scrip. Part of it is used to specify the   Master-ScripSecret (see definition below).
c) CustID: is an identifier of the customer. Part of it is used to specify the Mas-terCustomerSecret (see definition below).

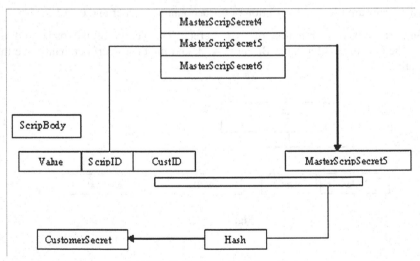

Fig. 3. CustomerSecret creation

MasterScripSecret: is the look-up value of the ScripID. It is used to produce the certificate (see definition below).

Certificate: is the signature of the scrip (Figure2). (The term "Certificate" is used with respect to the Millicents one.) It is used to verify that the scrip is valid. It is produced by hashing the concatenation of the ScripBody and the MasterScripSecret: Hash (ScripBody|MasterScripSecret).

MasterCustomerSecret: is the look-up value of the CustID. It is used to produce the CustomerSecret.

CustomerSecret: is used to prove ownership of the scrip. It is produced by hashing the concatenation of the CustID and the MasterCustomerSecret: Hash (CustID||MasterCustomerSecret) (Figure 3).

3 Public Key Cryptography

The proposed architecture is based on public key cryptography, thus a mechanism is needed to authenticate the public keys. That is why, it is assumed that certification authority (CA) has the private keys and other parties involved hold its public counterpart. For the sake of simplicity, it is assumed that for the rest of the paper that there is single CA and that is Bank.

In proposed architecture, the bank has a public key, which enables signing and encryption. Its public counterpart that enables signature verification and encryption is held by each accredited customer/merchant. As in current operation, the bank stores (in a database) the customers' and merchants' BankSecrets and has their Ids, is trusted to all parties involved, keeping these secrets confidential.

4 Threats and Adversaries in Internet Payment System

Three different adversaries are considered:

a)   Eavesdropper: listen to messages and tries to learn secrets. (e.g. bank account numbers, IDs)
b)   Active Attacker: introduces modification of the data stream or creation of a false stream.
c)   Insider: is either a legitimate party or one who learns the party's secret.

Internet is a heterogeneous network, without single ownership of the network resources and functions. One can't exclude the possibility that messages between the legitimate parties would not pass through a maliciously controlled computer. Furthermore, the routing mechanisms in the Internet are not designed to protect against malicious attacks. Therefore, neither confidentiality nor authentication over the Internet can be assumed. Hence cryptographic mechanisms are employed.

Also it is difficult to consider the trustworthiness of the merchants as well as of the customers over the Internet. It is very easy for anyone to pretend as authorize merchants and offers products to different customers in order to get customer's secret

[11]. While two possible attacks are possible from customer's side, namely double spending and scrip forgery.

- **Double Spending:** as already mentioned, scrip is concatenated with two secrets the master_scrip_secret and the master_customer_secret. These secrets are only to the producer of the scrip i.e. bank. Each time scrip is used, its secrets are deleted from the banks look up tables, ensuring that the scrip cannot be reused in another transaction.
- **Scrip Forgery:** scrip consists of the scrip body, which contains the information of the scrip and a certificate, which is the signature of the scrip. Any alteration of the information contained in the scrip body can be detected by verifying the scrip's certificate.

5 Security Requirements

5.1 Bank Requirements

The bank is assumed to enjoy some degree of mutual trust with its customers/merchants i.e. account holders. Also an infrastructure between them is ready in place enabling secure communications between them. Therefore, respective requirements of banks are unified with respect to customers and merchants.

- *Proof of transaction Authorization by the Customer:* When bank records a debit from any of its account with certain amount, it asks corresponding account holder about the authorization of this payment. This proof must not be repayable or usable as proof for any other transaction. Note also, that I this context it is considered that the merchant may be adversary; such a seller must not be able to generate fake transaction.
- *Proof of transaction Authorization by specific Merchant:* When bank authorizes a payment to certain merchant, the bank must be in possession of an unforgeable proof that customer has asked to start a payment transaction with this merchant and also that this merchant is legitimate.

5.2 Merchant Requirements

- *Proof of transaction Authorization by Bank:* The merchant needs an unforgeable proof that the bank has authorized the transaction.
- *Proof of transaction Authorization by Customer:* Before the merchant receives the transaction authorization from the bank, the merchant needs an unforgeable proof that the customer has authenticated it. Furthermore, before the merchant sends the information message to the bank about a payment, s/he must be certain that this specific customer requested it.

5.3 Customer Requirements

- *Anonymity:* Customer often does not want any of his/her information (personal or impersonal) get leaked out to anyone even to merchants during any transaction. All the transaction details are between bank and customer. Merchants are only aware of the authenticity of the customers.

- *Privacy:* Privacy is the foremost requirement of any of the online payment system. It is demanded from both customers' as well as merchants' side. The proposed architecture respects the customer's privacy of order and payment information. For example, investor purchasing information on certain stocks may not want competitors to be aware of the stocks s/he is interested in. All information is kept intact within the cloud framework.
- *Impossibility of Unauthorized Payment:* It must be impossible to charge a customer's bank account without possession of the bank account number, ID and account holder's digital signature. Thus, neither Internet nor malicious merchants must be able to generate spurious transactions, which end up approved by the bank.
- *Authentication of Merchant:* Customer may need proof that the merchant is a legitimate user of the payment system. If merchant already has an account in the bank then this requirement is partly fulfilled by the bank itself.

6 Payment Processing

In the following subsections, how the overall payment processing is done through Cloud Bank is discussed in detail. It is assumed that there is imaginary electronic market of second hand sold products. These steps are needed so that a trusted relationship between merchant and customer is established. Through the "Obtain electronic cash from the CloudBank" transaction step the customer purchases from the bank electronic cash. That amount is trickle down in his account by the bank i.e. its bank account is credited with that amount of electronic cash. Then through the "Buying Item" transaction step, firstly the amount of electronic cash present in the customer's account is checked whether it is enough to carry on the transaction further or not. If yes, the amount of cash that customer has to pay to the merchant is debited from the customer account and merchant account is credited with that amount. Otherwise a bank asks customer to more electronic cash so as to complete the transaction or drop the transaction depending upon whether s/he is willing to buy the electronic cash or not.

6.1 Obtain Electronic Cash from the CloudBank

A customer that desires to buy products sold in the electronic market needs to have enough in his/ her account so as to pay for that product. If s/he doesn't possess enough electronic cash, he has to buy it from the CloudBank. This is achieved through this transactional step; s/he establishes a connection to the CloudBank and buys, using real money, the desirable electronic cash. Having received the payment the bank credits the account of customer with that amount of money being generated by CloudBank.

In M0, the combination of the ID, customer bank account number and customer's digital signature provide the strong proof to the bank that the customer authorized the transaction. Further, the use if nonce ensures that the message is not replayable. Moreover, the message is encrypted so as to eliminate the exposure of customer's ID, account number and ensures the bank that message is not altered.

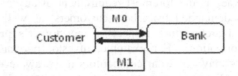

Fig. 4. Obtain electronic cash from the bank

If the information received in this message and processed is valid, the CloudBank creates the requested electronic cash (e-cash). Furthermore, bank records the information of the transaction. The recorded information can be used in the case of a dispute. Bank credits the amount generated in the customer's account and sends the message M1 to the customer. In this message, the digital signature of the bank ensures the customer that the bank authorized the transaction and amount demanded by him is credited into his account. Further, the received nonce offers him/her proof that the message doesn't come from a replay attack. Finally, encryption ensures confidentiality of the information sent.

When the customer receives the M1, s/he decrypts it, verifies its signature and checks if the amount credited into his/her account is requested one or not.

6.2 Buying Item

The customer that owns appropriate electronic cash for purchasing a desired item from the merchant should approach the bank to complete the transaction. This step initiated the transaction.

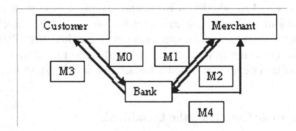

Fig. 5. Buying Item from merchant and making payment from the bank

In M0, the digital signature, customer ID, nonce and bank account number sends to bank as a proof that customer authorizes the transaction. Further s/he should send a request about the amount of electronic cash that should be credited into the merchant's account and merchant's account number. If merchant doesn't have bank account in the CloudBank, then bank asks merchant to open account in the bank first. In this scenario we assumed that both customer and merchant have their bank account in the bank. The nonce ensures that the message is not product of replay attack. Finally, encryption ensures authentication of the customer and proof that message is not altered.

The bank decrypts the message element and verifies the signature of the message. This ensures that the customer authorizes the transaction. So, if the received message is valid, bank sends message M1 to merchant and asks him/her to authorize the transaction. Merchant sends it's ID, its account number along with digital signature and amount that customer has to pay to merchant in message M2 to bank. It proves that the merchant authorizes the transaction.

Merchant encrypts this message before sending it to bank so as to provide the confidentiality.

The bank receiving the message decrypts is and verifies its signature. Further bank verifies the account number of the corresponding account holder and verifies if it belongs to that merchant or not. Finally, bank checks if the amounts send by both the customer and merchant are equal or not. If the amounts are unequal bank asks both of them about the confliction of the amount and correct it. If the information is valid, bank reduces the value of the scrip of the customer i.e. debits the account of the customer and increases the value the scrip in the merchant's account. If merchant's account has nil balance then bank generates the appropriate amount of scrip and credits the account of merchant. After that bank forms two messages, one for the customer (M3) and one for the merchant (M4) about information of whole transaction. And updates the account of the both of the account holders (customer/merchant) as well as corresponding log file of the transaction.

Merchant and customer can further communicate with bank to check if the amounts are correct or not.

7 Conclusion

In this paper, a novel architecture is presented. This architecture can be used in any kind of online payment but its purpose is to provide the security to all the transactions which take place over the unsecured Internet environment. Both the steps of the payment process," Obtain Electronic cash from the CloudBank" and "Buying Item", are considered to be necessary steps so as to establish a trustworthy business relationship between customer and merchant. Also in this architecture the role of the mediator i.e. broker has been removed completely so as to reduce the communication that takes place between "broker and merchant" and "broker and customer" which largely consume the bandwidth during any of the payment transaction. In this architecture, a centralized cloud maintains all the transaction logs so to provide more security as different benefits of the cloud computing architecture can be easily exploited in this architecture. Further, the new architecture is compliant to all parties' requirements involved in a transaction and offers confidentiality and full anonymity to the customers. Finally, it establishes a framework for enabling secure payment transaction.

References

1. IAIK Java Group. IAIK Java Crypto Software,
   http://jce.iaik.tu-graz.ac.at/
2. Amazon.com, Inc., http://www.amazon.com/

3. eBay, Inc., http://www.ebay.com/
4. Wal-Mart, http://www.walmart.com/
5. Glassman, S., Manasse, M., Abadi, M., Gauthier, P., Sobalvarro, P.: The Millicent protocol for inexpensive electronic commerce. In: Proceeding of the 4th International World Wide Conference, pp. 603–618 (1995)
6. Executive Summary on Electronic Commerce, http://www.big-world.org/upload/cahp1.htm
7. Armbrust, M., Fox, A., Griffith, R., et al.: Above the Clouds: A Berkeley View Cloud Computing, Technical Report No. UCB/EECS-2009-28, http://www.eecs.berkeley.edu/Pubs/TechRpts/2009/EECS-2009-28.html
8. Lee, Z.Y., Yu, H.C., Kuo, P.J.: An analysis and comparison of different types of electronic payment systems. In: Management of Engineering and Technology, PICMET 2001, vol. 2, pp. 38–45 (2001)
9. Netscape Inc., SSL Protocol, http://home.netscape.com/newsref/std/SSL.html
10. Nentwich, F., Kirda, E., Kruegel, C.: Secure Systems Lab, Technical University Vienna: Practical Security Aspects of Digital Signature Systems. Technical Report (2006)
11. Wallish, P.: Cyber view: How to steal millions in champ change, pp. 32–33. Science American
12. Rivest, R.: The MD5 Message-Digest Algorithm, IETF RFC 1321, http://gopher://.ds2.internic.net/00/rfc/rfc1321.txt
13. National Institute for Standards and Technology (NIST), Secure Hash Standard, FIPS PUB 180-1: Secure Hash Standard (April 1995), http://csrc.ncsl.nist.gov/fips/fip180-1.txt

Alignment Model and Training Technique in SMT from English to Malayalam

Mary Priya Sebastian, K. Sheena Kurian, and G. Santhosh Kumar

Department of Computer Science,
Cochin University of Science and Technology, Kerala, India
{marypriyas,sheenakuriank}@gmail.com,
san@cusat.ac.in

Abstract. This paper investigates certain methods of training adopted in the Statistical Machine Translator (SMT) from English to Malayalam. In English Malayalam SMT, the word to word translation is determined by training the parallel corpus. Our primary goal is to improve the alignment model by reducing the number of possible alignments of all sentence pairs present in the bilingual corpus. Incorporating morphological information into the parallel corpus with the help of the parts of speech tagger has brought around better training results with improved accuracy.

Keywords: Alignment, Parallel Corpus, PoS Tagging, Malayalam, Statistical Machine Translation.

1 Introduction

In SMT [1], by using statistical methods, a learning algorithm is applied to huge volumes of previously translated text usually termed as parallel corpus. By examining these samples, the system automatically translates previously unseen sentences. The statistical machine translator from English to Malayalam as discussed in [2], uses statistical models to acquire an appropriate Malayalam translation for a given English sentence.

A very large corpus of translated sentences of English and Malayalam is required to achieve this goal. In the current scenario there exist only very few numbers of such large corpora and the sad part is that they do not come with word to word alignments. However, there are techniques by which the large corpora is trained to obtain word to word alignments from the non-aligned sentence pairs [6].

In training the SMT, sentence pairs in the parallel corpus are examined and alignment vectors are set to identify the alignments that exist between the word pairs. A number of alignments is present between any pair of sentence. As the size of the corpus and the length of the sentence vary, the process of building the alignment vectors for sentence pairs becomes a challenging task. Moreover in training, representing the alignments using alignment vectors takes up major part of the working memory.

It has been observed that many of the alignments in a sentence pair are insignificant and carry little meaning. By removing these insignificant word alignments from

S. Ranka et al. (Eds.): IC3 2010, Part I, CCIS 94, pp. 305–315, 2010.

the sentence pairs, the quality of training is enhanced. In this paper a discussion is done about the alignment model which uses morphological information for removing the irrelevant alignment pairs. The training technique adopted to find the word to word translation in SMT is also discussed. The paper also highlights the changes occurring in the training process when morphological knowledge is introduced into the corpus.

The rest of this paper is organized as follows: In Section 2 the motivation to initiate this work is portrayed. Section 3 presents the details of the training performed in the parallel corpus. In Section 4, the method of incorporating morphological knowledge into the corpus and the modified alignment model is presented. The observations and the outcomes achieved by adopting the new alignment model is discussed in Section 5. Finally, the work is concluded in Section 6.

2 Motivation

Owing to the fact that English and Malayalam belong to two different language families, various issues are encountered when English is translated into Malayalam using SMT. The issues start off with the scarcity in the availability of English/Malayalam translations required for training SMT. The functioning of SMT completely rely on the parallel corpus. Less number of these resources in the electronic form adds on to the difficulty of implementing SMT.

Moreover in the bilingual translations available, a one to one correspondence between the words in the sentence pair is hard to find. The reason behind this occurrence is solely the peculiarity of Malayalam language. Due to the agglutinative nature of Malayalam [8], a linguist when asked to translate sentences into Malayalam, have a wide range of options to apply. The words "daily life" is translated as "നിത്യേനയുള്ള ജീവിതം "(nithyenayulla jeevitham) or "നിത്യജീവിതം" (nithyajeevitham) according to the will of the linguist. Even though the two translations share the same meaning, there is a difference of latter being a single word. Scope of occurrence of such translations cannot be eliminated and hence certain sentence pairs may lack a one to one mapping between its word pair.

In training, the entire corpus is examined and statistical methods are adopted to extract the appropriate meaning for a word. An alignment model is defined in training which sets all the possible alignments between a sentence pair. The amount of memory required to hold these alignments is a problem which cannot be overlooked. Lengthy sentences worsen the situation since word count of the sentence is the prime factor in determining alignments. In the pre-processing phase suffixes are separated from the Malayalam words in the corpus. Suffix separation results in further increase of sentence length which in turn increases the number of word alignments.

Certain suffix doesn't have a correct translation when they stand alone in the corpus. Hence setting alignments for such suffixes doesn't have any significance in training. Eliminating them from the corpus before the training phase brings down the word count of the sentences and thereby the number of alignments too.

Similarly many insignificant alignments is avoided by scrutinizing the structure of the sentence pair. Close observation reveals the fact that many words belonging to different categories are mapped together when alignment vectors are figured out. The English word that forms the subject of a sentence need not be aligned with the 'kriya' (verb) in Malayalam. Likewise verbs in English have little chance to get associated with words that forms 'karthavu'(subject) and 'karmam' (object) in Malayalam.

Insignificant alignments take up time and space in training. Methods were identified to strengthen the parallel corpus with more information so that only the relevant alignment is included in calculating translation probabilities. It is found that when the corpus is linked with a parts of speech tagger, many irrelevant alignments are eliminated. Also, training technique is further enhanced and better results are achieved.

3 Training the Parallel Corpus

In the training process, the translation of a Malayalam word is determined by finding the translation probability of a English word for a given Malayalam word. The corpus considered is a sentence aligned corpus where a sentence in Malayalam is synchronized with its equivalent English translation. The aligned sentence pairs are subjected to training mechanism which in turn leads to the calculation of translation probability of English words. The translation probability is the parameter that clearly depicts the relationship between a word in Malayalam and its English translation. It also shows how closely a Malayalam word is associated with an English word in the corpus. The translation probability for all the English words in the corpus is estimated. This results in generating a collection of translation options in English with different probability values for each Malayalam word. Of these translation options the one with the highest translation probability is selected as the word to word translation of the Malayalam word.

3.1 Alignments and Alignment Vectors

The corpus with aligned sentence pairs needs to be pre-processed to obtain the word to word alignments. In each sentence pair all the possible alignments of a Malayalam word is identified. The nature of the alignment truly depends on the characteristics of the language chosen. Since Malayalam with suffix separation holds a one to one mapping with words in the English sentence, only one to one alignment vectors are considered.

The Malayalam corpus is pre-processed and suffix separation [7] is done before pairing with English sentences. The suffix separated Malayalam sentence aligned with its English translation is given in Fig. 1. For a sentence pair all the possible alignments have to be considered in the training process. Depending upon the word count of the Malayalam sentence, the number of alignments varies. The number of alignments generated for any sentence pair is equal to the factorial of the number of words in the sentence. The alignment vector for the sentence pair is obtained by placing the position of the aligned Malayalam word in place of the corresponding English word in the sentence pair. The length of the alignment vector of an English sentence depends on its word count.

നമ്മൾ	ഇന്ത്യ	ഇൽ	താമസിക്കുന്നു
(nammal	india	il	thammasikkunnu)
m0	m1	m2	m3

	We	live	in	India
	e0	e1	e2	e3

Fig. 1. Malayalam English sentence pair

In the above example, the Malayalam word 'നമ്മൾ' (nammal) is aligned with any of the English word in the sentence. The word നമ്മൾ is positioned as [m0,-,-,-], [-,m0,-,-], [-,-,m0,-] and [-,-,-,m0] in the alignment vector where m0 denotes the Malayalam word in the 0th position. The alignment vector of the alignment shown in Fig. 2 is [m0, m3, m2, m1].

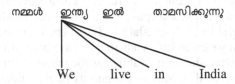

Fig. 2. Alignments of the word നമ്മൾ (Nammal)

3.2 Finding Translation Probability

The EM Algorithm, as discussed in [3], defines a method of estimating the parameter values of translation for IBM model1 [4]. By this algorithm there is equal chance for a Malayalam word to get aligned with any English word in the corpus. Therefore, initially the translation probability of all English words is set to a uniform value. Suppose there is N number of English words in the corpus, the probability of all Malayalam words to get mapped to an English word is 1/N. To start with the training process this value is set as the Initial Fractional Count (IFC) of the translation probability. Alignment weight for a sentence pair is calculated by observing the IFC of all the word pairs present in the alignment vector. The Alignment Probability (AP) of all the sentences is calculated by multiplying the individual alignment weight of each word pair in the sentence pair. The calculated alignment probability of the sentence pairs is then normalized to get Normalized Alignment Probability (NAP).

Fractional count for a word pair is revised from the normalized alignment probabilities. A word in Malayalam may be aligned to a same English word in many

Table 1. IFC of the word 'ഇന്ത്യ'(India)

Id	Possible translations	IFC
e0	We	0.25
e1	live	0.25
e2	in	0.25
e3	India	0.25

sentences. Therefore when the fractional count of a word pair is recomputed, all sentence pairs are analyzed to check whether it holds that particular word pair. If it is present in any pair of sentence, the alignment probabilities of the alignment vectors holding that word pair are added up to obtain the Revised Fractional Count (RFC). By normalizing the revised fractional counts (NFC) new values of translation probability is obtained.

Table 2. A view of alignment vectors and the alignment probabilities

SP	Alignment vectors corresponding to [e0,e1, e2,e3]	Alignment Weights of e_i given m_i				AP	NAP
	[m0,m1, m2,m3]	t(e0/m0) = 0.25	t(e1/m1) = 0.12	t(e2/m2) = 0.25	t(e3/m3) = 0.25	0.0019	0.02
	[m0,m1, m3,m2]	t(e0/m0) = 0.25	t(e1/m1) = 0.12	t(e2/m3) = 0.25	t(e3/m2) = 0.25	0.0019	0.02
S P 1	[m0,m2, m1,m3]	t(e0/m0) = 0.25	t(e1/m2) = 0.25	t(e2/m1) = 0.12	t(e3/m3) = 0.25	0.0019	0.02
	[m0,m2, m3,m1]	t(e0/m0) = 0.25	t(e0/m2) = 0.25	t(e0/m3) = 0.25	t(e0/m1) = 0.63	0.0098	0.11
	...	...	...	...	...	...	..
S P 2	[m0]	t(e0/m0) = 0.25	-	-	-	0.25	1

Table 3. Revised fractional count of the word 'ഇന്ത്യ'(India)

Id	Possible translations	RFC
e0	We	ΣNAP of t(e0|ഇന്ത്യ) from SP1 = 0.12
e1	Live	ΣNAP of t(e1|ഇന്ത്യ) from SP1= 0.12
e2	in	ΣNAP of t(e2|ഇന്ത്യ) from SP1= 0.12
e3	India	ΣNAP of t(e3|ഇന്ത്യ) from SP1 + ΣNAP of t(e0|ഇന്ത്യ) from SP2= 1.66

Hopefully the new values achieved are better since they take into account the correlation data in the parallel corpus. Equipped with these better parameter values, new alignment probabilities for the sentence pairs are computed. From these values a set of even-more-revised fractional counts for word pairs is obtained. Repeating this process over and over helps fractional counts to converge to better values.

The translational probability of the English word given a Malayalam word is found to determine the best translation of a Malayalam word. It is achieved by comparing the translation probabilities of English words associated with it and picking the one with highest probability value. The method of collecting fractional counts and setting alignment probabilities is illustrated with corpus1 having two sentence pairs (SP).

SP1:   നമ്മൾ   ഇന്ത്യ   ഇൽ   താമസിക്കുന്നു
       (nammal   india   il   thammasikkunnu)
       We live in India
SP2:   ഇന്ത്യ
       India

SP1 has 4 words and the total number of alignments is 4!. SP2 is a sentence with a single word and hence there is only one alignment defined for it. The total number of distinct English words in the corpus is four and initially any of these English words can be the translation of any Malayalam word in the corpus. Consider the word ഇന്ത്യ (India) that happens to appear in both the sentence pairs. To find the translation probability of English words in the corpus given the word ഇന്ത്യ (India), t(English word| ഇന്ത്യ), the IFC of ഇന്ത്യ is to be calculated. The IFC of ഇന്ത്യ is given in Table 1.

Table 4. Normalized fractional count of 'ഇന്ത്യ'(India)

Id	Possible translations	NFC
e0	We	RFC(e0|ഇന്ത്യ)/ Σ{RFC(e0|ഇന്ത്യ), RFC(e1|ഇന്ത്യ), RFC(e2|ഇന്ത്യ),RFC(e3|ഇന്ത്യ)} = 0.06
e1	Live	RFC(e1|ഇന്ത്യ)/ Σ{RFC(e0|ഇന്ത്യ), RFC(e1|ഇന്ത്യ), RFC(e2|ഇന്ത്യ), RFC(e3|ഇന്ത്യ)} = 0.06
e2	in	RFC(e2|ഇന്ത്യ)/Σ{RFC(e0|ഇന്ത്യ),RFC(e1|ഇന്ത്യ), RFC(e2|ഇന്ത്യ),RFC(e3|ഇന്ത്യ)} = 0.06
e3	India	RFC(e3|ഇന്ത്യ)/Σ{RFC(e0|ഇന്ത്യ),RFC(e1|ഇന്ത്യ), RFC(e2|ഇന്ത്യ),RFC(e3|ഇന്ത്യ)} = 0.82

The alignment probabilities of the sentence pairs are then calculated. The values of AP for all alignments of a sentence pair are equal in the first iteration and later it varies with revised fractional counts. The alignment probabilities and the normalized values calculated for the sample corpus after second iteration is shown in Table 2. Revised fractional count for the word ഇന്ത്യ(India) after second iteration is given in Table 3 and its normalized fractional count is given in Table 4. By doing this process again and again, the translation of 'ഇന്ത്യ' converges to the word 'India' as t(India|ഇന്ത്യ) has the highest probability value.

4 Integrating Morphological Information into Parallel Corpus

On introducing the training method described earlier into the parallel corpus, a large number of alignment vectors are obtained. Out of it a major share belongs to the group of insignificant alignments. An example of an unwanted alignment is shown in Fig. 3.

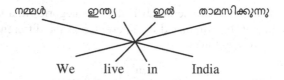

Fig. 3. Insignificant alignments

Presence of these unwanted ones complicates the training mechanism. Most of these alignments hold little meaning and is useless in building up the fractional count. To get rid of the alignments which have no significance and to reduce the burden of calculating the fractional count and alignment probabilities for every alignment of sentence pairs, the morphological information is incorporated into the corpora. The bilingual corpus is tagged and then subjected to training. Tagging is done by considering the parts of speech entities of a sentence.

4.1 Tagging the Corpus

By tagging the corpus extra meaning is embedded into each word which definitely helps in the formation of reasonably good alignments. The structure of the Malayalam sentence is analyzed and the different Parts of Speech (PoS) categories are identified. In a sentence there may be many words belonging to the same PoS category. After the tagging process, a word that doesn't have an exact translation in Malayalam may be deleted to improve the efficiency of the training phase. The English sentence is tagged in the same manner and paired with its tagged Malayalam translation. The word to word alignments are found only for the words that belong to the same PoS category of both languages. There is little chance for the words belonging to two different categories to be translations of each other and hence they need not be aligned. This helps to bring down the total number of alignments to a greater extent.

Without tagging, when all the words in a sentence are considered, the number of alignments, N_A, generated is equal to the factorial of its word count and is shown as

$$N_A = \text{factorial}(Ws) . \tag{1}$$

where Ws is the number of words in the sentence. The same corpus when tagged produces less number of alignments than factorial(Ws). By tagging, the number of categories present in a sentence is identified. There may be many words with the same tag in a sentence. Categorizing the sentence leads to grouping of words that belong to the same tag. The number of alignments for words belonging to same category is factorial(Wc) where Wc is the number of words in a category. Therefore the total number of alignments of a sentence formed by tagging, N_AT, results in

$$N_AT = \prod_{i=1}^{m} factorial(Wc_i) . \tag{2}$$

alignment vectors, where m is the number of PoS categories in a sentence pair. The insignificant alignment, I_A, eliminated is represented as the difference between Equation 1 and 2 and is given below:

$$I_A = factorial(Ws) - \prod_{i=1}^{m} factorial(Wc_i) . \tag{3}$$

By this method the number of alignment vector for the sentence pair SP1 is just one instead of twenty four. The steps involved in eliminating the insignificant alignments from the corpus are given below.

Step1: Tag all sentences in English and Malayalam corpus based on its parts of speech category.

Step2: Separate the suffixes from the Malayalam corpus and remove the suffix that doesn't have an equivalent English translation.

Step3: Generate the alignment vectors corresponding to each sentence pair by considering the category tags.

Step4: For the Malayalam word mw_i, initialize the fractional count as 1/number of words present in mw_i's category .

Step5: For all sentence pair in the parallel corpus calculate the alignment probability and normalize it.

Step6: For all words find the revised fractional count and normalize it

Step7: Repeat steps 5 and 6 until convergence

The training technique with tagged corpus is analyzed with corpus2 containing two sentences.

SP1: നമ്മൾ   ഇന്ത്യ   ഇൽ   താമസിക്കുന്നു
      (nammal India   il thammasikkunnu)
      We live in India

SP2: ന്യൂഡൽഹി   ഇന്ത്യയുടെ   തലസ്ഥാനം   ആണ്
      (Newdelhi indiayude thalasthaanam aanu)
      NewDelhi is the capital of India

In SP2 the tagged sentence structure is NewDelhi/NNP is/VBZ the/DT capital/NN of/IN India/NNP. The sentence pairs with its category are shown in Table 5.

Table 5. PoS category of corpus2

Category	id	Word
Proper Noun	m0	ഇന്ത്യ(India)
	m1	ന്യൂഡൽഹി (Newdelhi)
Noun	m2	തലസ്ഥാനം thalasthaanam)
Verb, 3rd ps.sing.present	m3	ആണ്(aanu)
Personal pronoun	m4	നമ്മള് (nammal)
Verb,non-3rd ps.sing.present	m5	താമസിക്കുന്നു thaamasikunnu)

Table 6. IFC of the word 'ഇന്ത്യ' in tagged corpus

Id	Possible translations	IFC
e0	India	0.5
e1	NewDelhi	0.5

Trying to find the word translation for the word ഇന്ത്യ(India), it is well understood that ഇന്ത്യ(India) may no longer be associated with all the English words in the corpus. It need to be associated only with the proper nouns (NNP) in the parallel corpus. To find the translation for the word ഇന്ത്യ t(Proper Nouns | ഇന്ത്യ) is considered and the IFC of ഇന്ത്യ is calculated as 1/ Total number of Proper Nouns in the corpus. Table 6 gives the IFC of word 'ഇന്ത്യ' in the tagged corpus. The alignment probabilities of the sentence pairs and the revised fractional count for the word ഇന്ത്യ are calculated with the new IFC.

In corpus1 and corpus2 the word ഇന്ത്യ (India) occur twice and therefore they are compared and analyzed to identify the advantages of the tagging method. The alignment probability and the normalized fractional count of the word 'ഇന്ത്യ'(India) after adopting the tagged corpus is given in Table 7and 8 respectively.

Table 7. Alignment vectors and alignment probabilities of tagged corpus

SP	Alignment vectors	Alignment Weights of e_i given m_i				AP	NAP
SP1	[m4,m5, m0]	$t(e0/m4)$ $= 1$	$t(e1/m5)$ $= 1$	$t(e3/m0)$ $= 0.75$	-	0.75	1
SP2	[m0,m3, m2,m1]	$t(e0/m4)$ $= 0.25$	$t(e1/m4)$ $= 1$	$t(e3/m4)$ $=1$	$t(e5/m4)$ $=0.5$	0.13	0.25
	[m1,m3, m2, m0]	$t(e0/m4)$ $= 0.5$	$t(e1/m4)$ $= 1$	$t(e3/m4)$ $= 1$	$t(e5/m4)$ $= 0.75$	0.38	0.75

Table 8. RFC of words in Proper Noun category

Proper Noun	Possible translations	RFC
ഇന്ത്യ	India	0.88
	NewDelhi	0.13
ന്യൂഡൽഹി	India	0.25
	NewDelhi	0.75

5 Observations and Results Achieved by Tagging the Parallel Corpus

By enhancing the training technique, it is observed that the translation probabilities calculated from the corpus shows better statistical values of translation probability. The end product of the training phase is obtained much faster. In the iterative process of finding the best translation, it takes less number of rounds to complete the training process.

Imparting the parts of speech information into the parallel corpus has made it rich with more information which in turn helps in picking up the correct translation for a given Malayalam word. It has reduced the complexity of the alignment model by cutting short the insignificant alignments. The meaningless alignments have a tendency to consume more space and time thereby increasing the space and time complexity of the training process. It has been observed that the rate of generating alignment vectors have fallen down to a remarkably low value as shown by Equation 2. Here the alignment vector is directly proportional to the number of words in the PoS category and not to the number of words in the sentence pair. Utmost care has to be taken while tagging the corpus, since wrong tagging leads to the generation of absurd translations.

By tagging the corpus better translations for English words are obtained and it has enhanced the final outcome of the SMT. These results are evaluated using WER, F measure and BLEU metrics and is discussed in [11].

6 Conclusion

An alignment model and a training technique mostly suited for statistical machine translators from English to Malayalam have been put forward. Using the parts of speech tags as an additional knowledge source, the parallel corpus is enriched and it contains more information to select the correct word translation for a Malayalam word. The alignment model with category tags is useful in diminishing the set of alignments for each sentence pair and thereby simplifying the complexity of the training phase. This technique helps to improve the quality of word translations obtained for Malayalam words from the parallel corpus.

References

1. Lopez, A.: Statistical Machine Translation. ACM Computing Survey, Article 8, 40(3) (2008)
2. Mary, P.S., Sheena, K.K., Santhosh, K.G.: Statistical Machine Translation from English to Malayalam. In: Proceedings of National Conference on Advanced Computing, Alwaye, Kerala (2010)
3. Brown, P.F., Pietra, S.A.D., Pietra, V.J.D., Jelinek, F., Lafferty, J.D., Mercer, R.L., Roossin, P.S.: A Statistical Approach to Machine Translation. Computational Linguistics 16(2), 79–85 (1990)
4. Brown, P.F., Pietra, S.A.D., Pietra, V.J.D., Mercer, R.L.: The Mathematics of Statistical Machine Translation: Parameter Estimation. Computational Linguistics 19(2), 263–311 (1993)
5. Dempster, A.P., Laird, N.M., Rubin, D.B.: Maximum Likelihood from Incomplete Data Via The EM Algorithm. Journal of the Royal Statistical Society 39(B), 1–38 (1999)
6. Knight, K.: A Statistical MT Tutorial Work Book (1999) (unpublished), http://www.cisp.jhu.edu/ws99/projects/mt/wkbk.rtf
7. Ananthakrishnan, R., Hegde, J., Bhattacharyya, P., Shah, R., Sasikumar, M.: Simple Syntactic and Morphological Processing Can Help English-Hindi Statistical Machine Translation. In: International Joint Conference on NLP, Hyderabad, India (2008)
8. Sumam, M.I., Peter, S.D.: A Morphological Processor for Malayalam Language. South Asia Research 27(2), 173–186 (2008)
9. Ueffing, N., Ney, H.: Using POS Information for Statistical Machine Translation into Morphologically Rich Languages. In: Proceedings of the 10th Conference on European Chapter of the Association for Computational Linguistics, vol. 1 (2003)
10. Sanchis, G., Sńchez, J.A.: Vocabulary Extension via PoS Information for SMT. In: Proceedings of the NAACL (2006)
11. Mary, P.S., Sheena, K.K., Santhosh, K.G.: A Framework of Statistical Machine Translator from English to Malayalam. In: Proceedings of Fourth International Conference on Information Processing, Bangalore, India (accepted 2010)
12. Jurafsky, D., Martin, J.H.: Speech and Language Processing: An Introduction to Natural Language Processing, Speech Recognition and Computational Linguistics, 2nd edn. Prentice-Hall, Englewood Cliffs (2008)
13. Allen, J.F.: Natural Language Understanding, 2nd edn. Pearson Education, London (2002)

Emotion Classification Based on Speaking Rate

Shashidhar G. Koolagudi, Sudhin Ray, and K. Sreenivasa Rao

School of Information Technology,
Indian Institute of Technology Kharagpur, Kharagpur - 721302, West Bengal, India
koolagudi@yahoo.com, sudhinray@gmail.com, ksrao@iitkgp.ac.in

Abstract. In this paper, vocal tract characteristics related to speaking rate are explored to categorise the emotions. The emotions considered are anger, disgust, fear, happy, neutral, sadness, sarcastic and surprise. These emotions are grouped into 3 broad categories namely normal, fast and slow based on speaking rate. Mel frequency cepstral coefficients (MFCC's) are used as features and Gaussian Mixture Models are used for developing the emotion classification models. The basic hypothesis is that the sequence of vocal tract shapes in producing the speech for the given utterance is unique with respect to the speaking rate. The overall classification performance of emotions using speaking rate is observed to be 91% in case of single female utterances.

Keywords: Emotion categorization, Fast speech, Gaussian mixture models, IITKGP-SESC, IITKGP-Speaking Rate Speech Corpus, Normal speech, Slow speech, Speaking rate.

1 Introduction

Speaking rate is normally defined as the number of words spoken per minute. The speaking rate of around 130-200 words per minute is treated as normal. Generally addition/removal of around 40 words per every minute to/from the normal speech makes it fast or slow. The speaker unknowingly changes speaking rate attributes of his speech such as pause and vowel durations, according to the situation [1], [2]. During natural contexts, one can compress or expand the speech duration to the maximum level of around 20%, because of physiological limitations of human speech production system. But during emotional contexts the variations in speaking rates is very high due to hormonal activities. For instance speaking rate of an angry person is nearly one and a half times in comparison to his speech in neutral contexts. The same for sad speech is nearly halved.

In general speaking rate is characterized by different parameters of speech. The varied rates of articulatory movements, inclusion of deliberate pauses between spoken words, varying duration of these pauses, expressing sudden emotions, stressing certain words or syllables while speaking, being more imperative during conversation and so on [3], [4], [5]. Several investigations are done on the relationship between speaking rate variation and articulator behavior in terms of

S. Ranka et al. (Eds.): IC3 2010, Part I, CCIS 94, pp. 316–327, 2010.

their displacement, gesture duration, velocity of movements, etc. [6], [3]. Changing velocity of articulator movement causes abrupt switching from one vocal tract(VT) shape to the other. The transition is so fast that the duration of VT shape being in a steady state is very less. So it especially affects the prominence of higher formants. Abrupt change in VT shape also results in reduced spectral tilt. Pause and their durations inserted in between the spoken words mostly contribute towards prosodic aspects. Emotional state or specific psychological state of the speaker will also involuntarily influence one's speaking rate variations. As this speaking rate is mainly due to VT activities, we have decided to use vocal tract features for modeling speaking rate. The sequence of vocal tract shapes is mostly unique for the speech spoken with specific rate.

Effect of speaking rate on the production of sound units is a matter of great interest. Its influence on perception is studied in detail by Jack *et al* [7]. Different analytical studies are conducted to observe the behavior of vocal tract while producing speech with varying rates [7]. The change in the prosodic parameter F0 and its contours, observed to be clearly distinctive as the speaking rate changes [7]. Intelligibility of speech is also considerably affected by changing the speaking rate. Jan Von Doorn reported that the mean intelligibility scores are reduced by 5-6%, when speaking rate is increased [4]. He also showed that varying the duration of pauses has least influence on intelligibility. But in this study emphasis is given to the involuntary change in the speaking rate, that represents the emotional state of the speaker. For instance if a person is in anger or aroused, his speaking rate automatically increases, where as a person in sad mood normally speaks in very low voice with reduced speaking rate. So speaking rate may act as an important cue to assess speaker's emotional state. Speech perception is not much affected, when there is a natural change in speaking rate. But its analysis helps to understand the intension of the speaker, which does not normally expressed through text.

speaking rate variability is found to be significant during speech and speaker recognition tasks, especially when there is a considerable speaking rate variation between training and testing data. The concept of human-like, man -machine speech interface is aimed at modeling day-to-day speaking rate variations, occurring due to emotional expressions. In this paper Gaussian Mixture Models are used to discriminate the emotional speech utterances based on their speaking rate.

The next section briefly discusses the design and collection emotional speech database IITKGP-SESC. Section 3 explains the motivation behind this study. Explanation of experimental setup and analysis of results is done in section 4. The paper is concluded with summary and scope for future work.

2   Indian Institute of Technology Kharagpur - Simulated Emotion Speech Corpus (IITKGP:SESC)

For analyzing speaking rate to recognize emotional categories, two speech databases have been used. One is exclusively collected with varying speaking rates and the other is with different emotions. This section discusses the details of emotional speech corpus. The database is recorded using 10 (5 male and 5 female) professional artists from All India Radio (AIR) Vijayawada, India. The artists have sufficient experience in expressing the desired emotions from the neutral sentences. All the artists are in the age group of 25-40 years, and have professional experience of 8-12 years. The eight emotions considered for recording this database are anger, disgust, fear, happy, neutral, sadness, sarcastic and surprise. Fifteen emotionally neutral, Telugu sentences are chosen as text prompts for the database. Each of the artists have to speak the 15 sentences in 8 given emotions in one session. The number of sessions recorded for preparing the database is 10. The total number of utterances in the database is 12000 (15 *sentences* × 8 *emotions* × 10 *artists* × 10 *sessions*). Each emotion has 1500 utterances. The number of words and syllables in the sentences vary from 3-6 and 11-18 respectively. The total duration of the database is around 7 hours. The speech samples are recorded using SHURE dynamic cardioid microphone C606N. The speech signal is sampled at 16 kHz, and each sample is represented as 16 bit number. The sessions were recorded on alternate days to capture the variability of the human speech production system. The recording was done in such a way that each artist had to speak all the sentences at a stretch in a particular emotion. This provides the coherence among the sentences for a specific emotion category. The entire speech database was recorded using single microphone at the same location, in a quiet room, without any obstacles in the recording path. The proposed speech database is the first one developed in an Indian language for analyzing the basic emotions. This database is sufficiently large to analyze the emotions in view of speaker, gender, text and session variability [8].

3   Motivation

To analyse the influence of speaking rate on emotion expression, speech features may be extracted from different levels of speech signal, like source, system and prosodic. Excitation source features - representing vocal folds' vibration pattern, spectral features representing - the characteristics of vocal tract system, prosodic features representing - broader level speech and speaker dynamics, may be used as knowledge sources. Any one of the above three or combination of them may be explored for the studies. To study the characteristics of speaking rate, a specific speech database is collected at Indian Institute of Technology, Kharagpur. The basic aim of this study is to explore classification of speech utterances on the basis of rate with which those are spoken. The speaking rate database is recorded using 5 female and 5 male research students of IIT Kharagpur. Ten neutral Hindi sentences are used as the text for recording. Each of them uttered all 10 sentences in 5 different rates namely super-slow, slow, normal, fast and super-fast. So the database contains 50 male and 50 female utterances in each of the speaking rate categories. This database is named as IITKGP-Speaking Rate Speech Corpus Database (IITKGP-SRSC). In this study, spectral features of the speech signal are used to characterize the speaking rate. Speaking rate being one of the important speech features, gets manifested and manipulated mainly by the articulator activities. By varying the speed of movement of articulator organs and period of articulator's gesture, one can artificially produce the speech with different rates. Speech with slow rate basically gets sufficient time for articulation, and there will be a smooth and gradual transition from one shape of the vocal tract to the other. Hence leading to clear prominence of the formant frequencies. Fig.1 shows the spectra for one of the frames of the steady region of the vowel from the syllable 'maa' in the utterance 'maataa aur pitaa kaa aadar karanaa chaahiye'.

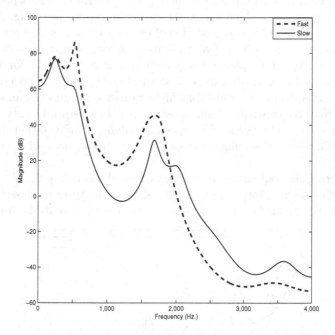

Fig. 1. The spectra of a frame from a steady region of the syllable *maa*, taken from the utterance *maataa aur pitaa kaa aadar karanaa chaahiye*

The two spectra represent the steady portion of the same vowel of fast and slow utterances uttered by the same male speaker. The formant frequencies are very prominent and clearly observable from the spectrum of slow utterance, where as sharpness of spectrum is less for the formants in case of fast expression. Some spurious peaks are also observed in the spectra (sharp peak seen immediately after the first formant in case of fast utterance). It is also evident from the visual observation that faster spectral roll-off is observed in case of fast speech (slope of line joining of F_2 and F_3), indicating abrupt change in the vocal tract shapes. The difference in the spectral energies of F_2 and F_3 is less in case of slow speech compared to that of fast speech. This also indicates the emotion specific information present in spectral features. From the duration analysis of emotional sentences shown in Table 2, one can clearly observe that the time taken to utter the same sentence in different emotions by varying the duration is mainly due to the variation in speaking rate. This is the motivation to take up this study. Similar observations are also evident from the spectra of the steady regions of the same vowel spoken in different emotions.

The speed of vocal folds' vibration manipulates the behavior of the vocal tract to produce a sound unit in a specific way. The phenomenon of opening of vocal folds is observed to be more or less same due to their tensile/ muscular restriction. But it is observed from the literature that, there is a considerable variation during vocal folds' closure. It is also known that abrupt closure of vocal folds makes the spectrum more flat causing less spectral tilt. This phenomenon, perceptually increases the loudness of the speech unit produced. Fig. 2 shows the spectra obtained from the steady portion of the syllable segment expressed in five selected emotions. From Fig. 2, fear and anger emotions show less tilt indicating more energy in higher frequency components. The spectral tilt for happy and neutral seems to be sharp. It can be measured as the slope of spectral roll-off. It is also observed from the figure that higher order formants (F_3 and F_4) found to be more distinctive with respect to emotions. In this study only F_1 and F_2 analysis is shown as they generally represent phonetic information. It is known that the variation in speaking rate, causes the unique way of producing the phoneme.

For capturing the sequential information of vocal tract shapes, MFCC features are used in this study. Motivation for using spectral features to classify emotions on the basis of speaking rate comes from the formant analysis done on slow

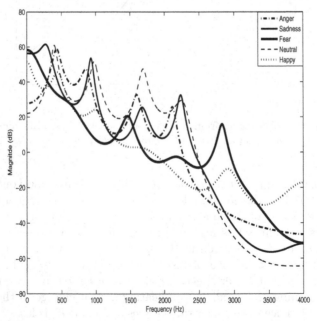

Fig. 2. The spectra of a frame from a steady region of the syllable *tha*, taken from the utterance *thallithandrulunu gouravincha valenu*

and fast speech utterances of IITKGP-SRD. Fig. 3 shows the distribution of F_2 values for the utterance 'maataa aur pitaa kaa aadar karanaa chaahiye', uttered in slow and fast rates. F_2 values for slow utterance have occupied lower frequency range from around 1400 Hz. to 1600 Hz., where as the same for fast utterance are distributed from above 1600 Hz. It is also evident from Fig. 3, that the range of F_2 for slow utterance is narrow (around 200 Hz.: 1400 Hz.-1600 Hz.), where as the same for fast utterance is wider (around 1100 Hz. : 1600 Hz.- 2700 Hz.) F_2 values for fast utterance are shown only upto 150 frames as the duration is lesser compared to that of slow utterance.

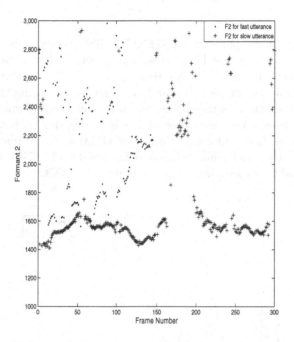

Fig. 3. F_2 values for fast and slow utterances for the text *maataa aur pitaa kaa aadar karanaa chaahiye*

The histogram of F_2 values drawn for fast and slow speech also depicts the clear distinction of F_2 distribution. Mostly all F_2 values for slow speech occupy the range of 1400-1600 Hz, whereas the range of the same for fast speech is wider with 1600-2600 Hz. The details are shown in Fig. 4. Nonlinear scale is chosen along X axis depending upon the density of the points.

Similarly F_1 Vs F_2 for slow and fast utterances are plotted in Fig. 5. One can clearly observe the cluster patterns of F_1- Vs- F_2 values. Here also points for slow utterance occupy distinguishable region on the initial part of the graph upto 300 Hz., where as the same for fast utterance occupy later portion above 250 Hz.

In this task GMM classifiers are used to classify the utterances on the basis of speaking rate [9]. Initially Gaussian Mixture Models are trained using the

Table 1. classification of speech utterances based on the speaking rate. Average : 82%. Database : IITKGP-SRSC.

	Super slow	Slow	Normal	Fast	Super fast
Super-slow	53	33	14	0	0
Slow	20	63	10	07	00
Normal	00	00	97	03	00
Fast	00	00	03	97	00
Super-fast	00	00	00	00	100

utterances of one male speaker from IITKGP-SRSC. The database contains the sentences with 5 varying speaking rates, namely super-slow, slow, normal, fast, super-fast. In each category there are 10 sentences of different text. Out of these, 8 are used for training the models and 2 are used for validating them. Each test utterance is sliced into 3 equal pieces. So there are totally 6 speech utterances for validation, in each category. One GMM is trained for each of the 5 speaking rate categories. Different configurations of GMM are experimented, and 82% average classification performance was accomplished for the GMM's with 4 components, iterated 25 times towards convergence. 13 MFCC values are extracted

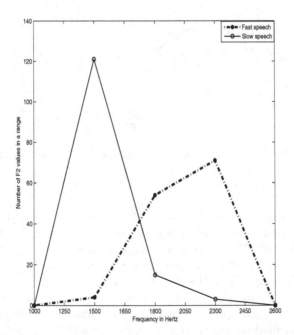

Fig. 4. Histogram of F_2 values for fast and slow utterances for the text *maataa aur pitaa kaa aadar karanaa chaahiye*

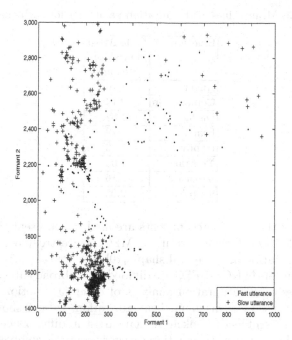

Fig. 5. F_1-Vs-F_2 values for fast and slow utterances for the text *maataa aur pitaa kaa aadar karanaa chaahiye*

from every speech frame of 20 ms. and a standard 10 ms. frame shift is used to compute feature vectors. This technique of overlapping frames is used to capture continuously varying signal characteristics. The classification performance of the experiment is shown in Table 1. The diagonal elements in the matrix show the correct classification performance, whereas the other entries in each row indicate the percentage of miss-classified utterances. It is clear from the table that machine can understand faster utterances better compared to the slower ones.

The analysis of formants shown in Fig. 3 and Fig. 5, the results tabulated in Table 1, motivated the task of categorising the emotions on the basis of speaking rate.

4   Classification of Emotions on Speaking Rate

MFCC features are effectively used for speech and speaker recognition. Variation of articulation rate results in variation of speaking rate. Change in phoneme duration is a major cause for this variation. Expression of emotions mainly depends upon the speaker. MFCC features use human perceptual mechanism during their computation. Therefore MFCC features are used in this study to characterize the speaking rate and the emotions. Inverse Fourier transform of log spectrum is known as cepstrum. The cepstrum computed after non-linear frequency wrapping onto a perceptual frequency scale (mel-scale) gives mel frequency cepstral

Table 2. Mean values of the duration parameter for each emotion

Emotion	Male Artist Duration (Seconds)
Anger	1.76
Compassion	2.13
Disgust	1.62
Fear	1.79
Happy	2.03
Neutral	1.93
Sarcastic	2.16
Surprise	2.05

coefficients. Only the first few coefficients are used to represent the frame of 20 ms. In this task 13 coefficients are used. MFCC's are treated as efficient and compact representation of a spectral shape [10].

Eight emotions of IITKGP-SESC are divided into 3 broad categories as active, normal and passive. The duration analysis of different emotions, obtained on IITKGP-SESC is used for this manual categorization. Table 2 shows the average duration of all the sentences, spoken by male artist in different emotions. Based on this study, 'slow' or 'passive' emotion category contains compassion (sadness) and sarcastic. 'Fast' or 'active' category contains anger, fear and disgust, where as neutral, happy and surprise are grouped into normal. Though 3 broad emotional categories are assumed, based on speaking rate, in practice it is very difficult to categorise them only on the basis of duration values. Fig. 6 shows the histogram of duration values for 4 emotions. The overlap of emotions may be observed from the figure, which may lead to mis-classification.

Three GMM's are trained to capture the characteristic properties of 3 categories. In each category 80% of the utterances are used to train the models and remaining 20% are used for testing them. IITKGP-SESC contains 150 utterances recorded for each emotion, by each speaker (15 *sentences* × 10 *sessions*). Out of 150, 120 utterances are used for training. It means - the model for slow emotion is trained with 240 utterances (120 *sentences per emotion* × 2 *emotions*). The model for fast emotions is trained using 360 (120 *per emotion* × 3 *emotions*) utterances and the normal emotion model is trained with 360 utterances (120 *per emotion* × 3 *emotions*). All the models are tested with 30 utterances of respective categories. The best classification performance was achieved by the models with 32 Gaussian components, converged after 30 iterations. The average categorization performance is found to be 91.33% for single female speaker utterances. Table 3 shows the percentage emotion classification performance based on speaking rate for a single female speaker. Columns of the table indicate the trained models and rows indicate the percentage of test utterances classified under different categories. The diagonal elements show the correct classification, whereas other elements in the row show the miss-classification among the different models. Inter miss-classification of slow emotions as normal is quite obvious and expected considering the overlapping of emotions in their duration plane.

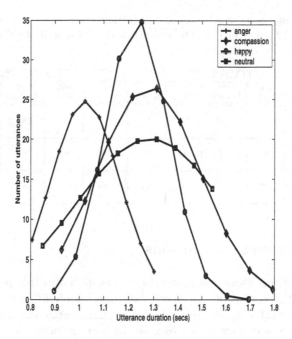

Fig. 6. Distribution of the durations for different emotions of the female artist

The effect of speaking rate on expression of emotions is studied from various viewpoints. The role of speaker specific information, gender related characteristics are studied in detail. The effect of higher order MFCC values on classification of emotions based on speaking rate is also studied. Table 4 shows the average emotion classification performance for different studies using 13 and 21 MFCC values. It is evident from the table that the emotion recognition performance for active and normal emotions is better compared to that of passive emotions (See rows 3 and 4). The emotions expressed by females are well recognised compared to the emotions expressed by males (See columns 2 and 3). Keen observation of results, also reveals that higher order MFCC's are better for speaker and gender independent emotion classification (See columns 6 and 11). This shows that lower order spectral features preserve phoneme and speaker specific information, whereas higher order features may help to capture the broader information like emotions.

Table 3. Emotion classification performance based on the speaking rate. Speaker : Single female. Database : IITKGP-SESC.

	Fast	Normal	Slow
Fast	93	07	00
Normal	00	97	03
Slow	03	13	84

Table 4. Performance of the emotion recognition systems developed by using (1) 13 MFCC's and (2) 21 MFCC's. The entries in the table indicate the percentage of recognition.

	13 MFCC's					21 MFCC's				
	Single female	Single male	Five females	Five males	5 fe. 5 ma.	Single female	Single male	Five females	Five males	5 fe. 5 ma.
Active emotions (fast)	93	83	87	77	74	93	87	87	80	83
Normal emotions (normal)	97	87	77	93	57	100	84	80	93	63
Passive emotions (slow)	84	87	77	70	64	80	83	80	77	74

5   Summary and Conclusions

Analysis of emotions using speaking rate was proposed in this paper. IITKGP-Speaking Rate Speech Corpus, a speech database with 5 different speaking rates is recorded. Spectral features are exploited to characterize the speaking rate, as the variation in vocal tract activities is an important cause for speaking rates. Gaussian Mixture Models are explored as classifiers. Later the concept is extended to categorization of emotions in 3 broad groups namely active, normal and passive emotions, using the database IITKGP-SESC. The prosodic analysis of IITKGP-SESC helped us to manually categorise 8 emotions into 3 groups. After validating the trained models we observed 82% of classification performance in case of classification of utterances based on speaking rate and 91.33 % is achieved in case of emotion categorization using speaking rate.

The experiments and results presented in this paper are obtained from single female speaker's utterances. The data corpus is also very small. More general observations may be derived by collecting gender independent, larger speech database, which may also be used to text independent experiments. Better non-linear classifiers like artificial neural networks may be explored to improve the classification performance. It is pointed in the literature that, duration of pauses is the major factor getting influenced by the change in speaking rate. We have removed the pauses before building the models, as they do not contribute positively to the spectral features. Prosodic features including pause pattern modeling may be studied as an extended work.

References

1. Sreenivasa Rao, K., Yegnanarayana, B.: Modeling durations of syllables using neural networks. Computer Speech and Language 21, 282–295 (2007)
2. Agwuelea, A., Harvey, M.S., Lindblom, B.: The Effect of Speaking Rate on Consonant Vowel Coarticulation. Phonetica 65, 194–209 (2008)

3. Martinez, J.F., Tapias, D., Alvarez, I.: Toward speech rate independence in large vocabulary continuous speech recognition. In: International Conference on Signal and Speesh Processing, pp. 725–728 (1998)
4. Van Doorn, J.: Does artificially increased speech rate help? In: 8th Aust. International Conference on Speech Science and Technology, pp. 750–755 (2000)
5. Goldman Eisler, F.: The significance of changes in the rate of articulation. Language and Speech 4, 171–175 (1961)
6. Wang, D., Narayanan, S.: Speech rate estimation via temporal correlation and selected sub-band correlation. In: International Conference on Acoustics, Speech, and Signal Processing (2000)
7. Gandour, J., Tumtavitikulc, A., Satthamnuwongb, N.: Effects of Speaking Rate on Thai Tones. Phonetica 56(3-4), 123–134 (1999)
8. Koolagudi Shashidhar, G., Sudhamay, M., Kumar, V.A., Saswat, C., Sreenivasa Rao, K.: IITKGP-SESC: Speech Database for Emotion Analysis. In: Communications in Computer and Information Science. LNCS. Springer, Heidelberg (2009), ISSN: 1865-0929
9. Duda, R.O., Hart, P.E., Stork, D.G.: Pattern Classification. John Wiley, Chichester (2001)
10. Rabiner, L.R., Juang, B.H.: Fundamentals of Speech Recognition. Prentice-Hall, Englewood Cliffs (1993)

A Vulnerability Metric for the Design Phase of Object Oriented Software

A. Agrawal and R.A. Khan

Department of Information Technology,
BBA University, Vidya Vihar, Raebareli Road, Lucknow, India
alka_csjmu@yahoo.co.in, khanraees@yahoo.com

Abstract. Unlike quality, quantitative estimation of security at design phase of object oriented software is largely missing. The work examines that coupling is one of the object oriented design characteristic responsible for propagation of vulnerabilities in the design of software. A metric is proposed to determine whether the design of one version of a software system is more vulnerable than another with respect to propagation of vulnerability. Unlike, counting bugs at the code level or counting vulnerability reports at system level, the proposed metric measures the overall propagation of vulnerabilities in an object oriented design.

Keywords: Object-oriented, Design Phase, Software Security, Vulnerability Propagation, Design Characteristics, Coupling.

1 Introduction

Software security is concerned with maintaining confidentiality, integrity and availability of data managed by the software [16]. A software failed to offer the three attributes of security is termed as vulnerable software [16]. Vulnerabilities are the defects introduced in the software during its development [9]. These vulnerabilities are the only reason behind confidentiality, integrity and availability breach of the software. That is why less vulnerable software which may protect an organization's assets from attacks, is in high demand among security seekers. This has given birth to the development of strict security mechanisms. But merely applying security mechanisms does not solve the problem. Strict security mechanisms badly affect usability and also no security mechanism guarantees complete security [1]. The problem becomes worse when the vulnerabilities are propagated from one component of the software to the other. The reason behind is simple; increasing availability of a vulnerable entity would also increase the vulnerability [13].

Design phase of the software development is the first step towards solution of the problem. Structure of the software is produced during this phase. Vulnerabilities introduced in this phase may manifest themselves in the subsequent phases of software development life cycle. Despite of the fact that concentrating on design vulnerabilities reduces cost and rework [10], the phase is largely ignored [1]. The literature available on software vulnerabilities generally revolve around code level vulnerabilities and system level vulnerabilities. G. McGraw [1] strongly believes that a vulnerable design

S. Ranka et al. (Eds.): IC3 2010, Part I, CCIS 94, pp. 328–339, 2010.

may never produce secure software. Though, few efforts have been done to produce secure design [10, 15]. But without any quantitative estimation, how one is able to judge

- Whether newer design of software is more secure than the older one.
- Which design is more vulnerable among designs of different software?

The proposed work tries to address the above mentioned difficulties utilizing the facts that

- In order to minimize vulnerabilities, the propagation of vulnerabilities must be controlled [13].
- Similar to quality, design characteristics, the means by which vulnerability propagation are made, need to be analyzed to make appropriate decision regarding the same.

As coupling has been identified as one of the means responsible for the quality degradation of an object oriented design [3], a humble attempt has been made to investigate the impact of coupling on propagation of vulnerabilities for object oriented design.

Rest of the paper is organized as: next section discusses about approach for measuring Coupling Induced Vulnerability Propagation Factor (CIVPF). Section 3 discusses about interesting results of the approach and their interpretation. In section 4, a comparative case study of two versions of Automated Teller Machine (ATM) has been carried out to validate the claim. Section 5 compares the existing approaches with proposed one. Advantages and limitations of the approach are listed in section 6. Paper concludes at section 7.

2   Development of Vulnerability Metric

An object oriented design (OOD) is centered on key entities as objects, attributes, methods and classes. These entities are arranged to form the design of software through design characteristics including Inheritance, Coupling, Cohesion, Encapsulation, polymorphism etc. In order to measure and minimize Vulnerabilities and their propagation, design characteristics must be investigated to find out whether they propagate vulnerability or restrict its propagation. Vulnerability minimization may be carried out by avoiding the use of characteristics causing vulnerability propagation and by encouraging the use of characteristics restricting the vulnerability propagation.

Coupling is the dependency of an entity to the other. Considerable research has been made to identify and assess the effect of Coupling on quality. As security is an attribute of quality, it becomes necessary to examine the effect of coupling on security too. Studies have been proven that higher coupling has negative impact on quality [3]. On the basis of the results [3] following hypothesis is made for security.

Hypothesis. As coupling increases, vulnerability propagation increases and hence security decreases.

At the same time, it has also been realized that development of large and complex systems can not be possible without Coupling. It is an unavoidable design decision.

Whether it is quality or security, Coupling can not be ignored at all. So, when it comes to security, instead of minimizing overall Coupling, the main focus should be on minimizing coupling of security related entities.

2.1 Terminology Used

Vulnerable Attribute and Vulnerable Method

Software vulnerability is defined as 'susceptibility to attack', i.e. every entity in the software which is attack prone is considered to be vulnerable. Hence, an attribute is considered to be vulnerable if it possesses one or more of the following characteristics [2]:

- Provides entry points for external application
- Processes confidential information
- Involves in internal network communication
- Allows user authentication and control

A method is considered to be vulnerable if it uses a vulnerable attribute.

Root Vulnerable Class

A class is termed as root vulnerable class if it declares at least one vulnerable attribute.

Induced Vulnerable Class

A class is termed as Induced Vulnerable Class if it is coupled with root vulnerable class through a vulnerable attribute or is coupled with one or more induced vulnerable classes.

Coupling Induced Vulnerability Propagation (CIVP)

If a class A is a Root Vulnerable Class and class B is defined in such a way that

- Class B is inheriting a vulnerable attribute of class A or
- A vulnerable method of class A is called by some method of class B or
- A vulnerable attribute of A is passed as parameter to some method of B or
- Vulnerable class A is the type of an attribute of class B.

Then A and B would said to have Coupling Induced Vulnerability Propagation and class B would be called an Induced Vulnerable Class. The phenomenon is termed as Strong Vulnerability Propagation or First Level Propagation.

However, if a class A is an Induced Vulnerable Class and B is a class such that one of the attribute of class B is of type A, then this type of Coupling Induced Vulnerability Propagation would be Weak Vulnerability Propagation or Second/ Higher Level propagation. The term 'weak' has been taken for the propagation because in this type of propagation, classes declaring the attribute of type induced vulnerable class, may or may not use vulnerable attribute.

The hypothesis and claim in above definition may be proved by transitivity property of relational algebra. Suppose there are three classes A, B and C. A is a root vulnerable class and R is a relation such that

A R B ⟹ A is related to B through a vulnerable attributes or methods.

B R C ⟹ B is related to C through a vulnerable attributes or methods.

Hence, A R C ⟹ A is related to C through a vulnerable attribute or methods, and the propagation goes on with the coupling of vulnerable attributes or methods.

2.2 Measuring Coupling Induced Vulnerability Propagation of an OOD

The aim of the work is to investigate how vulnerabilities are propagated from root vulnerable classes to others. All the classes communicating with root vulnerable class through its vulnerable attribute will be strong vulnerable. The other classes in design communicating with strong vulnerable classes are weak vulnerable and the vulnerability propagation becomes weaker and weaker for the next levels of communication. If there are p vulnerable attributes and M classes are root vulnerable because of these p attributes ($p \geq$ M, as a class may have more than one vulnerable attributes), computation of Coupling Induced Vulnerability Propagation Factor may be performed as:

Let Li represents the total Coupling Induced Vulnerability Propagation from a root vulnerable class Ci to the others, then overall Coupling Induced Vulnerability Propagation in an OOD due to p vulnerable attributes may be given as:

CIVPOOD= L1 + L2 + ...+ Lp

Hence,

$$CIVPOOD= \sum_{i=1}^{p} Li \tag{1}$$

So, Coupling Induced Vulnerability Propagation Factor comes out as:

$$CIVPF = IVPOOD/ N= \sum_{i=1}^{p} Li / N \tag{2}$$

Where, N is the total number of classes in OOD. An algorithm computing CIVPF has been described in the next subsection.

The Algorithm. If M classes out of N classes in an OOD are root vulnerable classes, an algorithm has been proposed to compute overall CIVP using which it computes Coupling Induced Vulnerability Propagation Factor (CIVPF). The algorithm takes as input a list class_list[1..N], and a queue VUL[1..M]. class_list[1..N] contains the classes present in the design and VUL[1..M] consists of the root vulnerable classes. The algorithm produces Induced Vulnerable trees corresponding to all vulnerable attributes present in the design. Roots of the Induced Vulnerable Trees are root vulnerable classes. Since a root vulnerable class may have more than one vulnerable attributes, hence it may appear in the roots of more than one induced vulnerable trees. The algorithm also produces Coupling Induced Vulnerability Propagation Factor (CIVPF) of an OOD. The algorithm maintains several additional data structures including three lists namely, parent_list, atr_list, atr_type and a queue IVC. The parent_list contains all the parent classes of an induced vulnerable class. atr_list is the list of all attributes (own, inherited and imported) corresponding to a class. The list atr_type of a class C consists of all the types, the class C declares to its attributes. The queue IVC contains all induced vulnerable classes.

```
1.     civp= 0
2.     for[i = 1; i≤ N; i++]
3.         parent_list [i] ← Ø
4.     for[i = 1; i≤ M; i++]
5.         vul ← head (VUL)
6          for each vul_atr € vul
7.             vul_link← 0
8.             for each class C € class_list[1..N] − vul
9.                 if vul_atr € atr_list[C] or vul € atr_type [C]
10.                then parent_list[C] ←vul
11.                    vul_link ← vul_link +1
12.                    insert[IVC, C]
13.        while IVC ≠ Ø
14.            ivc← head (IVC)
15.            for each class C € class_list[1..N] − ivc
16.                if ivc ∉ parent_list [C] and ivc € atr_type [C]
17.                then parent_list [C] ←ivc
18.                    insert[IVC, C]
19.                    vul_link ← vul_link +1
20.            dequeue (IVC)
21.        dequeue (VUL)
22.        civp ← civp + vul_link
23.    civpf ← civp/ N
```

Working. The working of CIVPF algorithm is as follows: Initially, variable civp is set as 0 and since there is no vulnerability propagation so parent_list of each class is set as Ø. From line 4 to 12 of the algorithm, every time a root vulnerable class is taken from the head of queue VUL. For each vulnerable attribute of class vul all the classes which have vulnerable attribute vul_atr in their atr_list or class vul in their atr_type are inserted into the queue IVC. Class vul is inserted into their parent_list. The variable vul_link is incremented for each induced vulnerable class showing vulnerability propagation. From steps 13 to 19 of the algorithm, the class in the head of the queue IVC is assigned to variable ivc till the queue is empty. For each ivc, if it is not present in the parent_list of any class C and is present in the atr_type of C, then C is inserted into the queue IVC. The class ivc is put into the parent_list of C. vul_link is incremented to reflect that a more vulnerable link is added because of coupling. In steps 19 and 20, IVC and VUL are de queued, as propagation of vulnerability for the classes present in their head is now calculated. In step 22, the overall vulnerability propagation in the form of vul_link is added with civp to give overall Coupling Induced Vulnerability Propagation. Finally, civp is divided by N to yield Coupling Induced Vulnerability Propagation Factor of a given object oriented design.

3   Interpretation and Discussion

The two extreme cases may be there. In first case, vulnerable classes do not communicate with other classes through their vulnerable attributes. In this case

$Li = 0$, for each root vulnerable class

No induced vulnerability propagation is made in such case and $CIVP_{OOD}$ will be min. therefore, numerator of equation (2) will be

$$CIVP_{OOD}(min) = \sum_{i=1}^{p} Li = 0 \qquad (3)$$

In second extreme case, a root vulnerable class may induce vulnerability in remaining of the N-1 classes making them strongly induced vulnerable classes. These induced vulnerable classes, except their parent vulnerable classes, may propagate weak vulnerability among them. The case may be more clearly understood by referring figure-1. Class C1 is a root vulnerable class which induces strong vulnerability to classes C2, C3, and C4. Now, C2 may propagate vulnerability to C3, and C4. C3 again may propagate vulnerability to C4. Therefore, Li may be calculated as:

$Li = N*(N-1)/2$, for each root vulnerable class

In this case, IVPOOD will be max and numerator of equation (2) will be

$$CIVPOOD(max) = \sum_{i=1}^{p} Li = p* N*(N-1)/2 \qquad (4)$$

Equation (3) and (4) are summarized to yield the inequality

$$0 \le CIVPOOD \le p* N*(N-1)/2$$

Using the above inequality, the range of CIVPF of equation (2) comes out to be

$$0 \le CIVPF \le p* (N-1)/2 \qquad (5)$$

Since, it is assumed that p>0, and $N \ge 1$ for any object oriented design. Hence, the interpretation about CIVPF may be drawn as:

"The higher the CIVPF of a design, the higher vulnerable the design is."

By minimizing the CIVPF of a design, its vulnerability can be minimized. Two given designs may also be compared on the basis of their CIVPF. Again, for the purpose of discussion, inequality in equation (5) may be written in another way as:

$$0 \le CIVPF \le (\sum_{i=1}^{p} Li) max / N \qquad (6)$$

From the inequality (5) and (6), it is clear that CIVPF depends upon vulnerable attributes p, number of classes N and overall number of vulnerable links Li. Neither the number of vulnerable attributes can be minimized nor the number of classes in a design. Hence, when it comes to minimize Vulnerability of a given design Li must be reduced to get a better design.

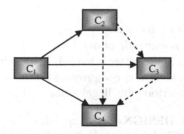

Fig. 1. Extreme highest case of CIVP

The Induced Vulnerable Trees corresponding to each vulnerable attribute produced by the algorithm show the direction of vulnerability propagation from one class to the others. The propagation becomes weaker and weaker when traversing from root class to leaf classes of the Induced Vulnerable Tree. By carefully inspecting the trees, unnecessary coupling may be avoided. Hence, the trees may prove to be an aid to minimize vulnerability and come up with a better design.

The Induced Vulnerable Trees corresponding to each vulnerable attribute produced by the algorithm show the direction of vulnerability propagation from one class to the others. The propagation becomes weaker and weaker when traversing from root class to leaf classes of the Induced Vulnerable Tree. By carefully inspecting the trees, unnecessary coupling may be avoided. Hence, the trees may prove to be an aid to minimize vulnerability and come up with a better design.

4   An Application of CIVPF

To prove the claim that CIVPF may be used to compare designs of different versions of the same object oriented software as well as designs of different object oriented software. Designs of two versions of Automated Teller Machine (ATM) have been considered. These two designs, 1999 version and 2002 version, are object oriented designs developed by Russell C. Bjork [14]. For the sake of simplicity, these two versions are denoted as DESIGN-1 and DESIGN-2. From the available detailed design documents, it is found that Design-1 and design-2 respectively has 15 and 22 classes, which are listed as:

DESIGN-1=   (ATM,   CardReader,   Display,   Keyboard, ReceiptPrinter,OperatorPannel, Session, transaction, withdrawal, transfer, enquiry, deposit, CashDispensor, Envelopeacceptor, Bank)

DESIGN-2 = (ATM, CustomerConsole, Receipt, ReceiptPrinter, session, transaction, withdrawal, transfer, enquiry, deposit, status, message, money, balances, log, cashDispensor, NetworkToBank, OperatorPanel, CardReader, card, AccountInformation, Envelopeacceptor)

For implementation of the proposed approach any type of documents including Collaboration Diagrams, Sequence Diagrams, State Diagrams and Class Hierarchy are not required. The only thing needed is the detailed design of classes showing all the methods and attributes. All that needed to prepare separate attribute list atr_list of each class and attribute type atr_type used in each class. Since there is only one vulnerable attribute i. e. pin, in both designs which possesses the causes of being vulnerable mentioned as:

- It provides an entry point for the user.
- It checks whether a user is authentic or not.
- It works as a communication interface/ channel between user and ATM machine.
- An attacker will have to somehow compromise pin in order to know the details of others account and hence perform the illegal actions as transfer, withdraw, inquiry etc.

CIVPF computation for DESIGN-1. On applying the algorithm for calculating CIVPF for the ATM DESIGN-1 (version-1), the following results are obtained:

1. civp= all the vulnerable links = 7 (calculated using algorithm)
2. Total number of classes in design= 15 (given)
3. civpf= 7 /15= 0.466

Since there is only one vulnerable attribute, there will be only one induced vulnerable tree produced by the algorithm. The induced vulnerable tree corresponding to DESIGN-1 is given in figure-2.

CIVPF computation for DESIGN-2. The algorithm calculates CIVPF for the ATM DESIGN-2 (version-2) as follows:

1. civp= all the vulnerable links = 23 (calculated using algorithm)
2. Total number of classes in design= 22 (given)
3. civpf= 23 /22= 1.05

As for DESIGN-1, a single vulnerable attribute PIN will lead to produce a single induced vulnerable tree in DESIGN-2. The tree is shown in figure-3.

Relative Results. A comparative analysis for both versions of ATM design is presented in Table-1. Quantitative figures obtained from both designs show that DESIGN-2 is more vulnerable than DESIGN-1 on the basis of vulnerability propagation. However, close observation of induced vulnerable trees produced for both designs and design documents reveals that there is no difference in terms of facility offered to user, unnecessary coupling has produced this extent of difference.

5 Relevant Work

Though quantitative assessment of software security is very tough [4], it is not new to security researchers. The research on software security quantification is carried on for years. F. Copigneaux et al(1988) introduced a systematic approach for security evaluation of non functional attributes of software. The approach is based on McCall's factor, criteria and metric approach [5]. J. Alves-Foss et al (1995) developed a method called as System Vulnerability Index (SVI). The SVI is a mechanism that can help assess the susceptibility of computer system to common attacks. It helps system administrators to assess the starting point for security policy [6]. C. Wang et al (1997) presented a framework for security measurement. Of course, it is not a universal measure, but it provides a systematic way for assessing security strength of a system [4]. A cost-benefit approach called SAEM is developed by S.A. Butler (2002) assesses multi attribute risk. On the basis of that risk prioritization is performed [7]. J. Hallberg et al (2005) developed a framework for system security assessment. They claimed that the framework was able to categorize existing security assessment methods. To support their claim, they proposed CAESAR method to calculate overall system security values [8]. O. H. Alhazmi et al (2005) introduced a metric called vulnerability density. It is a relative metric and defined as the number of vulnerabilities per unit size of code. It is used to distinguish that which version of given software is more vulnerable [9].

All the methods discussed above quantify security on system level. They either require code or system's characteristics such as the environment where the system is installed for computation etc. However, attack surface metric [11] developed by P.

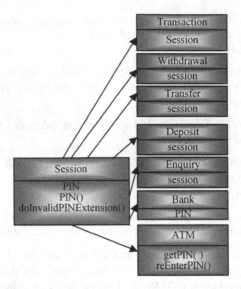

Fig. 2. Induced vulnerable tree corresponding to Design-1

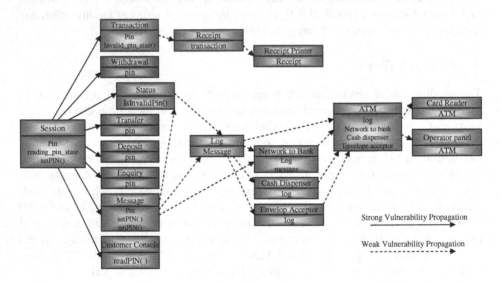

Fig. 3. Induced vulnerable tree corresponding to Design-2

Manadhata et al strikes at design level of a system. The work presented in the paper is some how analogous to attack surface metric but it is better in some aspects as:

- Attack surface metric require code for computation whereas CIVPF just requires parts of the detailed design documents.
- The definition of attackability in attack surface metric is based on intuition and experience, whereas it is already proven fact that increasing availability of anything vulnerable (vulnerability propagation), would increase its vulnerability [12].

- Knowledge of the usage scenario of the system is also required along with the attack surface measurement to determine whether one version of software is more secure than the other. CIVPF alone is capable of comparing two object oriented design on the basis of overall vulnerability propagation of the designs.
- Like other approaches, attack surface metric also relies on applying security mechanisms on entry points and exit points of a system to reflect back the attacks. On the contrary, CIVPF relies on developing an attack resistant design by the fullest use of object oriented design characteristics.
- Attack surface metric is a security metric which lies above level of code but below the level of entire system. CIVPF is a pure design phase security metric.
- Since CIVPF is a design phase metric so if CIVPF of a design is found to be higher than expected, an alternative design may be developed at the phase itself, whereas it is not possible with attack surface metric.

Table 1. A comparative Analysis of Designs of Version-1 and Version-2

Analysis → ATM Design ↓	Classes (N)	Vulnerable Attributes(p)	Root Vulnerable Classes (M)	CIVP $(\sum_{i=1}^{p} Li)$	CIVPF $\sum_{i=1}^{p} Li/ N)$	Concluding Remarks
Version-1(1999)	15	1	1	7	0.466	Version-1 is less vulnerable than Version-2
Version-2(2002)	22	1	1	23	1.05	

6 Advantages and Limitations

CIVPF is the only metric of its kind. Unlike quality, no similar work is identified considering the contribution of object oriented design characteristics in security. It is a relative metric which may be used to compare designs of object oriented software. Since it is an automated approach, it is quick, effective and practical to implement.

It may be treated as absolute measure of vulnerability too. CIVPF is may be used as a readymade solution to protect assets and security critical entities by minimizing their coupling. Hence, an existing design may be made less vulnerable by avoiding unnecessary coupling of vulnerable attributes. Also, with slight modification, the approach may be implemented for procedural design too.

Contribution of other design characteristics has been ignored when computing vulnerability propagation. Impact of inheritance on vulnerability propagation has already been covered in the work [13]. The effect of remaining design characteristics on vulnerability propagation has been left as future work.

7 Conclusion

Design phase prepares foundation of software under development. A weak foundation never tends to produce vulnerability resistant software. In absence of any tool/ approach [16], it is hard to predict the security of an object oriented design. A metric, CIVPF, has been proposed and the algorithm for automatic calculation of the metric has also been designed. The metric calculates relative vulnerability of two object oriented designs of same software as well as designs of different object oriented software. To prove the claim, two versions of ATM are also compared for their vulnerability.

Acknowledgment. This work is sponsored by University Grant Commission (UGC), New Delhi, India, under F. No. 34-107\ 2008(SR).

References

1. McGraw, G.: From the ground up: The DIMACS software security workshop. IEEE Security & Privacy 1, 59–66 (2003)
2. Zadeh, J., DeVolder, D.: Software Development and Related Security Issues. In: SoutheastCon 2007, pp. 746–748. IEEE Press, USA (2007)
3. Briand, L.C., Daly, J.W., Wust, J.K.: A Unified Framework for Coupling Measurement in Object Oriented Systems. IEEE Trans. on Software Eng. 25, 91–121 (1999)
4. Wang, C., Wulf, W.A.: A Framework for Security Measurement. In: National Information System Security Conference, Baltimore, MD, pp. 522–533 (1997)
5. Copigneaux, F., Martin, S.: Software Security Evaluation Based On A Top Down McCall-Like Approach. In: Fourth Aerospace Computer Security Applications Conference, pp. 414–418. IEEE Press, USA (1988)
6. Alves-Foss, J., Barbosa, S.: Assessing Computer Security Vulnerability. ACM SIGOPS Operating Systems Review 29, 3–13 (1995)
7. Butler, S.A.: Security Attribute Evaluation Method: A Cost-Benefit Approach. In: International Conference on Software Engineering, pp. 232–240. ACM Press, USA (2002)
8. Hallberg, J., Hunstad, A., Peterson, M.: A Framework for System Security Assessment. In: 6th Annual IEEE System, Man and Cybernetics (SMC) Information Assurance Workshop, pp. 224–231. IEEE Press, New York (2005)
9. Alhazmi, O.A., Malaiya, Y.K., Ray, I.: Security vulnerabilities in software systems: A quantitative perspective. In: Jajodia, S., Wijesekera, D. (eds.) Data and Applications Security 2005. LNCS, vol. 3654, pp. 281–294. Springer, Heidelberg (2005)
10. Torr, P.: Demystifying the threat-modeling process. IEEE Security & Privacy 3, 66–70 (2005)
11. Manadhata, P., Wing, J. M.: An Attack Surface Metric. CMU-CS-05-155 (July 2005), http://www.cs.cmu.edu/%7Ewing/publications/CMU-CS-05-155.pdf
12. Kaomea, P.: Beyond security: A Data Quality Perspective on defensive Information Warfare. In: 1996 International Conference on Information Quality (MIT IQ Conference) Sponsored by UC Berkeley CITM, USA, pp. 172–187 (1996)
13. Agrawal, A., Chandra, S., Khan, R.A.: An Efficient Measurement of Object Oriented Vulnerability. In: 4th International Conference on Availability, Reliability and Security, pp. 618–622. IEEE Press, Japan (2009)

14. An Example of Object oriented Design: ATM Simulation,
    http://www.math-cs.gordon.edu/courses/cs211/ATMExample/
15. Meland, P.H., Jensen, J.: Secure Software Design in Practice. In: 3rd International Conference on Availability, Reliability and Security, pp. 1164–1171. IEEE Press, Spain (2008)
16. Chandra, S., Khan, R.A., Agrawal, A.: Security Estimation Framework: Design Phase Perspective. In: 6th International Conference on Information Technology: New Generations, pp. 254–259. IEEE Press, Las Vegas (2009)

A Framework for Synthesis of Human Gait Oscillation Using Intelligent Gait Oscillation Detector (IGOD)

Soumik Mondal, Anup Nandy, Anirban Chakrabarti,
Pavan Chakraborty, and G.C. Nandi

Robotics & AI Lab, Indian Institute of Information Technology, Allahabad
{soumik,anup,anirban,pavan,gcnandi}@iiita.ac.in

Abstract. The main objective of this paper illustrates an elementary concept about the designing, development and implementation of a bio-informatics diagnostic tool which understands and analyzes the human gait oscillation in order to provide an insight on human bi-pedal locomotion and its stability. A multi sensor device for detection of gait oscillations during human locomotion has been developed effectively. It has been named "IGOD", an acronym of the "Intelligent Gait Oscillation Detector". It ensures capturing of different person's walking pattern in a very elegant way. This device would be used for creating a database of gait oscillations which could be extensively applied in several implications. The preliminary acquired data for eight major joints of a human body have been presented significantly. The electronic circuit has been attached to IGOD device in order to customize the proper calibration of every joint angle eventually.

Keywords: Intelligent Gait Oscillation Detector, Bio-informatics, Bi-pedal locomotion, Human gait oscillation, Lissajous curve.

1 Introduction

Learning to walk is a daunting task for a human baby. It takes close to a year for a human baby to stand on its two legs, balance and then learn to walk. The human bi-pedal locomotion, which we commonly known as simple "walking", involves a high amount of balancing and stability along with complex synchronous oscillation of its different joints of the body. These oscillations not only provide the required motion, but also the stability and balance. A combination of rhythmic activities of a nervous system composed of coupled neural oscillators and the rhythmic movements of a musculoskeletal system including interaction with its environment [1] produces the stable gait.

An in depth study the human bipedal motion through different oscillations of its body limbs holds great potential in understanding the dynamic human body. It is to be noted, that the upper body oscillation is in synchronicity with the lower body to provide a smooth and stable gait cycle. Our aim is to acquire these oscillation angles of different limbs of the human body, in real time.

There have been many attempts in acquiring the limb movements for training humanoid robots. One such method is using image processing on real time video. Su and

S. Ranka et al. (Eds.): IC3 2010, Part I, CCIS 94, pp. 340–349, 2010.

Huang [2] have proposed computer vision techniques using feature extraction process from the binarized silhouette of a walking person for automatic human gait recognition, analysis and classification. Cunado, Nixon and Carter [3] have used Fourier series to describe the motion of the upper leg and apply temporal evidence gathering techniques to extract the moving model from a sequence of images. Riley et al [4] have represented a method for enabling humanoid robots to acquire movements by imitation. A 3D vision has been used for perceiving the movements of a human teacher, and then estimating the teacher's body postures using a fast full-body inverse kinematics method that incorporates a kinematics model of the teacher. This solution is then mapped to a robot and reproduced in real-time. These image processing methods require laboratory conditions with well placed cameras and high computational facility. Such techniques used for training humanoid robots could in principle be implemented for obtaining the human gait oscillation data. However the techniques described, works well over a restricted space under controlled laboratory conditions, where the cameras are positioned in specific locations and the projections of the subject on the images are fixed. A controlled illumination of the subject will also be required. In our case such controlled conditions will be difficult. Our subject would need to walk some distance on a straight path without rotation to obtain his natural gait pattern. We would also like to obtain his gait pattern over different environment such as Staircase climbing.

Jihong Lee and Insoo Ha [5],[6] have proposed a motion capture system, based on low cost accelerometers, which is capable of identifying the body configuration by extracting gravity-related information from the sensors data. They applied a geometric fusion technology to cope with the uncertainty of sensor data. A practical calibration technique was also proposed to handle errors in aligning the sensing axis to the coordination axis. Similar work has also been done by Barbieri, et al. [7],[8] using accelerometers. This technique is good but requires elaborate calibration. The biomechanical system proposes [9] a stable human waling technique.

In our work we plan to acquire the time dependent oscillation angles of different limbs of the human body in a simple straightforward and elegant manner. To study the limb oscillation we require a multi-sensor device which could in real time measure variation of joint angles of a human body. In this paper we describe the design and development of such a multi-sensor device. This device is strap-on equipment, comprising rigid links interconnected by revolute joints, where each joint angle is measured by rotational sensors (single turn encoders). We name this strap-on suit as the "Intelligent Gait Oscillation Detector" (IGOD). The intelligence implies for the acquisition of accurate gait oscillations and provides flexibility to wear it in order to further classification of different person's gait patterns. This instrument enables us to simultaneously measure the oscillations of the human body (i.e. Oscillations of the shoulders, elbows, hips and knees joints) in real time on a remote computer. We have discussed the specification of Phidget electronic circuit and rotation sensor for capturing the different joint oscillations synchronously. The proper calibration of rotation sensor has been done in order to check in linearity measurement. In later section, extensive analysis of gait synthesis for full human body oscillations along with the significance of lissajous figures has been emphasized elaborately.

2 Primary Intention and Requirement of IGOD

Primarily intention and requirement of IGOD is to create a bioinformatics data base of human gait oscillations. The gait oscillations will be classified along with other information of the subjects such as gender (Male/Female), age, height, weight and "environment" of the gait. By "environment" we mean; the condition under which the gait patterns were measured. Such as walking on smooth terrain, rough terrain, stair case and slope climbing, walking with a load, to mention a few. We also intent to record the gait pattern at different gait speeds (i.e. slow fast and run conditions).

We intend to use this bioinformatics database to classify the training gait pattern for a prosthetic patient who has lost one of his/her leg (knee above) and for whom we are developing an Adaptive Modular Active Leg (AMAL) [10,15]. A patient with an amputated leg would have forgotten his natural gait pattern. The patient's most probable natural gait pattern will be reconstructed by comparing the bioinformatics database with the patient's weight height, age, etc. The required parameters for this gait pattern will be fed to AMAL for training the patient to walk.

3 Implication of IGOD Technology

We see a strong implication of IGOD technology in other projects as well.

3.1 Medical Implication

We believe that the bioinformatics data base of the human gait oscillations will have a strong medical implication. We know that every human being has an intrinsic gait pattern which depends on his or her childhood training and environments. It also depends on the inherited and inherent diseases the subject has. A medical classification of the database and the use of IGOD can be a new medical diagnostic tool. There for we would like to latter expand the scope of IGOD so that along with body limb oscillations, other medical diagnostics such as ECG is performed in real time.

3.2 Robotic Implication

Our plan to make simultaneous measurements of the human body joint oscillations using multi sensor in real time, and acquisition of the data on a remote computer, will also allow us to use the IGOD suit, to train a Humanoid Robot to mimic and copy. We expect IGOD to be a strong training and programming tool for Humanoid Robots.

3.3 Human Computer Interaction Implication

We can assure that IGOD could be used as an input sensing device in Human Computer Interaction implication which would be considered as an active agent to exchange information with computer in order to perform several applications.

4 Stages of Development of IGOD

The development of IGOD emerges a new dimension for synthesis and analyze of human gait oscillation [11] in a very intelligent way. It has been developed and fabricated with rigid links made by aluminum, steel and rotation sensor [13]. The framework of IGOD contains proper placements of rotation sensor on different joints of human body. A mechanical engineering approach has been adopted for the construction of IGOD in order to generate biological motion so that the signature of different persons could be retrieved effectively. The recognition of walking pattern deals with the characteristic of different person behaviors with stability. The IGOD implies the multisensory device to collect the different joint oscillations synchronously. As per the fabrication mechanism is concerned we have kept eight rotation sensors (potentiometer) on different major joints of our body.

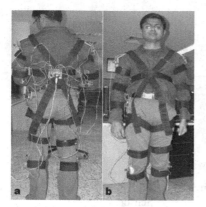

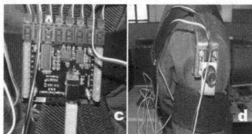

Fig. 1. (a) Rear (b) Front view of IGOD   **Fig. 2.** (c) Interface Kit (d) Pivot point of Rotation Sensor

Fig.1 indicates the both rear and front view of IGOD wearing suit where rotation sensor has been deployed on shoulder, elbow, hip and knee for left and right part of our body. The real time oscillation data of different joint angles has been captured synchronously during several walking modes like slow walking, brisk walking, running and also jumping. Fig.2(c) explores the integration of eight rotation sensor values of different joint angles using the phidget interface kit [12] that has been described in next section. Every sensor is having a pivoting point for their respective joints which is connected by rigid links tightly as shown in fig.2(d).

5 Sensor and Interface Kit Specification

The fabrication of IGOD deals with rotation sensor which is being integrated with Phidget interface kit. The sensor has been deployed in eight major joints of human body (both shoulders, both elbows, both knees and both hips) respectively. Each sensor is being connected with steel or aluminum rigid links in a very efficient manner. The sensor specification has been described in fig.3 where power supply voltage varies from 3.5VDC to 5 VDC with 10kΩ output impedance [13]. The rotation sensor has been opted for 0 to 300 degree resolution as per specification is concerned [13]. It implies a significant way for data acquisition technique from several joints of human body synchronously. The analog voltage is being generated accurately for every assigned joint of human body during bipedal locomotion. The output voltage is connected with Phidget interface kit for digitization and calibration of data effectively. The electronic circuit of Phidget interface kit has been presented in fig. 4. It illustrates the measurement of analog value from the rotation sensor and produces the digital counts as output between 0 to 1000 ranges [12]. It deals with both analog and digital inputs significantly. The calibration curve of sensor value has been depicted in fig.5 where least square fit is applied in order to check the linearity of the rotation sensor. The input voltage to interface kit is considered as sensor value of rotation sensor

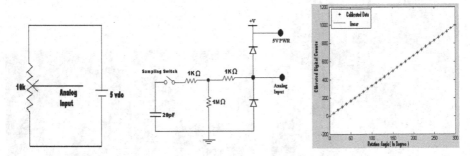

Fig. 3. Rotation Sensor   **Fig. 4.** Interface Kit circuit   **Fig. 5.** Calibration Curve for Sensor

The transformation of analog data into digital counts has been carried out with 10 bit internal ADC circuit along with sampling rate 65 samples/sec [12]. In order to seek the linear relationship between the observed data and calibrated data the least square fitting has been employed in the following equation.

$$\theta = 3.3335 \times count \ (\pm \ 0.020161)$$

It has been observed in fig.3 that calibrated data points are presented with '*' sign. The curve describes the linear relationship between the rotation angle and the calibrated digital counts. The equation illustrates that the first component which is being associated with digital count meets the Phidget originated observed data with the same coefficient value being calculated by maximum range of digital counts i.e. 1000 and maximum resolution of sensor value i.e. 300 degree.

6 Analysis of Full Human Gait Oscillation

The entire gait oscillation of different joint angle has been presented to discuss the characteristic of individual's walking pattern extensively [20]. Initially, for each gait pattern of respective joint a zero correction has already been done by collecting α_0 represented in the form of digital counts. The initial digital counts are subtracted from the current digital count which is being interpolated by joint angle values in degree for each oscillation. The movement of each oscillation for a particular joint is manipulated in terms of degree which is being calculated by the following method.

$$desired\ angle(degree) = (current\ digital\ count - initial\ count\ ) \times \frac{300}{1000}$$

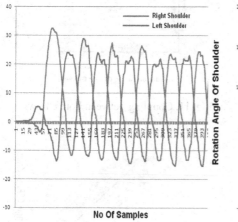

Fig. 6. Gait pattern of both shoulder joints

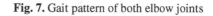

Fig. 7. Gait pattern of both elbow joints

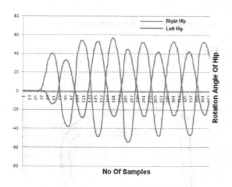

Fig. 8. Gait pattern of both hip joints

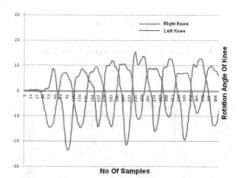

Fig. 9. Gait pattern of both knee joints

The gait patterns of a single person have been shown in the above figures (6,7,8,9). We have captured the walking patterns in normal walking mode only. Each gait oscillation consists of both swing and stance phase respectively. The generated pattern for both left limb and right limb implies the variation of calibrated angle values over the period of oscillation. The X axis of the each pattern corresponds to number of samples and Y axis refers to the rotation angle in degree. The period T of each oscillation for a particular pattern can be calculated using the following manner.

346   S. Mondal et al.

$$T = \frac{Total\ no\ of\ samples\ in\ a particular\ oscillation}{sampling\ rate} = \frac{64(Approx.)}{65} = 1\ sec\ (approx.).$$

where sampling rate is 65 samples/sec per detector.

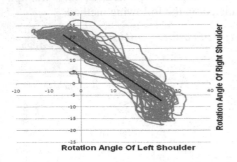

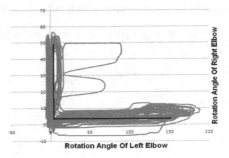

Fig. 10. Coupling between both shoulders

Fig. 11. Coupling between both elbows

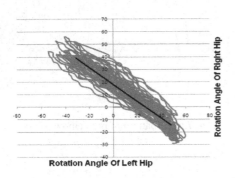

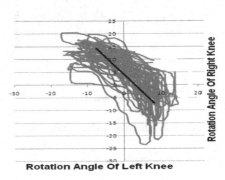

Fig. 12. Coupling between both hips

Fig. 13. Coupling between both knees

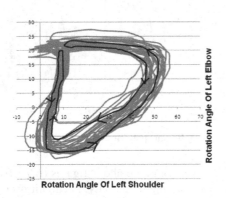

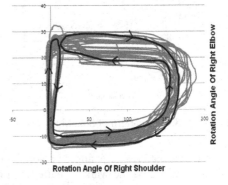

Fig. 14. Coupling between left elbow & shoulder

Fig. 15. Coupling between right elbow & shoulder

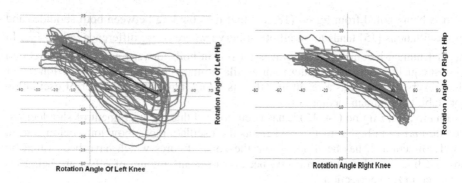

Fig. 16. Coupling between left hip & knee   **Fig. 17.** Coupling between right hip & knee

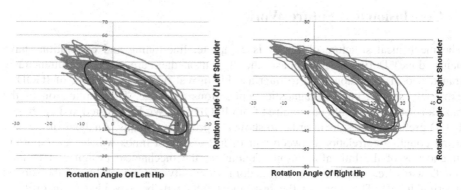

Fig. 18. Coupling between left shoulder & hip **Fig. 19.** Coupling between right shoulder & hip

The correlation and coupling between significant joints of human body during locomotion have been shown elaborately in the above figures. To understand the correlation and coupling of those joint oscillations, we have compared them with an oscillation equation of the form:

$$X(t) = a \sin(\omega_1 t + \varphi), \qquad Y(t) = b \sin(\omega_2 t)$$

Where ω_1 and ω_2 are frequencies of oscillation and φ the relative phase difference between $X(t)$ and $Y(t)$. The plot $X(t)$ v$_s$ $Y(t)$ provides us the lissajous curve [14] and enables us to determine the coupling parameters ω_1, ω_2 and φ. It has been observed in the fig no (10, 12, 13, 16 and 17) that phase difference φ from the fitting between two gait oscillation is $|\varphi| = \pi$ and $\omega_1 = \omega_2 = \omega$.

It is natural and understandable that a phase difference between 2 hip joints (fig 12) and 2 shoulder joints (fig 10) is $|\varphi| = \pi$ and has the same $\omega = \frac{2\pi}{T} = 2\pi$. This criterion is the basic requirement for the stability of human locomotion.

Fig no 11 shows that coupling between both the elbow joint oscillations. It shows an interesting oscillation of an envelope in the shape of an 'L'. This indicates when one elbow oscillates the other is practically static. This happens because of the elbow locking in the reverse cycle.

It is being noted from fig no (18, 19) that the coupling between both shoulder and hip oscillations [15] tends to an elliptical curve where phase difference $|\varphi| = \frac{5\pi}{4}$. In normal human locomotion hip joint is moved in both forward and reverse direction almost equally where as shoulder joint oscillates maximum in forward direction rather than reverse direction as a result an offset is being introduced in center of oscillation for stability of human locomotion.

Finally, from fig no (14, 15) it has been noticed that the movement of shoulder oscillation arises in both directions where as the oscillation of elbow joint belongs to in single direction. It has been noted that the above figures which have been fitted by straight lines are shifted from origin because of small amount of offset are being introduced in zero correction.

7 Conclusion and Future Work

The mechanical structure of IGOD is complete, fine-tuning and calibrations have being done. During testing phase the 8 sensor data are being simultaneously transferred in an analog form to interface kit in real time. The concept of IGOD is extremely simple, but its diagnostic implications are huge. The implication of the bioinformatics data could be acquired from IGOD suit. We have tested and calibrated IGOD preliminary results in order to show the promising results. Analysis of the data using coupling correlation between pair of left and right limbs will be an important diagnostics of the bio information. Tuning up the mechanical design and making IGOD wires free will improve the freedom, flexibility and movability of the subject wearing IGOD. The scope of the instrument later will be expended to incorporate other bio-information. So far we have studied the extensive human gait oscillations for eight major joints of human body. Additional sensors measuring ECG [16], EEG and EMG [17] could be added to the real-time gathering of the bio-information. The only problem that we foresee is from the Nyquist's sampling condition, since the signals from different sensors are time multiplexed. Addition of these bio information will help us correlate gait oscillation with the rhythmic activity of the human nervous systems. This will be the future extension of our work. The complete information of a human body in motion [18] and creation of the database and its classification [19] will be the final aim of IGOD.

References

1. Taga, G., Yamaguchi, Y., Shimizu, H.: Self-organized control of bipedal locomotion by neural oscillators in unpredictable environment. Biological Cybernetics 65(3), 147–159 (1991)
2. Su, H., Huang, F.-G.: Human gait recognition based on motion analysis. Proceedings of International Conference on Machine Learning and Cybernetics 7(18-21), 4464–4468 (2005)
3. Cunado, D., Nixon, M.S., Carter, J.N.: Automatic extraction and description of human gait models for recognition purposes. Computer Vision and Image Understanding 90(1), 1–41 (2003)

4. Riley, M., Ude, A., Wade, K., Atkeson, C.G.: Enabling real-time full-body imitation: a natural way of transferring human movement to humanoids. In: Proceedings of IEEE International Conference on Robotics and Automation, vol. 2(14-19), pp. 2368–2374 (2003)
5. Lee, J., Ha, I.: Real-Time Motion Capture for a Human Body using Accelerometer. In: Robotica, vol. 19, pp. 601–610. Cambridge University Press, Cambridge (2001)
6. Lee, J., Ha, I.: Sensor Fusion and Calibration for Motion Captures using Accelerometers. In: Proceedings of IEEE International Conference on Robotics and Automation, vol. 3, pp. 1954–1959 (1999)
7. Barbieri, R., Farella, E., Benini, L., Ricco, B., Acquaviva, A.: A low-power motion capture system with integrated accelerometers (gesture recognition applications). In: Consumer Communications and Networking Conference, vol. 1(5-8), pp. 418–423 (2004)
8. Hafner, V.V., Bachmann, F.: Human-Humanoid walking gait recognition. In: Proceedings of 8th IEEE-RAS International Conference on Humanoid Robots, pp. 598–602 (2008)
9. Au, S.K., Dilworth, P., Herr, H.: An ankle-foot emulation system for the study of human walking biomechanics. In: Proceedings of IEEE International Conference on Robotics and Automation, pp. 2939–2945 (2006)
10. Nandi, G.C., Ijspeert, A., Nandi, A.: Biologically inspired CPG based above knee active prosthesis. In: Proceedings of IEEE/RSJ International Conference on Intelligent Robots and Systems, pp. 2368–2373 (2008)
11. Lugo-Villeda, L.I., Frisoli, A., Sandoval, G.O.O., Bergamasco, M., Parra-Vega, V.: A mechatronic analysis and synthesis of human walking gait. In: Proceedings of IEEE International Conference on Mechatronics, pp. 1–6 (2009)
12. Phidget Interface kit,
    http://www.phidgets.com/products.php?category=0&
    product_id=1018
13. Phidget Rotation Sensor,
    http://www.phidgets.com/products.php?category=1&
    product_id=1109
14. Lissajous_curve, http://en.wikipedia.org/wiki/Lissajous_curve
15. Nandi, G.C., Ijspeert, A., Chakraborty, P., Nandi, A.: Development of Adaptive Modular Active Leg (AMAL) using bipedal robotics technology. Robotics and Autonomous Systems 57(6-7), 603–616 (2009)
16. Yi, Z., Shayan, A., Wanping, Z., Tong, L., Chen, T.-P., Jung, J.-R., Duann, M.S., Chung-Kuan, C.: Analyzing High-Density ECG Signals Using ICA. IEEE Transactions on Biomedical Engineering 55(11), 2528–2537 (2008)
17. Yang, Q., Siemionow, V., Yao, W., Sahgal, V., Yue, G.H.: Single-Trial EEG-EMG Coherence Analysis Reveals Muscle Fatigue-Related Progressive Alterations in Corticomuscular Coupling. IEEE Transactions on Neural Systems and Rehabilitation Engineering 18(2), 97–106 (2010)
18. Marzani, F., Calais, E., Legrand, L.: A 3-D marker-free system for the analysis of movement disabilities - an application to the legs. IEEE Transactions on Information Technology in Biomedicine 5(1), 18–26 (2001)
19. Green, R.D., Ling, G.: Quantifying and recognizing human movement patterns from monocular video Images-part I: a new framework for modeling human motion. IEEE Transactions on Circuits and Systems for Video Technology 14(2), 179–190 (2004)
20. Dejnabadi, H., Jolles, B.M., Aminian, K.: A New Approach for Quantitative Analysis of Inter-Joint Coordination During Gait. IEEE Transactions on Biomedical Engineering 55(2), 755–764 (2008)

Detection of Significant Opinionated Sentence for Mining Web Users' Opinion

K.M. Anil Kumar and Suresha

University of Mysore,
Mansagangothri, Mysore, Karnataka, India
{anilkmsjce,surehabm}@yahoo.co.in

Abstract. In this paper we present an approach to identify a significant sentence from an opinionated text and use the significant sentence to classify web user's opinion into positive or negative. Today, most of web users document their opinion in opinionated sites, shopping sites, personal pages etc., to express and share their opinion with other web users. The opinion expressed by web users may be with respect to politics, sports, products, movie etc. These opinions will be very useful to others such as, leaders of political parties, selection committees of various sports, business analysts and other stake holders of products, directors and producers of movies as well as to the other concerned web users. We use semantic based approach to find both significant sentence and users opinion. Our approach first detects subjective phrases and uses these phrases along with semantic orientation score to identify a significant sentence and user's opinion from such a significant sentence. Our approach provides better results than the other approaches reported in literature on different data sets.

Keywords: Sentiment Analysis, Data Mining, Opinion Mining, Product Analysis, affective computing.

1 Introduction

The fast development of web and its related technologies have fueled the popularity of the web with all sections of society. The web has been used by many firms such as governments, business houses, industries, educational institutions etc., to make them familiar and accessible globally. An individual web user is provided with an opportunity to obtain and share knowledge.

The web is the origin of many research activities and one interesting area of research is to mine users opinion from web on diverse topics like politics, movies, educational institutions, products etc. The study of opinions is useful to both producers and consumers of the topic. The producers can be manufacturers of automobiles, movie producers, editor of news article, digital product manufactures etc., who are very much interested to find opinion of a user. The consumers are individual users who express their opinion and want to share it with other web users.

S. Ranka et al. (Eds.): IC3 2010, Part I, CCIS 94, pp. 350–359, 2010.

In this paper, we attempt to find opinion of the users by identifying a significant sentence from the opinionated texts. Our intuition is that the opinion in a significant sentence reflects user's opinion on a subject. The other sentences of the opinionated text will have opinion on features of a subject.

An opinionated text discussing on digital camera may have sentences with an overall opinion of the digital camera as well as opinion on features of digital camera such as lens, battery backup, size etc. It becomes critical to identify the significant sentence from a cluster of sentences, detect opinion of the web user's and classify it as positive or negative. For example, consider the following opinionated texts of web users obtained from an opinionated site reviewcentre [10]. The collected opinionated texts were retained the same, no attempt was made to correct the grammatical mistakes of web users from these opinionated texts.

Example 1. *Did a lot of research on 1080 televisions and this one was the **best**. The **picture quality** when viewing non-HD television stations is a **little grainy**. The **design** looks **bad** for 21st century.*

Example 2. *I bought this cam thinking it would be **great**, I've owned quite a few. Indoor shots especially at night are **horrible** though, even at 7.2PM they come out blurry and dark. Outside shots are **OK** but for the price of this cam I am **very disappointed**. The **stylish design** sold me. The **video quality** in FINE mode however is **excellent**, **best** I've seen on any camera to date. But then again, most of my shots I take at night so it's basically **useless** to me.*

Example 3. *Takes too much time to change **screen displays**, even to switch off or on. Still **pictures** resolution is **bad**. I **won't recommend** for this phone. No auto **Keypad lock**. **Speaker phone** is **not clear and loud**.*

Example 1 refers to an opinion of a user on television product. The overall opinion of a user is positive along with a few negative opinions on some features of the product. The words in Bold refer to opinionated words and words in Bold and Underlined refer to a feature of the product.

We observe from the afore mentioned examples and other opinionated texts, users document their overall opinion in a sentence and uses other sentences to expresses opinion on different features of the product. We believe that it is important to identify such a significant sentence that provides an overall opinion of the users. The opinion obtained from such a significant sentence is considered as the actual opinion of a web user. In this paper, we focus on finding opinion of web users only on products using significant opinionated sentence.

The remainder of this paper is organized as follows: In Section 2 we give a brief description of related work. Then, in Section 3, we discuss our methodology. In Section 4, the experiments and results are discussed. Conclusion is discussed in Section 5.

2   Related Work

Opinion mining is a recent sub discipline of information retrieval which is not about the topic of a document, but with the opinion it expresses [1] [20]. In literature, opinion mining is also known as sentiment analysis [7], sentiment classification [8], affective classification [20] and affective rating [16]. It has emerged in the last few years as a research area, largely driven by interests in developing applications such as mining opinions in online corpora, or customer relationship management, e.g., customer's review analysis [20].

Hatzivassiloglou and McKeown [18] have attempted to predict semantic orientation of adjectives by analyzing pairs of adjectives (i.e., adjective pair is adjectives conjoined by and, or, but, either-or, neither-nor) extracted from a large unlabelled document set.

Turney [14] has obtained remarkable results on the sentiment classification of terms by considering the algebraic sum of the orientations of terms as representative of the orientation of the document. Turney and Littman [15] have bootstrapped from a seed set, containing seven positive and seven negative words, and determined semantic orientation according to Pointwise Mutual Information-Information Retrieval (PMI-IR) method.

Wang and Araki [19] proposed a variation of the Semantic Orientation-PMI algorithm for Japanese for mining opinion in weblogs. They applied Turney method to Japanese webpage and found results slanting heavily towards positive opinion. They proposed balancing factor and neutral expression detection method and reported a well balanced result.

Opinion observer [6] is the sentiment analysis system for analyzing and comparing opinions on the web. The product features are extracted from noun or noun phrases by the association miner. They use adjectives as opinion words and assign prior polarity of these by WordNet exploring method. The polarity of an opinion expression which is a sentence containing one or more feature terms and one or more opinion words is assigned a dominant orientation. The extracted features are stored in a database in the form of feature, number of positive expression and number of negative expression.

Kamps et al [12] have focused on the use of lexical relations defined in WordNet. They defined a graph on the adjectives contained in the intersection between the Turney's seed set and WordNet, adding a link between two adjectives whenever WordNet indicate the presence of a synonymy relation between them. The authors defined a distance measure d (t1, t2) between terms t1 and t2, which amounts to the length of the shortest path that connects t1 and t2. The orientation of a term is then determined by its relative distance from the seed terms good and bad.

Our work differs from the afore mentioned studies, by finding opinion of a user only with significant opinionated sentence from a document. We do not consider opinion of all other sentences found in a document. Our work uses adjectives and also other part-of-speech like verb, adverb etc., to capture opinionated words for efficient opinion detection.

3   Methodology

We collected three data sets for our work. The first data set consist of 250 opinionated texts on five different products, collected from results of various search engines. The web search engines used are Google search, Altavista, Google Product search, MSN Live search and Exalead search. The advanced search options of search engines were used to issue queries and collect manually the opinionated texts. The second data set is collection of 400 opinionated texts obtained manually from different opinionated sites like Amazon, CNet, review centre, bigadda, rediff etc. The third data set consisting of 140 opinionated texts on product is obtained from [3]. These data sets contained 50 % positive and 50 % negative opinionated texts, it can be made available to researchers on request to the authors.

In our approach we pass an opinionated text to a sentence splitter program. The sentences obtained from the program were input to a part of speech tagger. The tagger used in our approach is Monty Tagger [11]. Extraction patterns are applied to the tagged opinionated sentences to obtain opinionated phrases that are likely to contain user's opinion. Table 1 shows a few extraction patterns used to obtain opinionated phrases from opinionated sentences. From the Table 1, JJ represent adjective and NN/NNS, VB/VBD/VBN/VBG, RB/RBR/RBS represent different forms of noun, verb and adverb. These phrases are subjected to Sentiment Product Lexicon (SPL) for capturing only subjective or opinionated phrases. This is necessary as some phrases obtained after application of extraction patterns may be non subjective.

Table 1. Extracted patterns

Slno.	First Word	Second Word	Third Word
1	JJ	NN or NNS	anything
2	RB,RBR or RBS	JJ	not NN nor NNS
3	JJ	JJ	not NN nor NNS
4	NN or NNS	JJ	not NN or NNS
5	RB,RBR or RBS	VB,VBD,VBN or VBG	anything

Sentiment Product Lexicon is collection of General lexicon and Domain lexicon. General lexicon will maintain a list of positive and negative words by collecting opinion words that are positive or negative from sources like General Inquirer [9], Subjective clues [17] and list of adjectives [13]. Domain lexicon will maintain a list of positive or negative words from the domain context. We found words like cool, revolutionary etc., appeared in negative list of General lexicon. These words were used to express positive opinion by web user's. Hence we created a domain lexicon to have opinion words from the domain perspective. The details of construction of General lexicon and Domain lexicon are made available in [4].

In this paper we use these lexicons to identify neutral phrases. Sentiment product lexicon can be expressed as

$$SPL = \{GL_P, GL_N, DL_P, DL_N\} \qquad (1)$$

Where
GL_P : Positive words in General lexicon
GL_N : Negative words in General lexicon
DL_P : Positive words in Domain lexicon
DL_N : Negative words in Domain lexicon

For example, consider an opinionated sentence "*This is a bad phone.*" When the tagger is applied to input sentence, we get the following tagged sentence "*This/DT is/VBZ a/DT bad/JJ phone/NN ./.*". Application of extraction patterns from Table 1 will obtain **bad/JJ phone/NN** as opinion word from the sentence. Sentiment Product Lexicon is used to detect neutral phrases. We consider the extracted phrases or words namely word1 and word2 from an opinionated sentence as neutral if none of the words extracted are found in Sentiment Product Lexicon.

From the above example word1 is bad and word2 is phone. We find whether word2 is in positive or negative list of Domain lexicon. If word2 is present in any one of the list in Domain lexicon, polarity of the word will be similar to polarity of list in which it is found. If it is not in positive or negative list of Domain lexicon, then positive and negative list of General lexicon is consulted to find the polarity of a word.

If word2 is neither present in Domain lexicon nor in General lexicon, we assume word2 to have neutral polarity, in such a case we use word1 instead of word2, and find polarity of word1 similar to polarity of word2 afore discussed. If polarity is found, then polarity is for the phrase consisting of both word1 and word2. If polarity is not found, we assume both word1 and word2 to be neutral.

If a word, either word1 or word2, is present in both Domain lexicon and General lexicon, polarity of word will be similar to polarity of Domain lexicon. If word1 is a negator such as 'not', the polarity of word2 will be opposite to an earlier obtained polarity of word2. For example the phrase "not good", here word1 is 'not' and word2 is 'good'.

The polarity of word2 is positive, since word2 is prefixed by word1 i.e. 'not'. The polarity of phrase is negative. We retain only those phrases that have a polarity and discard phrases that are neutral. We compute the strength of semantic orientation of phrases using the Equation 2 as described in [5].

$$SO(phrase) = log_2\left[\frac{hits(ws_{10}(phrase, excellent)).hits(poor)}{hits(ws_{10}(phrase, poor)).hits(excellent)}\right] \qquad (2)$$

Our intuition is that, a phrase can be judged as positive or negative based on its association with positive and negative seed words. SO is the Semantic Orientation. We use excellent and poor as seed words, as they are a part of five star review rating system. SO is computed by finding association of these phrases with seed words from web corpus. It is found by querying the search engine and recording the number of hits returned by search engine for phrases that are closer to seed words in a window size (ws) of ten words. We used Google search engine, as it indexes more web pages, to find semantic orientation of the extracted phrases and compute average semantic orientation of opinionated sentences.

From the above example, we obtain SO (bad phone) = 4.20. The actual polarity of the phrase is negative, but SO value obtained is positive. We shift the polarity of the phrase in consultation with Sentiment Product Lexicon. We multiply the strength of semantic orientation of phrases by +1, if the phrases are positive, and -1, if phrases are negative. The new value for our example will be SO (bad phone) = - 4.20.

We compute the average semantic orientation of all phrases in an opinionated sentence. This is done for all the opinionated sentences in an opinionated text. We consider an opinionated sentence to be a significant opinionated sentence, if the average semantic orientation of a sentence is greater than the other opinionated sentences in an opinionated text.

An opinionated text is classified as positive, if the average semantic orientation of significant opinionated sentence is greater than a Threshold and negative when average semantic orientation of significant opinionated sentence is less than a Threshold. The Threshold used to classify opinionated sentences as positive or negative is 0.

4   Experiments and Results

We use our approach afore discussed to find an opinion from significant opinionated sentence. The result of our approach is compared with voting approach [6] and an approach discussed in [14]. Voting approach is sentence based approached similar to an approach discussed in [6]. We implemented this approach by considering not only adjectives, but also other part-of-speech tags to find a significant sentence and opinion of a user. We also implemented an approach discussed in [14] to find opinion of a user. We did not implement the approach discussed in [3], but use only the result reported on same data set.

The Table 2 shows the results of our approach along with other approaches on data set 1, data set 2 and data set 3. It also shows the result obtained by [3] on data set 3. We have used the result for comparing the accuracy of our approach on the same data set. We found the result obtained by our approach is better than the result documented in [3]. We compute the classification accuracy using

$$Accuracy = \frac{True\ Positive + True\ Negative}{Total\ Number\ of\ OpinionatedTexts\ to\ be\ Classified}$$

True Positive represent number of opinionated texts classified correctly as positive, Similarly True Negative represent number of opinionated text classified correctly as negatives.

The Figures 1, 2 and 3 show accuracy of our approach on different data sets. Figure 1 shows 78.15% positive accuracy and 65.55% negative accuracy

Table 2. Results of Our Approach

Slno.	Approach	Data sets	Accuracy
1	Turney [14]	Data set 1	71.85%
2	voting [6]	Data set 1	68.6%
3	**Our Approach**	**Data set 1**	**75.71%**
4	Turney [14]	Data set 2	65.75%
5	voting [6]	Data set 2	61.5%
6	**Our Approach**	**Data set 2**	**80.86%**
7	Turney [14]	Data set 3	65.71%
8	voting [6]	Data set 3	62.80%
9	Alistair [3]	Data set 3	69.3%
10	**Our Approach**	**Data set 3**	**71.33%**

for turney approach labeled as 1, 81.75% positive accuracy and 55.5% negative accuracy for voting method, labeled as 2, and 80.25% positive accuracy and 73.50 % negative accuracy for our approach, labeled as 3, on data set 1.

Similarly, Figures 2 and 3 show positive accuracy and negative accuracy obtained by our approach on data set 2 and data set 3. We found the accuracy obtained by our approach is better than the other two approaches.

Our approach extracts potential opinionated phrases, detects and eliminates neutral phrases among the extracted phrases. The neutral phrases may be extracted by patterns due to part of speech tagging error, grammatical discrepancies etc. For example, consider a positive opinionated text such as

I have nothing but good to say about this one! The updates that Apple is issuing are adding features or enhancing the existing ones. The synch works great! The map application is outstanding for finding

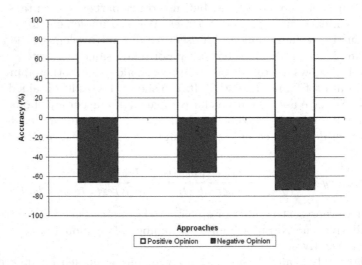

Fig. 1. Accuracy of different approaches on Data Set 1

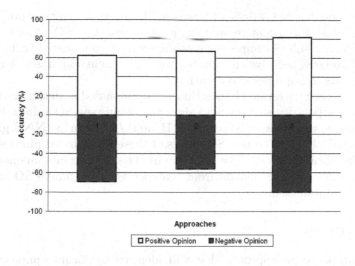

Fig. 2. Accuracy of different approaches on Data Set 2

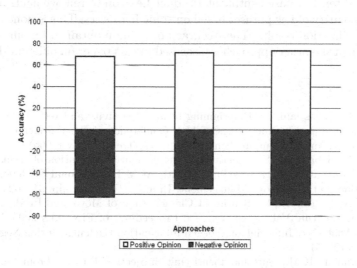

Fig. 3. Accuracy of different approaches on Data Set 3

places and getting directions to them! The weather application is really neat the way it shows the current temperature and updates it when the app is launched. Yeah, it is not 3G, but I don't mind. I'm not going to a fire!

We obtain phrase like current/JJ temperature/NN, n't/RB mind/VB, not/RB going/VBG, really/RB neat/JJ works/NNS great/JJ as opinionated phrase. The phrases like current/JJ temperature/NN, n't/RB mind/VB, not/RB going/VBG are found to be neutral phrases using SPL. Turney [14] and Voting [6] approaches consider all extracted phrases and finds their SO, it is quite possible SO values of phrases like current temperature, not going etc., to be too negative and may dominate the SO values of other phrases. These results in improper classification of opinionated text lessen its accuracy. Similarly, negative opinionated texts with neutral phrases that are too positive results in improper classification.

In our approach we retain phrases that are opinionated as determined by SPL and perform a polarity shift to SO values to obtain new SO values. From the above example, we obtain only **really/RB neat/JJ works/NNS great/JJ** as opinionated phrase. The new SO values of these opinionated phrases provide a better classification result. The accuracy of classification of opinionated texts increases by determining opinion from sentence with maximum SO value also known as significant sentence.

5   Conclusion

We have proposed an approach that will identify significant opinionated sentence based on the average SO value from a cluster of sentences composed in an opinionated text. We use Sentiment Product Lexicon to remove neutral phrases and shift polarity of few phrases based on some heuristics. This is done to obtain better classification results. The Accuracy of opinion obtained by our approach is better than the other approaches discussed in this paper on different data sets.

References

1. Esuli, A., Sebastiani, F.: Determining term subjectivity and term orientation for opinion mining. In: Proceedings of 11th Conference of the European Chapter of the Association for Computational Linguistics, Trento, Italy (2006)
2. Esuli, A., Sebastiani, F.: Determining the semantic orientation of terms through gloss classification. In: Proceedings of 14th ACM International Conference on Information and Knowledge Management, Bremen, Germany, pp. 617–624 (2005)
3. Kennedy, A., Inkpen, D.: Sentiment Classification of Movie and Product Reviews Using Contextual Valence Shifters. In: Proceedings of FINEXIN 2005, Workshop on the Analysis of Informal and Formal Information Exchange during Negotiations, Canada (2005)
4. Anil Kumar, K.M., Suresha: Identifying Subjective Phrases From Opinionated Texts Using Sentiment Product Lexicon. International Journal of Advanced Engineering & Applications 2, 63–271 (2010)
5. Anil Kumar, K.M., Suresha: Detection of Neutral Phrases and Polarity Shifting of Few Phrases for Effective Classification of Opinionated Texts. International Journal of Computational Intelligence Research 6, 43–58 (2010)
6. Liu, B., Hu, M., Cheng, J.: Opinion Observer: Analyzing and Comparing Opinions on the Web, Chiba, Japan (2005)
7. Pang, B., Lee, L.: A sentimental education: Sentiment analysis using subjectivity summarization based on minimum cuts. In: Proceedings of 42nd Meeting of the Association for Computational Linguistics, Barcelona, Spain, pp. 271–278 (2004)
8. Pang, B., Lee, L., Vaithyanathan, S.: Thumbs up? sentiment classification using machine learning techniques. In: Proceedings of 7th Conference on Empirical Methods in Natural Language Processing, Philadelphia, US, pp. 79–86 (2002)

9. General Inquirer, http://www.wjh.harvard.edu/~inquirer/
10. Review contre, http://www.reviewcentre.com/
11. Hugo: MontyLingua: An end-to-end natural language processor with common sense (2003)
12. Kamps, J., Marx, M., Mokken, R.J., De Rijke, M.: Using wordnet to measure semantic orientation of adjectives. In: Proceedings of 4th International Conference on Language Resources and Evaluation, Lisbon, Portugal, pp. 1115–1118 (2004)
13. Taboada, M., Grieve, J.: Analyzing appraisal automatically. In: Proceedings of the AAAI Symposium on Exploring Attitude and Affect in Text: Theories and Applications, California, US (2004)
14. Turney, P.D.: Thumbs up or thumbs down? Semantic orientation applied to unsupervised classification of reviews. In: Proceedings of 40th Annual Meeting of the Association for Computational Linguistics, Philadelphia, US, pp. 417–424 (2002)
15. Turney, P.D., Littman, M.L.: Measuring praise and criticism: Inference of semantic orientation from association. ACM Transactions on Information Systems, 315–346 (2003)
16. Owsley, S., Sood, S., Hammond, K.J.: Domain specific affective classification of document. In: Proceedings of AAAI 2006 Spring Symposium on Computational Approaches to Analyzing Weblogs, California, US (2006)
17. Wilson, T., Wiebe, J., Hoffmann, P.: Recognizing Contextual Polarity in Phrase-Level Sentiment Analysis. In: Proceedings of HLT/EMNLP, Vancouver, Canada (2005)
18. Hatzivassiloglou, V., McKeown, K.R.: Predicting the semantic orientation of adjectives. In: Proceedings of 35th Annual Meeting of the Association for Computational Linguistics, Madrid, Spain, pp. 174–181 (1997)
19. Araki, W.: Modifying SO-PMI for Japanese Weblog Opinion Mining by Using a Balancing Factor and Detecting Neutral Expressions. In: Proceedings of NAACL HLT 2007, New York, US, pp. 189–192 (2007)
20. Kim, Y., Myaeng, S.H.: Opinion Analysis based on Lexical Clues and their Expansion. In: Proceedings of NTCIR-6 Workshop Meeting, Tokyo, Japan, pp. 308–315 (2007)

Hyperspectral Data Compression Model Using SPCA (Segmented Principal Component Analysis) and Classification of Rice Crop Varieties

Shwetank[1,*], Kamal Jain [2], and Karamjit Bhatia[3]

[1] Vidya College of Engineering, Meerut (UP), India
shwetank_arya@rediffmail.com
[2] IIT, Roorkee, Uttarakhand, India
[3] Gurukul Kangri Vishwavidyalaya, Haridwar, Uttarakhand, India

Abstract. Hyperspectral Image Processing System (HIPS) is a good source of vegetation detection and identification. This work presents a spectral classification of rice crop using EO-1 Hyperion Hyperspectral image. In HIPS the traditional classification methods have major limitations due to high dimensionality. The Principal Component Analysis (PCA) is a well established data compression tool that can be applied on Hyperspectral data to reduce its dimensionality for feature extraction and classification. Now PCA has become a traditional tool of data compression in HIPS. This research proposes a new approach of data compression based on Segmented Principal Component Analysis (SPCA). The outcomes of our analysis led to a conclusion that the SAM classification of PCA_{NIR} (671.02-925.41nm) discriminates RICE crop varieties RICE 1[Ratan (IET-1411)], RICE 2[CSR-10 (IET-10349/10694)], RICE 3[Haryana Basmati-1(IET-10367)], RICE 4[HKR-126] and RICE 5[CSR-13 (IET-10348)] better than traditional $PCA_{VNIR-SWIR}$ and PCA_{VIR}, PCA_{SWIR-1}, PCA_{SWIR-2}, PCA_{SWIR-3} segments. Results of this research work have shown that the overall classification accuracy of PCA_5 in PCA_{NIR} segment is achieved 80.24% with kappa coefficient 0.77, however RICE4 and RICE5 varieties are classified 100% and RICE1 (72.73%), RICE2 (85.71%) and RICE3 (91.67%) are classified more accurately than other classification results.

Keywords: Hyperspectral, PCA, SAM (Spectral Angle Mapper).

1 Introduction

In Digital Image Processing (DIP) dimensionality of the imagery data is a constraint for pattern reorganization and information extraction. Many algorithms are evolved to reduce dimensionality of high volume Hyperspectral Satellite Data such as MNF (Minimum Noise Fraction) [1], DWT (Discrete Wavelet Transform) [2], End member Selection [3], Band Moment [4] and DSA (Derivative Spectral Analysis) [5]. However some amendments are required to improve these traditional methods of

---

* Vidya College of Engineering, Vidya Knowledge Park, Baghpat Road, Meerut-250002, India.

S. Ranka et al. (Eds.): IC3 2010, Part I, CCIS 94, pp. 360–372, 2010.

compression. In digital image processing the Principal Component Analysis (PCA) is a traditional tool of image compression which is frequently used in dimension reduction, preservation of variance in the image transformation. It minimizes mean square errors and generation of uncorrelated coefficients. In Principal Component Analysis the new image layers are developed with known components. This process is regarded as data compression in which a number of bands are extracted into higher order components and first few PC bands account for maximum information in the dataset, often high as 95-98%. In the present study EO-1 Hyperion Hyperspectral dataset of 155 bands is compressed by PCA; based on covariance and correlation matrices. Further, the compressed image is classified using SAM classifier to discriminate rice crop varieties. The preliminary results of classification using compressed satellite image is not enough to discriminate rice crop varieties and mixing. Therefore a new method of data compression, known as Segment Principal Component Analysis (SPCA), has been evolved to discriminate rice crop varieties with maximum accuracy. Finally, we focus on building a solid intuition for how and why PCA works.

2 Study Area

The research work is carried out in Bapauli town, northeast part of district Panipat in Haryana. It is situated in North-East, 70 km of the national capital. Bapauli is a healthy vegetated area in district Panipat of Haryana state in India, as shown in Figure 1. This is part of the lower great region of Yamuna basin. The study area is lying between $29°21'14''$-$29°16'15''$ N and $77°3'35''$-$77°7'2''$E with area of 176.26 hectares.

3 Data Used

The Hyperspectral image data is acquired on September 2, 2005. It has 242 bands covering a spectral region from 355nm to 2577nm with ground resolution of 30m within the same vegetation period of the EO-1 satellite, ground truth data has been collected by detailed mapping of land use and crop types across a major part of the area imaged by the sensor. The local framers and government organization also provided useful statistical information.

4 ROI-End Member Selection

The 253 multiple pixels or ROIs (region of interest) with unique color composition are selected in respect of sixteen land cover classes- RICE (RICE 1, RICE 2, RICE 3, RICE 4 and RICE 5), WATER (WATER 1 and WATER 2), POND, MOISTURE, VEG (VEG 1 and VEG 2), BUSHES, HABITATION, OPEN FIELD, BARONLAND and SAND for SAM classification listed in Table 1. The training pixels are mapped to the appropriate classes with reference Google image and ground training points.

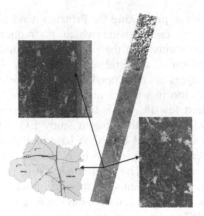

Fig. 1. False color image subset (192 x 306 pixels) of Bapauli town and its nearby region by Hyperion with a spectral resolution of 30 meter/pixel

Table 1. Rice Crop Varieties with Sixteen land cover classes and training pixels class with color composition

Table 2. Result of PCA showing the percentage of variability explained by different PCs of Hyperion dataset

S.No.	Class Type	No. of pixels Training Site	Class Color	Color Composition
1.	Rice 1	11	Green	
2.	Rice 2	07	Green 1	
3.	Rice 3	12	Green 2	
4.	Rice 4	26	Green 3	
5.	Rice 5	16	Seagreen	
6.	Water 1	64	White	
7.	Habitation	66	Cyan 3	
8.	Pond	04	Blue	
9.	Veg 1	02	Magenta	
10.	Veg 2	01	Maroon	
11.	Open field	07	Cyan	
12.	Moisture	05	Purple	
13.	Sand	08	Red	
14.	Water 2	02	Blue 2	
15.	Bushes	20	Yellow	
16.	Baron Land	02	Coral	
Total Sample Pixels		253		

Principal Components	Percentage Variability	Cumulative Percentage
PC-1	67.56	67.56
PC-2	25.87	93.43
PC-3	1.95	95.37
PC-4	1.59	96.96
PC-5	0.83	97.79
PC-6	0.61	98.40
PC-7	0.19	98.59
PC-8	0.15	98.74
PC-9	0.08	98.82
PC-10	0.07	98.89
PC-11	0.06	98.95
PC-12	0.06	99.00
PC-13	0.05	99.05
PC-14	0.04	99.10
PC-15	0.04	99.14
PC-16	0.04	99.18

5 Material and Methodology

5.1 Image Pre-processing

Pre-processing is necessary not only to remove the sensor errors during the acquisition but for the corrections of the display, band selection and to minimise the computational complexity. Out of the calibrated bands of Hyperion in the high water absorption range from 1400nm to 1900nm and bands which deemed to have water absorption streaking have been removed from further processing. Hence, 155 (8-57, 83-119, 135-164 and 183-220) bands from the 196 unique bands are selected to separate rice crop and its varieties from the other land cover classes. These selected bands are visually inspected for bad columns to eliminate the striping pixel errors. Two Hyperion multi band images having two scaling factors individually for VNIR and SWIR bands are developed and combined [6]. The atmospheric correction is performed using FLAASH (Fast Line-of-sight Atmospheric Analysis of Spectral Hypercubes) method complemented by Empirical Flat Field Optimal Reflectance Transformation (EFFORT) an image smoothing statistical correction method shown. EFFORT is also used to remove remaining instrument noise introduced by instrument and atmospheric effects from the Hyperion dataset by providing gain and offset value.

5.2 Traditional $PCA_{VNIR-SWIR}$ and SAM Classification

Dimensionality reduction refers to the process by which the main components, attributing to the spectral variance of the data set, are identified and removed reducing the dimensionality of the data. This is also refers to removal of noise and data redundancy. Traditional $PCA_{VNIR-SWIR}$ (Principal Component Analysis in VNIR-SWIR region) transformation, with covariance matrix, is applied in the study to accomplish this task. Once applying $PCA_{VNIR-SWIR}$ on 155 bands, new 155 PCA bands are obtained. The image pixels are represented by eigenvalues, the dimensionality of the data is determined by examining these values as shown in Figure 2 and Figure 3. In this data of 155 components, 67.56% of the data variance is explained by first principal component (PC1). Another 30.24% is covered in next four PCs. The first sixteen PCs contribute more than 99% of information in the dataset as shown in Table 2. It is also found that the dimensionality of data is around 4, since each of the first 4 PCs explains more than 1 percent variance in the data. Six $PCA_{VNIR-SWIR}$ (PCA_3-PCA_8) combinations, using 3 to 8 PC at a time starting from 1-3 then 1-4 and so on upto 1-8, are taken and classified using SAM classifier as shown in Figure 4. It is seen that the classification performance of RICE crop varieties is decreasing as number of PC bands in combination increases as shown in Table 3.

5.3 Segmented Principal Component Analysis (SPCA)

As mentioned previously, the compressed EO-1 dataset obtained by traditional $PCA_{VNIR-SWIR}$ is not enough to assist classification of rice crop varieties. PCA recognizes data according to their co-variances. Because of the slight differentiations among the five varieties of rice crop in the study area, traditional $PCA_{VNIR-SWIR}$ failed to notice healthy information that are helpful to the discrimination of different

PC1   PC2   PC3   PC4   PC5   PC6

Fig. 2. The consequential six PCs (Principal Components) out of 155 bands having maximum eigenvalues (LEFT to RIGHT) PC1, PC2, PC3, PC4, PC5 and PC6

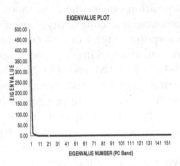

Fig. 3. PC$_{VNIR-SWIR}$ eigenvalues plots of Hyperion data set

PCA$_3$ PCA$_4$ PCA$_5$ PCA$_6$ PCA$_7$ PCA$_8$

Fig. 4. SAM classification of six iterations of novel PCA$_{VNIR-SWIR}$

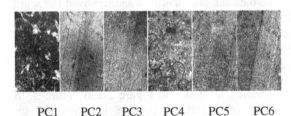

PC1   PC2   PC3   PC4   PC5   PC6

Fig. 5. PCA$_{VIR}$ band images for Hyperion data. (LEFT to RIGHT) PC1, PC2, PC3, PC4, PC5 and PC6

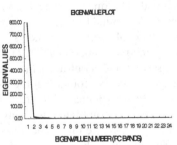

Fig. 6. PC$_{VIR}$ eigenvalues plots of Hyperion data set

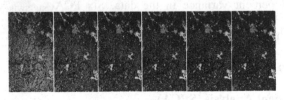

PCA$_3$ PCA$_4$ PCA$_5$ PCA$_6$ PCA$_7$ PCA$_8$

Fig. 7. SAM classification of six iterations of novel PCA$_{VIR}$

PC1   PC2   PC3   PC4   PC5   PC6

Fig. 8. PCA$_{NIR}$ band images for Hyperion data. (LEFT to RIGHT) PC1, PC2, PC3, PC4, PC5 and PC6

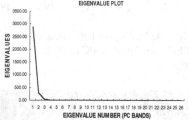

Fig. 9. PCA$_{NIR}$ eigenvalues plots of Hyperion data set

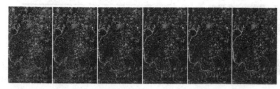

PCA$_3$ PCA$_4$ PCA$_5$ PCA$_6$ PCA$_7$ PCA$_8$

Fig. 10. SAM classification of six iterations of novel PCA$_{NIR}$

PC1   PC2   PC3   PC4   PC5   PC6

Fig. 11. PCA$_{SWIR-1}$ band images for Hyperion data (LEFT to RIGHT) PC1, PC2, PC3, PC4, PC5 and PC6

Fig. 12. PCA$_{SWIR-1}$ eigenvalues plots of Hyperion data set

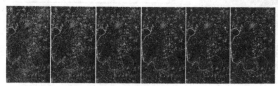

PCA$_3$ PCA$_4$ PCA$_5$ PCA$_6$ PCA$_7$ PCA$_8$

Fig. 13. SAM classification of six iterations of novel PCA$_{SWIR-1}$

PC1   PC2   PC3   PC4   PC5   PC6

Fig. 14. PCA$_{SWIR-2}$ band images for Hyperion data (LEFT to RIGHT) PC1, PC2, PC3, PC4, PC5 and PC6

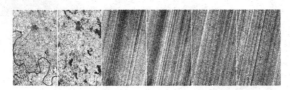

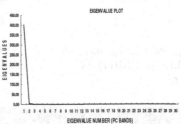

Fig. 15. PCA$_{SWIR-2}$ eigenvalues plots of Hyperion data set

PCA$_3$ PCA$_4$ PCA$_5$ PCA$_6$ PCA$_7$ PCA$_8$

Fig. 16. SAM classification of six iterations of novel PCA$_{SWIR-2}$

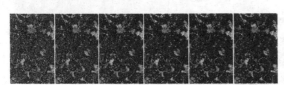

PC1   PC2   PC3   PC4   PC5   PC6

Fig. 17. PCA$_{SWIR-3}$ band images for Hyperion data (LEFT to RIGHT) PC1, PC2, PC3, PC4, PC5 and PC6

Fig. 18. PCA$_{SWIR-3}$ eigenvalues plots of Hyperion data set

PCA$_3$ PCA$_4$ PCA$_5$ PCA$_6$ PCA$_7$ PCA$_8$

Fig. 19. SAM classification of six iterations of novel PCA$_{SWIR-3}$

varieties. Therefore, Segmented Principal Component Analysis (SPCA), a new method of data compression, is developed, where 155 spectral bands are divided into five segments based on reflectance properties of vegetations over different wavelength as shown in Table 4.

Table 3. Assessment of classification accuracy of six PCA$_{VNIR-SWIR}$ using SAM classifier

S. NO.	PCA iterations	CROP	RICE1	RICE2	RICE3	RICE4	RICE5
1	PCA$_3$ (61.66%)	Un Classified	9.09	0.00	16.67	0.00	0.00
		RICE 1	54.55	42.86	33.33	0.00	0.00
		RICE 2	9.09	14.29	25.00	0.00	0.00
		RICE 3	0.00	0.00	8.33	0.00	6.25
		RICE 4	18.18	0.00	0.00	84.62	25.00
		RICE 5	9.09	42.86	16.67	15.38	68.75
2	PCA$_4$ (54.54%)	Un Classified	72.73	57.14	41.67	11.54	18.75
		RICE 1	9.09	14.29	25.00	0.00	0.00
		RICE 2	9.09	14.29	8.33	0.00	0.00
		RICE 3	9.09	0.00	16.67	0.00	6.25
		RICE 4	0.00	0.00	0.00	84.62	12.50
		RICE 5	0.00	14.29	8.33	3.85	62.50
3	PCA$_5$ (52.96%)	Un Classified	81.82	71.43	58.33	15.38	18.75
		RICE 1	9.09	14.29	0.00	0.00	0.00
		RICE 2	9.09	14.29	0.00	0.00	0.00
		RICE 3	0.00	0.00	41.67	0.00	0.00
		RICE 4	0.00	0.00	0.00	80.77	18.75
		RICE 5	0.00	0.00	0.00	3.85	56.25
4	PCA$_6$ (48.22%)	Un Classified	100.00	85.71	58.33	15.38	31.25
		RICE 1	0.00	14.29	0.00	0.00	0.00
		RICE 2	0.00	0.00	8.33	0.00	0.00
		RICE 3	0.00	0.00	41.67	0.00	0.00
		RICE 4	0.00	0.00	0.00	80.77	12.50
		RICE 5	0.00	0.00	0.00	3.85	56.25
5	PCA$_7$ (45.84%)	Un Classified	100.00	85.71	66.67	38.46	43.75
		RICE 1	0.00	14.29	0.00	0.00	0.00
		RICE 2	0.00	0.00	0.00	0.00	0.00
		RICE 3	0.00	0.00	33.33	0.00	0.00
		RICE 4	0.00	0.00	0.00	61.54	0.00
		RICE 5	0.00	0.00	0.00	15.38	56.25
6	PCA$_8$ (53.76%)	Un Classified	81.82	71.43	58.33	15.38	18.75
		RICE 1	9.09	14.29	0.00	0.00	0.00
		RICE 2	9.09	14.29	0.00	0.00	0.00
		RICE 3	0.00	0.00	41.67	0.00	0.00
		RICE 4	0.00	0.00	0.00	80.77	12.50
		RICE 5	0.00	0.00	0.00	3.85	68.75

Table 4. Five-group segmentations for PCA

S. No.	Segment	Wavelength	No. of Bands
1.	VIR	467.82-660.85nm	24
2.	NIR	671.02-925.41nm	26
3.	SWIR-1	972.99-1326.05nm	37
4.	SWIR-2	1497.63-790.19nm	30
5.	SWIR-3	1981.86-2355.21nm	38

PCA$_{VIR}$ and SAM Classification

In VIR (Visible Infrared) the reflectance and transmittance are relatively low because of high absorption of chlorophyll in pigments of crop leaf tissues [6-8]. A segment of 24 spectral bands (467.82-660.85nm) in VIR region is selected for PCA$_{VIR}$ (principal component analysis in VIR region) with covariance matrix. The first six PCs (principal components) from PC1 to PC6, having maximum information, are shown in Figure 5. However, PC4 band is acceptable image with less noise than PC2 and PC5. The dimensionality of the dataset has been determined by examining eigenvalues as explored in Figure 6. Six PCA$_{VIR}$ (PCA$_3$-PCA$_8$) combinations, using 3 to 8 PC at a time starting from 1-3 then 1-4 and so on upto 1-8, are taken and classified using SAM classifier as shown in Figure 7 and Table 5. However classification performance of RICE crop varieties is decreased due to mixed and unclassified pixels.

PCA$_{NIR}$ and SAM Classification

In NIR (Near Infrared) reflectance and transmittance are both relatively high because of multiple internal reflections in foliage structures; the reflectance of the vegetation is very strong in this region [9]. A segment of 26 spectral bands (671.02-925.41nm) in NIR region, is selected for PCA$_{NIR}$ (principal component analysis in NIR region) with covariance matrix. The first six PCs (principal components), from PC1 to PC6 acquire maximum information are shown in Figure 8. However, PC1, PC2, PC3, PC5 and PC6 bands are acceptable image with less noise than PC4. The dimensionality of the dataset has been determined by examining eigenvalues as shown in Figure 9. Six PCA$_{NIR}$ (PCA$_3$-PCA$_8$) combinations, using 3 to 8 PC at a time starting from 1-3 then 1-4 and so on upto 1-8, are taken and classified using SAM classifier as shown in

Table 5. Assessment of classification accuracy of six PCA$_{VIR}$ using SAM classifier

S. NO.	PCA Iterations	CROP	RICE1	RICE2	RICE3	RICE4	RICE5	S. NO.	PCA Iterations	CROP	RICE1	RICE2	RICE3	RICE4	RICE5
1	PCA$_3$ (35.18%)	Un Classified	9.09	0.00	16.67	46.15	25.00	4	PCA$_6$ (41.89%)	Un Classified	72.73	0.00	50.00	96.15	50.00
		RICE 1	54.55	28.57	0.00	0.00	12.00			RICE 1	18.18	14.29	0.00	0.00	0.00
		RICE 2	9.09	28.57	0.00	3.85	0.00			RICE 2	9.09	85.71	0.00	0.00	0.00
		RICE 3	0.00	0.00	25.00	7.69	12.50			RICE 3	0.00	0.00	41.67	0.00	6.25
		RICE 4	0.00	0.00	41.67	34.62	6.25			RICE 4	0.00	0.00	0.00	3.85	0.00
		RICE 5	0.00	0.00	16.67	7.69	43.75			RICE 5	0.00	0.00	8.33	0.00	43.75
2	PCA$_4$ (33.59%)	Un Classified	27.27	0.00	16.67	76.92	50.00	5	PCA$_7$ (41.89%)	Un Classified	72.73	0.00	66.67	96.15	50.00
		RICE 1	45.45	28.57	0.00	0.00	0.00			RICE 1	18.18	14.29	0.00	0.00	0.00
		RICE 2	18.18	14.29	0.00	0.00	0.00			RICE 2	9.09	85.71	0.00	0.00	0.00
		RICE 3	0.00	0.00	41.67	3.85	0.00			RICE 3	0.00	0.00	33.33	0.00	6.25
		RICE 4	0.00	0.00	16.67	7.69	6.25			RICE 4	0.00	0.00	0.00	3.85	0.00
		RICE 5	0.00	0.00	25.00	7.69	43.75			RICE 5	0.00	0.00	0.00	0.00	43.75
3	PCA$_5$ (42.29%)	Un Classified	54.55	0.00	50.00	88.46	50.00	6	PCA$_4$ (41.11%)	Un Classified	72.73	0.00	75.00	100	50.00
		RICE 1	36.36	14.29	0.00	0.00	0.00			RICE 1	18.18	14.29	0.00	0.00	0.00
		RICE 2	9.09	71.43	0.00	0.00	0.00			RICE 2	9.09	85.71	0.00	0.00	0.00
		RICE 3	0.00	0.00	33.33	0.00	6.25			RICE 3	0.00	0.00	25.00	0.00	6.25
		RICE 4	0.00	0.00	8.33	11.54	0.00			RICE 4	0.00	0.00	0.00	0.00	0.00
		RICE 5	0.00	0.00	8.33	0.00	43.75			RICE 5	0.00	0.00	0.00	0.00	43.75

Table 6. Assessment of classification accuracy of six PCA$_{NIR}$ using SAM classifier

S. NO.	PCA Iterations	CROP	RICE1	RICE2	RICE3	RICE4	RICE5	S. NO.	PCA Iterations	CROP	RICE1	RICE2	RICE3	RICE4	RICE5
1	PCA$_3$ (69.96%)	Un Classified	0.00	0.00	0.00	0.00	0.00	4	PCA$_4$ (82.21%)	Un Classified	0.00	0.00	0.00	0.00	0.00
		RICE 1	72.73	14.29	25.00	0.00	0.00			RICE 1	72.73	14.29	16.67	0.00	0.00
		RICE 2	27.27	71.42	33.33	0.00	0.00			RICE 2	27.27	85.71	0.00	0.00	0.00
		RICE 3	0.00	14.29	41.67	0.00	0.00			RICE 3	0.00	0.00	83.33	0.00	0.00
		RICE 4	0.00	0.00	0.00	96.15	6.25			RICE 4	0.00	0.00	0.00	100.00	6.25
		RICE 5	0.00	0.00	0.00	3.85	100.00			RICE 5	0.00	0.00	0.00	0.00	93.75
2	PCA$_4$ (71.93%)	Un Classified	0.00	0.00	0.00	0.00	0.00	5	PCA$_7$ (81.42%)	Un Classified	0.00	0.00	0.00	0.00	0.00
		RICE 1	72.73	14.00	16.67	0.00	0.00			RICE 1	72.73	14.29	16.67	0.00	0.00
		RICE 2	18.18	85.71	0.00	0.00	0.00			RICE 2	27.27	85.71	0.00	0.00	0.00
		RICE 3	9.09	0.00	83.33	0.00	0.00			RICE 3	0.00	0.00	83.33	0.00	0.00
		RICE 4	0.00	0.00	0.00	100.00	0.00			RICE 4	0.00	0.00	0.00	100.00	6.25
		RICE 5	0.00	0.00	0.00	0.00	100.00			RICE 5	0.00	0.00	0.00	0.00	93.75
3	PCA$_5$ (80.23%)	Un Classified	0.00	0.00	0.00	0.00	0.00	6	PCA$_4$ (82.61%)	Un Classified	0.00	0.00	0.00	0.00	0.00
		RICE 1	72.73	14.29	8.33	0.00	0.00			RICE 1	72.73	14.29	8.33	0.00	0.00
		RICE 2	27.27	85.71	0.00	0.00	0.00			RICE 2	27.27	85.71	0.00	0.00	0.00
		RICE 3	0.00	0.00	91.67	0.00	0.00			RICE 3	0.00	0.00	91.67	0.00	0.00
		RICE 4	0.00	0.00	0.00	100.00	0.00			RICE 4	0.00	0.00	0.00	100.00	6.25
		RICE 5	0.00	0.00	0.00	0.00	100.00			RICE 5	0.00	0.00	0.00	0.00	93.75

Table 7. Assessment of classification accuracy of six PCA$_{SWIR-1}$ using SAM classifier

S. NO.	PCA Iterations	CROP	RICE1	RICE2	RICE3	RICE4	RICE5	S. NO.	PCA Iterations	CROP	RICE1	RICE2	RICE3	RICE4	RICE5
1	PCA$_3$ (54.15%)	Un Classified	9.09	0.00	8.33	3.85	6.25	4	PCA$_6$ (58.10%)	Un Classified	9.09	28.57	16.67	3.85	6.25
		RICE 1	72.73	28.57	25.00	0.00	0.00			RICE 1	72.73	28.57	25.00	0.00	0.00
		RICE 2	27.27	28.57	33.33	23.08	0.00			RICE 2	27.27	42.86	8.33	7.69	0.00
		RICE 3	0.00	0.00	16.67	15.38	0.00			RICE 3	0.00	0.00	41.67	26.92	0.00
		RICE 4	18.18	28.57	0.00	34.62	25.00			RICE 4	18.18	0.00	0.00	38.46	25.00
		RICE 5	0.00	14.29	16.67	23.08	68.75			RICE 5	0.00	0.00	8.33	23.08	68.75
2	PCA$_4$ (56.13%)	Un Classified	9.09	0.00	8.33	3.85	6.25	5	PCA$_7$ (60.87%)	Un Classified	9.09	14.29	8.33	7.69	6.25
		RICE 1	72.73	28.57	25.00	0.00	0.00			RICE 1	72.73	14.29	16.67	0.00	0.00
		RICE 2	27.27	28.57	33.33	23.08	0.00			RICE 2	27.27	71.43	8.33	0.00	0.00
		RICE 3	0.00	0.00	16.67	11.54	0.00			RICE 3	0.00	0.00	50.00	23.08	0.00
		RICE 4	18.18	28.57	8.33	38.46	25.00			RICE 4	18.18	0.00	0.00	42.31	25.00
		RICE 5	0.00	14.29	8.33	23.08	68.75			RICE 5	0.00	0.00	16.67	26.92	68.75
3	PCA$_5$ (55.73%)	Un Classified	9.09	0.00	8.33	3.85	6.25	6	PCA$_4$ (61.06%)	Un Classified	9.09	28.57	8.33	7.69	6.25
		RICE 1	72.73	28.57	25.00	0.00	0.00			RICE 1	72.73	14.29	16.67	0.00	0.00
		RICE 2	27.27	28.57	25.00	15.38	0.00			RICE 2	27.27	57.14	8.33	0.00	0.00
		RICE 3	0.00	28.57	25.00	19.23	0.00			RICE 3	0.00	0.00	58.33	7.69	0.00
		RICE 4	18.18	14.29	8.33	38.46	25.00			RICE 4	18.18	0.00	0.00	57.69	25.00
		RICE 5	0.00	0.00	8.33	23.08	68.75			RICE 5	0.00	0.00	8.33	26.92	68.75

Figure 10 and Table 6, where classification performance of RICE crop varieties increased as compared to that of PCA$_{VNIR-SWIR}$. PCA$_5$ transformation shows RICE 1 exhibits major confusion with RICE 2 (27.27%), RICE 2 and RICE 3 classes exhibit confusion with RICE 1 (14.29% and 8.33%). The RICE 4 and RICE 5 classes classified 100% accuracy and do not exhibit any confusion with other land cover classes.

PCA_SWIR-1 and SAM Classification

In SWIR-1 (Shortwave Infrared - Segment 1) reflectance and transmittance are both relatively not high because of liquid water absorption in the plant strictures; the reflectance of the vegetation is not strong in this region [10-11]. A segment of 37 spectral bands (972.99-1336.05nm) in SWIR-1 region is selected for PCA_SWIR-1 (principal component analysis in SWIR-1 region) with covariance matrix. The first six PCs (principal components) from PC1 to PC6 acquire maximum information are shown in Figure 11. However, PC1 and PC2 bands are acceptable components with less noise than PC3, PC4, PC5 and PC6. The dimensionality of the dataset has been determined by examining eigenvalues as explored in Figure 12. Six PCA_SWIR-1 (PCA3-PCA8) combinations 3 to 8 PC at a time, starting from 1-3 then 1-4 and so on upto 1-8, are taken and classified using SAM classifier as shown in Figure 13 and Table 7, where classification performance of RICE crop varieties is decreased due to mixed and unclassified pixels.

Table 8. Assessment of classification accuracy of six PCA_SWIR-2 using SAM classifier

S. NO.	PCA Iterations	CROP	RICE1	RICE2	RICE3	RICE4	RICE5	S. NO.	PCA Iterations	CROP	RICE1	RICE2	RICE3	RICE4	RICE5
1	PCA3 (43.08%)	Un Classified	90.91	42.86	58.33	80.77	50.00	4	PCA6 (54.15%)	Un Classified	100.00	100.00	83.33	92.31	93.75
		RICE 1	0.00	0.00	0.00	0.00	0.00			RICE 1	0.00	0.00	0.00	0.00	0.00
		RICE 2	9.09	0.00	0.00	0.00	0.00			RICE 2	0.00	0.00	0.00	0.00	0.00
		RICE 3	0.00	0.00	16.67	7.69	6.25			RICE 3	0.00	0.00	16.67	0.00	0.00
		RICE 4	0.00	0.00	8.33	3.85	0.00			RICE 4	0.00	0.00	0.00	3.85	0.00
		RICE 5	0.00	28.57	16.67	7.69	12.50			RICE 5	0.00	0.00	0.00	3.85	6.25
2	PCA4 (47.43%)	Un Classified	100.00	85.71	66.67	88.46	75.00	5	PCA7 (54.54%)	Un Classified	100.00	100.00	83.33	96.15	93.75
		RICE 1	0.00	0.00	0.00	0.00	0.00			RICE 1	0.00	0.00	0.00	0.00	0.00
		RICE 2	0.00	0.00	0.00	0.00	0.00			RICE 2	0.00	0.00	0.00	0.00	0.00
		RICE 3	0.00	0.00	25.00	3.85	6.25			RICE 3	0.00	0.00	16.67	0.00	0.00
		RICE 4	0.00	0.00	0.00	3.85	0.00			RICE 4	0.00	0.00	0.00	3.85	0.00
		RICE 5	0.00	0.00	8.33	3.85	12.50			RICE 5	0.00	0.00	0.00	0.00	6.25
3	PCA5 (53.35%)	Un Classified	100.00	85.71	66.67	88.46	87.50	6	PCA8 (53.75%)	Un Classified	100.00	100.00	83.33	100.00	100.00
		RICE 1	0.00	0.00	0.00	0.00	0.00			RICE 1	0.00	0.00	0.00	0.00	0.00
		RICE 2	0.00	0.00	0.00	0.00	0.00			RICE 2	0.00	0.00	0.00	0.00	0.00
		RICE 3	0.00	0.00	25.00	3.85	0.00			RICE 3	0.00	0.00	16.67	0.00	0.00
		RICE 4	0.00	0.00	0.00	3.85	0.00			RICE 4	0.00	0.00	0.00	0.00	0.00
		RICE 5	0.00	0.00	8.33	3.85	12.50			RICE 5	0.00	0.00	0.00	0.00	0.00

Table 9. Assessment of classification accuracy of six PCA_SWIR-3 using SAM classifier

S. NO.	PCA Iterations	CROP	RICE1	RICE2	RICE3	RICE4	RICE5	S. NO.	PCA Iterations	CROP	RICE1	RICE2	RICE3	RICE4	RICE5
1	PCA3 (27.67%)	Un Classified	81.82	42.86	50.00	42.31	56.25	4	PCA6 (30.04%)	Un Classified	100.00	100.00	91.67	88.46	87.50
		RICE 1	0.00	0.00	0.00	3.85	0.00			RICE 1	0.00	0.00	0.00	0.00	0.00
		RICE 2	0.00	14.29	0.00	3.85	0.00			RICE 2	0.00	0.00	0.00	0.00	0.00
		RICE 3	0.00	0.00	0.00	0.00	6.25			RICE 3	0.00	0.00	0.00	0.00	6.25
		RICE 4	0.00	0.00	8.33	7.69	18.75			RICE 4	0.00	0.00	0.00	11.54	0.00
		RICE 5	0.00	0.00	0.00	0.00	0.00			RICE 5	0.00	0.00	0.00	0.00	6.25
2	PCA4 (32.41%)	Un Classified	81.82	71.43	83.33	80.77	81.25	5	PCA7 (29.25%)	Un Classified	100.00	100.00	100.00	92.31	87.50
		RICE 1	0.00	0.00	0.00	0.00	6.25			RICE 1	0.00	0.00	0.00	0.00	0.00
		RICE 2	0.00	14.29	0.00	3.85	0.00			RICE 2	0.00	0.00	0.00	0.00	0.00
		RICE 3	0.00	0.00	0.00	0.00	6.25			RICE 3	0.00	0.00	0.00	0.00	6.25
		RICE 4	0.00	0.00	0.00	15.38	0.00			RICE 4	0.00	0.00	0.00	7.69	0.00
		RICE 5	0.00	0.00	0.00	0.00	0.00			RICE 5	0.00	0.00	0.00	0.00	6.25
3	PCA5 (31.62%)	Un Classified	81.82	100	83.33	84.62	87.50	6	PCA8 (0.00%)	Un Classified	100.00	100.00	100.00	100.00	100.00
		RICE 1	0.00	0.00	0.00	0.00	0.00			RICE 1	0.00	0.00	0.00	0.00	0.00
		RICE 2	0.00	0.00	0.00	0.00	0.00			RICE 2	0.00	0.00	0.00	0.00	0.00
		RICE 3	0.00	0.00	0.00	0.00	6.25			RICE 3	0.00	0.00	0.00	0.00	0.00
		RICE 4	0.00	0.00	0.00	0.00	0.00			RICE 4	0.00	0.00	0.00	0.00	0.00
		RICE 5	0.00	0.00	0.00	0.00	6.25			RICE 5	0.00	0.00	0.00	0.00	0.00

PCA_SWIR-2 and SAM Classification

In SWIR-2 (Shortwave Infrared - Segment 2) reflectance and transmittance are both relatively not high than SWIR-1 because of liquid water and wax/oil absorption in the plant strictures; the reflectance of the vegetation is not strong in this region [10-11]. A segment of 30 spectral bands (1497.63-1790.19nm) in SWIR-2 region is selected for PCA_{SWIR-2} (principal component analysis in SWIR-2 region) with covariance matrix. The first six PCs (principal components) from PC1 to PC6 acquire maximum information which shown in Figure 14. However, PC1 and PC2 bands are acceptable image with less noise than PC3, PC4, PC5 and PC6. The dimensionality of the dataset has been determined by examining eigenvalues graph as explored in Figure 15. Six PCA_{SWIR-2} (PCA_3-PCA_8) combinations 3 to 8 PC at a time starting from 1-3 then 1-4 and so on upto 1-8, are taken and classified using SAM classifier as shown in Figure 16 and Table 8. However, classification performance of RICE crop varieties is decreased due to mixed and unclassified pixels.

PCA_{SWIR-3} and SAM Classification

In SWIR-3 (Shortwave Infrared - Segment 3) reflectance and transmittance are both relatively not high as compared to SWIR-1 and SWIR-2 because of nitrogen, protein and soil properties (clay) and absorption in the plant strictures. The reflectance of the vegetation is not strong in this region [12-15]. Therefore, a Hyperion dataset segment of 38 spectral bands (1981.86-2355.21nm) in SWIR-3 region is selected for PCA_{SWIR-3}. The first six PCs (Principal Components) from PC1 to PC6 acquire maximum information are shown in Figure 17.The dimensionality of the dataset has been determined by examining eigenvalues as explored in Figure 18. Six PCA_{SWIR-2} (PCA_3-PCA_8) combinations 3 to 8 PC at a time starting from 1-3 then 1-4 and so on upto 1-8, are taken and classified using SAM classifier as shown in Figure 19 and Table 9, where classification performance of RICE crop varieties is decreased due to mixed and unclassified pixels.

6   Result and Analysis

The 155 spectral bands are dimensionally compressed by regular $PCA_{VNIR-SWIR}$ (principal component analysis) and classified using SAM classifier in VNIR-SWIR region. The classification of $PCA_{VNIR-SWIR}$ image (layers) produces intermixed and unclassified pixels. As well as more pixels are classified as non objective classes. A check with referenced data indicates that a lot of rice grown area is misclassified. In PCA_{VIR}, PCA_{NIR}, PCA_{SWIR-1}, PCA_{SWIR-2} and PCA_{SWIR-3} segments, the PCA_{NIR} produces excellent classification of RICE crop varieties. PCA_{NIR} obtained maximum classification accuracy in six combinations PCA_3, PCA_4, PCA_5, PCA_6, PCA_7 and PCA_8 respectively. The PCA_5 image is classified using SAM classifier with first five PCs (Principal Components). The overall accuracy of PCA_5 is 80.24% with 0.77 Kappa Coefficient, in which RICE4 and RICE5 are classified 100% accuracy as well as RICE1 with 72.73% accuracy, RICE2 with 85.71% accuracy and RICE3 with 91.67% accuracy thus these varieties are classified more accurately than other combinations. The SAM classification of PCA_{NIR} segment has, in fact, effectively picked up more distinguishing information than other segments.

7 Conclusion

While hyperspectral data are very rich in information, but processing the hyperspectral data poses several challenges regarding computational requirements, information redundancy removal, relevant information identification, and modelling accuracy. This study demonstrates the capability of Segmented Principal Component Analysis (SPCA) methodology of hyperspectral data compression over traditional Principal Component Analysis (PCA) to classify RICE crop and its immersive varieties Ratan (IET-1411), CSR-10 (IET-10349/10694), Haryana Basmati-1(IET-10367), HKR-126 and CSR-13 (IET-10348) using SAM classifier. In this study, a segmented principal component analysis scheme, reducing dimensionality of Hyperion imagery data, retaining useful information, has been developed for detecting specific RICE plant species over different wavelength regions-VIR (24-bands), NIR (26-bands), SWIR 1(37-bands), SWIR 2(30-bands) and SWIR 3(38-bands). The outcome of our analysis led to a conclusion that the SAM classification of PCA_{NIR} (671.02-925.41nm) discriminates RICE crop varieties better than $PCA_{VNIR-SWIR}$, PCA_{VIR}, PCA_{SWIR-1}, PCA_{SWIR-2}, PCA_{SWIR-3} segments among 16 land cover classes. The PCA_5, a combination of first five PCs (Principle Components) of PCA_{NIR} segment has been selected to make supervised classification using SAM algorithm. The classification accuracy of SAM classification after PCA_{NIR} is 80.2% with 0.77 Kappa Coefficient in which RICE4 and RICE5 are classified with 100% accuracy as well as RICE1 with 72.73%, RICE2 with 85.71% accuracy and RICE3 with 91.67% accuracy. Thus these varieties are classified more accurately than other segments.

References

1. Green, A.A., Berman, M., Switzer, P., Craig, M.D.: A transformation for ordering multispectral data in terms of image quality with implications for noise removal. IEEE Transactions on Geoscience and Remote Sensing 26(1), 65–74 (1988)
2. Bruce, L.M., Koger, C.K., Li, J.: Dimensionality reduction of hyperspectral data using discrete wavelet transform feature extraction. IEEE Transaction Geoscience and Remote Sensing 40(10), 2318–2338 (2002)
3. Acito, N., Gorsini, G., Diani, M.: An unsupervised algorithm for selection of selection of end members in Hyperspectral images. In: Proceeding 2002 IEEE Geoscience and Remote Sensing Symposium (IGARSS 2002), vol. 3, pp. 1673–1675 (2002)
4. Staenz, K.: Classification of a hyperspectral agricultural data set using band moments for reduction of the spectral dimensionality. Canadian Journal Remote Sensing 23(3), 248–257 (1996)
5. Laba, M., Tsai, F., Ogurcak, D., Smith, S., Richmond, M.E.: Field determination of optimal dates for the discrimination of invasive wetland plant species using derivative spectral analysis. Photogrammetric Engineering & Remote Sensing 71(5), 603–611 (2005)
6. EO-1 User Guide: USGS Earth Resources Observation System Data Centre, EDC (2003)
7. Devlin, R.M., Baker, A.V.: Photosynthesis. Van Nostrand Reinhold, New York (1971)
8. Woolley, J.T.: Reflectance and transmittance of light by leaves. Plant Physiol. 47, 656–662 (1971)

9. Zarco-Tejada, P.J., Miller, J.R., Mohammed, G.H., Noland, T.L., Sampson, P.H.: Estimation of chlorophyll fluorescence under natural illumination from hyperspectral data. International Journal of Applied Observation and Geoinformation 3, 321–327 (2001)
10. Tucker, C.J., Garrat, M.W.: Leaf optical system modelled as a stochastic process. Appl. Opt. 16, 635–642 (1977)
11. Gupta, R.K., Vijayan, D.: New hyperspectral vegetation characterization parameters. Advance Space Research 28, 201–206 (2001)
12. Jacquemound, S., Baret, F.: Prospect: A model of leaf optical properties spectra. Remote Sensing Environment 34(2), 75–92 (1990)
13. Asner, G.P., Lobell, D.B.: A bio geophysical approach for automated SWIR unmixing of soils and vegetation. Remote Sensing and Environment 74, 99–112 (2000)
14. Clark, R.N., Roush, T.L.: Reflectance spectroscopy: Quantitative analysis techniques for remote sensing applications. Journal of Geophysics and Research 89, 6329–6340 (1984)
15. Clark, R.N., King, T.V.V., Klejwa, M., Swayze, G., Vergo, N.: High spectral resolution reflectance spectroscopy of minerals. Journal of Geophysics and Research 95, 12653–12680 (1990)
16. Clark, R.N., Swayze, G.A., Gallagher, A., Gorelick, N., Kruse, F.: Mapping with imaging spectrometer data using the complete band shape least-squares algorithm simultaneously fit to multiplespectral features from multiple materials. In: Proc. 3rd Airborne Visible/Infrared Imaging Spectrometer (AVIRIS) Workshop, JPL Publication, pp. 91–28, 2–3 (1991)

Impulse Noise Removal from Color Images Using Adaptive Neuro–fuzzy Impulse Detector

Umesh Ghanekar[1], Awadhesh Kumar Singh[2], and Rajoo Pandey[1]

[1] Department of Electronics and communication Engineering, National Institute of Technology, Kurukshetra, India
[2] Department of Computer Engineering, National Institute of Technology, Kurukshetra, India
ugnitk@rediffmail.com, aksinreck@rediffmail.com,
rajoo_pandey@rediffmail.com

Abstract. In this paper, we present a filtering scheme based on adaptive neuro-fuzzy inference system (ANFIS) for restoration of color images. The adaptive neuro-fuzzy impulse noise detector provides a reliable detection of noisy pixels in the noisy images. The filtering stage combines the best features of both component-based as well as vector-based approaches to restore the pixel value. The proposed scheme, thus, performs both brightness and color correction. Efficacy of the proposed method is verified through computer simulations which indicate that the present filtering scheme outperforms several other filters used in the study.

Keywords: ANFIS, Color image filtering, Impulse noise.

1 Introduction

Digital images are often corrupted by impulse noise which usually results due to a noisy sensor or transmission errors. An ideal filtering method must suppress the noise in such a way that the detail information and edges are not affected [1]. The color image filtering schemes can be classified component-wise filtering method or vector filtering method [2]. It is widely accepted that vector filtering methods are more appropriate than component-wise filtering methods which can generate color artifacts. Among vector filtering methods, vector median filter [3], vector directional filter [4] and directional distance filters are the most commonly used filters for noise removal in the color images. These filters, however, do not distinguish between noisy and noisy-free pixels and apply the filtering unconditionally across the entire image, removing the signal details of uncorrupted pixels. Therefore, to discriminate the noise-free pixels from the noisy ones, an impulse detector is often used prior to filtering. Filtering schemes based on separate noise detection include high performance detection (HPD) filter [5], directional weighted median (DWM) filter [6] and switching vector median filter based on CIELAB color space [7].

Recently, there has been an emphasis on fuzzy logic based filtering schemes such as local self adaptive fuzzy filter [8], adaptive fuzzy systems for filtering of multichannel images [9] and [10]. Since, in some portions of an image the local conditions can be evaluated only vaguely, a filtering system should possess the capability of reasoning with vague and uncertain information. Thus, the fuzzy

S. Ranka et al. (Eds.): IC3 2010, Part I, CCIS 94, pp. 373–380, 2010.

techniques are inherently well suited for image filtering [11]. Among the neuro-fuzzy based approaches, adaptive neuro-fuzzy (NF) operator [12] and genetic learning-based neuro-fuzzy filters [13] have been proposed. These filters adopt fuzzy-reasoning to model the noise removal process. The adaptive neuro-fuzzy inference system (ANFIS) [14,15] have been shown to produce excellent results as impulse noise detector and filter for gray-level images. In this paper, an ANFIS based impulse detection scheme is extended for detection of noise in color images. This is followed by a filtering method which takes into consideration the color and brightness information to restore the noisy pixels. The performance of the filtering scheme is measured in terms of peak signal to noise ratio (PSNR), mean absolute error (MAE) and normalized color difference (NCD). The paper is organized as follows. The impulse detector for color images is formulated in section 2. Section 3 describes the filtering framework. Section 4 provides the experimental results obtained through computer simulations. Finally, section 5 concludes the overall findings.

2 Proposed Algorithm

The impulse detection is performed for each channel separately. Let $\mathbf{x_{i,j}} = (x_{i,j}^{(1)}, x_{i,j}^{(2)}, x_{i,j}^{(3)})$ denote a multichannel pixel in the RGB space at location (i, j) of image I, which is corrupted by impulse noise. Let us also define $w_{n \times n}^{(k)}$ as $(n \times n)$ filtering window for channel k with center pixel $x_{i,j}^{(k)}$.

2.1 Structure

The general structure of the neuro-fuzzy detector is shown in fig1. It consists of four neuro-fuzzy sub-systems each having 3-inputs and 1-output. Each input has the generalized bell type membership functions. In a (3×3) window $w_{3 \times 3}^{(k)}$, the pixel values in four directions (vertical, horizontal and two diagonals) form the inputs to the neuro-fuzzy sub systems. Let the three inputs of the ANFIS be $x_{(1)}^{(k)}$, $x_{(2)}^{(k)}$, $x_{(3)}^{(k)}$ and $Y^{(k)}$ denots its output for k^{th} channel.

Each possible combination of inputs and their associated membership functions is represented by a rule in the rule base of the ANFIS. In each ANFIS subsystem there are 8 (2^3) rules described as follows:

1. if $(x_1^{(k)}$ is $M_{11})$ and $(x_2^{(k)}$ is $M_{21})$ and $(x_3^{(k)}$ is $M_{31})$ then $R_1 = f_1(x_1^{(k)} x_2^{(k)} x_3^{(k)})$

2. if $(x_1^{(k)}$ is $M_{11})$ and $(x_2^{(k)}$ is $M_{21})$ and $(x_3^{(k)}$ is $M_{32})$ then $R_2 = f_2(x_1^{(k)} x_2^{(k)} x_3^{(k)})$

3. if $(x_1^{(k)}$ is $M_{11})$ and $(x_2^{(k)}$ is $M_{22})$ and $(x_3^{(k)}$ is $M_{31})$ then $R_3 = f_3(x_1^{(k)} x_2^{(k)} x_3^{(k)})$

4. if $(x_1^{(k)}$ is $M_{11})$ and $(x_2^{(k)}$ is $M_{22})$ and $(x_3^{(k)}$ is $M_{32})$ then $R_4 = f_4(x_1^{(k)} x_2^{(k)} x_3^{(k)})$

5. if $(x_1^{(k)}$ is $M_{12})$ and $(x_2^{(k)}$ is $M_{21})$ and $(x_3^{(k)}$ is $M_{31})$ then $R_5 = f_5(x_1^{(k)} x_2^{(k)} x_3^{(k)})$

6. if $(x_1^{(k)}$ is $M_{12})$ and $(x_2^{(k)}$ is $M_{21})$ and $(x_3^{(k)}$ is $M_{32})$ then $R_6 = f_6(x_1^{(k)} x_2^{(k)} x_3^{(k)})$

7. if $(x_1^{(k)}$ is $M_{12})$ and $(x_2^{(k)}$ is $M_{22})$ and $(x_3^{(k)}$ is $M_{31})$ then $R_7 = f_7(x_1^{(k)} x_2^{(k)} x_3^{(k)})$

8. if $(x_1^{(k)}$ is $M_{12})$ and $(x_2^{(k)}$ is $M_{22})$ and $(x_3^{(k)}$ is $M_{32})$ then $R_8 = f_8(x_1^{(k)} x_2^{(k)} x_3^{(k)})$

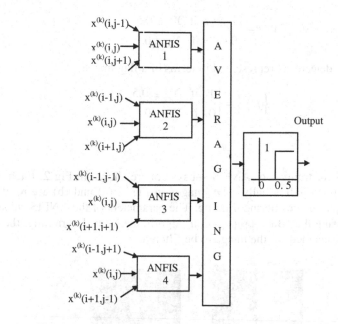

Fig. 1. The general structure of the neuro-fuzzy impulse detector

The input membership functions are described by

$$M_{rs} = \frac{1}{1 + \left|\dfrac{x - a_{rs}}{b_{rs}}\right|^{2c_{rs}}} \quad ; \quad r = 1, 2, 3 \ \& \ s = 1, 2 \tag{1}$$

And the output membership functions are linear combinations of inputs as given by

$$f_n(x_1^{(k)} x_2^{(k)} x_3^{(k)}) = d_{n1} x_1^{(k)} + d_{n2} x_2^{(k)} + d_{n3} x_3^{(k)} + d_{n4}; \quad n = 1, 2, ..., 8 \tag{2}$$

The parameters characterizing the input membership functions of antecedent parts and the input membership functions are adapted during the training phase of ANFIS. The outputs of the ANFIS subsystems are given by :

$$Y_i = \frac{\sum_{n=1}^{8} \omega_n R_n}{\sum_{n=1}^{8} \omega_n} \quad ; i = 1, 2, ...4 \tag{3}$$

Where ω_n representing the firing strength of nth rule in the rule base is determined by using the product operator.

The final output of the impulse detector is obtained by   thresholding the average value of outputs of four ANFIS subsystems.

$$Y_{av} = \frac{1}{4} \sum_{i=1}^{4} Y_i \tag{4}$$

$$Y^{(k)} = \begin{cases} 1 & \text{if } Y_{av} \geq 0.5 \\ 0 & \text{if } Y_{av} < 0.5 \end{cases} \tag{5}$$

The output of the detector is represented in terms of a flag image

$$\left\{ f_{i,j}^{(k)} \right\} = \begin{cases} 1 & \text{if } Y_{av} \geq 0.5 \\ 0 & \text{if } Y_{av} < 0.5 \end{cases} \tag{6}$$

2.2 Training

The images used for training of ANFIS subsystem are shown in Fig 2. Each ANFIS subsystems is trained individually. The images in Fig. 2 (a) and (b) are used as the target and the input images during training. The parameters of the ANFIS subsystems are adapted by using the 'Back-propagation' algorithm. After the training, the output of the detector is obtained for the image to be filtered.

(a)   (b)

Fig. 2. Images used for the training of ANFIS based impulse detector

3 Image Filtering

Only noisy pixels are replaced by filtering operation which consists of two phases. In the first phase of filtering to restore the brightness, a directional weighted scheme, as used in [6], is considered. The weight of a pixel is decided on the basis of standard deviation in four pixel directions (vertical, horizontal and two diagonals). The brightness of the noisy pixel $\left(f_{i,j}^{(k)} = 1 \right)$ is restored as:

$$y_{l,m}^{(k)} = med \left\{ w_{l,m} \Diamond x_{l,m}^{(k)} \right\} ; \text{ for all } l \text{ and } m \text{ such that } x_{l,m} \in w_{3 \times 3}^{(k)}$$

where operator $\Diamond$ denotes repetition operation and weights $\{w_{l,m}\}$ are defined as:

$$w_{l,m} = \begin{cases} 2 ; \text{if } x_{l,m}^{(k)} \in S \\ 1 ; \text{otherwise} \end{cases} \tag{7}$$

Here S denotes the set of pixels in the direction with minimum standard deviation. Now, the brightness restored multi-channel pixel is represented as $\mathbf{u_{i,j}} = \left(u_{i,j}^{(1)}, u_{i,j}^{(2)}, u_{i,j}^{(1)} \right)$ where

$$u_{i,j}^{(k)} = \begin{cases} y_{i,j}^{(k)} \text{ if } f_{i,j}^{(k)} = 1 \\ x_{i,j}^{(k)} ; \text{ otherwise} \end{cases} \text{ for } k = 1, 2, 3 \tag{8}$$

In the second phase of filtering, colour of the $\mathbf{x}_{i,j}$ is restored by using the colour information obtained from VDF. The output $\mathbf{v}_{i,j} = \left(v_{i,j}^{(1)}, v_{i,j}^{(2)}, v_{i,j}^{(3)} \right)$ of the VDF is obtained from a 3×3 filtering window by considering noise free-pixels. A 5×5 is window is used if the number of noise-free pixels is less than four in 3×3 window. The final output after colour restoration is given as $\mathbf{z}_{i,j} = \left(z_{i,j}^{(1)}, z_{i,j}^{(2)}, z_{i,j}^{(3)} \right)$ where

$$z_{i,j}^{(k)} = \begin{cases} v_{i,j}^{(k)} \times \left\| \mathbf{u}_{i,j} \right\| / \left\| \mathbf{v}_{i,j} \right\| \; ; \text{ if } f_{i,j}^{(k)} = 1 \\ u_{i,j}^{(k)} \; ; \qquad\qquad\qquad \text{otherwise} \end{cases} \tag{9}$$

4 Implementation and Simulation

To assess the performance of the proposed method, we compare it with several methods including VMF, VDF, DWM, HPD and that of Jin et al. [6]. The test images used in

Table 1. Comparison of restoration results for 'Lena' image

Method	Noise percentage					
	10		20		30	
	PSNR	MAE	PSNR	MAE	PSNR	MAE
VMF	31.1	3.99	26.1	5.41	20.1	8.81
VDF	29.1	4.57	21.9	7.42	16.2	14.97
Jin [6]	31.9	2.02	26.2	8.63	20.1	8.46
HPD	34.3	1.05	30.3	2.24	24.6	24.61
DWM	35.2	1.01	31.8	2.02	28.5	3.46
Proposed	39.9	0.64	36.2	1.36	31.5	2.46

Table 2. Comparison of restoration results for 'Boat in Lake' image

Method	Noise percentage					
	10		20		30	
	PSNR	MAE	PSNR	MAE	PSNR	MAE
VMF	29.2	4.48	24.5	6.41	19.3	10.32
VDF	26.9	5.32	21.0	8.63	15.6	16.61
Jin [6]	30.0	2.60	24.6	5.53	19.3	10.11
HPD	30.5	1.89	26.6	3.76	21.7	7.27
DWM	31.3	1.66	29.6	3.28	26.0	5.15
Proposed	39.5	0.61	35.4	0.36	31.6	2.43

Table 3. Comparison of NCD at different noise percentages for 'Lena' and 'Boat in Lake' image

Method	Lena			Boat in Lake		
	10	20	30	10	20	30
VMF	.0031	.0110	.0499	.0030	.0137	.0601
VDF	.0040	.0226	.0848	.0038	.0240	.0928
Jin [6]	.0020	.0106	.0498	.0023	.0128	.0594
HPD	.0034	.0103	.0318	.0070	.0247	.0714
DWM	.0027	.0072	.0164	.0089	.0105	.0206
Proposed	.0008	.0021	.0055	.0013	.0031	.0071

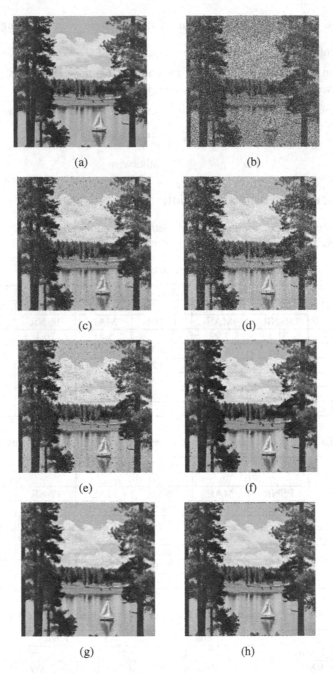

Fig. 3. Restoration performance of 'Boat in Lake' image a) Original (b) Noisy (c) VMf (d) VDF (e) Jin et al. [6] (f) DWM (g) HPD (h) Proposed

simulations are 'Lena' and 'Boat in Lake' each of size 512×512. The test images are corrupted with 50% correlated random valued impulse noise with noise density varying from 10% to 30%. The criteria used to compare the performance of various filters are PSNR (dB), MAE and NCD. The restoration results of various filters for subjective visual qualities are shown in the Fig. 3 for 'Boat in Lake' image. The PSNR and MAE resulting from various experiments are presented in Table 1 and 2 for 'Lena' and 'Boat in Lake' images, respectively. Table 3 presents the NCD comparison with various filters for both the images. From these tables, it is observed that the proposed method outperforms the other methods at all noise levels in terms of PSNR, MAE and NCD.

5 Conclusion

A filtering scheme based on adaptive-neuro fuzzy detection of impulse noise is presented for restoration of noisy color images. The fundamental advantage of the proposed method over other methods is that the detection of corrupted pixel is very efficiently performed by the ANFIS-based impulse detector. This efficient detection is translated into significantly improved performance of the filtering system which corrects only the corrupted pixel values by taking into consideration the brightness and color information for restoration of noisy images. The efficacy of the proposed scheme is demonstrated by experimental results which shows the significant improvement over several other methods.

References

1. Gonzales, R.C., Woods, R.E.: Digital Image Processing, 2nd edn. Addison Wesley, Reading (2002)
2. Karakos, D.G., Trahanias, P.E.: Generalized multichannel image-filtering structures. IEEE Trans. Image Process. 6(7), 1038–1045 (1997)
3. Astola, J., Haavisto, P., Neuov, Y.: Vector median filters. Proc. IEEE 78(4), 678–689 (1990)
4. Trahanias, P.E., Venetsanopoulos, A.N.: Vector directional filters - a new class of multichannel image processing filters. IEEE Trans. Image Process. 2(4), 528–534 (1993)
5. Awad, A.S., Man, H.: High performance detection filter for impulse noise removal in images. Electronics Letters 44(3), 192–194 (2008)
6. Dong, Y., Xu, S.: A new directional weighted median filter for removal of random-valued impulse noise. IEEE Signal Process. Lett. 14(3), 193–196 (2007)
7. Jin, L., Li, D.: A switching vector median filter based on the CIELAB color space for color image restoration. Signal Process. 87(6), 1345–1354 (2007)
8. Farbiz, F., Menhaj, M.B., Motamedi, S.A., Hagan, M.T.: A new fuzzy logic filter for image enhancement. IEEE Trans. Syst. Man and Cybern. Part B 30(1), 110–119 (2000)
9. Yuksel, M.E.: A simple neuro-fuzzy method for improving the performance of impulse noise filter for digital images. Int. J. Electron. Commun. (AEU) 59, 463–472 (2005)
10. Yuksel, M.E., Basturk, A.: A simple generalized neuro-fuzzy operator for efficient removal of impulse noise from highly corrupted digital images. Int. J. Electron. Commun. (AEU) 59, 1–7 (2005)

11. Russo, F.: Noise removal from image data using recursive neurofuzzy filters. IEEE Trans. on Instrumentation and Measurements 49(2), 307–314 (2000)
12. Jang, J.-S.R., Sun, C.-T., Mizutani, E.: Neuro-Fuzzy And Soft Computing, PHI (2002)
13. Ghanekar, U., Singh, A.K., Pandey, R.: Noise removal from images using adaptive neuro-fuzzy impulse detector. In: Int. Conf. on IT, H.I.T(W.B.) India, pp. 531–535 (March 2007)
14. Plataniotis, K.N., Androutsos, D., Venetsanopoulos, A.N.: Adaptive Fuzzy Systems for Multichannel Signal Processing. Proceeding of the IEEE 87(9), 1601–1622 (1999)
15. Morillas, S., et al.: Local self- adaptive fuzzy filter for impulse noise removal in color images. Signal Processing 88, 390–398 (2008)

Measuring of Time-Frequency Representation (TFR) Content – Using the Kapur's Entropies

Priti Gupta[1] and Vijay Kumar[2]

[1] Professor, Deptt. of Stat., Maharishi Dayanand University, Rohtak
[2] Sr. Lecturer in Mathematics, Delhi College of Tech.& Mgt., Palwal
sudansonu2@yahoo.com

Abstract. The generalized entropies of Kapur inspire new measures for estimating signal information and complexity in the time-frequency plane. When applied to a time-frequency representation (TFR) from Cohen's class or the affine class, the kapur's entropies confirm closely to the concept of complexity as discussed in theorem 2.2.1 and 2.2.2. In this paper, we study the properties of the Kapur's entropies, with emphasis on the mathematical foundations for quadratic TFRs. In particular, for the Wigner distribution we establish some results that there exist signals for which the measures are not well defined.

Keywords: Kapur's entropy, Renyi's entropy TFRs, Cohen's Class, Wigner distribution.

1 Introduction

The term *component* is encountered in the signal processing. In general, a component is a concentration of energy in some domain, but it is very difficult to translate this concept into a quantitative concept explained by Williams [1], Orr [2] and Cohen [3]. In other words, the concept of a signal component may not be clearly defined and this term is particularly used in the analysis of time-frequency. Time-frequency representations (TFRs) generalize the concept of the time and frequency domains to a function $C_s(t, f)$. Cohen [4] give the concept that how the frequency of a signal s changes over a time t.

In this paper, we will discuss some important theorems and its validity. Baraniuk [10] using Renyi's entropy for measuring TFRs and give some results. Here, we are using Kapur's entropy and finds that it will give us much better results for measuring TFRs than Renyi's entropy.

Let us consider $|s(t)|^2$ and $|s(f)|^2$ be the unidimensional densities of signal energy in time and frequency. It is very difficult for TFRs to act as bidimensional densities of signal energy in time-frequency.

In particular, there exist some marginal properties of TFRs parallel to those of probability densities:

$$\int C_s(t, f) \, df = |s(t)|^2, \quad \int C_s(t, f) \, dt = |s(f)|^2 \quad (1)$$

S. Ranka et al. (Eds.): IC3 2010, Part I, CCIS 94, pp. 381–390, 2010.

$$\iint C_s (t, f) \, dt \, df = \int |s(t)|^2 \, dt = \|s\|_2^2 \tag{2}$$

The quadratic TFRs of the large and useful Cohen's Class [4] can be obtained by convolution as:

$$C_s (t, f) = \iint W_s (u, v) \, \Phi(t - u, f - v) \, du \, dv = (W_s * \Phi) (t, f) \tag{3}$$

Where Φ is a kernel function

The Wigner distribution W_s of the signal is as:

$$W_s (t, f) = \int s\left(t + \frac{\tau}{2} \right) s^*\left(t - \frac{\tau}{2} \right) e^{-j2\pi\tau f} \, d\tau \tag{4}$$

The classical Shannon Entropy for unit-energy signals:

$$H(C_s) = - \iint C_s (t, f) \log_2 C_s (t, f) \, dt \, df \tag{5}$$

Eq.(5) is a measure for the complexity of a signal through TFRs.

Here, complexity measure (Shannon Entropy) is only applied to TFRs, which acts as a probability density function not on a signal or process. The peaky TFRs of signals consists of small numbers of elementary components would give small entropy values, where as the diffuse TFRs of more complicated signals would give large entropy values.

However, the negative values taken by most of the TFRs (including all fixed-kernel Cohen's class TFRs satisfying (1)) are unable to give the application of the Shannon entropy due to the logarithm in (5). Baraniuk [10] using the concept of Renyi's entropy to sideline the issue of negativity. In order to keep the same thing in mind, we are employing the generalized entropies of Kapur of order α and type β [11] (again for unit-energy signals)

$$H_{\alpha,\beta}(C_s) = \frac{1}{\beta - \alpha} \log_2 \left(\frac{\iint C_s^\alpha (t, f) \, dt \, df}{\iint C_s^\beta (t, f) \, dt \, df} \right), \alpha \neq \beta, \ \alpha, \beta > 0 \tag{6}$$

In the limiting case, when $\alpha \to 1 \ and \ \beta = 1$, $H_{\alpha,\beta}(C_s)$ reduces to $H(C_s)$

and when $\beta = 1$, (6) reduces to Renyi's Entropy.

The class of information measures is obtained by taking the mean value property of the Shannon entropy from an arithmetic to an exponential mean.

In several empirical studies, Williams, Brown, and Hero[1] found that the appearance of negative TFR values invalidate the Shannon approach, the 3rd-order Renyi's entropy seemed to measure signal complexity. Since Kapur's entropy of order α and type β is the limiting case of Renyi's entropy.

In our study, we are using the generalized Kapur's entropy of order-3 and type β to measure signal complexity. Also, We will discuss in detail the properties and some applications of the Kapur time-frequency information measures (6), which emphasis on the quadratic TFRs.

After reviewing these measures, we will examine their existence and show that for odd α and even β or vice-versa and for $\alpha \neq \beta$, there exist signals s for which (6) is not defined

due to $\left(\dfrac{\iint C_s^\alpha (t,f)\, dt\, df}{\iint C_s^\beta (t,f)\, dt\, df} \right) < 0$.

Also, for odd integers $\alpha, \beta \geq 1$, (6) is defined for the 1st order Hermite function.

Using Renyi's entropies, Baraniuk's [10] fails for sufficiently large order α, but while using kapur's entropy for measuring TFRs, we get some results as discussed in theorem 2.2.1 and 2.2.2

The 3rd-order entropy is defined for a broad class of distributions including those taking locally negative values.

The properties of the Kapur time-frequency information measure is similar to that of Renyi's as explained by Baraniuk [10] are as:

(i) $H_{\alpha,\beta}(C_s)$ counts the number of components in a multi component signal.

(ii) For odd orders $\alpha, \beta > 1$, $H_{\alpha,\beta}(C_s)$ does not count the no. of components, due to asymptotically invariant to TFR cross- components.

(iii) The range of $H_{\alpha,\beta}(C_s)$ values is bounded from below. For Wigner distribution, a single Gaussian pulse attains the lower bound.

(v) The values of $H_{\alpha,\beta}(C_s)$ are invariant to time and frequency shifts of the signal.

Since $H_{\alpha,\beta}(C_s)$ is the limiting case of Renyi's entropy. Thus, for more general invariances, kapur's entropy takes not only the TFRs of the affine class but also the generalized representations of the unitarily equivalent Cohen's and affine classes.

2 The Kapur's Entropies

2.1 Shannon's Measure of Entropy of Kapur's Generalized Probability Distributions

Since Kapur's entropy is the limiting case of Shannon's and Renyi's entropy.

According to Renyi's [8], the axiomatic derivative of Kapur's Entropy based on incomplete probability mass distributions $p = \{p_1, p_2, p_3, \ldots\ldots, p_n\}$ whose total probability $\omega(p) = \sum_{i=1}^{n} p_i$. We have $0 < \omega(p) \leq 1$, where $\omega(p)$ is the weight of the distribution.

Generally, the weight of an ordinary (complete) distribution is equal to 1. A distribution having weight less than 1 will called an incomplete distribution.

It is observed that the Shannon entropy $H(p)=\dfrac{-\sum\limits_{i=1}^{n} p_i \log_2 p_i}{\omega(p)}$ uniquely

satisfies the property of symmetry, continuity, normality, expansibility, recursivity, decisivity, maximality, additivity. In addition to this, it also satisfies mean value condition as:

$$H(p\cup q) = \frac{\omega(p)\,H(p) + \omega(q)\,H(q)}{\omega(p) + \omega(q)} \tag{7}$$

Where p and q are incomplete densities such that $\omega(p) + \omega(q) \leq 1$ and $p\cup q$ satisfies the composite density $\{p_1, p_2, \ldots\ldots, p_n, q_1, q_2, \ldots\ldots, q_m\}$.

In other words, the entropy of the union of two incomplete distributions is the weighted mean value of the entropies of the two distributions, where the entropy of each component is weighted with its own weight. The advantage of defining the entropy for incomplete distributions is that this mean value condition is much simpler in the general case.

If $\omega(p) + \omega(q) > 1$, then $p\cup q$ is not defined. If there exists a strictly monotonic and continuous function $y = m(x)$ such that $\omega(p) + \omega(q) \leq 1$, we have

$$H^K(p\cup q) = m^{-1}\left(\frac{\omega(p)\,m\!\left(H^K(p)\right) + \omega(q)\,m\!\left(H^K(q)\right)}{\omega(p) + \omega(q)}\right) \tag{8}$$

$H_{\alpha,\beta}(C_s)$ is only compatible with two types of functions of m with the properties of Shannon's entropy as:

(i) $m_1(x) = ax + b$ with $a \neq 0$, is compatible with the additivity and gives the

$H(p) = -\sum\limits_{i=1}^{n} p_i \log_2 p_i$, known as the Shannon entropy.

(ii) $m_2(x) = 2^{\left(\frac{\alpha-1}{\beta-1}\right)x}$, $\alpha, \beta > 0$ and $\alpha, \beta \neq 1$ \hfill (9)

is an exponential function and gives the

$$H_{\alpha,\beta}^{K}(p) = \frac{1}{\beta - \alpha} \log_2 \left(\frac{\sum\limits_{i=1}^{n} p_i^{\alpha}}{\left(\sum\limits_{i=1}^{n} p_i^{\beta} \right) \left(\sum\limits_{i=1}^{n} p_i \right)} \right) \tag{10}$$

known as the Kapur's Entropy of order α and type β.

If $m_1(x) = m_2(x)$, it satisfies all the properties of Shannon's entropy

In limiting case, $\underset{\substack{\alpha \to 1 \\ \beta = 1}}{lt} \ H_{\alpha,\beta}^{K}(p) = H(p)$

The Kapur's Entropy to continuous-value bivariate densities $p(x, y)$ is:

$$H_{\alpha,\beta}^{K}(p) = \frac{1}{\beta - \alpha} \log_2 \left(\frac{\iint p^{\alpha}(x, y) \, dx \, dy}{\left(\iint p^{\beta}(x, y) \, dx \, dy \right) \left(\iint p(x, y) \, dx \, dy \right)} \right) \tag{11}$$

Since the Shannon entropy is a class of Kapur's Entropy. It consists of mean value property from an arithmetic mean to exponential mean. $H_{\alpha,\beta}^{K}(p)$ behaves like as $H(p)$.

2.2 Kapur's Entropy of Time-Frequency Representation

The main theme of this paper is the application of entropy measures to TFRs to measure the complexity and information content of non stationary signals in time-frequency plane.

Primarily, the TFR tools lie in Cohen's class [4], which is expressed in (3) as the convolution between the wigner distribution an a real valued kernel $\Phi \in L^1(\Re^2)$. To avoid confusion, we restrict ourself only to the wigner distribution and all the TFRs obtained from (3).

Since we are interested only in odd powers of TFRs, the kernel Φ and its inverse fourier transform ϕ completely determine the properties of the corresponding TFR.

For example, a fixed kernel TFR possesses the energy preservation property (2) provided $\phi(0,0) = 1$ and the marginal properties (1) provided $\phi(\theta,0) = \phi(0,\tau) = 1, \forall \ \theta, \tau$

Where ϕ is uncertainty function of the time-reversed window function and $\phi(\theta,\tau) = h_1(\theta) h_2(\tau)$ is the smoothed pseudo-wigner distribution.

The similarity between TFRs and bidimensional probability densities discussed in the introduction ceases at at least two points:

(i)   The TFR of a given signal is non unique, due to the choice of kernel function.
(ii) Most Cohen's class TFRs are non positive and thus cannot be interpreted strictly
      as densities of signal energy, because here we consider only quadratic TFRs.
      There must exist non quadratic classes of TFRs which satisfy (1) and (2).

These locally negative values creates a confusion with the logarithm in the Shannon
entropy (5), while the Kapur's entropy (6) makes interesting and encouraging the
applications of TFRs[1,5,6,9]. It is indeed a point of discussion, whether these
measures deal successfully the locally negative of Cohen's class TFRs.

From (6), we need $C_S^\alpha(t,f), C_S^\beta(t,f)$ to be real for a signal s changes over a
time t such that

$$\left(\frac{\iint C_S^\alpha(t,f)\, dt\, df}{\iint C_S^\beta(t,f)\, dt\, df} \right) > 0 \tag{12}$$

For non integer $\alpha, \beta, C_S^\alpha(t,f), C_S^\beta(t,f)$ possess complex values and have limited

utility. Also, for even integer $\alpha, \beta, C_S^\alpha(t,f), C_S^\beta(t,f)$ always possess positive

values and pose no such hazards. But, odd integer orders are not so strong in giving

the positive value of $C_S^\alpha(t,f), C_S^\beta(t,f)$.

For each odd integer $\alpha, \beta \geq 3$, there exist signals in $L^2(\Re)$ and TFRs such that
(12) is not satisfied and by virtue of this (6) is not defined. Here, we develop some
results in the form of theorems for the wigner distribution $W_S(t,f)$, which invalidate
the proofs of existence in the time-frequency plane based on kapur's entropy.

For any odd integer $\alpha, \beta \geq 3$, a signal s for the wigner distribution $W_S(t,f)$ such
that

$$\left(\frac{\iint W_S^\alpha(t,f)\, dt\, df}{\iint W_S^\beta(t,f)\, dt\, df} \right) < 0 \tag{13}$$

For such signal s, $H_{\alpha,\beta}(W_S)$ is not defined.

The nth order Hermite function is:

$$h_n(t) = (-1)^n\, 2^{1/4}\, (n!)^{-1/2}\, (4\pi)^{-n/2}\, e^{\pi t^2} \left(\frac{d}{dt} \right)^n e^{-2\pi t^2} \tag{14}$$

The nth order Hermite function has a wigner distribution that can be expressed in
terms of a Laguerre polynomial as:

$$W_n(t,f) = W_{h_n}(t,f) = 2(-1)^n\, e^{-2\pi t^2}\, L_n(4\pi r^2) \tag{15}$$

Where $r^2 = t^2 + f^2$ and $L_n(x) = \sum_{j=0}^{n} C^n_j \frac{(-x)^j}{j!}$ (16)

is the nth order Laguerre polynomial.

It is well known that, the Hermite function has wigner distribution as:

(i)   When the order n is odd, Hermite function is strongly peaked at the origin, with a negative sign.

(ii)   When origin has radius larger than $\left(\frac{\left(n+\frac{1}{2}\right)}{\pi}\right)^{1/2}$, Hermite function has

        small but non-negligible values away from the origin but inside the circle.

(iii)   Hermite function has negligibly small values outside the circle.

Therefore, the odd-order Hermite functions are giving negative values in (13).

Theorem 2.2.1. For sufficiently large order α, β, (12) is not satisfied for odd α and even β and vice-versa and for $\alpha \neq \beta$ for smooth, rapidly decaying odd signal.

Proof. Let s be a smooth, rapidly decaying odd signal of unit energy, then $W_s(t, f)$ is smooth and rapidly decaying as $t^2 + f^2 \to \infty$ and

$$|W_s(t, f)| < 2 = -W_s(0,0), \quad (t, f) \neq (0,0)$$ (17)

It can be done by Cauchy-Schwarz inequality.

As $\alpha, \beta \to \infty$, the asymptotic behavior of (13) is determine by the behavior of $W_s(t, f)$ at $(t, f) = (0,0)$.

Since $\dfrac{\partial W_s}{\partial t} = \dfrac{\partial W_s}{\partial f} = \dfrac{\partial^2 W_s}{\partial t\,\partial f} = \dfrac{\partial^2 W_s}{\partial f\,\partial t} = 0$ (18)

$$\frac{\partial^2 W_s}{\partial t^2} = 8\left\| s^* \right\|^2 \quad , \quad \frac{\partial^2 W_s}{\partial f^2} = 32\pi^2 \left\| t\, s(t) \right\|^2$$ (19)

As $(t, f) = (0,0)$, we have

$$\log\left(-\frac{1}{2} W_s(t, f)\right) = -2t^2 \left\| s^* \right\|^2 - 8\pi^2 f^2 \left\| t\, s(t) \right\|^2 + O(t^2 + f^2)$$ (20)

As $t^2 + f^2 \to 0$, we have

$$\frac{\iint W_s^\alpha(t,f)\,dt\,df}{\iint W_s^\beta(t,f)\,dt\,df} = \frac{(-2)^\alpha \iint \exp\left(\alpha\log\left(-\frac{1}{2}W_s(t,f)\right)\right)}{(-2)^\beta \iint \exp\left(\beta\log\left(-\frac{1}{2}W_s(t,f)\right)\right)} = \frac{\dfrac{(-2)^\alpha}{4\alpha\|s\|^*\|t\,s(t)\|}}{\dfrac{(-2)^\beta}{4\beta\|s\|^*\|t\,s(t)\|}}$$

$$= (-2)^{\alpha-\beta}\frac{\beta}{\alpha} \qquad (21)$$

Eq. (13) is satisfied for large odd integer α and even β and vice-versa and for $\alpha \neq \beta$ for smooth, rapidly decaying odd signal s.

Theorem 2.2.2. For odd integers $\alpha, \beta \geq 1$, (12) is satisfied for the 1st order Hermite function.

Proof. Let s be the 1st order Hermite function with wigner distribution as:

$$s(t) = h_1(t) = 2^{\frac{5}{4}}\pi^{\frac{1}{2}}t\,e^{-\pi t^2}, \qquad t \in \Re$$

$$W_s(t,f) = -2\,e^{-2\pi(t^2+f^2)}(1 - 4\pi(t^2 + f^2))$$

Using polar coordinates, we have for $\alpha, \beta \geq 1$

$$\frac{\iint W_s^\alpha(t,f)\,dt\,df}{\iint W_s^\beta(t,f)\,dt\,df} = \frac{\dfrac{2^{\alpha-1}}{\alpha}(-1)^\alpha \displaystyle\int_0^\infty e^{-x}\left(1 - \frac{2x}{\alpha}\right)^\alpha dx}{\dfrac{2^{\beta-1}}{\beta}(-1)^\beta \displaystyle\int_0^\infty e^{-x}\left(1 - \frac{2x}{\beta}\right)^\beta dx} \qquad (22)$$

For odd $\alpha \geq 1$, We have

$$\int_0^\infty e^{-x}\left(1 - \frac{2x}{\alpha}\right)^\alpha dx = \int_0^{\alpha/2} e^{-x}\left(1 - \frac{2x}{\alpha}\right)^\alpha dx - \int_{\alpha/2}^\infty e^{-x}\left(\frac{2x}{\alpha} - 1\right)^\alpha dx \qquad (23)$$

The first term on the right hand side of the eq.(23), increases in $\alpha \geq 1$. The second term decreases in $\alpha \geq 1$ and can be evaluated as:

$$\int_{\alpha/2}^\infty e^{-x}\left(\frac{2x}{\alpha} - 1\right)^\alpha dx = \left(\frac{4}{e}\right)^{\alpha/2}\frac{\alpha!}{\alpha^\alpha}.$$

Thus (23) increases for odd $\alpha \geq 1$.

For odd $\beta \geq 1$, We have

$$\int_0^{\infty} e^{-x} \left(1 - \frac{2x}{\beta}\right)^{\beta} dx = \int_0^{\beta/2} e^{-x} \left(1 - \frac{2x}{\beta}\right)^{\beta} dx - \int_{\beta/2}^{\infty} e^{-x} \left(\frac{2x}{\beta} - 1\right)^{\beta} dx \quad (24)$$

The first term on the right hand side of the eq.(24), increases in $\beta \geq 1$. The second term decreases in $\alpha \geq 1$ and can be evaluated as:

$$\int_{\beta/2}^{\infty} e^{-x} \left(\frac{2x}{\beta} - 1\right)^{\beta} dx = \left(\frac{4}{e}\right)^{\beta/2} \frac{\beta!}{\beta^{\beta}}$$

Thus (24) increases for odd $\beta \geq 1$.

Since

For $\alpha = \beta = 1$: $\int_0^{\infty} e^{-x} (1 - 2x)\, dx = -1$

For $\alpha = \beta = 3$: $\int_0^{\infty} e^{-x} \left(1 - \frac{2x}{3}\right)^3 dx = -\frac{1}{9}$ and

For $\alpha = \beta = 5$: $\int_0^{\infty} e^{-x} \left(1 - \frac{2x}{5}\right)^5 dx = \frac{127}{625}$

We can see that (22), is positive for all odd integers $\alpha, \beta \geq 5$.

Thus, for odd integers $\alpha, \beta \geq 1$, (12) is satisfied for the 1st order Hermite function.

Also, in order to balance the fact, we will assume that all the signals under consideration are such that the kapur's entropies is well-defined.

The pre-normalization of the signal energy before raising the TFR to the power α and β are:

$$H_{\alpha, \beta}(C_S) = \frac{1}{\beta - \alpha} \log_2 \iint \left(\frac{\left(\dfrac{C_S(t, f)}{\iint C_S(u, v)\, du\, dv} \right)^{\alpha}}{\left(\dfrac{C_S(t, f)}{\iint C_S(u, v)\, du\, dv} \right)^{\beta}} \right) dt\, df \quad (25)$$

The pre-normalization of the signal energy is equivalent to normalization and is related by

$$H_{\alpha, \beta}^{K}(C_S) = H_{\alpha, \beta}(C_S) - \log_2 \|s\|_2^2 \quad (26)$$

Therefore, $H_{\alpha, \beta}^{K}(C_S)$ varies with the signal energy.

3 Conclusion

In this paper, we studied a new class of signal analysis tool - the Kapur's entropies. The Kapur's entropy measure shows great promising results for estimating the complexity of signals via the time frequency plane as mentioned in the theorem 2.2.1 and 2.2.2.

References

1. Williams, W.J., Brown, M.L., Hero, A.O.: Uncertainty, information, and time-frequency distributions. In: Proceeding of SPIE Int. Soc. Opt. Eng., vol. 1566, pp. 144–156 (1991)
2. Orr, R.: Dimensionality of signal sets. In: Proc. SPIE Int. Soc. Opt. Eng., vol. 1565, pp. 435–446 (1991)
3. Cohen, L.: What is a multi component signal? In: Proc. IEEE Int. Conf. Acoust., speech, Signal Processing, vol. V, pp. 113–116 (1992)
4. Cohen, L.: Time-Frequency Analysis. Prentice-Hall, Englewood Cliffs (1995)
5. Baraniuk, R.G., Flandrin, P., Michel, O.: Information and complexity on the time-frequency plane. In: 14 EME Collogue GRETSI, pp. 359–362 (1993)
6. Flandrin, P., Baraniuk, R.G., Michel, O.: Time-Frequency complexity and information. In: Proc. IEEE Int. Conf. Acoust., Speech, Signal Processing, vol. III, pp. 329–332 (1994)
7. Shannon, C.E.: A mathematical theory of communication. Bell Sys. Tech. J. 27, 379–423 (1948)
8. Renyi's, A.: On measures of entropy and information. In: Proc. 4th Berkeley Symp. Math. Stat. and Prob., vol. 1, pp. 547–561 (1961)
9. Williams, W.J.: Reduced interference distributions. Proc. IEEE Biological Applications and Interpretations 84, 1264–1280 (1996)
10. Baraniuk, R.G., Janssen, A.J.E.M.: Measuring time-frequency information content using the Renyi's entropies. IEEE Transactions on Information Theory 47(4), 1391–1409 (2001)
11. Kapur, J.N.: Generalization entropy of order α and type β. The Mathematical Seminar 4, 78–84 (1967)
12. Ash, R.: Information Theory. Interscience Publishers, New York (1965)

An Ontology Based Framework for
Domain Analysis of Interactive System

Shrutilipi Bhattacharjee, Imon Banerjee, and Animesh Datta

Dept. of Information Technology, NIT Durgapur
shrutilipi.2007@gmail.com, imonban@gmail.com,
animeshrec@gmail.com

Abstract. Understanding user requirement is an integral part of information system design and is critical to the success of interactive systems. It is now widely understood that successful systems and products begin with an understanding of the needs and requirements of the users. There are several purposes for modeling and analyzing the problem domain before starting the software requirement analysis. First it focuses on the problem domain so that the domain users could be involved easily. Secondly a comprehensive description on the problem domain will advantage getting a comprehensive software requirement model. This paper model an ontology based framework to satisfy the criteria mainly organizational structure, multi agents' interaction, goal achievement.

Keywords: Ontology, Domain analysis, Interactive System, Modeling, Requirement Specification.

1 Introduction

Several surveys indicate that a significant percentage of software fail to meet business objectives or are outright failure. One of the reasons for this is that requirement analysis is typically overlooked in real life software projects. Good requirement practices can accelerate software development. The process of defining business requirements aligns the stakeholders with shared vision, goals and expectations. Substantial user involvement in establishing and managing changes to agreed upon requirements increases the accuracy of requirements, ensuring that the functionality built will enable users to perform essential business tasks. Software requirement engineering encompasses the two major sub domains of requirement definition and requirement management.

Requirement definition is the collaborative process of collecting, documenting and validating a set of requirements that constitute an agreement among key project stackholders. Requirements definition is further subdivided into the critical process areas of elicitation, analysis, specification and validation process. From a paragmatic perspective, requirement definition strives for requirements that are user validated and clear enough to allow the team to proceed with design, construction and testing at an acceptable level of risks.

Requirement management involves working with a defined set of product requirements throughout the product's development process and its operational life. It also

S. Ranka et al. (Eds.): IC3 2010, Part I, CCIS 94, pp. 391–402, 2010.

includes managing changes to that set of requirements throughout the project lifecycle. An effective requirement definition and management solution creates accurate and complete system requirements. While helping organization communications in an effort to better align IT with business needs and objectives.

The paradigm shifts from mainframes in the 1950s-1970s to the personal computer technology of the 1980s and the networked computing devices of the 2000s can be conceptually modeled by paradigm shifts from algorithms to sequential interaction and then to distributed(multiagent,collaborative) interaction. Interactive models provide a domain independent unifying view of the design space for software intensive systems. The key dimension of change in software-intensive systems is interactiveness. Whereas at one time computing was mostly batch the execution of algorithms, with all input data supplied a priori and all output generated afterword-today ongoing interaction is ubiquitous. This interaction differs semantically from iterated batch computing in that each computing entity maintains a persistent state that evolves and enables computations to be driven by their entire input/output histories.

Accordingly, the design issues of greatest interest relate broadly to the management of interaction rather than the development of algorithms. While disciplines like human-computer interaction, networking and the physical sciences have a place in the science of design, a domain-independent study of interaction will be an essential element of such systems. One popular application "Teleteaching" is fundamentally interactive and can not be properly understood until more research is done on domain-independent models and on the principles of interactions.

The requirements of a software system are often ambiguous, incomplete, redundant and variant at the requirement analysis phase of a system. Requirement generated by different stackholders may be inconsistent since different stackholders and users may have different perspective on the system. This may bring about the same term is applied to different concepts and different terms are used to denote the same entity. A suitable solution was the use of ontology which can make sure that different designers have a common understanding of the term to be used.

Ontology was originally concept from philosophy. It describes the essence and composition of the world, as said by the philosophers. In computer science, ontology is mainly used for knowledge representation and defining the concept of the system It provides a means for knowledge sharing which is very much necessary for large scale, complex real software projects. For the last few years more and more software engineers become interested in the research system designing using ontology concept [1]. The five points presented in the paper [2] for using ontology in requirement analysis are:

- Make relations as independent knowledge units.
- Organize the objects in ontologies.
- Take objects as basic components of ontologies.
- Let ontologies form their own inheritance hierarchies.
- Allow ontologies to be nested.

For the same reason we are also interested to design a semi formal conceptual framework to specify the requirements of different stakeholders for a large complicated interactive system. Our paper is structured as follows. In section2, it describes the related works and surveys of this area. Section3 gives the formal definition of ontology. In section4,an innovative semi formal framework is proposed for requirement specification of interactive software system. In section5 as a case study of our proposed framework, a very popular example of teleteaching systems is shown. Section6 concludes our work.

2 Related Works

As software become more and more complicated and large scale, the requirement analysis phase plays an important role in the software development. [3] It is generally accepted that the ultimate quality of the delivered software depends on the requirements upon which the system has been built. [4,5] studies performed at many companies have measured and assigned cost to correct defects in software discovered at various phases of the life cycle. Generally, the later in the software lifecycle a defect is discovered the more expensive it is to rectify [6, 7]. Modern software projects require fast delivery and changes their requirements even after developing requirement specification; they must be continued through out the whole process of the system development [8]. There are still no efficient tools for automated acquisition and analysis of early software requirement [9]. As early informal requirements are written in natural languages, many problems occur in their handling. Still the informal requirements is one of the important way of communication between the system analyst and their clients[10]. The lack of formalization and formal framework from informal requirements makes it difficult to efficiently handle them. Informal requirements collected in the early requirements elicitation phase should be classified into their identification, priority, feasibility, risk, source and type before analyzing them [11]. New requirements and viewpoints are continuously created and frequently changed, the classification of the requirements is a difficult task in negotiation, in trade-off and in viewpoints approach such as Win Win Negotiation model[12 13], ABAS (Attribute Based Architecture style) [14], and Viewpoint approaches[15].

The requirements of a complex, large scale interactive systems [16] are often ambiguous, incomplete and redundant, they are also changed frequently during the design process due to the changes of technology and customer's objective[17]. To make sure that different analyst and designers have a common understanding of the term to be used, the ontology oriented requirements approach was presented in [2, 18, 19]. An ontology[20, 21] is a collection of definitions of concepts and the shared understanding[22]. The requirement ontology is a part of a more general ontology to capture engineering design knowledge[1, 23]. The formalization of requirement ontology was described in [2, 17], but their abilities of reasoning were inefficient and undecidable particularly for complex interactive system. As the system grows in scale and complexity, the requirement analysis process must balance expressivity and inferential power with the real demands of requirement ontologies construction, maintenance, performance and comprehensibility. In this paper we propose an ontology based conceptual framework for requirement specification of a large and complex interactive system.

3 Ontology

In computer science and information science, ontology is a formal representation of a set of concepts within a domain and the relationships between those concepts. It is used to reason about the properties of that domain, and may be used to define the domain.

3.1 Conceptualization

Conceptualization can be defined as structure consisting of domain D and their inter relationship R and can be written as <D,R>. It actually refers to the ordinary mathematical relation on D that is extensional relation. But the main difference of ordinary and conceptual relation lies in the working space of those. While ordinary relations are defined on a certain domain and conceptual relations are defined on a *domain space*. We shall define a domain space as a structure <D, W>, where D is a domain and W is a set of maximal states of affairs of such domain. Now a *conceptual relation* ρ^n of arity n on <D, W> as a total function $\rho^n:W \rightarrow 2^{D^n}$ from W into the set of all n-ary (ordinary) relations on D. A *conceptualization* for D can be now defined as an ordered triple $\mathbf{C}$ = <D, W, Ŕ>, where Ŕ is a set of conceptual relations on the domain space <D, W>. We can say therefore that a conceptualization is a set of conceptual relations defined on a domain space. Let $\mathbf{C}$ = <D, W, Ŕ > be a conceptualization. For each possible world $w \in$ W, the intended structure of w according to $\mathbf{C}$ is the structure $\mathbf{S}_{wC}$ = <D, $\mathbf{R}_{wC}$>, where $\mathbf{R}_{wC}$={ρ (w) | $\rho \in$ Ŕ } is the set of extensions (relative to w) of the elements of Ŕ. We shall denote with $\mathbf{S}_C$ the set {$\mathbf{S}_{wC}$ | $w \in$ W} all the intended world structures of $\mathbf{C}$.

3.2 Formal Ontology

An ontology defines the basic terms and relation comprising the vocabulary of a topic area as well as the rules for combining terms and relation to define extension to the vocabulary[24].Ontology basically define as a formal specification of shared conceptualization. Shared reflects the notation that an Ontology captures consensual knowledge that is, it is not private of some individual but accepted by a group.

Ontology is a logical theory which gives an explicit and partial account of conceptualization. For a conceptualization C, Let O is a ontology with language L where Ontological commitment K=<C,Γ>.

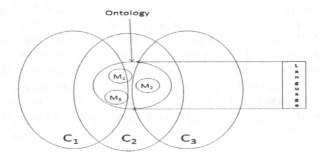

Fig. 1. Formal Ontology

Conceptualization = $\{C_1, C_2, C_3\}$
Model = $\{M_1, M_2, M_3\}$

3.3 Ontology Components

- Individuals: instances or objects (the basic or "ground level" objects)
- Classes: sets, collections, concepts, types of objects, or kinds of things.
- Attributes: aspects, properties, features, characteristics, or parameters that objects (and classes) can have
- Relations: ways in which classes and individuals can be related to one another
- Function terms: complex structures formed from certain relations that can be used in place of an individual term in a statement
- Restrictions: formally stated descriptions of what must be true in order for some assertion to be accepted as input
- Rules: statements in the form of an if-then (antecedent-consequent) sentence that describe the logical inferences that can be drawn from an assertion in a particular form
- Axioms: assertions (including rules) in a logical form that together comprise the overall theory that the ontology describes in its domain of application. This definition differs from that of "axioms" in generative grammar and formal logic. In those disciplines, axioms include only statements asserted as *a priori* knowledge. As used here, "axioms" also include the theory derived from axiomatic statements.
- Events: the changing of attributes or relations

4 Ontology for Requirement Specification

Although many requirement analysis techniques have been used so far for softwar engineering field, yet many are not upto the mark as they are not able to specify the system requirements from the perspectives of Interactive System. So here we need to use an information technology tool which can map our requirement in the interactive system in a efficient way.

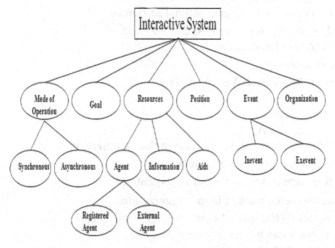

Fig. 2. Ontology Based Architechture of interactive System

Ontology hierarchically describes the system and model each requirement in a structured way. Here we can also describe the interactive behavior of the system in efficient way. Ontology can also provide a facility that we can explicitly add extra feature or tuple to describe the system according to the user need after building the total system structure in the requirement analysis phase.

Interactive systems can be defined as the class of systems whose operations involve a significant degreeof user interaction .It is a system with Back-and-forth dialog between user and computer, contrast with batch system. Here we construct an ontology in figure 2 for the requirement specification of an interactive system.

4.1 Concept Types

Mode: It is the mode of operation between the two actors or an actor with the system. The mode can be of synchronous operation or asynchronous operation.

Goal: It is a target objectives that to be achieved by an organization, actor, entity.

Resources: It is an actor or agent which some activity to achieve organizational goal Resources may be machineries, raw material, tools, information, databases which are used, consumed to achieve the organizational goal.

Position: It is a concept used to assign role to an agent in an organization.

Event: the changing of attributes or relation.

Organization: It is a social/corporate organization consisting of some actor, entity with some definite goal.

Schema:

Entity: Registered_Agent.

Class: Registered_Agent$\in$ Organization.Agent.

Attributes: Agent.Registration $\leftrightarrow$ Registered_Agent.

Relation:

i)(Registered_Agent $\cup$ External_Agent) $\subseteq$ Organisation.Agent.

ii) Registered_Agent $\cap$ External_Agent= ϕ.

Function: i) $P_1(x)$: x is triggering an event.

$\forall$ Registered_Agent P_1(Registered_Agent) $\rightarrow$ Event

ii) $P_2(y)$: y is accessing some organizational resources.

$\forall$ Registered_Agent P_2(Registered_Agent) $\rightarrow$ True.

 Restriction: i) Agent.Event $\subseteq$ Event.

ii)$P_3(x,y)$: y can accesss x.

$\exists$ Event P_3(Event,Registered_Agent) $\rightarrow$ True.

Schema:

Entity: External_Agent.

Class: External_Agent$\in$ Agent.

Attributes: $P_1(x)$: x has registered himself in the organization.

$\neg$ ($\forall$ Agent P_1(Agent))=External_Agent.

Relation: i) Registered_Agent $\cap$ External_Agent= ϕ.

ii) $P_2(x)$: x has registered himself in the organization.

$\forall$ External_Agent P_2(External_Agent) $\rightarrow$ Registered_Agent.

Function: i) $P_3(x)$: x can trigger an external event.

$\forall$ External_Agent P_3(External_Agent) $\rightarrow$ True.

ii) $P_4(x)$: x can trigger an internal event.

$\forall$ External_Agent P_4(External_Agent) $\rightarrow$ False.

Restriction: $P_5(x)$: x can access internal event.

$\neg$ ($\forall$ External_Agent P_5(External_Agent)) $\rightarrow$ True.

Schema:

Entity: Information.

Class: Information$\in$ Organization.Resource.

Attributes: $P_1(x)$: x is private to the organization.

$P_2(x)$: x can access.

$\forall$ Information P_1(Information) $\rightarrow$ $\forall$ Registered_Agent P_2(Registered_Agent)

Function: $P_3(x)$: x is triggered.

Event.Information $\rightarrow$ $\exists$ Event P_3(Event).

Restriction: $P_4(x)$:x is accessed by external agent.

$\forall$ private Information P_4(private Information)$\rightarrow$False.

Schema:

Entity: Aids.

Class: Aids$\in$ Organization.Resource.

Attributes:$P_1(x)$: x is accessed by Registered_Agent.

$\forall$ Aids P_1(Aids) $\rightarrow$ True.

Function: $P_2(x)$: x is supported by External_Agent.

$\exists$Event P_2(Event) $\rightarrow$ True.

Restriction: $P_3(x)$: x is accessed by External_Agent.

$\forall$ Aids P_3(Aids) $\rightarrow$ False.

Schema:

Entity: Exevent.

Class: Exevent $\subseteq$ Event.

Attributes: $P_1(x)$: x can access.

Exevent $\rightarrow$ $\forall$ Agent P_1(Agent).

$P_2(x)$: on triggering x is generated.

Exevent $\rightarrow$ $\exists$ Exevent P_2(new(Exevent)).

Relation: Exevent $\cap$ Inevent= ϕ.

Mode.Exevent $\rightarrow$ Asynchronous.

Restriction: $P_3(x)$: On triggering x.

$\neg\exists$Exevent P_3(External_Agent.Exevent) $\rightarrow$ Inevent.

Schema:

Entity: Inevent.

Class: Inevent $\subseteq$ Event.

Attributes: $P_1(x)$: x can access.

Inevent $\rightarrow$ $\forall$ Regietered_Agent P_1(Registered_Agent).

$P_2(x)$: on triggering x is generated.

Inevent $\rightarrow$ $\exists$ event P_2(new(event)).

Relation: Exevent $\cap$ Inevent= ϕ.

Mode.Inevent $\rightarrow$ (Synchronous $\cup$ Asynchronous).

Restriction: $P_3(x)$: On triggering x .

$\neg \exists$Inevent P_3(External_Agent.Inevent) $\rightarrow$ Event.

Schema:

Entity: Goal.

Attributes: $P_1(x)$: x will achieve.

$\forall$ Registered_Agent P_1(Registered_Agent) $\rightarrow$ Goal.

Relation: ($\forall$ inevent)($\exists$ Goal).

Restriction: Goal $\neq \phi$.

Schema:

Entity: Position.

Attributes: $P_1(x)$: x is in a position of organization.

$\forall$ Regitered_Agent P_1(Registered_Agent) $\leftrightarrow$ Organization.Position.

Relation: $P_2(x)$: x will achieve.

$\forall$ Position P_2(Position) $\leftrightarrow$ Organization.Gaol.

Restriction: i) $P_3(x)$: x will achieve.

$\neg$ $\forall$ External_Agent P_3(External_Agent) $\rightarrow$ Organization.Position.

ii)Organization.Position $\neq \phi$.

Schema:

Entity: Synchronous mode.

Class: Synchronous mode$\in$ Mode of operation.

Attributes: $P_1(x,y)$: y can occur at x.

$\exists$time $\forall$ Synchronous event P_1(time,Synchronous event) $\rightarrow$ True.

Relation: i) Synchronous mode $\cup$ Asynchronous mode= Mode of operation.

ii) $P_2(x)$: Registered_Agent only can works on x.

$\forall$ Synchronous mode P_2(Synchronous mode) $\rightarrow$ True.

Restriction: i) $P_3(x)$: External_Agent can works on x.

$\forall$ Synchronous mode P_3(Synchronous mode) $\rightarrow$ False.

ii) $P_4(x)$: Synchronous event can occur only at x.

$\exists$predefined time schedule P_4($\neg$ predefined time schedule) $\rightarrow$ False.

Schema:

Entity: Asynchronous mode.

Class: Asynchronous mode$\in$ Mode of operation.

Attributes: $P_1(x,y)$: y can occur at any x.

$\forall$ time $\forall$ Asynchronous event P_1(time, Asynchronous event) $\rightarrow$ True.

Relation: i) Asynchronous mode $\cup$ Synchronous mode= Mode of operation.

ii) $P_2(x)$: Agent can works on x.

$\forall$ Asynchronous mode P_2(Asynchronous mode) $\rightarrow$ True.

Models: Modeling is a part of Formal Ontology designing tool for concepts and mutual relations describing the structure of organization. Models are the detail view of the concept space according to the necessity of the user.

Interaction Model:

Depends on: Synchronous $\rightarrow$ (Time$\times$Agent).

Depends on: Asynchronous $\rightarrow$ (Agent$\times$Resources)

Mode of Operation: Synchronous $\cup$ Asynchronous.

Operates on: Synchronous→Inevent.
              Asynchronous→Exevent ∪ Inevent.
Resource Management Model:
Node: Aids ∪ Information ∪ Agent.
Depends on: Resource→(Event.Agent).
Supports: Inevent ∪ Exevent.
Beloangs to: Resource→Organization.
Goal Model:
Goal: Organization_Goal ∪ Agent_Goal.
Node: Goal ∪ Organization ∪ Agent.
Achieved by: Goal→(Organization ∪ Agent)×Event.
 Event Activity Flow Model:
Node: Event ∪ Agent ∪ Interaction ∪ Information.
TriggerLink: (Agent×Interaction)→Event.
              (Information×Agent×Event)→Event.
Depends on: Event→Mode of operation(Asynchronous×Synchronous)

4.2 Concept Space

Concept space is a formal graph of terms occurring within objects linked to each other
by the frequency with which they occur together. Concept Space of the organization

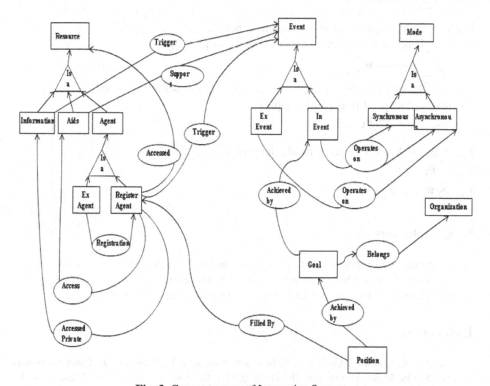

Fig. 3. Concept space of Interactive System

contains abstract model for modeling and analyzing the problem domains. This model makes the organizational structure explicit.

4.3 Formalization of Concept Space

Concept space C_s is consisting of 7 tuples, i.e.
$C_s = (C, A, R, E_{CR}, E_{CA}, E_{AC}, E_{RC})$.
C = Concept:

A=Association: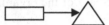

R= Relation:

E_{CR} =   Set of edges from concept to relation.
Edge in which concept is related by a specific relation. It is an [1:1] mapping.

E_{CA} =   Set of edges from concept to association. Edge in which concept is achieved by hierarchical relationship. It is an [n:1] mapping.

E_{AC} =   Set of edges from association to concept.
It is a [1:1] relationship from association to concept.

E_{RC} =   Set of edges from relation to concept.Edge in which any relation is related to a specific concept. It is an [1:1] mapping

$E_{AC} \wedge E_{CA} \wedge A \wedge C \rightarrow$ Hierarchical relationship.
$E_{AC} \cap E_{CA} = \phi$
$E_{RC} \cap E_{CR} = \phi$

5   Conclusion

In this paper, we proposed a formal ontological framework and approach for Interactive System. This paper can be used as a basic research framework and tool for domain analysis for any system which require a high degree of interaction.

References

1. Abran, A., Cuadrado-Gallego, J.J., García-Barriocanal, E., Mendes, O., Sánchez-Alonso, S., Sicilia, M.A.: Engineering the Ontology for the Swebok: Issues and Techniques. In: Calero, C., Ruiz, F., Piattini, M. (eds.) Ontologies for Software Engineering and Software Technology, pp. 103–112. Springer, New York (2006)

2. Lu, R., Jin, Z., Chen, G.: Ontology-Oriented Requirements Analysis. Chinese Journal of Software 11(8), 10090–11017 (2000)
3. van Axel, L.: Handling obstacles in goal-oriented requirements engineering. IEEE Transactions on Software Engineering 26(10), 978–1005 (2000)
4. Brooks, F.P.: No Silver Bullet: Essence and Accidents of Software Engineering. IEEE Computer 20(4), 10–19 (1987)
5. Hrones, J.: Defining Global Requirements with Distributed QFD. Digital Technical Journal 5(4), 36–46
6. James, W.: Effectiveness of Elicitation techniques in distributed requirements Engineering. In: Proceedings of the IEEE Joint International Conference on RE (2002)
7. Davis, A.M.: Software Requirements: Objects, Functions, and States. Prentice-Hall, Englewood Cliffs (1993)
8. Sommerville, I.: Integrated requirements engineering: A tutorial. IEEE Software 22(1), 16–23 (2005)
9. Cybulski, J.L., Reed, K.: Computer-Assisted Analysis and Refinement of Informal Software Requirements Documents. In: Proceedings of the fifth Asia-Pacific Software Engineering Conference (APSEC 1998), Taipei, Taiwan, pp. 128–135 (December 1998)
10. Davis, A.M.: Predictions and farewells. IEEE Software 15(4), 6–9 (1998)
11. IEEE Std IEEE-Std-1233-1998, IEEE Guide for Developing System Requirements Specifications, IEEE Computer Society Press (1998)
12. Boehm, B., Abi-Antoun, M., Port, D., Kwan, J., Lunch, A.: Requirements Engineering, Expectations Management and the Two Cultures. In: Proceedings of 4th International Symposium on Requirement Engineering, pp. 14–22 (1999)
13. Boehm, B., Egyed, A.: WinWin Negotiation Process: A Multi-Project Analysis. In: Proceedings of the 5th International Conference on Software Process, pp. 125–136 (1998)
14. Klein, M.H., Kazman, R., Bass, L., Carriere, J., Barbacci, M., Lipson, H.: Attribute-Based Architectural Style. In: Proceedings of the First Working IFIP Conference on Software Architecture(WICSA1), San Antonio, TX, pp. 225–243 (1999)
15. Sommerville, I., Sawyer, P.: Viewpoints: principles, problems and a practical approach to requirements engineering. Annals of Software Engineering 3, 101–130 (1997)
16. Goldin, D., Keil, D.: Interactive Models for Design of Software-Intensive Systems. ENTCS. Elsevier, Amsterdam (2005)
17. Jinxin, L., Mark, S.F., Taner, B.: A Requirement Ontology for Engineering Design. Concurrent Engineering: Research and Application 4(3), 279–291 (1996)
18. Lu, R., Jin, Z.: Formal Ontology: Foundation of Domain Knowledge Sharing and Reusing. Chinese Journal of Computer Science and Technology 17(5), 535–548 (2002)
19. Jin, Z.: Ontology-Based Requirements Elicitation. Chinese Journal of Computers 23(5), 486–492 (2000)
20. Guarino, N.: Formal Ontology: Conceptual Analysis and Knowledge Representation. International Journal of Human-Computer Studies 43(5/6), 625–640 (1995)
21. Gruber, T.R.: Towards Principles for the Design of Ontologies Used for Knowledge Sharing. Int. Journal of Human-Computer Studies 43(5/6), 907–928 (1995)
22. Baader, F., Horrocks, I., Sattler, U.: Description Logics as Ontology Languages for the Semantic Web. In: ICCS 2003. LNCS (LNAI). Springer, Heidelberg (2003) (to appear)

23. Dutta, A., Dasgupta, R., Bhattacharya, S.: A group synchronization algorithm for VoIP conferencing. In: Proceedings of the 8th WSEAS International Conference on Software Engineering, Parallel and Distributed Systems, Cambridge, UK, pp. 84–89 (2009)
24. Dutta, A., Mittal, N.: Goal Oriented Requirement Analysis for Teleteaching System. In: International Conference on Recent Trends in Information Telecommunication and Computing ITC 2010, Kochi, Kerala, India (2010)
25. Dutta, A., Bhattacharjee, S., Banerjee, I.: Formal Design of Teleteaching Interactivity. In: International Conference on Recent Trends in Information Telecommunication and Computing, ITC 2010, Kochi, Kerala, India (2010)

Entropy Based Clustering to Determine Discriminatory Genes for Microarray Dataset

Rajni Bala[1] and R.K. Agrawal[2]

[1] Deen Dayal Upadhyaya College, University of Delhi,
Delhi, India
[2] School of Computer and System Science, Jawaharlal Nehru University,
New Delhi, India

Abstract. Microarray datasets suffers from curse of dimensionality as they are represented by high dimension and only few samples are available. For efficient classification of samples there is a need of selecting a smaller set of relevant and non-redundant genes. In this paper, we propose a two stage algorithm GSUCE for finding a set of discriminatory genes responsible for classification in high dimensional microarray datasets. In the first stage the correlated genes are grouped into clusters and the best gene is selected from each cluster to create a pool of independent genes. This will reduce redundancy. We have used maximal information compression to measure similarity between genes. In second stage a wrapper based forward feature selection method is used to obtain a set of informative genes for a given classifier. The proposed algorithm is tested on five well known publicly available datasets . Comparison with other state of art methods shows that our proposed algorithm is able to achieve better classification accuracy with less number of features.

Keywords: Cancer Classification, Microarray, Hierarchical Clustering, Representative Entropy, Maximal Information Compression index, Gene Selection.

1 Introduction

DNA microarrays have provided the opportunity to measure the expression levels of thousands of genes simultaneously. Distinguishing cancerous samples from non-cancerous samples by comparing gene expression level is one of the most common applications of microarray. However, gene expression data is characterized by high dimension, high noise and small sample size. This offers difficulty in building an efficient classifier for gene expression. Due to high dimension and small sample size, one of the main challenges is to determine a set of highly discriminatory genes which helps in classification of different types of samples. Gene/feature Selection is the process of finding a set of highly discriminatory genes by removing irrelevant, redundant and noisy genes. This will not only help to increase the performance of the classifier but will also decrease the computational time required to train the model. It will also help doctors to identify a

S. Ranka et al. (Eds.): IC3 2010, Part I, CCIS 94, pp. 403–411, 2010.
© Springer-Verlag Berlin Heidelberg 2010

small subset of biologically relevant genes associated with a particular cancer as well as designing less expensive experiments by targeting only a small number of genes.

Various feature selection methods proposed in literature broadly fall into two categories[1]: filter and wrapper methods. Most filter methods employ statistical characteristics of data for feature selection which requires less computation time. Here relevance of features is measured without involving any classifier. The features subset so obtained may contain many correlated gene. Besides being an additional computational burden, it can also degrade the performance of the classifier. On the other hand, wrapper methods directly use the classification accuracy of some classifier as the evaluation criteria. They tend to find features better suited to the learning algorithm resulting in better performance. However, it is computationally more expensive since the classifier must be trained for each candidate subset. The conventional wrapper methods have been applied for feature selection on small or middle scale datasets. But, due to large computation time, it is difficult to apply them directly on high dimensional datasets. Reducing the search space for wrapper methods will decrease the computation time. This can be achieved by selecting a set of non-redundant features from the original set of features without losing any informative feature.

In this paper, we have proposed a two stage algorithm for selecting a set of discriminatory genes that can classify the data well. In the first stage we aim to reduce redundancy by grouping correlated genes. So we propose to carry out gene clustering before gene selection. We have used a divisive hierarchical clustering and maximal information compression index as the similarity measure. The clusters so obtained are evaluated for further splitting using representative entropy. In the second stage a Sequential Forward feature selection method is applied to the set of genes obtained in the first stage for further selecting a smaller set of discriminatory genes.

This paper is organized as follows Section 2 present outline of our proposed algorithm for gene selection using clustering based on entropy(GSUCE). Experimental results on five publicly available datasets presented in Section 3. Section 4 contains conclusions

2   Gene Selection Using Clustering Based on Entropy

Most of the microarray data are represented by a large number of genes i.e. in thousands. However, the number of samples available is very few i.e in hundreds. Due to this it suffers from curse of dimensionality[2]. Hence there is need to reduce the dimension. Many genes in the dataset may be redundant, irrelevant and noisy. There is need to determine a smaller set of relevant genes from a given set of genes which can provide better classification. A variety of gene selection techniques have been proposed to determines relevant genes. Among them, gene ranking method is commonly used technique for microarray datasets. It assigns a score for each gene which approximates the relative strength of the gene and returns a set of top ranked genes on which a classifier is built. Golub et al.[3]

used correlation measure to determine relationship between expression levels in samples with its class label to select top genes. In literature [4] and [5], many approaches are suggested that adopt the same principle with some modifications and enhancements. A subset of genes selected using ranking method may contain many correlated genes. Also, the selected subset so obtained may not perform well on a given classifier as we are not using a classifier while selecting such subset. It is observed that wrapper approaches, which involve a classifier, perform better on small and middle dimensional data. However, it cannot be applied directly on high dimensional microarray dataset as it requires huge computation. We can overcome this by determining a smaller set of genes for wrapper approach. This is possible if we can group correlated or similar genes into clusters and then select a representative gene from each cluster. The collection of these representative genes of each cluster can provide us a reduced set of independent genes. Wrapper method can then be applied to this reduced set of genes to get a set of discriminatory genes for better classification.

In literature many diverse clustering techniques have been used for grouping such correlated or similar genes. Self-organized- maps (SOM)[6], Hierarchical[7] and K-means clustering[8] are some of the most widely used clustering techniques. Each technique is associated with certain advantages and disadvantages. A large number of similarity or distance measures have been used for determine similarity or distance between two genes in clustering. In general Euclidean distance is used as the distance or similarity measure. However, when Euclidean distance is applied to measure the similarity between genes, it is not suitable to capture functional similarity such as positive and negative correlation and interdependency[9]. It is also pointed out that it is suitable only for a data which follows a particular distribution[10]. Pearsons correlation coefficient is another commonly used similarity measure among research community. It is pointed out[11] that Pearson coefficient is not robust to outliers and it may assign a high similarity score to a pair of dissimilar genes. Also both these measures are sensitive to scaling and rotation. A similarity measures called maximal information compression index[12] is suggested in literature for measuring redundancy between two features. The maximal information compression index $\lambda_2(x_1, x_2)$ for two random variables x_1 and x_2 is defined as

$$\lambda_2(x_1, x_2) = \frac{\sigma_1 + \sigma_2 + \sqrt{((\sigma_1 + \sigma_2)^2 - 4\sigma_1\sigma_2(1 - \rho(x_1, x_2)^2)}}{2} \qquad (1)$$

where σ_1, σ_2 are the variance of x_1, and x_2 respectively and $\rho(x_1, x_2)$ is the correlation between x_1 and x_2.

The value of λ_2 measures dependency between x_1 and x_2 and is zero when the features are linearly dependent. It increases as the amount of dependency decreases. The measure λ_2 possesses several desirable properties such as symmetry, sensitivity to scaling and invariance to rotation. Some of these properties are not present in the commonly used Euclidean distance and correlation coefficient. Hence λ_2 may be a good choice for measuring similarity or redundancy between the two features.

Divisive hierarchical clustering[13] is based on top-down strategy which starts with all objects in one cluster. It subdivides the cluster into smaller cluster until it satisfies certain termination condition, such as a desired number of clusters is obtained or the diameter of each cluster is within a certain threshold. For clustering correlated genes, splitting of a cluster from a set of available clusters can be decided on the basis of representative entropy measure. Representative entropy measures the amount of redundancy among genes in a given cluster. For a cluster containing p genes with covariance matrix Σ, representative entropy, H_R of a cluster is given by

$$H_R = -\Sigma_{l=1}^{p}\overline{\lambda_l}log(\overline{\lambda_l}) \tag{2}$$

where $\overline{\lambda_l} = \frac{\lambda_l}{\Sigma_{l=1}^{p}\lambda_l}$ and $\lambda_l, l = 1, 2, \ldots, p$ are the eigenvalues of the matrix Σ.

H_R attains a minimum value(zero) when all the eigenvalues except one are zero, or in other words when all the information is present along a single direction. If all the eigenvalues are equal, i.e. information is equally distributed among all the genes, H_R is maximum. High value of H_R represents low redundancy in the cluster. Since we are interested in partitioning the original subspace into homogeneous clusters, each cluster should have low H_R. So we split a cluster which has maximum H_R among a given set of clusters as it contains more non-redundant genes.

The first phase of our proposed algorithm GSUCE involves partitioning of the original gene set into some distinct subsets or clusters so that the genes within a cluster are highly correlated to each other while those in different clusters are less correlated. Two genes which are highly independent are selected and are placed in two different clusters. The remaining genes are then distributed into these two clusters based on their similarity measure. To choose which cluster to further split from the existing set of clusters, representative entropy of each cluster is calculated and the cluster with the maximum entropy (low redundancy) is selected. This process is repeated till we get the required number of cluster. After the genes are clustered, best gene from each cluster is selected using t-statistics to create a set of non-redundant genes. In the second phase a Sequential Forward feature selection(SFS) method is applied to select a set of discriminatory genes giving maximum accuracy. The criterion used in the SFS is the accuracy of the classifier. Since the number of samples is very less in microarray datasets, the LOOCV accuracy is calculated. The outline of the proposed algorithm is:

GSUCE Algorithm (Gene Selection Using Clustering based on Entropy)

Input : Initial Set of genes, Class Labels C, Classifier M,
          Cluster_Size
PHASE 1 // to determine a subset independent genes S

   1. Intialization : Set C=initial set of genes ;
   2. S = empty set /*Set of Selected Attributes*/
   3. Calculate the dissimilarity Matrix S using maximal information compression index

4. Choose the two genes with maximum dissimilarity
5. Split the original clusters into two clusters C1 and C2
6. No_of_clusters=2;
7. While (no_of_clusters≤Cluster_Size)
8. Begin
9. For each cluster calculate the representative entropy H_R
10. Choose the Cluster C_i having the maximum H_R
11. Split C_i into two clusters
12. No_of_clusters=No_of_clusters+1
13. End
14. S=empty set
15. For each cluster
16. Find the informative gene g_i from cluster C_i using t-statistics
17. S=S U g_i
18 end for

PHASE 2 // to determine subset of genes which provides max accuracy

1.Initialization R=empty set
2.For each $x_j \in S$ calculate classification accuracy for classifier M.
3.$[x_k, max\_acc] = max_j\ Classification\_accuracy(x_j)$;
4.$R = R \cup x_k; S = S - x_k; R\_min = R$
5. For each x_j calculate classification_accuracy of $R \cup x_j$ for classifier M
6. $[x_k, new\_max\_acc] = max_j\ Classification\_accuracy(R \cup x_j)$;
7. $R = R \cup x_k; S = S - x_k$
8. If new_max_acc ≥ max_acc then R_min=R;max_acc=new_max_acc;
9. Repeat 5-9 until max_acc=100 or S = empty set
10. Return R_min, max_acc

3 Experimental SetUp and Results

We have applied our algorithm GSUCE on five well known publicly available datasets. The details of these datasets are given in Table 1. Prostate, Colon, Leukemia and LungCancer datasets were taken from Kent Ridge Biomedical Data Repository[14]. SRBCT dataset has been taken from [15]. During preprocessing we normalized the datasets using Z-score i.e. mean and variance of each gene was made zero and one respectively.

Table 1. Datasets Used

Dataset	Samples	Genes	Classes
Colon	62	2000	2
SRBCT	83	2308	4
Prostate	102	5967	2
Leukemia	72	7128	3
LungCancer	181	12534	2

During the first phase of the algorithm the original gene set is partitioned into k clusters using hierarchical clustering and then from each cluster the most relevant gene was selected using t-statistics. Thus a pool of k independent genes is created The experiment was conducted for different cluster sizes (k). The cluster sizes were taken as 30, 40, 50 and 60. During the second phase a Sequential Forward Feature Selection method is applied to obtain a set of discriminatory genes which provides maximum accuracy. Classification accuracy of the classifier is used as a criterion in forward feature selection. The different classifiers used in our experiments are linear discriminant classifier(LDC), quadratic discriminant classifier(QDC), k-nearest neighbor (KNN) and support vector machine(SVM). For KNN the optimal value of k is chosen. In SVM linear kernel is used.

Table 2. Maximum classification accuracy along with number of genes for different classifiers using different cluster size methods

No.of Clusters	LDC	QDC	KNN	SVM
30	90.32(10)	95.16(23)	91.93(4)	91.93(12)
40	90.32(10)	96.77(12)	98.38(12)	93.54(22)
50	91.93(13)	95.16(8)	93.54(5)	95.16(24)
60	93.54(6)	95.16(7)	95.16(23)	95.16(19)

a. Colon dataset

No.of Clusters	LDC	QDC	KNN	SVM
30	100(7)	96.38(14)	100(6)	100(7)
40	100(11)	96.38(18)	100(11)	100(7)
50	100(12)	96.36(13)	100(9)	100(6)
60	100(12)	100(18)	100(12)	100(6)

b. SRBCT dataset

No.of Clusters	LDC	QDC	KNN	SVM
30	97.22(8)	95.83(2)	98.61(5)	98.61(5)
40	97.22(5)	100(8)	98.61(5)	98.61(5)
50	97.22(5)	100(8)	100(22)	100(7)
60	97.22(5)	98.61(8)	98.61(5)	98.61(3)

c. Leukemia dataset

No.of Clusters	LDC	QDC	KNN	SVM
30	96.07(14)	97.05(8)	97.05(16)	96.07(3)
40	96.07(16)	97.05(10)	97.05(1)	99.01(19)
50	95.09(4)	98.03(9)	97.05(14)	97.05(12)
60	97.05(36)	98.03(7)	99.01(1)	97.05(5)

d. Prostate dataset

No.of Clusters	LDC	QDC	KNN	SVM
30	100(4)	100(3)	100(2)	100(3)
40	100(4)	100(3)	100(2)	100(3)
50	100(4)	100(4)	100(3)	100(3)
60	100(4)	100(4)	100(3)	100(3)

e. LungCancer dataset

The maximum classification accuracy along with the number of genes obtained by GSUCE for different cluster sizes are shown in Table 2. The following observation can be made from Table 2:

1. For Colon dataset a maximum accuracy of 98.38% is achieved with 12 genes for KNN classifier. For QDC a maximum accuracy of 96.77% is achieved with 12 genes. A maximum accuracy of 95.16% is achieved with 19 genes with SVM.

2. For SRBCT dataset maximum classification accuracy of 100% is achieved with all classifiers using GSUCE. It was achieved with 7, 18, 6 and 6 genes for LDC, QDC, KNN and SVM respectively.

3. For Leukemia dataset a maximum accuracy of 100% is achieved with 8 , 7 and 22 genes with QDC , SVM and KNN classifier respectiely. For LDC a maximum accuray of 97.22% is achieved with 5 genes.

4. For prostate dataset maximum classification accuracy of 99.01% is achieved with 19 and 1 gene with SVM and KNN classifier respectively. For QDC maximum accuracy of 98.03% is achieved with 7 genes. Maximum accuracy of 97.05% is achieved for LDC with 36 genes.

5. For Lungcancer dataset a maximum accuracy of 100% is achieved with 4, 3, 2 and 3 genes with LDC, QDC, KNN and SVM respectively.

Table 3. Comparison of Maximum Classification accuracy and number of genes selected with other state of art methods

SRBCT	LUNGCANCER	LEUKEMIA
Proposed Method 100(6)	Proposed Method 100(2)	Proposed Method 100(7)
GS2+SVM [4] 100(96)	GS2+KNN [4] 93.1(44)	GS2+KNN[4] 98.6(10)
GS1+SVM [4] 98.8(34)	GS1+SVM[4] 98.6(4)	GS1+SVM[4] 98.6(4)
Chos+SVM[4] 98.8(80)	Chos+SVM[4] 98.6(80)	Chos+SVM[4] 98.6(80)
Ftest + SVM[4] 100(78)	Ftest + SVM[4] 98.6(94)	Ftest + SVM[4] 98.6(33)
Fu and Liu [16] 100(19)	Shah , Kusiak[23] 100(8)	Fu and Liu[16] 97.0(4)
Tibsrani [21] 100(43)	PSO+ANN[4] 98.3	Guyon[24] 100(8)
Khan [17] 100(96)	Yuechui ,Yaou[22] 98.3	Tibsrani[21] 100(21)

COLON	PROSTATE
Proposed method 98.38(12)	Proposed Method 99.02(1)
PSO+ANN[4] 88.7	GAKNN[18] 96.3(79)
Yuechui and Yaou [22] 90.3	BIRS[19] 91.2(3)
BIRSW [19] 85.48(3.50)	
BIRSF [19] 85.48(7.40)	

It is observed that our proposed algorithm is able to achieve a high classification accuracy with small number of genes. In Table 3, we have also compared performance of our proposed method in terms of classification and number of genes with some already existing gene selection methods in literature[4], [16], [17], [18], [19], [20], [21], [22], [23],[24]. From Table 3, it can be observed that the performance of our proposed algorithm is significantly better in terms of both classification accuracy and number of genes selected.

4   Conclusion

In this paper, we have proposed a two stage algorithm GSUCE for finding a set of discriminatory genes for building an efficient classifier for high dimensional microarray datasets. Since microarray datasets contains many correlated genes, the proposed approach first determine correlated genes, group them and then select an informative gene from each of group. This helps in reducing redundancy. We have used a different similarity measure maximal information compression index which is not used before for microarray datasets. The size of this set obtained after first stage is small. This allows us to use wrapper approach at the second stage. The use of wrapper method at the second stage gives a better subset of genes. Experiments results show that our proposed method GSUCE is able to achieve a better accuracy with a small number of features. In case of Lungcancer and SRBCT 100% accuracy is achieved with 2 and 6 features respectively. For other datasets, the method provides competitive accuracy. Comparisons with other state of art methods show that our proposed algorithm is able to achieve better or comparable accuracy with less number of genes for all the datasets used.

References

1. Guyon, I., Elisseeff, A.: An Introduction to Variable and feature Selection. Journal of Machine Learning Research (3), 1157–1182 (2003)
2. Bellman, R.: Adaptive Control Processes. In: A Guided Tour. Princeton University Press, Princeton (1961)
3. Golub, T.R., Slonim, D.K., Tamayo, P., Huard, C., Gaasenbeek, M., Mesirov, J.P., Coller, H., Loh, M.L., Dowing, J.R., Caligiuri, M.A., Bloomfield, C.D., Lander, E.S.: Molecular classification of cancer: Class discovery and class prediction by gene expression monitoring. Science 286, 531–537 (1999)
4. Yang, K., Cai, Z., Li, J., Lin, G.H.: A stable gene selection in microarray data analysis. BMC Bioinformatics 7, 228 (2006)
5. Cho, J., Lee, D., Park, J.H., Lee, I.B.: New gene selection for classification of cancer subtype considering within-class variation. FEBS Letters 551, 3–7 (2003)
6. Kohonen, T.: Self-organizing maps. Springer, Berlin (1995)
7. Eisen, M.B., Spellman, T.P., Brown, P.O., Botstein, D.: Cluster analysis and display of genome-wide expression patterns. Proc. Natl. Acad. Sci. USA 95(25), 14863–14868 (1998)
8. Tavazoie, S., Huges, D., Campbell, M.J., Cho, R.J., Church, G.M.: Systematic determination of genetic network architecture. Nature Genet., 281–285 (1999)

9. Jiang, D., Tang, C., Zhang, A.: Cluster Analysis for gene expression data: A survey. IEEE Trans. Knowledge and Data Eng. 16, 1370–1386 (2004)
10. Yu, J., Amores, J., Sebe, N., Tian, Q.: Toward Robust Distance Metric analysis for Similarity Estimation. In: Proc. IEEE Int'l Conf. Computer Vision and Pattern Recognition (2006)
11. Heyer, L.J., Kruglyak, S., Yooseph, S.: Exploring Expression Data: identification and analysis of coexpressed genes. Genome Research 9, 1106–1115 (1999)
12. Mitra, P., Murthy, C., Pal, S.K.: Unsupervised feature selection using feature similarity. IEEE Trans. Pattern Analysis and Machine Intelligence 24(3), 301–312 (2002)
13. Han, J., Kamber, M.: Data Mining: Concepts and Techniques (2000)
14. Kent Ridge Biomedical Data Repository, http://datam.i2r.a-star.edu.sg/datasets/krbd/
15. http://research.nhgri.nih.gov/Supplement/
16. Fu, L.M., Liu, C.S.F.: Evaluation of gene importance in microarray data based upon probability of selection. BMC Bioinformatics 6(67) (2005)
17. Khan, J., Wei, S., Ringner, M., Saal, L.H., Ladanyi, M., Westermann, F.: Classification and diagnosis prediction of cancers using gene expression profiling and artificial neural networks. Nat. Med. 7, 673–679 (2001)
18. Li, L., Weinberg, C.R., Darden, T.A., Pedersen, L.G.: Gene Selection for sample classification based on gene expression data: Study of sensitivity to choice of parameters of the GA/KNN method. Bioinformatics 17(12), 1131–1142 (2001)
19. Ruiz, R., Riquelme, J.C., Aguilar-Ruiz, J.S.: Incremental wrapper based gene selection from microarray data for cancer classification. Pattern Recognition 39(12), 2383–2392 (2006)
20. Hong, J.H., Cho, S.B.: The classification of cancer based on DNA microarray data that uses diverse ensemble genetic programming. Artif. Intell. Med. 36, 43–58 (2006)
21. Tibsrani, R., Hastie, T., Narasimhan, B., Chu, G.: Diagnosis of multiple cancer types by shrunken centriods of gene expression. Proc. Natl. Acad. Sci. USA 99, 6567–6572 (2002)
22. Yuechui, C., Yaou, Z.: A novel ensemble of classifiers for microarray data classification. Applied Soft Computing (8), 1664–1669 (2008)
23. Shah, S., Kusiak, A.: Cancer gene search with Data Mining and Genetic Algorithms. Computer in Biology Medicine 37(2), 251–261 (2007)
24. Guyon, I., Weston, J., Barnhill, S., Vapnik, V.: Gene Selection for cancer classification using support vector machine. Machine Learning (46), 263–268 (2003)

A Framework for Incremental Domain-Specific Hidden Web Crawler

Rosy Madaan, Ashutosh Dixit, A.K. Sharma, and Komal Kumar Bhatia

YMCA University of Science & Technology Faridabad, Haryana India 121006
madaan.rosy@gmail.com,
{dixit_ashutosh,ashokkale2,komal_bhatia1}@rediffmail.com

Abstract. Hidden Web's broad and relevant coverage of dynamic and high quality contents coupled with the high change frequency of web pages poses a challenge for maintaining and fetching up-to-date information. For the purpose, it is required to verify whether a web page has been changed or not, which is another challenge. Therefore, a mechanism needs to be introduced for adjusting the time period between two successive revisits based on probability of updation of the web page. In this paper, architecture is being proposed that introduces a technique to continuously update/refresh the Hidden Web repository.

Keywords: WWW, Hidden Web, Surface Web, Search Engine, Crawler.

1 Introduction

WWW [1, 12, 16] can be broadly divided into two parts: Surface Web and Hidden Web [2, 6, 10]. The Surface Web refers to the part of the Web that can be crawled and indexed by general purpose search engines [3], while the hidden Web refers to the abundant information that is "hidden" behind the query interfaces and not directly accessible to the search engines. Hence, there is need to access the Hidden Web through their query interfaces. UUIC survey indicates that there are more than 300,000 Hidden Web databases [2,6,10] and 450,000 query interfaces available on the Web. The contents on Hidden Web are not only increasing but also spanning well across all topics.

The main characteristics of the Hidden Web are as follows:

- It has Broad, relevant Coverage,
- It contains High quality contents, and
- Its contents exceed all printed contents.

The existing web crawlers can retrieve only Surface web pages ignoring the large amounts of high quality information 'hidden' behind search forms that need to be filled manually by the user. A search interface consists of many forms elements like textboxes ,labels ,buttons etc. and the user is expected to provide data in at least one of them before submitting the form in order to obtain the response pages containing the results of the query.

S. Ranka et al. (Eds.): IC3 2010, Part I, CCIS 94, pp. 412–422, 2010.

In order to download the Hidden Web contents from the WWW the crawler needs a mechanism for Search Interface Interaction i.e. it should be able to download the search interfaces in order to automatically fill them and submit them to get the Hidden Web pages as shown in Fig. 1.

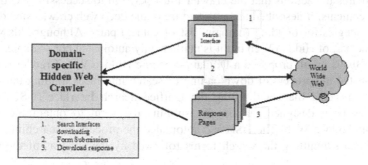

Fig. 1. Crawler Search Interface Interaction

The retrieved Hidden web documents are thereof stored in a repository. The Indexing function is performed by the Indexer [3] module of the Search engine. User provides a query on the query interface of the Search engine, the index is then searched for finding out a corresponding match, if any and the results are returned to the user.

In this paper, a framework has been proposed that updates the repository of search engine by re-crawling the web pages that are updated more frequently. The paper has been organized as follows: Section 2 describes the current research that has been carried out in this area; section 3 describes the proposed work to crawl the hidden web documents incrementally; section 4 shows the performance of proposed work and last section concludes the proposed work.

2 Related Work

The notion of a Hidden (or Deep or Invisible) Web has been a subject of interest for a number of years. A number of researchers have discussed the problems of crawling the contents of hidden Web databases [3, 8, 12, 9, 10, 11 12, 14, 16] as follows.

Raghavan and Garcia-Molina [14] proposed HiWE, a task-specific hidden-Web crawler, the main focus of this work was to learn Hidden-Web query interfaces. Lin and Chen's [10] built a catalogue of small search engines located in sites and choose which ones were more likely to answer the query. However, forms with more than a text field was not treated. Wang and Lochovsky [9] described a system called, DeLa, which reconstructed (part of) a "hidden" back-end web database, and it used the HiWE. There are other approaches that focused on the data extraction. Lage et al. [12] claimed to automatically generate agents to collect hidden web pages by filling HTML forms. Liddle et al [12] performed a study on how Valuable information could be obtained behind web forms, but did not include a crawler to fetch them. Barbosa and Freire [11] experimentally evaluated methods for building multi-keyword queries that could return a large fraction of a document collection.

Xiang Peisu et al. [16] proposed model of forms and form filling process that concisely captures the actions that the crawler must perform to successfully extract Hidden Web contents. It described the architecture of the deep web crawler and described various strategies for building (domain, list of values) pairs. Although this work extracts some part of Hidden Web but it is neither fully automated nor scalable.

In [7], Bhatia at. al. proposed a Domain–Specific Hidden Web Crawler (DSHWC) that automated the process of downloading of search interfaces, finding the semantic mappings, merging them and filling the Unified Search Interface (USI) produced thereof has been designed that finally submits the form to obtain the response pages from Hidden Web. The DSHWC automated the process of searching, viewing, filling in and submitting the search forms followed by the analysis of the response pages.

Since the Hidden Web has broad and relevant coverage of dynamic [16] and high quality contents, there is a need to refresh/update the local collection of Hidden web documents incrementally [4,11,13,17],so as to maintain document collection or repository updated with the latest information.

However, a critical look at the available literature [4,6,11,12,14,16,17] indicates that although the Hidden Web crawling enables the crawler to download Hidden Web but none of the work has been done for the purpose of maintaining the document collection of Hidden Web pages updated with the latest information. So, there is a need of some mechanism to keep the repository fresh. For the purpose, it is required to verify whether a web page has been changed or not. Therefore, a mechanism needs to be introduced for adjusting the time period between two successive revisits of the crawler based on probability of updation [5,15]of the web page.

3 Proposed Work

The architecture of an Incremental Hidden Web Crawler (shown Fig. 2.) has been proposed that introduces a technique to continuously update/refresh the Hidden Web repository. It uses a mechanism for adjusting the time period between two successive revisits of the crawler based on probability of the web page [5,11,15].

The proposed architecture consists of the following functional components:

1. Domain-Specific Hidden Web Crawler (DSHWC)
2. URL Extractor
3. Revisit Frequency Calculator
4. Update Module
5. Dispatcher

The description of each functional component with required data structures is given below.

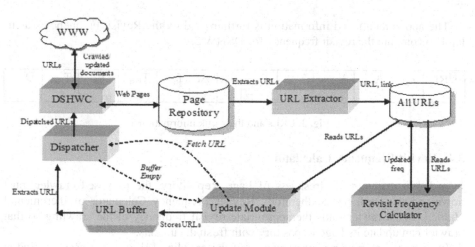

Fig. 2. Architecture of an Incremental Hidden Web Crawler

3.1 Domain Specific Hidden Web Crawler (DSHWC)

DSHWC [7] is a fully automated crawler that downloads search interfaces, finds the semantic mappings, merges them and fills the Unified Search Interface (USI) produced thereof. Finally, the DSHWC submits the form to obtain the response pages from Hidden Web [2,6,10].

After obtaining response pages, the DSHWC stores the downloaded pages into Page repository that maintains the documents crawled/updated by the DSHWC along with their URLs.

3.2 URL Extractor

It extracts the URLs along with their link information from the above repository and stores them in the AllURLs. The details of link information stored in AllURLs have been discussed in next section.

3.3 AllURLs

It records all URLs that the crawler has discovered, along with their link information as contained in the Page Repository. The AllURLs contains the URLs and their corresponding link information (see Fig. 3.) as follows:

$\lambda_{low}, \lambda_{mid}, \lambda_{upper}$: boundary conditions for change frequency of pages.

λ_{prev} : change frequency of page at the previous visit

$\lambda_{current}$: current change frequency of page

f_n : current revisit frequency

Δf :change in the frequency of the page

f_{n+1}: adjusted crawler revisit frequency

$D_{last\ crawl}$: date of their last crawl

$T_{last\ crawl}$: time of their last crawl

D_{curr} : current date

T_{curr} : current time

The above mentioned information is further used by the Revisit Frequency Calculator to compute the revisit frequency for DSHWC.

URL	λ_{low}	λ_{mid}	λ_{upper}	λ_{prev}	λ_{curr}	f_n	Δf	f_{n+1}	T_{last} crawl	D_{last} crawl	T_{curr}	D_{curr}

Fig. 3. URLs and their link information

3.4 Revisit Frequency Calculator

In order to maintain the freshness of Page Repository, the proposed crawler must download the fresh pages, therefore, Revisit Frequency Calculator of Incremental Hidden Web Crawler finds the appropriate revisit frequency of the crawling so that crawler can update its Page Repository with fresh documents.

In order to compute revisit frequency of the crawling [3], it is necessary to find at which rate crawler needs to visit each page. The rate of revisit of a page should increase for the pages that change more often. However, this may not be the conclusion as frequent revisits of a page, mayn't always provide the updated information. So, there is a need to modify the revising rate of a page. It has been observed from Fig. 4. that the revisiting frequency of the crawler is proportional to the change frequency [5,15] of the page up to a certain threshold value ($\lambda_{middle)}$, after the threshold it remains constant up to the next threshold (λ_{upper}) and then decrease, with increase in the change frequency of the page after the second threshold (λ_{upper}).

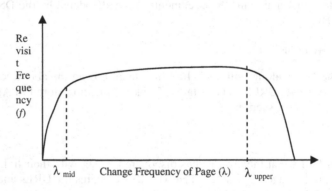

Fig. 4. Change frequency of page vs. Revisit frequency

This functional component reads AllURLs and for each URL_i, it computes the Revisit frequency of the crawler by using the following equation:

$$f_{n+1=}f_n + \Delta f, \tag{1}$$

where

$$\Delta f = [\{f_n \times (\lambda_{current}/\lambda_{previous} -1) \times u\ (\lambda_{current} - \lambda_{lower})\ \times u\ (\lambda_{middle} - \lambda_{current}) \times u\ (\lambda_{upper} - \lambda_{current}) + \{f_n \times (1 - \lambda_{current}/\lambda_{upper}) \times u(\lambda_{current} - \lambda_{upper}) \times u(1 - \lambda_{current})\}], \tag{2}$$

A unit step function u(x) has been employed,
Where

$$u(x) = \begin{cases} 1, \text{ if } x > 0 \\ 0 \text{ otherwise.} \end{cases}$$

On the calculation of the adjusted crawler revisit frequency, AllURLs needs to be updated. Also, Δf, f_n, $\lambda_{previous}$, $\lambda_{current}$ needs to be updated. The algorithm for the Revisit frequency calculator is given below.

```
RevisitFrequencyCalculator( )
{
For each URLi in AllURLs
{
        compute Δf;
        compute (fn+1 = fn +  Δf);
        fn = fn+1 ;
        λprev = λcurr ;
        update AllURLs with (Δf,fn,fn+1,λprev,λcurr);
    }
}
```

For each URL in AllURLs, the revisit frequency f_{n+1} has been computed by using the above mentioned method. This revisit frequency is further overwritten by the calculator in AllURLs to previous frequency i.e. f_n.

3.5 The Update Module

Update module one by one fetches the URLs and their updated link information (with updated revisit frequencies) from the AllURLs. After fetching an URL from AllURLs, it finds the time, denoted as τ (computed as inverse of revisit frequency), after which crawler should revisit the same web page and compare it with a threshold time T. If τ of a given URL is greater than T, then the web page needs to be recrawled and this URL is further stored in URL Buffer thereof, otherwise this URL is discarded and will not be stored in URL Buffer but it will exist in AllURLs. In this way, the URLs of all the web pages that need to be recrawled will be placed in the URL Buffer. When this buffer will become full, the Update Module will send a signal called Fetch URL signal to Dispatcher. After getting the Fetch URL signal from Update Module, the Dispatcher will start fetching the URLs one by one and forward it to the crawler to download the web page again so that the freshness of Page repository can increase. When URL Buffer will become empty, the Dispatcher will in turn send Buffer Empty signal to Update Module. Buffer Empty signal signifies that currently the buffer is empty and after receiving this signal Update Module will process and add more URLs in the URL Buffer. The algorithm given below describes how the Update Module makes the decision of recrawling of the selected URLs which in turn maintains the repository fresh.

```
Update ( )
{
    wait (Buffer Empty);
    fetch URLs and their link info from AllURLs;
    for each fetched URL do
        {
            if (τ >= T) then
                add URL in URL Buffer;
            else
                continue;
                If full(URL Buffer) then
                signal (fetch URL);
        }
}
```

Consider In the following example, the revisit frequency for URL www.sample.com has been computed by assuming the following values.

$\lambda_{lower} = 0.1$, $\lambda_{middle} = 0.6$ and $\lambda_{upper} = 0.8$, $D_{last\ crawl}$ = 13-01-2010
$T_{last\ crawl}$ = 14:00

Now consider the data given below:
Initial frequency of revisit f_i = 10 times/unit time.
Current change frequency of page $\lambda_{current}$ = 0.15 and $\lambda_{previous}$ = 0.1
Computing Δf as given below:
$\Delta f = [\{10 \times (0.15 / 0.1 -1) \times u\ (0.15 - 0.1) \times u\ (0.6- 0.15) \times u\ (0.8- 0.15)\} + \{10 \times (1- 0.15/ 0.1) \times u\ (0.15 - 0.8) \times (1-0.15)\}]$.
= 5
Now, the new revisit frequency can be computed as follows:
f_{n+1} = 10+5 = 15 times/unit time
Let the basic unit of revisit be 24 hours and T (threshold time) =2 hours.
Calculating τ (time) =2(approx.).
It means that the crawler will revisit the corresponding web page every 2 hours (i.e. after a time period of 2 hours).
Now, τ is compared with T. If τ is greater than or equal to T, then the corresponding web page needs to be recrawled otherwise not. Since, for the above example τ is equal to T, so the web page needs to be recrawled and is further added in the URL Buffer.

3.6 Dispatcher

Dispatcher waits for the *fetch URL* signal and upon receiving this signal, it fetches an URL from the URL Buffer so that DSHWC in turn can download the corresponding web page. However, if dispatcher finds the URL Buffer empty during this operation, then it sends Buffer Empty signal to the Update Module so that it can add more URLs in the URL Buffer. The algorithm for Dispatcher is given below.

```
Dispatcher ( )
{
wait (fetch URL);
while (not (empty URL Buffer)
    {
        fetch URL from URL Buffer;
        forward URL to DSHWC to download web page;
    }
signal (Buffer Empty);
}
```

4 Implementation/Performance Evaluation

With the increase in the availability of hidden web pages, the major problem faced by
the current search engines [3] is difficulty in fresh or updated information retrieval. It
is problematic to identify the desired information from amongst the large set of web
pages resulted by the search engine. With further increase in the size of the Hidden
Web [2,6,10] contents, the problem grows exponentially. The number of web pages
which have gone under updation increases [1, 12, 16], with the increase in web size.
As discussed above, the proposed incremental hidden web crawler downloads the
fresh hidden web contents incrementally to make the search engine repository updated. The proposed incremental Hidden Web crawler has been implemented using
.Net technology on Windows platform and the snap shot for the incremental hidden
web crawler has been shown in Fig.5. Several experiments were conducted over the
Books and *Airline* following domains and the initial results were very promising.

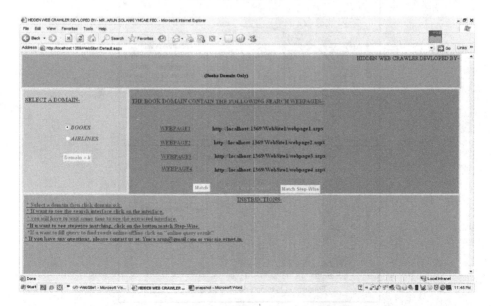

Fig. 5. Snapshot for Domain-specific Hidden Web Crawler

The proposed incremental hidden web crawler updates the hidden web pages that are already crawled by the hidden web crawler and makes the repository fresh. Therefore, to evaluate the proposed work two performance metrics i.e. *freshness of database* and *age of database* are taken in to the consideration and several experiments were conducted evaluate freshness and age of database.

Freshness of database D at time t is computed as

$$F(D, t) = 1/N\sum F(e_i, t),$$ (3)

where

$$F(e_i, t) = \begin{cases} 1, \text{ if page ei is up-to-date at time} \\ 0, \text{ otherwise} \end{cases}$$

and N is total number of web pages in D.

Similarly, Age of database D at time t is computed as

$$A(D, t) = 1/N\sum A(e_i, t),$$ (4)

where

$$A(e_i, t) = \begin{cases} 0, \text{ if page } e_i \text{ is up-to-date at time t} \\ t, \text{Modification time of } e_i, \text{ otherwise} \end{cases}$$

and N is total number of web pages in D.

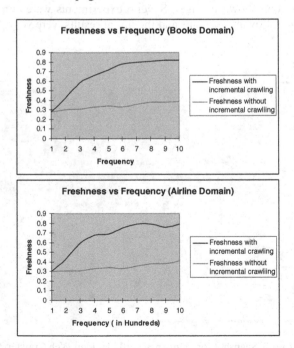

Fig. 6. (a) & (b) Freshness vs Frequency for Book and Airlines Domain

As discussed above, that proposed incremental hidden web crawler updates the repository created by the hidden web crawler, therefore, freshness and age of the updated database has been verified and analyzed. The observations show that as more fresh pages are crawled by the proposed crawler, the freshness of the database increases and the age of the database decreases with increase in time i.e. the database become fresher as the updated hidden web pages are recrawled by the incremental hidden web crawler.

Therefore, it may be concluded that the age of the database decreases as freshness of the database has been increased. The observation has been shown in form of graphs for both the domains in Fig. 6 (a). and (b).

5 Conclusion

The proposed architecture overcomes the limitation of the traditional DSHWC by continuously updating/refreshing the Hidden Web repository. It is based on adjusting the time period between the two successive revisits of the crawler based on probability of updation of the web page.

References

1. Arasu, A., Cho, J., Garcia-Molina, H., Paepcke, A., Raghavan, S.: Searching the Web. ACM Transactions on Internet Technology (TOIT) 1(1), 2–43 (2001)
2. Bergman, M.K.: The deep web: Surfacing hidden value. Journal of Electronic Publishing 7(1) (2001)
3. Brin, S., Page, L.: The anatomy of a large-scale hypertextual Web search engine. Computer Networks and ISDN Systems 30(1-7), 107–117 (1999)
4. Cho, J., Garcia-Molina, H.: The Evolution of the Web and Implications for an Incremental Crawler. In: Proceedings of the Twenty-Sixth VLDB Conference, pp. 200–209 (2000)
5. Cho, J., Garcia-Molina, H.: Estimating Frequency of Change. Technical report, DB Group, Stanford University (2001)
6. Czajkowski, K., Fitzgerald, S., Foster, I., Kesselman, C.: Grid Information Services for Distributed Resource Sharing. In: 10th IEEE International Symposium on High Performance Distributed Computing, pp. 181–184 (2001)
7. Bhatia, K.K., Sharma, A.K.: A Framework for an Extensible Domain-specific Hidden Web Crawler (DSHWC). Communicated to IEEE TKDE Journal (December 2008)
8. Bhatia, K.K., Sharma, A.K.: A Framework for Domain-Specific Interface Mapper (DSIM). International Journal of Computer Science and Network Security (2008)
9. Bhatia, K.K., Sharma, A.K.: Merging Query Interfaces in Domain-specific Hidden Web Databases. Accepted in International Journal of Computer Science (2008)
10. Bhatia, K.K., Sharma, A.K.: Crawling the hidden web resources. In: Proceedings of NCIT 2007 (2007)
11. Dixit, A., Sharma, A.K.: Self Adjusting Refresh Time Based Architecture For Incremental Web Crawler. International Journal of Computer Science and Network Security (IJCSNS) 8(12) (2008)
12. Burner, M.: Crawling towards Eternity: Building an archive of the World Wide Web. Web Techniques Magazine 2(5) (1997)

13. Cho, J., Garcia-Molina, H.: The evolution of the web and implications for an incremental crawler. In: Proceedings of the 26th International Conference on Very Large Databases
14. Sharma, A.K., Gupta, J.P., Agarwal, D.P.: A novel approach towards management of Volatile Information. Journal of CSI 33(1), 18–27 (2003)
15. Cho, J., Garcia-Molina, H.: Estimating Frequency of Change. Technical report, DB Group, Stanford University (2001)
16. Brewington, B.E., Cybenko, G.: How dynamic is the web. In: Proceedings of the Ninth International World-Wide Web Conference, Amsterdam, Netherlands (2000)
17. Edwards, J., McCurley, K., Tomlin, J.: An Adaptive Model for Optimizing Performance of an Incremental Web Crawler

Impact of K-Means on the Performance of Classifiers for Labeled Data

B.M. Patil*, R.C. Joshi, and Durga Toshniwal

Department of Electronics and Computer Engineering,
Indian Institute of Technology, Roorkee, Uttarakhand, India 247667
{bmp07dec,rcjosfec,durgafec}@iitr.ernet.in

Abstract. In this study a novel framework for data mining in clinical decision making have been proposed. Our framework addresses the problems of assessing and utilizing data mining models in medical domain. The framework consists of three stages. The first stage involves preprocessing of the data to improve its quality. The second stage employs k-means clustering algorithm to cluster the data into k clusters (in our case, k=2 i.e. cluster0 / no, cluster1 / yes) for validation the class labels associated with the data. After clustering, the class labels associated with the data is compared with the labels generated by clustering algorithm if both the labels are same it is assumed that the data is correctly classified. The instances for which the labels are not same are considered to be misclassified and are removed before further processing. In the third stage support vector machine classification is applied. The classification model is validated by using k-fold cross validation method. The performance of SVM (Support Vector Machine) classifier is also compared with Naive Bayes classifier. In our case SVM classifier outperforms the Naive Bayes classifier. To validate the proposed framework, experiments have been carried out on benchmark datasets such as Indian Pima diabetes dataset and Wisconsin breast cancer dataset (WBCD).These datasets were obtained from the University of California at Irvine (UCI) machine learning repository. Our proposed study obtained classification accuracy on both datasets, which is better with respect to the other classification algorithms applied on the same datasets as cited in the literature. The performance of the proposed framework was also evaluated using the sensitivity and specificity measures.

Keywords: Classification, Performance measure, Pima Indian diabetes data, k-Means, k-fold cross-validation.

1 Introduction

In the 21st century, diabetes is one of the most challenging health problems. In most of the developed countries, diabetes is fourth or fifth leading cause of death. Complications from diabetes such as coronary artery disease, peripheral vascular disease, stroke, diabetic neuropathy, amputations, renal failure and blindness are

---

* Corresponding author.

S. Ranka et al. (Eds.): IC3 2010, Part I, CCIS 94, pp. 423–434, 2010.
© Springer-Verlag Berlin Heidelberg 2010

resulting in disability and reduced life expectancy [1]. As a consequence, data mining for clinical decision making has received a great importance in the research community. There are two main classes of diabetes which are diagnosed by the severity of insulin deficiency. Type-1 diabetes is usually diagnosed in children and adolescents when pancreas is unable to produce insulin. Insulin is a hormone which ensures that the body energy needs are met. Type-1 diabetes is always treated with insulin intake. Type-2 diabetes is caused by relative insulin deficiency. InType-2 diabetes pancreas produces insufficient insulin to control blood glucose [2].

Several classification models are built using various machine learning and statistical algorithms to predict the presence of disease on UCI diabetes dataset. Michie et al. in [3], used 22 distinct algorithms to classify diabetes data and reported the accuracy to lie between 69% to 77%. Boich et al. demonstrated how Bayesian approach can improve the predictive performance of neural network. Standard neural networks are universal approximators and are able to model non-linear regularities in the data. However, they face the problem of overfitting i.e. a good fit on the training data and a poor generalization on the test data. To overcome this problem Bayesian approach has been used. In their study they removed 16 instances having zero attribute values for glucose and Body Mass Index (BMI) and remaining 752 instances were used for classification. Out of these 752 instances, 500 were used for training and the remaining 252 were used for testing. The accuracy of 79.5% is reported [4]. Carpenter G.A. and Markuzon, N proposed Predictive Adaptive Resonance Theory Instance Counting (ARTMAP-IC) algorithm for classification on the same dataset. The instance counting algorithm is added to basic fuzzy (ARTMAP) system. The added capabilities allowed ARTMAP-IC to encode predictions of inconsistent cases in the training set. It gave good performance on Indian Pima Diabetes data with the reported accuracy of 81%. Deng et al. obtained a classification accuracy of 78.4% with 10-fold cross-validation using evolving Self-Organizing Maps (ESOM) [6].

Kayaer et al. applied General Regression Neural Network (GRNN) to Pima Indian diabetes and it obtained accuracy of 80.21%. Polat et al. proposed a system that used Principal Component Analysis (PCA) for dimension reduction in first stage. PCA reduced the features from 8 to 4. In second stage, a neuro-fuzzy inference system was used. Overall accuracy of 89.47% has been reported [8]. Polat et al. proposed a cascade learning system based on Generalized Discriminant Analysis (GDA) and Least Square Support Vector Machine (LS-SVM) and reported the accuracy of 82.05%. Humar et al. proposed a hybrid system using Artificial Neural Network (ANN) with Fuzzy Neural Network (FNN) and obtained an accuracy of 84.24%.

None of the above mentioned techniques used the validation of class labels, which affect the predictive performance of classification methods. Our study proposes a novel frame work which uses simple K-means clustering algorithm aimed at validating the class label of given data. The incorrectly classified instances are removed before further processing. Both support vector machine and Navie Bayes classifiers are applied separately to the dataset by using the k-fold cross validation method.

The proposed framework has been used to accurately classify type-2 diabetic patients. The study is limited to patients who are pregnant women. They are classified into a group that is likely to develop diabetes or into a group that will not develop diabetes. The performance of proposed framework has also been tested on breast cancer dataset for classification of benign or malignant tumors. These datasets were obtained from the University of California at Irvine (UCI) machine learning repository [11].

The rest of the paper is organized as follows: In Section 2, we briefly discuss the proposed method (k-Means clustering, SVM & Navie Bayes Classifiers). The performance measures used the results obtained are presented in section 3. The conclusions are discussed in section 4.

2 Proposed Methodology

The block diagram of proposed framework for classification shown in Fig. 1 consists of the different stages – data preprocessing, pattern extraction (clustering) and classification. In preprocessing stage data normalization is performed. Second stage, uses clustering method for validation of class labels associated with data. Finally we applied SVM on reduced dataset for classification. The proposed framework was also tested with Navie Bayes Classifier.

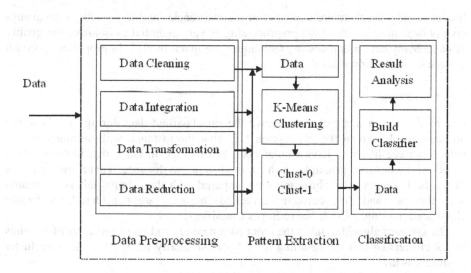

Fig. 1. Proposed framework for classification

2.1 Datasets

Pima Indian Diabetes dataset and WBCD (Wisconsin Breast Cancer Dataset) obtained from UCI machine learning repository [11].

2.1.1 Pima Indian Diabetes Dataset
A study was conducted on 768 randomly selected Pima Indian female patients whose age was at least 21. The dataset includes parameters, like number of times of pregnancy and age in years. Some other important parameters like plasma glucose concentration every 2 hours in an oral glucose tolerance test, diastolic blood pressure

(mm Hg), triceps skin fold thickness (mm), 2-Hour serum insulin (mu U/ml), body mass index (weight in kg/(height in $(mm)^2$), and diabetes pedigree function which are closely related to diabetes were also included.

2.1.2 WBCD (Wisconsin Breast Cancer Dataset)

WBCD – 1 (Wisconsin Breast Cancer dataset) consists of 699 samples that were collected by Dr. W.H. Wolberg at the University of Wisconsin—Madison Hospitals taken from needle aspirates from human breast cancer tissue (Setiono, 2000). The WBCD consists of nine features obtained from fine needle aspirates, each of which is ultimately represented as an integer value between 1 and 10. The measured variables are as follows: (1) Clump Thickness (x1); (2) Uniformity of Cell Size (x2); (3) Uniformity of Cell Shape (x3); (4) Marginal Adhesion (x4); (5) Single Epithelial Cell Size (x5); (6) Bare Nucleoi (x6); (7) Bland Chromatin (x7); (8) Normal Nucleoi (x8); and (9) Mitoses (x9). Out of total 699 samples belong 458 belong to benign class and remaining 241 samples belong to malignant class.

2.2 Data Preprocessing

In real world data, there are a number of inconsistencies and low-quality data always give poor mining results. Data preprocessing is very essential to improve the quality of data. Many data preprocessing techniques are given in [12]. In proposed approach z-score normalization is used.

2.3 Clustering

Our motivation in this paper to remove the misclassified data during the clustering procedure is based on the assumption [12] that the instance with similar attribute values is more likely to have similar class label as the instance that is closest to it based on the distance principle, such as, the Euclidean distance. Therefore the labels of all the instances after clustering are compared with the original labels associated with the data and only correctly classified instances are considered for further classification using SVM & Naïve Bayes Classifiers.

The k-means algorithm takes the input parameter, k, and partitions a set of N points into k clusters so that the resulting intracluster similarity is high but the intercluster similarity is low.

The steps in the k-means method are as follows [13]:

1. Select k random instances from the training data subset as the centroids of the clusters $C_1, C_2, \ldots C_k$
2. For each training instance X:
   a. Compute the Euclidean distance
      $$D(C_i, X), i = 1,\ldots, k$$
      Find cluster that is closest to X.
   b. Assign X to Cq. Update the centroid of Cq. (The centroid of a cluster is the arithmetic mean of the instances in the cluster)
3. Repeat Step 2 until the centroids of clusters $C_1, C_2,\ldots,C_k$ stabilize in terms of mean-squared error Criterion.

K-means clustering method was used to validate the class label associated with the data before classifying. The reason behind choosing k-means is because it produces good validation results. A similar method, K-medoids was also tried for clustering but the misclassification rate was as high as 50% and hence was not considered. The clustering process will group the data based on intrinsic properties of data and without considering actual class labels of the data. The validation is done based on the concept that if the class label given by clustering method and the actual class label are same it is correctly classified else it is considered to be misclassified. Data in cluster1 indicates diabetes may occur (yes) and cluster0 indicates that diabetes will not occur (no). K-means clustering algorithm was tested 20 times to check for any variation in the misclassification rate. It was observed that the misclassification rate was almost constant i.e. 33.21% in case of diabetes dataset and the same was 4.29% in case breast cancer dataset.

Table 1. Misclassified instances after K mean clustering

Datasets	Cluster Attribute	Instances	Incorrectly classified	Error (%)
1. Pima Indian diabetes data	Cluster1(Yes)/ Cluster0 (No)	768	255	33.21
2. WBCD (Wisconsin Breast Cancer dataset)	Cluster1 (malign) / Cluster0 (begin))	699	30	4.29

2.4 Support Vector Machine (SVM)

Sequential Minimal Optimization (SMO) algorithm of SVM implementation available in WEKA tool is used for classification [14].In Pima Indian Diabetes data and Wisconsin breast cancer dataset (WBCD) the total number of instances correctly classified after comparison with output of clustering are 512 and 669 respectively.The Classification was performed using SVM–RBF kernel method with 10-fold cross validation. The parameter gamma was set to 0.9 after rigorous tuning. The classification accuracy achieved on diabetes and breast cancer datasets are 97.47 % and 99.41 respectively.

2.5 Naive Bayes

The simple Naive Bayes algorithm [17] is used in this study. Navie bayes algorithm is assumed to be class-conditionally independent. It has often performed well on real data. If the features are not redundant then this algorithm will yield best accuracy. If features are redundant, the result given by the algorithm is misleading. Langley et al. reported that the performance of Naive Bayes classifier improves when redundant features are removed. Posterior probability of each class is calculated based on given attribute value present in the tuple. The navie bayes was used with 10-fold cross validation and classification accuracy of 96.29% and 97.76% was achieved on diabetes and breast cancer dataset respectively.

3 Results

3.1 Performance Measures

The performance of proposed framework was evaluated by using 10-fold cross validation method. The data set was divided in 10 equal subsets. The method was repeated 10 times and each time one subset is used for testing and other nine subsets are used for training [19]. The measures true positive (TP) and true negative (TN) are correct classifications. A false positive (FP) occurs when the outcome is incorrectly predicted as YES (positive) when it is actually NO (negative). A false negative (FN) occurs when the outcome is incorrectly predicted as NO (negative) when it is actually YES (positive). Actual results obtained by our framework on both the datasets are shown in Table 2 and Table 3

Table 2. Confusion matrix, accuracy, sensitivity and specificity by SVM & Navie Bayes on Pima Indian diabetes dataset

Classifiers	Confusion matrix		Accuracy %	Sensitivity %	Specificity %
Navie Bayes	130	02	96.29	88.43	99.45
	17	364			
SVM	122	10	97.47	97.6	97.42
	03	378			

Table 3. Confusion matrix, accuracy, sensitivity and specificity by SVM & Navie Bayes on WBCD (Wisconsin Breast Cancer Dataset)

Classifiers	Confusion matrix		Accuracy %	Sensitivity %	Specificity %
Navie Bayes	432	14	97.76	96.87	99.76
	01	222			
SVM	445	02	99.41	99.55	99.09
	02	220			

The performance is measured by using accuracy, sensitivity and specificity measures. They are calculated using equations 1, 2 and 3 as given below:

$$\text{Accuracy} = \frac{TP + TN}{TP + TN + FP + FN} \tag{1}$$

$$\text{Sensitivity} = \frac{TP}{TP + FN} \tag{2}$$

$$\text{Specificity} = \frac{TN}{TN + FP} \tag{3}$$

As shown in Table 4, the Naive Bayes and SVM classification accuracy, sensitivity and specificity obtained by proposed framework on Indian Pima Diabetes are 96.29%, 88.43% and 99.15% and 97.47%, 97.6%, and 97.42% respectively which are better as compared to recent prediction systems by Potal et al, [8] and Humar et al, [10]and it also shown in Fig 2.The Naive Bayes and SVM classification accuracy, sensitivity and specificity obtained by proposed framework on WBCD is compared with [21] and it is given in Table 5.The graphical representation is shown in Fig 3.

The proposed framework obtained better results in classifying the type-2 diabetes patients compared to other classifiers on the same dataset as presented in Table 7. Our method is efficient than Hybrid Prediction System [8], the generalized discriminator analysis, least square Support Vector Machine (GDA) - (LSSVM) [9],and Principle Component Analysis and Adaptive Neuro-Fuzzy Inference System (ANFIS) [10].

Table 4. Comparisons of accuracy, sensitivity and Specificity of proposed method with other recent method in the literature on Pima Indian Diabetes data

Measures	ANN-Neuro-fuzzy	PCA-Neuro-fuzzy	K-means +Bayes (Proposed study)	k-means + SVM(Proposed Study)
Accuracy	84.2	89.47	97.76	97.47
Sensitivity	80	86.71	88.43	97.6
Specificity	87.3	92.00	99.45	97.42

Table 5. Comparisons of accuracy, sensitivity and Specificity of proposed method with other recent method in the literature on WBCD

Measures	LS-SVM Potal et al. 2007	K-means +Bayes (Proposed study)	k-means + SVM (Proposed Study)
Accuracy	97.08	97.47	99.41
Sensitivity	97.87	96.87	99.55
Specificity	97.77	99.76	99.09

The performance of the proposed method is also evaluated using Kappa statistics. The kappa value is calculated by equation (4) where P(A) is percentage of agreement and P(E) is chance of agreement calculated by equation (5) and (6). N is the total number of instances. Kappa value is calculated using the values in the confusion matrix presented in Table 6. It can define the prediction agreement between the classifier data and real world data. A kappa statistic of 0.7 or higher is generally regarded as a good statistic correlation. The higher the value, the better is the correlation.

$$K = [P(A) - P(E)] / [1 - P(E)] \qquad (4)$$

Where

$$P(A) = (TP + TN)/N \tag{5}$$

$$P(A) = [(TP + FN)*(TP + FP)*(TN + FN)]/N \tag{6}$$

The method has been evaluated against other important parameters which defined below [20]. 'p' is the predicted value and 'a' is the actual value.

Mean absolute error is the average of the differences between predicted and actual value in all test cases. It is the average prediction error. The mean absolute error is calculated refer to equation (7).

$$\frac{\left|p_i - a_i\right| + ... + \left|p_n - a_n\right|}{n} \tag{7}$$

Root mean-squared error: is one of the most commonly used measures of success for numeric prediction. This value is computed by taking the average of the squared differences between each predicted value (p_i) and its corresponding correct value (a_i). The root mean-squared error is simply the square root of the mean-squared-error. The root mean-squared error gives the error value of the same dimensionality as the actual and predicted values. Root mean square error is given equitation (8)

$$\sqrt{\frac{(p_i - a_i)^2 + ... + (p_n - a_n)^2}{n}} \tag{8}$$

Relative absolute error is just the total absolute error, with the same kind of normalization. The errors are normalized by the error of the simple predictor that predicts average values. Relative absolute error can be calculated based on refer to equation (9)

$$\frac{\left|p_i - a_i\right| + ... + \left|p_n - a_n\right|}{\left|a_i - \overline{a}\right| + .. + \left|a_n - \overline{a}\right|} \tag{9}$$

Root relative squared error is the average of the actual values from the training data. The relative squared error takes the total squared error and normalizes it by dividing by the total squared error of the default predictor. By taking the square root of the relative squared error one reduces the error to the same dimensions as the quantity being predicted refer to equation (10)

$$\sqrt{\frac{(p_i - a_i)^2 + ... + (p_n - a_n)^2}{(a_1 - \overline{a})^2 + ... + (a_n - \overline{a})^2}} \tag{10}$$

Table 6. General error output on Pima Indian diabetes data

Performance measure	Navie Byes	SVM
Correctly classified instances	494	500
Incorrectly classified instances	19	13
Kappa statistics	0.9066	0.9325
Mean absolute error	0.0517	0.0253
Root mean square error	0.1792	0.1593
Relative absolute error	0.1352	0.06621
Root relative squared error	0.4098	0.36141

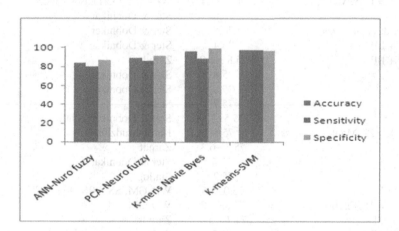

Fig. 2. Comparison result on Pima Indian diabetes data with Polat [8] and Humar [10]

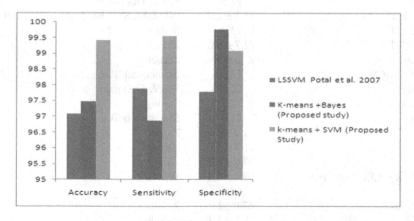

Fig. 3. Comparison result on WBCD with Polat et al. [21]

Table 7. Classification accuracies of Proposed Model and other classifier for the Pima Indian diabetes

Method	Accuracy %	Reference
K-mean +SVM	**97.47**	**Proposed Study**
k-means +Navie Bayes	**96.29**	" "
Hybrid model	84.5	Humar Kahramanli
Logdisc	77.7	Statlog
IncNet	77.6	Norbert Jankowski
DIPOL92	77.6	Statlog
Linear Discr. Anal.	77.5–77.2	Statlog; Ster & Dobnikar
SMART	76.8	Statlog
GTO DT (5 ×CV)	76.8	Bennet and Blue
kNN, k =23, Manh, raw , W	76.6 ±3.4	WD-GM, feature weighting 3CV
kNN, k = 1:25, Manh, raw	76.6 ±3.4	WD-GM, most cases k = 23
ASI	76.6	Ster & Dobnikar
Fisher discr. analysis	76.5	Ster & Dobnikar
MLP + BP	76.4	Ster & Dobnikar
MLP + BP	75.8 ± 6.2	Zarndt
LVQ	75.8	Ster & Dobnikar
LFC	75.8	Ster & Dobnikar
RBF	75.7	Statlog
NB	75.5±3.8	Ster & Dobnikar; Statlog
kNN, k = 22, Manh	75.5	Karol Grudzinski
MML	75.5 ±6.3	Zarndt
SNB	75.4	Ster & Dobnikar
BP	75.2	Statlog
SSV DT	75.0±3.6	WD-GM, SSV BS, node 5CV MC
kNN, k = 18, Euclid, raw	74.8± 4.8	WD-GM
CART DT	74.7 ± 5.4	Zarndt
CART DT	74.5	Stalog
DB-CART	74.4	Shang & Breiman
ASR	74.3	Ster & Dobnikar
SSV DT	73.7 ± 4.7	WD-GM, SSV BS, node 10CV strat
C4.5 DT	73.0	Stalog
C4.5 DT	72.7 ± 6.6	Zarndt
Bayes	72.2 ± 6.9	Zarndt
C4.5 (5 ×CV)	72.0	Bennet and Blue
CART	72.8	Ster & Dobnikar
Kohonen	72.7	Statlog
kNN	71.9	Ster & Dobnikar
ID3	71.7 ±6.6	Zarndt
IB3	71.7 ± 5.0	Zarndt
IB1	70.4 ± 6.2	Zarndt
kNN, k = 1,Euclides, raw	69.4 ± 4.4	WD-GM
kNN	67.6	Statlog
C4.5 rules	67.0 ±2.9	Zarndt
OCN2	65.1 ± 1.1	Zarndt
QDA	59.5	Ster, Dobnikar

4 Conclusions

In the proposed framework, it has been observed that the impact of k-means clustering on validation of labeled data results is better classification accuracy for disease diagnosis. Both SVM and Navie Bayes were tested. SVM outperformed Navie Bayes for both the benchmark datasets. The proposed framework is more efficient and gives better results specifically for binary classification problems. The reason for improving accuracy of these classifiers is due to the clustering procedure. It will work based on the assumption that the instance with similar attribute values is more likely to have similar class label as the instance that is closest to it based on the distance principle, such as, the Euclidean distance. The grouping of instances is carried out by clustering process based on feature associated with instances however it is not based on the label associated with data.

References

1. Gan, D.: Diabetes atlas, Brussels: International diabetes Second Eds,
   http://www.eatlas.idf.org/Atlaswebdata/docs/2003Summary.pdf
   (assesed 24/04/2009)
2. Acharya, U.R., Tan, P.H., Subramanian, T., et al.: Automated identification of diabetic type 2 subjects with and without neuropathy using wavelet transform on pedobarograph. J. Medical Systems 32(1), 21–29 (2008)
3. Michie, D., Spiegelhalter, D.J., Taylor, C.C.: Machine learning, neural and statistical Classification. Ellis Horwood, NJ (1994)
4. Bioch, J.C., Meer, O., Potharst, R.: Classification using bayesian neural nets. In: Int. Conf. Neural Networks, pp. 1488–1149 (1996)
5. Carpenter, G.A., Markuzon, N.: ARTMAP-IC and medical diagnosis: Instance counting and inconsistent cases. Neural Networks 11, 323–336 (1998)
6. Deng, D., Kasabov, K.: On-line pattern analysis by evolving self-organizing maps. In: Proc. 5th Biannual Int. Conf. Artificial Neural Networks and Expert System (ANNES), pp. 46–51 (2001)
7. Kayaer, K., Yıldırım, T.: Medical diagnosis on Pima Indian diabetes using general regression neural networks. In: Proc. Int. Conf. Artificial Neural Networks and Neural Information Processing (ICANN/ICONIP), pp. 181–184 (2003)
8. Polat, K., Gunes, S.: An expert system approach based on principal component analysis and adaptive neuro-fuzzy inference system to diagnosis of diabetes disease. J. Digital Signal Processing 17(4), 702–710 (2007)
9. Polat, K., Gunes, S., Aslan, A.: A cascade learning system for classification of diabetes disease: Generalized discriminant analysis and least square support vector machine. Expert Systems with Applications 34(1), 214–221 (2008)
10. Humar, K., Novruz, A.: Design of a hybrid system for the diabetes and heart diseases. J. Expert Systems with Application 35, 82–89 (2008)
11. Newman, D., Hettich, J.S., Blake, C.L.S., Merz, C.J.: UCI Repository of machine learning databases. University of California, Department of Information and Computer Science, Irvine (1998),
    http://www.ics.vci.edu/~mleasn/MLRepository.html
    (last assessed: 1/5/2009)

12. Han, J., Kamber, M.: Data mining: Concepts and techniques, pp. 47–94. Morgan Kaufmann Publisher, San Francisco (2006)
13. Shekhar, R., Gaddam, V., Phoha, V., Kiran, S.: K-Means+ID3 A Novel Method for Supervised Anomaly Detection by Cascading K-Means Clustering and ID3 Decision Tree Learning Methods. IEEE Trans. Knowledge AND Data engineering 19(3), 345–354 (2007)
14. Witten, I.H., Frank, E.: Data mining Practical Machine Learning Tools and Techniques, pp. 363–423. Morgan Kaufmann, San Fransisco (2005)
15. Plat, J.: Fast training of support vector machine using sequential minimal optimization in Advance kernel support vector machine learnining. In: Shoelkopf, B., Burges, C., Somolo, A. (eds.), pp. 61–74. MIT Press, Cambridge (1998)
16. Keerti, S.S., Shevade, S.K., Bhattachayra, C., Murthy, K.R.K.: Improvements to Plato'SMO Algorithmfor SVM classifiere design. Neural Computation 13(3), 637 (2001)
17. John, G.H., Langley, P.: Estimating continuous distributions in Bayesian classifiers. In: Int. Conf. Uncertainty in Artificial Intelligence, San Mateo, pp. 338–345 (1995)
18. Langley, P., Sage, S.: Induction of selective Bayesian classifiers. In: Int. Conf. Uncertainty in Artificial Intelligence. Morgan Kaufmann, Seattle (1994)
19. Delen, D., Walker, G., Kadam, A.: Predicting Breast Cancer Survivability: a Comparison of Three Data Mining Methods. J. Artificial Intelligence in Medicine 34(2), 113–127 (2005)
20. Thora, J., Ebba, T., Helgi, S., Sven, S.: The feasibility of constructing a predictive outcome model for breast cancer using the tools of data mining. J. Expert Systems with Applications 34, 108–118 (2008)
21. Polat, K., Gunes, S.: Breast cancer diagnosis using least square support vector Machine. Digital Signal Processing 17(4), 694–701 (2007)

Digital Watermarking Based Stereo Image Coding

Sanjay Rawat[1], Gaurav Gupta[2], R. Balasubramanian[1], and M.S. Rawat[2]

[1] Department of Mathematics, Indian Institute of Technology Roorkee,
Roorkee-247667, Uttarakhand, India
[2] Department of Mathematics, Hemwati Nandan Bahuguna Garhwal University
Srinagar-246 174, Uttarakhand, India
{sanjudma,guptagaurav.19821,balaiitr,hnbrawat}@gmail.com

Abstract. In this paper, we present a novel stereo-image coding approach using digital watermarking based on discrete cosine transform (DCT) and singular value decomposition (SVD). Disparity obtained from the stereo pair is used as watermark, and is embedded into the left image of the stereo pair. By embedding into one image (left-image) the information needed to recover the other image (right-image), the storage requirements are halved. Instead of applying SVD on whole image, block based SVD scheme is used to embed the data, which increases the robustness of the scheme. A reliable watermark extraction scheme is developed for the extraction of disparity from the distorted images. Extracted disparity can be used to recover the right image of stereo pair as well as recovering 3D information of the scene. A series of experiments are conducted to prove the fidelity and robustness property of the scheme. Error analysis is done after extracting the disparity from the distorted images. The experimental results show that our scheme is highly reliable and is also robust against various attacks.

Keywords: Disparity, Digital watermarking, Discrete cosine transform, Singular value decomposition.

1 Introduction

The advent of the Internet and the wide availability of computers, scanners, and printers make digital data acquisition, exchange, and transmission simple tasks. However, making digital data accessible to others through networks also creates opportunities for malicious parties to make salable copies of copyrighted content without permission of the content owner. Digital watermarking represents a viable solution to the above problem, since it makes possible to identify the author, owner, distributor or authorized consumer of a document [1, 2]. Digital watermarking is based on the science of data hiding. Digital watermarking is a technique of embedding some data into the given media, which can be later extracted or detected for variety of purposes. The data embedded is called as watermark and the given media is called as host or cover media.

On the other hand, stereo vision is used in many applications of 3-D video applications and machines vision. Typically, the transmission or the storage of a stereo image

S. Ranka et al. (Eds.): IC3 2010, Part I, CCIS 94, pp. 435–445, 2010.
© Springer-Verlag Berlin Heidelberg 2010

sequence requires twice as much data volume as a monocular vision system. In this context, digital watermarking can be helpful to transmit the information of stereo images in a secure and robust manner, with equal requirements of monocular image data storage and transmission rate. In the other words, digital watermarking shows a great applicability in the process of secure and robust stereo image coding. Recently, stereo vision has been applied for image coding and security with the help of disparity map. Aydinoglu *et al.*[3] have proposed a region-based stereo image coding algorithm. They have considered three types of regions: occlusion, edge, and smooth regions. The non occluded region is segmented into edge and smooth regions. Each region is composed of fixed size blocks. The disparity for each block in a nonoccluded region is estimated using a block-based approach. The estimated disparity field is encoded by employing a lossy residual uniform scalar quantizer and an adaptive arithmetic coder based on segmentation. Jiang *et al.*[4] have proposed a wavelet-based stereo image pair coding algorithm. The wavelet transform is used to decompose the image into an approximation and detail images. A new disparity estimation technique is developed for the estimation of the disparity field using both approximation and edge images. To improve the accuracy of estimation of wavelet images produced by the disparity compensation technique, the wavelet-based subspace projection technique is developed. Coltuc [5] proposed a stereo-embedding technique using reversible watermarking. Their scheme investigates the storage and bandwidth requirement reduction for stereo images. Instead of compression of stereo pair, they have relied on the embedding of reversible watermarking. The main advantage of their scheme was that the content of images remains available without additional manipulations.

In this paper a robust stereo image coding algorithm using digital watermarking, based on DCT and SVD [6, 7] is presented. Disparities are calculated by two methods, Sum of square difference (SSD) and Gradient method. Final disparity is obtained by taking linear combination of both the disparities. Left image from the stereo pair is used as host image and this disparity is used as watermark in the proposed algorithm. Host image and the disparity map are divided into 16×16 blocks. Blocks of the host image are transformed into frequency domain by applying discrete cosine transform on all the blocks. Disparity map is embedded in the host image by modifying the singular values of the transformed blocks with the singular values of the disparity map blocks. At the receiver's end disparity map is extracted by a reliable extraction scheme. Extracted disparity can be used to recover the right image of stereo pair as well as recovering the 3D information of scene/object.

Rest of the paper is organized as follows. A brief description about disparity estimation, disparity enhancement, discrete cosine transform and singular value decomposition is given in section 2. Proposed watermarking scheme is explained in section 3. Experimental results are given in section 4. Finally conclusions are drawn in section 5.

2 Preliminaries

2.1 Disparity Estimation

In this approach, the initial disparity maps are obtained by applying two local methods simultaneously, sum of square difference (SSD) and gradient. In SSD, for each pixel in the left image (reference image I_l), similarity scores are computed by comparing a finite small window of size 3×3 centered on the pixel of a window in the right image (I_r) by shifting along the corresponding horizontal scan line. The traditional sum-of-squared-differences (SSD) algorithm is described as [8]:

1. The matching cost is the squared difference of intensity values.
2. Aggregation is done by summing up the matching cost over square windows with constant disparity.
3. Disparities are computed by selecting the minimal (winning) aggregated value at each pixel.

$$C_S(u,v,d) = \sum_{(u,v) \in W(u,v)} [I_l(u,v) - I_r(u+d,v)]^2 \qquad (1)$$

where I_l and I_r represent the left and right images of stereo pair and d denotes the disparity at a point (u,v) in the right image.

One of the main drawbacks of SSD is its high sensitivity to radiometric gain and bias. In order to remove this we have used gradient based method which is insensitive to radiometric gain and bias. Gradient based method seeks to determine small local disparities between two images by formulating a differential equation relating motion and image brightness [9]. The disparity by gradient based methods is calculated as follows:

$$C_G(u,v,d) = \sum_{(u,v) \in W_u(u,v)} [\nabla_u I_l(u,v) - \nabla_u I_r(u+d,v)]^2 + \sum_{(u,v) \in W_v(u,v)} [\nabla_v I_l(u,v) - \nabla_y I_r(u+d,v)]^2 \qquad (2)$$

where $W(u,v)$ represent the 3×3 surrounding window at position (u,v).

We used the linear combination of SSD and Gradient method to obtain the final disparity map as follows:

$$E(u,v,d) = C_S(u,v,d) + \lambda * C_G(u,v,d), \ 0 \le \lambda \le 1 \qquad (3)$$

where C_s and C_G are the disparities obtained by SSD and gradient method respectively.

2.2 Disparity Enhancement

In this section, a cross-checking algorithm eliminating unreliable disparity estimation is used for increasing reliability of the disparity map. Cross-checking algorithm is very efficient to remove outlier as used in [10, 11]. Let the pixel (u',v') in the matching image is corresponding to the pixel (u,v) in the reference image. The initial disparities are $d(u',v')$ and $d(u,v)$ in the matching and reference image respectively. If $d(u,v) \ne d(u',v')$, the pixel (u,v) is considered as an outlier. Here we are just comparing left-to-right and right-to-left disparity maps. The reliable correspondence is filtered out by applying a cross-checking technique.

The winner-take-all optimization (WTA) is used to find the optimal disparity map [12]. WTA algorithm takes the lowest (aggregated) matching cost as the selected disparity at each pixel whereas the other algorithms like dynamic programming (DP), graph cut (GC) etc require (in addition to matching cost) the smoothness cost. A limitation of this approach is that the uniqueness of matches is only enforced for one image (the reference image), while points in the other image might get matched to multiple points. Furthermore, In order to obtain better disparity, a mode filter is adopted for preserving boundary of image and effective removal of noise. Mode filter is applied to obtained disparity after cross-checking test.

2.3 Discrete Cosine Transformation

The discrete cosine transform (DCT) represents an image as a sum of sinusoids of varying magnitudes and frequencies. Discrete cosine transform and inverse discrete cosine transform calculation are the bridges that connect the spatial domain and the DCT domain. The equations for the two dimensional DCT and Inverse DCT (IDCT) are as follows:

$$F(m,n) = \frac{2}{\sqrt{MN}} C(m)C(n) \sum_{x=0}^{M-1}\sum_{y=0}^{N-1} f(x,y) \times \cos\frac{(2x+1)m\pi}{2M}\cos\frac{(2y+1)n\pi}{2N} \qquad (4)$$

$$f(x,y) = \frac{2}{\sqrt{MN}} \sum_{m=0}^{M-1}\sum_{n=0}^{N-1} C(m)C(n)F(m,n) \times \cos\frac{(2x+1)m\pi}{2M}\cos\frac{(2y+1)n\pi}{2N} \qquad (5)$$

where $C(m), C(n) = 1/\sqrt{2}$ when $m; n = 0$; otherwise $C(m), C(n) = 1 \cdot f(x,y)$ is the pixel value in the spatial domain, $F(m,n)$ is the pixel value in the DCT domain. M and N represents the block size or image size. The coefficient at the top left corner of the frequency domain matrix stands for the DC value of the image's frequency domain, and the remaining parts are the AC values with the absolute value of the AC in each position representing the magnitude of the energy.

2.4 Singular Value Decomposition (SVD)

Let A be a general real (complex) matrix of order $m \times n$. The singular value decomposition (SVD) of A is the factorization

$$A = U \times S \times V^T \qquad (6)$$

where U and V are orthogonal (unitary) and $S = diag(\lambda_1, \lambda_2, \ldots \ldots \lambda_r)$ where $\lambda_i, i = 1 : r$ are the singular values of matrix A with $r = \min(m, n)$ and satisfying

$$\lambda_1 \geq \lambda_1 \geq \lambda_1 \geq \ldots \ldots \ldots \geq \lambda_r \qquad (7)$$

The first r columns of V are the *right singular vectors* and the first r columns of U are the *left singular vectors* of A. Each singular value specifies the luminance of the image layer while the corresponding pair of singular vectors specifies the geometry of the image layer. For majority of the attacks, change in the largest singular value is very small.

3 Proposed Watermarking Scheme

The proposed watermarking scheme is based on DCT and SVD. Block diagram of the proposed scheme is shown in figure 1. Let us assume that I is the host image of size $M \times N$ and W is the watermark of size $m \times n$. The watermark embedding and extraction algorithms are described next.

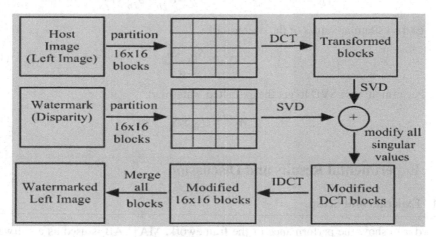

Fig. 1. Block Diagram of Proposed Scheme

3.1 Watermark Embedding Algorithm

1. Divide the host image into non overlapping 16×16 blocks.

2. Apply discrete cosine transform on each block. Let us denote it by I_D

3. Apply SVD on all blocks $\qquad I_D = U_{I_D} \times S_{I_D} \times V_{I_D}^T$ $\qquad\qquad$ (8)

4. Divide the watermark image W into non overlapping 16×16 blocks.

5. Apply SVD on all blocks $\qquad W = U_W \times S_W \times V_W^T$ $\qquad\qquad$ (9)

6. Modify the singular values of I_D as

$$\overline{S_{I_D}} = S_{I_D} + \alpha S_W \qquad\qquad (10)$$

where α is the watermark strength.

7. Perform inverse SVD to get all the modified blocks of I_D.

8. Perform inverse discrete cosine transform on each modified block and then merge all the blocks to get the watermarked image.

3.2 Watermark Extraction Algorithm

The extraction of watermark is inverse process of embedding. Let us denote watermarked image by $\overline{I}$.

1. Divide the watermarked image into non overlapping 16×16 blocks.

2. Apply discrete Cosine transform on each block. Let us denote it by $\bar{I}_D$.

3. Apply SVD on I_D and $\bar{I}_D$

$$I_D = U_{I_D} \times S_{I_D} \times V_{I_D}^T , \quad \bar{I}_D = U_{\bar{I}_D} \times S_{\bar{I}_D} \times V_{\bar{I}_D}^T \qquad (11)$$

4. Extract singular values of the watermark

$$S_{W^{ext}} = \frac{S_{\bar{I}_D} - S_{I_D}}{\alpha} \qquad (12)$$

5. Perform inverse SVD to get the extracted watermark

$$W^{ext} = U_W \times S_{W^{ext}} \times U_W^T \qquad (13)$$

4   Experimental Results and Discussion

4.1   Experimental Setup

In order to show the performance of the framework, MATLAB is used as a software tool. Two different stereo image pairs, namely, Aerial and Tsukuba, shown in figure 2 are used in our experimental study. Aerial and Tsukuba images are of size 400×400 and 288×288 respectively. The Tsukuba images are taken from the www.middle-bury.edu/stereo and aerial images are taken from http://isprs.ign.fr./packages/pack-ages_en.htm. Disparities are calculated by two local methods, Sum of square difference (SSD) and Gradient method. A linear combination of the disparities thus obtained is used as final disparity in our algorithm. This disparity is used as water-mark and the left image of the stereo pair is used as host image. Strength factor α is set to 0.1 for aerial image and 0.2 for Tsukuba image.

(a)   (b)

Fig. 2. (a) Aerial image stereo pair, (b) Tsukuba image stereo pair

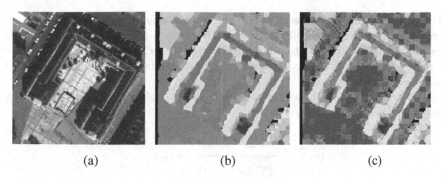

(a)   (b)   (c)

Fig. 3. (a)Watermarked image, (b) obtained disparity and (c) extracted disparity

PSNR (peak signal-to-noise ratio), is used in this paper to analyze the visual quality of the watermarked image $\bar{I}$ in comparison with the original image I. PSNR is defined as:

$$PSNR = 20 \log_{10}\left(\frac{255}{RMSE}\right) \quad dB \tag{14}$$

where
$$RMSE = \sqrt{\frac{1}{m*n}\sum_{i=1}^{m}\sum_{j=1}^{n}\left[I(i,j)^2 - \bar{I}(i,j)^2\right]}$$

The higher the *PSNR* value is, less distortion is there to the host image. PSNR value of the watermarked Aerial image and watermarked Tsukuba image is 41.85782 dB and 43.3849 dB respectively. Watermarked aerial image, obtained disparity and extracted disparity images are shown in figure 3.

4.2 Results and Discussion

To test the robustness of our algorithm we have performed several attacks on the test images. Results for the Ariel image are shown in this paper. The results show that the extracted watermarks are still recognizable despite the images being seriously distorted. The attacks are described as follows:

Filtering Attack: Filtering is the most common manipulation in digital images. We tested our images by applying average filter and median filter with 3×3 window. Results are shown in figure 4.

Blurring and Sharpening Attacks: We tested our algorithm against blurring and sharpening attack. We blurred the image with 3×3 window and increased the sharpness of image by 50. Results are shown in figure 5.

Cropping and Resizing Attacks: We tested our algorithm against resizing and cropping. For resizing, first the size of watermarked images is reduced to 200×200 and then again carried back to original size i.e. 400×400. For cropping attack, watermarked image is cropped from both sides. Results are shown in figure 6.

JPEG Compression: We compressed the watermarked images by JPEG with compression ratio 15:1, 30:1, 50:1 and 80:1. The extracted watermarks are still visually recognizable and are also having high correlation coefficient. Results are shown in figure 7 and 8. From these results we can say that the proposed scheme is robust under JPEG compression.

The performance of the extracted watermarks is evaluated by calculating the correlation coefficient, which is given by

$$\rho\left(w, \overline{w}\right) = \frac{\sum\limits_{i=1}^{r} w(i) \ \overline{w}(i)}{\sqrt{\sum\limits_{i=1}^{r} w(i)} \ \sqrt{\sum\limits_{i=1}^{r} \overline{w}(i)}} \tag{15}$$

where w denotes the singular values of the original watermark, and $\overline{w}$ denotes the singular values of the extracted watermark and $r = \min(m, n)$

Mean of disparity error: The extract disparity and embedded disparity have been normalized in a range [0, 1]. The mean of absolute difference between the normalized extract disparity and embedded disparity has been calculated.

Standard disparity error: extract disparity and embedded disparity have been normalized in a range [0, 1]. The standard deviation of absolute difference between the normalized extract disparity and embedded disparity has been calculated.

The correlation coefficient, mean error and standard deviation error of the extracted watermarks, are given in table 1.

Table 1. Correlation coefficient, mean and standard deviation error between original and extracted watermark (disparity)

Images		Correlation Coefficient		Mean Error		Standard Deviation Error	
		Aerial	Tsukuba	Aerial	Tsukuba	Aerial	Tsukuba
Without attack		0.9956	0.9969	0.0409	0.0910	0.0331	0.0463
Average filtering		0.5520	0.4187	0.3661	0.4443	0.1953	0.1821
Median filtering		0.6854	0.5915	0.3645	0.4405	0.1940	0.1777
Blurring		0.5851	0.4372	0.3682	0.4453	0.1929	0.1814
Sharpening		0.6287	0.6274	0.3437	0.3989	0.1845	0.1864
Cropping		0.8291	0.8289	0.3702	0.4417	0.1777	0.1729
Resizing		0.8182	0.6067	0.3539	0.4365	0.1791	0.1784
JPEG compression	15:1	0.9533	0.9010	0.3355	0.4033	0.1634	0.1633
	30:1	0.9277	0.8755	0.3456	0.4075	0.1700	0.1666
	50:1	0.8901	0.8137	0.3354	0.4213	0.1698	0.1726
	80:1	0.8281	0.7593	0.3528	0.4233	0.1781	0.1749

(a)   (b)   (c)   (d)

Fig. 4. (a)Watermarked image after average filtering (b) extracted disparity (c) Watermarked image after median filtering (d) extracted disparity

(a)   (b)   (c)   (d)

Fig. 5. (a)Watermarked image after blurring (b) extracted disparity (c) Watermarked image after sharpening (d) extracted disparity

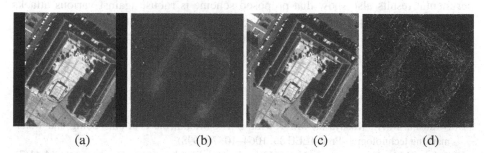

(a)   (b)   (c)   (d)

Fig. 6. (a)Watermarked image after cropping (b) extracted disparity (c) Watermarked image after resizing (d) extracted disparity

(a)   (b)   (c)   (d)

Fig. 7. (a) Watermarked image after JPEG compression (b) extracted disparity (c) Watermarked image after JPEG compression (d) extracted disparity

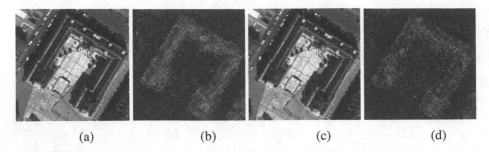

(a)   (b)   (c)   (d)

Fig. 8. (a) Watermarked image after JPEG compression (b) extracted disparity (c) Watermarked image after JPEG compression (d) extracted disparity

5 Conclusion

In this paper a watermarking based stereo image coding is presented. A linear combination of the disparities obtained by two methods is used as final disparity. The disparity thus obtained holds the quality of both the techniques and enhances its quality in terms of sensitivity against radiometric gain and bias. A reliable embedding and extraction scheme based on DCT and SVD is presented. Mean error and standard deviation error between embedded disparity and extracted disparity is calculated. The errors show that the distortion between embedded and extracted disparity is very less, hence 3D information of the scene can be obtained using the extracted disparity. Experimental results also show that proposed scheme is robust against various attacks including JPEG compression. The advantage of our scheme is that it reduces the storage capacity and it is also useful in many applications such as, image security, rightful ownership protection, copyright protection etc..

References

1. Swanson, M.D., Kobayashi, M., Tewfik, A.H.: Multimedia data embedding and watermarking technologies. Proc. IEEE 86, 1064–1087 (1998)
2. Acken, J.M.: How watermarking adds value to digital content. Commun. ACM 41(7), 74–77 (1998)
3. Aydinoglu, H., Kossentini, F., Jiang, Q., Hayes, M.H.I.: Regionbased stereo image coding. In: Proc. of IEEE Int. Conf. on Image Processing, vol. 2, pp. 57–61 (1995)
4. Jiang, Q., Leet, J.J., Hayes, M.H.I.: A wavelet based stereo image coding algorithm. In: Proc. of IEEE Int. Conf. on Acoustics, Speech, and Signal Processing, vol. 6, pp. 3157–3160 (1999)
5. Coltuc, D.: On stereo embedding by reversible watermarking. In: Int. Symp. on Signals, Circuits and Systems (ISSCS 2007), Iasi, Romania, vol. 2, pp. 1–4. IEEE, Piscataway (2007)
6. Ganic, E., Eskicioglu, A.M.: Robust embedding of visual watermarks using DWT-SVD. J. Electron. Imaging 14(4), 043004 (2005)
7. Chandra, D.V.S.: Digital image watermarking using singular value decomposition. In: Proc. of IEEE 45th Midwest Symposium on Circuits and Systems, vol. 3, pp. 264–267 (2002)

8. Scharstein, D., Szeliski, R., Zabih, R.: A taxonomy and evaluation of dense two-frame stereo correspondence algorithms. In: IEEE Workshop on Stereo and Multi-Baseline Vision, pp. 131–140 (2001)
9. Brown, M.Z., Burschka, D., Hager, G.D.: Advances in Computational Stereo. IEEE Trans. on Pattern Analysis and Machine Intelligence (PAMI) 25(8), 993–1008 (2003)
10. Hong, L., Chen, G.: Segment-based stereo matching using graph cuts. In: CVPR, pp. 74–81 (2004)
11. Klaus, A., Sormann, M., Karner, K.: Segment-Based Stereo Matching Using Belief Propagation and a Self-Adapting Dissimilarity Measure. In: International Conference on Pattern Recognition, ICPR 2006 (2006)
12. Zhang, Y., Gong, M., Yang, Y.H.: Local stereo matching with 3D adaptive cost aggregation for slanted surface modeling and sub-pixel accuracy. In: International Conference on Pattern Recognition, Tampa, Florida, Oral Presentation (2008)

Content Based Multimodal Retrieval for Databases of Indian Monuments

Aman Agarwal and Vikas Saxena

Jaypee Institute of Information Technology
A-10, Sector 62, Noida, India 201 307
aman.netaddress@gmail.com, vikas.saxena@jiit.ac.in
http://www.jiit.ac.in

Abstract. With the explosion of multimedia content online image search
has become a viable way of retrieving relevant images. However, current
methods of image search use textual cues to retrieve images and do not
take into account the visual information they contain. In this paper we
aim to crawl and build multimodal image search engines that take into
account both the textual and visual content relevant to the images. We
intend to use off the shelf text search engines to accomplish the above
task, making the construction of image retrieval systems extremely easy.
We build visual models by using the bag of words paradigm and propose
and validate through experimentation a combined multiple vocabulary
scheme that outperforms normal vocabularies.

Keywords: Multimodal retrieval, text and image crawler, focused
crawler, object classification, image filtering.

1 Introduction

The explosion of multimedia content online is making it harder to find relevant
images online. Though image search helps, its current reliance on textual cues
alone to retrieve images is detrimental to performance. The current estimates
state more than 3.6 million images on Flickr, 10 billion images on Facebook,
and even a much greater number in the Google image database. Although image
search engines enable accessing this data a facile task, but they are limited by
the poor precision of the search results. Figure 1 gives the precision statistics
of over 1000 images returned by Google Image search for 10 object classes. The
precision is as low as 46% for one of the classes tested here (Golden Temple) and
averages to about 67%.

Crawling and collecting the relevant dataset is the primary job of any image
search engine. The vastness of the multimedia data available out there makes
focused crawling a very vital task. In this paper we begin by collecting our
dataset by focused crawling using textual cues and refining them using visual
models. Most of the previous work has primarily focused only on collecting image databases, thus leaving us without a standard database having both images
and their corresponding text. Li et al. [4] overcame the download restriction by

S. Ranka et al. (Eds.): IC3 2010, Part I, CCIS 94, pp. 446–455, 2010.
© Springer-Verlag Berlin Heidelberg 2010

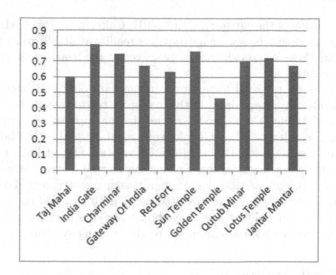

Fig. 1. Google Image Search Precision. Precision over 1000 images returned by Google Image search for 10 specific object classes. Class 'Golden Temple' has the lowest precision of 46%. Average precision is 67%.

the search engines by generating multiple related queries using a standard lexical database and also translating their queries into several languages, reaching out to the regional websites of the search engines. Fergus et al.[5,6] re-ranked images obtained from Google image search using visual algorithms. Berg et al. [7] aims to automatically construct image datasets for several animal categories. They gather images from the 1000 web pages returned by querying Google text search. They use LDA (Latent Dirichlet Allocation) [8] to identify a number of latent topics and corresponding exemplary images from the crawled set. These exemplary images are labeled by the user as relevant or background; this labeled set is used to train their voting classifier. Their classifier incorporates textual, shape, color, and texture features. The Tiny Image technical report [9] focuses on collecting a large number of tiny images, not merely to achieve high accuracy for each keyword. They have succeeded in collecting about 80 million images for 75,062 non-abstract nouns in English. On a similar approach ImageNet [3] uses the hierarchal structure of WordNet to populate their dataset. As of present, they have collected 3.2 million images for 5247 synsets. But they rely on human intervention to verify each candidate image collected for a given synset. To collect a large number of images, they append their query with the word from their parent synsets. Schroff et al. [2] use text information to rank retrieved images. The top ranked images hence obtained form a training dataset for the visual classifier. A similar process termed OPTIMOL, used by Li et al. [1] uses the first 5-10 images returned from Google image search to train their classifier. OPTIMOL classifies images as either background or relevant. If the image is classified as relevant, the classifier uses incremental learning to refine its model. As the classifier accepts more images, these images allow the classifier to obtain a richer description of the category. Caltech101, Caltech256, PASCAL, LabelMe, Lotus Hill are amongst the few image datasets readily available over the internet. Over the years these datasets have widely served as the benchmarks of computer vision applications.

Current work on retrieval focusses on image data only and hence, all these datasets provide only image data. In this paper we try to remedy this by collecting an image dataset for multimodal retrieval. Our approach features querying Google image search as well as Google web search to gather candidate results and populate a seeding set. By crawling the vast amount of links in the seeding set we populate a huge database of images as well as text data relevant to the image. Our system essentially gathers a vast image and text database from the internet. These images are represented using both text and the bag of visual words model. Multimodal text and image based search is performed on the entire dataset with high precision as compared to the existing systems.

2   Proposed Approach

This section describes in detail the following stages of the system in their entirety:

Stage 1 - Data Collection: Downloading the initial set of seed images and expanding the crawling system to acquire images and their relevant text and other relevant information and index the text to the text search database.

Stage 2 - Filtering retrieved images: Removing those images from the database which are small in size or are dominated by human faces.

Stage 3 - Text and Image Retrieval: Extraction of SIFT features, perform K Means and populate the *bag of words* model for each image file and index these to the search engine system and hence, perform text and image based retrieval on the system.

For the purpose of classifying images and measuring precision statistics, we currently focus on images of Indian monumental sites over the internet, taking in account the following 10 classes : Taj Mahal, India Gate, Gateway of India, Red Fort, Jantar Mantar, Konark Sun Temple, Charminar, Golden Temple, Qutub Minar, Lotus Temple.

The stages involved in the processing of the system are explained as follows:

2.1   Data Collection

We begin by querying the Google Image search database with the query phrase. Since only the first 1000 results can be obtained from each, we have with us a pool of web links specific to the query phrase. This pool of web links serve the purpose of a seeding set. By seeding to the links, images are downloaded along with their relevant text, from the web page where the seed image originated. Secondly we also query the Google Web Search with the same query word. The obtained 1000 results again serve as the seeding set, wherein all the images on these web pages

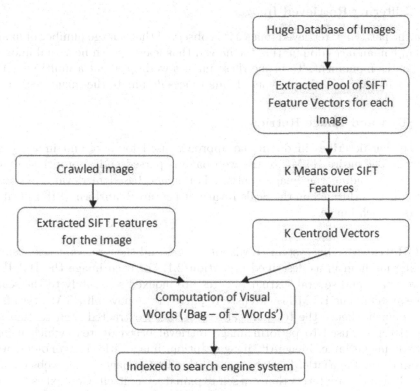

Fig. 2. General Preprocessing Framework. Visual words i.e., ''bag-of-words' are computed with the help of precomputed K Means centroids. These visual words are indexed to the search engine system.

are downloaded. Through this approach we overcome the 1000 results restriction barrier by Google search. In general, most of the web pages contain more than a single image; hence we have with us more than thousand images for a single query word. Small images i.e., with resolution 120 x 120 pixels or less are discarded. In all cases, the image text tags, HTML tags and the text surrounding the image are extracted. We therefore have with us a dataset that contains several thousand images for each class along with the relevant text for each image. Over time our system crawls for new or updated web pages and updates the database for any new images. Table 1 gives the precision statistics over 1000 images returned by the Google Image search for the ten monumental categories.

The great diversity of images present over the internet makes it an onerous task to access, manage and rightly classify the data. Polysemy also highly affects the precision for the retrieved results over the internet. For example, for a query taj mahal, several results include brand names (taj mahal tea) or hotel names (Taj Mahal hotel) etc. Due to this, it is of utmost importance to have an efficient image retrieval system and robust object classification system to manage the data correctly.

2.2   Filtering Retrieved Images

From the pattern of retrieved images it is observed that a large number of images contain human faces dominating the image, thus leaving with no visual information for the monument. To prune these images we implement a multi-view face detector to filter out images where human faces dominate the image region.

2.3   Text and Image Retrieval

This section describes in detail the approach used for text and image based retrieval. The entire HTML of the web page is parsed and appropriate text is extracted including the image context. For image based retrieval a K-Means clustering is performed on the Scale Invariant Feature Transform (SIFT) feature vectors of each image.

Text Retrieval. Our system crawls for images and their relevant text using a crawling mechanism as described in section 2.1. For each image the HTML of the web page and several textual features are indexed separately to the search engine system. The HTML is extensively parsed to remove all HTML tags from the document, hence the textual features used are extracted. Ten textual features [10,2] are used to perform image retrieval based on text which include Context, imageName, imageAlt, imageCaption, imageTitle, imageFolder, websiteName, webPageTitle, hyperlink and otherText. ImageName, websiteName and websiteTitle are terms that are self explanatory in itself. Context is the textual data that is 200 characters on either side of the image on the HTML page. ImageFolder is the location name (folder name on the server) where the image is stored, imageAlt and imageTitle is a property in the IMG HTML tag. Although HTML does not have a reserved caption for an image, the HTML of the web page where the image is located can signal an image caption located near the image. Often, images are placed on web pages as hyperlinks to other web pages, hyperlink property refers to the URL of the hyperlink. OtherText refers to the text on the entire HTML apart from the context. Since a considerable number of images are now present over the internet, and an massive number of these are being uploaded daily, image type (bmp, gif, jpeg etc) serve no purpose of providing valuable information of any sorts, hence are neglected. A standard list of stop words [11] is used to expurgate the words during text parsing. The text search engine system creates several different search indexes for different text tags. Different criteria of searches are developed based on these indexes.

Image Retrieval. To perform image based image retrieval, we make use of local SIFT feature vectors for all images in the dataset. We prefer using the SIFT feature [12] vectors because SIFT features are invariant to image scaling, translation, and rotation, and partially invariant to illumination changes. Features are extracted through a staged filtering process that identifies stable points in scale space. Each SIFT feature vector is a 128 dimensional vector of the form $x_i = (a_1, a_2, a_3, ..., a_{128})$ wherein $a_1, a_2, a_3, ..., a_{128}$ are the 128 dimensions of a

SIFT feature vector. Along with the feature vector following four values are also associated with each feature vector $y_i = (X, Y, Scale, Orientation)$. Here (X, Y) are the relative coordinates in the image where the feature is present. Each image is resized to a size of 400px * 400px in size. On an average for a 400px * 400px image we are able to extract 1400 SIFT features in about 2 seconds time. For the purpose of building a reliable image model for later image retrieval, K Means algorithm is used to cluster the feature vector space. K means clustering algorithm is a method to cluster the data, thus partitioning into n observations. K means measures the Euclidian distance of each vector to the current cluster and associates the vector to the nearest cluster. K means model is built using a dataset of 1100 images (having 1177049 feature vectors) for 5000, 20000 and 30000 means. For each image added to the database, visual words are calculated for its features using the cluster vectors, which were a result of the k means clustering. For each image we obtain a bag of words which are indexed to the search engine system and used for the process of image retrieval. The final image retrieval features a combined vocabulary model which is built by combining the vocabularies from all 3 clustering models i.e., from 5000, 20000 and 30000 means into a single file, each model words distinguished by a unique identifier. Our results demonstrate that this combined vocabulary model performs better than the models built from individual vocabularies.

3   Results

3.1   Crawling

Figure 3 gives the statistics for the average number of accurate images retrieved for the process during crawling web pages. It can be observed that more number of images are retrieved for the first 100 links crawled. As the seeding set is acquired

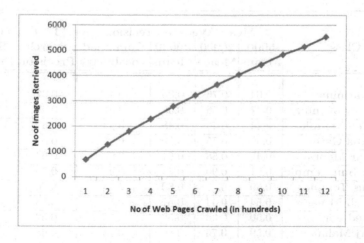

Fig. 3. Statistics for the number of retrieved images during the crawling process

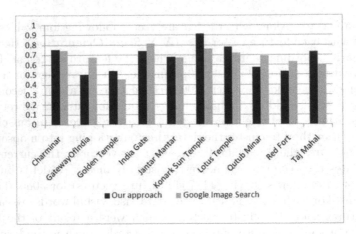

Fig. 4. Precision comparison statistics. Comparison of precision of our approach with the Google Image Search. Our system performs better in most of the classes while performs slightly lower in a few classes.

from the Google search database, it is eminent to have more accurate images for the first few results used as the seeding set. The number of images retrieved henceforth decreases for the next 300 web links and come to a standing value after.

3.2 Image Retrieval

Comparison with Google Image Search. A detailed comparison with Google results makes it evident that our system performs better than Google Image.

Table 1. Comparison Statistics between text and image retrieval of our system versus Google Image Search

Class	Mean Average Precision				Text Search Precision	Google Image Search Precision
	5000 Means	20000 Means	30000 Means	Combined Vocabulary		
Charminar	0.64	0.75	0.80	0.81	0.67	0.74
Gateway of India	0.47	0.56	0.59	0.61	0.57	0.67
Golden Temple	0.44	0.46	0.48	0.53	0.39	0.45
India Gate	0.59	0.75	0.79	0.74	0.67	0.81
Jantar Mantar	0.47	0.58	0.61	0.68	0.62	0.67
Konark Sun Temple	0.91	0.90	0.88	0.91	0.79	0.67
Lotus Temple	0.69	0.77	0.80	0.78	0.70	0.72
Qutub Minar	0.54	0.54	0.57	0.57	0.53	0.69
Red Fort	0.50	0.56	0.58	0.53	0.52	0.63
Taj Mahal	0.59	0.76	0.80	0.73	0.68	0.60

Table 1 compares the precision between our system and Google Image Search over the web. From the results, it is observed that though our system provides lower precision than Google image search for object classes such as India Gate and Qutub Minar, it out rightly performs better than the latter in object classes like the Konark Sun Temple. The lower precision of our system in the two above mentioned classes is accounted to the poor ranking of the image results within the search system, which leave us with a below par result set. For a more detailed comparison, Table 1 provides a comprehensive in depth precision comparison among the 2 systems for each object class. We compare the precision of the results retrieved from Google Image Search and our approach at 100 image recall. It is rightly observed that our approach performs better than Google image search. For certain classes such as Jantar Mantar, our results are at par with Google.

3.3   Comparison with Text Search

Table 1 clearly displays that image input search method performs better than the text search methods. This is primarily because text search is based on the metatags and other relevant textual information associated with the image. On

Class	Text Based Retrieval	Image Based Retrieval
Taj Mahal		
Gateway of India		

Fig. 5. Comparison of retrieved results with text as well as image query. Images in red boxes signify erronious result for the monument.

the contrary, Image search is based on visual cues and text has no role to play in this approach.

3.4 Mean Average Precision for Different K Means Model

Table 1 gives the precision statistics for all k means model with means = 5000, 20000, 30000. The best precision is obtained when we combine all the different vocabularies into one.

Text and Image based Retrieval. Figure 5 compares the results obtained based on a text query as well as image query. Precision is improved when an input query to the search system is an image. This is primarily because text incorporates errors due to polysemy, which are removed through efficient image algorithms. It is observed that for an input query of taj mahal, we retrieve an image of a tea stall named as taj mahal or the Taj Mahal hotel, instead of the actual monument. On giving an image as input to the system, only those images are retrieved as results which share common features to the input image, hence the precision increases greatly.

4 Future Work

Future work would focus on building an incremental classifier learning model that learns itself to the newly in-class retrieved images. Hence the object model strengthens itself at each iteration. This not only increases the precision at each iteration but makes manual human intervention negligilble.

References

1. Li, L.-J., Wang, G., Fei-Fei, L.: OPTIMOL: automatic Online Picture collection via Incremental Model Learning. In: Computer Vision and Pattern Recognition, CVPR, Minneapolis (2007)
2. Schroff, F., Criminisi, A., Zisserman, A.: Harvesting Image Databases From The Web. In: Proceedings of the 11th International Conference on Computer Vision, Rio de Janeiro, Brazil (2007)
3. Deng, J., Dong, W., Socher, R., Li, L.-J., Li, K., Fei-Fei, L.: ImageNet: A Large Scale Hierarchical Image Database. In: Computer Vision and Pattern Recognition, CVPR, Miami (2009)
4. Collins, B., Deng, J., Li, K., Fei-Fei, L.: Towards scalable dataset construction: An active learning approach. In: Proceedings of the 10th European Conference on Computer Vision, ECCV, Marseille, France (2008)
5. Fergus, R., Fei-Fei, L., Perona, P., Zisserman, A.: Towards scalable dataset construction: An active learning approach. In: Proceedings of the 10th International Conference on Computer Vision, ICCV, Beijing, China (2005)
6. Fergus, R., Perona, P., Zisserman, A.: A Visual Category Filter for Google Images. In: Proceedings of the 8th European Conference on Computer Vision, ECCV, Prague, Czech Republic (2004)
7. Berg, T.L., Forsyth, D.A.: Animals on the Web, Computer Vision and Pattern Recognition, CVPR, New York (2006)

8. Blei, D.M., Ng, A.Y., Jordan, M.I.: Latent Dirichlet Allocation. Journal of Machine Learning Research 3, 993–1022 (2003)
9. Torralba, A., Fergus, R., Freeman, W.T.: 80 Million Tiny Images: a Large Database for Non-Parametric Object and Scene Recognition. IEEE PAMI 30, 1958–1970 (2008)
10. Frankel, C., Swain, M.J., Athitsos, V.: Webseer: An Image Search Engine for the World Wide Web. In: Computer Vision and Pattern Recognition, CVPR, San Juan, Puerto Rico (2007)
11. Onix Text Retrieval Toolkit,
    http://www.lextek.com/manuals/onix/stopwords1.html
12. Lowe, D.G.: Object Recognition from Local Scale-Invariant Features. In: International Conference on Computer Vision, Corfu, Greece, pp. 1150–1157 (2009)

Evolutionary Based Automated Coverage Analysis for GUI Testing

Abdul Rauf, Sajid Anwar, Naveed Kazim, and Arshad Ali Shahid

Department of Computer Science,
National University of Computer & Emerging Sciences (NUCES), Islamabad, Pakistan
{a.rauf,sajid.anwar,naveed.kazim,arshad.ali}@nu.edu.pk

Abstract. In recent times, software industry has seen the immense expansion in its popularity. Graphical user interface (GUI) is of the most important and ground breaking factor behind the exponential growth of acceptance of software systems. Beside this popularity, software organizations are trying best to optimize the quality of delivered products. In software development life cycle, software testing is one major phase having focus towards improved software quality. Increased attention towards GUI in development helped in materialization of GUI testing as a vital branch of software testing. Manual efforts to test GUI have revealed a lot of problems, which, ultimately led towards automation of GUI testing. This paper presents a novel approach towards automation of GUI test coverage analysis based on an evolutionary algorithm, Particle Swarm Optimization (PSO). Another objective that has been tried to achieve is keeping number of test cases at minimum side.

Keywords: GUI Testing; Multi-objective optimization; Coverage Criterion; Coverage Analysis; Multi Objective PSO.

1 Introduction

Software testing, being one of the most crucial phases of software development life cycle, deserves a major focus and attention. Hence a growing concern of software development organizations is effective and thorough software testing. But manually testing software can cost for about 67% of the total cost of software development [1]. Because of this time consuming and effort demanding nature, manual software testing is now being discouraged. Increase of test execution speed, ease in repetition to run tests, and obtaining a high coverage of functionality are some of the reported benefits of automated testing and hence automation of software test activity is getting very high popularity.

Graphical user interface (GUI) has made software applications very easy and efficient to use [2]. GUI design is now being considered as one of critical success factor in the software marketplace of today's software programs. GUI design is being focused a lot while developing a software, but it is very difficult to thoroughly test GUI. Manually testing a GUI application is a nightmare as GUI provides high flexibility while interacting with them. Freedom offered by GUI can be presumed by the fact that a user can access a particular component in a software system by following multiple itineraries of events. A lot of efforts have been put to overcome the problems

S. Ranka et al. (Eds.): IC3 2010, Part I, CCIS 94, pp. 456–466, 2010.

incurred by manual testing of GUIs. Many frameworks and approaches have been suggested and developed to minimize the efforts required for GUI testing and to achieve the confidence in quality of GUI applications. Recently, evolutionary algorithms (EAs) have been tried to solve problems faced by automated software testing. There are two major types of evolutionary algorithms that have been used for software testing: Single objective evolutionary algorithms and multiple objective evolutionary algorithms. A general single-objective optimization problem is defined as minimizing (or maximizing) f(x) subject to $g_i(x) \leq 0$, i = {1,2, 3. . . , m}, and $h_j(x) = 0$, j = {1,2,3 . . . , p} $x \in \Omega$. A solution minimizes (or maximizes) the scalar f(x) where x is a n-dimensional decision variable vector x = $(x_1,x_2. . . , x_n)$ from some universe Ω [4]. Evolutionary algorithm works on single objective optimization principle. EA can be used for finding out optimized test suite for GUI testing as well as it can be used for coverage analysis [3]. In case of GUI testing, evolutionary algorithm searches for optimal test parameter combinations that satisfy a predefined test criterion. This test criterion is represented through a "coverage function" that measures how much of the automatically generated optimization parameters satisfies the given test criterion.

In this paper we are proposing GUI test automation by multi objective PSO based on event flow nature of GUI. We have set following objectives for our multi-objective optimization problem:

- To minimize the number of event based GUI test cases.
- To maximize the coverage of GUI test cases.

The major contributions of our proposed technique are following:

- Test coverage analysis is fully automated by using MO-PSO
- Optimization of test cases is through evolutionary algorithm MO-PSO.
- One indigenous application [calculator] was selected to experiment with.
- Results of the experiments are very encouraging and promising comparing to previous approach.

The remainder of the paper is organized as follows: in next Section, we discuss related work in field of software testing, GUI testing and optimization techniques. Section 3 describes problem modeling. Section 4 describes proposed method while section 5 presents results of experiments related to test case optimization and maximizing coverage. In section 6, some future directions have been presented and conclusion of the paper has also been presented in this paper.

2 Related Work

GUI testing is quite a different practice than software testing. It involves many unique features that are quite different from the common practices of software testing. Although many of the conventional software testing techniques are being implied in GUI testing but their success rate is quite lesser than expected.

While evolutionary techniques, are well researched for software testing, relatively little research has been done in the area of evolutionary GUI testing. Evolutionary testing is distinguished in a sense that it uses meta-heuristic search for software testing. An example of evolutionary algorithms is Genetic Algorithms (GA). There have been a number of studies that use genetic algorithms (GA's) for software testing.

Jones et al proposed a technique to generate test-data for branch coverage using GA [16, 17]. This technique has shown good results with number of small programs. Pargas et al used a GA based on the control dependence graph to search for test data that give good coverage [18]. They used the original test suite developed for the SUT as the seed for the GA. They compare their system to random testing on six small C programs. For the smallest programs, there is no difference, but for the three largest programs, the GA-based method outperforms random testing. Tracey et al presents a framework for test-data generation based on optimization algorithms for structural testing [19]. Yongzhong Lu et al presented a new GUI automation test model based on the event-flow graph modeling [20]. Wasif Afzal et al [21] have presented a systematic mapping study to present a broad review of primary studies on the application of search-based optimization techniques to non-functional testing. This study puts an effort to identify the gaps in the application of search-based optimization techniques to different types of non-functional testing.

Another example of evolutionary algorithms is Particle Swarm Optimization (PSO). Andreas Windisch et al [28] used Particle Swarm Optimization to investigations particle swarm optimization (PSO) as a heuristic search technique to search for adequate test data. Authors performed experiments with 25 small artificial test objects and 13 more complex industrial test objects taken from various development projects. Authors believe that higher effectiveness and efficiency generally attributed to PSO helps in conclusion that it will improve evolutionary structural testing. The results of the experiments show that particle swarm optimization is competitive with genetic algorithms and even outperforms them for complex cases [28]. Even though the genetic algorithm yields a covering test case faster than particle swarm optimization in some cases, the latter is much faster than the genetic algorithm in the majority of the cases [28]. Khin Haymar Saw Hla proposed particle swarm optimization (PSO) algorithm to prioritize the test cases automatically based on the modified software units [29]. The goal was to prioritize the test cases to the new best order, based on modified software components, so that test cases, which have new higher priority, can be selected in the regression testing process [29]. The empirical results show that by using the PSO algorithm, the test cases can be prioritized in the test suites with their new best positions effectively and efficiently [29].

3   Problem Modeling

In this section we are going to discuss some technical terms related to multi objective optimization problems and working of PSO. Also modeling of our problem, as a multi-objective optimization problem is presented in this section.

In recent times, evolutionary algorithms have become popular in the field of software testing and several approaches to software testing have been published. Genetic algorithms and Particle swarm optimization are two popular approaches used in evolutionary algorithms. Kennedy J. and Eberhart R.C. drew the world's attention towards particle swarm optimization (PSO) inspired by the sequence of steps of a bird flock in 1995 [26]. PSO has shown a high convergence speed in multi-objective optimization. In particle swarm optimization, the system is initialized with a population of random solutions, called particles. Each particle preserves its own recent position and velocity as well as its personal best position investigated (discovered) so far. Besides retaining these personal values, each swarm keeps track of global best position achieved by all of the members. The iterative application of updating position and velocity through certain rules leads to an optimization of these parameters. During the process of optimization each of the particles explores certain space, whereas their neighbors and the whole swarm, also has explored a certain other regions. This leads to further explorations of regions that turned out to be profitable. In particle swarm optimization, personal best for a particle refers to the best previous position of that particle *while global best points to the* best previous position of the entire population.

To illustrate the working of our algorithm to optimize the coverage function, Let us take a simple run of simple PSO to our work. This example is just to illustrate the working of evolutionary algorithm to problem of GUI test coverage. Dataset of event sequences, we have chosen for simple run is being shown in table 1.

Table 1. Dataset of Event Sequences

1,2
1,3,2
1,4,2
1,4,3,2
1,4,3,5,2

For the sake of simplicity, we suppose inertia w = 0.1; and $c_1r_1 = c_2r_2 = 0.2$

We have taken three particles, p1, p2, p3 having event ID's as dimensions and fitness of each particle is calculated based on number of event sequences (shown in table 1) being followed by each particle.

P1= 2, 1,5,4,3 0/5
P2= 1, 4,4,5,1 0/5
P3= 1, 4,5,1,3 0/5

Each of the given particles is representing its local best and let's supposes that P1 is the global best for the given iteration. To keep things simple, velocity of each dimension of every particle is being initialized from 1 as shown below:

$V_1 = [1.1.1.1.1]$
$V_2 = [1.1.1.1.1]$
$V_3 = [1.1.1.1.1]$

After updating the velocity of each particle, we will get following updated velocity for particle 1.

$V_1 = [0.1, 0.1, 0.1, 0.1, 0.1]$

With the change in velocity of particle1, its position will be updated according to the following:

$P_1 = [2.1, 1.1, 5.1, 4.1, 3.1]$

As we got continuous values, we will round off the position of each particle and it will be:

$P_1 = [2, 1, 5, 4, 3]$ as there is no change in dimensions of P_1 (comparing to initial dimensions of P1), so its fitness function will remain 0/5, hence, local best for particle one will remain the previous local best.

Updating velocity and position of particle2, we will get following results:

V_2 = 0.3, -0.5, 0.3, -0.1, 0.5 [Velocity Update]
P_2 = 1.3, 3.5, 4.3, 4.9, 1.5 [Position update]
P_2 = 1, 4, 4, 5, 2 [Position Round Off]

Updated particle P2 has fitness function of 2/5, as it is covering 2 paths of test data. Having better fitness than previous iteration, local best of P2 will be updated.
Similarly updating particle 3, we will get following:

V_3 = 0.3, -0.5, 0.1, 0.7, 0.1 [Velocity Update]
P_3 = 1.3, 3.5, 5.1, 1.7, 3.1 [Position update]
P_3 = 1, 4, 5, 2,3 [Position Round Off]
P_3 has an updated fitness function of 2/5 so it will be the local best for P_3. As P_2 and P_3, both have fitness function 2/5 so any of them can be global best. Let's say P_2 is having the global best.
Similarly after having one more iteration, we will get the following updated values.

V_1 = -0.19, 0.61, -0.19, 0.21, -0.19 [Velocity Update]
P_1= 1.81, 1.61, 4.81, 4.21, 2.81 [Position update]
P_1 = 2, 2, 5, 4,3 [Position Round Off]
V_2 = 0.03, -0.05, 0.03, - 0.01, 0.05 [Velocity Update]
P_2= 1.03, 3.95, 4.03, 4.99, 2.05 [Position update]
P_2 = 1, 4, 4, 5, 2 [Position Round Off]
V_3 = 0.03, -0.5, -0.19, 0.67, -0.19 [Velocity Update]
P_3= 1.3, 3.95, 4.81, 2.67, 2.81 [Position update]
P_3 = 1, 4, 5, 3, 3 [Position Round Off]
P_1 has a fitness function of 0/5, P_2 has a fitness function of 2/5 and P_3 has a fitness function of 0/5. So these will be no change in local best or global best of any particle.

Similarly the experiment will continue, unless stopping criterion is met or required coverage (fitness function) is achieved.

The position and velocity of each particle are updated according to following equations [30]:

$$x_i(t) = x_i (t-1) + v_i(t) . \tag{1}$$

$$v_i(t) = W * v_i(t-1) + c_1 r_1 (X_i^{pb} - X_i(t)) + c_2 r_2 (X_i^{gb} - X_i(t)) \tag{2}$$

where $X_i(t)$ is the position of particle P_i at time t and $V_i(t)$ is the velocity of particle P_i at time t. w is the inertia factor; c_1 represents the self confidence of the particle; c_2 represents particle's confidence in its society or swarm; r_1 and r_2 are constants whose values are randomly chosen between 0 and 1. X_i^{pb} is the ith dimension of the personal best position reached so far by the particle under consideration. X_i^{gb} is the ith dimension of the global best position reached so far by the entire swarm. In equation 2, the first term, $W*V_i(t-1)$ is the current motion of the particle, while the second term $c_1 r_1 (X_i^{pb} - X_i(t))$ represents particle's memory influence and last term $c_2 r_2 (X_i^{gb} - X_i(t))$ represents the influence of swarm on the particle.

The multiobjective optimization problem can be defined as "a vector of decision variables which satisfies constraints and optimizes a vector function whose elements represent the objective functions" [5]. These functions form a mathematical description of performance criteria which are usually in conflict with each other. Hence, the term "optimizes" means finding such a solution which would give the values of all the objective functions acceptable to the decision makers [5].

Our problem has two objectives, maximizing the coverage for GUI testing and minimizing the number of test cases to optimize the cost. Both of these objectives are clearly in an inverse relation, as increasing coverage of testing demands more test cases and vice versa.

4   Proposed Method

To test GUI and analyze the coverage, we have proposed a method based upon Multi Objective Particle Swarm Optimization (MOPSO). For this purpose we have used a multi objective PSO based upon the concept of maintaining dominated tree.

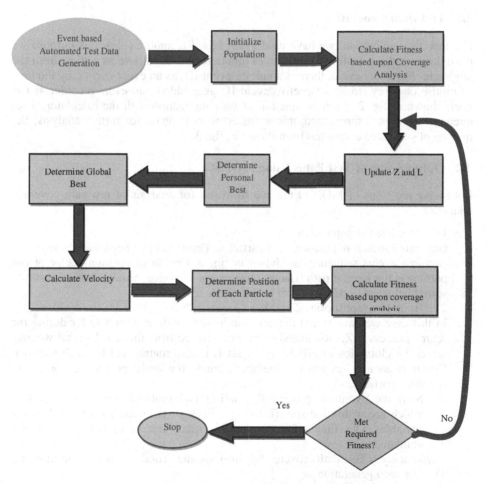

Fig. 1. Block Diagram of Multi-Objective PSO

Dominated tree is constructed in such a way that final composite point dominates all other composite points. The selection of the global best for an individual in the swarm is based upon its closeness to an individual in the non dominated set. For any member of the swarm, x_i, a composite point c_j is chosen such that c_j is not dominated by x_i and x_i dominates c_{j-1}. The global best for an individual x_i is that archive member of c_j contributing the vertex which is less than or equal to the corresponding objective in x_i. A set of local best solutions L is also maintained for each swarm member. Local best position for each member is selected uniformly from this set.

The used MOPSO algorithm has been explained with the help of a block diagram in fig. 1. We have divided our proposed system into two major blocks.

- Test data [Test Cases] generation
- Optimization [minimization] of test paths [cases] using MOPSO

4.1   Test Data Generation

For test data generation, we have used event based techniques. For this purpose we have developed a calculator that receives inputs both from mouse as well as from the keyboard. For every event, there is a unique event ID, as an event occurs, by the help of mouse or a key stroke, respective event ID gets added into event recorder as has been shown in fig. 2. After completion of user interaction with the calculator, a sequence of events is formulated, this is passed to next phase for further analysis. Sequence of generated events has been shown in fig. 3.

4.2   Optimization of Test Paths Using MOPSO

Following are steps of MOPSO that we followed for analysis of test path coverage analysis:

1)   Initialize the population
Generate random population of n particles. Particles have been formed from the captured events sequences as shown in fig. 3. Length of position vector of our particle is the longest path (Longest test case). We have initialized these chromosomes between 1 and maximum length of the test case.
2)   Build two repositories Z and L
In this case we have stored the non dominated solutions found so far during the search process in Z. Dominated tree is constructed from this set Z so that we may select the global leader efficiently. A set L is also maintained for each member. Currently each L has just one member namely the initial position of the corresponding particle..
3)   Start the evolution process Population is initialized with random values which are within the specified range. Each particle consists of the decision variables. Our fitness function is how much test cases have successfully validated?
      Accuracy = Test Paths covered by chromosome/ Total number of chromosome
4)   For each generation
      a)   Update the velocity of each particle.
            Calculate the new velocity for each particle according to equation no 2.
      b)   Update the position of each particle.

Determine the new position for each particle according to equation no 1. Since the position vector in continuous PSO usually consists of real values, we have rounded off the values to the nearest integer. In this way the algorithm was made to work on discrete data. We have also made it sure that the resulting position is in the specified interval for each dimension.

c)   Update non dominated global set Z.

If the solution found is non dominated with respect to members of Z, add it to Z. If the solution dominates any member of Z, then we have deleted that member from Z and then included the current solution in Z. The composite points in dominated tree will also be updated if an updating occurs in Z. By using dominated tree, we have selected the global best for each particle based upon its closeness to non dominated members stored in Z.

d)   Update local set L of each particle.

Since there is comparatively small number of Pareto solutions stored locally than globally, local best position for each particle is selected uniformly from the corresponding updated L.

5)   End

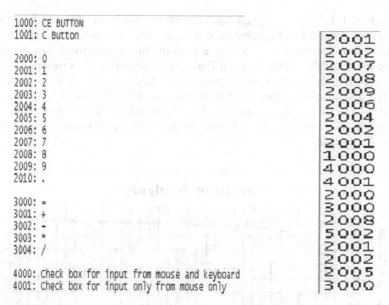

```
1000: CE BUTTON
1001: C Button                          2001
                                        2002
2000: 0                                 2007
2001: 1                                 2008
2002: 2                                 2009
2003: 3                                 2006
2004: 4                                 2004
2005: 5                                 2002
2006: 6                                 2001
2007: 7                                 1000
2008: 8                                 4000
2009: 9                                 4001
2010: .                                 2000
                                        3000
3000: =                                 2008
3001: +                                 5002
3002: -                                 2001
3003: *                                 2002
3004: /                                 2005
                                        3000
4000: Check box for input from mouse and keyboard
4001: Check box for input only from mouse only
```

Fig. 2. Event ID's of Calculator Application   **Fig. 3.** Sequence of Generated Events

5 Results and Discussion

We have used a multi objective PSO based upon the concept of maintaining dominated tree. Our system generates multiple solutions to the origin and optimizes the solution using multi objective PSO. The solutions are then checked against the many predefined quality measures. Solutions are selected to build Pareto Front. Table 2 shows the coverage achieved by the number of generations for which the experiments

Table 2. Coverage achieved according to Number of Generations

Number of Generations	Coverage Achieved
300	65%
325	70%
350	76%
375	81%
400	85%
425	88%
450	91%
475	92%
500	92%

were conducted. In the fig. 4. graph has been shown for Pareto front formed by plotting coverage achieved and number of test cases. Fig. 4. shows that while trying to maximize one objective, we are facing a tradeoff in form of minimization in other objective function. Therefore, we must find a good compromise between maximizing the dual objective, according to the requirements and conditions. Also the results have shown the overall effectiveness and improvement that our proposed technique has achieved in effective coverage analysis. We are in the process of generating further test cases for other applications to further examine the performance of our approach for coverage analysis.

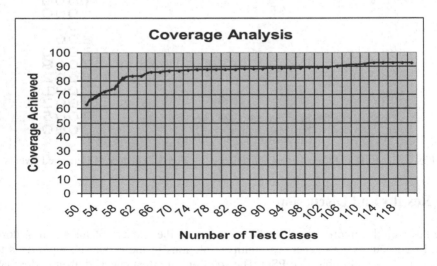

Fig. 4. Coverage analysis of proposes technique

6 Conclusion and Future Work

Graphical User Interface testing has always been considered a critical element of overall testing paradigm for software applications. In this paper, we have proposed a multi objective PSO based technique for coverage analysis of GUI testing. The technique has been subjected to extensive testing. And the experiments have shown encouraging results. The results have also shown enhanced coverage increase in number of generations. The proposed technique offers an exciting new area of research which can be applied using different other artificial intelligence techniques. Our aim is to extend this technique in such a way that it is automatically able to generate correct test data for the complete test coverage.

Acknowledgments. The first author, Abdul Rauf (042-320110Eg2-317) is sponsored by Higher Education Commission of Pakistan, Government of Pakistan, and wishes to acknowledge HEC for funding.

References

1. Hackner, D.R., Memon, A.M.: Test case generator for GUITAR. In: Companion of the 30th International Conference on Software Engineering, ICSE Companion 2008, pp. 959–960. ACM, New York (2008)
2. Memon, A.M.: An event-flow model of GUI-based applications for testing. Software Testing, Verification and Reliability 17(3), 137–157 (2007)
3. Rauf, A.: Automated GUI Test Coverage Analysis using GA. In: Seventh International Conference on Information Technology (ITNG 2010) Las Vegas, Nevada, USA (2010)
4. Coello Coello, C.A., Lamont, G.B., Van Veldhuizen, D.A.: Evolutionary Algorithms for Solving Multi-Objective Problems. Springer, New York (2006)
5. Osyczka, A.: Multicriteria optimization for engineering design in Design Optimization, pp. 193–227. Academic Press, London (1985)
6. Memon, A.M., Pollack, M.E., Soffa, M.L.: Hierarchical GUI test case generation using automated planning. IEEE Transactions on Software 27(2), 144–155 (2001)
7. Xie, Q., Memon, A.M.: Using a pilot study to derive a GUI model for automated testing. ACM Transactions on Software Engineering and Methodology 18(2-7) (2008)
8. Memon, A.M.: A Comprehensive Framework for Testing Graphical User Interfaces. Doctoral Thesis. University of Pittsburgh (2001)
9. Memon, A.M., Xie, Q.: Studying the fault-detection effectiveness of GUI test cases for rapidly evolving software. IEEE Transactions on Software Engineering 31(10), 884–896 (2005)
10. Memon, A.M., Soffa, M.L., Pollack, M.E.: Coverage criteria for GUI testing. In: Proceedings of the 8th European Software Engineering Conference, Vienna, Austria (2001)
11. Kasik, D.J., George, H.G.: Toward automatic generation of novice user test scripts. In: Proceedings of the SIGCHI Conference on Human Factors in Computing Systems, Vancouver, British Columbia, Canada (1996)
12. White, L., Almezen, H., Alzeidi, N.: User-based testing of GUI sequences and their interaction. In: Proceedings of the International Symposium on Software Reliability Engineering, pp. 54–63. IEEE Computer Society Press, Piscataway (2001)

13. White, L., Almezen, H.: Generating test cases for GUI responsibilities using complete interaction sequences. In: Proceedings of the International Symposium on Software Reliability Engineering, pp. 110–121. IEEE Computer Society Press, Piscataway (2000)
14. Memon, A.M., Pollack, M.E., Soffa, M.L.: Using a goal-driven approach to generate test cases for GUIs. In: Proceedings of the 21st International Conference on Software Engineering, pp. 257–266. ACM Press, New York (1999)
15. Memon, A.M., Soffa, M.L., Pollack, M.E.: Coverage criteria for GUI testing. In: Proceedings of the 8th European Software Engineering Conference, Vienna, Austria, pp. 256–267. ACM, New York (2001)
16. Jones, B.F., Eyres, D.E., Sthamer, H.H.: A strategy for using Genetic Algorithms to automate branch and fault-based testing. The Computer Journal 41, 98–107 (1998)
17. Jones, B.F., Sthamer, H.H., Eyers, D.E.: Automatic structural testing using genetic algorithms. The Software Engineering Journal 11, 299–306 (1996)
18. Pargas, R., Harrold, M.J., Peck, R.: Test-data generation using genetic algorithms. Journal of Software Testing, Verification and Reliability 9(4), 263–282 (1999)
19. Tracey, N., Clark, J., Mander, K., McDermid, J.: Automated test-data generation for exception conditions. Software Practice and Experience 30(1), 61–79 (2000)
20. Lu, Y., Yan, D., Nie, S., Wang, C.: Development of an Improved GUI Automation Test System Based on Event-Flow Graph. In: Proceedings of the 2008 International Conference on Computer Science and Software Engineering. IEEE Computer Society, Washington (2008)
21. Afzal, W., Torkar, R., Feldt, R.: A Systematic Review of Search-based Testing for Nonfunctional System Properties. Information and Software Technology 51, 957–976 (2009)
22. Ferligoj, A., Batagelj, V.: Direct multicriterion clustering. J. Classification 9, 43–61 (1992)
23. Coello Coello, C.A.: Theoretical and Numerical Constraint-Handling Techniques used with Evolutionary Algorithms: A Survey of the State of the Art. Computer Methods in Applied Mechanics and Engineering 191(1112), 1245–1287 (2002)
24. Coello Coello, C.A., Lamont, G.B. (eds.): Applications of Multi-Objective Evolutionary Algorithms. World Scientific, Singapore (2004)
25. Van Veldhuizen, D.A.: Multiobjective Evolutionary Algorithms: Classifications, Analyses, and New Innovations. Doctoral thesis. Air Force Institute of Technology, Wright-Patterson AFB, Ohio (1999)
26. Kennedy, J., Eberhart, R.C.: Particle swarm optimization. In: Proc. IEEE International Conference on Neural Networks, Perth, pp. 1942–1948 (1995)
27. Coello, C.A.C.: Evolutionary multiobjective optimization: A historical view of the field. IEEE Computational Intelligence Magazine, 28–36 (2006)
28. Windisch, A., Wappler, S., Wegener, J.: Applying particle swarm optimization to software testing. In: Proceedings of the 9th Annual Conference on Genetic and Evolutionary Computation, pp. 1121–1128. ACM, New York (2007)
29. Hla, K.H.S., Choi, Y.S., Park, J.S.: Applying Particle Swarm Optimization to Prioritizing Test Cases for Embedded Real Time Software Retesting. In: IEEE 8th International Conference on Computer and Information Technology, pp. 527–532 (2008)
30. Kennedy, J., Eberhart, R.C.: Particle Swarm Optimization. In: Proceedings of IEEE Int. Conference on Neural Networks, pp. 1942–1948 (1995)

Online Signature Classification Using Modified Fuzzy Min-Max Neural Network with Compensatory Neuron Topology

B.M. Chaudhari[1], Rupal S. Patil[1], K.P. Rane[1], and Ulhas B. Shinde[2]

[1] E&TC Dept. GF's Godavari College of Engg. Jalgaon
Maharashtra (India)
bhupendra_scorpion29@rediffmail.com,
rupalmore@gmail.com,
kantiprane@rediffmail.com
[2] Savitribai Phule Women's Engineering College Aurangabad
Maharashtra (India)
drshindeulhas@gmail.com

Abstract. An Efficient signature recognition system is proposed in this paper. A new approach of application of krawtchouk moment method is used to estimate a set of feature vector which is an informative subset and is used as a input data for MFMCN classifier. Preprocessing step uses Krawtchouk moment, which automatically identifies the useful and common features consistently existing within different signature images of the same person. They are also invariant to shift, rotation, and scale. This moment method reduces the dimensionality of the input signature pattern by eliminating features containing low information or high redundancy. These features are used to recognize the signature using Modified Fuzzy Min –Max Neural Network with Compensatory Neuron (MFMCN). The proposed approach is applied to online signature recognition and experimentally it shows that it produces the excellent result by reducing the computational burden of the recognition system and provides high recognition rates.

Keywords: Signature Recognition, Invariant Krawtchouk Moments, MFMCN.

1 Introduction

Signature recognition system is classified as online and offline system. In early days for the offline signature recognition systems [1], [2], [3], the previously written signatures are captured by scanning or by other biometric system as a static image and then the recognition are carried out. Recently, more research carried on the online signature recognition, where signatures are acquired during the writing process with a special instrument, such as pen tablet. For online signature Recognition, Artificial Neural Networks (ANN) [5],[6], Dynamic Time Warping (DTW) [7],[8], the Hidden Markov Models (HMM) [9],[10], etc methods are widely used by number of researcher. Multiple known signature samples are required to learn the style of writing person and to classify a given test signature sample as a signature belonging to the writer or not. This type of learning approach is called writer dependent approach. There are always small variations between the signature of a person and major

S. Ranka et al. (Eds.): IC3 2010, Part I, CCIS 94, pp. 467–478, 2010.

variation between the similar signatures made by different person. So specific features are required to extract, these feature are called consistent features. It requires multiple signatures of a person which are used as training samples.

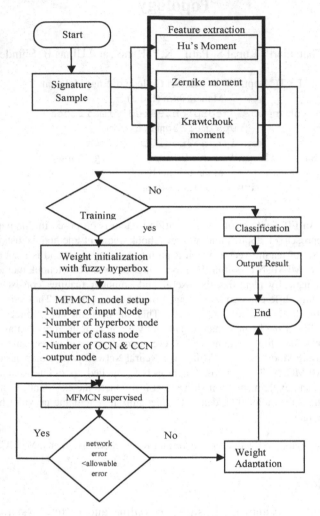

Fig. 1. Signature recognition system

If the numbers of training samples are limited, the determination of threshold is very challenging as the rejection and acceptance depends on it. To overcome this problem, we use invariant krawtchouk moments [11], which extract optimal object feature depending on maximum entropy principal as a selection criteria, because of this the dimensionality of input signature pattern is reduced by eliminating features with low information content or high redundancy with respect to other features. It is also invariant to shift, rotation, and scale provided that the signature pattern is in the proper format for classification. In classification phase the Modified Fuzzy Min-Max Neural Network with Compensatory Neuron (MFMCN) algorithm is proposed. This neural network is devised from Fuzzy Min-Max Neural Network with Compensatory Neuron designed by Nandelkar and Biswas [17]. The result shows that MFMCN is capable to learn data online in a single pass also it reduce classification and gradation error. The MFMCN's performance is less dependent on the initialization of expansion coefficient because the compensatory neuron can handle the hyperbox overlap and containment. These neuron are added in neural network framework as the hyperboxes are overlapped and contained so that MFMCN are capable to approximate the complex data in better manner than FMMN. So it provides high accuracy and less computational complexity in training and testing phase of the system. The Fig. 1 shows the basic building block of the recognition system.

2   Preprocessing and Feature Extraction

The signature sample is acquired from the pen tablet and conditioned to get required signature pattern for feature extraction using preprocessing technique. The preprocessing include binarization, noise elimination, signature outline calculation, thinning. These quality steps facilitate pattern description and responsible for quality of system.

The feature extraction method is a most important step in online signature recognition. Using MFMCN, the system performance can be strongly enhanced by the quality of the representation of the signature sample, which includes accuracy, required learning time and necessary number of samples.

For feature extraction purpose, we use Krawtchouk Moments [11],[12],[13]. It extract optimal feature from the signature sample depending on the Maximum Entropy Principle which reduces the input dimensionality of feature vector by eliminating some features with low specified criteria. Krawtchouk moment invariant [11] [12] have desirable properties of being invariant under image scaling, translation, rotation, and shear as shown in fig.2 and fig 3.

The geometrical moment of order $(n+m)$ for an image with intensity function $f(x,y)$ is defined as,

$$M_{nm} = \sum_{x=0}^{N-1} \sum_{y=0}^{N-1} x^n y^m f(x,y) \tag{1}$$

Where the parameter N is substituted with $N-1$ to match the $N \times N pixel$ point of an image. Then the standard set of geometric moment invariants, which are independent to rotation, scaling and translation can be written as,

$$V_{nm} = M_{00}^{-y} \sum_{x=0}^{N-1} \sum_{y=0}^{N-1} [(x - \bar{x})cos\theta + (y - \bar{y})sin\theta]^n \times [(y - \bar{y})cos\theta + (x - \bar{x})sin\theta]^m f(x,y)$$

Where

$$\gamma = \frac{n+m}{2} + 1 \,, \bar{x} = \frac{M_{10}}{M_{00}} \,, \bar{y} = \frac{M_{01}}{M_{00}} \,, \theta = \frac{1}{2} tan^{-1} \frac{2\mu_{11}}{\mu_{20} - \mu_{02}} \tag{2}$$

And μ_{nm} are the central moments defined as

$$\mu_{nm} = \int_{-\infty}^{\infty} \int_{-\infty}^{\infty} (x - \bar{x})^n (y - \bar{y})^m f(x,y)dxdy \qquad (3)$$

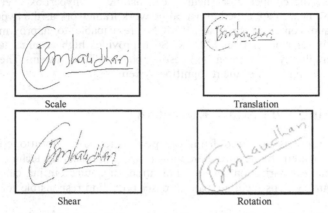

| Scale | Translation |

| Shear | Rotation |

Fig.2. Input Images Affine Transformation

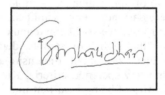

Fig. 3. Original Image

The value of θ is limited to $-45^0 \le \theta \le 45^0$. if intensity function is modified as $(\tilde{f}(x,y) = [w(x)w(y)]^{-1/2}f(x,y)$.

The normalized image with V_{nm} does not fall inside the domain of $[0, N-1] \times [0, N-1]$ as required by krawtchouk moments so it is required to modify. This krawtchouk moment can be written in terms of geometric moment as

$$Q_{nm} = \sum_{x=0}^{N-1}\sum_{y=0}^{N-1} \overline{k_n}(x)\overline{k_n}(y)\tilde{f}(x,y) = [\rho(n)\,\rho(m)]^{-\frac{1}{2}}\sum_{x=0}^{N-1}\sum_{y=0}^{N-1} k_n(x)\,k_m(y)f(x,y)$$

$$= [\rho(n)\,\rho(m)]^{-\frac{1}{2}}\sum_{i=0}^{N-1}\sum_{j=0}^{N-1} a_{i,n,P_1}a_{j,m,P_2}M_{ij} \qquad (4)$$

Where $\{a_{k,n,p}\}$ are coefficient $\rho(n)$ & $\rho(m)$ are n^{th} and m^{th} discrete polynomial. Hence Q_{nm} is a linear combination of geometric moments, *(Mij)* up to order $i = n$ *and* $j = m$, weighted by coefficients $\{a_{k,n,p}\}$. Orthogonal geometric moments is found to form the non orthogonal krawtchouk moments. So orthogonality has to be achieved.

$$\overline{V_{nm}} = \sum_{x=0}^{N-1}\sum_{v=0}^{N-1}\frac{N^2/2}{M_{00}}f(x,y) \times \left\{ \left[(x-\bar{x})cos\theta + (y-\bar{y})sin\theta \sqrt{\frac{N^2/2}{M_{00}}+\frac{N}{2}} \right] \right.$$

$$\left. \times \left\{ \left[(y-\bar{y})cos\theta + (x-\bar{x})sin\theta \sqrt{\frac{N^2/2}{M_{00}}+\frac{N}{2}} \right]^m \right\} \right. \tag{5}$$

Which can be written in terms of $\{V_{nm}\}$ as

$$\overline{V_{nm}} = \sum_{p=0}^{n}\sum_{q=0}^{m}\binom{n}{p}\binom{m}{q}\left(\frac{N^2}{2}\right)^{\frac{p+q}{2}+1} \times \left(\frac{N}{2}\right)^{n+m-p-q} V_{pq} \tag{6}$$

The new set of moments can be formed by replacing the regular geometric moments $\{M_{nm}\}$ by their invariant counterparts $\{\widetilde{V_{nm}}\}$ we have,

$$\tilde{Q} = [\rho(n)\rho(m)]^{-\frac{1}{2}}\sum_{i=0}^{n}\sum_{j=0}^{m}a_{i,n,p1}\,a_{j,m,p1}\widetilde{V_{ij}} \tag{7}$$

Note that the new set of moments is rotation, scale and translation invariant. We shall designate this set of moments as krawtchouk moment invariants some examples of them are,

$$\tilde{Q}_{00} = \Omega_{00}\tilde{V}_{00}$$

$$\tilde{Q}_{10} = \Omega_{10}\left[\tilde{V}_{00} - \frac{1}{(N-1)P_1}\tilde{V}_{10}\right] \tag{8}$$

$$\tilde{Q}_{01} = \Omega_{01}\left[\tilde{V}_{00} - \frac{1}{(N-1)P_2}\tilde{V}_{01}\right] \tag{9}$$

$$\tilde{Q}_{11} = \Omega_{11}\left[\tilde{V}_{00} - \frac{1}{(N-1)P_1}\tilde{V}_{10}\right] - \Omega_{11}\left[\frac{1}{(N-1)P_2}\tilde{V}_{01} + \frac{1}{(N-1)^2 P_1 P_2}\tilde{V}_{11}\right]$$

Where $\Omega_{nm} = [\rho(n; P_1, N-1)\rho(n; P_2, N-1)]^{-1/2}$ \tag{10}

The use of krawtchouk moments discriminate the original sample in the decision space, collecting the required information for representing the sample. It also minimize the computational time and complexity of the classifier because the feature vector obtained from the sample signature determines the size of the classifier (MFMCN).

3 MFMCN Topology

The proposed MFMCN is an online classifier which learns the data online in a single pass and based on the hyperbox fuzzy set class concept, it uses the compensatory neuron topology. This compensatory neuron are produced in the learning process and handles hyperbox overlap and containment process which enables MFMCN to approximate the data in better manner and makes initialization of expansion coefficient less critical. Removal of these two processes makes the learning algorithm is very simple. Also result shows that MFMCN can avoid the dependency of the classifier on the learning parameter in a great manner.

The proposed topology of MFMCN is shown in Fig 4.Architecture is made from four layers and it is divided into the three subsections as Main section, overlap compensation neuron section (OCN),and containment compensation neuron section (CCN) as it called compensatory neuron compensation block.

The feature vector extracted from the input signature pattern is considered as input vector for the neural network. This input vector is applied to the input layer for the neural network and number of nodes in the input layer is equal to the dimension of applied input vector A_h. Where the $A_{h1}, A_{h2},....A_{hn}$ are the input sample belongs to the pattern area I^n. And $A_1, A_2,....A_n$ are the corresponding input nodes. The second layer neuron called hyperbox nodes $B_1, B_2,....B_j$ are created at the training time, which represents the Min-Max points of the hyperbox and are stored into the (V, W) matrix.

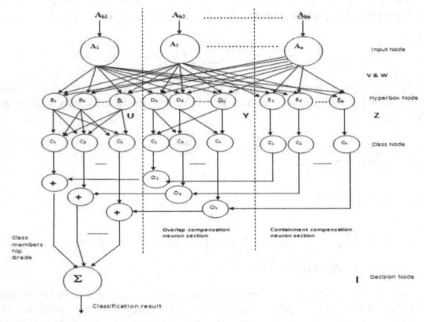

Fig. 4. Topology of MFMCN

3.1 Main Section

The activation function of main section hyperbox neural node B_j is proposed by A.V.Nandelkar and Biswas [17] and given as follows.

$$B_j = \{A_h, V_j, W_j \ f(A_h, V_j, W_j)\} \qquad (11)$$

Where $A_h \in I^n$

- $V_j = (V_{ji}, V_{j2}......V_{jn})$ are the Min point of jth Hyperbox.
- $W_j = (W_{ji}, W_{j2}......W_{jn})$ are the Max point of jth Hyperbox.

- $A_h = (A_{hi}, A_{h2} \ldots \ldots A_{hn})$ are the input vector of jth Hyperbox.
- And n- is Number of dimension.

So from above equation, we can say that the membership function for the jth hyperbox is

$$0 \leq B_j (A_h, V_j, W_j) \leq 1$$

In the recognizing process, decision making criteria are always depends upon the confidence limit of the input vector as this confidence limit will increase the accuracy. In this classifier, we assume that the degree of membership of input vector A_h for the hyperbox B_j is one if A_h is in or within the hyperbox B_j and the degree of membership decreases as A_h moves away from the hyperbox B_j.

It should be noted that neither the membership function [14] nor the membership value [15] satisfies this assumption. It is shown that even for patterns that are far from the hyperbox, the membership values are large. It can also be observed that the membership values do not decrease steadily with increasing distance from the hyperbox. To meet these required criteria, a new membership function Gabrys and Bargiela [16] have discussed and proposed a new activation function for a neuron. Hence, the activation function used for the neuron is given as follows.

$$b_j = (A_h V_j W_j) = \min(\min\left[\left(1 - f(a_{hi} - w_{ji}, \gamma)\right), \left(\left(1 - f(v_{ji} - h_i, \gamma)\right)\right)\right])$$

$$for \ i = 1 \ldots n \tag{12}$$

$$f(x, \gamma) = \begin{cases} 1, & if \ x\gamma > 1 \\ x\gamma & if \ 0 \leq x\gamma \leq 1 \\ 0 & if \ x\gamma < 0 \end{cases} \tag{13}$$

Where $\gamma = (\gamma_1, \gamma_2, \ldots \ldots \gamma_n)$ is sensitivity parameters regulating how fast the membership values decrease. This activation function is assigned if a input sample is within the hyperbox. Otherwise its membership function calculation is based on the distances between Min-Max points of the pattern A. Hyperbox nodes in Main Section are created if training sample belongs to a class. This has not been encountered that the existing hyperboxes of that class cannot be expanded further to accommodate it. The connections between hyperbox node and class node in main section are represented by matrix U and hence the learning process is improved. The OCN takes over the control from the overlapped hyperboxes and assigns membership to the test sample depending upon its distance from the min-max points. Note that unit step function with threshold one prevents the neuron from being active if test data is outside the overlapped region. If the test sample belongs to the overlapped region, the classifier section will allocate membership grade "1" for both classes. In such a case, the activation function of a compensatory neuron compensates the dispute and adds the respective membership grade.

The hyperbox nodes in middle layer OCN section are created whenever the network faces problem of overlap or containment. The OCN section takes care of the overlap problem. The connections between hyperbox and class nodes in OCN section are represented by matrix Y. The connection weight from neuron d_p is representing the overlap between the ith and j^{th} class hyperbox.

A connection between hyperbox nodes to a class node is adjusted by the following equation.

$$u_{ij} = \begin{cases} 1 \ if \ \{b_j \in c_i\} \\ 0 \ if \ \{b_j \in c_i\} \end{cases} \tag{14}$$

3.2 Overlap Compensation Neuron Section (OCN)

The neuron represent in this subsection is a hyperbox of size equal to the overlap region between two hyperboxes belonging to different classes. OCN Produces two outputs, one each for the two overlapping classes. OCN is active only when a test sample belongs to the overlap region. The activation function is given by

$$d_{jp} = U(b_j(A_h V_j W_j) - 1) \times \left(-1 + \frac{1}{n} \sum_{i=1}^{n} max\left(\frac{a_{hi}}{w_{pi}}, \frac{v_{pi}}{a_{hi}} \right) \right) \tag{15}$$

The Activation function of this neuron is such that it protects the class of the min and max point of overlapped hyperboxes

The class node in OCN section is given by

$$y_{ip} \ and \ y_{jp} = \begin{cases} 1, \ if\{d_p \in c_i \cap c_j, i \neq j\} \\ 0, \qquad\qquad otherwise \end{cases} \tag{16}$$

3.3 Containment Compensation Neuron Section (CCN)

The CCN is trained to handle the overlap in the pattern area. CCN represents a overlapping region in the hyperbox from different classes. This neuron is active only when test data sample falls inside the containment region. The output of this neuron is connected to the class that contains the hyperbox of other class.

The activation function of this neuron is

$$e_j = -1 \times U(b_j(A_h V_j W_j) - 1) \tag{17}$$

Whenever hyperbox of the class is contained within a hyperbox of another class, the hyperbox node in CCN section is created. The connection between the hyperbox and class node are represented by Z matrix. The connection weight of neuron in this subsection is given as,

$$z_{iq} = \begin{cases} 1, \quad if \ c_j \ is \ contained \ fully \ or \ partially \ by \ c_i, i \neq j \\ 0, \qquad\qquad\qquad\qquad\qquad Otherwise \end{cases} \tag{18}$$

The number of third layer nodes in main section is same as the number of classes learned. The number of class nodes in CCN and OCN section depends on the nature of overlap the network faces during the training process. The forth layer of this neural network directly provides the result that the pattern is in class or not. The sum of activations of the hidden nodes that are connected to the particular class is computed by each class node & forward this sum to a decision node. The decision node outputs the class with sigmoid activation function as in equation 19. The unity connection weight of neuron gives proper decision.

$$Y = \frac{1}{1+e^{-x}}$$ (19)

4   Training Algorithm

The training algorithm has mainly two step process:hyperbox creation and expansion/creation of compensatory neuron if overlap exits [17]. Let the training starts with the input sample is A_h .The hyperbox is created for a ordered pair and if the pattern is not fall in the hyperbox then existing hyperbox is expanded with the criteria,

$$n\theta \geq \sum_{i=1}^{n} \left(max(w_{ij}, a_{hi}) - min(v_{ij}, a_{hi}) \right)$$ (20)

where θ is expansion coefficient

Also if the hyperbox is not overlapping with any previous hyperbox of different classes. Then the min-max point of hyperbox is adjusted as described in [17].

The second step is a creation of compensatory neuron. The isolation test is carried out which checks ($w_{ij} < v_{ki}$) or($w_{ki} < v_{ji}$) for any value of i, indicates that two hyperbox (b_j, b_k) are isolated. So no compensation is needed and takes new signature sample for training. Otherwise the containment test will be carried out. In this containment test if $(v_{ij} < v_{ki} < w_{ki} < w_{ji})$ or $(v_{ki} < v_{ji} < w_{ji} < w_{ki})$, then we can say that the hyperbox b_j contained in hyperbox b_k or hyperbox b_k contained in hyperbox b_j respectively.

Then a new CCN node is created in the neural network and hyperbox min-max points are calculated as,

$$V_{ci} = max(v_{ki}, v_{ji}) \quad for\ i = 1,2, \ldots n$$ (21)

And

$$W_{ci} = min(w_{ki}, w_{ji}) \quad for\ i = 1,2, \ldots n$$ (22)

Then take a new signature sample for training and if this condition is not satisfied, the overlap compensation neuron is created because the hyperbox is not isolated or contained. The dimension for hyperbox representing the compensatory neuron are given by,

$$V_{oi} = max(v_{ki}, v_{ji}) \quad for\ i = 1,2, \ldots n$$ (23)

And

$$W_{oi} = min(w_{ki}, w_{ji}) \quad for\ i = 1,2, \ldots n$$ (24)

5   Implementation and Result

The proposed signature recognition system is implemented using MATLAB. The system is trained and tested using 56 signature database used by [20] . The proposed system is evaluated on two performance criteria. The feature extraction stage and the overall recognition rate for achieving high recognition performance in signature recognition system is highly influenced by the selection of efficient feature vector. In this paper, we evaluate three different feature extraction methods like Hu's moment [18] Zernike moment [19], and Krawtchouk moments [11], [12], [13] for signature recognition system.

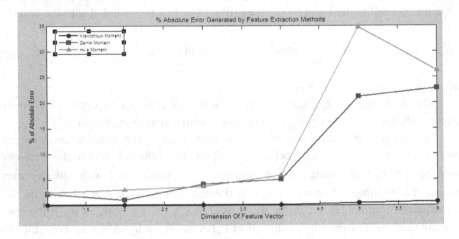

Fig. 5. Comparison of Feature Extraction Method

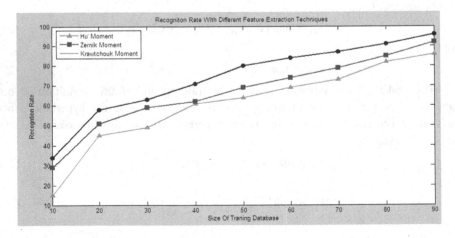

Fig. 6. Comparison of Recognition Rate Using Different Method

These systems are tested using two characteristics of the feature extraction techniques, which are invariance and reconstruct-ability Features. The performance of these feature extraction techniques is calculated using the percentage of absolute error produced in their original data with their counterpart's variations. Original feature vectors produced from three different moment invariant techniques are applied for signature features extraction from the binary images of the signature and absolute percentage error with the dimension of the feature vector is calculated as shown in Fig.5.The overall performance of the signature recognition system is calculated. Signature pattern database is used to train the MFMCN neural network. As shown in the graph the overall recognition rate of Krawtchouk Moment is increased because the techniques ensures the minimum information redundancy in the feature vector. This also reduces the computation time required for the signature recognition system.

6 Conclusion

We demonstrate the techniques that can be applied to classify the signature pattern. In this paper, orthogonal moments using Invariant Krawtchouk moments is used to extract the global shape feature of signature pattern, while MFCN is used as a classifier. The result shows that Krawtchouk moment, producing the feature vectors are more invariant against scaling translation and rotation. Also Krawtchouk moments gives highest classification rate as compared to the Hu's and Zernike moment because it reduces the input dimensionality of classification by eliminating features with low information content or high redundancy with respect to other features exaction algorithm. It substantially reduces the computational burden from the classifier stage in terms of number of nodes produced for MFMCN Neural network for every input signature pattern.

References

1. Yingyong, Q., Hunt, B.R.: Signature Verification Using Global and Grid Features. Pattern Recognition, Great Britain 22(12), 1621–1629 (1994)
2. Drouhard, J.P., Sabourin, R., Godbout, M.: A neural network approach to off-line signature verification using directional PDF. Pattern Recognition 29(3), 415–424 (1996)
3. Rigoll, G., Kosmala, A.: A Systematic Comparison Between On-Line and Off-Line Methods for Signature Verification with Hidden Markov Models. In: 14th International Conference on Pattern Recognition, Australia, vol. II, p. 1755 (1998)
4. Plamondon, R., Lorette, G.: Automatic signature verification and writer identification-The state of the Art. Pattern Recognition 22(7), 107–131 (1989)
5. Martens, R., Claesen, L.: On- Line Signature Verification by Dynamic Time-Warping. In: IEEE Proceedings of ICPR 1996 (1996)
6. Wu, Q.-Z., Joe, I.-C., Lee, S.-Y.: On-Line Signature Verification Using LPC Cepstrum and Neural Networks. IEEE Transactions on Systems, Man, and Cybernetics–Part B: Cybernetics 27(1), 148–153 (1997)

7. Mautner, P., Rohlik, O., Matousek, V., Kempp, J.: Signature Verification Using ART-2 Neural Network. In: Proceedings of the 9th International Conference on Neural information Processing (ICONIP'OZ), vol. 2, pp. 636–639 (2002)
8. Jain, A., Griess, F., Connell, S.: On-line signature Verification. Pattern Recognition 35(12) (2002)
9. Nelson, W., Turin, W., Hastie, T.: Statistical methods for on-line signature verification. International Journal of Pattern Recognition and Artificial Intelligence 8 (1994)
10. Kashi, R., Hu, J., Nelson, W.L., Turin, W.: A hidden markov model Approach to online handwritten signature verification. International Journal on Document Analysis and Recognition 1(1) (1998)
11. Krawtchouk, M.: On interpolation by means of orthogonal polynomials. Memoirs Agricultural Inst. Kyiv 4
12. Yap, P.T., Raveendran, P., Ong, S.H.: Krawtchouk moments as a new set of moments for image reconstruction. In: Proc. IJCNN 2002, vol. 1, pp. 908–912 (2002)
13. El affar, A., Ferdous, K., Cherkaoui, A., El fadili, H., Qjidaal, H.: Krawtchouk Moment Feature Extraction for Neural Arabic Handwritten Words Recognition. IJCSNS International Journal of Computer Science and Network Security 9(1) (January 2009)
14. Simpson, P.K.: Fuzzy min-max neural network-Part I: Classification. IEEE Trans. Neural Netw. 3(5), 776–786 (1992)
15. Simpson, P.K.: Fuzzy min-max neural network—Part II: Clustering. IEEE Trans. Fuzzy Syst. 1(1), 32–45 (1993)
16. Gabrys, B., Bargiela, A.: General fuzzy min-max neural network for clustering and classification. IEEE Trans. Neural Netw. 11(3), 769–783 (2000)
17. Nandedkar, A.V., Biswas, P.K.: A Fuzzy Min-Max Neural Network Classifier with Compensatory Neuron Architecture. IEEE Transactions on Neural Networks 18(1) (January 2007)
18. Hu, M.K.: Visual pattern recognition by moment invariants. IRE Trans. Inform. Theory IT-8, 179–187 (1962)
19. Khotanzad, A., Hong, Y.H.: Invariant image recognition by Zernike moments. IEEE Trans. Patt Anal. Mach. Intell. 12, 489–497, doi:10.1109/34.55109
20. Chaudhari, B.M., Barhate, A.A., Bhole, A.A.: Signature Recognition Using Fuzzy Min-Max Neural Network. In: Proceeding of International Conference of Control Automation Communication & Energy Conversation, pp. 242–249, ISBN 978-81-8424-439

Multifaceted Classification of Websites for Goal Oriented Requirement Engineering

Sangeeta Srivastava[1] and Shailey Chawla[2]

[1] Bhaskaracharya College of Applied Sciences, Sector-2, Dwarka, Delhi-110075, India
[2] Department of Computer Science, University of Delhi, Delhi-110007, India
sangeeta.srivastava@gmail.com, shaileychawla@gmail.com

Abstract. Access to Internet and web applications has become a part of everyone's chores be it for personal, corporate or business use. Web applications too have evolved a great deal from static web pages to interactive web services. It has thus become important to engineer these applications methodologically. As in ISD, detailed requirement analysis for web applications has many benefits. Also, Incorporation of goals form the early stages maximizes the product quality and prevents giving "requirements" amiss. We propose a multifaceted classification of websites based on different criteria. It helps in creation and validation of requirement models for variety of websites. Also how the classification would bind to the goal model for engineering websites has been explained.

Keywords: Goal oriented Requirement engineering, Web engineering, Web site Classification.

1 Introduction

Web sites are being built not only as repository of information but also for business purposes. It is becoming the staple source for sharing information. Today, web applications represent the business itself, rather than only supporting the business. Hence, during the requirement engineering process the business and technology issues are tangled in such a way that these can't be considered in isolation and an integrated approach is required for web system development. Whatever the kind of websites, their development has to be based on an integration of the goal of the website and the technical issues. It becomes important to take notice that web community is enormous in size and several families of web applications exist which may be classified according to different criteria like domain, goals, content etc. However, a classification base on which the models for requirement engineering can be applied doesn't formally exist.

Requirement engineering is given much attention in the ISD community but not so in web. Web applications are mostly designed and not engineered. That leads to fancy designing but less of functionality and goal achievement The functional and non functional requirements, if detected early in the phase lead to properly engineered product. Left out requirements or loopholes if detected later my cost both time, cost and effort. It therefore becomes imperative to devote enough consideration to this

S. Ranka et al. (Eds.): IC3 2010, Part I, CCIS 94, pp. 479–485, 2010.

phase in web development. Also application of goal oriented methodologies from the early stages would result in the desired product that is closest to the stakeholders aspirations. For engineering the web applications many initiatives have been taken in both academia and industry. UWE, NDT, WEBML, WSDM, AWARE[5] are amongst many models that have been developed to systematically develop these applications. We focus on the less researched area of goal oriented web requirement engineering.

Organization of Paper
In this paper we provide the classification of web sites based on different criteria. Then we provide the need of web classification in goal oriented web requirement engineering. Further, we present a model for the development of web applications. The paper concludes with a discussion and an outlook on future work.

2 Website Taxonomy

The classification of web sites is a highly intricate procedure because the web sites belong to various domains and there are overlapping/tangling criterion. There is no doubt that the classification would be multidimensional and multifaceted. Web is ever evolving so there is also room for new entries and dimensions. We have categorized various web sites according to three different criterion(Fig. 1.):

a) **Content:** The content here refers to type and management of the content.
b) **Service:** The service the website is rendering and the goal is the criteria here.
c) **Technology:** The design and pubishing techniques also keep evolving. This criteria classifies websites according to the technical aspects.

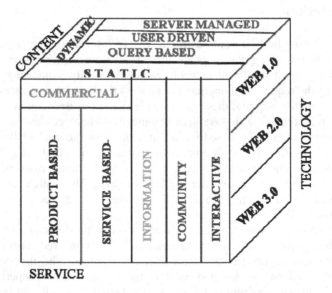

Fig. 1. Website Multifaceted Taxonomy

2.1 Content

Web sites have evolved profoundly. In early stages of evolution of world wide web the intenet was mainly a repository of information. The information was collected and posted on the internet so that the reach of information is wide spread. Now, it's the age of rich internet applications and semantic web.

a) Static: Wikipedia definition of static web page is a web page that always comprises the same information in response to all download requests from all users. Contrast with Dynamic web page. It displays the same information for all users, from all contexts, providing the classical hypertext, where navigation is performed through "static" documents. Static pages are mostly for providing information to users and nothing else. These include personal web pages, corporate information web pages, weather information pages, etc.

b) Dynamic: A dynamic web page is a hypertext document rendered to a World Wide Web user presenting content that has been customized or actualized for each individual viewing or rendition or that continually updates information as the page is displayed to the user. Content (text, images, form fields, etc.) on a web page can change, in response to different contexts or conditions. There are two ways to create this kind of effect:

Using client-side scripting to change interface behaviors within a specific web page, in response to mouse or keyboard actions or at specified timing events. Or, Using server-side scripting to change the supplied page source between pages, adjusting the sequence or reload of the web pages or web content supplied to the browser.

Most of the internet pages existing nowadays are dynamic in nature. Further refinement on how the change in content is managed results in further categorization:

Managed at the server: The content of the web site is managed at the server. Owing to the changeable nature of the content the content keeps on changing. Example of such web pages are stock market websites, weather or news websites.

User driven: The content of the web pages is managed by the users. Community websites like discussion forums, usegroups, chatrooms, socializing websites are very good examples of such web pages. Here except for the basic design of the web sites the contents are managed by the users. Also personalized pages provided by various portals like yahoo and google (aka igoogle.com) are also user driven.

Query based web sites: The content of the web page in this case is in response to the query posted by the user. The main example being the search engine. Within other websites also like shopping or information oriented websites some web pages are a result of query based interaction with the user.

Special note- Database driven Websites: The contents of the website are driven by the databases. This category can overlap with any of the above websites. The contents of shopping/banking/search engine/information oriented websites are mostly database driven. The criteria of database is important here but since it overlaps the above categories it has not kept as separate class. It can however be taken as a criteria for further refinement of dynamic websites, if required.

2.2 Service

The second criteria for classifying the website is goal with which the website is being created. The purpose of web application development and the utilization of the web site come under this perspective. Though the list is expandable, we have classified the website based on its utility into the following:

a) **Information.** The website main purpose is to provide information. The information can be in any format including multimedia or textual. Information can be received in response to queries like search engines. The personal or corporate web pages that only provide information about the entity also come under this category. Website containing articles from magazines, newspapers or any domain knowledge also fall in this class.

b) **Commercial.** All e-commerce web sites have a commercial motive. The business here can be based on either product or services. Hence there is scope of refinement in this category. Shopping web sites come under the product based business. Banking, stock market websites are service based businesses. Most of the commercial websites involve transaction oriented interaction, where in there is transfer of money through some means. Here advanced technology for security is used.

c) **Community.** The community web sites provide platforms for socializing, discussions forums, blogs, networking etc. These are for bringing people around the world closer who share common interests.

d) **Interactive.** These web sites are for live interaction, though other website categories also have some form of interaction but it has been kept as separate category keeping in mind the web sites being build specifically for live interactions like online gaming, video conferencing wherein people from different parts of world can play the same game. Also the response of the web site is spontaneous for various actions. This category may also include the service tools that provide some interactive services to the users like file conversion etc.

2.3 Technology

The third criteria has been chosen to classify the websites according to the techniques used for publishing and installing the websites. Depending upon the usage of the website the technology of its creation also differs. Also with time the technologies have evolved and the way internet is used has also made a magnificent shift. The websites fall under the category of the categories Web 1.0, Web 2.0 or Web 3.0. These three terms represent the evolution of web in terms of technology and usage.

a) **Web 1.0.** That initial world wide web era was all about read-only content and static HTML websites. People preferred navigating the web through link directories of Yahoo! and dmoz. The applications here are native internet applications using HTML, XHTML, and basic javascript and vbscript etc. Web 1.0 is a retronym that refers to the state of the Web, and any website design style used before the advent of the Web 2.0 phenomenon [8].

b) Web 2.0. This is about user-generated content and the read-write web. People are consuming as well as contributing information through blogs or sites like Flickr, YouTube, Digg, etc. The line dividing a consumer and content publisher is increasingly getting blurred in the Web 2.0 era[8]. The technologies used are flash, java etc.

c) Web 3.0. This is a new concept. This will be about semantic web (or the meaning of data), personalization (e.g. iGoogle), intelligent search and behavioral advertising among other things.The term was coined by Tim Oreilly who coined the term web 2.0 as well[7][9]. Active research is going on in this area for converting the world wide web into a semantic web database, this will increase the utility of web manifolds[9].

3 Goals and Web Applications

A *goal* is defined as "something that some stakeholder hopes to achieve in the future" [10]. To capture declarative, behavioural and interactive aspects of systems, goal-oriented requirements analysis have been proposed [6]. Using goals as the main requirement constructs, these analysis methods allow exploration of alternatives, decision spaces, and tradeoffs by considering questions such as "why", "how" and "how else" instead of only considering functional concerns. The amalgamation of Goal oriented requirement engineering with web applications has enormous benefits. It is apparent that web applications are a necessity for every business. The incorporation of goal oriented approach for engineering such applications will reap assorted benefits and the final product will be fairly closer to the stakeholders expectations. There are models for building business applications like in [1]. In our context, a web application can be build with a combination of mainly three models: *Information model, Design model and Process model.* A perspective of a goal model in development of all the above models would result in a finer product that meets mass expectations of users and business owners.

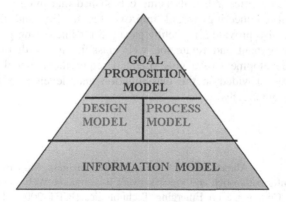

Fig. 2. Website Development Model

A Goal Proposition Model can be build over these models so that the web application also suffice soft goals along with the basic functionalities. The website development model can be seen in Fig. 2.

Depending on the web application being developed the website development model can be build on the basis of the website taxonomy. The website can be placed in the multidimensional, multifaceted model and accordingly different parameters can be checked. The Goal proposition model can be mainly based on the service dimension. The information model can be based on the content dimension. Also, the design and process model can be linked with technology and service dimension.

The above web site classification model helps in identifying the type of website that the user is asking for. The website category can be chosen for all the three dimensions according to the requirements. The web applications can be a hybrid category as well.

Example: If a web application has to be developed that has to perform search then first of all its category should be decided based on the three dimensions. In this case for different dimensions:

Content:- Dynamic / Query based
Service:- Information
Technology:- Web 2.0

Further detailing of each dimension can also be done. The detailing would describe how in each category the requirement engineering can be semi-automated. We are doing further work on this area.

4 Conclusion and Future Work

The contribution made by this paper is the taxonomy of websites that can be taken as a reference for any kind of research based on the web applications. We maintain that web is ever evolving and there is scope of improvement and addition of new dimensions and categories. Also, its being established that integration of goals with web requirement engineering would improve the quality and usability of web applications. We also provide a modeling pyramid for integrating goals with the web application development and relate the web classification with the model. Future work includes development of a goal oriented requirement model that suffices all kinds of websites provided in the classification and develop its tool support for engineering it automatically.

References

1. Azam, F., Li, Z., Ahmad, R.: Introducing VIP Business Modeling Framework for Innovative, Information-rich and Process-aware E-commerce Web Applications. In: IEEE International Conference on Emerging Technologies (ICET 2006), Peshawar, Pakistan (2006)
2. Bolchini, D., Paolini, P., Randazzo, G.: Adding Hypermedia Requirements to Goal-Driven Analysis. In: Proceedings of the 11th IEEE International Conference on Requirements Engineering, p. 127 (2003)

3. van Lamsweerde, A.: Goal-Oriented Requirements Engineering: A Guided Tour. In: Proc. RE 2001: 5th Intl. Symp. Req. Eng. (2001)
4. Gordijn, J., Yu, E., van der Raadt, B.: e-Service Design Using i* and e3value Modeling. IEEE Software 23(3), 26–33 (2006)
5. Koch, N., Escalona, M.: Requirements Engineering for Web Applications – A Comparative Study. Journal of Web Engineering 2(3), 193–212 (2004)
6. Mylopoulos, J., Chung, L., Yu, E.: From object-oriented to goal-oriented requirements analysis. Communications of the ACM 42(1), 31–37 (1999)
7. Oreilly, T.: What is Web 2.0: Design Patterns and Business Models for the Next Generation of Software. Communications & Strategies 1, 17 (2007)
8. Cormode, G., Krishnamurthy, B.: Key differences between Web 1.0 and Web 2.0 (First Monday, 2008)
9. Lassila, J.H.: Embracing Web 3.0, IEEE Internet Computing (2007)
10. Plihon, V., Ralyté, J., Benjamen, A., Maiden, N.A.M., Sutcliffe, A., Dubois, E., Heymans, P.: A reuse oriented approach for the construction of scenario based methods. In: Proceedings of the International Software Process Association's 5th International Conference on Software Process (ICSP 1998), Chicago, Illinois, USA, pp. 14–17 (1998)

A Simplified and Corroborative Approach towards Formalization of Requirements

Ram Chatterjee and Kalpana Johari

Academic Block, CDAC, Noida, B-30, Sector-62, Institution Area, Noida-201307, India
chatterjee.ram@gmail.com,
kalpanajohari@cdacnoida.in

Abstract. This manuscript elucidates a simplified and corroborative approach towards Formalization of Requirements. The discussion implicates Use Cases, Scenarios and State Transition Diagrams as a basis for automating the process of formalization, which is achieved via a self-developed tool "STATEST 1.0.0" that exemplifies the underlying concept and illustrates the ease of automation.

Keywords: Formalization, Requirements, Use Cases, Scenarios, State Transition Diagrams.

1 Introduction

The topic under scrutiny primarily focuses on the aspect of testing software in the absence of source code and is oriented towards Specification based testing. In the scenario, devoid of the source code, the Requirements Specification and the dynamic black box testing of the program depicting its dynamic behaviour are the only pioneers to demonstrate the characteristic features of the software under test.

For the sake of completeness, we prefer to state that there exists a distinct difference between requirements and specifications. A requirement is a condition needed by a customer to solve a problem or achieve an objective. However, a specification is a manuscript that specifies the requirements, design, behavior, or other properties of a system. To exemplify we refer the need of a GUI interface to be user friendly as a requirement whereas the relevant specification to achieve it would include details on design aspects of the GUI like proper placement of controls, use of alternative methods of entry of information in the interface under consideration etc. Requirements Specification is a document stating the requirements of the customer and is quoted informally in simple English language at the first place. From the perspective of this research we identify Requirements Specification as an informal document mentioning customer's needs, which is subject of formalization by the tool STATEST 1.0.0 and is expected to implicate pre-conditions and post-conditions as well, in its formalized representation.

Readers may be acquainted that source code may not be available under following circumstances [3]. Firstly, the third party programs (COTS) that promote reusability are devoid of source code and are only accompanied with binary files and few reference documents. Secondly, the components that are developed for confidential clients like military, nuclear power plant etc. have forbidden access to their source code to

S. Ranka et al. (Eds.): IC3 2010, Part I, CCIS 94, pp. 486–496, 2010.

prevent malicious manipulations of the code. Lastly, at times, access to source code to the test team is deliberately prohibited to encourage independence in testing so that the ITG (Independent Test Group) don't get baffled by the logic of the code and thus design "best of the breed" test cases that lie beyond the scope of the program under test, which in turn improvises testing the robustness of the program under test.

Veteran software engineers seem to be congenial with the industry analysis that suggests "Specification" as the prime source of bugs due to the reason that specification is usually rushed, frequently changed or not well communicated. The other reasons for presence of bugs have been traced to Design, followed by Code and other reasons comprising false positives, interpretations of illusive bugs etc. [7].

The rest of this paper has been portrayed as follows. Section 2 describes the need and significance of Formalization with supportive literature survey concentrating on Techniques to aid Formalization of Requirements, Techniques to achieve Formalization of Requirements and Approaches of Automating Formalization of Requirements. Section 3 elaborates the discussion in the perspective of self-developed tool "STATEST 1.0.0" that automates a given Requirements Specification narrated in the form of Use Cases into state charts as medium to Formalization. Finally, Section 4 concludes with discussion on pros and cons of the demonstrated tool with notification on future work.

2 Formalization Pragmatics

The act of formalization refers to transforming the representation of the informally written requirement in a formal form complying with some rationale. Our objective is concerned with automated formalization of the requirements specification in an apt form that lends itself easily into generation of test cases from the formalized form.

2.1 Techniques to aid Formalization of Requirements [12]

This refers to various methods that facilitate formalization. We begin with discussion on the role play of scenarios. At the initiation of the development the scenarios play three different roles viz.

- Identify anomalies existing in the current system which the new system has to solve.
- Render visions of how the new system might operate.
- Forms the basis for description of user and system behaviour.

Two RE (Requirements Engineering) methods have placed considerable importance on the role of scenarios. ScenIC proposes a schema of scenario related knowledge. Goals are classified into achieving, maintaining or avoiding states.

The figure (Fig. 1) given below demonstrates the basis for deciding scenarios. A Scenario is composed of Episodes which in turn is composed of Actions. The Goal, Obstacle, Objective, Task and Actor represent the schema of the scenario. Few of the scenarios chosen must represent obstacles that would prohibit the goal from being achieved or would slow down the task. The actions must represent those actions too that prevent the task from being accomplished.

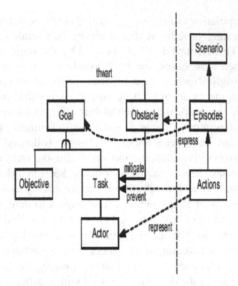

Fig. 1. Schema of Scenario related knowledge [12]

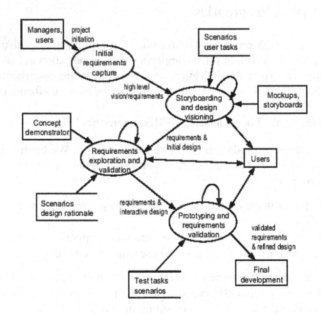

Fig. 2. Process road map of the SCRAM method [12]

The second RE method has been discussed below:

Fig.2 describes the SCRAM (Scenario based Requirement Analysis Method):

1. Implicates conventional interviewing and fact finding techniques.
2. Creates early visualization of the required system.

3. Uses concept demonstrators and early prototypes to present more detailed design for probing.
4. Involves development of fully functional prototypes and refinement of requirements unless and until agreed by all users.

The above discussion signifies the importance and necessity of various scenarios, its representation and role in requirements and design.

2.2 Techniques to achieve Formalization of Requirements [9] [10]

This part concentrates on utilizing formalization to test programs in the absence of source code [3]. In such a case the Interface scenarios represented in terms of sequence of inputs and corresponding outputs forms basis for formalization and facilitates 'consistency' of formalized specification with program interface for effective testing. The interface scenario can be discovered from the informal requirements and/or dynamic black box testing.

Steps for Formalization:

- For each interface scenario it is needed to relocate the corresponding requirements description in informal specification.
- The work proceeds by forming an operation whose signature is derived from the scenario and the informal document.
- The previous step is followed by writing pre- and post-conditions for the operation using a formal specification language (SOFL).

Finally the test case generation and test result analysis follows. The test cases should cover all the specification scenarios.

The combination of natural language, graphical notations and formal methods address following RE issues: Requirements Specification format should be easily comprehensible by non technical users. Formal methods must help developers identify inconsistencies. The natural language format & formal version of requirements must be synchronized.

In the figure given below (Fig. 3), it may be noted that changes as a result of analysis shown follow the sequence A, B, C. The typified text alongside has been bulleted to depict refinement of requirement, in ascending order. The crux to be noted is that as gradually the process of refinement progresses, the description becomes more and more precise, complete and comprehensible.

The above narration and the Fig. 3 depicted below states process of refining requirement with an example which helps in understanding how better formalization can be emulated.

This narrative won't be complete without a decipherable description of "Borg Tool" shown in Fig. 3 below. Borg is a specialized implementation of the architecture analogous to Circe's, which focuses on generating formal models from textual and graphical requirements. Further detail regarding the tool is available in [9].

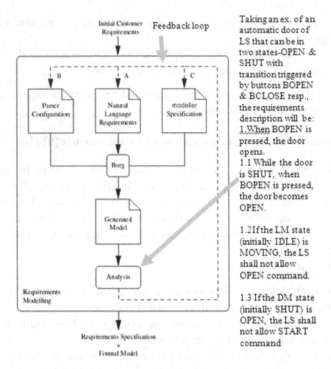

(*Legend: LS: Lift System, LM: Lift Module, DM: Door Module*)

Fig. 3. Requirements modelling in detail with example of analysis [9]

2.3 Approaches of Automating Formalization of Requirements [7] [11] [13]

This sub section elaborates on approaches of automating the formalization of requirements. The Formalization can be achieved via assimilation of any Formal Language available like – 'Z', 'B', 'SOFL', 'OCL', to name a few. However, the tedious characteristic of these languages prohibit its wide application in the industry, OCL, gaining the highest acceptability, but, via an indirect implementation.

The figure below (Fig. 4) shows the tedious process of transforming the Natural Language Requirements into Executable Models.

In addition to the above mentioned mind-numbing characteristic of formal languages and convoluted process shown in Fig. 4, there are many other anomalies associated with formal methods viz. [2]

The Requirements Issue: This can be explained via the often repeated aphorism – "You cannot go from the informal to formal by formal means". In other words, formal methods are capable to verify a system, but not to validate a system.

Physical Implementation Issue: Formal Methods confirms its application with reference to a specification on an idealized abstract machine, but not on a physical machine. For instance, an abstract machine might be assumed to have an infinite memory, while every actual machine is bounded by some upper limit.

Implementation Issues: The disparity between users' intentions and formal specifications and between physical implementations and abstract proofs are reasons for

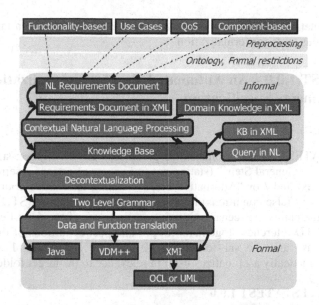

Fig. 4. From Natural Language Requirements translation into Executable Models [11]

inherent limitations to formal methods, irrespective to how much they may be developed in the future. The point to probe is, however, whether formal methods are yet suitable for full-scale implementation. They are most well-developed for addressing issues of functionality, safety, and security, but even for these mature methods, serious questions exist about their ability to scale up to large applications. This issue of scaling plays a vital role as a deciding factor in the choice of a method.

The above mentioned facts signify the need to adopt a different approach towards Formalization of Requirements Specification such that the design and development of the automated tool to achieve the purpose gets simplified enough.

In the context of the topic of discussion we further proceed to understand the significance of use cases that represents the requirements textually and is comprised of scenarios [13]. It is vital to clear the difference between these two. The use case is a possible collection of scenarios between the system under discussion and the external actors of the system, while a scenario represents a linear sequence of interactions

Table 1. List of various Tools for Formalization

Name	Characteristic
AgroUML	Non Automated
BoUML	Non Automated
StarUML	Non Automated
Visual Paradigm for UML	Non Automated
UCEd	Automated

between external actors and the system. Above, we have presented a table (Table 1) depicting various tools for formalization.

3 STATEST 1.0.0 – An Automated Tool for Formalization of Requirements Specification

3.1 Nitty-Gritty of the Tool

The tool "STATEST 1.0.0" automates the given scenario description stated as steps, categorized into "General Steps" (stating general course of actions resembling normal / true conditions) and / or "Alternative Steps" (stating alternative course of actions resembling error / false conditions) into State Transition Diagram (STD). A database "Use Cases" maintains the scenario descriptions in terms of requisite fields including "steps" and "STD reference" together with pre and post conditions of the STD. Note that the database and the sub-folders of "Executable STATEST 1.0.0\STATEST 1.0.0*.*" automatically acclimatizes itself in relevance to the target folder.

3.2 Analysis of STATEST 1.0.0

In this section some distinguishing features of the designed and developed application tool is being discussed to highlight the operation of the application in light of various circumstances.

■ The application tool is able to handle situations of "if and else" statements, for both the circumstances viz. when if and / or else is followed by a single statement – "goto step <'step_id'>", and / or when if and / or else is followed by a multiple statements ending with a – "goto step <'step_id'>".

Table 2. Comparison of STATEST 1.0.0 with UCEd 1.6.2

STATEST 1.0.0	UCEd 1.6.2
The tool is intended to facilitate Specification Based Testing.	The tool is intended to facilitate Require-ments Engineering Process.
The tool has an inbuilt database (maintained by the Requirements Engineer), from where it picks the input. The presence of database facilitates the tester in using the tool without having to enter the inputs manually for a new scenario.	The tool mandates the need to enter the in-puts manually by the end user for every new scenario, even though the end user is a tester.
The STDs are labelled with pre and post conditions.	Pre and post conditions aren't described in STD.
The STD generated depicts "start" and "end" states.	Here only "start" state is shown.
Each STD transition is labelled descriptively.	STD transitions aren't descriptive.
The tool is expected to automate test suite generation from Scenario Description, in relevance to Specification Based Testing.	This isn't focused towards test suite generation.

- The next point of observation is that every backward branch in a STD, indicated by a "goto step <'step_id'>", has been shown in terms of respective "state node id" rather than a backward arrow entering the concerned state. One of the reasons for adopting this method of representation is ease of programming and the other reason is related to avoid the cluttering of the application contents.
- Another fact revealed by careful observation of the STDs is the absence of labels indicating the "state" of the system under consideration. The system states have not been labelled for the reason that relates to the avoidance of cluttering of the application contents and to avoid terminology bias.

3.3 Glimpse of Screen Snapshot of STATEST 1.0.0

Note the following details with reference to Fig. 7:

- The absence of end state in UCEd 1.6.2 shown above doesn't manifest the next state the system under consideration will assume after reaching state s2, s3 or s5. This connotes a dilemma of the next state to be either an end state or error state or even a hangover state.
- The absence of any pre-condition doesn't justify the state s0 to be always in a ready state. In other words what conditions are mandatory for the system to operate are absent.
- Also, the absence of any post-condition doesn't warrant the system of having attained the objective when the end of the STD is reached.

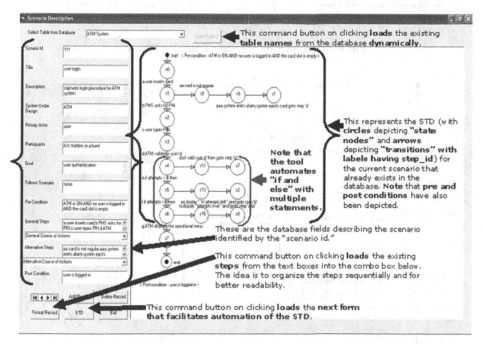

Fig. 5. Screen snapshot of Scenario Description

3.4   Implementation Details with an Example

To exemplify, let us consider an ATM system with functionalities of user authentication, money withdrawal, dispensing of mini-statement etc. Here each scenario description is comprised of an individual functionality. Given below is a scenario description for user authentication with field names described in parenthesis:

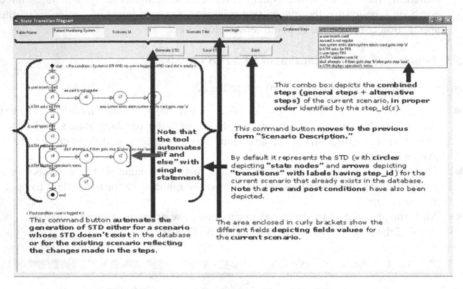

Fig. 6. Screen snapshot of State Transition Diagram

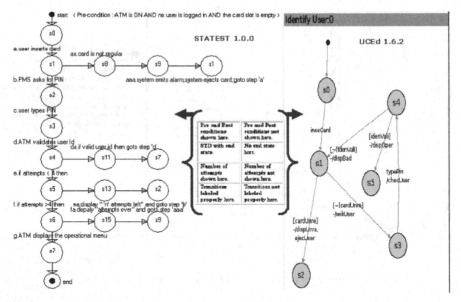

Fig. 7. Screen snapshot on comparison of STATEST 1.0.0 vs. UCEd 1.6.2

The tool initially reads the field details of the selected table as has been shown in Fig. 5. The "Format Record" button (Fig. 5) arranges the gen_steps and alt_steps, described above as ordered set of steps with respect of the associated step_id(s). The "Generate STD" button when clicked automates the STD from the relevant description as shown in Fig.6 and the relevant file name is stored in the "path" field of Use Cases database as spelled in the dialog box that appears on click of the "Save STD" button (Fig.6).

Table 3. Record values of STATEST 1.0.0

Field Names	Value
sid:	111
title:	user login
description:	captures login procedure for ATM system
sud: (system under detection)	ATM
pa: (primary actor)	User
participants:	A/c holders in a bank
goal:	user authentication
follows_scen:(follows scenario)	None
pre_cond: (pre conditions)	ATM is on AND no user is logged in AND the card slot is empty
gen_steps: (normal course of actions)	a.user inserts card,b.ATM asks for PIN,c.user types PIN,d.ATM validates user Id,e.if attempts < 4 then,f.if attempts >4 then
alt_steps: (alternative course of actions)	aa.card is not regular,aaa.system emits alarm;system ejects card;goto step <a>,da.if valid user id then display operational menu and await user response,ea.display "'n' attempts left" and goto step <b>,fa.dispaly "attempts over" and goto step <aaa>;goto step <a>
post_cond: (Post condition)	user is logged in
path: (name of the file containing scenario diagram)	ATMSystem_Login

4 Conclusion and Future Work

As has been discussed, the tool STATEST 1.0.0 achieves formalization by using scenario descriptions written in structured English, a form that lends itself into automation logic leading to transformation of the scenario into state transition diagram. We thus have been able to overcome the difficulties relevant to formalization discussed in this paper and the convoluted process which was a hard nut to crack.

The future work holds the task of automating test suit from the formalized representation i.e. State Transition Diagram (STD), which will be implicated in the enhanced version of the tool as STATEST 1.1.0 which is under development presently.

References

1. Model Based Test Generation Tools, Agedis Consortium, http://www.agedis.de
2. Formal Methods,
   http://www.ece.cmu.edu/~koopman/des_s99/formal_methods
3. Liu, S.: Utilizing Formalization to Test Programs without Available Source Code. In: Proceedings of the Eighth International Conference on Quality Software (2008)
4. Jayaraman, P.K., Whittle, J.: A Tool for Simulating Use Case Scenarios. In: Companion to the Proceedings of the 29th International Conference on Software Engineering, pp. 43–44 (2007)
5. Fernandez, L., Lara, P.J., Cuadrado, J.J.: Efficient software quality assurance approaches oriented to UML models in real life, pp. 385–426. Idea Group Pulishing (2007)
6. Liu, S., Nagoya, F., Chen, Y.: An Empirical Study on a Specification-Based Program Review Approach. In: Proceedings of the International Conference on Dependability of Computer Systems DEPCOS-RELCOMEX 2006 (2006)
7. Patton, R.: Software Testing, 2nd edn. SAMS Publication (2005)
8. Liu, S., Nagoya, F., Chen, Y.-T., Goya, M., McDermid, J.A.: An Automated Approach to Specification–Based Program Inspection. In: Lau, K.-K., Banach, R. (eds.) ICFEM 2005. LNCS, vol. 3785, pp. 421–434. Springer, Heidelberg (2005)
9. Fernande, R., Cowie, A.J.: Capturing Informal Requirements as Formal Models. In: Proceedings of 9th Australian Workshop on Requirements Engineering (2004)
10. Iwu, F., Galloway, O., Toyn, A., McDermid, J.A.: Practical Formal Specification for Embedded Control Systems. In: INCOM 2004, 11th IFAC Symposium on Information Control Problems in Manufacturing (2004)
11. Bryant, B.R., Lee, B.S., Cao, F., Zhao, W., Gray, J.G., Burt, C.C., et al.: From Natural Language Requirements to Executable Models of Software Components (2003)
12. Sutcliffe, A.: Scenario Based Requirements Engineering. In: Proceedings of the 11th IEEE International Conference on Requirements Engineering (2003)
13. Somé, S.: Beyond Scenarios: Generating State Models from Use Cases. In: Scenarios and State Machines: Models, Algorithms, and Tools SCESM 2002 (2002)
14. Jacobson, I., Booch, G., Rumbaugh, J.: The Unified Software Development Process. Addison-Wesley Professional, Reading (1999)

Robust Multiple Watermarking Using Entropy Based Spread Spectrum

Sushila Kamble, Vikas Maheshkar, Suneeta Agarwal, and Vinay Shrivastava

Motilal Nehru National Institute of Technology,
Computer Science & Engineering department, Allahabad-211004, India
sushila@mnnit.ac.in, v_maheshkar@yahoo.com,
suneeta@mnnit.ac.in, vinay@mnnit.ac.in

Abstract. Nowadays; information hiding has become a significant topic of computer science due to the increasing popularity of the Internet and the essential need of data security. With respect to the general information hiding problem, a tradeoff is involved between robustness, visibility and capacity. There are many watermarking techniques and models and each of them has some advantages and disadvantages. Mostly used in conjunction with spread spectrum watermarking, perceptual shaping refers to the idea of adjusting the strength of the watermark based on the perceptual sensitivity of a region in the image. All these methods use some model that assigns weights to various regions of the image. This weight determines the strength of the watermark that is added to that part of the image. This paper offers a way of embedding watermarks in a manner that increases robustness and reduces perceptual degradation and computational complexity. After an image is segmented, the entropy is calculated for each segment and only those segments that have entropy above some thresholds are considered for watermarking. This reduces the number of segments that are watermarked thereby economizing on computation and perceptual degradation. The choice of high entropy segments ensures that the method is robust, as low entropy segments would be more sensitive to attacks.

Keywords: watermarking; entropy; spread spectrum; scalar-quantization.

1 Introduction

The availability of digital data such as multimedia services on the internet leads to exponential growth of multimedia traffic (image, text, audio, video, etc). With the ease of editing and perfect reproduction in digital domain, the protection of ownership and the prevention of unauthorized tampering of multimedia data become important concerns. Digital watermarking has been proposed as a generic technique to solve various problems associated in the area of Digital Right Management (DRM) and multimedia security. Watermarking is defined as the practice of imperceptibly altering a work to embed a message about the work [5]. In general, a watermarking system consists of an embedder and a detector. The embedder takes two inputs, one is the message we want to encode as a watermark, and the other is the cover work in which we want to embed the mark. The output of the watermark embedder is typically

S. Ranka et al. (Eds.): IC3 2010, Part I, CCIS 94, pp. 497–507, 2010.

transmitted or recorded. Later that work is presented as input to the watermark detector. Most detectors try to determine whether a watermark is present, and if so, output the message encoded by it. The embedding and extraction of watermark is given in the Figure 1.

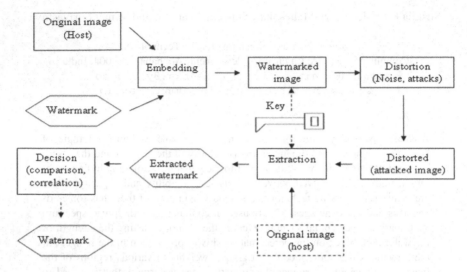

Fig. 1. Embedding and Extraction of Watermarking

If we embed more than one watermark in the cover image to increase the robustness, then it is also termed as multiple watermarking techniques [3, 9]. These are broadly classified as composite, segmented and successive (Re-watermarking).

A variety of practical approaches to data hiding with a focus on scalar quantization schemes shows that these schemes are superior to spread spectrum hiding schemes [1, 2, 6, and 7] which simply add a spread version of the hidden data to the host. To limit the distribution while embedding the watermark, the watermarking scheme must use image-adaptive criteria in addition to statistical criteria. The use of local criteria to choose where to embed the watermark can provide robustness against a variety of attacks [8].

The rest of this paper is organized as follows: section II explains the scalar quantization based techniques in detail. Section III gives the terminology used in the paper. Section IV gives the proposed technique. The experimental results are given in the section V. The paper is concluded in section VI followed by the references.

2   Scalar Quantization Based Watermarking Techniques

There are two major techniques to be considered for scalar quantization based watermarking viz. ET (Entropy) scheme and SEC (Selective Embedding in Coefficients) scheme [8].

2.1 ET (Entropy Based) Scheme

2.1.1 Embedding of Watermark

- The image is divided into 8X8 non- overlapping blocks and block processing of 8x8 DCT of the block is taken
- The accumulated entropy of each block is computed.
- DC coefficient is neither used for entropy calculation nor for information embedding because JPEG uses predictive coding for DC coefficient.
- The block whose entropy E is greater than a predefined threshold is selected for information embedding.
- Low frequency coefficients are used to embed in qualifying blocks (i.e. blocks that satisfy the entropy test).

2.1.2 Extraction of Watermark

- The hidden coefficient is reverse scanned to form an 8X8 matrix.
- Inverse DCT is taken to get the original image coefficients.

2.2 SEC (Selectively Embedding in Coefficients) Scheme

Instead of deciding where to embed at the block level, we do a coefficient by coefficient selection with the goal of embedding in those coefficients that cause minimal perceptual distortion.

2.2.1 Embedding of Watermark

- 8x8 DCT of no overlapping blocks is taken and the coefficients are divided by JPEG quantization matrix at design quality factor.
- Quantization is done using JPEG quantization matrix.
- Coefficients are scanned in zig zag way and only a predefined low frequency band is considered for hiding.
- Quantize those coefficient values to nearest integers and take their magnitude.
- Embed in a given coefficient only if resulting value exceeds a positive integer threshold t. Embedding is again done using the choice of scalar quantizers.

2.2.2 Extraction of Watermark

- The hidden coefficients are reverse scanned to get 8X8 matrix.
- Multiply by JPEG quantization matrix
- Take inverse DCT

As the threshold increases, fewer coefficients qualify for embedding, and hence, less data can be hidden which provides a trade off between hiding rate and perceptual quality. For thresholds $t \geq 2$, it becomes difficult for a human observer to distinguish between the original and composite image while embedding reliably at fairly higher rate.

3 Terminology

3.1 Quantization

Quantization is defined as division of each DCT coefficient by its corresponding quantizer step size, followed by rounding to the nearest integer. In this step the less important DCT coefficients are wiped out. This (lossy) transformation is done by dividing each of the coefficients in the 8x8 DCT matrices by a weight taken from a quantization table. If all the weights are equal, the transformation does nothing but if they increase sharply from origin, higher spatial frequencies are dropped quickly. Most existing compressors start from a sample table developed by the ISO JPEG committee. Subjective experiments involving the human visual system have resulted in the JPEG standard quantization matrix. With a quality level of 50, the matrix renders both high compression and excellent decompressed image quality [4].

16	11	10	16	24	40	51	61
12	12	14	19	26	58	60	55
14	13	16	24	40	57	69	56
14	17	22	29	51	87	80	62
18	22	37	56	68	109	103	77
24	35	55	64	81	104	113	92
49	64	78	87	103	121	120	101
72	92	95	98	112	100	103	99

Fig. 2. JPEG standard quantization matrix for quality factor (QF) =50

If however, another level of quality and compression is desired, scalar multiplies of the JPEG Standard quantization matrix (QM) may be used. For a quality level greater than 50 (less compression and higher image quality), the standard QM is multiplied by (100-quality level)/50. For a quality less than 50 (more compression, lower image quality), the standard QM is multiplied by 50/quality level. The scaled QM is then rounded and clipped to have positive integer values ranging from 1 to 255. For example, the following QM yields quality levels of 10 and 90.

$$Q_{10} = \begin{bmatrix} 80 & 60 & 50 & 80 & 120 & 200 & 255 & 255 \\ 55 & 60 & 70 & 95 & 130 & 255 & 255 & 255 \\ 70 & 65 & 80 & 120 & 200 & 255 & 255 & 255 \\ 70 & 85 & 110 & 145 & 255 & 255 & 255 & 255 \\ 90 & 110 & 185 & 255 & 255 & 255 & 255 & 255 \\ 120 & 175 & 255 & 255 & 255 & 255 & 255 & 255 \\ 245 & 255 & 255 & 255 & 255 & 255 & 255 & 255 \\ 255 & 255 & 255 & 255 & 255 & 255 & 255 & 255 \end{bmatrix} \quad Q_{90} = \begin{bmatrix} 3 & 2 & 2 & 3 & 5 & 8 & 10 & 12 \\ 2 & 2 & 3 & 4 & 5 & 12 & 12 & 11 \\ 3 & 3 & 3 & 5 & 8 & 11 & 14 & 11 \\ 3 & 3 & 4 & 6 & 10 & 17 & 16 & 12 \\ 4 & 4 & 7 & 11 & 14 & 22 & 21 & 15 \\ 5 & 7 & 11 & 13 & 16 & 12 & 23 & 18 \\ 10 & 13 & 16 & 17 & 21 & 24 & 24 & 21 \\ 14 & 18 & 19 & 20 & 22 & 20 & 20 & 20 \end{bmatrix}$$

Fig. 3. JPEG standard quantization matrix for quality factor 10 and quality factor of 90

3.2 PSNR (Peak Signal to Noise Ratio)

The PSNR computes the peak signal-to-noise ratio, in decibels, between two images. This ratio is often used as a quality measurement between the original and a compressed image. The higher the PSNR, the better is the quality of the compressed or reconstructed image.

The Mean Square Error (MSE) and the Peak Signal to Noise Ratio (PSNR) are the two error metrics used to compare image compression quality. The MSE represents the cumulative squared error between the compressed and the original image, whereas PSNR represents a measure of the peak error. The lower the value of MSE, the lower is the error.

To compute the PSNR, first calculates the mean-squared error using the following equation:

$$MSE = \frac{\sum_{M,N}[I_1(m,n) - I_2(m,n)]^2}{M \times N} \tag{1}$$

M and N are the number of rows and columns in the input images, respectively. The PSNR is given by the following equation:

$$PSNR = 10\log_{10}\left[\frac{R^2}{MSE}\right] \tag{2}$$

R is the maximum fluctuation in the input image data type. For example, if the input image has a double-precision floating-point data type, then R is 1. If it has an 8-bit unsigned integer data type, R is 255, etc.

Logically, a higher value of PSNR is good because it means that the ratio of Signal to Noise is higher. Here, the 'signal' is the original image, and the 'noise' is the error in reconstruction. So, if you find a compression scheme having a lower MSE (and a high PSNR), you can recognize that it is a better one. Usually PSNR of more than 35 dB is considered good quality.

4 Proposed Algorithm

In this paper, a multiple watermarking technique based on spread transform is proposed, which has good performance in validity and capacity. The watermark is embedded in the DCT block based on the predefined threshold of the entropy of the block. In this section the embedding and extraction methods of watermarking are introduced, and its performances are analyzed.

4.1 Watermark Embedding Method

- Firstly, the image is block processed using 8 × 8 DCT
- Now find the entropy of each 8*8 block. Entropy (E) is a statistical measure of randomness that can be used to characterize the texture of the input image. Entropy is defined as

$$E = - \text{sum}(p.*\log(p)) \tag{3}$$

- The embedding of the watermark is done in only those blocks for which the threshold exceeds predefined value of the entropy. This step achieves additional compression losslessly by encoding the quantized DCT coefficients more compactly based on their statistical characteristics.

Consider for example Lena (512*512) grayscale image. If the threshold for entropy is set to 5.65, we get block nos. 1321, 1330, 1396, 1464, 2716 having entropy greater than 5.65. The entropy for these blocks is 5.7188. These highest threshold blocks are selected for embedding of watermark as it indicates that these blocks are having the most important information of the cover image. Hence the security is increased in case of filtering or compression attacks. However, if we choose the lowest entropy blocks for selection, then we get the improved quality of watermark image but it will not resist the filtering or the compression attacks. Hence, we had preferred the highest entropy blocks for embedding to increase the security against attacks.

- The watermark is now segmented into parts to embed into different entropy selected blocks. The division of watermark is four for simplicity.
- Performing the DCT on the entropy qualified blocks, a simple piecewise division by the quantization matrix obtains the quantized matrices needed for the next step. The design QF determines the maximum JPEG compression that hidden image will survive.
- Let $c_{i,j}$ = DCT coefficients of block processed image
- $M_{i,j}^{QF}$ = quantization matrix entry for particular QF

$$\tilde{C}_{i,j} = \frac{C_{i,j}}{M_{i,j}^{QF}} \ \forall \ i, j \in \{0, 1, 2, .., 7\} \tag{4}$$

- Scan these DCT coefficients in the zigzag order
- The coefficient with zero frequency in both dimensions is called the "DC coefficient" and the remaining 63 coefficients are called the "AC coefficients."
- The coefficients $\tilde{C}_{i,j}$ are scanned in zigzag fashion to get one dimension vector $\tilde{C}_k$ where $0 \le k \le 63$.
- The first n of these coefficients are used for hiding after excluding the DC coefficient (k = 0) term. Thus, low frequency coefficients are used for embedding.
- Quantize these coefficient values $\tilde{C}_k$ to nearest integers and take their magnitude to get r_k.
- Embed in a given coefficient only if r_k exceeds a positive integer threshold t. Embedding is again done using the choice of scalar quantizers. We send either $Q_0 (\tilde{C}_k)$ or $Q_1 (\tilde{C}_k)$ depending on incoming bit.

$$\tilde{d}_k = \begin{cases} Q_{bl}(\tilde{c}_k) & ,if \ 1 \le k \le n \\ r_k & ,r_k = t \\ c_k & ,otherwise \end{cases} \tag{5}$$

Where bl is the message and Q_{bl} is the quantizer Q_0 or Q_1 depending upon the message. If after embedding $\tilde{d}_k$ −t then the same message is embedded into the next qualified coefficient to have synchronization with the decoder.

4.2 Watermark Extraction

The watermarking extraction process is the exactly reverse process of the embedding.

- The hidden coefficient $\tilde{d}_k$ is reverse scanned to form an 8X8 matrix.
- It is multiplied by JPEG quantization matrix to obtain DCT coefficients.
- Inverse DCT is taken which yields the hidden image intensity values $a'_{i,j}$ for that block.

5 Experimental Results

This multiple watermarking technique is implemented using MATLAB 7.0. The watermark is embedded in the DCT block based on the predefined threshold of the entropy of the block. Grayscale images are used as the cover works, and binary images are used as the watermark signals. Firstly, the image is divided in blocks of 8 × 8 pixels. The entropy of each 8X8 block is calculated. The decision of where to embed the watermark will totally base on the entropy of the individual block. A predefined threshold is considered to embed the watermark. Only those blocks whose entropy is more than this threshold will be considered for embedding. As the pre-processing of blocks for embedding is done only on selected blocks, this method reduces the computational complexity. Finally, the watermark information is embedded into the corresponding qualified blocks.

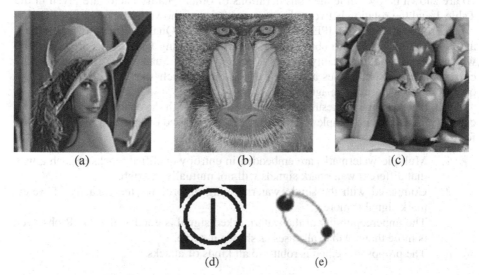

(a) (b) (c)

(d) (e)

Fig. 4. (a-c) Cover Images (d) watermark1 (e) watermark2

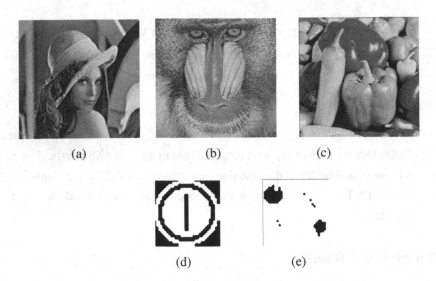

(a)   (b)   (c)

(d)   (e)

Fig. 5. (a) Watermarked image (b-c) Extracted watermark1 & watermark2

Many experiments are carried out under different cover images and different entropy threshold. Due to limited space, we only give the experimental results when using grayscale Lena, Mandrill, and Pepper images as the cover work (as shown in Fig 4) having dimension 512*512. These images are taken from the standard image dataset of test images. The two watermarks namely watermark1 and watermark2 are used for embedding. Both the watermarks are binary images having dimension 32*32.

The corresponding watermarked images after applying the technique along with the extracted watermarks are shown below. Due to the limitation of the space the watermarked images considering step size of quantizer as 40 and Quality Factor of 50 are shown below while the considerations of other Quality Factor are given in the Table 1 and the relation between these constraints are shown in the graphs of Fig. 6

The robustness against JPEG is tested using plot of Quality factors 10, 40, 50, 60 and 90. The bit error ratio obtained for the corresponding watermarks are compared with the corresponding quality factors. The step size of quantizer is fixed at 40. The corresponding PSNR values are given in the table which shows that the perceptual quality of the watermark image is good.

From the experimental results shown above, along with the analysis in section 5, we can conclude that the multiple watermarking method based on spread transform has the following characteristics:

1. Multiple watermarks are embedded in entropy qualified blocks in such a way that different watermark signals will not mutually interfere.
2. Compared with the single watermarking algorithms, the capacity of watermark signal is more.
3. The imperceptibility of the watermarked signal is good as the PSNR observed is more than 40db in all cases as shown in table.
4. The proposed method is robust to all kinds of attacks.

Table 1. Robustness test against JPEG using Quality factor Vs. PSNR plot

Images	Step Size of Quantizer	PSNR	QF	BER1	BER2
LENA	40	41.9346	10	0.5977	0.6211
			40	0.6846	0.9053
			50	0.6836	0.9063
			60	0.6836	0.9063
			90	0.6836	0.9063
MANDRIL	40	41.8537	10	0.6299	0.6514
			40	0.6846	0.9043
			50	0.6836	0.9063
			60	0.6836	0.9063
			90	0.6836	0.9063
PEPPER	40	41.8956	10	0.5713	0.6016
			40	0.6846	0.9102
			50	0.6836	0.9063
			60	0.6836	0.9063
			90	0.6836	0.9063

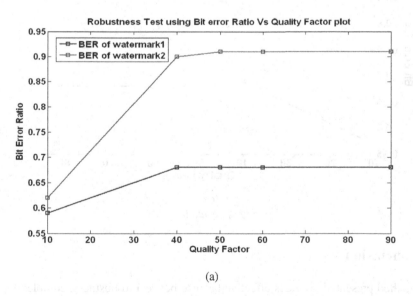

(a)

Fig. 6. (a-c) Robustness against JPEG using quality factor Vs. Bit Error Ratio plot

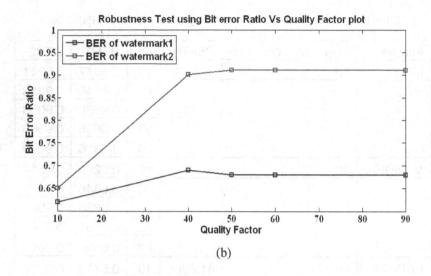

(b)

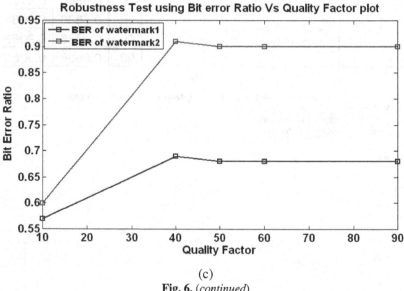

(c)

Fig. 6. (*continued*)

5 Conclusion

The method presented provides effective balance between robustness, complexity, and image quality. The embedding of the watermark is done in only those blocks for which the threshold exceeds predefined value of the entropy. This step achieves additional compression losslessly by encoding the quantized DCT coefficients more compactly based on their statistical characteristics. The local criterion to decide where to embed data gives the choice for scalar quantization without compromising robustness. The proposed method is very flexible and its mathematical background is clear. This method can avoid many drawbacks of existing multiple watermarking methods. It can be designed to be robust or fragile watermarking algorithms accordingly, and the capacity of each watermark is the same as the common singular watermarking algorithms.

References

1. Chen, B., Wornell, G.W.: Quantization Index Modulation Methods for Digital Watermarking and Information Embedding of Multimedia. J. VLSI Signal Processing Systems 27, 7–33 (2001)
2. Chen, B., Wornell, G.W.: Quantization Index Modulation: A Class of Provably Good Methods for Digital Watermarking and Information Embedding. IEEE Transaction on Information Theory 47, 1423–1443 (2001)
3. Mintzer, F., Braudaway, G.W.: If one watermark is good, are more better? In: International Conference on Accoustics, Speech, and Signal Processing, pp. 2067–2070. IEEE Computer Society, Washington (1999)
4. Wallace, G.K.: The JPEG Still Picture Compression Standard. Communications of the ACM 34, 30–44 (1991)
5. Cox, I.J.: Digital watermarking and steganography. Morgan Kaufmann, San Francisco (2002)
6. Cox, I.J., Kilian, J., Leighton, T.: Secure spread spectrum watermarking for multimedia. IEEE Transaction on Image Processing 6, 1673–1687 (1997)
7. Xiao, J., Wang, Y.: Multiple Watermarking Based on Spread Transform. In: 8th International Conference on Signal Processing, China (2006), ISBN: 0-7803-9736-3
8. Solanki, K.N., Jacobsen, N., Madhow, U., Manjunath, B.S., Chandrasekaran, S.: Robust image-adaptive data hiding using erasure and error correction. IEEE Transaction on Image Processing 13, 1627–1639 (2004)
9. Sheppard, N.P., Safavi-Naini, R., Ogunbona, P.: On multiple watermarking. In: Workshop on Multimedia and Security at ACM Multimedia, Canada, pp. 3–6 (2001)

Application of Adaptive Learning in Generalized Neuron Model for Short Term Load Forecasting under Error Gradient Functions

Chandragiri Radha Charan[1,*] and Manmohan[2,*]

[1] EEE Department, Sreenidhi Institute of Science and Technology,
Hyderabad, Andhra Pradesh, India
crcharan@gmail.com
[2] Electrical Department, Faculty of Engineering,
Dayalbagh Educational Institute, Agra, Uttar Pradesh, India
a.manmohan@yahoo.co.in

Abstract. Artificial Neural Networks (ANN's) have huge difficulties such as large training time, large number of nodes, hidden nodes can cause training difficulties, more training patterns, more complexity of model, least flexibility. Generalized Neuron Model (GNM) has less training time, no hidden layer, and more flexibility, less complexity. In this paper non adaptive learning, adaptive learning in GNM for short term load forecasting (STLF) is trained and tested for different error gradient functions.

Keywords: Adaptive Learning, Artificial Neural Network, Error Gradient Functions, Generalized Neuron Model, Short Term Load Forecasting.

1 Introduction

Load forecasting plays a prominent role in power system planning, operation and control. Short term load forecasting, medium term load forecasting and long term load forecasting are three types of load forecasting. Short term load forecasting is usually done for an hour. Medium term load forecasting is done few months ahead. Long term load forecasting is done few year ahead demands.

Short term load forecasting is required for control, unit commitment, security assessment, optimum planning of power generation, and planning of both spinning reserve and energy exchange, also as inputs to load flow studies and contingency analysis. Medium term load forecasting planning is done for seasonal peak winter, summer. Long term load forecasting is used to determine the capacity of generation, transmission and distribution in system planning, annual hydrothermal maintenance scheduling etc.

---

* Chandragiri Radha Charan, Dr. Manmohan is working under Soft Computing, Load Forecasting.

S. Ranka et al. (Eds.): IC3 2010, Part I, CCIS 94, pp. 508–517, 2010.

1.1 Short term Load Forecasting with Different Techniques

In 1980-81 the IEEE load forecasting working group [1], [2] has published a general philosophy load forecasting on the economic issues. Some of the techniques are general exponential smoothing [3], state space and Kalman filter [4] and multiple regression [5].

In 1987 Hagan [6] proposed stochastic time series model for short term load forecasting. Load forecasting depends on weather according to ARMA mode[7], which falls under time series category. The combination of both these models gives the better performance. In 1990 Rahaman [8] and Ho [9] proposed the application of KBES. In 1991-92 Park [10] and Peng[11] used ANN for STLF, which did not consider the dependency of weather on load. In 1995 Kalra [12] incorporated the feature of weather dependency also for STLF. Later in 1996 Khincha [13] developed online ANN model for STLF.

In artificial neural networks the drawbacks are limited to accuracy, large training time, huge data requirement, relatively large number of hidden layer to train for non-linear complex load forecasting problem. So the fuzzified neural network approach for load forecasting, D. K. Chaturvedi et al [14] has been developed in 2001. In-order to train the total number of neurons, it requires large amount of time. In 2002, Man Mohan, et al [15] proposed a generalized neuron model (GNM) for training and testing of short-term load forecasting.

In order to reduce local minima and other deficiencies, the training and testing performances of the models have been compared by Chaturvedi D. K. et al in 2003 [16]. In ANN, the training time required training the neurons, size of hidden layer can cause training difficulties, size of training data, learning algorithm is comparatively large. Here an attempt has been made to develop new neuron model, which is using neuro-fuzzy approach by Man Mohan et al in 2003 [17]. By having all these difficulties with ANN, so a new neuron model with development for short term load forecasting has been done in 2003 by Man Mohan et al [18]. In 2009 C Radha Charan, Manmohan have predicted the relation between RMS testing error, maximum testing error, minimum testing error and time elapsed during testing with error functions [19].

1.2 Major Reasons for Development of Short Term Load Forecasting

The deterministic models provide only the forecast values, not a measure for the forecasting error. The stochastic models provide the forecast as the expectation of the identified stochastic process. They allow calculations on statistical properties of the forecasting error. Regression models are among the oldest methods suggested for load forecasting which are quite insensitive to occasional disturbances in the measurements.

The stochastic time series models have many attractive features. The properties of the model are easy to calculate. The model identification is also relatively easy. Moreover, the estimation of the model parameters is quite straightforward, and the implementation is not difficult.

The weakness in the stochastic models is in the adaptability. In reality, the load behavior can change quite quickly at certain parts of the year. While in ARMA models the forecast for a certain hour is in principle a function of all earlier load values, the model can not adapt to the new conditions very quickly, even if model parameters are estimated recursively.

If the load behavior is abnormal on a certain day, this deviation from the normal conditions will be reflected in the forecasts into the future. A possible solution to the problem is to replace the abnormal load values in the load history by the corresponding forecast values. In order to improve the accuracy of model, better modeling result, include the feature of adaptivity, an artificial neural network (ANN) has been used for STLF. But the drawback of ANN model is the requirement of large training time which depends on size of training file, type of ANN, error functions, learning algorithms, hidden nodes.

2 Generalized Neuron Model

Generalized Neuron Model over comes the above draw backs. The GNM has less number of unknown weights. The number of weights in the case of GNM is equal to twice the number of inputs plus one, which is very low in comparison to a multi layered feed forward ANN. By reducing number of unknown weights, training time can be reduced. The number of training patterns required for GNM training is dependent on the number of unknown weights. The number of training patterns must be greater or equal to number of GNM weights. The number of GNM weights are lesser than multilayered ANN, hence the number of training patterns required is also lesser.

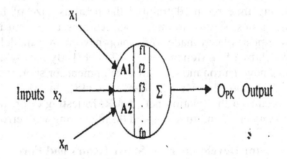

Fig. 1. Generalized Neuron Model

In GNM usage of flexible neuron model reduces the total number of neurons, less training time, no hidden layer is required and a single neuron is capable to solve most of the problems. The complexity of GNM is less as compared to multi layered ANN. The flexibility of GNM has been improved by using more number of activation functions and aggregation functions.

In this the model of Fig.1.GNM, contains sigmoid, gaussian, straight line activation functions, with two aggregation functions summation ($\sum$), product ($\prod$).The summation and product of an aggregation function have been incorporated and aggregated output passes through non-linear activation function.

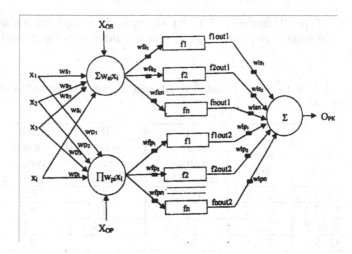

Fig. 2. Structure of Generalized Neuron Model

In Fig.2., the output of generalized neuron is

$$Opk = f1out1 \times w1s1 + f2out1 \times w1s2 + ... + fnout1 \times w1sn +$$

$$f1out2 \times w1p1 + f2out2 \times w1p2 + ... + fnout2 \times w1pn \quad (1)$$

Here f1out1, f2out1,.... ,fnout1 are outputs of activation functions f1,f2,...,fn related to aggregation function $\sum$, and f1out2, f2out2,...., fnout2 are outputs of activation functions f1,f2,...,fn related to $\prod$. Output of activation function $f1$ for aggregation function, $\sum f1out1 = f1(ws1 \times sumsigma)$. Output for activation functions $f1$ for aggregation function of π, $f1out2 = f1(wfp1 \times product)$.

2.1 Data for Short Term Load Forecasting

Data for the short term load forecasting has been taken from Department of Electricity and water supply, Dayalbagh and Dayalbagh science museum, Agra, India. Different types of conditions have been considered which are mentioned below as different types. The data consists of load of different weeks, weather conditions (maximum temperature in ° C, minimum temperature in ° C and humidity in percentage) have been considered for the month of January 2003.

Normalization value: $[(Y_{max} - Y_{min}) * (\dfrac{L - L_{min}}{L_{max} - L_{min}})] + (Y_{min}) \quad (2)$

where: $Y_{max}=0.9$, $Y_{min}=0.1$, $L=$ values of variables, $L_{min}=$ minimum value in that set, $L_{max}=$ maximum value in that set.

Data is tabulated in three types where in the inputs are six and output is one. Type I consists of I, II, III weeks loads, I, II, III weeks average temperatures as inputs and IV week load as output. Type II consists of I, II III weeks load, III week maximum temperature, III week minimum temperature, III week humidity as inputs and IV week load as output. Type III consists of I, II, III weeks load, average maximum temperature, average minimum temperature, and average humidity as inputs and IV week load as output.

Table 1. Type I (I, II, III weeks of load, I, II, III week average temperature as input and IV week load as output)

I week load	II week load	III week load	I week average temperature	II week average temperature	III week average temperature	IV week load
2263.2	2479.2	2166	10.75	8	7.25	2461.2
2238	3007.2	2227.2	12	8	8.5	2383.2
2482.2	3016.8	2802	11.5	7.75	8.25	2025.6
2384.4	3285.6	2022	9.5	7	7.5	2557.2
2196	2295.6	2014.8	9.5	7.5	6.75	2548.8
2678.4	2286	3087.6	8.5	8	7.75	2560.8
2887.6	2458.8	2618.4	9.5	8.75	9.25	2800.8
Normalized Data						
I week load	II week load	III week load	I week average temperature	II week average temperature	III week average temperature	IV week load
0.17	0.25	0.20	0.61	0.55	0.26	0.54
0.14	0.67	0.25	0.90	0.55	0.66	0.46
0.43	0.68	0.68	0.78	0.44	0.58	0.10
0.31	0.90	0.10	0.32	0.10	0.34	0.64
0.10	0.10	0.09	0.32	0.32	0.10	0.63
0.65	0.10	0.90	0.10	0.55	0.42	0.65
0.90	0.23	0.54	0.32	0.90	0.90	0.90

Table 2. Type II (I, II, III weeks load, III week maximum temperature, III week minimum temperature, III week humidity as inputs and IV week load as output)

I week load	II week load	III week load	III week maximum temperature	III week minimum temperature	III week humidity	IV week load
2263.2	2479.2	2166	9.5	5	95	2461.2
2238	3007.2	2227.2	11	6	99	2383.2
2482.2	3016.8	2802	10.5	6	98	2025.6
2384.4	3285.6	2022	10	5	88	2557.2
2196	2295.6	2014.8	8.5	5	92	2548.8
2678.4	2286	3087.6	10.5	5	90	2560.8
2887.6	2458.8	2618.4	13.5	5	81	2800.8

Table 2. (*continued*)

Normalized Data						
I week load	II week load	III week load	III week maximum temperature	III week minimum temperature	III week humidity	IV week load
0.17	0.25	0.20	0.26	0.10	0.72	0.54
0.14	0.67	0.25	0.50	0.90	0.90	0.46
0.43	0.68	0.68	0.42	0.90	0.85	0.10
0.31	0.90	0.10	0.34	0.10	0.41	0.64
0.10	0.10	0.09	0.10	0.10	0.58	0.63
0.65	0.10	0.90	0.42	0.10	0.50	0.65
0.90	0.23	0.54	0.90	0.10	0.10	0.90

Table 3. Type III (I, II, III weeks load, average maximum temperature, average minimum temperature, average humidity as inputs and IV week load as output)

I week load	II week load	III week load	Average maximum temperature	Average minimum temperature	Average Humidity	IV week load
2263.2	2479.2	2166	11.5	5.83	87	2461.2
2238	3007.2	2227.2	12	6.66	95	2383.2
2482.2	3016.8	2802	11.5	6.83	88.6	2025.6
2384.4	3285.6	2022	10.83	5.16	95	2557.2
2196	2295.6	2014.8	10.16	5.66	90	2548.8
2678.4	2286	3087.6	10.5	6.33	90	2560.8
2887.6	2458.8	2618.4	12.5	5.83	85.6	2800.8
Normalized Data						
I week load	II week load	III week load	Average maximum temperature	Average minimum temperature	Average Humidity	IV week load
0.17	0.25	0.20	0.55	0.42	0.21	0.54
0.14	0.67	0.25	0.72	0.81	0.90	0.46
0.43	0.68	0.68	0.55	0.90	0.35	0.10
0.31	0.90	0.10	0.32	0.10	0.90	0.64
0.10	0.10	0.09	0.10	0.33	0.64	0.63
0.65	0.10	0.90	0.21	0.66	0.47	0.65
0.90	0.23	0.54	0.90	0.42	0.10	0.90

2.2 Error Gradient Functions

The mathematical expression for the sum squared error gradient function:

$$\frac{\delta E}{\delta Wsi} = -sum((D - Opk) * \frac{\delta opk}{\delta Wsi} \tag{3}$$

The mathematical expression for Cauchy error gradient function:

$$\frac{\delta E}{\delta Wsi} = -sum(((cauchy^2) * \frac{error}{(cauchy^2 + error^2)}) * \frac{\delta opk}{\delta Wsi}) \tag{4}$$

The mathematical expression for mean fourth power error gradient function:

$$\frac{\delta E}{\delta Wsi} = -sum(4 * ((D - opk)^3 * (\frac{\delta opk}{\delta Wsi}))) \tag{5}$$

where δE=change in error, δWsi= change in weights, opk= actual output, δopk= change in output ,D = desired output, Cauchy = 2.3849.

3   Results of Short Term Load Forecasting with Generalized Neuron Model

The generalized neuron model has been applied to train the network with the sum squared error gradient function using Equation (3), Cauchy error gradient function using Equation (4) and mean fourth power error gradient function using equation (5) for comparing root mean square(RMS) testing error, maximum testing error and minimum testing error with MATLAB 7.0.

Table 4. GNM with the sum squared error gradient function without adaptivity

Type of load data	RMS testing error	Maximum testing error	Minimum testing error
I	0.0420	0.0486	-0.0738
II	0.0685	0.1059	-0.1146
III	0.0175	0.0236	-0.0233

Table 5. GNM with Cauchy error gradient function without adaptivity

Type of load data	RMS testing error	Maximum testing error	Minimum testing error
I	0.0429	0.0499	-0.0754
II	0.0686	0.1061	-0.1150
III	0.0177	0.0239	-0.0237

Table 6. GNM with mean fourth power error gradient function without adaptivity

Type of load data	RMS testing error	Maximum testing error	Minimum testing error
I	0.2273	0.3941	-0.4047
II	0.1849	0.3312	-0.3264
III	0.2183	0.3833	-0.3904

4 Application of Adaptive Learning and Momentum Factor Using Generalized Neuron Model for Short Term Load Forecasting

Short term load forecasting with the sum squared error gradient function, Cauchy error gradient function, mean fourth power error gradient function has been studied. In that, III type of load in the sum squared error gradient function in which root mean square testing error is 0.0175, maximum testing error is 0.0236, minimum testing error is -0.0233 is the minimum error. By applying adaptability, the error gradient in III type of load in the sum squared error gradient function will further decrease by varying learning factor, η, momentum factor, α with respect to training epochs. The

adaptive learning Equation is $\quad \eta = \eta_{old} \times \left[\dfrac{\delta E / \delta t_{old}}{\delta E / \delta t_{new}} \right]$ (6)

Table 7. GNM using short term load forecasting with load and weather parameters under the sum square error gradient function of type III

	Without adaptive learning and momentum factor, $\alpha = 0.95$	With adaptive learning and momentum factor, $\alpha = 0.95$
Root mean square testing error	0.0175	5.2307×10^{-15}
Maximum testing error	0.0236	9.992×10^{-15}
Minimum testing error	-0.0233	-5.8845×10^{-15}

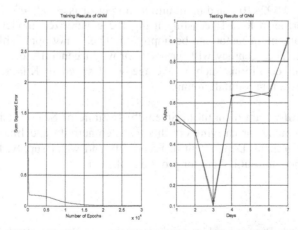

Fig. 3. Type III: GNM using short term load forecasting under the sum squared error gradient function with learning rate, $\eta = 0.001$, momentum factor, $\alpha = 0.95$, gain scale factor $= 1.0$, tolerance$= 0.002$, all initial weights $= 0.95$, training epochs$= 30,000$, without adaptive learning.

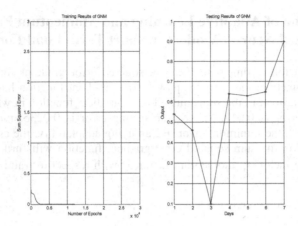

Fig. 4. Type III: GNM using short term load forecasting under the sum squared error gradient function with learning rate, η=0.001, momentum factor, α= 0.95, gain scale factor =1.0, tolerance= 0.002, all initial weights = 0.95, training epochs= 30,000, with adaptive learning

5 Conclusion

The variations of short-term load forecasting with the generalized neuron model with the sum squared error gradient function, Cauchy error gradient function, mean fourth power error gradient functions has been simulated. The sum square error gradient function without adaptive learning with momentum factor, $\alpha = 0.95$ gives as root mean square testing error is = 0.0175, maximum testing error is = 0.0236 and minimum testing error is = -0.0233 which is minimum result. By including adaptive learning , momentum factor ,$\alpha = 0.95$ of the sum square error gradient function with III type of load will give the root mean square testing error is =5.2307×10^{-15}, maximum testing error is = 9.992×10^{-15} and minimum testing error is = -5.8845×10^{-15}. The accuracy of the short-term load forecasting using the generalized model with adaptive learning and momentum factor can be improved. This is not applicable to long term load forecasting. The accuracy will further improve in generalized neuron model by considering other conditions such as average wind speed in Km/hr, average wind direction in degree, total rainfall in mm.

Acknowledgments. I am thankful to Sreenidhi Institute of Science and Technology, Ghatkesar, Hyderabad for carrying out this research activity and financial support. I would also like to thank Department of Electricity and water supply, Dayalbagh and Dayalbagh science museum, Agra for providing the data.

References

1. IEEE Committee Report: Load Forecasting Bibliography, Phase 1. IEEE Trans. on Power Apparatus and Systems PAS-99(1), 53–58 (1980)
2. IEEE Committee Report: Load Forecasting Bibliography, Phase 2. IEEE Trans. on Power Apparatus and Systems PAS-100(7), 3217–3220 (1981)

3. Christiaanse, W.R.: Short term load forecasting using General Exponential Smoothing. IEEE Trans. in Power Apparatus and System PAS-90(2) (1971)
4. Sharma, K.L.S., Mahalanabis, A.K.: Recursive Short Term Load Forecasting Algorithm. IEE Proc. 121(1), 59 (1974)
5. Mathewmann, P.D., Nicholson, H.: Techniques for Load Prediction in Electric Supply Industry. IEE Proc. 115(10) (1968)
6. Hagan, M.T.: The Time series Approach to Short Term Load Forecasting. IEEE Trans. on Power System 2(3), 785 (1987)
7. Galiana, F.D.: Identification of Stochastic Electric Load Models from Physical Data. IEEE Trans. on Automatic Control ac-19(6) (1974)
8. Rahaman, S.D., Bhatnagar, R.: Expert Systems Based Algorithm for Short Term Load Forecasting. IEEE Trans. on Power Systems 3(2), 392 (1988)
9. Ho, K.L.: Short Term Load Forecasting Taiwan Power System Using Knowledge Based Expert System. IEEE Trans. on Power Systems 5(4), 1214 (1990)
10. Park, D.: Electric Load Forecasting Using an Artificial Neural Network. IEEE Trans. on Power Systems 6, 442 (1991)
11. Peng, T.M.: Advancement in Application of Neural Network for Short Term Load Forecasting. IEEE Trans. on Power Systems 7(1), 250 (1992)
12. Kalra, P.K.: Neural Network- A Simulation Tool. In: National Conference on Paradigm of ANN for Optimization Process Modeling and Control. IOC, Faridabad (1995)
13. Khincha, H.P., Krishnan, N.: Short Term Load Forecasting Using Neural Network for a Distribution Project. In: National Conference on Power Systems, p. 17. Indian Institute of Technology, Kanpur (1996)
14. Chaturvedi, D.K., Satsangi, P.S., Kalra, P.K.: Fuzzified neural network approach for load forecasting. Engineering Intelligent Systems 8(1), 3–9 (2001)
15. Man Mohan, D.K., Chaturvedi, A.K., Saxena, P.K.: Short Term Load Forecasting by Generalized Neuron Model. Inst. of Engineers (India) 83, 87–91 (2002)
16. Chaturvedi, D.K., Mohan, M., Singh, R.K., Kalra, P.K.: Improved generalized neuron model for short-term load forecasting. Soft Computing 8(1), 10–18 (2003)
17. Man Mohan, Chaturvedi, D.K., Satsangi, P.S., Kalra, P.K.: Neuro - fuzzy approach for developing of a new neuron model. Soft Computing 8(1), 19–27 (2003)
18. Man Mohan, Chaturvedi, D.K., Kalra, P.K.: Development of New Neuron Structure for Short Term Load Forecasting. Int. J. of Modeling and Simulation, ASME periodicals 46(5), 31–52 (2003)
19. Radha Charan, C., Manmohan: Joint International Conference on Applied Systems Research and XIII National Systems Conference, Agra, India, pp. 372–375 (2009)
20. Chaturvedi, D.K.: Soft Computing Techniques and its Applications in Electrical Engineering, pp. 93–94. Springer, Heidelberg (2008)

Intelligent Schemes for Indexing Digital Movies

R.S. Jadon[1] and Sanjay Jain[2]

[1] Department of Compter Applications, MITS Gwalior, India-474005
[2] Department of Compter Applications, ITM Gwalior, India-474020
rsjadon@hotmail.com, sanjayjainitm@gmail.com

Abstract. In this paper we have proposed a set of computable audio visual features of movies and have developed methods to estimate them. These features are global in nature and are extracted using whole sequence; therefore, they do not require any object detection, tracking and classification. These features include video shots, average shot length, motion, color dominance and lighting key as visual features and time domain, pitch based, frequency domain, sub band energy and MFCC as audio features. We have then developed a movie classifier that can parse a given movie clip into predefined genre categories using both the extracted audio and visual features of the movie clips. The movie classifier is designed using multi layer Feed forward neural network with back propagation learning algorithm and tested the classifier for characterization of movies into action, comedy, drama, horror, and musical genres. We achieved about 87% successful classification.

Keywords: movie classification, semantic features, audio-visual contents, neural net based learning.

1 Introduction

Recent advances in multimedia compression technology, the significant increase in computer performance and the growth of Internet, have led to the widespread use and availability of digital video. The availability of audio-visual data in the digital format is increasing day by day. This data includes documents, audio-visual presentation, home made video and professionally created contents such as TV shows and movies. Movies constitute a large portion of the entertainment industry. With the digital technology getting inexpensive and popular, there has been a tremendous increase in the volume and availability of movies through cable and Internet such as video on demand. Currently several web sites host movies and provide users with the facility to browse and watch online movies.

In film theory, genre refers to the primary method of movie categorization. A "genre" generally refers to movies that share similarities in the narrative elements from which they are constructed. Directors often follow rules pertaining to the specific genre of a movie. Such rules are referred as Film Grammar or cinematic principles in the film literature. By following these principles, camera movements, sound effects, and lighting we can create mood and atmosphere, induce emotional reactions, and convey

S. Ranka et al. (Eds.): IC3 2010, Part I, CCIS 94, pp. 518–529, 2010.
© Springer-Verlag Berlin Heidelberg 2010

information to the viewers. Although, different directors use these principles differently, movies of the same genre have a lot of features in common [4] [15][19].

Movie genres are various forms or identifiable types, categories, classifications or groups of movies that have similar, familiar or instantly recognizable patterns, filmic techniques or conventions that include one or more of the following: settings, content, themes, plot, narrative events, motifs, styles, structures, situations, icons, characters (or characterizations), and stars. Three main types are often used to categorize film genres; setting, mood, and format. The film's location is defined as the setting. Movies belong to such type are- crime, fantasy, film noir, historical, science fiction, sports, teen war and westerns. The emotional charge carried throughout the movie is known as its mood. Movies belong to such type are- action, adventure, comedy, drama, horror, mystery, romance and thriller.

It is feasible to classify movies at the time of making a movie. Once movie is created, it is very difficult to classify it. So, we need a system that automatically gives the idea of the genre of the movie. This could help peoples to choose movie based on personal preferences.

Rest of the paper is organized as follows: Related work is reviewed in section 2. Section 3, describes the proposed methodology of our work. In section 4, we describe extraction process of various visual features. Section 5, describes the extraction process of various audio features. In section 6, we describe the designing of neural network based movie genres classifier. Implementation and experimental results are given in section 7. Section 8 concludes the paper.

2 Related Work

Automatic genre classification of movies is an important task. People have tried to use the video part for classification. Vasconcelos et al. proposed a feature-space based approach in [13]. In this work, two features of the previews, average shot length and shot activity, were used. An extension of their approach was presented by Nam et al. [10], which identified violence in previews. They attempted to detect violence using audio and color matching criteria. Zeshan[30] demonstrated the combination of visual cues and cinematic principles for genre categorization. Recently several researchers have started to investigate the potential of analyzing the accompanying audio signal for video scene classification [3, 9, 23, 28, 33]. Liu et al [34,36] present two approaches for TV genre classification. They investigate a range of statistical time and frequency features extracted from audio. M. Xu. et al. [11] detect audio emotional events from comedy and horror movies. Simon et al. [12] developed an algorithm for the detection of sound energy and affect events for extraction horror scenes.

Obviously, audio information alone may not be sufficient for understanding the scene content, and in general, both audio and visual information should be analyzed. Our aim is to analyze both audio-visual cues from the movie clips and make an educated guess about its genre. In this work, we have extracted various audio visual features of various movie clips and then designed movie genres classifier using feed forward neural network with back propagation learning algorithm and tested the classifier for the characterization of movie clips into action, horror, comedy, musical, and drama genres[16].

3 Proposed Methodology

The overall schematic diagram for our approach is shown in figure 1. The input to the system is a movie clip, while the output is a genre of the defined types. We perform the shot segmentation of video using normalized Image Histograms intersection and pixel difference of two consecutive frames. We then extract the visual features average shot length, motion color dominance and lighting key from the segmented video part and audio based features time domain, pitch, frequency domain, sub band energy, and MFCC form the audio part.

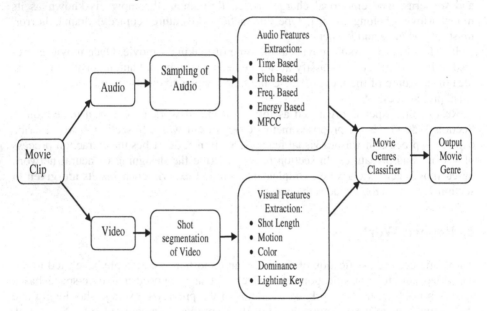

Fig. 1. Schematic diagram for movie genres characterization system

Once we extracted the audio-visual features from various movie clips. We then compute the expected outcomes of the movie genre based on listening and watching the movies clip and store them in a separate text file. Finally, we supply the extracted audio visual features and their expected outcomes to the movie genres classifier. The classifier is implemented using MATLAB's Neural Networking toolbox. The classifier is a feed forward neural network with back propagation learning algorithm. Once the classifier is trained we simulate the classifier and get the movie genres characterization.

4 Visual Features Extraction

We first segment the movie clip into shots and then low level visual features average shot length, motion, color dominance, and lighting key are extracted. We have reported this work in [21,22].

4.1 Shot Segmentation

Shot segmentation is performed by extracting frames from movie sequence. Several features have been suggested for the purpose of video segmentation. These features include Histogram Intersection, Pixel Difference, edge pixel count and Optical Flow etc. No particular feature is general enough to capture all possible types of changes in video data. Therefore, we have used combined approaches of pixel difference and image histogram interaction. These features were also reported by Jadon et al.[18] for video segmentation using fuzzy theoretical approach. Shot boundaries are detected by setting a threshold. We have used static threshold values based on experimental results. There are many schemes available for threshold selection. We have used this approach because of its robustness. Table 1 shows recall and precision of shot segmentation result of some movie clips of 60 seconds.

Table 1. Shows the shot segmentation results

Movie Name	Recall	Precision
American Pie2	91.07%	100%
Bad Boys	100%	100%
Batman Begins	93.54%	96.66%
Fearless	88.88%	99.96%
Final Terror	83.33%	93.33%
La Bam bola Assa2	92.85%	96.29%
Madonna	86.66%	68.42%
Razor back	100%	91.66%
Revelation	100%	100%
Rolling Stone	100%	87.88%
Shakespeare In Love	100%	100%
The Boondocks Saint's	91.17%	93.93%

4.2 Average Shot Length Computation

This feature was first proposed by N. Vasconcelos and A. Lippman [13]. The average shot length is computed by dividing the total number of frames by the total number of shots in the preview [31]. Semantically this feature characterizes the pace of the movie [4]. Experiments show that slower paced films have larger average shot length as they have many dialogue shots, whereas action movies appear to have shorter shot lengths because of rapidly changing shots.

4.3 Motion Computation

Motion computation is performed by comparing the frames of the movie clip. Since, we are comparing frames with each others; we will have to always keep one frame as a reference for comparison. Comparing 24-bit images will generate too much difference between frames since 2^{24} values could change between one frame and the next, therefore we should compare grayscale images with 256 or less shades of gray [20].

The algorithm for motion detection is works on single frames, these come in arrays of bytes containing the 8-bit value of each color. The algorithm takes the input frames one by one and compares it to the reference frame. If there is a difference between the input and reference frames calculate the motion in the frame, otherwise, ignore it. This process is repeated to all the frames of the movie. If the reference frame is too old then store a new reference frame. We then calculate the standard deviation of the motion distribution. Experiments show that, action films would have higher values for such a measure, and less motion value for the other genres.

4.4 Color Dominance

The effectiveness of the color histogram feature depends on the color coordinate used and the quantization method. Zettl observes in, [7], "The expressive quality of color is, like music, an excellent vehicle for establishing or intensifying the mood of an event." Wan and Kuo [16] studied the effect of different color quantization methods in different color spaces including RGB, YUV, HSV, and CIE L*u*v*.

We use RGB space for its simplicity and effectiveness. Based on color histogram, we detect the dominant color (DC) of flame and fire the dominant color of flame is yellow, orange, and/or red. Mean (E) and standard deviation (σ) of the dominant color within one clip are used as clip level color features. This feature is helpful for detecting flame and fire which is mostly available in action movie.

$$E_i = 1/n \sum_{j=1}^{n} p_{ij} \tag{1}$$

$$\sigma_i = \left[1/n \sum_{j=1}^{n} \left(p_{ij} - E_i \right)^2 \right]^{1/2} \tag{2}$$

4.5 Lighting Key

Lighting is an important dramatic agent. Movie directors often used multiple light sources to balance the amount and direction of light while shooting scene. Lighting can also be used to direct the attention of the viewer to certain area of importance in the scene. It can also affect viewer's feeling directly regardless of the actual content of the scene. There are many ways to illuminate a scene; we adopt a scene lighting quality to achieve this characteristic which is defined as

$$\zeta_i = \mu_i \bullet \sigma_i \tag{3}$$

where μ and σ denote the mean and standard deviation of i'th key frame [14, 32].

In film literature, two major lighting methods are used to establish a relation between the context and the mood of the viewer, called low key lighting and high key lighting. In high key lighting frames, the light is well distributed which results in larger values for the standard deviation and the mean and in low key lighting frames, these measures have smaller value[33]. Figure 2 (a), (b), (c) and (d) shows the distribution of gray scale pixel values in low key frame of movie "Final Terror", its histogram, high key frame of movie "A Christmas Story" and its histogram, respectively.

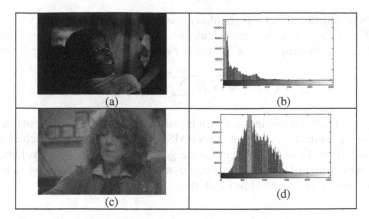

Fig. 2. Distribution of gray scale pixel values

Table 2 shows the results of visual features Average Shot Length (ASL), Color Dominance Mean (CDM), Color Dominance Standard Deviation (CDSD), Lighting Intensity(LI), Motion Mean(MM) and Motion Standard Deviation(MSD) extraction of various movie clips.

Table 2. Extracted visual features of various movie clips

Movie Name	ASL	CDM	CDSD	LI	MM	MSD
Bad Boys	40	2.68	36.37	0.06	2.75	6.23
Batman Begins	46.45	0	0	0.03	2.45	4.85
Fearless	43.63	0	0	0.05	10.32	8.36
Shakes Pear in Love	72	0.07	0.31	0.04	2.65	2.75
White Mans Burden	160	0	0	0.02	1.00	1.53
My Part in his Downfall	360	0.28	1.12	0.11	4.68	6.00
Ali	120	0.08	0.34	0.10	3.24	5.45
Always	144	0	0	0.06	2.44	2.71
Royskatt	96	0	0	0.06	1.62	3.89
Final Terror	144	0	0	0.03	2.45	3.70
Razorback	57.6	0	0	0.02	0.81	2.10
Revelation	130.91	0.01	0.12	0.05	1.90	2.88
Rolling stone	45	0.44	0.84	0.09	7.73	6.59
Under oath	9.72	0.54	1.36	0.10	12.15	14.10

5   Audio Features Extraction

Liu et al[34,35] investigate a range of statistical time and frequency based audio features. We have extracted time domain, pitch, frequency domain, sub band energy, and MFCC based audio features. We have reported this work in [21, 22].

5.1   Volume Based Features

Volume is a reliable indicator for silence detection; therefore, it can be used to segment audio sequence and determine clip boundaries [8, 25]. In electronic sound, the physical quantity is amplitude, which is particularly characterized by the sample value in digital signals. Therefore volume is often calculated as the *Root-Mean-Square (RMS)* of amplitude [6,24,29]. Volume of the nth frame is calculated, by the following formula:

$$v(n) = \sqrt{1/N \sum_{i=0}^{N-1} S_n^2(i)} \tag{4}$$

where $S_n(i)$ is the ith sample in the nth frame audio signal, and N is the total number of samples in the frame. Figure 3 plot the VRMS of five movie clips, which clearly indicate the difference between different movie genres. After calculating volume of each frame, volume standard deviation, volume dynamic range, zero crossing rate and salience ratio are extracted as clip level features.

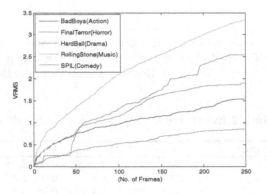

Fig. 3. Shows the vrms of five movie genres

5.2 Pitch Based Features

Pitch serves as an important characteristic of an audio for its robust classification. Pitch information helps derive 3 features, which help in a more accurate and better classification, as compared to other features. Average Magnitude Difference Function (AMDF) is used to determine the pitch of a frame, and is defined as:

$$A_m(n) = \frac{\sum_{i=0}^{N-n-1} |s_m(i+1) - s_m(i)|}{N-n} \tag{5}$$

where, $A_m(n)$ = AMDF for n^{th} sample in m^{th} frame, N = number of samples in a frame and $s_m(i)$ = i^{th} sample in m^{th} frame of an audio signal. AMDF is calculated for every sample of the frame. After computing pitch for each frame, clip level features pitch standard deviation, VMR, NUR are extracted.

5.3 Frequency Based Features

To obtain frequency domain features, spectrogram of an audio clip, in the form of short-time Fourier transform is calculated for each audio frame. Since time domain does not show the frequency components and frequency distribution of a sound signal[2] [26]. The spectrogram is used for the extraction of two features, namely frequency Centroid, and frequency bandwidth.

5.4 Sub-band Energies

The energy distribution in different frequency bands also varies quite significantly among different types of audio signals. The entire frequency spectrum is divided into four sub-bands at the same interval of 1 KHz. Each subband consists of six critical bands which represent cochlear filter in the human auditory model [17]. The Sub-band energy is defined as:

$$E_i = \sum_{w=w_{iL}}^{w_{iH}} |F(w)|^2 \quad 1 \le i \le 4 \tag{6}$$

Where W_{iL} and W_{iH} are lower and upper bound of sub-band i,

5.5 Mel Frequency Cepstral Coefficients(MFCC)

MFCCs are cepstral coefficients used for representing audio in a way that mimics the physiological properties of the human auditory system. MFCCs are commonly used in speech recognition and are finding increased use in music information recognition and comedy genre classification. The cepstrum of a signal is the Fourier transform of the logarithm (decibel) signal (with unwrapped phase) of the Fourier transform of a signal [1]. In the Mel frequency cepstrum, the frequencies are scaled logarithmically using the Mel scale. Table 3 shows the results of extraction of audio features Volume Standard Deviation (VSD), Volume Dynamic Range (VDR), Zero Crossing Rate (ZCR), Salience Ratio (SR), Pitch Standard Deviation (PSD), Voice Music Ratio (VMR), Noise Unvoice Ratio (NUR), Frequency Centroid (FC), Frequency Bandwidth (FB), and MFCC of various movie clips.

Table 3. Extracted audio features of various movie clips

Movie Name	VSD	ZCR	SR	VDR	PSD	VMR	NUR	FC	FB	MFCC
Bad Boys	0.76	0.05	0.01	0.99	0.06	0.94	0.06	0.39	1.39	18.90
Batman Begins	0.41	0.03	0.04	0.99	0.03	0.97	0.03	0.17	1.96	9.92
Fearless	0.93	0.03	0.07	0.99	0.09	0.95	0.05	0.33	1.56	13.79
Shakes Pear in Love	0.32	0.06	0.01	0.98	0.04	0.94	0.06	0.16	1.99	8.00
White Mans Burden	0.93	0.05	0.06	0.99	0.06	0.96	0.04	0.33	1.53	15.58
My Part in his Downfall	1.33	0.05	0.35	1.0	0.08	0.97	0.03	0.45	1.25	24.89
Ali	0.09	0.03	0.34	0.99	0.01	0.90	0.10	0.06	2.28	2.82
Always	2.21	0.04	0.01	1.0	0.17	0.93	0.07	1.37	0.04	51.61
Royskatt	2.31	0.06	0.03	1.0	0.16	0.97	0.03	1.35	0.05	63.76
Razorback	0.96	0.05	0.01	1	0.08	0.97	0.03	0.32	1.58	18.23

6 Designing of Movie Genres Classifier

We have designed the movie genres classifier using feed forward multilayer perceptron neural network with supervised back propagation learning algorithm. A MLP is

composed of layers of processing units that are interconnected through weighted connections. These layers are input, output and Intermediate layer called hidden layer.

The network is trained using back propagation with three major phases. In the first
phase an input vector is presented to the network which has audio-visual extracted
feature values in our case, which leads via the forward pass to the activation of the
network as a whole. This generates a difference (error) between the output of the network and the desired output. In the next phase error is computed for the output unit and
propagates this factor successively back through the network.

In the final phase we compute the changes for the connection weights by feeding the
summed squared errors from the output layer back through the hidden layers to the
input layer. This process is continued until the connection weights in the network have
been adjusted so that the network output has converged, to an acceptable level, with the
desired output. The trained network is then given the new data. We have five categories in the output: action, comedy, horror, drama and music.

7   Experimental Results

We have implemented this system on windows platform in Java and C#. Video part is
implemented by Java and audio part is implemented by the C#. We have conducted
extensive experiments on around two hundred movie clips. These clips were obtained
from the various sites. Our experiments show interesting structure within the feature
space, implying that a mapping does indeed exist between high-level classification and
low-level computable features. We identified five major genres, namely action, comedy, drama, horror and musical.

The easiest way of examining the accuracy of the trained classifier is by plotting the
output value of each output neuron for each movie clip. For the first twenty movie
clips, the first output neuron should be the most highly activated, for the second sixteen
movie clips, the second output neuron should be activated and so on.

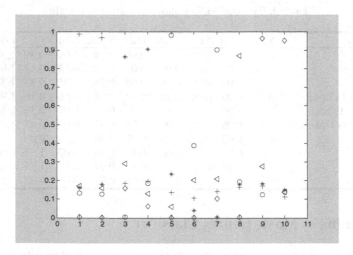

Fig. 4. Graph of the output values for ten output neuron

Figure 4 shows the graph of the output values for ten movie clips. These values are generated by the movie classifier. The table 4 shows the output values of neurons for ten movie clips generated by the movie classifier. The output neuron1 represent the action, neuron2 represent the comedy and so on. The table 5 summarizes the classification result of all the 72 movie clips. The result table contains the number of clips, their ground truth, generated results and the correctness of the result. The result shows that the system has correctly classified 56 movie clips, 05 are not classified in any of the given genre category, 03 are classified as multiple genres and 08 are false classified. The overall performance of the system is around 77%.

Table 4. Output values of neurons for ten movie clips

Movie Name	Ground Truth	Neuron1 (Action)	Neuron2 (Comedy)	Neuorn3 (Drama)	Neuron4 (Horror)	Neuron5 (Music)	Result Generated
Bad boys	Action	0.987	0.162	0.133	0.169	0.005	Action
The Bourne Identity	Action	0.967	0.179	0.127	0.159	0.002	Action
A Touch of Class	Comedy	0.185	0.864	0.003	0.292	0.159	Comedy
My Part In His Downfall	Comedy	0.196	0.904	0.184	0.129	0.063	Comedy
Always	Drama	0.137	0.234	0.981	0.060	0.001	Drama
Royskatt	Drama	0.106	0.040	0.388	0.202	0.004	Not classi.
Revelation	Horror	0.142	0.005	0.900	0.210	0.103	Drama
Final Terror	Horror	0.164	0.180	0.194	0.869	0.004	Horror
Madonna	Musical	0.169	0.182	0.124	0.275	0.962	Musical
Rolling Stone	Musical	0.112	0.150	0.138	0.137	0.951	Musical

Table 5. Result of Characterization of Movie Clips

Movie Name	No. of Clips	Ground Truth	Result Generated	Correctness
BadBoys	04	Action	4A	100%
Bounre Identity	04	Action	4A	100%
Fearless	04	Action	4A	100%
Matrix	04	Action	4A	100%
The Boondock Saints	04	Action	3A,1C	75%
A Touch of Class	04	Comedy	3C,1NC	75%
Shakespeare in Love	04	Comedy	1C,1D,2NC	25%
Hot To Trot	04	Comedy	4C	100%
MyPartin his Downfall	04	Comedy	3C,1CD	75%
Always	04	Drama	4D	100%
Royskatt	04	Drama	3D,1NC	75%%
Ali	02	Drama	2D	100%
Revelation	04	Horror	1H,3D	25%
Final Terror	04	Horror	2H,1D,1CH	50%%
Razor back	04	Horror	1H,2C,1CH	25%
LaBambolaAssa2	04	Horror	3H,1NC	75%
Underoath	03	Musical	3M	100%
Madonna	04	Musical	4M	100%
Rolling Stone	03	Musical	3M	100%

8 Conclusions

The results obtained for the classification of movie genres are quite promising. This has been in-spite of the fact that our training set has been fairly small and consists of movie clips of different semantic structures. This authenticates the choice of features that we have selected. The proposed system could overcome problems that are posed by purely audio and purely visual classifiers. This further established our hypothesis that a proper understanding of movie genres classification is possible only if we make use of both the audio as well as visual content.

We have trained our system for a fairly small database and the length of the movie clips is also small (60 seconds). An immediate concern would be to see how it scales to huge databases and full length of movies for it to have any commercial value. In the present system, we are only able to characterize movie in action, comedy, drama, horror and music genres. In Future work, we could further extend the work by including more movie genres for characterization in the existing system.

References

1. Adams, B., Dorai, C., Venkatesh, S.: Towards automatic extraction of expressive elements from motion pictures: tempo. In: IEEE International Conference on Multimedia and Expo., pp. 641–644 (2000)
2. Boas hash, B., Zoubir, A.M.: Digital signal processing, Brisbane: Queensland University of Technology, Signal Processing Research Centre (1995)
3. Saraceno, C., Leonardi, R.: Audio as a Support to Scene Change Detection and Characterization of Video Sequences in ICASSP 1997, vol. 4, pp. 2597–2600 (1997)
4. Arijon, D.: Grammar of the Film Language. Hasting House Publishers, New York (1996)
5. Wold, E., Blum, D., Keislar, D., et al.: Content-based classification, search, and retrieval of audio. IEEE Multimedia, 27–36 (1996)
6. Lu, G.J.: Multimedia database management systems. Artech House, Boston (1999)
7. Sight, H.Z.: Sound Motion: Applied Media Aesthetics, 2nd edn. Wadsworth Publishing Company, Belmont (1990)
8. Hao, J., Tong, L., Hong-Jiang, Z.: Video segmentation with the assistance of audio content analysis. In: ICME 2000, vol. 3, pp. 1507–1510 (2000)
9. Nam, J., Tewfik, A.H.: Combined Audio and Visual Streams Analysis for Video Sequence Segmentation. In: Proc. of ICASSP 1997, vol. 3, pp. 2665–2668 (1997)
10. Nam, J., Alghoniemy, M., Tewfik, A.H.: Audio-visual content based violent scene characterization. In: IEEE International Conference on Image Processing, pp. 353–357 (1998)
11. Xu, M., Chia, L.T., Jin, J.S.: Affective content analysis in comedy and horror videos by audio emotional event detection. In: ICME 2005, pp. 622–625 (2005)
12. Moncrieff, S., Venkatesh, S., Dorai, C.: Horror film genre typing and scene labeling via audio analysis. In: ICME 2003, vol. 2, pp. 193–196 (2003)
13. Vasconcelos, N., Lippman, A.: Statistical models of video structure for content analysis and characterization. IEEE Transactions on Image Processing, 3–19 (2000)
14. Cinematique, P.: Lighting in filmmaking, http://www.inpoint.org
15. Lyman, P., Varian, R.H.: School of Information Management and Systems. University of California, Berkeley (2000)

16. Presents a comprehensive list of genres,
    http://us.imdb.com/Sections/Genres/
17. Safranek, R., Jayant, N., Johnston, J.: Signal compression based on models of human perception. Proc. IEEE 81(10), 1385–1422 (1993)
18. Jadon, R.S., Chaudhary, S., Biswas, K.K.: A Fuzzy Theoretic Approach for Video Segmentation using Syntactic Features. In: Pattern Recognition Letters. Elsevier Press, Amsterdam (2001)
19. Ng, S.K., Lindblom, J., Tanskanen, A.: Motion Detection Report
20. Jain, S., Jadon, R.S.: Features Extraction for Movie Genres Characterization. In: Proceeding of WCVGIP 2006 (2006)
21. Jain, S., Jadon, R.S.: Audio Based Movies Characterization using Neural Network. International Journal of Computer Science and Applications 1(2), 87–91 (2008)
22. Jain, S., Jadon, R.S.: Audio-Visual Contents Based Movies Characterization. International Journal of Computer Science and Information Technology 1(2), 93–99 (2008)
23. Pfeiffer, S., Fischer, S., Feldberg, W.: Automatic Audio Content Analysis. In: Proc. ACM Multimedia, pp. 21–30 (1996)
24. Kientzle, T.: A programmer's guide to sound. Addison-Wesley Developers Press (1998)
25. Zhang, T., Kuo, J.C.: Audio content analysis for online audiovisual data segmentation and classification. IEEE Transactions on Speech and Audio Processing 9, 441–457 (2001)
26. Ingle, V.K., Proakis, J.G.: Digital signal processing using MATLAB. Brooks/Cole Pub., Pacific Grove (2000)
27. Wan, X., Kuo, J.C.: A new approach to image retrieval with hierarchical color clustering. IEEE Trans. on Circuits and Systems for Video Technology 8(5), 628–643 (1998)
28. Wang, Y., Huang, J., Liu, Z., Chen, T.: Multimedia Content Classification using Motion and Audio Information. In: Proc. of IEEE ISCAS 1997, vol. 2, pp. 1488–1491 (1997)
29. Wang, Y., Liu, Z., Huang, J.C.: Multimedia content analysis-using both audio and visual clues. IEEE Signal Processing Magazine 17, 12–36 (2000)
30. Rasheed, Z., Shah, M.: Movie genre classification by exploiting audio- visual features of previews. In: International Conference on Pattern Recognition (2002)
31. Rasheed, Z., Sheikh, Y., Shah, M.: Semantic Film Preview Classification Using Low-Level Computable Features. In: 3rd International Workshop on MDDE 2003, Berlin, Germany (2003)
32. Rasheed, Z., Sheikh, Y., Shah, M.: On the use of computable features for film classification. IEEE Trans. on Circuits and System for Video Technology 15(1), 52–63 (2005)
33. Liu, Z., Wang, Y., Chen, T.: Audio Feature Extraction and Analysis for Scene Segmentation and Classification. Journal of VLSI Signal Processing System (1998)
34. Liu, Z., Huang, J., Wang, Y., Chen, T.: Audio feature extraction & analysis for scene classification. In: IEEE MMSP 1998, pp. 343–348 (1998)
35. Liu, Z., Wang, Y., Chen, T.: Audio feature extraction and analysis for scene segmentation and classification. Journal of VLSI Signal Processing Systems for Signal, Image, and Video Technology 20(1/2), 61–79 (1998)
36. Liu, Z., Huang, J., Wang, Y.: Classification of TV programs based on audio information using hidden Markov model. In: IEEE MMSP 1998, pp. 27–32 (1998)

Fuzzy Reasoning Boolean Petri Nets Based Method for Modeling and Analysing Genetic Regulatory Networks

Raed I. Hamed[1], S.I. Ahson[2], and R. Parveen[1]

[1] Department of Computer Science, JMI, New Delhi-110025, India
raed.inf@gmail.com
[2] Bioinformatics and Computational Biology, Patna University - 800005, India

Abstract. We have developed a new algorithm for modeling and analyzing generic regulatory networks. This algorithm uses fuzzy Petri net to transform Boolean network into qualitative descriptors that can be evaluated by using a set of fuzzy rules. By recognizing the fundamental links between Boolean network (two-valued) and fuzzy Petri net (multi-valued), effective structural fuzzy rules is achieved through the use of well-established methods of Petri net. For evaluation, the proposed technique has been tested using real bacterium *E.Coli* which under the nutritional stress response and experimental results shows that the use of fuzzy Petri net based technique in gene expression data analysis can be quite effective.

Keywords: Boolean network; Fuzzy Petri net; Generic regulatory networks; Modeling and analysing.

1 Introduction

A major challenge of modeling biological systems is that conventional methods based on physical and chemical principles require data that is difficult to accurately and consistently obtain using either conventional biochemical or high throughput technologies, which typically yield noisy, semi-quantitative data (often in terms of a ratio rather than a physical quantity) [1]. The problem of modeling is concerned with searching for optimal (or near-optimal) models subject to a number of constraints. A review of modeling in genetic regulatory networks containing research on several techniques, such as differential equation [2], [3], fuzzy logic [4], Petri nets [5], [6], [7], Boolean networks [8], [9], Bayesian networks [10] and artificial neural networks [11]. The above-mentioned papers are dedicated to the applications of different methods to genetic networks and show that these methods are suitable to model special molecular biological systems.

However, differential equation models are widely accepted to express biological systems, but the drawback of this approach is the hardness to observe the regulation mechanism intuitively in the biological sense, also can be computationally expensive and sensitive to imprecisely measured parameters [12]. Modeling using stochastic Petri nets [13] or hybrid Petri nets [14] can not deal with vague or fuzzy information. On the other hand, Boolean network models have inadequate dynamic resolution to accurately describe the behavior of a biological network.

S. Ranka et al. (Eds.): IC3 2010, Part I, CCIS 94, pp. 530–546, 2010.

Petri net theory and fuzzy logic exhibit a graphical and mathematical formalism to model, and simulate the biological systems. Fuzzy Petri net (PN) is a successful tool for describing and studying information systems. Incorporating the fuzzy logic with Petri Nets has been widely used to deal with fuzzy knowledge representation and reasoning [15], [16], [17], [18]. It has also proved to be a powerful representation method for the reasoning of a rule-based system. FPN with rule- based system are a qualitative approach to modeling and simulating the dynamics of qualitative systems. Such an approach is appropriate for the case where a state of the modeled system corresponds to a marking of the associated FPN. The motivation for the development of the FPN model is to fuse the benefits of fuzzy logic (i.e. effectively manage uncertain or corrupted inputs, natural linguistic structure, etc.) with FPN techniques. The advantages of using FPNs in fuzzy rule-based reasoning systems include [17], [19]: (1) the graphical representation of FPNs model can help to visualize the inference states and modify fuzzy rule bases; (2) the analytic capability, which can express the dynamic behavior of fuzzy rule-based reasoning. Evaluation of markings is used to simulate the dynamic behavior of the system. The explanation of how to reach conclusions is expressed through the movements of tokens in FPNs [19].

In this paper, we modeled and analysed the genetic network by using fuzzy reasoning Boolean Petri nets (FRBPN) and describe the dynamical behavior of gene. We illustrate our FRBPN approach by presenting a detailed case study in which the genetic regulatory network for the carbon starvation stress response in the bacterium *E. coli* [20] is modelled and analysed. Using the case study of data provided in [20] we define the Boolean behaviour of the key regulatory entities involved using truth tables. However, understanding the molecular basis of the transition between the exponential and stationary phase of *E. coli* cells has been the focus of extensive studies for decades [21].

The organization of this paper is as follows: In Section 2, Boolean Networks are described. In Section 3, the fundamental properties of aggregation operations and formal definition of fuzzy Petri nets are presented. In Section 4, we explain the details of the membership functions for active and inactive state with Boolean tables are investigated in this Paper. Section 5 describes the proposed FRBPN modeling approach is presented. Section 6 describes the reasoning algorithm. Section 7 describes the experimental results. Finally, we presented the conclusions of our model in Section 8.

2 Boolean Network

In recent years Boolean Networks (BN) has become popular paradigms for modeling gene regulation. Boolean networks compose a class of discrete models where the expression levels of each gene are assumed to have two possible values: ON (*active*) or OFF (*inactive*) [22]. In this model, gene expression is functionally related to the expression levels of other genes using logical rules. A *Boolean network* is defined by a set of genes (nodes), $V = \{x_1, x_2, \ldots, x_n\}$ and a list of Boolean functions, $F = \{f_1, f_2, \ldots, f_n\}$. Given n genes, the activity level of gene i at time step t is denoted by $x_i(t)$, where $x_i(t) = 0$ indicates that gene i is not expressed and $x_i(t) = 1$ indicates that it is expressed. However, the overall expression levels of all the genes in the network at time step t is given by the state (row) vector $x(t) = [x_1(t), x_2(t), \ldots, x_n(t)]$. Gene i evolves from time t to $(t + 1)$ according to the Boolean function $x_i(t+1) = f_i(x(t), x(t), \ldots, x(t))$; $i = 1, 2,\ldots, n$, where the genes in the argument of f_i form the *regulatory set* for the gene x_i. The number k_i is called the *connectivity* to gene i and $K = max_i\ k_i$ is the maximum connectivity of a Boolean network. The *state transition* $x(t) \rightarrow x(t + 1)$ is governed by the n Boolean functions. The 2^n state transitions can fully characterize a Boolean network's dynamics. For instance, if a Boolean network has 3 nodes, its one-step state transitions will have 8 pairs of states, where the first pair consists of state 000 and its next state, the second pair consists of 001 and its next state, etc.

Given all the one-step state transitions, a directed graph $G(V,F)$, known as the *state transition diagram*, can thus be constructed for the Boolean network. V is a set of 2^n vertices, each vertex being a state of the Boolean network. An example of a state transition diagram with two attractors is shown in Fig.1, where the graph is composed of two disjoint subgraphs. In Fig.1 the states (0 0 0) and (1 1 0) with red color are both attractors, and the other states leading into them are their basins of attraction.

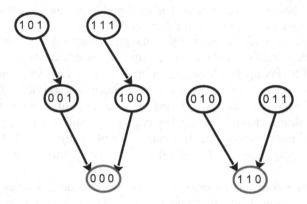

Fig. 1. The state transition diagram of a Boolean network with 3 genes

3 Fuzzy Petri Nets

3.1 Fundamental Properties of Aggregation Operations

The use of a fuzzy Petri net approach allows for an easily customizable model. Aggregation of information represented by membership functions is a central field in intelligent systems where fuzzy rule base and reasoning mechanism are applied. More specifically, the essence of data system can be captured in the form of AND and OR aggregation operations as illustrated in Fig. 2.

Given n places, $P_1, P_2 \ldots P_n$, where $P_i \in FPN$, let us assume an AND relationship exists among the P's, an integrated P is created with AND operation plotted in Fig.1. Using the AND operation, the single places $(P_{1,1}, P_{1,2},\ldots, P_{n,1})$ are linked into an integrated transition $T_{1,1}$ where all operations from each single place will be executed. The OR Operation allows single places to be combined into an integrated place allowing the choice of operations from each single place to be performed based upon predetermined conditions. Given n places, $P_1, P_2, \ldots, P_n$, where $P_i \in FPN$, let us assume an

OR relationship exists among the P's, an integrated P is created with OR operation plotted in Fig.2. The AND and OR aggregation operations can be represented by a variety of operations for relational computation. The most fundamental logic-based aggregation operations occur within the field of two-valued logic (binary data), where we have simple AND and OR gates for processing binary data [23]. t-norm is a function $T : [0,1]^2 \rightarrow [0,1]$ which is associative, increasing and commutative, and satisfies the boundary condition $T(1,x) = x$ for all $x \in [0,1]$. A t-conorm is an associative, commutative, increasing $S : [0,1]^2 \rightarrow [0,1]$ function, with boundary condition $S(1,x) = x$ for all $x \in [0,1]$.

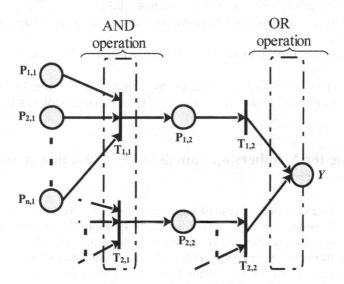

Fig. 2. Structure of a fuzzy Petri net model represented as an aggregation operations: AND and OR

3.2 Formal Definition of Fuzzy Petri Nets

The model was introduced by Looney [24] for the specification of rule-based reasoning using propositional logic. Places are interpreted as conditions having fuzzy truth values (tokens), while transitions represent the fuzzy decision values of rules. Reasoning in a FPN can be performed by iteratively maxing (OR operation) and mining (AND operation) transitions and fuzzy truth values of tokens, respectively. Formally, a fuzzy Petri net structure is defined as follows [25]: The tuple $FPN = (P, T, D, I, O, F, \alpha, \beta)$ is called a fuzzy Petri net if:

1. $P = \{p_1, p_2, ..., p_n\}$ is a finite set of places, corresponding to the propositions of FPRs;
2. $T = \{t_1, t_2, ..., t_n\}$ is a finite set of transitions, $P \cap T = \emptyset$, corresponding to the execution of FPRs;
3. $D = \{d_1, d_2, ..., d_n\}$ is a finite set of propositions of FPRs. $P \cap T \cap D = \emptyset$, $|P| = |D|$, d_i $(i = 1,2,..., n)$ denotes the proposition that interprets fuzzy linguistic variables, such as: very low, low, lnorm , eug , hnorm ,as in our model;

4. $I : P \times T \to \{0, 1\}$ is an $n \times m$ input incidence matrix defining the directed arcs from propositions (P) to rules (T). $I(p_i, t_j) = 1$, if there is a directed arc from p_i to t_j, and $I(p_i, t_j) = 0$; if there is no directed arcs from p_i to t_j, for $i = 1, 2, \ldots, n$, and $j = 1, 2, \ldots, m$.

5. $O : P \times T \to \{0, 1\}$ is an $n \times m$ is an output incidence matrix defining the directed arcs from rules to propositions. $O(p_i, t_j) = 1$, if there is a directed arc from t_j to p_i, and $O(p_i, t_j) = 0$; if there is no directed arcs from t_j to p_i, for $i = 1, 2, \ldots, n$, and $j = 1, 2, \ldots, m$.

6. $F = \{\mu_1, \mu_2, \ldots, \mu_m\}$ where μ_i denotes the certainty factor (CF $=\mu_i$) of R_i , which indicates the reliability of the rule R_i , and $\mu_i \in [0,1]$;

7. $\alpha : P \to [0,1]$ is the function which assigns a token value between zero and one to each place;

8. $\beta : P \to D$ is an association function, a bijective mapping from a set of places to a set of propositions.

Moreover, this model can be enhanced by including a function $Th: T \to [0, 1]$ which assigns a threshold value $Th(t_j) = \lambda_j \in [0, 1]$ to each transition t_j, where $j = 1, \ldots, m$.

4   Defining the Membership Functions for Active and Inactive State

In this section we consider the case of fuzzy set-based fuzzy model that is formed by using FRBPNs model. The fuzzy model is usually split into the identification activities dealing with the premise and consequence parts of the rules. In this study, we carry out the modeling using characteristics of experimental data of a genetic regulatory network [20]. However, we present a method to illustrate how a FRBPNs model can be applied to get the optimal result. The method involves a genetic regulatory network with seven genes: Inputs Fis; CRP; Cya; Sig; GyrAB; TopA; SRNA, and outputs Fis>; CRP>; Cya>; GyrAB>; TopA>; SRNA>; Sig>. These set of genes are given by the truth table in Table 1. In this example, we try to check the model is able to correctly switch between the exponential and stationary phases of growth control which is same as that in [20]. To make that the diagonal matrix B which can be got from the truth table for each gene in Table 1. Next the task is to construct the vector C_j. However, it is the sum of all the entries of the matrix B that denote transition to state j. To make the sum of all the entries in C_j, we need to use the following formula:

$$C(j) = \frac{1}{n} \sum_i [Dig(B)]_{i,j} \tag{1}$$

where n is the number of columns. As the vector $C(j)$ is determined, we need to calculate the finale value using the equation 2. After the value C_j is determined, we need to use this value for each gene as input to FRBPNs model corresponding on the membership degree. As the value C_j is determined for each gene, these values help us to identify the procedure of fuzzy model by using it as initial parameters in our fuzzy model. In principle any function of the form $A : X \to [0, 1]$ describes a membership function associated with a fuzzy set A tha t depends not only on the concept to be represented, but also on the context in which it is used [26]. However, in our problem the

$$C_i = \sum_i^n C(j) \qquad (2)$$

membership functions with two linguistic value of *active* and *inactive* and with overlap 0.5 are plotted in Fig.3. However, these membership functions are used to make the decision on the gene behavior. With a numeric value g_i existing in a particular continuous variable's universe of discourse, we calculate a series of gene expressions to fuzzy sets existing in the frame of cognition of the variable. Conferring the character of Boolean Network, so the regulatory gene can be judged if it is active or inactive by function 3 as following:

$$g_i = \begin{cases} 0\ (inactive) & 0 \le C_i < 0.35 \\ 1\ (active) & 0.35 \le C_i \le 1 \end{cases} \qquad (3)$$

It is noted that the membership functions of Fig. 3 is either 1 or 0, singly depending on the truth of facts represented by C_i. For this task, membership functions Fig. 3 appear to be quite suitable, offering both flexibility and simplicity. These membership functions exhibit two important properties: 1) overlap is equal to 0.5; note that we

Table 1. The truth table of each gene

Fis	CRP	Cya	Sig	CRP
0	0	0	0	1
0	0	0	1	1
0	0	1	0	1
0	0	1	1	1
0	1	0	0	1
0	1	0	1	1
0	1	1	0	1
0	1	1	1	1
1	0	0	0	0
1	0	0	1	0
1	0	1	0	0
1	0	1	1	0
1	1	0	0	0
1	1	0	1	0
1	1	1	0	0
1	1	1	1	0

CRP	Cya	Sig	CRP
0	0	0	1
0	0	1	1
0	1	0	1
0	1	1	1
1	0	0	1
1	0	1	1
1	1	0	1
1	1	1	0

GyrAB	TopA	Fis	GyrAB
0	0	0	1
0	0	1	0
0	1	0	1
0	1	1	0
1	0	0	0
1	0	1	0
1	1	0	1
1	1	1	0

Sig	Sig
0	0
1	1

Fis	CRP	Cya	Sig	GyrAB	TopA	Fis
0	0	0	0	0	0	0
0	0	0	0	0	1	0
0	0	0	0	1	0	1
0	0	0	0	1	1	0
.	.	.	.	.	.	.
.	.	.	.	.	.	.
.	.	.	.	.	.	.
.	.	.	.	.	.	.
1	1	1	1	0	1	0
1	1	1	1	1	0	0
1	1	1	1	1	1	0

Fis	SRNA
0	0
1	1

GyrAB	TopA	Fis	TopA
0	0	0	0
0	0	1	0
0	1	0	0
0	1	1	0
1	0	0	0
1	0	1	1
1	1	0	0
1	1	1	0

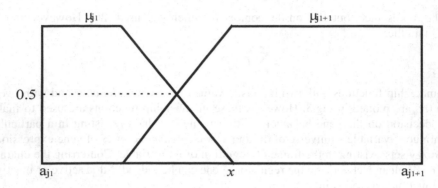

Fig. 3. The membership functions of active and inactive

keep them at 0.5 overlap, as is the norm seen in the literature [26], and 2) overlapping membership functions add up to 1 i.e.

$$\mu_{j_i}^i(x_i) = 1 - \mu_{j_i+1}^i(x_i) \tag{4}$$

The membership function is denoted as one-input–one-output will be studied to simplify the analysis so the rules will be as follows:

IF x is A_{j_i} THEN Z_{j_i} is inactive

IF x is A_{j_i+1} THEN Z_{j_i+1} is active

The expression for the function defined by the fuzzy system when the input lies on the interval $x \in [a_{j_i}, a_{j_i+1}]$ will be:

$$f(x) = \frac{Z_{j_i}\mu_{j_i}(x) + Z_{j_i+1}\mu_{j_i+1}(x)}{\mu_{j_i}(x) + \mu_{j_i+1}(x)}$$

$$= Z_{j_i}\mu_{j_i}(x) + Z_{j_i+1}\mu_{j_i+1}(x) \tag{5}$$

where the membership functions are parameterized as

$$\mu_{j_i}(x) = \frac{a_{j_i+1} - x}{a_{j_i+1} - a_{j_i}} \tag{6}$$

$$\mu_{j_i+1}(x) = \frac{x - a_{j_i}}{a_{j_i+1} - a_{j_i}} \tag{7}$$

According to the system state represented by the place, the membership functions, designating the degree of truth of the state, of the related fuzzy variables are determined. As soon as a token arrives at the place, the fuzzy marking of the token will be determined through the assigned AND and OR operations on the fuzzy variables, the AND and OR operations which are to be further addressed in the sequel.

5 The Proposed FRBPN Modeling Approach

By means of the basic FPN modeling techniques mentioned in Section 3, the proposed FRBPN-based knowledge representation algorithm for the genetic regulatory network of the *Escherichia coli* cells is described in this section. However, in order to identify the FRBPNs model we determine such a structure as the number of input variables (genes), input genes being selected and the number of the membership functions standing in the premise part and the order of polynomial in conclusion part. A more powerful idea is that the token has a linguistic value, such as, *low*, *medium* and *high*, defined as a membership function for a linguistic variable. This function also determines the degree of membership in a particular place, or the truth value of that proposition. However, our main goal here is to construct semantically meaningful fuzzy model, allowing us to attach intuitive linguistic fuzzy sets such as *low*, *medium*, and *high*, each describing a different level of gene concentration in genetic regulatory network of *E.coli* bacterium. For this purpose the triangular fuzzy membership functions with overlap ½ are plotted in Fig. 4.

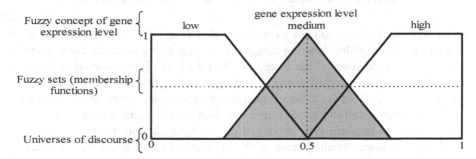

Fig. 4. The triangular fuzzy membership functions with respect to the biological concept (concentration)

In this study, each value of gene expression is normalized into a real number in the unit interval [0,1] the methods to deal with membership functions must be applied the following strict restrictions [27], [28]: 1) the membership degree of all linguistic labels must be complementary, i.e., its sum must be 1 in every point of the variable universe of discourse (X):

$$\forall x \in X, \quad \forall (A_0, A_1, ..., A_n) \in F(X), \quad \sum_{i=0}^{n} \mu_{A_i}(x) = 1 \qquad (9)$$

2) All linguistic terms must have the same basic shape (Triangular, Gaussian, Γ-function, etc.), and their membership functions must cross with their neighbours when $\mu = 1/5$. However, for these membership functions in order for error-free reconstruction of all possible numeric output values in the data, purely triangular membership functions used for fuzzification. The fuzzy model follows the fundamentals of fuzzy Petri net modeling. As advocated in [25], fuzzy Petri net modeling is realized at the conceptual level of the system formed by a collection of semantically meaningful information granules defined in each variable. These are also regarded as linguistic

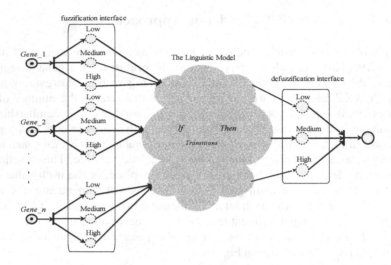

Fig. 5. FRBPNs: illustrate is a case of the *n*-input single-output system

fuzzy sets whose choice implies a certain point of view of the data under process. As a result, the membership function values (i.e. degrees of truth) of the fuzzy variables VC_i depend on the states of the place, and then the token is transmitted to the place. Definition of VC_i is depcted in Fig. 5 and described as follows: $VC_i = [\mu_{low}\_C_i, \mu_{medium}\_C_i, \mu_{high}\_C_i]^T$, That is, a 3-d membership vector for the fuzzy sets *low, medium,* and *high* corresponding to fuzzy gene expression value is generated and is given by VC_i. In order to measure these input and output metadata universally, we normalize them into the same standard scale of [0, 1]. The values of linguistic variables are fuzzified to obtain the membership degree by membership function. For example, $\mu_{low}\_\text{Fis}=(0.109) = 1$, $\mu_{medium}\_\text{Fis}=(0.109) = 0.0$, and $\mu_{high}\_\text{Fis}=(0.109)= 0.0$ means the value, 1 belongs to low with confidence value (i.e. truth degree) of 100% while 0% belongs to medium and high. Here, in our model the number of input genes is limited by n, where n is the number of inputs of truth tables defining the Boolean behaviour of each regulatory entity in the nutritional stress response network for carbon starvation. More specifically, we have the following inputs and outputs: Inputs Fis; CRP; Cya; Sig ; GyrAB; TopA; RNA, and outputs Fis>; CRP>; Cya>; GyrAB>; TopA>; RNA>; Sig>. Our FRBPNs model Fig. 5 has two fundamental functional components: (a) input and output interfaces and (b) a set of fuzzy rules as inference process. The interfaces allow interaction between the conceptual, logic-driven structure of the FRBPNs model and the physical world of measured gene expression level. More specifically, the input interface realizes perception, where input genes are transformed into an internal format of fuzzy sets formed by a set of rules, which can be expressed as rules of type:

IF Antecedent$_1$ is A$_1$ AND Antecedent$_2$ is A$_2$ AND . . . Antecedent$_n$ is A$_n$ THEN Consequent is C$_i$,

6   The Reasoning Algorithm

Starting with giving a token to each of the places of the FRNPN model, the following step-by-step algorithm is employed to derive the final value for each entity. For clarity of description, the GyaAB entity is taken for example of the proposed reasoning algorithm.

The reasoning steps for FRBPNs are described as follows:

Step1) Described a set of truth tables defining the Boolean behaviour of all the entities in a genetic network.

Step2) Based on truth tables calculate the probabilities of all entities from the diagonal matrices B_j. Then obtain the final value C_i for each entity.

Step3) Evaluate all entities in the genetic network based on C_i,

$$g_i = \begin{cases} 0 & 0 \le C_i < 0.35 \\ 1 & 0.35 \le C_i \le 1 \end{cases}$$

Stap4) Obtain the membership degree (μ_i) for each C_i, is generated and is given by

$$VC_i = [\mu_{low\_}C_i, \mu_{medium\_}C_i, \mu_{high\_}C_i]^T,$$

Stap5) The knowledge base is described by rules for genetic network problem.

- ❖   create a set P of places;
- ❖   create a set T of transitions;
- ❖   create a set I of input arcs;
- ❖   create a set O of output arcs;
- ❖   FPN structure (every transition, with its input and output places), and the name of the goal place.

Stap6) The fuzzy reasoning Boolean Petri net (FRBPN) of rules in the knowledge base is modeled for genetic regulatory networks.

Stap7) Obtain the enable transition set T based on initial marking in the step 4.

Stap8) Compare the marking value with the threshold value of the transition, to which the places as input are connected. If the marking value exceeds the threshold, then the token $\alpha(p_i)$ is passed on to the output places of the transition.

Stap9) Fire all the enable transitions, and calculated new markings M' of places p_i. Update the current set of the places p_i the token has traveled along,

Stap10) Obtain the new enable transitions set T_i. Fire the transitions and remove the tokens from input places.

Stap11) Check if the final place is reached. If it is reached, output the information brought by the winner token (with maximum fuzzy marking); otherwise, go back to Step 4 and proceed with the traveling process of the tokens. The information brought by the winner token consists of the path of traveled places, which imply the adequate switching operations for service restoration.

Following this procedure, we can extract a compact representation of the regulatory relationships between entities. The parameters of the proposed FRBPNs system are determined. The FRBPNs can be viewed as a formal representation of a fuzzy rule based system. Each antecedent parts of a fuzzy rule, and its label, and truth degree defines the consequent part (goal place).

7 Experimental Studies

Here we conduct a case study on the genetic regulatory network of the transition between the exponential and stationary phase of *E. coli* cells. It concerns a description of real estate in the *E. coli* which under normal environmental conditions, when nutrients are freely available, is able to grow rapidly entering an exponential phase of growth [21]. On the other hand, as important nutrients become depleted and scarce the bacteria experiences nutritional stress and respond by slowing down growth, eventually resulting in a stationary phase of growth. However, many people have become aware that the genetic regulatory network is not linear quadratic and that many situations can not be modeled accurately by mathematically tractable equations.   This given us good estimate to use fuzzy Petri nets to model fuzzy reasoning with propositional logic. Our ultimate goal is to model the genetic regulatory network responsible for the carbon starvation nutritional stress response in *E. coli* cells based on the comprehensive data collated in [20]. The genes (*crp, cya, fis, gyrAB, topA,* and *rrn*) and their interactions believed to play a key role in the process, make up six modules, corresponding to the truth tables defining the Boolean behaviour of each regulatory entity in the nutritional stress response network for carbon starvation. Following the approach in [20], the level of *cAMP.CRP* and DNA supercoiling are not explicitly modelled as entities in our model. We initialise the model to a set of values representing the expression level of each gene. Starting from the initial conditions representing exponential growth the system is perturbated with an activate signal.

For illustration of the algorithm, we use a model shown in Fig. 5. The net contains twenty seven transitions T_1, T_2,...,T_{27} (representing twenty seven production rules of the entity *GyrAB*) with appropriate input and output places representing the propositions forming the antecedents and consequents of the corresponding rules. However, assume that the certainty factor value CF = 1, and the knowledge base of a rule-based system defining the behavior of the entity *GyrAB* has been conceded. For example, according to the diagonal matrix GyaAB, we need to calculate the value of C_i. Thus,

$$Dig(\text{GyaAB}) \begin{pmatrix} 1\,0\,0\,0\,0\,0\,0\,0 \\ 0\,0\,0\,0\,0\,0\,0\,0 \\ 0\,0\,1\,0\,0\,0\,0\,0 \\ 0\,0\,0\,0\,0\,0\,0\,0 \\ 0\,0\,0\,0\,0\,0\,0\,0 \\ 0\,0\,0\,0\,0\,0\,0\,0 \\ 0\,0\,0\,0\,0\,0\,1\,0 \\ 0\,0\,0\,0\,0\,0\,0\,0 \end{pmatrix}$$

Here,
$C(1) = 0.125$ $C(2) = 0$ $C(3) = 0.125$ $C(4) = 0$ $C(5) = 0$ $C(6) = 0$ $C(7) = 0.125$
$C(8) = 0$

After the matrix C_i is determined, the value of $C(\text{GyaAB})$ will be $C(\text{GyaAB}) = 0.375$.

Table 2 shows the value and state for seven entities. The degree of truth of input propositions is shown in Table 2, and we wants to ask what degree of truth of the end proposition might have, then the rules and the fact can be modeled by the fuzzy reasoning Boolean Petri net model as shown in Fig. 5.

Table 2. The value and state obtained for each gene

Gene name	CRP	Cya	Fis	GyaAB	TopA	Sig	SRNA
Value	0.5	0.875	0.109	0.375	0.125	0.5	0.5
State	active	active	inactive	active	inactive	active	active

The membership degrees of these input data are calculated by triangular membership functions. These membership function value can be used as the truth degree of each antecedent proposition in our FRBPN model. However, the degree of truth of all input propositions proposition listed as:

CRP = 0.5
$\mu_{CRP\_Low}(0.5) = 0.0$
$\mu_{CRP\_Medium}(0.5) = 1$
$\mu_{CRP\_High}(0.5) = 0.0$

Cya = 0.875
$\mu_{Cya\_Low}(0.875) = 0.0$
$\mu_{Cya\_Medium}(0.875) = 0.0$
$\mu_{Cya\_High}(0.875) = 1$

Fis = 0.109
$\mu_{Fis\_Low}(0.109) = 1$
$\mu_{Fis\_Medium}(0.109) = 0.0$
$\mu_{Fis\_High}(0.109) = 0.0$

GyrAB = 0.375
$\mu_{GyrAB\_Low}(0.375) = 0.5$
$\mu_{GyrAB\_Medium}(0.375) = 0.5$
$\mu_{GyrAB\_High}(0.375) = 0.0$

TopA = 0.125
$\mu_{TopA\_Low}(0.125) = 1$
$\mu_{TopA\_Medium}(0.125) = 0.0$
$\mu_{TopA\_High}(0.125) = 0.0$

Sig = 0.5
$\mu_{Sig\_Low}(0.5) = 0.0$
$\mu_{Sig\_Medium}(0.5) = 1$
$\mu_{Sig\_High}(0.5) = 0.0$

SRNA = 0.5
$\mu_{SRNA\_Low}(0.5) = 0.0$
$\mu_{SRNA\_Medium}(0.5) = 1$
$\mu_{SRNA\_High}(0.5) = 0.0$

Determine the marking value of the token after being passed to the output place (i.e. firing fuzzy production rules can be considered as firing transitions) according to the indicated operations required by the transition. For example, the following operations are executed by the AND and OR transitions.

AND transition: $\quad M'_{\Omega\alpha_i \in output\_place} = \underset{\alpha_j input\_place}{Min}$

OR transition: $\quad M'_{\Omega\alpha_i \in output\_place} = \underset{\alpha_j input\_place}{Max}$

where Ω is the current set of the places which the token has traveled along, and the token value in a place p_i, $p_i \in P$, is denoted by $\alpha(p_i) \in [0, 1]$. With these definitions on hand for the proposed FPN model, we can proceed to develop an inferencing scheme for making the final decision on the switching between the exponential and stationary phase of *E. coli* cells. We may then illustrate the reasoning or the calculation of the output as follows. Since we are dealing with rules that have the AND connector, we get an output that is a minimum of the n inputs, i.e. the output set S for Rule1 is cut at the membership value of MIN ($\mu_{GyrAB\_low}(0.375) = 0.5$, $\mu_{TopA\_low}(0.125) = 1$, $\mu_{Fis\_low}(0.109) = 1$). The reasoning for all Rules is similar. For example, with *GyaAB* input data the firing strength of each activated rule is calculated by the *MIN* and *MAX* composition operator, respectively. It yields

FR_1 : *MIN*(GyaAB_low= 0.5, TopA _low= 1, Fis_low= 1) = 0.5,
FR_2 : *MIN*(GyaAB_low= 0.5, TopA _low= 1, Fis_medium= 0.0) = 0.0,
FR_3 : *MIN*(GyaAB_low= 0.5, TopA _low= 1, Fis_high= 0.0) = 0.0,
FR_4 : *MIN*(GyaAB_low= 0.5, TopA _medium= 0.0, Fis_low= 1) = 0.0,
FR_5 : *MIN*(GyaAB_low= 0.5, TopA _ medium = 0.0, Fis_ medium = 0.0) = 0.0,
FR_6 : *MIN*(GyaAB_low= 0.5, TopA _ medium = 0.0, Fis_high= 0.0) = 0.0,
FR_7 : *MIN*(GyaAB_low= 0.5, TopA _ high = 0.0, Fis_low= 1) = 0.0,
FR_8 : *MIN*(GyaAB_low= 0.5, TopA _ high = 0.0, Fis_medium= 0.0) = 0.0,
FR_9 : *MIN*(GyaAB_low= 0.5, TopA _ high = 0.0, Fis_high= 0.0) = 0.0,
FR_{10} : *MIN*(GyaAB_medium= 0.5, TopA _low= 1, Fis_low= 1) = 0.5,
FR_{11} : *MIN*(GyaAB_medium= 0.5, TopA _low= 1, Fis_medium= 0.0) = 0.0,
FR_{12} : *MIN*(GyaAB_medium= 0.5, TopA _low= 1, Fis_high= 0.0) = 0.0,
FR_{13} : *MIN*(GyaAB_medium= 0.5, TopA _medium= 0.0, Fis_low= 1) = 0.0,
FR_{14} : *MIN*(GyaAB_medium= 0.5, TopA_ medium = 0.0, Fis_ medium = 0.0) = 0.0,
FR_{15} : *MIN*(GyaAB_medium= 0.5, TopA_ medium = 0.0, Fis_high= 0.0) = 0.0,
FR_{16} : *MIN*(GyaAB_medium= 0.5, TopA_high= 0.0, Fis_low= 1) = 0.0,
FR_{17} : *MIN*(GyaAB_medium= 0.5, TopA_high= 0.0, Fis_ medium = 0.0) = 0.0,
FR_{18} : *MIN*(GyaAB_medium= 0.5, TopA_high= 0.0, Fis_high= 0.0) = 0.0,
FR_{19} : *MIN*(GyaAB_high= 0.0, TopA_low= 1, Fis_low= 1) = 0.0,
FR_{20} : *MIN*(GyaAB_high= 0.0, TopA_low= 1, Fis_ medium = 0.0) = 0.0,
FR_{21} : *MIN*(GyaAB_high= 0.0, TopA_low= 1, Fis_high= 0.0) = 0.0,
FR_{22} : *MIN*(GyaAB_high= 0.0, TopA_medium= 0.0, Fis_low= 1) = 0.0,
FR_{23} : *MIN*(GyaAB_high= 0.0, TopA_medium= 0.0, Fis_medium = 0.0) = 0.0,
FR_{24} : *MIN*(GyaAB_high= 0.0, TopA_medium= 0.0, Fis_high= 0.0) = 0.0,
FR_{25} : *MIN*(GyaAB_high= 0.0, TopA_high= 0.0, Fis_low= 1) = 0.0,
FR_{26} : *MIN*(GyaAB_high= 0.0, TopA_high= 0.0, Fis_ medium = 0.0) = 0.0,
FR_{27} : *MIN*(GyaAB_high= 0.0, TopA_high= 0.0, Fis_high= 0.0) = 0.0,

When we are dealing with two or more rules, we have an OR operation between all the rules. Therefore we "maximize" all the fired rules to a single set. It yields

Low: $MAX(FR_1, FR_2, FR_3, FR_4, FR_5, FR_6, FR_{10}, FR_{11}, FR_{12}, FR_{13}, FR_{19}, FR_{20})$ = $MAX(0.5, 0, 0, 0, 0, 0, 0.5, 0, 0, 0, 0)$ = 0.5, Medium: $MAX(FR_7, FR_8, FR_9, FR_{14}, FR_{15}, FR_{16}, FR_{21}, FR_{22}, FR_{23}, FR_{24})$ = $MAX(0, 0, 0, 0, 0, 0, 0, 0, 0, 0)$ = 0.0, High: $MAX(FR_{17}, FR_{18}, FR_{25}, FR_{26}, FR_{27})$ = $MAX(0, 0, 0, 0, 0)$ = 0.0,

According to the result of *max* composition operation the defuzzification of output is used to make a final decision. We adopt the "center of gravity" method in [29] to solve this problem. Then, the defuzzification of GyaAB, is calculated as GyaAB = 0.2 by the centroid of the aggregate output membership function in the FRBPN model. Following the steps of the reasoning process, the final winning rule in GyaAB FRBPN model is FR_{10} (*IF GyaAB is Medium and TopA is Low and Fis is Low THEN the GyaAB is Low*), which indicates that the "GyaAB is Low". In the following, the Mamdani fuzzy method of the MATLAB tools is also used to compare the inference results under the same conditions (same inputs, same linguistic values, and same ranges). As shown in Fig. 6, the fuzzy rules of GyaAB entity are aggregated and

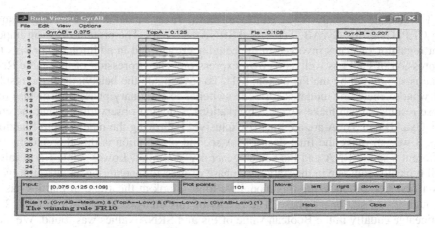

Fig. 6. Final decision of a GyaAB FRBPN model

defuzzied to have a crisp value of GyaAB = 0.207. By using the membership functionsFig.3 which indicate the μ_{j1} is the winner function. As the value of GyaAB = 0.207, belong to μ_{j1} so the final decision will be "0". By calculating the centroid, which indicates the rule FR_{10} is the winner. In reference to the consequent proposition of FR_{10}, "GyaAB is Low" is thus inferred for GyaAB entity. Through the comparative study between the methods [21], [20], [30] with the inferred results, all methods have the same reasoning outcomes. The table 3 shows the output data of the all genes. However, the first row represents the FRBPN models outcomes and each subsequent row the next state observed. Using our FRBPN model, we can say that the model correctly switches from the exponential to the stationary phase of growth. Comparing the results of the genetic regulatory network estimation between the FRBPN model and L.J. Steggles model [30], the similarity that we have discovered is that they both have a same results and a high level of agreement for the *E.Coli* cells. Here the number of fuzzy sets used for input and output interfaces were fixed to three, with the best performing configuration subjected. Any nominal genes encountered were encoded in the form 1-out-of-*n* input. The results expressed in Table 3 show that the FRBPN approach provides an optimal completion, while the model correctly switches from the exponential to the stationary phase of growth.

Table 3. Set of quantified rules description of *E.Coli* cells growth

If-condition							Then-condition	Confidence
CRP	Cya	Fis	GyaAB	TopA	Sig	SRNA	Growth	
High	High	Low					High	0.883
High	High						High	0.825
		Low	Medium	Low	High		Low	0.2
Medium	Medium	Low	Medium	Low	High		Low	0.120
		Low	Medium	Low	High		Low	0.101
		Low			High	Low	Low	0.01

To illustrate the analysis, we will focus on the fuzzy model at the Fis entity assuming CRP, Cya, Fis, GyrAB, TopA, and SRNA as inputs. The protein Fis is an important regulator of genes involved in the cellular growth and in addition, it controls the expression of CRP, as well as its own expression. The expression of the stable RNA gene is stimulated by the Fis protein [31]. To investigate the behaviour of the results, we want to check the model is correctly switches to stationary phase of growth. From these results we can make several observations. Our first observation is that the entities GyaAB and TopA are a mutually exclusive. Following the membership functions Fig. 3 we can make the final decision. A second observation is that the outcome for different a stable RNA and Fis values generally is similar. Lower stable RNA values will typically generate in the stationary phase of growth by entering an attractor cycle. As a first step in analyzing this model we took a look at the value of entities passed through to the stationary phase. The results of this analysis are shown in table 2. A noticeable equally in the Boolean value of Fis and SRNA values was found. We have compared the results of our analysis with a Boolean network Petri nets described in [30]. In the analysis of [30], only two states of expression were considered, "0" and "1", inferred from the data. While both analyses generate results consistent with known biology, fuzzy model analysis is more sensitive to small changes in concentration level, includes more details of functional relationships, and consequently fuzzy analysis can be potential alternative hypotheses. However, the biological systems are different from Boolean networks: entities in a Boolean network take binary values which are updated synchronously, whereas quantities of gene expressions in real cells are not binary and are changing continuously in time.

8 Conclusion

In this paper, we give a new method combined fuzzy Petri net and Boolean networks to modeling and analyzing genetic regulatory network. The fuzzy set theory and the fuzzy production rule method are used to establish the fuzzy rules for the modeling and analyzing. By transforming the Boolean values into linguistic terms, the proposed technique can discover fuzzy wining rules. As the Boolean networks lack effective analysis tools; and have problems capturing with incomplete information, the fuzzy reasoning Boolean Petri nets (FRBPN) algorithm apparently has higher computational complexity than a general Boolean networks , because it uses more places (i.e. P_i) and transitions (i.e. T_i) in the reasoning process and in the verification module. The motivation for using fuzzy Petri nets models is the ability to translate Boolean data into linguistic constructs that can then be easily converted into testable hypotheses. It is also worth remarking that the quality values assigned by fuzzy Petri net to determine confidence values for cell growth in the $E.coli$ are much more informative. We have shown here, that the FRBPN model is appropriate and can reach the same accuracy performance of available tool. The validation was achieved by comparing the results obtained with the FRBPN model and fuzzy logic using the MATLAB Toolbox; both methods have the same reasoning outcomes. It verifies that the confidence value of the cells growth can be successfully reasoned by the proposed FRBPN model. This process can be applied to other genetic regulatory networks algorithms as well, including those with more complex regulatory relationships.

Acknowledgement

The authors would like to acknowledge Dr. Bernd Eichenauer, Braunlage (Germany), and Dr. K. Mustafa for their help and encouragement in this project.

References

1. Fitch, J.P., Sokhansanj, B.: Genomic engineering moving beyond DNA sequence to function. Proc. IEEE 88, 1949–1971 (2000)
2. Novak, B., Csikasz-Nagy, A., Gyorffy, B., Chen, K., Tyson, J.J.: Mathematical model of the fission yeast cell cycle with checkpoint controls at the G1/S, G2/M and metaphase/anaphase transitions. Biophysical Chemistry 72, 185–200 (1998)
3. Chen, T., He, H.L., Church, G.M.: Modeling gene expression with differential equations. In: Pacific Symposium on Biocomputing 1999, New York, pp. 29–40 (1999)
4. Ressom, H., Natarjan, P., Varghese, R.S., Musavi, M.T.: Applications of fuzzy logic in genomics. J. of Fuzzy Sets and Systems 152, 125–138 (2005)
5. Matsuno, H., Doi, A., Nagasaki, M., Miyano, S.: Hybrid Petri net representation of gene regulatory network. In: Pacific Symposium on Biocomputing, vol. 5, pp. 338–349 (2000)
6. Matsuno, H., Fujita, S., Doi, A., Nagasaki, M., Miyano, S.: Towards Biopathway Modeling and Simulation. In: van der Aalst, W.M.P., Best, E. (eds.) ICATPN 2003. LNCS, vol. 2679, pp. 3–22. Springer, Heidelberg (2003)
7. Fujita, S., Matsui, M., Matsuno, H., Miyano, S.: Modeling and simulation of fission yeast cell cycle on hybrid functional Petri net. IEICE Transactions on Fundamentals of Electronics, Communication and Computer Sciences E87-A(11), 2919–2928 (2004)
8. Liang, S., Fuhrman, S., Somogyi, R.: REVEAL, a general reverse engineering algorithm for inference of genetic network architectures. In: Pacific Symposium on Biocomputing, New York, vol. 3, pp. 18–29 (1998)
9. Akutsu, T., Miyano, S., Kuhara, S.: Identification of genetic networks from a small number of gene expression patterns under the Boolean network model. In: Pacific Symposium on Biocomputing 1999, New York, pp. 17–28 (1999)
10. Husmeier, D.: Sensitivity and specificity of inferring genetic regulatory interactions from microarray experiments with dynamic Bayesian networks. Bioinformatics 19, 2271–2282 (2003)
11. Vohradsky, J.: Neural networks model of gene expression. J. FASEB 15, 846–854 (2002)
12. de Jong, H.: Modeling and Simulation of Genetic Regulatory Systems: A Literature Review. J. Comp. Biol. 9, 67–103 (2002)
13. Goss, P.J.E., Peccoud, J.: Analysis of the stabilizing effect of Rom on the genetic network controlling ColE1 plasmid replication. In: Pacific Symposium on Biocomputing 1999, New York, pp. 65–76 (1999)
14. Matsuno, H., Fujita, S., Doi, A., Nagasaki, M., Miyano, S.: Towards pathway modelling and simulation. In: van der Aalst, W.M.P., Best, E. (eds.) ICATPN 2003. LNCS, vol. 2679, pp. 3–22. Springer, Heidelberg (2003)
15. Garg, M.L., Ahson, S.L., Gupta, P.V.: A fuzzy Petri net for knowledge representation and reasoning. Information Processing Letters 39, 165–171 (1991)
16. Lukas, W., Ralf, Z.: Intuitive Modeling of Dynamic Systems with Petri Nets and Fuzzy Logic. In: German Conference on Bioinformatics, vol. 136, pp. 106–115 (2008)
17. Bostan-Korpeoglu, B., Yazici, A.: A fuzzy Petri net model for intelligent databases. Data & Knowledge Engi. 62, 219–247 (2007)

18. Fryc, B., Pancerz, K., Peters, J.F., Suraj, Z.: On Fuzzy Reasoning Using Matrix Represen-tation of Extended Fuzzy Petri Nets. Fundamental Informatics 60, 143–157 (2004)
19. Ahson, I.: Petri net models of fuzzy neural networks. IEEE. Trans. on. SMC 25, 926–932 (1995)
20. Ropers, D., de Jong, H., Page, M., Schneider, D., Geiselmann, J.: Qualitative Simulation of the Nutritional Stress Response in Escherichia coli. INRIA, Rapport de Reacherche, vol. 5412, pp. 1–39 (2004)
21. Hengge-Aronis, R.: The general stress response in Escherichia coli. In: Storz, G., Hengge-Aronis, R. (eds.) Bacterial Stress Responses, pp. 161–178. ASM Press, Washington (2000)
22. Kauffman, S.A.: Metabolic stability and epigenesis in randomly constructed genetic nets. The. Biol. 22, 437–467 (1969)
23. Pedrycz, W.: Fuzzy Sets Engineering. CRC Press, Boca Raton (1995)
24. Looney, C.G.: Fuzzy Petri nets for rule-based decision making. IEEE Trans. Systems Man and Cybernetics 18, 178–183 (1988)
25. Chen, S.M., Ke, J.S., Chang, J.F.: Knowledge Representation Using Fuzzy Petri Nets. IEEE Trans. on Knowledge and Data Engineering 2, 311–319 (1990)
26. Pedrycz, W., Gomide, F.: An Introduction to Fuzzy Sets: Analysis and Design. MIT Press, Cambridge (1998)
27. Carvalho, J.P., Tomé, J.A.: Rule Based Fuzzy Cognitive Maps—qualitative systems dy-namics. In: Proc. 19th International Conference of the North American Fuzzy Information Processing Society, NAFIPS 2000, Atlanta, pp. 407–411 (2000)
28. Carvalho, J.P., Tomé, J.A.: Interpolated linguistic terms: uncertainty representation in rule based fuzzy systems. In: Proc. 22nd International Conference of the North American Fuzzy Info. Proc. Society, NAFIPS 2003, Chicago, pp. 93–98 (2003)
29. Jian, Y., Jintao, L., Hongzhou, S., Xiaoguang, G., Zhenmin, Z.: A Fuzzy Petri Net Model towards Context-Awareness Based Personalized Recommendation. IEEE Transactions, FSKD (3), 325–330 (2008)
30. Steggles, L.J., Banks, R., Wipat, A.: Modelling and Analysing Genetic Networks: From Boolean Networks to Petri Nets. In: Priami, C. (ed.) CMSB 2006. LNCS (LNBI), vol. 4210, pp. 127–141. Springer, Heidelberg (2006)
31. Paul, B., Ross, W., Gaal, T., Gourse, R.: rRNA transcription in E. coli. Ann. Rev. Gen. 38, 749–770 (2004)

Mining the Blogosphere for Sociological Inferences

Vivek Kumar Singh

Department of Computer Science,
Banaras Hindu University, Varanasi-221005, U.P., India
vivek@bhu.ac.in

Abstract. The blogosphere, which is the name given to the universe of all blog sites, is now a collection of a tremendous amount of user generated data. The ease & simplicity of creating blog posts and their free form and unedited nature have made the blogosphere a rich and unique source of data, which has attracted people and companies across disciplines to exploit it for varied purposes. The large volume of data requires developing appropriate automated techniques for searching and mining useful inferences from the blogosphere. The valuable data contained in posts from a large number of users across geographic, demographic and cultural boundaries provide a rich opportunity for not only commercial exploitation but also for cross-cultural psychological & sociological research. This paper tries to present the broader picture in and around this theme, chart the required academic and technological framework for the purpose and presents initial results of an experimental work to demonstrate the plausibility of the idea.

Keywords: Blogosphere, Web Mining, Collective Intelligence, Social Computing, Cross Cultural Psychology.

1 Introduction

A weblog or blog is a website that allows one or more individuals to write about things they want to share with others. Others can make comments on these writings as well as create a link to them. A typical blog post can have text, images, and links to other media related to its topic. The individuals who author the blog posts are called bloggers. The blog sites display the posts by one or a community of users in reverse chronological order. Blogs can be individual blog sites, like personal diaries; or community blog sites, which are like discussion forums & collaborative platforms. Individual blogs are owned and maintained by an individual whereas community blogs are owned and maintained by a group of related people. The universe of all blog sites is referred to as the blogosphere.

The ease of creating blog posts, low barrier to publication, open standards of content generation and the free-form writing style allows large number of people to create their own blogs and post their contributions on community blog sites. People express their opinions, ideas, experiences, thoughts, and wishes through blog posts. It is very easy for people to create their own blogs or to post their thoughts and comments on different blog sites. Bloggers need not know any of the technical details behind the blogging phenomenon and yet post their content in a simple and easy to use manner.

S. Ranka et al. (Eds.): IC3 2010, Part I, CCIS 94, pp. 547–558, 2010.

The limited computer knowledge that a blogger may have does not restrain him from contributing to the blogging. Perhaps it is the ease of contributing which is to a large extent responsible for the tremendous amount of user posted data in the blogosphere. According to a statistics by a blog tracking company, Technorati, there were more than 112 million blogs as of September 2008 [1], with two blog posts created per second. Blogosphere is now a huge collection of discussions, commentaries and opinions on virtually every topic of interest. As the penetration of Internet will increase the number of blog posts will also increase tremendously.

The tremendous amount of valuable information contained within the blogs has attracted attention of people in academics as well in industry. Whether it be the much talked about strategy- to get early feedback about the newly released operating system Vista by Microsoft- by contacting influential bloggers in early 2007 and persuading them to share their experiences in return of Laptops as free gifts, or tacit marketing strategies by a number of companies; blogosphere is now a widely acknowledged platform for commercial exploitation. The huge amounts of data (mostly textual) in the blogosphere and its immense commercial potential have opened new areas of research in and around the blogosphere. The key areas of research in blogosphere nowadays include efforts to model the blogosphere [2], [3], [4], blog clustering [5], [6], [7], mining the blog posts [8], [9], community discovery [10], [11], [12], [13], searching influential bloggers [14], and filtering spam blogs [15], [16], [17], [18].

One aspect of the blogosphere that however remained relatively unexplored is that it is a rich and unique treasure house for cross-cultural psychological & sociological analysis. There are primarily two broad motivating observations behind this statement. First, the Internet has reduced the distance between people across the world and allowed them to express themselves and interact with others, irrespective of the geographical, demographic, religious and cultural boundaries. And secondly, the free form, unedited, first hand and relatively more emotionally laden expressions of various people on blog sites provide a rich source for cross cultural & sociological analysis. One may no longer be required to travel distances to get the cross cultural perspective on different issues. Experiments with blogosphere can result in at least interesting preliminary findings, if not a rigorous cross-cultural psychological one. And the other wonderful thing is that it uses a relatively more original data at a much lower cost. All analysis efforts of this type can then be subjected to rigorous experimentation and validation. This paper tries to identify and establish the core issues around this goal and demonstrate the viability of the idea through the initial results on one such experiment. Sections 2 and 3 describe the general framework & steps required in a search & analysis effort of this kind; section 4 presents the experimental work along with initial results; and the section 5 presents a short discussion of the relevant issues.

2 Searching the Blogosphere

With the number of blog posts about to touch the billion mark, efforts to search the blogosphere for required data and mine useful inferences is now an evolving and qualitative research area. Traditionally blogs have been seen by marketing companies as valuable source to track consumers' beliefs and opinions, to monitor their initial reactions to product launches, to understand the language of consumers and to track trends in consumer preferences. Recently blog sites have also become a platform for advertisers to disseminate information about variety of products and services. Selecting the blog site on to which an advertisement be placed is however not so easy and is itself a research area requiring largely automated solutions. There are now more than about fifty companies which track blog sites. Most of them keep track of what is being published on different blog sites and maintain important statistics including what new data has been posted, their titles, themes, important keywords and tags. The companies sometime also cluster them into various categories based on tags extracted from content or assigned by users. They may also use sophisticated crawlers to build and maintain the reference structure (similar to link structure of web sites) of the different blog posts.

The availability of large number of blog tracking companies, most of which provide free tracking service, can be used to obtain blog posts with high authority scores on any topic of interest. Searching the blogosphere for relevant posts on a topic can thus be done through a following four step process: (a) creating a query and submitting it to a blog searcher program, (b) blog searcher program translates the query into a format which can be understood by the blog tracking provider and sends this information using either HTTP Get or HTTP Post, (c) the blog tracking provider processes the request and sends back a response, generally in XML, and (d) the received response is parsed by the blog searcher program and results displayed [19]. While steps (a) and (d) originate and terminate, respectively, at the client site; steps (b) and (c) involve the blog tracking provider. Fig. 1 presents a clear picture of the steps and information interchanges involved in a typical content search process. One can also use an improved blog searcher program which instead of sending queries to a single blog tracking provider may send it to multiple trackers and then aggregate (or summarize) the results obtained from multiple trackers to have a probably bigger and wider information.

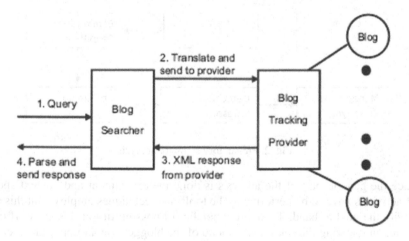

Fig. 1. Steps in searching the blogosphere (courtesy [19])

3 Analyzing the Collected Blog Data

Once the relevant blog posts are identified the main task is to use the collected data for detailed analysis & mining phase for extracting meaningful inferences. This usually involves a two phase process. The first phase is a generic phase which prepares the collected data into a suitable format which is then used by the second phase for application specific analysis, which varies with the goal of the experimenter. Since the data collected is largely textual in nature therefore before it can be subjected to actual mining task, first phase preprocessing is necessary. The preprocessing involves a number of preparatory steps, as discussed below. Once the first phase prepares the necessary data, a detailed experiment-specific analysis can be performed.

In the first phase, the text contained in different fields of each blog post, including its title, body, comments and/or user generated tags, is converted into a term vector (tag cloud) kind of structure with frequency of each term included in it. This is done for all blog posts collected. The tokens thus identified are normalized by converting them into lowercase. Thereafter they are accepted or discarded as valid tokens based on their frequency of occurrence in weighted sets of title, body and comment. Sometimes it also involves comparison with any user generated tags available. This is followed by eliminating stop words {such as and, or, not, to, is, can, the, their, all etc} from the sets of accepted tokens. Another step that is often required is to remove occurrences of the same term in multiple forms, for example 'user' and 'users'. This is termed as Stemming. The multi-word phrases which may have important role to play needs to be captured as well, making the use of appropriate technique for detecting relevant phrases necessary. This however may vary with the experiment at hand. Sometimes tokens are also to be classified into different groups such as nouns, verbs & adjectives; and synonyms may also need to be taken care of. All these activities, despite appearing to be simple and straightforward, have their inherent complexities and sophistications. Fig. 2 gives a pictorial representation of the sequence of steps.

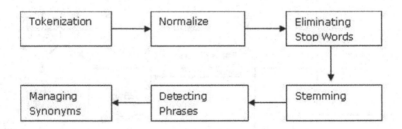

Fig. 2. Preparatory steps for analysis

Once the generic part of the analysis is done the experiment and context specific set of activities have to be performed. The tools and techniques employed at this stage vary with the goal at hand. There are a number of possibilities at this stage. If one is interested in knowing the sentiments/ mood of the bloggers on an important event, for which data might have been prepared as stated above, he can do a sentiment or mood analysis experiment. Many people have tried to mine sentiments in the blog posts and proposed tools and APIs for sentiment and mood analysis [20], [21], [22]. A more involved work could be to extract the opinion of bloggers expressed in the free-form writings in blog posts; and using them to make important inferences. Few attempts, though in early stages, have been made to devise tools and techniques for general opinion mining & analysis [23], [24]. Clustering blog posts of similar type is another active area of research and there are several generic platforms available which can be used for this purpose. The two popular open source frameworks for clustering are WEKA [25] and JDM [26], which provide various tools and APIs for classification and clustering of blog entries using generic techniques such as Regression and Artificial Neural Network based classifiers. Moreover, it is always open to the experimenter to write a customized program, with or without using available libraries and APIs, which can be used for analytical purposes. Most of the complex analytical tasks often require some kind of customization and re-integration of available libraries and APIs and/or creating new functions and APIs. However, there are hardly any APIs or libraries designed with specific focus on sociological analysis of the blogosphere.

4 Experimental Work

Over the past few months my research group has been working towards a systematic social-inference oriented analysis of the blogosphere. We are trying to develop an integrated framework for this kind of analytical goal, which can by and large be automated. In the first such experiment we have tried to carry out an event-based analysis experiment on the blogosphere [27]. The primary aim was to do a sentiment and opinion oriented analysis of blog posts on three related events (but in different demographic regions) and to identify the similarities and variations of opinions of bloggers, who are from these demographic regions. The assumption was that their blog posts and comments will have a common psychological & social context. The three events selected were of high social & political concern, which probably also involved high emotive elements. The initial findings has been improved and cross referenced since then and the broader framework employed has also changed a lot. The paper reports recent results of the improved version. There is however some more validation in the pipeline. In another experiment of similar nature, which aims to do a detailed analysis of the blog posts on political & constitutional developments in Nepal; we have obtained some interesting initial findings [28]. The results however need to be validated and organized in a more structured manner.

4.1 Collecting and Grouping the Event-Based Data

Since the goal was to observe the variations of opinions and sentiments of bloggers from different demographic & social groups on events of high social & political concern, three important and well discussed events which occurred in different demographic & social regions were chosen. The events selected were three terror events, namely 26/11/08 Mumbai hotel attack in India, the March 2009 twin terrorist attacks in Pakistan on Lahore hotel & on Srilankan cricket team, and the 9/11/01 attack on World Trade Centre in USA. These events were chosen due to their relevance, highly discussed nature, and the demographic & social variations of the three different societies in which they occurred. After selecting the events, the first step was to collect authority data on these events. Each collected data item includes the text in the blog post title, blog body and the comments of various users on the blog posts. To distinguish between the different social & political individual groups of bloggers, the comments on the blog posts were grouped in three categories, each broadly corresponding to the three demographic areas in which these events took place. These three groups were termed as IND, WAC and USE corresponding to bloggers belonging to India, West Asian Countries and United States & Europe (West) respectively. Table 1 summarizes the scheme of grouping the collected data. The three groups contained indexed aggregated data extracted from a good number of blog posts on the three events.

Table 1. Clustering the data into different groups

	Event 1	Event 2	Event 3
Blog Posts	Title & Body	Title & Body	Title & Body
Comments	IND	IND	IND
Comments	WAC	WAC	WAC
Comments	USE	USE	USE

4.2   Generating Tag Cloud

The blog posts along with comments on them were used to generate a summary using text summarizer [29], [30] and to compute a term frequency based tag cloud [31], in parallel. The aggregated set of tag cloud generated was grouped into four different groups: tag cloud of the blog post, tag cloud of the comments by IND group, tag cloud of comments by WAC group and tag cloud of the comments by USE group. This resulted into a total of twelve set of tag clouds, four set each for all the three events. Each set comprised of aggregated data of 20-25 selected blog posts. The candidate blog posts were selected manually based on the summary data generated in parallel. This was done to preserve the original content of the blog post, which would have been lost if summarized data would have been used to generate tag cloud. The twelve sets of tag clouds were also grouped, for later verification & validation, into three subgroups of nouns, verbs and adjectives by using WordNet for parts of speech tagging [32]. On one hand it can help to find important inferences about the keywords, such as role players in the event, victims of the event and nature of emotional reactions of different users, on the three events; and at the same time it could be used to correlate the findings of opinion & sentiment analysis through the qualitative words about the reasons attributed to be responsible for a particular event, by the three different groups, in a non-automated manner.

4.3   Analyzing the Data along Vertical and Horizontal Dimensions

The twelve sets of tag cloud were then subjected to analysis along both vertical and horizontal dimensions. Vertical analysis involved comparison of the four sets of tag cloud on the same event. For example comparing the tag cloud of comments of IND, WAC and USE groups with each other and with the tag cloud of the blog post on 26/11

Mumbai attack event. This would give an analytical perspective of the reactions of the different groups on a particular event. The resulting data was analyzed to find the similarity score of tag cloud of comments of each of the three groups IND, WAC and USE with respect to the tag cloud of the blog post. A mood & sentiment analysis [33], [34], [35] was also done in a similar manner.

Horizontal analysis involved comparing the comments of a particular group along three different events. For example comparison of the comment set of WAC group for all the three events. This would give the variation in opinion, sentiment and mood of a particular group along the three events. Similarity score in terms of nouns, verbs and adjectives was also computed. While vertical analysis could have important inferences about the difference in opinions of IND, WAC and USE groups on a particular event (say 26/11 Mumbai attack); horizontal analysis was expected to have implications about the variations of opinion of the same group along similar event but at different places (for example observing IND group's reaction on 26/11 Mumbai attack, Lahore bombing and 9/11 WTC attack).

4.4 Analysis Results

The vertical and horizontal analysis resulted in interesting findings. Similarity score computations along vertical dimension show that by and large the IND and USE groups tend to agree on the same set of opinionated words for a particular event and this was true for all the three events. WAC group's reaction was varied and differed a lot on the 26/11 Mumbai attack event, 9/11 WTC attack event and the twin events in Lahore. Also, similarity between tag clouds of the blog post and comment set was observed for twin events in Lahore. The findings were also supported by the mood analysis along vertical dimension. Table 2 shows the result of mood analysis based on aggregated blog and comment set of the three groups along 9/11 WTC attack event. The parallel categorization of tag clouds into nouns, verbs & adjectives and subsequent similarity score computations on them also showed similar findings.

The horizontal analysis showed varied opinions of the three groups on different events. While IND and USE group's opinions matched to some extent on the 26/11 Mumbai attack and 9/11 WTC attack, there was a slight degree of variation in case of Lahore twin terror attack event. WAC group on the other hand showed drastically different opinion on the three different events considered. The extracted sets of nouns,

Table 2. Mood analysis of the IND, WAC and USE groups on 9/11 WTC event in U.S.A.

Mood	Upset	Happy
Blog post	93.9%	6.1%
IND	85%	15%
WAC	36.6%	63.4%
USE	97.6%	2.4%

Table 3. Similarity score of the tag cloud of the comment set of IND, WAC and USE groups on 9/11 WTC event in U.S.A.

Group	IND	WAC	USE
IND (400)	400	46	92
WAC (254)	45	254	91
USE (620)	105	103	620

verbs and adjectives from all the twelve sets of tag clouds showed a moderately high similarity score, particularly in case of adjectives, in comment sets of IND and USE groups. The WAC group's reaction was slightly more varied. A snapshot of the similarity score along horizontal analysis is shown in Table 3. The number in brackets in first column is the total number of relevant words in the comment set of the group and entries in the table show number of similar words. An opinionated word analysis [36] was also close to these findings. Table 4 shows list of opinionated words of the post and comment set of the three groups on the 9/11 WTC attack event.

4.5 Inferences

The results obtained are very interesting. They portrayed an accurate picture of the variation of opinions in the three different political and social groups (rather societies) on a social & political phenomenon of high concern to them, as supported by the commonly held views and widely available writings on the topic. The similarity scores, mood analysis, word groupings and opinionated words, all taken together, make the results highly relevant and valuable. Most of the initial trends observed were in agreement with a non-automated inspection of the data. Moreover, it was similar to a larger extent to the popular writing and other contents available in other media. This analytical approach applied in a slightly modified form in another experiment on blogosphere analysis of constitutional and political developments in Nepal, obtained interesting initial results, which cross-validate the usefulness of this method of study.

The results clearly demonstrate that the blogosphere, which is now an extremely valuable source of information, can also be used for social inferences rather than be limited to commercial exploitation. Blogosphere has immense potential for sociological studies and research, which needs to be exploited in a useful manner. The geographical spread and culturally different background of bloggers provide a cross cultural perspective, which makes it an attractive source of study. Blogosphere can be studied to understand the formation, spread and variation of opinions across geographies and cultures. The free form and un-inhibited expressions makes the opinions expressed highly authentic and extremely useful. Collection of appropriate data will however always remain important and one has to be very careful about this issue.

Table 4. Opinionated words of the IND, WAC and USE groups on the 9/11 WTC event in U.S.A.

IND	WAC	USE
Aggressive	Attractive	Alone
Bad	Awesome	Affirmatively
Dominate	Continued	Biased
Inevitable	Dangerous	Blatantly
Islamic	Foolish	Burning
Ludicrous	Holy	Drastically
Passive	Lying	Faux
Putrid	Moral	Guilty
Superior	Pissed	Pathetic
		Subservient

5 Discussion

It is beyond doubt that the large amount of data in blogosphere is an extremely valuable source, which can be exploited for mining important commercial and sociological inferences. Whether it is to find initial reactions to a new product launch, or creating favourable opinion among prospective buyers/ users, finding the right audience for advertising, identifying different opinion clusters on various issues or studying the social networks of bloggers; blogosphere analysis has a lot to offer. The use of relatively unedited, free form writings, comments on them, the reference structure of blog posts and any user generated tags, for cross-cultural psychological & sociological analysis purposes is the most recent of the possibilities. It is a direction worth more exploration and experimentation [37].

Most of the contemporary work on blogosphere analysis, however, has a high usage of syntactical mechanisms. This is partly true about the present experimental work as well. The mechanisms involving similarity score computations, word groupings, finding opinionated words, and mood extraction, all involve some degree of syntactical manipulations. Though it is not an inherent limitation of the technological framework; rather it is due to the primarily textual nature of the content on blog sites and apparently the unstructured design schema of the World Wide Web itself. Though it would not be out of order to say that advances in research in natural language processing [38], [39] and web information retrieval techniques [40], [41] can improve the analytical results to a greater extent; but the inherent syntactical and unstructured content will always be a source of problem for any such analytical effort.

With significant developments and progress towards semantic web [42], more structuring will be incorporated into the web content. The Web content will then be more like semantic elements of a program, open to better manipulation and use. As this gains momentum, the techniques which are applied to derive intelligence from the

World Wide Web will become much simpler. Till the time this happens, most of the techniques to derive intelligence will be something in between the existing efforts of mining inferences from unstructured content as available on the web, to approaches of imposing structure on the content as it is gathered from users and then subjecting it to analysis [43], [44]. However, irrespective of the type and direction, what is more important is the necessity to understand the immense potential contained in the new forms of web applications, which are largely comprised of user generated content, and to devise appropriate methodologies and tools & techniques to harness the valuable information for various useful and productive purposes.

References

1. Technorati Blogosphere Statistics (2008),
   http://technorati.com/blogging/state-of-the-blogosphere/
2. Kritikopoulos, A., Sideri, M., Varlamis, I.: Bogrank: Ranking Weblogs based on connectivity and similarity features. In: AAA-IDEA 2006- Proceedings of the 2nd International Workshop on Advanced Architectures and Algorithms for Internet Delivery and Applications. ACM Press, New York (2006)
3. Leskovec, J., McGlohon, M., Faloutsos, C., Glance, N., Hurst, M.: Cascading Behaviour in Large Blog Graphs. In: SIAM International Conference on Data Mining (2007)
4. Kumar, R., Novak, J., Raghavan, P., Tomkins, A.: On the Bursty Evolution of Blogspace. In: Proceedings of 12th International Conference on World Wide Web, pp. 568–576. ACM Press, New York (2003)
5. Brooks, C.H., Montanez, N.: Improved Annotation of Blogosphere via Autotagging and Hierarchical Clustering. In: WWW 2006: Proceedings of 15th International Conference on World Wide Web, pp. 625–632. ACM Press, New York (2006)
6. Li, B., Xu, S., Zhang, J.: Enhancing Clustering Blog Documents by author/ reader comments. In: ACM-SE 45: Proceedings of 45th Annual Southeast Regional Conference, pp. 94–99. ACM Press, New York (2007)
7. Agarwal, N., Galan, M., Liu, H., Subramanya, S.: Clustering Blogs with Collective Wisdom. In: Proceedings of International Conference on Web Engineering (2008)
8. Gammon, M., Aue, A., Corston-Oliver, S., Ringger, E.: Pulse: Mining Customer Opinions from Free Text. In: Famili, A.F., Kok, J.N., Peña, J.M., Siebes, A., Feelders, A. (eds.) IDA 2005. LNCS, vol. 3646, pp. 121–132. Springer, Heidelberg (2005)
9. Liu, B.: Web Data Mining: Exploring Hyperlinks, Contents and Usage Data. Springer, Heidelberg (2006)
10. Blanchard, A., Markus, M.: The Experienced Sense of a Virtual Community- Characteristics and Processes. The DATA BASE for Advances in Information Systems 35(1) (2004)
11. Efimova, L., Hendrick, S.: In Search for a Virtual Settlement: An Exploration of Weblog Community Boundaries. IEEE Computer Society Press (2005)
12. Lu, Y., Lee, H.: Blog Community Discovery Based on Tag Data Clustering. In: 2008 Asia-Pacific Workshop on Computational Intelligence & Industrial Application. IEEE Computer Society Press, Los Alamitos (2008)
13. Chin, A., Chignell, M.: A Social Hypertext Model for finding Community in Blogs. In: HYPERTEXT 2006: Proceedings of Seventeenth Conference on Hypertext and Hypermedia, pp. 11–12. ACM Press, New York (2006)

14. Agarwal, N., Liu, H., Tang, L., Yu, P.S.: Identifying the Influential Bloggers in a Community. In: Proceedings of International Conference on Web Search and Web Data Mining, pp. 207–218. ACM Press, Palo Alto (2008)
15. Ntoulas, A., Najork, M., Manasse, M., Fetterl, D.: Detecting Spam Web Pages through Content Analysis. In: Proceedings of 15th International Conference on World Wide Web, WWW (2006)
16. Gyongyi, Z., Berkhin, P., Gracia-Molina, H., Pedersen, J.: Link Spam Detection Based on Mass Estimation. In: Proceedings of the 32nd International Conference on Very Large Databases, VLDB (2006)
17. Kolari, P., Finin, T., Joshi, A.: SVMs for Blogosphere: Blog Identification and Splog Detection. In: AAAI Spring Symposium on Computational Approaches to Analyzing Weblogs. AAAI, Menlo Park (2006)
18. Kolari, P., Java, A., Finin, T., Oates, T., Joshi, A.: Detecting Spam Blogs: A Machine Learning Approach. In: Proceedings of 21st National Conference on Artificial Intelligence (AAAI). AAAI, Menlo Park (2006)
19. Alag, S.: Collective Intelligence in Action. In: Manning, New York, pp. 111–144 (2009)
20. Online Sentiment Analysis: Free and Paid tools, http://www.rockyfu.com/blog/sentiment-analysis/ (reteieved August 2009)
21. Sood, S.O., Vasserman, L.: Esse: Exploring mood on the Web. In: Proceedings of International Conference on Weblogs and Social Media, Seattle (May 2009)
22. Godbole, N., Srinivasaiah, M., Skiena, S.: Large Scale Sentiment Analysis for News and Blogs. In: Proceedings of the International Conference on Weblogs and Social Media, ICWSM (2007)
23. Pang, B., Lee, L.: Opinion Mining and Sentiment Analysis. Journal of Foundation and Trends in Information Retrieval 2 (2008)
24. Esuli, A., Sebastiani, F.: SentiWordNet: A Publicly available lexical resource for opinion mining. In: Proceedings of the fifth Conference on Language Resources and Evaluation (LREC 2006), Geneva (2006)
25. WEKA- Waikato Environment for Knowledge Analysis, http://www.cs.waikato.ac.nz/ml/weka/ (retrieved May 2009)
26. JDM-Java Data Mining API 2.0, JSR 247, http://www.jcp.org/en/jsr/detail?id=247 (retrieved May 2009)
27. Singh, V.K., Jalan, R., Chaturvedi, S.K., Gupta, A.K.: Collective Intelligence Based Computational Approach to Web Intelligence. In: Proceedings of 2009 International Conference on Web Information Systems and Mining. IEEE Computer Society Press, Shanghai (November 2009)
28. Singh, V.K., Mahata, D., Adhikari, R.: A Clustering and Opinion Extraction Based Approach to Socio-political Analysis of the Blogosphere. In: Communicated to appear in 2010 IEEE International Conference on Computational Intelligence and Computing Research. IEEE Xplore, Coimbatore (December 2010)
29. Subject Search Summarizer tool, by Kryloff technologies, http://www.kryltech.com/summarizer.htm (retrieved April 2009)
30. Hovy, E., Marcu, D.: Automatic Text Summarization Tutorial. In: Proceedings of the Workshop on Intelligent Scalable Text Summarization, ACL/EACL Conference, Madrid, pp. 66–73 (1998)
31. TagCrowd Beta, Tag Cloud Generation tool, http://www.tagcrowd.com/ (retrieved April 2009)
32. Miller, G.A.: Wordnet: A Lexical Database for English. Communications of the ACM 38(11), 39–41 (1995), http://wordnet.princeton.edu

33. Uclassify Mood Analysis tool,
    http://www.uclassify.com/browse/prfekt/Mood (retrieved April 2009)
34. Mishne, G., Rijke, M.D.: MoodViews: Tools for Blog Mood Analysis. In: AAAI 2006
    Spring Symposium on Computational Approaches to Analyzing Weblogs, AAAI-CAAW
    2006 (March 2006)
35. Balog, K., Rijke, M.D.: Decomposing Bloggers' Moods. In: 3rd Annual Workshop on the
    Web blogging Ecosystem, at WWW 2006 (2006)
36. Attardi, G., Simi, M.: Blog Mining through Opinionated Words. In: Proceedings of Fif-
    teenth Text Retrieval Conference, TREC (2006)
37. Agarwal, N., Liu, H.: Data Mining and Knowledge Discovery in Blogs. Morgan & Clay-
    pool Publishers, San Francisco (2010)
38. Jones, K.S.: What is the Role of Natural Language Processing in Information Retrieval In
    Natural Language Information Retrieval. In: Strzalkowski, T. (ed.) Text, Speech and Lan-
    guage Technology. Springer, Heidelberg (1999)
39. Lease, M.: Natural Language Processing for Information Retrieval: the time is ripe (again).
    In: Proceedings of Conference on Information and Knowledge Management (2007)
40. Chakrabarti, S.: Mining the Web: Discovering Knowledge from Hypertext Data. Morgan
    Kaufmann, San Francisco (2002)
41. Manning, C.D., Raghavan, P., Schutze, H.: Introduction to Information Retrieval. Cam-
    bridge University Press, Cambridge (2008)
42. Greaves, M.: Semantic Web 2.0. IEEE Intelligent Systems 22(2) (2007)
43. Gruber, T.: Collective Knowledge Systems- Where the Social Web Meets the Semantic
    Web. Web Semantics (November 2007)
44. Singh, V.K.: Collective Intelligence Transforming the World Wide Web. CSI Communica-
    tions (2010) (in Press)

Modeling for Evaluation of Significant Features in siRNA Design

Chakresh Kumar Jain and Yamuna Prasad

Department of Biotechnology, Jaypee Institute of Informtion Technology University,
Noida, India
ckj522@yahoo.com
Department of Computer Science and Engineering, Indian Institute of Technology, Delhi, India
yprasad@cse.iitd.ernet.in

Abstract. RNAi is the most conserved phenomenon occurring in eukaryotes, where it controls the developmental process through gene regulation. Recently, exogenously generated siRNA mediated RNAi has drawn greater significance in functional genomics and therapeutic applications like cancer, HIV and neurodegenerative diseases specially in mammalian system. Computational designing of efficient sequence specific siRNAs against the gene of interest deploy many guidelines, which are based upon sequence to thermodynamic features as a pivotal determinants of effective siRNA sequences, but identification of optimal features needed for efficient designing are yet to be deciphered in the assurance of better efficacy. Till date many computational tools are available, but no tool provide the accurate gene specific siRNA sequences with absolute efficacy therefore study of suitable features of siRNA design is very smoldering issue to be solved in the present scenario. In the present work, we have applied ant colony optimization technique to indentify the features of siRNA up to considerable amount of accuracy and further the results are modeled using four independent models such as linear regression, ANCOVA, libSVM and liblinear with the conclusion that linear features are preferentially superior then thermodynamic features while both group of features are important in the efficacy prediction of siRNA. The results are highly coherence with prior investigations and highlight the importance of sequential features in effective siRNA design.

Keywords: RNAi, siRNA, ACO, LibSVM, RBF, Regression, ANCOVA.

1 Introduction

RNAi is naturally occurring phenomenon in eukaryotes to regulate and control the gene expression and initially identified in lower organism like fungi, plants and animals. The discovery of fire et. al. [1] in gene silencing by double stranded RNA in *C. elegans* has been proven the milestone in RNAi technology.

Elbashir and coworkers [2] have first time shown the application of 21(Base pair)bp (double stranded) ds-siRNA against mammalian cell line by suppressing the expression of endogenous and heterologous genes and provided a new tool for

S. Ranka et al. (Eds.): IC3 2010, Part I, CCIS 94, pp. 559–567, 2010.

studying gene function which opened the new vistas in the gene-specific therapeutics in mammalian cells. The recent literature reported it as the most promising technology in functional genomics and therapeutics, against diseases like HIV [4,5] and neurodegenerative disorder etc. In RNAi gene functions are disrupted through siRNA using ds-RNA which is endogenously or exogenously generated. The pathway is very complex and multi-enzymatic where ds-RNA(s) are cleaved by DICER; a RNAs III enzyme and generate endogenously 21-25 bp small, conserved and non-coding RNAs i.e. siRNA and miRNA, moreover these siRNA can be chemically synthesized exogenously with sequence specificity and ported in to the cellular environment by many delivery vehicles like viruses, nano-particles and plasmids [3]. Though there are still many challenges exist in the delivery of siRNA in to the mammalian cell. In the mechanism of cleavage the antisense strand (5'end)of small ds-RNA incorporate in to the RISC(RNA Induced Silencing Complex) with complementary mRNA, the association of argonaute proteins trigger the cleavage of mRNA, resulting knock down of the gene in cell. In the journey of tool development various criteria's were published by group of researchers [6, 7, 8, 9], mainly MPI (Max-Planck-Institute) guidelines and rational design rule sets for designing the effective siRNA.

The list of tools is available on public servers for siRNA prediction against gene of interest, but these tools generate the bunch of siRNAs with varied efficacy against the selected gene. A study [10] reveals the cause behind the large number of siRNA sequence design, because of biased dataset or small dataset or noise dataset or sometimes it is effected with over fitting problem [11,12]. Despite of continuous research work, till date, there is much scope in the algorithmic development and optimization of features with modeling [39].

In general optimal feature selection is intractable, and most of the feature selection problems are NP-hard problem [13, 40]. The Huesken dataset used as benchmark dataset in siRNA design was comprised of 110 features and revealed the NP hardness in the selection of suitable features [15]. In another work Nemati et. al.[41] have successfully mapped the protein function prediction problem into Feature selection problem and demonstrated it as a NP-hard and provided the solution through population based algorithm.

In this paper, we focus on to identify the significant features in siRNA design and their priorities with clustering by Ant Colony Optimization technique and modeled them through linear regression, ANCOVA, libSVM and liblinear for observing the linearity and non-linearity among the feature sets. Since identification of optimal features is the NP- hard problem [13], which can be solved by using heuristic based approaches like Genetic Algorithm (GA), ACO and clustering. Recently ACO seems to be most effective method of choice under heuristic applications [14], which has been successfully applied in the study of features selection of siRNA necessary in effective siRNA designing [15].

2   Methodology

A benchmark Huesken dataset [16] has been classified with sequential and thermodynamic features, simultaneously through ant colony optimization heuristic on the basis of euclidian distance in the multidimensional feature space. All the generated clusters have been modeled via linear regression, ANCOVA, LibSVM and Liblinear approaches. To find out their similarity and accuracy among different features Silhouette score was calculated. The proceeding subsection describes the data and techniques.

2.1 Dataset

In our work Huesken dataset[16] has been used which is applied by several researcher to validate their algorithm [15, 17,18].The dataset is comprised of 2431 siRNA sequences against 34 mRNA in human gene with 110 features besides to efficacy.

2.2 ACO

ACO is one of the meta-heuristic algorithms applied for optimization problems. The algorithm is entirely developed by Dorigo et. al. [14], conceptually based upon foraging behavior of ant. This algorithm utilizes the approximate methods to provide the good enough solution against hard combinatorial problems. Though there are other meta-heuristic algorithms exist like tabu search, simulated annealing etc. Based upon given siRNA features one has to recognize the significant features via grouping methods. Clustering is one of the approaches for partitioning or grouping the features in the given set of features based upon similarities among them, generally on measurable parameters [15]. Further the ant colony optimization heuristic [19, 14, 20, 21] has been applied to produce the efficient partitions of the siRNA features have been grouped using ACO and classification result has been validated using Silhouette score. Further each partition is analyzed for efficacy prediction. The detail of ACO algorithm for feature mapping can be seen in [15].

2.3 Linear Regression

We have applied the linear regression on the obtained sub-cluster of siRNA features on XLSTAT tool [24] on ms excel where the linearly related features were mapped against the efficacy. The details of the techniques are available [22]. The technique has been applied in many tools to verify the linearity among datasets [23].

2.4 ANCOVA

It is an amalgamation of two techniques which includes ANOVA (Analysis of Variance) and regression models for continuous variables. The general linear model can be written mathematically as below [25, 26]:

$$y = xb + u$$

Where y is a matrix with series of multivariate measurements, x is a matrix that might be a design matrix, b is a matrix containing parameters that are usually to be estimated and u is a matrix containing errors or noise. Basically it has been applied to analyze the significance and effect of certain factors on the outcome variable after removing the variance for which quantitative predictors (covariates) account. These models are applied in the study of statistical parametric mapping of brain scans, microarray data set evaluation of gene expression [27, 28].with observable quality.

In another study Chan et. al. [29] reported the superiority of in term of performance and accuracy with respect to other available approaches.

2.5 LibSVM-2.89

Patterns are of different kind in their dimensionalities and appearances which encompass from linearity to non-linearity in space. To identify these patterns machine learning approaches are very common in use. Currently, support vector machine method has attained much popularity because of its better classification accuracy which is based upon construction of maximal-margin in hyper-planes between the two datasets. Consequently, maximize the distance between data margin for the given input dataset as a vectors in multidimensional space. SVM has been developed by Vapnik 1963, and categorized as a group of supervised learning methods in machine learning. It has been extended to classify datasets from linear to non linear classification and regression [30, 31, 32].

LibSVM, a library for support vector machines, was developed by Chih-Chung Chang and Chih-Jen Lin [33]. Basically it is an integrated software for support vector classification, (C-SVC, nu-SVC), regression (epsilon-SVR, nu-SVR) and distribution estimation (one-class SVM). It mainly supports the different SVM formulations, efficient multi-class classification, probability estimations with automatic model selection and cross validation. These features made LibSVM an indispensible tool for classification and pattern recognition especially in complex dataset. Handling to our dataset LibSVM has mapped the selected cluster groups as input vector into multidimensional space with the efficient classification via radial basis function (RBF) kernel and performed the *fivefold* cross validation for the data validity with considerable accuracy. Results were collected and presented in the table 1.

2.6 LibLinear-1.33

Liblinear is an open source library for large-scale linear classification. It supports L2-regularized logistic regression (LR), L2-loss and L1-loss linear support vector machines (SVMs) [30]. Liblinear inherit many features from SVM [33] like simple usage, open source license etc. Moreover, liblinear is competitive with or even faster than state of the art linear classifiers such as Pegasos [34] and SVMperf [35]. Experiments demonstrate that liblinear is very efficient on large sparse data sets and highly useful for training the large scale problems.

3 Implementation and Results

We implemented the ACO method on linux platform using C. Experiments have been conducted on the Huesken data set [16] which is a benchmarking data set commonly used for experiments in efficacy prediction for siRNA. The tunable parameters in the ant-based clustering algorithm include number of iterations i, number of ants m, rate of decay , and the parameters α and β that control the bias on the pheromone trail. Parameter values for ACO have been set as in [15].

The table 1 stores the result generated from four independent models such as Linear Regression, ANCOVA, LibSVM and Liblinear, showing the correlations between the efficacies of predicted and experimental values for the optimized clusters i.e. 7 and 10.These optimized clusters were obtained after certain number of iterations when ACO was applied and shown the higher accuracy. In case of cluster 7, the higher accuracy i.e. 0.961817 and 0.961851 was achieved after iterations 3,5 and 8, while the cluster 10 has shown the range of higher accuracy from 0.95651 to 0.929055 after completion of iterations 30, 40, 50, 60 and 120 [15].

Table 1. All models with Accuracy

Partition /Cluster, subgroup	Features	Regression (Correlation between Predicted and Experimental)	ANCOVA (Correlation between Predicted and Experimental)	LibSVM-2.89 Accuracy	LibLinear-1.33 Accuracy
7, 2	*Thermo-dynamic and Sequence*	0.541568	**0.711253**	0.44672	0.41393
7,4	**Sequence**	**0.661479**	**0.710352**	**0.536885**	**0.536885**
10,4	*Thermo-dynamic*	0.534015	0.669194	0.47545	0.483607
10,5	Sequence	**0.661479**	0.661479	0.491803	0.512295

Both clusters 7 with its subgroup 2 and 4 i.e. ((7, 2) and (7, 4)) and 10 with its subgroup 4 and 5 i.e. ((10,4) and (10,5)) are presented in table 1. It has been observed that (7, 4) and (10, 5) are dominated with sequence based features, and shown highest correlation by linear regression model i.e. 0.661479, while (7, 2) is dominated with thermodynamics features has the highest correlation value i.e. .711253 in ANCOVA model. We can also observe the accuracy predictions by LibSVM and Liblinear model for cluster (7, 4) which is higher i.e. 0.536885 for sequence features. Further we have averaged the correlation values of both the models for (7, 2), (7, 4) and (10, 5) i.e. 0.6264105, 0.6859155 and 0.661479 respectively. From these observations one can reveals the significance of sequential features as compare to thermodynamic properties, which is shown by cluster (7, 4). The present analysis is evidenced with [10, 15]. Comparisons of all the four independent models reveals that except in ANCOVA rest all shows higher accuracy towards sequence features.

As it is depicted from fig.1 that sequence based features represented in red and deep blue bars for different clusters have shown comparatively higher correlation between predicted and experimental value, which concludes the preferential role of sequence based features over to thermodynamic features in efficacy prediction of siRNA designing. Present results show the coherence with Saetrom and Snøve work [10].

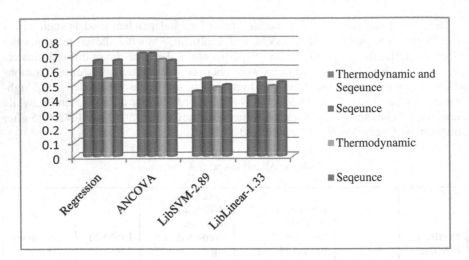

Fig. 1. Representing the differential accuracy with features for different clusters, as it illustrates that sequence features (Red and Deep blue bars) have attained maximum values in all except ANCOVA model

4 Conclusion

Our result from various models (Linear Regression, LibSVM and Liblinear) except ANCOVA have demonstrated the comparative significance with preferential importance of sequence or composition based features over to thermodynamic features in siRNA designing, which is supported by Saetrom and Snøve [10], while ANCOVA model has exclusively revealed the importance of both features i.e. sequence based and thermodynamic features with considerable accuracy and coherence with Lu and Mathews contribution [36].These proposed models are based upon the clusters of features obtained from ACO. Many groups [37, 38, 11] have advocated the importance of thermodynamic features and concluded their importance in siRNA efficacy. The significance of both features along with newly advent features will certainly enhance the designing effectiveness. Recently, accessibility of the target site is another suggested feature, to improve upon efficacy prediction model of siRNA.

Acknowledgement

We are thankful to Prof G.B.K.S Prasad, Coordinator, Department of Biotechnology, Jiwaji University, Gwalior for his academic suggestions, We are also thankful to Prof. K.K. Biswas, Department of Computer Science and Engineering, Indian Institute of Technology, New Delhi for his unending support during the entire research work and to Jaypee Institute of Information technology University, Noida for providing the necessary facilities. At the end we also thank to all our reviewers.

References

1. Fire, A., Xu, S., Montgomery, M., Kostas, S., Driver, S., Mello, C.: Potent and specific genetic interference by double-stranded RNA in Caenorhabditis elegans. Nature 391(6669), 806–811 (1998)
2. Elbashir, S.M., Harborth, J., Lendeckel, W., Yalcin, A., Weber, K., Tuschl, T.: Duplexes of 21-nucleotide RNAs mediate RNA interference in cultured mammalian cells. Nature 411(6836), 428–498 (2001)
3. Kim, S.H., Jeong, J.H., Cho, K.C., Kim, S.W., Park, T.G.: Target-specific gene silencing by siRNA plasmid DNA complexed with folate-modified poly (ethylenimine). Journal of Controlled Release 104, 223–232 (2005)
4. Surabhi, R.M., Gaynor, R.B.: RNA interference directed against viral and cellular targets inhibits human immunodeficiency Virus Type 1 replication. J. Virol. 76(24), 12963–12973 (2002)
5. Pai, S.I., Lin, Y.Y., Macaes, B., Meneshian, A., Hung, C.F., Wu, T.C.: Prospects of RNA interference therapy for cancer. Gene. Ther. 13(6), 464–477 (2006)
6. Tuschl, T., Zamore, P., Lehmann, R., Bartel, D., Sharp, P.: Targeted mRNA degradation by double-stranded RNA in vitro. Genes. Dev. 13(24), 3191–3197 (1999)
7. Reynolds, A., Leake, D., Boese, Q., Scaringe, S., Marshall, W.S., Khvorova, A.: Rational siRNA design for RNA interference. Nat. Biotechnol. 22(3), 326–330 (2004)
8. Ui-Tei, K., Naito, Y., Takahashi, F., Haraguchi, T., Ohki-Hamazaki, H., Juni, A., Ueda, R., Saigo, K.: Guidelines for the selection of highly effective siRNA sequences for mammalian and chick RNA interference. Nucleic Acids Res. 32(3), 936–948 (2004)
9. Amarzguioui, M., Prydz, H.: An algorithm for selection of functional siRNA sequences. Biochem. Biophys. Res. Commun. 316(4), 1050–1058 (2004)
10. Saetrom, P., Snove, O.: A comparison of siRNA efficacy predictors. Biochem. Biophys. Res. Commun. 321(1), 247–253 (2004)
11. Chalk, A.M., Wahlestedt, C., Sonnhammer, E.L.: Improved and automated prediction of effective siRNA. Biochem. Biophys. Res. Commun. 319(1), 264–274 (2004)
12. Gong, W., Ren, Y., Xu, Q., Wang, Y., Lin, D., Zhou, H., Li, T.: Integrated siRNA design based on surveying of features associated with high RNAi effectiveness. BMC Bioinformatics 7, 516 (2006)
13. He, M.: Feature Selection Based on Ant Colony Optimization and Rough Set Theory. In: International Symposium on Computer Science and Computational Technology (ISCSCT), vol. 1, pp. 247–250 (2008)
14. Dorigo, M., Maniezzo, V., Colorni, A.: The ant system: Optimization by a colony of cooperating agents. IEEE Transactions on Systems, Man, and Cybernetics - Part B 26(1), 29–42 (1996)
15. Jain, C.K., Prasad, Y.: Feature selection for siRNA efficacy prediction using natural computation. In: World Congress on Nature & Biologically Inspired Computing (NaBIC 2009), pp. 1759–1764. IEEE Press, Los Alamitos (2009)
16. Huesken, D., Lange, J., Mickanin, C., Weiler, J., Asselbergs, F., Warner, J., Meloon, B., Engel, S., Rosenberg, A., Cohen, D., Labow, M., Reinhardt, M., Natt, F., Hall, J.: Design of a genome-wide siRNA library using an artificial neural network. Nat. Biotechnol. 23, 995–1001 (2005)
17. Matveeva, O., Nechipurenko, Y., Rossi, L., Moore, B., Sætrom, P., Ogurtsov, A.Y., Atkins, J.F., Shabalina, S.A.: Comparison of approaches for rational siRNA design leading to a new efficient and transparent method. Nucleic Acids Res. 35, e63 (2007)

18. Vert, J.P., Foveau, N., Lajaunie, C., Vandenbrouck, Y.: An accurate and interpretable model for siRNA efficacy prediction. BMC Bioinform. 7, 520 (2006)
19. Zhou, D., He, Y., Kwoh, C., Wang, H.: Ant MST:An Ant-Based Minimum Spanning Tree for Gene Expression Data Clustering. In: Rajapakse, J.C., Schmidt, B., Volkert, L.G. (eds.) PRIB 2007. LNCS (LNBI), vol. 4774, pp. 198–205. Springer, Heidelberg (2007)
20. Lee, M., Kim, Y., Kim, Y., Lee, Y.K., Yoon, H.: An Ant-based Clustering System for Knowledge Discovery in DNA Chip Analysis Data. International Journal of Computational Intelligence 4(2) (Spring 2008)
21. He, Y., Hui, S.C., Sim, Y.: A Novel Ant-Based Clustering Approach for Document Clustering. In: Asia Information Retrieval Symposium, Singapore, pp. 537–544 (2006)
22. Everitt, B.S.: The Cambridge Dictionary of Statistics. CUP, Cambridge (2002), ISBN 0-521-81099-x
23. Ichihara, M., Murakumo, Y., Masuda, A., Matsuura, T., Asai, N., Jijiwa, M., Ishida, M., Shinmi, J., Yatsuya, H., Qiao, S., Takahashi, M., Ohno, K.: Thermodynamic instability of siRNA duplex is a prerequisite for dependable prediction of siRNA activities. Nucleic Acids Research 35(18), e123 (2007)
24. http://www.xlstat.com/en/download/?file=xlstat2009.exe (May 3, 2009)
25. http://www.statsoft.com/textbook/stbasic.html (June 14, 2009)
26. Mardia, K.V., Kent, J.T., Bibly, J.M.: Multivariate Analysis. Academic Press, London (1979), ISBN 0-12-471252-5
27. Friston, K.J., Holmes, A.P., Worsley, K.J., Poline, J.B., Frith, C.D., Frackowiak, R.S.J.: Statistical Parametric Maps in Functional imaging: A general linear approach. Human Brain Mapping 2, 189–210 (1995)
28. Liu, Q., Irina, D., Adewale Adeniyi, J., Potter John, D., Yutaka, Y.: Comparative evaluation of gene-set analysis methods. BMC Bioinformatics 8, 431 (2007)
29. Chan, S.H., Chen, L.J., Chow, N.H., Liu, H.S.: An ancova approach to normalize microarray data, and its performance to existing methods. Journal of Bioinformatics and Computational Biology 3(2), 257–268 (2005)
30. Boser, B.E., Guyon, I., Vapnik, V.: A training algorithm for optimal margin classifiers. In: Proceedings of the Fifth Annual Workshop on Computational Learning Theory, pp. 144–152. ACM Press, New York (1992)
31. Drucker, H., Burges Chris, J.C., Kaufman, L., Smola, A., Vapnik, V.: Support Vector Regression Machines. In: Advances in Neural Information Processing Systems, NIPS 1996, vol. 9, pp. 155–161 (1997)
32. Cortes, C., Vapnik, V.: Support-Vector Networks. Machine Learning 20 (1995), http://www.springerlink.com/content/k238jx04hm87j80g/
33. Chang, C.-C., Lin, C.-J.: LIBSVM: a library for support vector machines (2001), http://www.csie.ntu.edu.tw/~cjlin/libsvm
34. Shalev-Shwartz, S., Singer, Y., Srebro, N.: Pegasos, primal estimated sub-gradient solver for SVM. In: Proceedings of the 24th International Conference on Machine Learning, pp. 807–814 (2007)
35. Joachims, T.: Training Linear SVMs in Linear Time. In: Proceedings of the ACM Conference on Knowledge Discovery and Data Mining, KDD (2006)
36. Lu, Z.H., Mathews, D.H.: OligoWalk: an online siRNA design tool utilizing hybridization thermodynamics. Nucleic Acids Research 36(Suppl. 2), 104–108 (2008)
37. Poliseno, L., Evangelista, M., Mercatanti, A., Mariani, L., Citti, L., Rainaldi, G.: The energy profiling of short interfering RNAs is highly predictive of their activity. Oligonucleotides 14, 227–232 (2004)

38. Khvorova, A., Reynolds, A., Jayasena, S.D.: Functional siRNAs and miRNAs exhibit strand bias. Cell 115, 209–216 (2003)
39. Wang, X., Wang, X., Verma, R.K., Beauchamp, L., Magdaleno, S., Sendera, T.J.: Selection of hyperfunctional siRNAs with improved potency and specificity. Nucleic acid Research 37(22), e152 (2009)
40. Basiri, M.E., Ghasem-Aghaee, N., Aghadam, M.H.: Using Ant Colony optimization based selected features for predicting post synaptic activity in proteins. In: Marchiori, E., Moore, J.H. (eds.) EvoBIO 2008. LNCS, vol. 4973, pp. 12–23. Springer, Heidelberg (2008)
41. Nemati, S., Basiri, M.E., Aghadam, N.G., Aghadam, M.H.: A novel ACO-GA hybrid algorithm for feature selection in protein function prediction. Expert System With Applications 36, 12086–12094 (2009)

A Fast Progressive Image Transmission Algorithm Using Linear Bivariate Splines

Rohit Verma[1], Ravikant Verma[2], P. Syamala Jaya Sree[3], Pradeep Kumar[4],
Rajesh Siddavatam[5], and S.P. Ghrera[6]

[1,2,3,5,6] Department of Computer Science & IT,
[4] Department of Electronics and Communications
Jaypee University of Information Technology,
Waknaghat, Himachal Pradesh, 173215, India
email4rohit@gmail.com, ravikant.verma@juit.ac.in,
jayasree.syamala@gmail.com,
{pradeep.kumar,srajesh,sp.ghrera}@juit.ac.in

Abstract. Progressive image transmission provides a convenient User Interface when images are transmitted slowly. In this paper, we present a progressive image reconstruction scheme based on the multi-scale edge representation of images. In the multi-scale edge representation an image is decomposed into Most Significant Points which represent the strong edges and Insignificant Points which represent weak edges. Image re-construction is done based on the approximation of image regarded as a function, by a linear spline over adapted Delaunay triangulation. The proposed method progressively improves the quality of the reconstructed image till the desired quality is obtained.

Keywords: progressive image transmission, delaunay triangulation, linear Bivariate splines.

1 Introduction

With the emergence of the World Wide Web, images have become an important means of communicating information in the formerly text-only Internet. When people view an image through a low speed connection, for example, via a telephone line or via wireless networks, it will take much time to transmit the whole image. Even with increased bandwidth, transmitting large images such as pictures captured by digital cameras is still relatively slow. The desire to let mobile users participate in the Internet leads to the need to cope with even narrower bandwidth and smaller client displays. If the delay is too long user will feel irritated and will give up. In order to reduce the bandwidth required for transmitting a given image in a given time, image compression techniques are commonly used to encode images. The encoded results, instead of the original images, are transmitted over the Internet. After decoding, we can obtain the decoded images, which are similar to the original ones.

Rohit Verma and Siddavatam Rajesh [1],[2],[3] have developed a fast image reconstruction algorithms using second generation wavelets and splines. Image Compression and Reconstruction algorithms have been devloped by many researchers

S. Ranka et al. (Eds.): IC3 2010, Part I, CCIS 94, pp. 568–578, 2010.

Siddavatam Rajesh [4] has developed a fast progressive image sampling using B-splines. Carlos Vazquez et al, [7] has proposed interactive algorithm to reconstruct an image from non-uniform samples obtained as a result of geometric transformation using filters Delaunay triangulation [13],[16] has been extensively used for generation of image from irregular data points. The image is reconstructed by either by linear or cubic splines over Delaunay Triangulations of adaptively chosen set of significant points. This paper concerns with progressive triangulation of an image using standard gradient edge detection techniques and reconstruction using bivariate splines from adapted Delaunay triangulation until the desired quality of the reconstructed image is not obtained.

Although image compression provides an efficient and effective method to reduce the amount of data needed to represent an image, it oftentimes requires receivers to wait for the completely encoded results before reconstructing the image. If the decoded image is not the expected one, then receivers must transmit another image again. Progressive Image Transmission (PIT) techniques have been proposed to alleviate this problem by first sending a coarse version of the original image and then resending it progressively. Progressive image transmission can help reducing the latency when transmitting raster images over low bandwidth links. Often, a rough approximation (preview) of an image is sufficient for the user to decide whether or not it should be transmitted in greater detail. This allows the user to decide whether to wait for a more detailed reconstruction, or to abort the transmission. Progressive image transmission has been widely applied for many applications, such as teleconferencing, remote image database access and so on.

Existing approaches for PIT have adopted, explicitly or implicitly, the minimal distortion principle to decide the importance. For example, in the SPIHT algorithm [17], the coefficients with larger magnitude are considered more significant for they will cause larger distortion. The algorithm will therefore sort the coefficients by their magnitudes before transmission.

Some PIT techniques have adopted HVS (human visual system) weighting in spectral domain to improve the perceptual quality of the transmitted image [18],[19]. However, they did not consider the attention change in spatial domain. Popular image standards such as JPEG and JPEG2000 do support ROI coding, but they do not provide any mechanism for automatic ROI definition.

Section 2 describes the significant sample point selection and in section 3 the modeling of the 2D images using the Linear Bivariate splines is elaborated. Section 4 describes the reconstruction algorithm and it's complexity in is explained in section 5. In section 6 significant measures for reconstruction have been discussed. Experimental results along with comparison of the proposed method with APEL are discussed in section 7 and conclusions in 8.

2 Progressive Significant Sample Point Selection

This section provides a generic introduction to the basic features and concepts of novel Progressive Sample Point Selection algorithm.

Let M be a mXn matrix representing a grayscale image

The algorithm involves following steps:-

1) Initialization: initialization of variables
2) Edge Detection: Edge detection using sobel and canny filters.
3) Filtering: Passing the images/matrices through rangefilt.
4) First Phase Transmission: Transmission of strong edges resulting in a coarse image.
5) Second Phase Transmission: Transmission of weak edges resulting in a fine image.
6) Third Phase Transmission: Detailed transmission producing the original reconstructed image.

2.1 Initialization

$$X1=0; X2=0; X3=0 \quad x \in X1, X2, X3$$

$$Y1=0; Y2=0; Y3=0 \quad y \in Y1, Y2, Y3$$

$$Z1=0; Z2=0; Z3=0 \quad z \in Z1, Z2, Z3$$

X,Y,Z Matrices for representing x,y,z pixel co-ordinates
H The starting level for third phase retransmission
M The increment level for third phase retransmission The values of H and M represents on the network bandwidth used for image transmission
Count1=0; Count2=0; Count3=0;
Integers representing the number of points obtained for triangulation at successive phases of transmission
Xs Data Set (Sobel Filter) Xc Data Set (Canny Filter)

2.2 Edge Detection

An edge detector like sobel or canny takes a grayscale image as its input and returns a binary image of the same size, with 1's where the function finds edges in the original image and 0's elsewhere.

Fig. 1. Edge Detection 1 Sobel

The Sobel method finds edges using the Sobel approximation to the derivative. It returns edges at those points where the gradient of I is maximum. In this method all the edges that are not stronger than a default threshold value are ignored. We can also specify our own threshold value. So this method does not identify weak edges which can be seen clearly in the Figure-1. This method was giving too less points to get the required triangulation.

The Canny method finds edges by looking for local maxima of the gradient of image. The gradient is calculated using the derivative of a Gaussian filter. The method uses two thresholds, to detect strong and weak edges, and includes the weak edges in the output only if they are connected to strong edges. This method is therefore more likely to detect true weak edges. The result is the following image. But again this resulted in too many points for the required triangulation.

Fig. 2. Edge Detection 1 canny

2.3 Filtering

After identifying the edges, the resulting image is passed through a filter so that the edges become prominent and we get more points near the edges. In order to obtain good triangulations most significant points are chosen. Rangefilt filters an image with respect to its local range. It returns an array, where each output pixel contains the range value (maximum value - minimum value) of the 3-by-3 neighborhood around the corresponding pixel in the input image.

2.4 First Phase Transmission

Input: Original Lena Image I(x,y);

Step 1:   for k=1, 3, 5, 7...................2n-1
Step 2:   Locate a point P(x,y) such that P $(x,y) \in$ Xs,
Step 3:   Add P(x,y) to matrices X1, Y1 , Z1
Step 4:   count = count+1
Step 5:   end
Output: I (X1, Y1, Z1) $\in$ Xs

2.5 Second Phase Transmission

Input: X=0 ; Y=0; count=0 ; Z=0 I (X, Y)
        Step 1: for k= 1, 4,7,11....................3n-2
        Step 2:   Locate a point P(x,y) such that
        Step 3: $P(x,y) \in Xc$ and $P(x,y) \notin Xs$
        Step 4:   Add P(x,y) to matrices to X2, Y2 and Z2
        Step 5: count = count+1
        Step 6: end
Output: $I(X2, Y2, Z2) \in Xc \cup Xs$

2.6 Overview of Delaunay Triangulation

Delaunay Triangulation [14, 15, 16] is also popular due to its following properties:

1) It gives a unique set of triangles T, provided that no four points in S are co-circular,
2) It guarantees optimal triangulation according to the min-max angle criterion, i.e. the smallest angle is maximal.
3) It gives the smoothest piecewise linear approximation for a given data set.

In the Delaunay triangulation method [16], the location of the global nodes defining the triangle vertices and then produce the elements by mapping global nodes to element nodes. Element definition from a given global set can be done by the method of Delaunay Triangulation. The discretization domain is divided into polygons, subject to the condition that each polygon contains only on global node, and the distance of an arbitrary point inside a polygon from the native global node is smaller than the distance from any other node. The sides of the polygon thus produced are perpendicular bisectors of the straight segments connecting pairs of nodes.

2.7 Third Phase Transmission

To further improve the triangulations, in every triangle a point is inserted at the centroid of the triangle and triangles are formed including that point. This algorithm is useful for even those images having low gradient at the edges or weak edges.

Input: TRI(X1+X2, Y1+Y2)

        Step 1: T=Dataset (TRI)
        Step 2: for threshold=H to 0 step M
        Step 3:   for m=1, 2, 3, 4,5,6,7....................................N
        Step 4:   If Area > Threshold
        Step 5:   C(x,y)=Centroid of Triangle TN
        Step 6:   add C(x,y) to data set (X3,Y3,Z3)
        Step 7:   count = count+1
        Step 8:   end
        Step 9: end
        Step 10 : TRI = delaunay(X,Y)

Output: $I(X3, Y3, Z3) \in Xc \cup Xs$

3 Image Reconstruction Using Linear Bivariate Splines

The transmitted image as a result of the three phases of transmission is reconstructed at the receiver's end. The reconstruction is carried out based on the approximation of image regarded as a function, by a linear bivariate spline over adapted Delaunay triangulation.

The Linear Bivariate Splines are used very recently by Laurent Demaret et al [9]. The image is viewed as a sum of linear bivariate splines over the Delaunay triangulation of a small recursively chosen non uniform set of significant samples Sk from a total set of samples in an image denoted as Sn. The linear spline is bivariate and continuous function which can be evaluated at any point in the rectangular image domain in particular for non uniform set of significant samples denoted as Sk from a total set of samples in an image denoted as Sn.

If we denote Ω as the space of linear bivariate polynomials, for the above set Sk $\subseteq$ Sn, the linear spline space ΩL, containing all continuous functions over the convex hull of Sk denoted as [Sk].

Definition: If for any triangle $\Delta \in T(S^k)$ where $T(S^k)$ is the delaunay triangulation of S^k is in Ω defined as

$$\Omega_L = \{x : x \in [S^k]\} \forall \Delta \in T(S^k) \mid x \in \Omega \qquad (1)$$

then any element in ΩL is referred to as a linear spline over T(Sk). For a given luminance values at the points of S, {I(y): y $\in$ S} there is a unique linear spline interpolant L(S, I) which gives

$$L(S, I)(y) = I(y) \forall \ y \in S \qquad (2)$$

where I(y) denotes the image I with y samples that belong to S. Using the above bivariate splines and the concept of Significant Sample point selection algorithm discussed above the original image can be approximated and the reconstruction of the image can be done as per the algorithm given below.

4 Reconstruction Algorithm

The following steps are used to reconstruct the original image from set of regular points comprising of significant (S_K) and insignificant points (I_K):

INPUT:

1. Let S^N=data set $S \in S^K \cup I^K_i$
2. Z^0: luminance
3. S^0: set of regular data for initial triangulation

Step1. Use Delaunay triangulation and Linear Bivariate Splines to produce unique set of triangles and image.

574   R. Verma et al.

Step2. Use Progressive Significant sample point selection algorithm to find a set of new significant points (SP).
Step3. Get $S^K=S^{K-1}+SP$
Step4. Repeat steps 1 to 3 to get the image $I_R(y)$
Step5. Return S^K and $I_R(y)$
OUTPUT:
   Most Significant Sample Set (S^K) and Reconstructed Image $I_R(y)$

5 Algorithm Complexity

In general, the complexity of the non-symmetric filter is proportional to the dimension of the filter n2, where n * n is the size of the convolution kernel. In canny edge detection, the filter is Gaussian which is symmetric and separable. For such cases the complexity is given by n+1 [20]. All gradient based algorithms like Sobel do have complexity of O(n). The complexity of well known Delaunay algorithm in worst case is O(n^ceil(d/2)) and for well distributed point set is ~ O(n). N is number of points and d is the dimension. So in 2D, Delaunay complexity is O(N) is any case.

Step 1: Sobel Edge Detector: O(n)
Step 2: Canny Edge Detector: O(n)
Step 3: Filtering (rangefilt) : O(n)
Step 4: First Phase Transmission: O(2n-1)=O(n)
Step 5: Second Phase Transmission: O(3n-2)=O(n)
Step 6: Third Phase Transmission: O(n)
Step 7: Image Reconstruction: O(n)

Hence the total complexity of the proposed algorithm is O(n) which is quite fast and optimal.

6 Significance Measures for Reconstructed Image

Peak Signal to Noise Ratio:
A well-known quality measure for the evaluation of image reconstruction schemes is the Peak Signal to Noise Ratio (PSNR),

$$PSNR = 20 * \log 10 \ (b / RMS) \qquad (3)$$

where b is the largest possible value of the signal and RMS is the root mean square difference between the original and reconstructed images. PSNR is an equivalent measure to the reciprocal of the mean square error. The PSNR is expressed in dB (decibels). The popularity of PSNR as a measure of image distortion derives partly from the ease with which it may be calculated, and partly from the tractability of linear optimization problems involving squared error metrics.

7 Results and Discussions

We have used absolutely addressed Picture Element coding (APEL) [19] to compare the effectiveness of our proposed method. APEL is a robust, loss-less image coding technique, which transforms binary images into a tessellation of independent black picture elements. As the APEL technique operates on a binary level, the encoding of grey-scale images must employ a Bit Plane Coding (BPC) [18] stage. APEL interleaves and sends the larger pixels from each of the bit-planes immediately after the transmission has begun so that a coarse image can be encoded by the recipient. Subsequently, as further pixels arrive, a finer image can be decoded by the recipient. APEL decreases the visual impact of errors by rearranging the addresses of pixels in an ascending order and placing two contiguous pixels a considerable distance apart in the data-stream, the probability of both being destroyed by the same burst is decreased. Error can be detected and removed by removing the out-of-order addresses and consecutively transmitted non-neighbor pixels.

The proposed method transmits the image pixels as per increasing order of significance. Proposed method sends the pixels corresponding to the strong edges as soon as the transmission begins and enables the recipient to reconstruct a coarse image. In due course, pixels corresponding to weaker edges and other lesser significant pixels (second and third phase transmission) are send to the recipient which improves the definition of the reconstructed image. In our proposed method we define the reconstruction error as $\| I_O - I_R \| / \| I_O \|$, where I_O is the original image and I_R is the reconstructed image.

The reconstructed image at various levels of transmission for APEL coding scheme and proposed method are shown in figure 3.

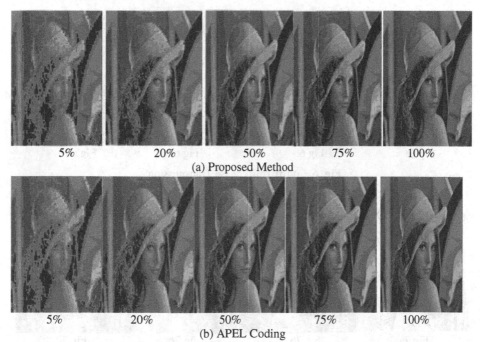

| 5% | 20% | 50% | 75% | 100% |

(a) Proposed Method

| 5% | 20% | 50% | 75% | 100% |

(b) APEL Coding

Fig. 3. Comparison of (b) APEL coding[19] and (a) proposed method at various levels of transmission

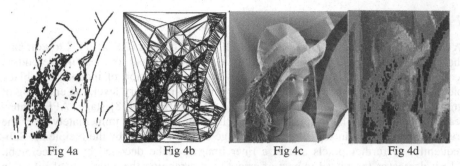

Fig. 4. (a)-(d)First phase Transmission

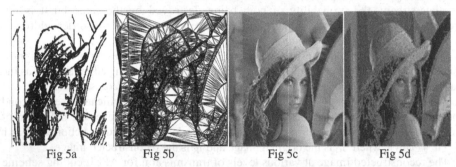

Fig. 5. (a)-(d) Second phase Transmission

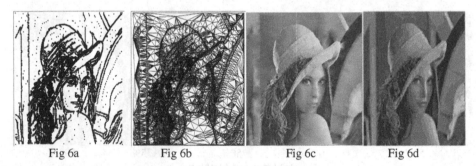

Fig. 6. (a)-(d) Third phase Transmission

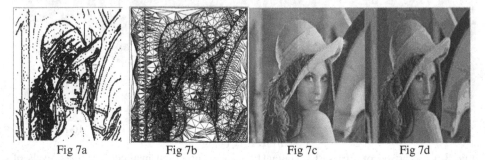

Fig. 7. (a)-(d) Fourth phase Transmission

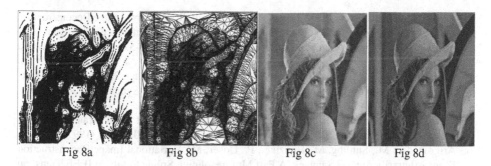

| Fig 8a | Fig 8b | Fig 8c | Fig 8d |

Fig. 8. (a)-(d) Fifth phase Transmission

Table 1. PSNR at various stages of transmission

S No	Progressive Transmission Phases	Proposed Method Fig (d) dB
1	First phase - Fig. 4 (a) – 4(d)	13.90
2	Second phase - Fig. 5 (a) – 5(d)	21.68
3	Third Phase - Fig. 6(a) – 6(d)	21.97
4	Fourth Phase -Fig. 7(a) – 7(d)	23.41
5	Fifth Phase - Fig. 8(a) – 8(d)	27.22

8 Conclusions

In this paper, algorithm based on significant point selection is applied for progressive image transmission. Experimental results on the popular image of Lena are presented to show the reconstructed image at various phases of transmission. Set of regular points are selected using Canny and Sobel edge detection and Delaunay triangulation method is applied to create triangulated network. The set of increasingly significant sample points are transmitted in each transmission phase. The gray level of each sample point is interpolated from the luminance values of neighbor significant sample point. The original image, sample points, Delaunay triangulation and its reconstruction results along with the error image are shown for LENA image.

The PSNR value goes on increasing towards the latter phases of transmission. Thus we can fairly approximate that the proposed Progressive Transmission technique can transmit the image progressively varying the image quality. This indicated by the range of the PSNR that varies from 13.9 to 27.22 dB.

References

1. Verma, R., Srivastava, G.K., Mahrishi, R., Siddavatam, R.: A Fast Image Reconstruction Algorithm Using Significant Sample Point Selection and Linear Bivariate Splines. In: IEEE TENCON, pp. 1–6. IEEE Press, Singapore (2009)
2. Verma, R., Srivastava, G.K., Mahrishi, R., Siddavatam, R.: A Novel Wavelet Edge Detection Algorithm For Noisy Images. In: IEEE International Conference on Ultra Modern Technologies, pp. 1–8. IEEE Press, St. Petersburg (2009)

3. Verma, R., Srivastava, G.K., Mahrishi, R., Siddavatam, R.: A Novel Image Reconstruction Using Second Generation Wavelets. In: IEEE International Conference on Advances in Recent Technologies in Communication and Computing, pp. 509–513. IEEE Press, Kerala (2009)

4. Siddavatam, R., Sandeep, K., Mittal, R.K.: A Fast Progressive Image Sampling Using Lifting Scheme And Non-Uniform B-Splines. In: IEEE International Symposium on Industrial Electronics, pp. 1645–1650. IEEE Press, Spain (2007)

5. Eldar, Y., Lindenbaum, M., Porat, M., Zeevi, Y.Y.: The Farthest Point Strategy For Progressive Image Sampling. IEEE Trans. Image Processing 6(9), 1305–1315 (1997)

6. Arigovindan, M., Suhling, M., Hunziker, P., Unser, M.: Variational Image Reconstruction From Arbitrarily Spaced Samples: A Fast Multiresolution Spline Solution. IEEE Trans. on Image Processing 14(4), 450–460 (2005)

7. Vazquez, C., Dubois, E., Konrad, J.: Reconstruction of Nonuniformly Sampled Images in Spline Spaces. IEEE Trans. on Image Processing 14(6), 713–724 (2005)

8. Cohen, A., Mate, B.: Compact Representation Of Images By Edge Adapted Multiscale Transforms. In: IEEE International Conference on Image Processing, Tessaloniki, pp. 8–11 (2001)

9. Laurent, D., Nira, D., Armin, I.: Image Compression by Linear Splines over Adaptive Triangulations. Signal Processing 86(4), 1604–1616 (2006)

10. Tzu-Chuen, L., Chin-Chen, C.: A Progressive Image Transmission Technique Using Haar Wavelet Transformation. International Journal of Innovative Computing, Information and Control 3, 6(A), 1449–1461 (2007)

11. Eldar, Y., Oppenheim, A.: Filter Bank Reconstruction of Bandlimited Signals from Non-Uniform and Generalized Samples. IEEE Trans. Signal Processing 48(10), 2864–2875 (2000)

12. Aldroubi, A., Grochenig, K.: Nonuniform Sampling and Reconstruction in Shift Invariant Spaces. SIAM Rev. 43, 585–620 (2001)

13. Wu, J., Amaratunga, K.: Wavelet Triangulated Irregular Networks. Int. J. Geographical Information Science 17(3), 273–289 (2003)

14. Barber, C.B., Dobkin, D.P., Huhdanpaa, H.T.: The Quickhull Algorithm for Convex Hulls. ACM Transactions on Mathematical Software 22(4), 469–483 (1996)

15. Preparata, F.P., Shamos, M.I.: Computational Geometry. Springer, New York (1988)

16. Rippa, S.: Minimal Roughness Property of the Delaunay Triangulation. Comput. Aided Geometric Des. 7, 489–497 (1990)

17. Said, A., Pearlman, W.A.: A New, Fast, and Efficient Image Codec Based on Set Partitioning in Hierarchical Trees. IEEE Trans. on Circuits and Systems for Video Technology 6(3), 243–250 (1996)

18. Bodson, D., McConnell, K.R., Schaphorst, R.: FAX: Facsimile Technology and Applications Handbook, pp. 195–199 (1992)

19. Paul, C., Bahram, H.: Progressive Robust Image Transmission. In: 6th International Workshop on Systems, Signals and Image Processing. Lancaster University, UK (1999)

20. Neoh, H.S., Hazanchuk, A.: Adaptive Edge Detection for Real-Time Video Processing using FPGAs. Global Signal Processing (2004)

Building Optimization

Rekha Bhowmik[1] and Pradeep Sharma[2]

[1] Computer Science Department, University of Texas, Dallas, USA
[2] IT Department, ABES Engineering College, Ghaziabad, India
rxb080100@utdallas.edu, pksharma26@rediffmail.com

Abstract. The goal of designing a facility layout is to minimize the communication cost between the facilities. The paper presents an approach for minimizing the communication cost while considering the functional constraints. We
present a nonlinear programming approach for the minimization of communication cost to determine the optimum room dimensions and demonstrate its application using an illustrative example. The problem is solved by Sequential
Linear Programming. The objective function and all the constraints are linear in
the neighborhood of the design point and an optimum obtained through simplex
algorithm.

Keywords: Optimization, Nonlinear Programming, Communication Cost
Sequential Linear Programming.

1 Introduction

Several algorithms are available which can be used for nonlinear programming problems. These can be classified into : i) Penalty function methods involving the transformation of constrained problem in sequential unconstrained minimization problems,
ii) Direct methods which handle the minimization of the objective function and satisfaction of constraints simultaneously. Some of the   algorithms are: i) Zontendijk's
method of feasible direction, ii) Rose's gradient projection method, and iii) Sequential
Linear Programming. Sequential Linear Programming was originally proposed by
Griffith and Stewart[7]. Bhavikatti[8] suggested several improvements to the method.
A good discussion of the earlier developments can be found in Himmelblaue[2] who
calls the method as Approximate programming.

A nonlinear programming approach is used for the minimization of total communication cost to determine the optimum room dimensions. This paper discusses the
optimization procedure.

This work deals with optimum dimensioning of architectural plans presented as
dimensionless layouts. The dimensionless layout is usually produced using Iterative
Heuristic algorithm[6]. Once a dimensionless layout is available the constraints on
walls, rooms, windows, doors can be stated so that the resultant dimensions produce
values which satisfy without violating the prescribed architectural constraints while
minimizing the cost.

S. Ranka et al. (Eds.): IC3 2010, Part I, CCIS 94, pp. 579–587, 2010.
Springer-Verlag Berlin Heidelberg 2010

2 Building Design Optimization Problem

Plan of a unit is available. Each room has restriction on wall, area, window, door of a room. The objective function is to minimize the communication cost based on wall, door, window, and area of a room. length, width and area.

Radford[1]suggested the building design optimization problem. The objective is to minimize the area of the house, while satisfying certain constraints. The constraints for are based on each room[4, 5]. The constraints are based on area, length, width, and aspect ratio of a room.

3 Building Design Optimization Using Improved Move Limit Method Sequential Linear Programming

3.1 Problem Formulation

The simplex method for solving LP problems is very powerful, therefore, a number of techniques for solving nonlinear programming problems are based on converting them to LP problems. An initial solution is to be selected to provide a base for the determination of the tangents of the constraints and of the objective.

Consider a finite set of variables x_1, x_2, ..., x_n The unit cost coefficients for the main constructional elements, namely, floor and walls are assumed and the construction cost function, $f(x)$ is to be minimized. This is generally a nonlinear function of the variables. The upper and lower limits on the length/width, ratios of the rooms, and the minimum area for each room constitute the constraints.

Thus, the problem is:

$$\text{minimize } f(x)$$
$$\text{subject to } g_j(x) \leq 0, \qquad\qquad\qquad j = 1,2, \dots, n \quad (1)$$

where x is the Consider the case of a building consisting of a single room with wall lengths w_1 and w_2, where we only specify minimum vector of design variables which constitute the optimum layout problem, n is a set of inequality constraints of the form $g_j(x) \leq 0$ ($j=1, 2, \dots, n$), and $x_i \leq 0$ ($i=1,2, \dots, k$), where k is a set of decision variables.

3.2 Objective Function

Consider the dimensionless layout shown in Fig. 1a. The problem is to determine the optimum values of the variables $(w_1, w_2, w_3, \dots, w_n)$which minimize the overall construction cost while satisfying the constraints. The values of the variables provide the room dimensions.

The total cost for i rooms is given by:

$$K_1 \sum_{i=1}^{n} (A_N + A_S + A_E + A_W) + K_5 \sum_{i=1}^{n} (A_{winN} + A_{winS} + A_{winE} + A_{wnW})$$
$$+ K_2 (K_3 \sum_{i=1}^{n} l_i + K_4 \sum_{i=1}^{n} w_i) \qquad\qquad (2)$$

This is the objective function to be minimized. Here, A_N, A_S, A_E, A_W are the areas of the walls and A_{winN}, A_{winS}, A_{winE}, A_{winW} are the areas of windows, K_1 and K_2 are constants depending upon the cost of floor/roof, cost of wall, and K_3, K_4 depend on the geometry of the layout, K_5 is the cost for windows.

It can be estimated easily that the values of K_3 and K_4 range from 1.5 to 2.0, depending upon the common wall between adjacent rooms. Initially a value of 1.5 is taken.

3.3 Constraints

The planning constraints are:
i) minimum area, $amin_i$, minimum length/width, $lmin_i$, and maximum length/width, $lmax_i$, can be set for each room as:

$lmin_i - l_i \leq 0$	minimum length
$l_i - lmax_i \leq 0$	maximum length
$lmin_i - w_i \leq 0$	minimum width
$w_i - lmax_i \leq 0$	maximum width

ii) minimum and maximum area for different rooms($amin_i$, $amax_i$) can be set for each room

$amin_i - l_i * w_i \geq 0$	minimum area
$l_i * w_i - amax_i \leq 0$	maximum area

iii) room length-to-width ratio can be set. The minimum ratio constraint consists of two constraints: the minimum width-to-length ratio and the minimum length-to-width ratio.

$rmin_i\, l_i - w_i \leq 0$	minimum length-to-width ratio
$rmin_i\, w_i - l_i \leq 0$	minimum width-to-length ratio
$w_i - rmax_i\, l_i \leq 0$	maximum width-to-length ratio
$l_i - rmax_i\, w_i - \leq 0$	maximum length-to-width ratio

iv) This constraint forces units into the building boundary. To force unit i inside unit j, the constraints are:

$$y_{Ni} \leq y_{Nj}$$
$$y_{Sj} \leq y_{Si}$$
$$x_{Ei} \leq x_{Ej}$$
$$x_{Wj} \leq x_{Wi}$$

v) The constraint to prevent two units from occupying the same space. To prevent unit i from intersecting unit j, one of the constraints must be satisfied:

$(x_{Wi} \geq x_{Ej})$ or $(x_{Wj} \geq x_{Ei})$ or $(y_{Si} \geq y_{Nj})$ or $(y_{Sj} \geq y_{Ni})$

This can be represented as:

$min(x_{Ej} - x_{Wi}, x_{Ei} - x_{Wj}, y_{Nj} - y_{Si}, y_{Ni} - y_{Sj}) \leq 0$

vi) The constraint used when spaces are forced to intersect to ensure access:

$$x_{Wi} \leq x_{Ej}$$
$$x_{Wj} \leq x_{Ei}$$
$$y_{Si} \leq y_{Nj}$$
$$y_{Sj} \leq y_{Ni}$$

These constraints also permit intersection at a point. To model an intersection that provides space for a door or an opening, at least one of the following conditions must be satisfied:

$y_{Nj} - y_{Si} \geq \max(door_i, \ door_j)$	(*i* overlaps north wall of *j*)
$y_{Ni} - y_{Sj} \geq \max(door_i, \ door_j)$	(*i* overlaps south wall of *j*)
$x_{Ej} - x_{Wi} \geq \max(door_i, \ door_j)$	(*i* overlaps east wall of *j*)
$x_{Ei} - x_{Wj} \geq \max(door_i, \ door_j)$	(*i* overlaps west wall of *j*)

where, $door_i$ is the minimum size for a door or opening in unit i. This set of constraints can be represented as:

$$\min\{\max(door_i, door_j) - x_{Ej} + x_{Wi},$$
$$\max(door_i, door_j) - x_{Ei} + x_{Wj},$$
$$\max(door_i, door_j) - y_{Nj} + y_{Si},$$
$$\max(door_i, door_j) - y_{Ni} + y_{Sj}\} \ \leq 0$$

vii) To force a room to a particular wall, one of the following constraints can be added:

$$y_{Ni} = y_{Nj}$$
$$y_{Si} = y_{Sj}$$
$$x_{Ei} = x_{Ej}$$
$$x_{Wi} = x_{Wj}$$

viii) If a room may require an external door, but it is not important which direction the door faces, then the following constraint can be added:

$$\min \{(x_{Ei} - x_{Ej})^2, (x_{Wi} - x_{Wj})^2, (y_{Si} - y_{Sj})^2, (y_{Ni} - y_{Nj})^2\} = 0$$

ix) This constraint is used to keep the construction cost below some value, C_{total}. Here, build cost is measured only in terms of material cost. Material costs for walls, k_{wall} and for windows, k_{window} are specified per square unit of material. The build cost constraint is calculated as:

$$k_{wall}(A_N + A_S + A_E + A_W) +$$
$$k_{window}(A_{winN} + A_{winS} + A_{winE} + A_{wnW}) \leq C_{total}$$

where A_N, A_S, A_E, A_W are the areas of the external walls and A_{winN}, A_{winS}, A_{winE}, A_{winW} are the areas of windows.

x) This constraint ensures that the window width cannot be larger than the wall it is on. Each window added to a room is given by the following constraint:

$win_{Ni} \leq l_i$, $win_{Si} \leq l_i$, $win_{Ei} \leq w_i$, or $win_{Wi} \leq w_i$

3.4 Improved Move Limit Method of Sequential Linear Programming

The problem, as formulated, is a nonlinear programming optimization problem. The optimization method used here is Sequential Linear Programming. This method can adequately handle this problem and has the advantage that it is simple to program. An outline of the formulation is given below.

A general nonlinear programming problem can be defined as:

minimize $Z = F(x)$
subject to
$G_j(x) \leq 0$, $j = 1, 2, ..., m$

where x is a design vector on n dimensions, $F(x)$ is the objective function and G_j's are constraints. A problem falls under the category of nonlinear programming if either $F(x)$ or any one of G_j's is a nonlinear function of the variables. In the neighborhood of the design vector x^k using Taylor's series expansion and retaining only up to linear terms, the objective function and constraints are approximated as

$F(x^{k+1}) = F(x^k) + \nabla F^T(x^k)(x^{k+1} - x^k)$
$G_j(x^{k+1}) = G(x^k) + \nabla G^T(x^k)(x^{k+1} - x^k)$

With these approximations, the problem reduces to a linear programming problem. The linear programming problem is solved with the following additional constraints on the movement of design variables

$| (x_i^{k+1} - x_i^k) | \quad \leq \quad M_i^k$

where x_i^{k+1}, x_i^k and M_i^k are the ith components of x^{k+1}, x^k and M^k. The vector M^k sets the move limits on the design variables.

If x^{k+1} is a feasible point, the objective function is checked for improvement [$F(x^{k+1}) < F(x^k)$]. The sequence of linear programming is continued from x^{k+1} if improvement is found in objective function. Otherwise, the new design point is selected by quadratic interpolation between the design points x^k and x^{k+1}.

If a linear programming solution enters infeasible region, it is steered to feasible region by moving in the gradient direction of most violated constraint.

In some problems the technique of steering to feasible region is to be used repeatedly to reach feasible region. If the number of repetitions required is large, recalculation of constraint derivatives is performed after predefined repetitions.

After steering the design vector to feasible region, if no improvement is found in the objective function, the usability of the direction is checked. The quadratic interpolation is resorted only if the direction is usable.

Economy and success of optimization depends to a large extent on the choice of move limits. If move limits are small the progress of optimization is slow, if large the design vector is likely to enter the infeasible region and it may take considerable time to reenter the feasible region.

3.5 Example

Consider the dimensionless floor plan as shown in Fig. 1a. This layout was obtained by Iterative Heuristic Technique as described in [6]. Here, cluster analysis technique is used to group closely related rooms. The layout procedure is carried out based on Iterative Heuristic technique. The dimensions are in 300 mm (1 ft) units. A program is developed to optimize nonlinear programming problems using Move Limit Method of SLP. The optimization proceeds as shown in Fig. 1. Nonlinear programming is used in conjunction with dimensional representations of floor plans to generate optimum layouts subject to cost criterion and functional constraints.

Improved Move Limit of   SLP has been used to obtain optimum dimension of the house. Fig. 1a shows the dimensionless plan showing the variables. The objective is to determine the values of the dimensions represented by w_1, w_2 ... w_{11} in order to minimize the overall cost, subject to the constraints on room dimensions, areas, doors and windows, and aspect ratios. 50 to 250% variations are set for the room areas and dimensions.

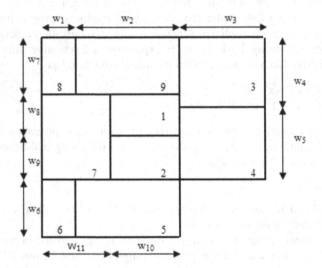

Fig. 1a. Functional Layout obtained before optimization

3.6 Program

The program developed involves the following steps:

1. Checks whether the initial values are feasible
2. Generates Simplex Table with the Move Limits
3. Determines the most violated constraint and its value
4. Determines the derivatives of the objective function and the constraint equations
5. Determines alpha with respect to the most violated constraint to steer to the feasible domain
6. Checks the usability of the direction and if it is not usable, then adopts quadratic interpolation to get a usable direction

7. Determines alpha by conventional method and steers the feasible domain
8. Checks for optimum, if not, uses quadratic interpolation and go back to Simplex Table
9. Conventional method of averaging the variables– displays the number of function evaluations, number of derivative evaluations.
10. Method for simplex table
11. Method to calculate the derivatives of the objective function and the constraints
12. Method to read the objective function and the constraints for optimization

4 Results

The layout dimensions which minimizes the construction cost may be determined using the optimization problem. The designer may want to know the near optimal results, and if there is more than one set of dimensions which produces the optimal results.

Fig. 1b presents the optimum result.

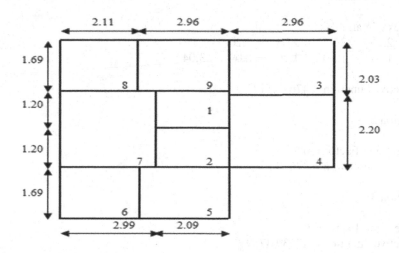

Fig. 1b. Layout after optimization

Stepl = 0.00001
Number of variables = 11
Number of constraints = 40

Lower Bound Values

1.00	2.50	2.50	2.00	2.00	
1.50	1.50	1.00	1.00	1.50	1.50

Upper Bound Values

3.00	3.50	3.50	2.50	2.50	
2.50	2.50	2.00	2.00	2.50	4.00

The Starting Point is:

$w_1 = 2.13$ $w_2 = 2.97$ $w_3 = 2.97$ $w_4 = 2.05$ $w_5 = 2.20$
$w_6 = 1.70$ $w_7 = 1.70$ $w_8 = 1.22$ $w_9 = 1.22$ $w_{10} = 2.05$
$w_{11} = 3.20$

Objective Function = 47939.1700

Iteration 1

Move Limit Factor = 0.5
Point is in Infeasible Region
Most Violated Constraint 25
Maximum Constraint Violation   0.001031

Violated Constraints Alpha
23   -0.000181
24   -0.000181

Values of Variables
2.11 2.96   2.96   2.20
1.69 1.69   1.90   1.20   2.09   3.04

Objective Function = 47639.5125

Iteration 2

Move Limit Factor = 0.5
Objective Function = 47639.47

Iteration 3

Move Limit Factor = 0.5
Objective Function = 47639.4759

Optimum Point(Values Of Variables)
$w_1 = 2.11$ $w_2 = 2.96$ $w_3 = 2.96$ $w_4 = 2.03$ $w_5 = 2.20$
$w_6 = 1.69$ $w_7 = 1.69$ $w_8 = 1.20$ $w_9 = 1.20$ $w_{10} = 2.09$
$w_{11} = 2.99$

Objective Function = 47639.4758
Number of Function Evaluations   0
Number of Derivative Evaluations   3

Thus, the number of variables are 11 and the number of constraints are 40. The costs of the rooms are derived from the costs of the walls and floors plus the costs of their finishes. Cost of the wall is assumed to be 850/sq unit and the cost of floor/roof is set as 100/sq unit. This includes the cost of finishing. Once all the constraints are specified, they are in the form of inequalities, it is possible to determine the optimal value of the dimensions. Improved Move Limit method of SLP is used for design optimization.

5 Conclusion

The problem of generating the optimized layout has been solved. Thus, given a topology, the dimensions of a layout can be obtained which satisfies a number of constraints while minimizing the construction cost. Improved Move Limit method of Sequential Linear Programming provides an efficient method to solve dimensioning problems.

References

1. Radford, A.D., Gero, J.S.: Design by Optimization in Architecture, Building and Construction, pp. 84–90. Van Nostrand Reinhold Company (1988)
2. Himmelblaue, D.M.: Applied Nonlinear Programming. McGraw Hill, New York (1972)
3. Carpentieri, G., Tooren, J.L.: Improving the Efficiency of Aerodynamic Shape Optimization on Unstructured Meshes. In: 44th AIAA Aerospace Sciences Meeting and Exhibit, Reno, NV (2006)
4. Michalek, J.J., Choudhary, R., Papalambros, P.Y.: Architectural Layout Design Optimization. Eng. Opt. 34(5), 461–484 (2002)
5. Mashford, J.S., Drogemuller, R.M., Stuckey, P.J.: Building Design Optimization using Constraint Logic Programming. In: INAP/ WLP Proc. of the International Conference on the Applications of Prolog, Potsdam, Germany (2004)
6. Bhowmik, R.: Allocating Clusters using Hierarchical Clustering Technique. In: Proc. of Hawaii International Conference on Computer Sciences, Hawaii (2004)
7. Griffith, R.E., Steward, R.A.: A nonlinear programming technique for the optimization of continuous processing systems. J. Mgmt. Sci. 7, 379–392
8. Bhavikatti, S.S.: Computational Efficiency of Improved Move Limit Method of Sequential Linear Programming for Structural Optimization. Computers and Structures 11(3), 191–196 (1980)

Adaptive Bacterial Foraging Optimization Based Tuning of Optimal PI Speed Controller for PMSM Drive

Ravi Kumar Jatoth[1] and A. Rajasekhar[2]

[1] Department of Electronics and Communication Engineering,
National Institute of Technology, Warangal-506004, Andhra Pradesh, India
[2] Department of Electrical and Electronics Engineering,
National Institute of Technology, Warangal-506004, Andhra Pradesh, India
ravikumar@nitw.ac.in, boni.simulator@gmail.com
http://www.nitw.ac.in

Abstract. Speed regulation with conventional PI regulator reduces the speed control precision because of disturbances in Motor and load characteristics, leading to poor performance of whole system. The values so obtained may not give satisfactory results for a wide range of speed. This paper implements, a new tuning algorithm based on the foraging behavior of E-coli Bacteria with an adaptive chemotaxis step, to optimize the coefficients of "Proportional-Integral" (PI) speed controller in a Vector-Controlled Permanent Magnet Synchronous Motor (PMSM) Drive. Through the computer simulations, it is observed that dynamic response of Adaptive bacterial foraging PI (ABF-PI) controller is quite satisfactory. It has good dynamic and static characteristics like low peak overshoot, low Steady state error and less settling time. The ABF technique is compared with "Gradient descent search" method and basic "Bacterial Foraging" Algorithm. The performances of these methods are studied thoroughly using "ITAE" criterion. Simulations are implemented using Industrial Standard MATLAB/SIMULINK.

Keywords: Permanent Magnet Synchronous Motor, PI speed controller, gradient descent, bacterial foraging, adaptive chemotaxis, ITAE.

1 Introduction

According to recent studies, with the advancement of Control theories, Power Electronics, Micro electronics in connection with new motor design and magnetic materials since 1980's electrical (A.C) drives are making tremendous impact in the area of variable speed control systems [1,2]. Among A.C drives newly developed Permanent Magnet Synchronous Motors with high energy permanent magnet materials like "Neodymium Iron Boron" ("Nd-Fe-B") provide fast dynamics and compatibility with the applications if they are controlled properly.

PMSM's are commonly used for applications like actuators, machine tools and robotics. This is due to some of its advantages, features such as high power-density, efficiency, reduced volume and weight, low noise and robustness [3].

S. Ranka et al. (Eds.): IC3 2010, Part I, CCIS 94, pp. 588–599, 2010.
© Springer-Verlag Berlin Heidelberg 2010

Now-a-days vector control technique has made it possible to apply the PMSM's in high-performance industrial applications where only D.C motor drives were previously available. In order to make the most of a motor performance, a very effective control system is needed. Although many possible solutions are available, eg., adaptive, intelligent control [4,5], PI based control system scheme still remains the more widely adopted solution because of the fact that although simple, a PI based control allows achieving of very high performances when optimally designed [6].

The PI controller has been widely used in industry due to its low steady state error and less maintenance cost [7]. However finding out the parameters K_p, K_i of controller is not any easy task because of motor dynamics and Load parameters. To get the controller parameters "Trail and Error" solution is very complex and doesn't guarantee optimal solution. So for finding optimal PI parameters, bio inspired tuning methods are used to tune the controller. In this paper a new algorithm based on the foraging behavior of bacteria with an adaptive chemotactic step is been used to optimize the K_p and K_i gains of PI controller. The basic BF optimization technique is proposed by "K.M.Passino" [8]. This paper also presents the tuning of PI speed controller with "Gradient Descent search" method, "Bacterial Foraging Optimization Algorithm" and compared with "Adaptive Bacterial Foraging Optimization algorithm".

2   Permanent Magnet Synchronous Motor

2.1   Structure of PMSM

PMSM with approximately sinusoidal back electromotive force can be broadly categorized in to two types 1) Interior Permanent Magnet Motors (IPMSM) 2) Surface mounted Permanent Magnet Motors (SPM). In this paper we considered "SPM". In this motor magnets are mounted on the surface.

Because the incremental permeability of magnets is 1.02-1.20 relative to external fields, the magnets have high reluctance and SPM can be considered to have large and effective uniform air gap. This property makes saliency negligible. Thus q-axis inductance of motor is equal to d-axis inductance i.e., $L_q = L_d$. As a result magnetic torque only can be produced by the motor which arises from the

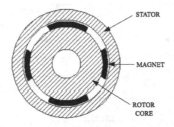

Fig. 1. Structure of Permanent Magnet Synchronous Motor [10]

interaction of Magnetic flux and quadrature axis current [9].The cross-sectional layout of a surface mounted permanent magnet motor is shown in Fig.1. The stator carries a three-phase winding, which produces a near sinusoidal distribution of magneto motive force based on the value of the stator current. The magnets have the same role as the field winding in a synchronous machine except their magnetic field is constant and there is no control on it [10].

In this paper following [11] assumptions are taken in to account for deriving the mathematical equations.

- Saturation is neglected.
- The back EMF is sinusoidal.
- Eddy currents and Hysteresis losses are negligible.

2.2   Mathematical Model of PMSM

Mathematical Model of PMSM can be defined in rotor frame (i.e., d-q frame) of reference using the following differential equations [11]. By these equations SIMULINK model of drive is obtained shown in Fig 2.

$$v_d = r_s i_d + p\lambda_d - \omega_e \lambda_q \tag{1}$$

$$v_q = r_s i_q + p\lambda_q + \omega_e \lambda_d \tag{2}$$

where v_d, v_q are d-q axis voltages, i_d, i_q are d-q axis currents,r_s is the stator resistance, p represents the differential operator. w_e is the electrical speed of motor. The linkage fluxes λ_d and λ_q can be expressed in the terms of stator currents, inductances and flux linkage due to the permanent magnets of the rotor linking the stator as

$$\lambda_d = L_d i_d + \lambda_m \tag{3}$$

$$\lambda_q = L_q i_q \tag{4}$$

here λ_m represents magnet mutual flux. By substituting Eqn(3),(4) into Eqn(1),(2) the following stator voltage equations are obtained

$$v_d = r_s i_d + L_d p i_d - \omega_e L_q i_q \tag{5}$$

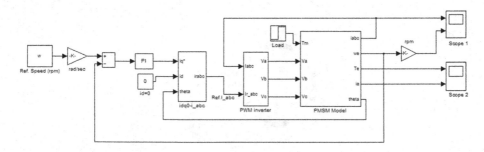

Fig. 2. SIMULINK Model of PMSM Drive

$$v_q = r_s i_q + L_q p i_q + \omega_e L_d i_d + \omega_e \lambda_m \qquad (6)$$

The Electromagnetic torque is

$$T_e = \frac{3}{2}\frac{P}{2}[\lambda_m i_q + (L_d - L_q)i_d i_q] \qquad (7)$$

For constant flux operation when i_d equals zero, in Field oriented control (FOC) [9,11] electric torque is modified as $T_e = \frac{3}{2}\frac{P}{2}[\lambda_m i_q] = K_t i_q$, where K_t is the motor torque constant. Hence in state space form

$$p i_d = (v_d - r_s i_d + \omega_e L_q i_q)/L_d \qquad (8)$$

$$p i_q = (v_q - r_s i_q - \omega_e L_d i_d - \omega_e \lambda_m)/L_q \qquad (9)$$

$$T_e = J\frac{2}{P}\frac{d\omega_e}{dt} + B\frac{2}{P}\omega_e + T_L \qquad (10)$$

$$\frac{d\omega_e}{dt} = \frac{1}{J}[\frac{P}{2}(T_e - T_L) - B\omega_e] \qquad (11)$$

$$\omega_e = P\omega_r/2 \qquad (12)$$

$$p\theta_r = \frac{2}{P}\omega_e \qquad (13)$$

T_L represents load torque, w_r is rotor speed and θ_r represents position of rotor. v_d and v_q are obtained from v_a, v_b and v_c through the abc to dq0 transformation defined below

$$\begin{bmatrix} v_q \\ v_d \\ v_0 \end{bmatrix} = \frac{2}{3}\begin{bmatrix} \cos(\theta) & \cos(\theta - \frac{2\pi}{3}) & \cos(\theta - \frac{2\pi}{3}) \\ \sin(\theta) & \sin(\theta - \frac{2\pi}{3}) & \cos(\theta + \frac{2\pi}{3}) \\ 1/2 & 1/2 & 1/2 \end{bmatrix}\begin{bmatrix} v_a \\ v_b \\ v_c \end{bmatrix}$$

To find the variables v_a, v_b and v_c we use dq0 to abc transformation stated below

$$\begin{bmatrix} v_a \\ v_b \\ v_c \end{bmatrix} = \begin{bmatrix} \cos(\theta) & \sin(\theta) & 1 \\ \cos(\theta - \frac{2\pi}{3}) & \sin(\theta - \frac{2\pi}{3}) & 1 \\ \cos(\theta + \frac{2\pi}{3}) & \sin(\theta + \frac{2\pi}{3}) & 1 \end{bmatrix}\begin{bmatrix} v_q \\ v_d \\ v_0 \end{bmatrix}$$

By using above equations and transformations Vector-Controlled Model of PMSM in d-q frame of reference is modeled using MATLAB/SIMULINK. Vector-Control is based on stator current control in the field of rotating reference using PMW inverter control. The model of PMSM in Fig 2. is making on the d-q reference and the machine is feed by a PWM inverter. The model uses park transformers, abc to d-q. A reference speed is given to PI controller which is implemented after the feedback and speed response of the speed vs. time graph can be seen in scope.

3   Problem Formulation

3.1   PI Speed Controller

Proportional Integral (PI) speed controller is the simplest in comparison with any other speed controller. The performance of drive depends on these parameters. It is difficult to find appropriate parameter gains for the controller by using "trial and error" solution. So, bio inspired tuning methods are used to get optimum values for the controller. Fig 3 shows the block diagram of PI controller.

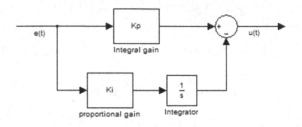

Fig. 3. Tuning of PI speed controller

The input of controller is given by

$$e(t) = \omega_{ref} - \omega_{act} \tag{14}$$

Here

$\omega_{ref}, \omega_{act}$ –reference, actual speed given to the motor

$e(t), u(t)$ –input and output of PI controller

Mathematically PI speed controller with proportional and integral gain constant is represented as

$$u(t) = K_p e(t) + K_i \int e(t)\, dt \tag{15}$$

Here Proportional gain (K_p) and integral gain (K_i) are functions of speed error e(t). When the speed error is large a large proportional gain is used to increase the control effect and hence accelerate or decelerate the motor speed to the desired value. When the speed error is small a large value of integral gain is used to overcome the steady-state error. So, optimum (K_i) and (K_p) values are obtained by using evolutionary computing tools like BFO and its variants.

The design requirements like Rise time (t_r), Settling time (t_s), peak overshoot (po) and Steady state error (e_{ss}) depends on these two gain constants. So, to get the good transient response controller is to be tuned properly.

4   Application of BFO and ABFO to Optimize PI Parameters

4.1   Bacterial Foraging Optimization

Bacterial foraging optimization is a new method based on foraging behavior of "Escherichia coli" *(E-coli)* bacterial present in the human intestine, and been already implemented to real world problems [12]. A group of bacteria move in search of food and away from noxious elements known as Foraging. BFO algorithm draws its inspiration from this foraging behavior. The control system of these bacteria that dictates how foraging should be proceed can be subdivided into four sections namely Chemotaxis, Swarming, Reproduction, and Elimination and Dispersal. Detailed mathematical derivations as well as the theoretical aspect of this concept are presented in [8,12,13].

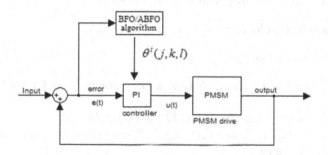

Fig. 4. Tuning of PI speed controller

The performance of PMSM varies according to PI gain values and it is judged by value of ITAE (Integral Time Absolute Error). ITAE is chosen as objective function because it has an advantage of producing smaller over shoots and oscillations [15]

$$ITAE = \int_0^\infty t|e(t)|\, dt$$

In this PI controller each parameter (i.e.,K_p, K_i) is assumed as bacteria and are set to random values. Each bacterium updates its values using the BFO principles so that objective function ITAE is minimized. Fig 4. shows the optimizing process, a reference input is given and the error obtained by the feedback is sent to ABFO/BFO algorithm block so that the it sends the appropriate parameters to the controller. Once the simulation is started, at each iteration the new bacteria (i.e. parameter values) are fed to the controller and the response is analyzed graphically with help of scope. Out of all the parametric values obtained the best fit values is shown as output which is best solution for optimizing function in given dimensional search space.

The BFO Algorithm

[Step 1] Initialize the parameters $p, S, N_c, N_s, N_{re}, N_{ed}, P_{ed}, C(i)(i = 1, 2, 3, \ldots, S), \theta^i$ where

p –Dimension of the search space;
S –Total number of bacteria in the population;
N_c –number of chemotactic steps;
N_s –Swimming length, always $N_c > N_s$;
N_{re} –number of reproduction steps;
N_{ed} –number of Elimination and dispersal events;
P_{ed} –Probability of elimination and dispersal;
θ^i –Location of the ith $(i = 1, 2, 3, \ldots, S)$ bacterium;
$C(i)$ –the size of the step taken in random direction, specified by the tumble.

[Step 2] Elimination and dispersal loop: $l = l + 1$

[Step 3] Reproduction loop: $k = k + 1$

[Step 4] Chemotaxis loop: $j = j + 1$

[substep 4.1] For $i = 1, 2, 3, \ldots, S$ take a chemotactic step for bacterium i as follows
[substep 4.2] Compute cost function, $ITAE(i, j, k, l)$.
[substep 4.3] Ler $ITAE_{last} = ITAE(i, j, k, l)$ save this value, since we may get better value via a run.
[substep 4.4] Tumble: generate a random vector $\Delta(i) \in \Re^p$, with each element $\Delta(i)_m$ $m = 1, 2, 3, \ldots, p$ a random number on range [-1 1]
[substep 4.5] Move: Let,

$$\theta^i(j + 1, k, l) = \theta^i(j, k, l) + C(i)\frac{\Delta(i)}{\sqrt{\Delta^T(i)\Delta(i)}} \tag{16}$$

This results in a step of size $C(i)$ in the direction of the tumble for bacterium i
[substep 4.6] Compute $ITAE(i, j + 1, k, l)$
[substep 4.7] Swim:

(i)   Let $m = 0$ (counter for swim length)
(ii)   while $m < N_s$ (if the bacteria have not climbed too long)

- Let $m = m + 1$;
- If $ITAE(i, j + 1, k, l) < ITAE_{last}$(if doing better), Let $ITAE_{last} = ITAE(i, j+1, k, l)$ and let $\theta^i(j+1, k, l) = \theta^i(j, k, l) + C(i)\frac{\Delta(i)}{\sqrt{\Delta^T(i)\Delta(i)}}$
  use this $\theta^i(j+1, k, l)$ to compute new cost function $ITAE(i, j+1, k, l)$
- Else, let $m = N_s$. This is the end of while statement

[substep 4.8] go to next bacterium $(i + 1)$ if $i \neq S$ (i.e., go to [substep 4.2]) to process next bacterium

[**Step 5**] If $j < N_c$, go to [**Step 4**]. In this case, continue chemotaxis Since the life of the bacteria is not over.

[**Step 6**] Reproduction:

[substep 6.1] For the given k and l and for each $i = 1, 2, 3, ..., S$ let $ITAE^i_{health} = \sum_{j=1}^{N_c+1} ITAE(i, j, k, l)$ be the health of the bacterium i (a measure of how many nutrients it got over its lifetime and how successful it was at avoiding noxious substances). Sort bacteria in order of ascending cost $ITAE_{health}$ (higher cost means lower health).

[substep 6.2] The $S_r = S/2$ bacteria with the highest $ITAE_{health}$ values die and remaining S_r with the best values split and this process is performed by the copies that are made are placed at same location as their parent.

[**Step 7**] If $k < N_{re}$, go to the [**Step 3**]. Since in this case the specified reproduction steps are not reached, start the next generation of the chemotactic loop.

[**Step 8**] Elimination-dispersal: For $i = 1, 2, ..., S$ with the probability P_{ed}, eliminate and disperse each bacterium, which results in keeping number of bacteria in the population constant. To do this, if a bacterium is eliminated, simply disperse another one to a random location on the optimization domain. If $l < N_{ed}$ then go to [**Step 2**], otherwise end;

4.2   Adaptive Bacterial Foraging Optimization

Chemotaxis is a foraging strategy that implements a type of local optimization where the bacteria try to climb up the nutrient concentration, avoid noxious substance and search for ways out of neutral media [13,14]. A chemotactic step size varying as the function of the current fitness value is expected to provide better convergence behavior as compared to a fixed step size. A simple adaption scheme for the step size for i^{th} bacterium given in following equation is employed to get better optimal controller parameters for PMSM drive.

$$C(i) = \frac{|j^i(\theta)|}{|j^i(\theta) + \psi|} = \frac{1}{1 + \frac{\psi}{|j^i(\theta)|}} \tag{17}$$

Where ψ is positive constant.

$j^i(\theta)$ –cost function of the ith bacterium

C_i –variable run length unit of ith bacterium

If $j^i(\theta) \rightarrow 0$, then $C(i) \rightarrow 0$ and when $j^i(\theta) \rightarrow large$, $C(i) \rightarrow 1$. This implies that the bacterium which is in the vicinity of noxious substance associates with higher cost function. Hence it takes larger steps to migrate to a place with higher nutrient concentration. Use of Eqn (17) in Eqn (16) is expected to give improved convergence performance compared to fixed step size due to the above phenomenon

The Adaptive BFO Algorithm for optimization of PI parameters

[**Step 1**]. Same as that of BFO based optimization.
[**Step 2-3**]. Same as that of BFO, but only difference is that while updating location in Eqn (16) (and also in swim) the adaptive run length unit, defined in Eqn (17) is used instead of fixed run length unit.
[**Step 5-8**]. Same as that of BFO based optimization technique.

5   Simulations and Results

5.1   Experimental Settings

Simulations are carried out for this drive by the following experimental settings

Variable	Actual meaning	Value	Units
r_s	Stator resistance	2.0	Ω
L_d	d-axis inductance	2.419	mH
L_q	q-axis inductance	2.419	mH
J	Moment of inertia	0.0034463	$kg.m^2$
λ_m	Magnet mutual flux	0.27645	$V/rad/sec$
B	Damping coefficient	0.0027715	$Nm/rad/sec$
P	Number of poles	8	

Design Specifications of drive are:-

- Peak-overshoot $(po\%) < 2\%$, Rise time $(t_r) < 0.01sec$
- Settling time $(t_s) < 0.6sec$, Steady state error $(e_{ss}) < 0.01rpm$

Simulation is done for a time $T = 1$ sec under a load torque $5 - Nm$ with a reference speed of 1300 rpm. The range for K_p is taken from 0 to 1 and for that of K_i is 0 to 10. Various parameters employed in the simulation study for BFO and ABFO are

$S = 10, N_c = 5, N_s = 4, N_{re} = 2, N_{ed} = 2, P_{ed} = 0.25, C(i) = 0.14, \psi = 9.$
The Gradient descent search method used for tuning, depends on design specifications and this method is implemented using "Gradient descent" method in MATLAB/SIMULINK. A maximum of 25 iterations are used to get optimum value. Step responses of various methods are shown in following figures.

5.2   Step Responses of PMSM Drive with Different Controllers

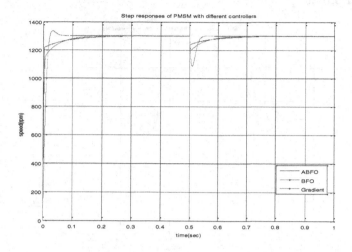

Fig. 5. Step response of gradient tuned PMSM

5.3   Step Responses of PMSM Drive with Different Controllers before Load

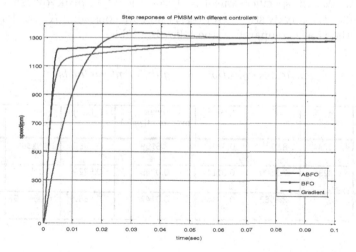

Fig. 6. Step responses of PMSM before load (T=0.1sec)

5.4 Step Responses of PMSM Drive with Different Controllers after Load

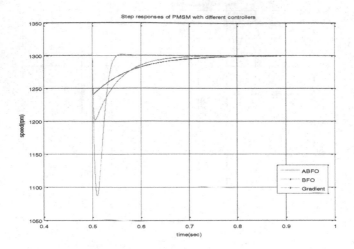

Fig. 7. Step responses of PMSM after load

From above figures we can confirm that rise time and peak overshoot ABFO tuned controller are very much improved compared to that of remaining tuned controllers. Design specifications like Rise-time (t_r), peak overshoot $(po\%)$, settling-time (t_s), steady state error (e_{ss}) and gain constants K_p, K_i for different tuning methods are compared in the following table.

Comparison of Design Specifications using different methods:-

Method	K_p	K_i	t_r(sec)	Peak overshoot($po\%$)	t_s(sec)	e_{ss}	Run time(sec)
Gradient descent	0.0734	8.9717	0.0144	2.6199	0.5456	0.01331	24.08sec
BFO	0.3236	7.5600	0.0114	0.0245	0.5729	0.009137	22.42sec
ABFO	0.6227	8.3562	0.0034	0.0147	0.5652	0.005275	20.58sec

6   Conclusions

In this paper BFO and Adaptive BFO are used for tuning PI controller of PMSM drive. From the above simulations and results we can conclude that ABFO based tuning of PI controller is performing better compared to that of BFO and Gradient descent method. The rise time and steady state error are much improved in ABFO tuned PMSM. Our future research include performance and analysis of "Fractional Order Proportional Integral" (FOPI) controller for the PMSM drive.

References

1. Bose, B.K.: Power Electronics and Motion Control-Technology Status and Recent Trends. IEEE Trans. Ind. App. 29, 902–909 (1993)
2. Lipo, T.A.: Recent Progress in the Development of Solid state AC Motor Drives. IEEE Trans. Power Electron. 3, 105–117 (1988)
3. Vas, P.: Sensorless Vector and Direct Torque Control, 1st edn. Oxford University Press, Oxford (1998)
4. Khorrami, F., Krishnamurthy, P., Melkote, H.: Modeling and Adaptive Nonlinear Control of Electric Motors. Springer, Heidelberg (2003)
5. Jain, L.C., De Silva, C.W., Jain, L.C.: Intelligent Adaptive Control: Industrial Applications. CRC, Boca Raton (1998)
6. Åström, K.J., Hägglund, H.: The future of PID control. Control Eng. Pract. 9(11), 1163–1175 (2001)
7. Tursini, M., Parasiliti, F., Zhang, D.: Real-Time Gain Tuning of PI Controllers for High-Performance PMSM Drives. IEEE Trans. Ind. App. 38(4) (2002)
8. Passino, K.M.: Biomimicry of Bacterial Foraging for Distributed Dptimization and Control. IEEE Control Systems Magazine, 52–67 (2002)
9. Song Chi, M.S.E.E.: Position-Sensorless Control of Permanent Magnet Synchronous Machine Over Wide Range Speed. PH.D Thesis, Ohio State University (2007)
10. Sebastian, T., Slemon, G.R.: Transient Modeling and Performance of Variable-Speed Permanent-Magnet Motors. IEEE Trans. Ind. App. 25(1), 101–106 (1986)
11. Pillay, P., Krishnan, R.: Modeling, Simulation, and Analysis of Permanent-Magnet Motor Drives, Part I: The Permanent-Magnet Synchronous Motor Drive. IEEE Trans. Ind. App. 25(2), 265–273 (1989)
12. Mishra, S., Bhende, C.N.: Bacterial Foraging Technique-Based Optimized Active Power Filter for Load Compensation. IEEE Trans. Power Delivery 22(1), 457–465 (2007)
13. Mishra, S.: A Hybrid Least Square-Fuzzy Bacteria Foraging Strategy for Harmonic Estimation. IEEE Trans. Evol. Comput. 9(1), 61–73 (2005)
14. Dasgupta, S., Das, S., Abraham, A., Biswas, A.: Adaptive Computational Chemotaxis in Bacterial Foraging Optimization: An Analysis. IEEE Trans. Evol. Comput. 13(4) (2009)
15. Schultz, W.C., Rideout, V.C.: Control System Performance Measures: Past, Present and Future. IRE Trans. Automatic Control AC-6, 22–35 (1961)

Missing Value Imputation Based on K-Mean Clustering with Weighted Distance

Bankat M. Patil, Ramesh C. Joshi, and Durga Toshniwal

Department of Electronics and Computer Engineering,
Indian Institute of Technology, Roorkee, Uttarakhand, India 247667
{bmp07dec,rcjosfec,durgafec}@iitr.ernet.in

Abstract. It is common to encounter databases that have up to a half of the entries missing, which is specifically true with medical databases. Most of the statistical and data mining techniques require complete datasets and obviously these techniques do not provide accurate results with missing values. Several methods have been proposed to deal with the missing data. Commonly used method is to delete instances with missing value attribute. These approaches are suitable when there are few missing values. In case of large number of missing values, deleting these instances results in loss of bulk of information. Other method to cope-up with this problem is to complete their imputation (filling in missing attribute). We propose an efficient missing value imputation method based on clustering with weighted distance. We divide the data set into clusters based on user specified value K. Then find a complete valued neighbor which is nearest to the missing valued instance. Then we compute the missing value by taking the average of the centroid value and the centroidal distance of the neighbor. This value is used as *impute value*. In our proposed approach we use K-means technique with weighted distance and show that our approach results in better performance.

Keywords: Pima Indian diabetes data, k-Means, Euclidian distance, Manhattan Distance.

1 Introduction

Handling Missing value imputation is a major issue in data mining, data warehousing and database management. Most of the real-world data set contains missing values especially those related with fields like medical, industrial etc. This may be due to the number of reasons like error in the equipment, denial of respondents from answering to certain queries regarding personal information or due to the improper data entry and so on. Thus quality of data is a major issue in data mining and other related areas as the absence of values in the data may affect on the quality of results. In [1] it is stated that if the quality of data is good then patterns extracted from data also provide significantly better performance. Several methods have been proposed in the literature to deal with missing values. The first approach is deleting the data instances which contain missing values. This approach is also called as complete data analysis because

S. Ranka et al. (Eds.): IC3 2010, Part I, CCIS 94, pp. 600–609, 2010.
Springer-Verlag Berlin Heidelberg 2010

here we are discarding (list wise deletion) those instances which have incomplete attribute values. Such type of default approach has been proposed while adopting statistical methods [2] [3].These approaches are suitable when there are few missing values. However, as the quantity of missing values increases we tend to loose significant information by deleting these instances. The other approach makes use of parameter estimation, in which *maximum likelihood procedures* are used to estimate parameters of model by making use of variants of the Expectation-Maximization algorithm [4]. The third approach is filling-up the missing values by using probable values based on information available in the database [5]. Mean imputation method has been most widely used in literature especially when the values are of numeric type. The mean of attributes of non-missing value is filled in as missing value attributes. If the data is categorical then the mode of non missing value is used as missing attribute. Let us assume that the value x_{ij} of the k-th class C_k is missing then it will be replaced by

$$x_{ij} = \sum_{i:x_{ij} \in c_k} \frac{x_{ij}}{n_k} \tag{1}$$

where n_k represents the number of non-missing values in the *j*-th feature of the k-th class. The limitation of this method is that, it will replace all missing values by the same value though definite variability is associated with real missing data. As consequence a statistical distribution of the data is changed and it will impact on quality of data. This is a simple and most frequently used approach in literature [6], [7]. However in [8] and [9] the authors have shown that mean imputation method has improved performance of classifier.

Conventional missing value imputation method can be classified as either parametric or non-parametric. Former is considered as better approach when the dataset is in parametric form. In case of linear regression, this method usually performs well for the continuous target attribute as it is a linear combination of the conditional attributes. This method predicts values derived from a regression equation based on variables in the dataset that contain no missing data. However, if we do not know the actual relationship between the conditional attributes and the target attribute the performance of this method is very found to be poor [10]. In cases where the distribution of data is unknown the results obtained using parametric method are found to be biased.

Non-parametric imputation algorithm offers a better choice when the users have no idea about the nature of data distribution. Non-parametric algorithm has proved effective when the relationship between the conditional attributes and the target attribute is initially unknown [11]. Clustering algorithm is also used for missing value imputation. This paper addresses the above issues by proposing a clustering-based weighted distances approach for dealing with the problem of missing value imputation. We make use cluster based k-means algorithm with weighted distance to compute the missing value by taking the average of the centroid value and the centroidal distance of the nearest neighbor.

2   Related Work

For relational databases various sophisticated techniques have also been used for imputing the missing data such as associative neural network [7], genetic algorithm [12] and supervised learning like C4.5 [1]. In the machine learning algorithm first step is to build the classifier model based on the training data. This model can then be used for testing data to predict class labels. In case of missing value imputataion method target attribute is missing value atrribute instead of class label. Bayesian methods have also been used to impute missing data as outlined in [13]. In [14] authors have proposed application of Bayesian method for estimating and imputing missing data based on prior knowledge about the data distribution primarily applicable to uni-variate missing data.

In [15] authors have used instance based learning approach for calculating k nearest neighbor value. For nominal values the most common value among the neighbours is choosen. Weighted imputation with K-Nearest neighbor selects the instances with similar values based on distance, so that it can impute as KNNI does. The calculated value now takes into account the different distances to the neighbors either using a weighted mean or the most repeated value according to the distance [16].

In [17] K-means Clustering Imputation (CMI) has been used to fill the missing values of set of objects by clustering carried out by dividing the data set into groups based on similarity of objects. This approach minimizes the intra-cluster dissimilarity. In K-means clustering, the intra-cluster dissimilarity is measured based on the sum of distances among the objects and the centroid of the cluster which they are assigned to. A cluster centroid represents the mean value of the objects in the cluster. When the clusters are formed by using k-mean the last step fill in all the non-reference attribute of each object by using cluster information. The object belonging to same cluster is chosen to replace missing data based on nearest neighbour algorithm.

3   Clustering Method Imputation with Weighted Distance (CMIWD)

Our inspiration for this study is based on the clustering algorithms by grouping instances according similarity on the basis of distance principle such as the Euclidean distance. In spite of the fact that K-means was proposed over 50 years ago and thousands of clustering algorithms have been published since then, K-means is still widely used [18]. We apply clustering method on whole data set in order to group the instances in cluster based on their distances. Then we make use of nearest neighbor algorithm to find nearest instance to missing value attributes instance in same cluster and use this distance as a weighted distance. We have taken average of centroid value and weighted distance to impute missing value attributes.

Let us consider a given set of N instances $D = (d_1, d_2, ..., d_N)$ where each instance has A set of attributes, we refer d_{ij} ($1 \leq i \leq N$ and $1 \leq j \leq A$) to indicate the value of attribute j in instance d_i. If instance d_i satisfies the condition $\{ d_{ij} \neq \phi \mid \forall \ 1 \leq j \leq A \}$ we can say that it is a complete instance. We call an instance as incomplete if $\{\, d_{ij} = \phi \ \exists\, |\, 1 \leq j \leq A\,\}$ and thus we can say that d_i has a missing value on attribute j. Let us consider $R = \{\, j\,|\,d_{ij} \neq \phi, 1 \leq j \leq A\}$ be the set of attributes whose value is present and call such attributes as reference attributes. Our main aim is to find the values of non reference attribute for incomplete instances.

In this article we propose using K- means as the clustering algorithm because of its simplicity and efficiency. The missing data imputation based on k-means clustering and weighted distances method consist four steps:

1. First step involves arbitrarily selecting K complete data instances as K centroids. Let C=$\{c_1, c_2, ..., c_K\}$ be centroid of K clusters, where $c_i(1 \leq i \leq K)$ refer to the centroid of cluster i and is also a vector in A-dimensional space.
2. In the second step we iteratively change the partition to reduce the sum of the distances of each instance from the centroid of the cluster to which the instance belongs. For distance calculation we use references attributes only. So for a complete instance all the attributes are taken as in Eq. 2. For missing valued instances, we simple remove the non- referenced attributes from calculation and use Eq. 3. The convergence will stop when the summation distance is less than the user specified threshold.
3. Third step is to find complete value instance that belong to the same cluster C_i and also is nearest to the missing value instance based on distance calculated using the referenced attributes only Eq. 3. Let R_i be that instance nearest to M_i, the missing value instance.
4. In fourth step, we calculate the distance of R_i from C_i .i.e. d (C_i, R_i). We refer to this distance as weighted distance $w_i\,(1 \leq i \leq N)$. Then take its average with C_{kj} value to compute M_{kj} the missing value of attribute j of instance M_i.

We use Manhattan distance when $p = 1$ (i.e., $L1$ norm) and Euclidean distance when $p = 2$ (i.e., $L2$ norm) to calculate distance from centroid to data instance as given in Eq. (4). Finally we fill the missing value by using the Eq. (5).

$$d(c_k, d_i) = \left(\sum_{j=1}^{A} |d_{i,j} - c_{k,j}|^p \right)^{\frac{1}{p}} \tag{2}$$

$$d(c_k, d_i) = \left(\sum_{j=1}^{R} |d_{i,j} - c_{k,j}|^p \right)^{\frac{1}{p}} \tag{3}$$

Weighted distance $w_i = d(c_k, R_i)$ \hfill (4)

$$M_{i,j} = \frac{w_i + c_{ij}}{2} \tag{5}$$

Based on the above discussions, the CMIWD algorithm is presented as follows:

```
Algorithm: CMIWD
Input: Incomplete dataset D, k;
Output: Complete dataset D';
   1. (C₁,C₂,...Cₖ)=k-means(D, k);
   2. FOR each cluster Cᵢ;
   3. FOR each missing-valued instance Mᵢ in cluster Cᵢ;
   4. Find instance Rᵢ nearest to Mi using Eq. (3);
   5. Calculate the distance of Rᵢ from Cᵢ using eq (2)and
      call it weighted distance Wᵢ using Eq. (4);
   6. fill missing value Mᵢⱼ using average of centroid at-
      tribute value and wᵢ Value using Eq.(5);
```

4 Experiment Analysis

In order to assess the efficiency of the proposed approach, we conducted an experimental study that compares it with two existing methods. The first one is the mean substitution method, which is widely used in accomplish for handling missing data. The second is the CMI method proposed by [17].

4.1 Data Set

We have used standard data set   from UCI machine learning depository [19] for our analysis. The data set contains total 768 instances described by 8 attributes and a predictive class. In this 268 instances belong to class '1' which indicate that they are of diabetic patients and 500 instances belong to class '0' means negative cases i.e. they are of healthy persons. All the patients in the dataset are more than 21 years old woman. Characteristics of the patients including number of times they were pregnant, age (in years) have been recorded. Some other important physical measures that might be closely related to diabetes have also been recorded. These measures are plasma glucose concentration a 2 hours oral glucose tolerance test, diastolic blood pressure (mm Hg), triceps skin fold thickness (mm), 2-Hour serum insulin (mu U/ml), body mass index (weight in kg/(height in (mm)^2) and diabetes pedigree function. Most of the records contain missing data. For example a variable pregnant has the 111 missing values, *plasma glucose* and *diastolic BP* have '0' value for 5 and 35 patients respectively. For *TricepsSFT* and *Serum-Insulin* 227 and 374 have '0' values. BMI for 11 patients have '0' value. List of missing value attributes has been tabulated in Table 1. We have carried out pre-processing on the original data and have eliminated those instances which have missing values. However in case of TricepsSFT and Se-rum-Insulin as missing values are significant, we have eliminated these attributes from all instances. After preprocessing we are left with 625 complete value instances for analysis purpose obtained from original 768 instances.

Analysis has been carried out on 625 complete instances each having 6 attributes. The reason for eliminating missing data record is that it is difficult to assess the origi-nal missing values to ascertain the performance of a missing value handling method.

Table 1. Numbers of zero in each variable

Variable	Number of zero values (missing values)
Pregnant	111
Plasma glucose	5
Diastolic BP	35
TricepsSFT	227
Serum-Insulin	374
BMI	11
DPF	0
Age	0
Class	0

For the evaluation purposes, we randomly set additional 5%, 10%, 15%, 20%, 25%, and 30 % of the total values in dataset to missing values. As their true values are known, it is easier to analyze the effectiveness of the proposed approach

4.2 Implementation

We use our proposed method on Pima Indian dataset. The dataset obtained from UCI machine learning repositories which are belongs to medical domain. We chosen one important task for performance evaluation is univariate summary statistics, which are used in most data imputation method applications. In this part, we use a measure called Root Mean Square Error (RMSE), based on a similar measure used in the [17], [20] defined as in Eq. (6).

$$RMSE = \sqrt{1/m \sum_{i=1}^{m} (e_i - \overline{e}_i)^2} \qquad (6)$$

where e_i is the original attribute value, $\overline{e}_i$ is the estimated attribute value, and m is the total number of missing values. In our experiment we have randomly removed the amount data from different attributes from instances to obtain the error value. Such analysis has been carried out fifteen times to obtain the error estimations. Further the error value obtained from each execution has been averaged out to estimate the mean error value.

4.3 Mean Imputation vs. Clustering Based Imputation (CMI)

In this study first we have carried out the analysis of mean imputation and clustering based on imputation method and is as shown in Fig.1 and Fig.2 having number of clusters k=3 and k=5 respectively. Every experiment was conducted 15 times and we observe that in both the figures k-mean imputation performs better than the mean imputation method. We have used the Manhattan distance formula to find the distance

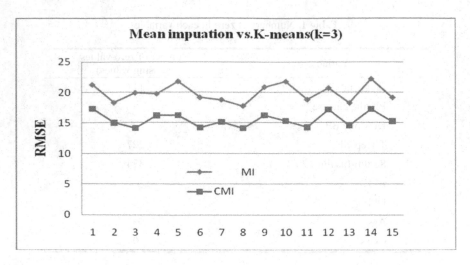

Fig. 1. Mean imputation vs. k-mean imputation where k=3

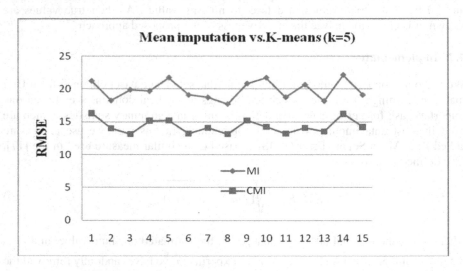

Fig. 2. Mean imputation vs. k-mean imputation where k=5

between two instances. The k-means imputation is based on the concept of finding out distance from centroid to nearest non-missing value instance that belongs to same cluster. This distance is used for filling missing value.

4.4   k-Mean Imputation vs. Clustering with Weighted Distance

In this section we present the comparison between basic K-means and proposed k-means with average of weighted distance and centroid value imputation algorithm. Fig.3, shown obtained results when the number of cluster are 3 and Fig.4, shown the results when the number of cluster are 5. It is evident that that our method provides

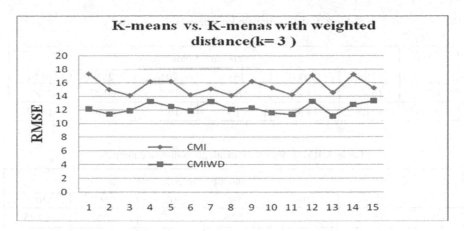

Fig. 3. k-mean imputation vs. clustering with weighted distance where k =3

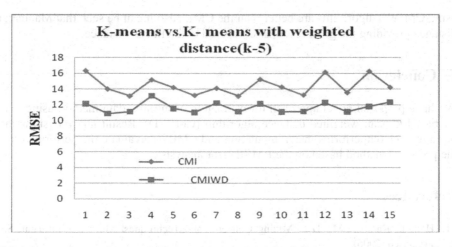

Fig. 4. k-mean imputation vs. clustering with avg of weighted distance and centroid where k=5

better estimation as compare to K-means algorithm. Further as discussed in the section 4.3, clustering method imputation method outperforms mean imputation. We have shown that our method out performs clustering method imputation method.

4.5 Evaluation Based on Percentage of Missing Data

The results obtained by varying the percentage of missing values in test data are as tabulated in the Table 2 and Table 3. These results are based on dissimilarity measure using Euclidean distance metric and Manhattan distance metric for cluster with k=4. In this analysis we observe that when percentage of missing value increases the error also increases in both the imputation methods. As the percentage of missing value increases, we tend to lose useful information. It also indicates those results obtained

Table 2. RMSE vary with Euclidean Distance metrics

	Euclidean Distance K=4					
	5%	10%	15%	20%	25%	30%
CMI	16.47	17.28	18.56	19.45	20.23	21.48
CMWD	13.28	14.88	15.42	16.34	17.88	18.67

Table 3. RMSE vary with manhattans distance metrics

	Manhattan Distance K=4					
	5%	10%	15%	20%	25%	30%
CMI	15.47	16.27	17.16	18.25	19.67	20.25
CMWD	12.46	13.44	14.28	15.34	16.38	17.61

using CMIWD algorithms are better than the CMI. Also it can be seen that Manhattan distance providing the good result, as compared to Euclidean distance.

5 Conclusion

We have proposed novel approach for estimation of missing data method using cluster based k-mean weighted distance algorithm (CMIWD). Result analysis show that our approach outperforms mean imputation and CMI. We evaluate the performance of the proposed method based on the RMSE error analysis.

References

1. Han, J., Kamber, M.: Data Mining Concepts and Techniques. Morgan Kaufmann, San Francisco (2006)
2. Quinlan, J.R.: C4.5 Programs for Machine Learning. Morgan Kaufmann, San Mateo (1993)
3. SAS Institute, Inc.: SAS Procedure Guide. SAS Institute Inc. Cary NC (1990)
4. Dempster, A.P., Laird, N.M., Rubin, D.B.: Maximum Likelihood from Incomplete Data via the EM Algorithm. J. Royal Statistical Society 82, 528–550 (1978)
5. Myrtveit, I., Stensrud, E., Olsson, U.H.: Analyzing Datasets with Missing Data: an Empirical Evaluation of Imputation Methods and Likelihood-Based Methods. IEEE Trans. on Software Engineering 27, 999–1013 (2001)
6. Pyle, D.: Data Preparation for Data Mining. Morgan Kaufmann, San Mateo (1999)
7. Michie, D., Spiegelhalter, D.J., Taylor, C.C.: Machine Learning, Neural, and Statistical Classification. Ellis Horwood, New York (1994)
8. Chan, S.L., Dunn, O.J.: The Treatment of Missing Values in Discriminant Analysis. J. American Statistical Association 67, 473–477 (1972)
9. Mundfrom, D.J., Whitcomb, A.: Imputing Missing Values: The effect on the Accuracy of Classification. Multiple Linear Regression Viewpoints 25(1), 13–19 (1998)

10. Beaumont, J.F.: On Regression Imputation in the Presence of Nonignorable Nonresponse. In: Proceedings of the Survey Research 570 Methods Section, ASA, pp. 580–585 (2000)
11. Lall, U., Sharma, A.: A Nearest-Neighbor Bootstrap for Resampling Hydrologic Time Series. Water Resource. Res. 32, 679–693 (1996)
12. Chen, S.M., Huang, C.M.: Generating Weighted Fuzzy Rules from Relational Database Systems for Estimating Null Values using Genetic Algorithms. IEEE Trans. Fuzzy Systems 11, 495–506 (2003)
13. Congdon, P.: Bayesian Models for Categorical Data. John Wiley & Sons, New York (2005)
14. Chiu, H.Y., Sedransk, J.: A Bayesian Procedure for Imputing Missing Values in Sample Surveys. J. Amer. Statist. Assoc., 5667–5676 (1996)
15. Batista, G.E.A.P.A., Monard, M.C.: An analysis of Four Missing Data Treatment Methods for Supervised Learning. J. Applied Artificial Intelligence 17, 519–533 (2003)
16. Troyanskaya, O., Cantor, M., Sherlock, G., Brown, P., Hastie, T., Tibshirani, R., Botstein, D., Altman, R.B.: Missing Value Estimation Methods for DNA Microarrays. Bioinformatics 17, 520–525 (2001)
17. Li, D., Deogun, J., Spaulding, W., Shuart, B.: Towards Missing Data Imputation: A Study of Fuzzy K-means Clustering Method. In: Tsumoto, S., Słowiński, R., Komorowski, J., Grzymała-Busse, J.W. (eds.) RSCTC 2004. LNCS (LNAI), vol. 3066, pp. 573–579. Springer, Heidelberg (2004)
18. Jain, A.K.: Data Clustering: 50 Years Beyond K-Means. J. Pattern Recognition Letters (2009)
19. Newman, D.J., Hettich, S., Blake, C.L.S., Merz, C.J.: UCI Repository of Machine Learning databases. University of California, Department of Information and Computer Science, Irvine (1998) (last assessed: 15/01/2010)
20. Chen, G., Astebro, T.: How to Deal with Missing Categorical data: Test of a Simple Bayesian Method. Organ. Res. Methods, 309–327 (2003)

Author Index